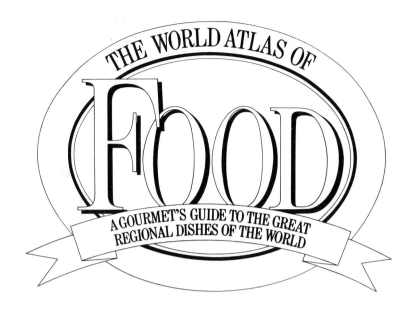

THE WORLD ATLAS OF FOOD

A GOURMET'S GUIDE TO THE GREAT REGIONAL DISHES OF THE WORLD

MAISON FONDÉE
MITCHELL BEAZLEY
EN 1969

THE WORLD ATLAS OF Food

A GOURMET'S GUIDE TO THE GREAT REGIONAL DISHES OF THE WORLD

Contributing Editor
Jane Grigson

Contributors

Maggie Angeloglou
Lynne Reid Banks
James Beard
Wina Born
Don Brothwell
Alan Davidson
Rotraud Michael-Degner
J. Audrey Ellison
Norman Gelb
Rachel Grenfell
Attia Habibullah
Arto der Haroutunian

Hugh Johnson
Kenneth Lo
Anna Macmiadhachain
Anica Mitrović
Paul Norbury
Elisabeth Lambert Ortiz
Rita Palmer
Jane Tressider
Lucia van der Post
Mollie E. C. Webster
Alwyne Wheeler
José Wilson
Edna Wood

The World Atlas of Food
was edited and designed
by Mitchell Beazley Publishers Limited
14-15 Manette Street, London WIV 5LB

Editor	Glorya Hale
Art Editor	Ed Day
Technical Advisors	Diane F. Harris
	Helena Radecka
Assistant Editor	Rachel Grenfell
Editorial Assistants	Joyce Becker
	Susanna Courtauld
	Marsha Lloyd
Researchers	Gillian Abrahams
	Ursula Whyte

Designers	Susan Casebourne
	Pat Gilliland
	Sheilagh Noble
Art Assistants	Pauline Faulks
	Nicole Fothergill
	Roger Hall
	Gail Howell-Jones
Editorial Director	Bruce Marshall
Managing Editor	Frank Wallis
Cartographic Consultant	Harold Fullard
Office Co-ordinator	Ethel Bottomley

ISBN 0 85533 038 4

Printed in the Netherlands
by de Lange/van Leer B.V., Deventer

Contents

Introduction

THE WORLD ATLAS OF FOOD is designed to be a lively reference book, a culinary atlas and a great cook book, but, above all, it is the aim of those who created it—writers, artists and editors—to bring to you the excitement and the sheer sensual pleasure of fine food, good cooking and educated eating around the world.

Cooking is the most ephemeral of the arts. At its simplest, it makes you savour a wedge of ripe cheese or delight in the aroma and flavour of good bread. At its most splendid, it is represented by great dishes which draw upon knowledge and techniques which have taken centuries to evolve and develop.

Man has been cooking for more than a quarter of a million years. Even before this, our primitive ancestors were already experimenting with the wide range of fascinating tastes available to them in the wild. But what we have eaten and how we have eaten it, changed through the ages almost beyond recognition. The search for food has followed a path from the simple to the bafflingly complex, from hunting and the haphazard collection of edible plants to advanced technology and the lavishness of the gourmet spread.

When fire came into use, a new range of enticing tastes was first discovered and this encouraged further experimentation. While men concerned themselves with hunting, women were probably the main collectors of fruits, nuts, roots and other flavoursome plants. But whatever pleasures these Stone Age peoples derived from eating, they were limited by other deficiencies. They had no pottery, no flavourings, no opportunity to trade meat for salt or spices or coffee. And although there may have been the occasional taboos for magico-religious reasons, they could not be selective in their food.

Population growth began to change human eating habits profoundly about ten thousand years ago. Just as in modern times over-population has resulted in the need to explore the possibility of synthetic foods, so earlier it led to the beginnings of agriculture. The young mammal brought in live from the hunt was cared for and tamed. Wild seed, scattered accidentally, gave a modest harvest the next year.

By 5000 BC farming had begun to spread throughout the Old World and parts of the Americas. The pig, sheep and goat came under domestic control. Probably the cultivation of rice in eastern Asia and of barley and wheat in western Asia and Europe began equally early.

Villages and towns sprang up. The early farmers began to use pottery. Salt was mined and traded. Boiling, braising and salting gave new taste dimensions to mixtures of meats and plants. The early use of herbs and spices is lost in antiquity, but by the fourth century BC, they were sought as keenly as any treasure.

In Graeco-Roman times there were not only regional cooking traditions and dishes, but the beginnings of a literature on the subject. Apicus, for example, produced a Roman version of Mrs Beeton for the upper classes, which included the most elaborate of sauces. Those were days of exotic eating, days when even dormice were fattened for the table.

Although the dignitaries of much earlier times may have banqueted sumptuously, the classical world saw the spread of gourmet eating on a much more general scale. At last food was becoming an aesthetic experience, not just the means of maintaining life.

Food widened the horizons of commerce, it led to wars, played an important role in the building of empires and motivated the discovery of faraway lands. Yet, the sources of all great food and drink have never changed. *The World Atlas of Food* takes you to the gardens and orchards, the grain fields and pastures, the rivers, lakes and oceans, that provide the good ingredients of all cuisines.

Then, region by region, with the help of an unique cartographic format, we explore the world of food, the special features of geography, climate and culture that influence regional cooking. We discover the ways in which different cultures use the same foods and why certain foods and food combinations are so satisfying that they occur over and over again in countries, oceans and languages apart.

We pinpoint each major gastronomic area and the foods for which it is noted and describe the fascinating natural and historical influences that have led to the development of the great dishes of every cuisine. And we have selected more than five hundred outstanding recipes—from everyday fare to *haute cuisine*—so that you can readily duplicate these mouth-watering and distinctive dishes in your own kitchen.

The World Atlas of Food is dedicated to the gourmet traveller, the adventurous cook and to all those who want to heighten their understanding of food and their joy in eating.

THE EDITORS

An Epicurean Journey with James Beard

New York, my city, is in many ways the most fascinating gastronomic centre in the world. Everything I would want to eat is practically at my doorstep. From the market in Chinatown I get fresh ginger root, bean sprouts, winter melon, the freshest of fish, ducks lacquered brown with soy sauce. Bleecker Street is for Italian *cotechino*, freshly made pasta and bread. Over on First Avenue, the Polish stores sell *kielbasa*, ham loaf and huge round loaves of dark bread.

In the German markets of Yorkville, the pork stores bulge with *mettwurst*, *weisswurst* and *teawurst*, the confectioners sell marzipan, luscious pastries and *torten*. There are Greek stores on Ninth Avenue for *phyllo* leaves, Syrian and West Indian markets in Brooklyn, Indian stores on Lexington Avenue, the sprawling, cacophonous uptown Spanish-American market—just about every food you could think of within a small radius. Right around the corner from my house, my favourite neighbourhood store, the Jefferson Market, offers the best America can produce, from one coast to another.

New York excites. Here, one dines internationally, too. Hunger for *carpaccio* and tender *tortellini* takes me to Trattoria da Alfredo. The Coach House comforts me with American black bean soup and corn sticks, striped bass and asparagus, huge

double lamb chops, pecan pie and, my particular passion in desserts, bread-and-butter pudding. Hunan's fiery Chinese cooking suits another mood. Lutèce is all French elegance—pâté of pike and salmon, sweetbreads in the fashion of the chef, André Soltner. Quo Vadis serves a *bollito misto* more authentic than any you could find in Italy today. At Maxwell's Plum I munch a giant bacon cheeseburger and watch the activity at the bar.

What better springboard could there be than this from which to launch ourselves on a gastronomic odyssey that will take us across North America to the Far East, then to the Middle East, Europe and back home again? So come with me as we leave New York and head south.

We begin our explorations in America's greatest stronghold of traditional country food, the Pennsylvania Dutch region, with its Muscovy ducks, smoked sausage and Lebanon bologna. We pause at Betty Groff's farmhouse restaurant in Mount Joy, Lancaster County, for dinner at tables laden with country-cured ham, roast beef and chicken Stoltzfus, Harvard beets, sugar peas, tiny new potatoes, chow chow pickles and pepper relish and shoofly pie.

We turn north again—up the coast to New England for flounder on Nantucket, Cape Cod for sweet sea scallops and roast duckling at Chillingsworth-on-the-Cape. On to Maine for native lobsters from those icy waters, and farther north to Prince Edward Island and Nova Scotia for Malpeque oysters, more lobster, smoked salmon. Through Quebec, eating *tourtière* on the way. Back over the border for meat-stuffed pastries in the Copper Country of Michigan's Upper Peninsula. A stop at Harbor Springs, where enchanting miniature vegetables are grown for the summer tourist trade—a rarity in this country of giantism. Then

down to Detroit and a supper of spaghetti with oyster sauce at Lester Gruber's London Chop House with a California Pinot Chardonnay from the excellent wine list.

Over to Lena, Illinois, where they make a Brie that rivals that of France. On to Iowa, for the equally impressive Maytag Blue, and sweet-corn from those vast plains. Then to Minnesota for pike and Wisconsin for more cheese—Longhorn, a native Cheddar.

Down through Ohio and a stop at the Golden Lamb in Lebanon, near Cincinnati, for Shaker sugar pie. Then across the Ohio River to Louisville, Kentucky, home of wonderful, aged country hams, Bibb lettuce and America's own whiskey, bourbon.

Back to the Eastern shore for oysters and blue crabs in Virginia, south to Florida for mangoes, hearts of palm and those tiny oranges called calamondins. Dinner with friends in Palm Beach—stone crab, pompano, huge strawberries bathed in orange juice. In Tampa, we eat Spanish-American food at the Columbian. Then off to the South's most famous city, New Orleans, and oysters Rockefeller and crawfish bisque at Galatoire's, breakfast at Brennan's of *absinthe suissenesse* and eggs Sardou, shrimp Saki in the Caribbean Room of the Pontchartrain Hotel and a fried oyster sandwich in the French Quarter. A trip into Cajun country, Avery Island, where Tabasco is made, for crawfish, Tabasco fried chicken, fragrant Creole gumbo. Into the southern states to eat catfish-head soup and fried catfish with hush puppies.

A swing through Texas—Roquefort mousse and ham balls at Neiman-Marcus's Zodiac Room in Dallas. Over the border into Mexico. *Mole poblano* in Pueblo. The fantastic crush of people, colour, noise and vitality in Mexico City's Central Market, where stalls are heaped with tropical and subtropical fruits and vegetables. At Circolo

de Surestes we munch a *taco* and refresh ourselves with a tequila sour. A *seviche* bar proffers a dozen different kinds of lime-marinated fish.

Back across the border and through New Mexico to Colorado to eat Basque bread, lamb and mountain trout, wild coral mushrooms and cèpes. On to Idaho for lentils and the best baking potatoes in the world. Across the State of Washington—the famous Walla-Walla onions. Dinner at The Farm House on the northernmost tip of the Olympic Peninsula—fresh rockfish, superb Columbia River salmon, Pacific razor clams, Dungeness crab, originally from the village of Dungeness, but now to be found all up and down the coast.

A ferry ride to Seattle. On the waterfront is Pike Street Market, one of the last real farmers' markets in the United States, where there are precise arrangements of dewy fresh vegetables. Lunch is delicious at a little stand where we can order practically any fish on sale in the market, cooked to our liking.

On to Olympia for those fabulous tiny oysters, fast disappearing, to be enjoyed while they last. Then to the Oregon coast for sturgeon, fresh caviar and a dinner of crab thighs at Hara's in Seaside. Down to Newport for a bowl of Mrs Mo's razor clam chowder. Dinner with friends in Portland— rare wild duck, fresh apple sauce, a Cabernet Sauvignon, one of the new Oregon wines from around Roseburg.

Down into northern California for more Dungeness crab at Ondine in Sausalito. A trip to the Napa Valley to taste another superb Cabernet Sauvignon, Robert Mondavi's and Blanc Fumé and to sip the exquisitely light, dry blanc de blancs champagne made by Jack Davies of Schramsberg. Across to the Sonoma Valley and a visit to the Sebastiani winery with a stop in the old Spanish mission town of Sonoma for sourdough French bread from the bakery, which is even better than that in San Francisco, and Teleme and Monterey Jack from the cheese factory.

Next to San Francisco. Lunch at Jack's— sand dabs, rex sole, tiny bay shrimp dashed with home-made tarragon vinegar—a subtle contrast of flavours. To Chinatown for a special dinner prepared by chef Pui of Helen Kan's—barbecued lamb, Peking duck, glorious dishes made with clams and with crab.

9

A flight over the great fruit and vegetable valleys of California—vast panoramas of beds of tender green asparagus, hundreds on hundreds of acres of artichokes, uncountable heads of iceberg lettuce, the universal American salad ingredient, much maligned, but crisp and well-flavoured nevertheless. We are sucked into the whirling, spreading hugeness of Los Angeles, a city that seems to live on hamburgers. We prefer to dine on Mexican food in Olvera Street or oysters with fresh ginger at New Hung Far.

Up the coast, flying over the tuna fishers and over to Hawaii to breakfast on fresh ripe papaya and pineapple. We dine on the roof of the Hilton, the Pacific stretching away before us. We eat *lomi-lomi*, salt salmon massaged to a tender pulp, and that splendid local fish, *mahi-mahi*.

We whisk away to Japan for *sushi*, *sashimi*, *tempura*, the famous Kobe beef, prepared in so many ways, just one of them, *sukiyaki*, a profusion of game fish and birds. On a terrace overlooking a magnificent stone garden we eat game caught by falcons and prepared by Buddhist monks—vegetables and flowers cooked *tempura*-style in batter. Then to Kyoto and a restaurant near the Kabuki theatre for a remarkable and fascinating meal of but one thing—*tofu*, from the fresh white bean curd to the aged and amber-coloured, which has the bouquet of an old, matured cheese.

Off again to Hong Kong—the most enormous variety of restaurants with food in the style of every province of China, from the hot spiciness of Hunan and Szechwan to the subtleties of Canton and Shanghai. We try beggar's chicken, popular but much overrated. At the night market, where you can pick out your own snake, eel or dog, we sample a ragoût of snake and find it good. Chopsticks high, awash with Chinese wine, we blissfully anticipate the next stage of our gastronomic odyssey.

A long leap from Hong Kong and we touch down in Teheran. We feast on caviar—pressed caviar, fresh caviar from pink to delicate grey—on kebabs of sturgeon and lamb, on ripe apricots and cherries—fruits with an intensity of flavour almost forgotten, a sweet shock to the palate. Then to Beirut and baked *kibbe* and those seductive little appetizers called *mezze*. On to Istanbul—pistachio nuts, ripe figs, chicken with sauces of fruits or nuts, *döner kebab*—great mounds of lamb, revolving on a spit, thinly sliced, pinkly rare, tucked in an envelope of

pitta to eat right there on the street. More *mezzes* from little shops huddled in the bazaars and sips of sweet Turkish coffee.

On to Greece, where we eat *barbounia* grilled over coals with a touch of olive oil, lemon juice and oregano. We drink ouzo and nibble *mezedakia*—stuffed grape leaves, tiny, crisp fried whitebait, olives, *taramasalata*, little triangular pillows of flaky *phyllo* pastry stuffed with meat, with cheese, with spinach.

Another take-off and then we land in Rome. We dash to El Toula for soup of *cannolicchi*, little razor clams, to be picked from their shells and eaten with sips of the aromatic broth, a salad of blush-red *radiccio*. A halt in the Piazza Navona for the chocolate truffle at Tre Scalini, the richest of all frozen desserts. In the markets we buy zucchini blossoms for friends to put in a luncheon *frittata*.

Then on to Alba. It is the season for white truffles, completely unrelated in flavour to their black brothers. We sniff their strange, garlic-like odour in the air. We dine with friends who own truffle-producing land and eat home-made pasta, glossy with butter and perfumed with thin shavings of this unique tuber.

Off to Milan. Sensational pasta at Giannino's. We visit the famous bakeries and the *salumerias*. Here hang huge, spice-scented salami, each slice like a mosaic of rose and white marble. We glory in the Milanese hams and the creamily ripe, deeply blue-veined Gorgonzola.

We drive to Parma for one of the most famous of all hams—*prosciutto del Parma*, mild, sweet and delicate—for candied violets and the venerable Parmesan cheese. In Canterelli, a country restaurant, we lunch on ham, *risotto*, kid roasted to perfection and served with the tiniest fresh vegetables.

Bologna welcomes us with veal, turkey breast sautéed in the Bolognese fashion, pasta with the sauce of the city, *ragù Bolognese*. We press on to Venice, everyone's dream city. A sea bonanza of clams and mussels—*cannolicchi*, *cozze*, *telline*—*aragosta*, the spiny lobster, and the true *scampi* of the Adriatic. We lunch on the extraordinary sandwiches at Harry's Bar, nibble pastries in the Piazza San Marco, watching the world go by. We buy tiny red blood oranges in the fruit market. We savour a most unusual dish of pasta with a creamy sauce of tomato and *aragosta* on the terrace of the Gritti Palace. For the finale, we go to Al Graspo

de Ua, where we eat tiny wild strawberries, spiced with champagne vinegar, sugar and freshly ground black pepper, a fantastic and exciting combination of flavours.

From Venice on to Nice, still touched by the Italian influence. In the great market, a shadow of its former glory, but still a marvel, we spy enormous sheets of *pissaladière*, Provençal first cousin to *pizza*. We buy a slice of *socca*, that strange flat cake of chick-pea flour and oil that seems to exist nowhere but here. The fish market dazzles with undulating heaps of fish, freshly caught and glistening.

through France—the gourmet's paradise...

At La Coquille, in Cannes, we encounter the unforgettable, robust cooking of Provence—*soupe de poissons*, thick, aromatic, eaten with garlic-scented toast and grated Parmesan. A detour inland to Grasse—a glory of flowers in this perfume capital. Stalls in the farmers' market in the Place aux Aires spill over with vegetable still lifes—baby courgettes, their golden blossoms still intact; deep-purple aubergines; tiny, exquisite *haricots verts*; long strings of fresh garlic. *Charcuterie* tempts, we fall and buy a thick *tranche* of whole baby pig, stuffed with pâté and pieces of pork.

We lunch at the Moulin de Mougins—terrine of *rascasse* with a haunting undertone of lemon, thin slices of rare duck breast, the legs grilled separately, and fat asparagus, Charentais melons, the lightest of pastries

Back to Cannes and the Rue d'Antibes for the world's most magnificent *glacé* fruits—whole peeled melons, pineapples, apricots and figs—soft to the bite, intoxicating to the palate. Then off along the coast to Marseilles. The fish market is in the centre of town—shining piles of fresh sardines, anchovies, *rougets*, *daurades*. A great tumult of fishwives screaming their wares. We hurry our sharpened appetites to l'Escale at Carry-le-Rouet. M Berot prepares for us the greatest

bouillabaisse and *bourride* to be found in all Provence. We eat on a terrace overlooking the Mediterranean, relaxed in voluptuous languor.

We visit towered Carcassonne, Castelnaudary and Toulouse, the triumvirate of cities in Languedoc blessed with the lore of *cassoulet*, that inspired melange of beans, sausage, meats and *confit d'oie*. Close to Toulouse, we are in the country of Armagnac, a superb aged brandy, rough to the tongue, but a joy to the palate. At the Hotel de France in Auch we dine on grilled breast of duck, juicy and rare.

In Bordeaux we visit the great châteaux. We find the food overshadowed by the wines, except perhaps for *cèpes à la Bordelaise*, *pré salé* lamb, the Gironde caviar. Tradition rules here. Never is wine served with asparagus, with artichokes. Surprisingly, we find the honeyed frappé sweetness of Chateau d'Yquem a perfect foil for the caviar and for *foie gras*, better even than with dessert.

On to Cognac, stopping en route for oysters, mussels and periwinkles at La Rochelle. The food does not enchant, but we breathe the heady bouquet of old unblended Cognac and find the trip worth while.

Then to Tours. Loire salmon is on the menu Chez Barrier. With it we drink a fresh, brisk young Muscadet, the perfect partner for fish or *poulet d'Angevine*, chicken braised in the wine of the region. Up to Brittany we go for oysters, scallops and lobsters with Gros Plant, close to Muscadet, but a meatier wine. Turning our backs on the chic hotels of Deauville, we seek out the Sailor's Brasserie in Trouville. At tables covered with paper cloths, we eat the finest mussels.

Finally, we are in Paris. An extravaganza of food and restaurants. At Tour d'Argent we have featherlight *quenelles*, and eschew the famous pressed duck for one simply roasted. We are enraptured by Jean Senderens's skilful reconstructions of the noble dishes of other centuries at l'Archestrates—by the inventive cooking of Claude Peyrot at Vivarois. Lunch at Prunier—French caviar, oysters, *oursins*, all the great shellfish and fish.

In the Place Madeleine, the windows of Fauchon draw us—a fabulous still life. Inside there are displays of fruit from all over the world and a pride of pâtés. Across to the pastry shop to taste pastries and savouries and sip expresso at the counter. On the other side of the square, Hédiard offers Oriental foods, every kind of spice,

green peppercorns from Madagascar. Up-
stairs at Caviar Kaspia we sample a variety
of caviars with icy vodka, smoked eel,
borscht, freshly made blini.

We follow our noses to Androuet, the
world's greatest cheese shop. We dine on
cheese dishes, talk cheese with M Androuet,
sniff the tantalizing aromas from the cellars
—over five hundred varieties of cheese in all
stages of ripeness. A craving for sweets
takes us to the Boulevard St Honoré—
chocolates from Mary's, a Pithiviers from
the pastry shop of Le Notre. In Paris, eating
is exciting, inexhaustible.

Leaving the city of temptations we go
north to Strasbourg. *Choucroute* and beer,
foie gras en brioche at the Auberge de l'Ill—
local *eaux-de-vie*, the distilled soul of fruit—
the young, fresh Alsatian vines, as accom-
modating to hearty *charcuterie* as to suavely
sauced salmon. Across the Rhine to Baden-
Baden. Wild boar and wild berries from the
Black Forest at the Brenner's Park Hotel. A
jump to Holland to breakfast on cheese and
sausage and to seek out the street markets
where we buy delicious snacks of fresh
herring, smoked eel, little packets of crisp
fried potatoes with mustard mayonnaise.

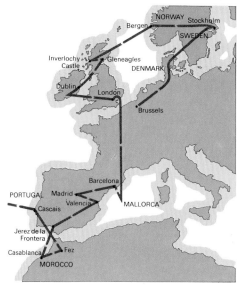

In the more refined atmosphere of Brussels we dine at Ravenstein on sole from the North Sea, *anguilles au vert*, the pieces of eel nestled in a deep-green sauce of herbs, and *rognons de veau à la Liegoise*, veal kidneys subtly flavoured with gin and juniper berries. We linger for the autumn Mushroom Fair, a great and glorious display of many curious and fascinating varieties.

We cross to Denmark to sample the excellent beer and hams, but for the greatest of *smörgåsbords* we must go to Sweden and the Opera Kellern, where Tore Wretman presides. We feast on the specially cured salmon, *gravlax*, sliced thin, fresh or grilled. In Norway, the fish markets of Bergen are bursting with cod—to be boiled with potatoes, accompanied by red wine. We acquire a liking for *lefka* and the Norwegian flatbread.

Making our way to Scotland we dine at Inverlochy Castle on local crayfish, Angus beef. We drink unblended straight-malt Scotch. At Gleneagles Castle we breakfast on finnan–haddie cooked with cream and a touch of tomato and on Arbroath smokies.

A quick trip across the sea to Ireland—Irish whiskey and stout in the pubs—superlative Galway Bay oysters and Dublin Bay prawns at Snaffles in Dublin.

London beckons—the splendours of the Covent Garden vegetable market, the straw-hatted porters of Billingsgate, insouciantly toting towers of fish-filled baskets on their heads. In Harrod's great Food Hall we linger in that most impeccable of all meat and game departments. Here are both French and English butchers, everything from pheasant, grouse and venison to the British banger—a pale, plump pork sausage.

Like New York, London eats internationally. Shezan in Knightsbridge serves perhaps the finest Indian food one can find anywhere. But for now we choose to revisit old haunts and new favourites where we can taste the best of Britain's produce. Bentley's plies us with Dover sole, prepared in innumerable ways. We go to the Savoy Grill for potted shrimp and Scotch smoked salmon, to Simpson's for roast sirloin and Yorkshire pudding, to the Berkeley for haddock mousse, to The Garden for *crudités*, baskets of hand-picked raw vegetables from nearby Covent Garden, to the grill room of the Capital Hotel for perfectly poached turbot and thin, thin slices of calves' liver wreathed with bacon.

Weekending with friends, we request an English tea—crumpets toasted in front of the fire and slathered with butter, scones with blackcurrant jam, mustard-and-cress sandwiches, maids of honour with their rich, almondy insides. For Sunday lunch we have that most time-honoured of sturdy British dishes, steak and kidney pudding.

Once again we feel the pull of the Mediterranean. We take flight for Mallorca and André Surmain's Foc i Fum to lunch on refreshing *gazpacho* and *poulet au vinaigre*.

Crossing to Barcelona, we seek out the Sole Antico in the old part of the city—suckling pig with *ailloli*, the Spanish version of this garlic-laden mayonnaise, a brilliant contrast to the crispness and softness of the pork. At Los Caracoles we eat snails, winkling them from their shells while the life of the city surges around us and follow them with *langosta*. We leave for Madrid. *Angulas*, baby eels sautéed in oil and garlic, at Botin—smoked swordfish at the Jockey with Marques de Riscal wines. Down to Valencia for the prototype of *paella*. On to Jerez de Frontera for sherry in the *bodegas* with *tapas* of olives, ham, cheese and *percebes*, those strangely bunched dark barnacles that look like a miniature elephant's foot.

Morocco is so near and irresistible. We fly across for *couscous* and *bstilla* at Al Mounia in Casablanca, a *tajine* of chicken and *mechoui* in Fez.

Portugal rounds out our odyssey. We eat lobsters steamed in seaweed at Cascais, pork with clams in the Alentejo, grilled sardines in Setubal, countless versions of *bacalhau* in the country *pousadas*. We picnic on local hams, bread, cheese and *vinho verde*. We go north for the matchless ports, south to the Algarve for those desserts, rich with eggs and sugar, on which the Portuguese dote.

So ends our gastronomic revels, a globe-circling trip that returns us to New York with much food for thought, tastes to be remembered, dishes to be reconstructed in the kitchen and a reinforcement of a long-held belief that the best of all ways to travel is on one's stomach.

Fish of the Deep

THE EVENING SUN catches the shore, while a white liner glides down the darkening waters of the Bosphorus from the Black Sea. The fish restaurant is simple, the proprietor eager as he presents a grilled *palamut*, young bonito, in which the savour of the sea is charcoal tinged. At such a moment it is excusable to think that the fish of the sea exist for man's pleasure and nourishment.

But fish supply food for each other on a far greater scale than they do for man. When the Third Fisherman in Shakespeare's *Pericles* marvels how the fishes live in the sea, the First Fisherman explains, "Why, as men do on land; the great ones eat up the little ones." The fish which we eat are only some of the links in a long chain which begins when the action of the sun produces phytoplankton in the sea. This nourishes zooplankton, on which some fish feed before being devoured by bigger fish, which in turn are devoured by still bigger fish. Man is by no means the only predator to draw nourishment from the sea, but he is becoming more and more exacting in the toll which he takes of marine resources.

Fish have always been an important source of protein for man. Once he had found means of preserving them and of sailing beyond the horizon to catch them, his harvesting of the seas began in earnest. But there were no fundamental changes from classical times until the nineteenth century, when the introduction of trawling, of railway transport and of canning produced a leap forward to a new pattern and scale in both fisheries and marketing. Now, in the twentieth century, we have taken another great leap, based on the new techniques of freezing, of ocean-going fleets and of air transport.

These new factors, together with the population explosion, imbalances in economic development around the world and regional differences in eating habits, are beginning to make the consumption of fish a global rather than a regional matter. The fisheries revolution is of interest to the gourmet, since it lifts the variety of fish available to him on to a new plane.

Since there are tens of thousands of species of fish in the seas, and hundreds of these are consumed by man in large quantities, this particular area of gastronomy might seem unmanageably large. Fortunately, the complications are less than one would think. Some important species, such as swordfish, tuna and bonito, range right around the world, and many of the great families are represented by closely related species in different parts of the world. The cod of the North Atlantic, for example, is matched by the cod of the North Pacific. The famous anchovy of the Mediterranean has numerous and abundant relations elsewhere, especially in South American waters.

The closeness of these relationships may be obscured by misleading vernacular names, which are due, in part, to the faulty ichthyological knowledge of early colonial settlers. Thus, what English settlers in South Africa called salmon and Dutch settlers called *kabeljou* (after the Dutch name for cod) is neither a salmon nor a cod, but a member of the family *Sciaenidae*, familiar in Australia as the jewfish or mulloway and in North America as croakers. Even when the names are not misleading, the differences between languages may baffle people. Many think that the famous rouget of the Mediterranean (the fish for which Romans in classical times paid the equivalent of more then twenty dollars a pound) is a Mediterranean speciality. But the same species, the red mullet, occurs in the Atlantic, as far north as southern England, and similar species, usually known as goatfish, are widely distributed in the Indo-Pacific region.

If such connections could be generally comprehended the results would be rewarding. In North America the anglerfish (goose-fish), for example, is not marketed. At best it goes to feed pets or to make fish meal. Yet in Venice the tail end of this same uncouth fish is highly prized as *coda di rospo*, and rightly so since it consists of admirably firm white flesh which might even pass for lobster.

The British eat fewer varieties of fish than people in the Mediterranean, and North Americans fewer than people in the Caribbean. This is partly because the colder waters contain relatively few species (although they often contain these in enormous quantities), while warmer waters have a proliferation of species. So it is not entirely fair to charge the northerners with being too conservative in their fish-eating habits. These have, after all, changed considerably over the centuries, partly as a result of changes in the available supplies.

It is reasonable to hope that in the future man will find a way of increasing many-fold the populations of the most delicious fish, of whatever kind.

John Dory

Halibut

Marine Miniatures

(*Left to right*), adult herring, pilchard, sardine, young herring, young sprat and anchovy are all tiny but tasty fish. Herring can be eaten fresh or cured in a number of ways. Pilchards, usually canned, are at their best when eaten fresh, but sardines—the same fish at a younger age—improve in flavour after canning in oil. Young sprats and young herring make up whitebait, best when fried and eaten as soon as they are caught. The anchovy, which the Ancient Greeks made into sauce, is today made into a paste or used in pizzas and salads.

Bass

Haddock

Swordfish

Red snapper

Sole

Herring

Winting

Bonito tuna

Turbot

The Japanese Tiger Fish

The most violent form of fish poisoning is produced by puffers or blowfish. Eating one which has not been properly prepared can be fatal. Yet some of these fish are delicious and many epicures in Japan, where they are known as *fugu,* regard them, particularly the *toro* (tiger) *fugu,* as the best fish of all. Eaten at a good restaurant, where proper care is taken to remove the liver and ovaries, the fish should be safe as well as delicious.

Mackerel

Dogfish

Shellfish and Unusual Seafood

At this New England clambake, the clams were buried in a pit. Lobster and sweet-corn were arranged on top, and everything was covered with a tarpaulin and steamed.

THE FISH of the deep share the seas and inland waters of the world with a remarkably diverse assortment of creatures upon which man has dined for a long time. Excavation of prehistoric sites has revealed that crabs, mussels and other shellfish graced man's meals well before he took to eating those meals off tables.

The first encounter with shellfish must have been on a beach or river bank where an ebbing tide left its deposit of molluscs, as it does today. Some time later, man daringly penetrated first shallow, then deep water to bring back inhabitants of swamps, estuaries and then oceans which tended to stay clear of the water's edge or surface. He discovered not only that they were good to eat, but that they had superb flavours and textures which could not be duplicated by the food of the land.

Today there is a virtually insatiable demand for many of the non-fish seafoods, particularly lobsters, shrimp, prawns, oysters and scallops. Octopus and squid are intrinsic elements of the cuisines of China, Japan, Southeast Asia and regions of the Pacific. They are popular as well, along with shellfish, in Italy, Spain and Portugal. The American clambake, which usually includes lobsters, is halfway between a feast and a festival.

Street stands and fishmongers throughout Britain offer fresh cockles, whelks and winkles by the pint, as well as jellied eel. In Paris, in the winter, fishmonger tables are set up outside better restaurants for the epicure to choose from a tantalizing display of clams, oysters, sea cucumbers and related appetizers, to begin a meal with style.

Non-fish seafood can be divided into two primary groups—the molluscs, including oysters, mussels, clams, octopus and squid, and crustaceans, which include lobsters, crawfish, shrimp and crabs.

The lobster (the regal *homarus americanus* of New England and its somewhat more modestly turned-out European cousin) is generally regarded as the king of crustaceans because of its lordly appearance, relative scarcity and substantial, firm, delicious white flesh. The main ingredient in a great number of special recipes (newburg, thermidor and *americaine* are among the best known), the lobster is so much in demand that the full resources of modern technology have been brought into play for lobster "farming" in America, France and other countries.

King James I of England is reported to have said, early in the seventeenth century, "He was a bold man who first swallowed an oyster." Such boldness evidently was contagious. Oysters were imported from Britain to satisfy a hunger for them in Ancient Rome. No less are they treasured in much of the world today, to such an extent that, like lobsters, oysters are specially cultivated in American, European, Japanese and Australian "beds".

There is no need, as yet, to establish "beds" or nurseries for crabs. They abound in great numbers, are comparatively easy to harvest and are, therefore, relatively cheap, although Alaskan king crab (sometimes called Japanese crab) and the giant crab of Tasmania are much prized. The American Atlantic blue crab and Pacific Dungeness crab are also deservedly popular. Nevertheless, crabs do not elicit the kind of devotion and appreciation in the West that they do in parts of Asia and Polynesia.

Probably because of their grotesque, tentacled appearance, squid and octopus have also failed to make much of an impression on the cuisines of North America and of Europe, except for the Mediterranean shore, but someone who has tasted the *polpetielli* of Naples or the *calamar* of Tarragona or the cuttlefish as it is prepared in any good Chinese restaurant is not likely to dismiss these cephalopods as too unpleasant in appearance to be consumed with pleasure. They are part of the huge relatively untapped resources of the ocean's deep, one of the great potential sources of food for the future.

The Major Shellfish

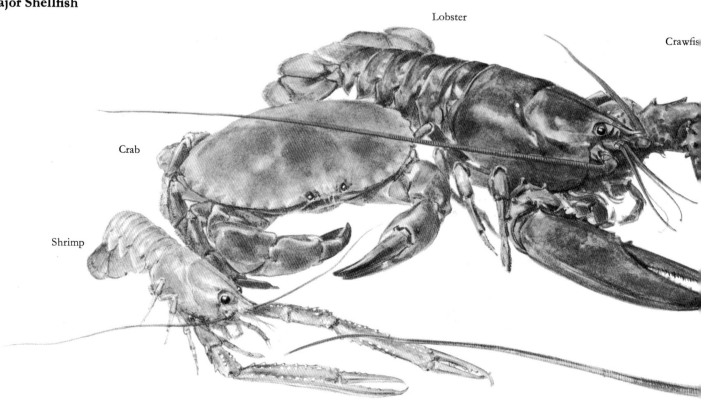

Lobster

Crawfis

Crab

Shrimp

Edible shellfish fall into four main classes. The crab (**1**) is a Crustacean, a class which includes lobsters, shrimp and crayfish. The scallop (**2**), like clams and mussels, is two-shelled, a Bivalve.

Gastropods cling to rocks on their stomachs and form beautiful shells. Only a few, like the whelk (**3**), are eaten. Squid (**4**), octopus and cuttlefish are shell-less, soft-bodied Cephalopods.

I

2

3

4

Unusual Seafood

The meat of the green sea turtle (*top*) is fatty and has a greenish tint. An excellent soup can be made from the meat, which can also be dried or smoked. The *figue de mer* (*centre*), a delicacy in France, is a leathery creature which lives attached to a rock. Only the inner yellow part, which looks rather like scrambled egg, is edible. The sea slug (*bottom*), also called sea cucumber or *bêche de mer*, is made into a popular dish in the Orient. Before it can be gutted, boiled and then dried.

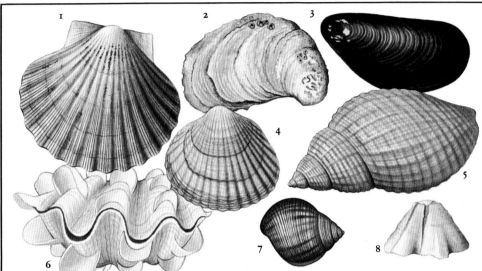

The shell of the scallop (**1**), a popular decorative motif since Roman times, was the emblem of pilgrims to the church of St James of Compostela. In France scallops are still known as *coquilles St Jacques*.
Oysters (**2**) were the food of the poor in nineteenth-century Europe. Today, oysters are an expensive delicacy, usually eaten raw or smoked. Oysters Rockefeller, a New Orleans speciality, or a classic English oyster stew are two excellent oyster dishes.
Mussels (**3**) are regarded by many to be the poor man's shellfish of today, an unfortunate mistake. The French appreciate the pleasant sweetness of the mussel and use them in soups, stews and salads.
Cockles (**4**) are often referred to as poor man's oysters. Like oysters, they are delicious eaten raw, and, they can also be cooked in soups and stews.

Whelks (**5**) are usually used by fishermen as bait for other fish, although they can be made into a tasty soup.
Clam shells (**6**) were used as a currency by American Indians. One of the most versatile of shellfish, clams can be eaten raw or fried, or they can be made into stews, soups, sauces and the traditional clam chowder.
Winkles or periwinkles (**7**) can be prepared like any other shellfish, but they are usually eaten raw. A straight pin is used to extract the tiny fish from its spiral shell. The fish is dipped into a spicy sauce and swallowed whole.
Limpets (**8**) usually fix themselves solidly to rocks. If they can be pried away, the flesh can be used to make a delicately flavoured soup.

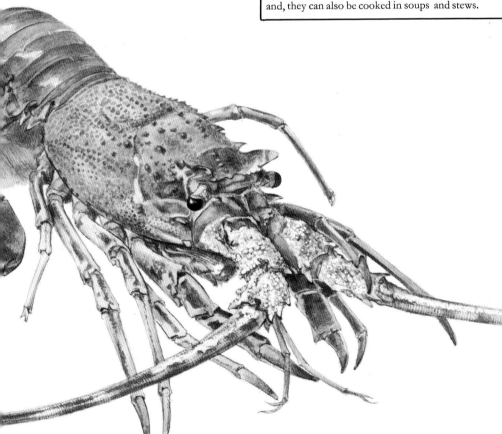

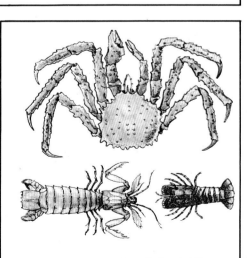

The king crab or Kamchatka crab, *Paralothides camschatica* (*top*), is fished off the shores of the North Pacific and is canned on a large scale. The mantis shrimp, *Squilla mantis* (*left*), and the French delicacy *petite cigale*, *Scyllarides latus* (*right*), each provide the base for an excellent soup. The *cigale* can also be prepared and served like lobster, if it is large enough.

Fish of Ponds and Rivers

CARP BONES have been recovered by archaeologists from Stone Age sites in Greece, pike skeletons have been found in Danish peat bogs with bone arrowheads embedded in them and sturgeon remains have been recovered from sixth-century sites at Lake Ladoga, near the Baltic. These finds all date from the hunter-fisher stage of human development, when fresh-water fish provided a vital source of food for people living in inland areas.

The appreciation of fresh-water fish as a delicacy, however, is largely a development of northern America and Europe, mainly because the Northern Hemisphere is inhabited by some of the best food fish known to man. The salmon family, for example, which includes the trout, char and whitefish, as well as the salmons, is naturally distributed across the Arctic and temperate regions of the Northern Hemisphere. And sturgeons, while best represented in Europe and the Black Sea basin, also occur in North America.

Other parts of the world, while lacking these well-known food fish, have native species of high quality. The whitebait of New Zealand rivers, juveniles of various *Galaxias* species, are a seasonal delicacy,

and a native perch of Australia, the callop or golden perch, is an excellent food fish. The fresh waters of both New Zealand and Australia have also been enriched by such non-native species as trout and carp.

The carp is one of the best-known fresh-water fish delicacies, particularly esteemed in Europe and Asia. It belongs to a family which numbers about fifteen hundred species, and although many are small, there are also some huge ones, among them the delicious *pla kaho*, a ten-foot-long inhabitant of the rivers of Thailand and Indochina. In North America, although carp are well represented in terms of numbers of species, they are mostly small and of little culinary importance.

The most highly regarded fresh-water food fish of Africa are the cichlids, perch-like fish known as breams in southern Africa.

It is ironic that the Northern Hemisphere, which once had the greatest wealth of fresh-water fish, has also been the scene of its greatest destruction. Many fresh-water species, such as the Atlantic and European sturgeons, have been overfished, so that they are rare where they once abounded.

The Atlantic salmon has shown a dramatic decline during the twentieth century, due partly to overfishing, but also to industrial pollution.

To some extent, the worst consequences of this have been overcome by restocking rivers with young fish raised from the egg in hatcheries, or by fish farming. Fish farming has long been practised in Asia, where various fish are raised to an edible size in small ponds enriched with animal waste, or as a by-product in paddy fields. Although the Western world was relatively late in starting, great progress has been made in the intensive culture of fish for the table.

In Europe and elsewhere, carp have been widely cultured, especially in the warmer inland regions, for marketing at around their third summer, when they weigh about three pounds. Carp are relatively tolerant of water quality, do not require large quantities of water, and are thus ideal for farming in relatively natural conditions.

Members of the salmon family, on the other hand, require large quantities of cool, clean, well-oxygenated water and are rather

Lake trout
Powan
Brown trout
Sockeye salmon
Inconnu
Rainbow trout
Perch
Large-mouth black bass
Mirror ca
Chub
Burbot
Golden perch
Char
Dolly Varden trout
Brook trout
Bream

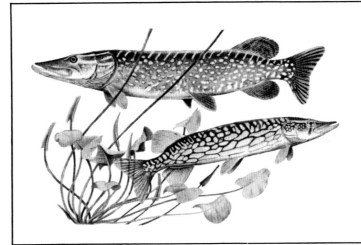

Pike—Ancient Carnivore

Pike are members of the ancient family *Esocidae,* the oldest surviving species of fish. They thrive equally well in lakes and in rivers. A vicious carnivore, the pike is often ignored as a food fish, but in some countries, particularly in France, its firm white flesh is considered a delicacy.

more difficult to rear. Within recent years, however, the right techniques have been developed. Whitefish, brown trout, brook trout and, in particular, rainbow trout, are now reared successfully either for release into natural lakes for later capture, or for rearing to table size in concrete ponds.

The delicious small fresh-water crayfish is also reared in captivity and fished commercially in Europe, North America and Australia. Unfortunately, the native European species was severely affected by a fungal disease in the nineteenth century, and although an American species was introduced, it is smaller and of poorer quality.

Fresh-water eels are found in all the temperate regions of the world except for South America and the western parts of North America. All the known species are fine food fish with rich, oily flesh which is particularly delicious when it is smoked. In Japan, the culture of eels has been raised to a fine art and large numbers are also captured each year in parts of Europe. On the whole, however, eels remain one of the most underexploited fresh-water delicacies of the world.

The Carp Family

The carp, a fine food fish, is found all over the world. Carp, which thrive in small lakes and do not require very clean water, can also survive for a long time out of water, thus ensuring freshness at the market. In Japan, the golden carp is a symbol of masculine strength. The carp's courage in struggling upstream to spawn is admired greatly, and it is believed that some of this bravery is acquired when the flesh is eaten.

Only the tribulations, wanderings and nostalgia of Odysseus can compare with the saga of the salmon, which will travel up to 3,000 miles from the sea back to the stream in which it was spawned.

The salmon is known by various names during the stages of its life cycle. When it emerges from the egg it is called a fingerling. In two years it reaches a length of six inches and is a parr.

Making its way downstream it grows into a smolt, and lingers in the estuary before setting out into the ocean as a grilse. There it matures into a salmon.

Within four years, having fully matured, the salmon returns. It navigates by the sun until it reaches its home river, which it recognizes by the smell. It takes no food during the journey upstream, and it will exhaust itself leaping over any obstacle in its path.

After the eggs have been laid by the female and fertilized by the male, the salmon turns dull grey and is known as a kelt. Most salmon die after spawning, with only a few returning to the sea and undertaking the journey again.

Fish–Smoked, Dried and Cured

It is still a necessity in the hot climates of the Orient to preserve fish. A fish seller in Singapore (*below*) displays several varieties of dried fish. In Southeast Asia, (*top right*), fish are spread out on bamboo mats on poles over the water to sun-dry. In the West, modern methods of refrigeration have made it unnecessary to preserve fish, but they are considered a delicacy. To smoke salmon (*bottom right*) the fish are suspended over a slow-burning wood fire.

FISH, an important part of the human diet, and its major component in some places, is highly perishable. For storage, it has to be preserved against the putrefying ravages of even brief periods of time. Consequently, since prehistoric times, methods for its preservation have been devised.

Today, fish can be most efficiently preserved by canning or freezing. Older techniques of preservation are, however, very much in use not only in parts of Africa and Asia where modern methods are not readily accessible, but also in other places where they are maintained largely because of desired taste sensations which they produce. Salted dried cod, for example, has a wide appreciative market in southern Europe. Smoked salmon is one of the unparalleled delicacies of Europe and North America. Bombay duck, a dried fish called *bombil*, is an inexpensive source of protein and is extensively eaten in India. Dried shark's fin, or sawfish fin, is the key ingredient of the Chinese speciality, shark's fin soup.

Having extracted fish from water, man discovered that one of the simplest ways of preserving it was to extract water from fish. Water is essential to life, including the life of the bacteria which are responsible for fish spoilage. When the water content is removed, or sharply reduced, most of the destructive bacteria are removed as well. Fish with a low fat content and which are thin or capable of being opened flat can be dried in the sun or the wind.

Often, however, the elements alone cannot do the job adequately and a salting process must be employed. The preservative powers of salt were well known to the Ancient Egyptians who used it, among other things, for embalming, as well as for food preservation. By the time the Roman Empire had stretched across the Mediterranean, there was already a brisk trade in salted fish. Many subtle techniques of salting fish were lost during the Dark Ages after the collapse of the Roman Empire. In Europe, people resorted to the laborious and expensive method of stuffing fish into barrels of salt to preserve them, a practice permitted to lapse when it was apparent that fish would last equally well when coated with salt.

The requirements of Lent, when Christians abstained from meat, dramatized the importance of salted fish. With the growing availability of salt, there developed a massive inland market in the pre-Easter period, a market which today relies mostly on frozen fish.

Salting and drying methods are often used to supplement each other, but even together they are insufficient to preserve fatty fishes, for which only smoking and pickling, among the old techniques, suffice.

The discovery of the smoking process was probably completely fortuitous. Very likely, a fish was suspended over a smoky fire to be cooked or dried and, wonder of wonders, it developed an intriguing new flavour. Although smoking is a very effective means of preserving fish, today smoked salmon, sturgeon, trout, kippers, eels and other fish are in great demand because of the flavour imparted to them in the smoking process, rather than because they have been preserved by that process.

Smoking fish is an elaborate art. The quality of the finished product is influenced by, among other things, the type of wood used. Shavings and sawdust of hardwoods generally produce a gentler flavour than soft woods. Peat is sometimes added to sawdust to get a somewhat more pungent taste. Some "smokers" are partial to cedar, juniper, eucalyptus and other special woods which contribute their own special flavours.

Like smoking, the method of preserving by pickling is used almost exclusively for fatty fish. To remove it from contact with air, the fish is immersed in brine, or in a marinade of vinegar and salt to which various spices can be added. Bismarck herring and roll-mops are pickled in a vinegar brine spiced with black pepper, mustard seed and sliced onions. Pickling has a "cooking" effect on the fish, tenderizing it, as well as preserving it and giving it a strong, distinctive flavour.

The Major Preserved Fish

Fish can be preserved by pickling, drying or smoking. Herring are preserved in many different ways. With the exception of the smoked haddock (**11**), this selection of fish shows some of the varieties of preserved herrings. They include dried undyed kipper (**1**), smoked red herring (**2**), pickled roll-mops (**3**), smoked and ungutted bloaters (**4**), Bismarck herring fillets (**5**), whole pickled herring (**6**), dried dyed kipper (**7**), salted *matjes* herring (**8**), cured and smoked buckling (**9**) and smoked golden herring (**10**).

Caviar and Other Roes

Sevruga, the smallest sturgeon, yields the smallest grained caviar.

Salmon caught during their sea-going phase yield large red eggs.

The roe of the Osetrova sturgeon may be grey or, very rarely, golden.

White roe from the whitefish or lumpfish is dyed to resemble caviar.

Grey Beluga caviar is of high quality equal to that of the black caviar.

Pressed caviar is made from the damaged eggs of various sturgeons.

The finest caviar is the large black eggs of the giant Beluga sturgeon.

Golden salmon roe is taken from salmon caught in fresh water.

The roes most commonly eaten are those of *(top to bottom)* lumpfish, salmon, sturgeon, grey mullet and cod.

Hard roe from the female cod is smoked or made into cod-roe pâté.

Smooth, creamy soft cod's roe is the sperm of the male fish.

Roe from the grey mullet is used in *taramasalata* and pressed into *Boutargue*.

Strange Delicacies

STRANGE DELICACIES always belong to somebody else, to another nation or to past history. While they seem odd to outsiders, to the society which enjoys them they are often no more than rare or expensive dishes. Today, when people travel freely and widely, strangeness is qualified. People who would have, for example, scorned snails and frogs' legs only ten years ago, now eat them as a pleasurable treat.

Sometimes strange-seeming delicacies are part of the culinary repertoire of a small section of society. Hedgehogs, for example, which are said to taste like suckling pigs, are much appreciated by the gypsies of Britain. They bake them in clay or roast them over a fire. The former method is more practical as the spines and skin adhere to the clay and peel off with it when the hedgehog is cooked. Hedgehogs should never be killed for food: they do a useful job keeping down the insect population. But many of these creatures are hit by fast cars as they amble off to their winter quarters, or take a nap on the sun-warmed roads, and these are the ones to take home for an experimental supper.

In Australia, sugar ants are regarded as a delicacy by the Aborigines. A type of ant called *melophorus inflatus*, or swollen honey-bearer, stores so much honey in its belly that it swells up to the size of a grape. The belly is bitten off and is said to have a strong, sweet flavour with a hint of tartness.

Kangaroos provide Australians with another delectable dish. The tail is chopped into pieces, marinated and made into a rich ragoût or soup. In the outback, kangaroo legs are boiled or roasted.

Camel meat has always been popular with the Arabs. Although most parts of the camel may be eaten, it is the hump and the feet of the young animal which delight desert gastronomes. The hump is usually marinated, then roasted. The feet are cooked in the same way as calves' feet and should be served with a vinaigrette sauce.

In the past, cocks' combs threaded on to *attelets*, ornamental skewers, were used by French chefs to decorate dishes for grand dinners. *Crêtes de coq* are still used to garnish meat dishes in expensive French restaurants, although *attelets* are no longer fashionable. Cocks' combs, either plain or stuffed with forcemeat, *foie gras* or a vegetable purée, can also be coated with egg and breadcrumbs, fried and served as hot *hors d'oeuvre*. They should be brought to the table sandwiched between two grilled mushrooms and placed on a slice of fried bread.

Snails are undoubtedly the most renowned French delicacy. The tradition of eating these rubbery creatures goes back as far as the Middle Stone Age, when the people of the Pyrenees devoured them by the thousand. Two varieties of snails are eaten: the prized and beautifully marked *Helix pomatia*, or *gros Bourgogne*, which grows fat on a diet of vine leaves, and the smaller *Helix aspersa*, or *petit gris*, the common garden snail of France, England and North America. Either type may be used to make the best-loved snail dish, *escargots à la bourguignonne*, which comes to the table on a dimpled plate, sizzling with garlic butter.

Frogs' legs are generally thought to be a particularly French dish, but since the Second World War they have become more and more popular in North America, England and the rest of Europe. Often the deep-frozen frogs' legs in speciality grocery shops will have come originally from eastern Europe or Turkey. The hibernating frogs are sent from all over the world to Luçon in the Charente. (Local frogs ran out twenty years ago from a mixture of enthusiasm and bad frosts.) The legs are cut off in one piece above the thigh muscle, skinned, trimmed and spiked on to wooden skewers for local sale, or frozen for re-export. They are quick to cook and have a delicate flavour, reminiscent of good chicken. A creamy, rich sauce is usually served with them.

In Guinea and Central and South America, iguana meat is sautéed, then casseroled; it is considered a gastronomic treat by local gourmets. Only the back of this tree-loving lizard is eaten.

Rook pie is an old English dish. Today in Britain it can be tasted only when an irate farmer, seeing his crops being ruined by a flock of rooks, takes out his gun and brings back half a dozen of the great pompous birds for the cooking pot. Only the breasts are eaten; the rest of the meat is too bitter and tough. The breasts, with slices of onion and sherry-flavoured gravy, are put between two thick slices of steak and the pie is covered with a pastry crust.

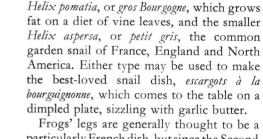

For centuries, bear paw and steak have been highly prized in China, Russia and eastern Europe. Bear meat is difficult to obtain now, but a recipe for cooking bear paws in a modern Romanian cook book gives instructions for removing the hair and skin with hot water and a knife. The paws are then simmered in stock, boned, stuffed with mushrooms and chopped ham and baked. The skimmed stock is flavoured with

Some of the world's most exotic foods are gathered together at Monsieur Corcellet's shop in Paris. Customers are greeted by four painted figures representing Chinese, Mexican, African and Indian nationalities, who hold our baskets of their specialities. Moroccan sweetmeats, called *courabies,* candied fruits, and little Chinese cakes are displayed on the counter. But the real oddities, for example, braised elephant's trunk, which tastes like ox tongue and is served with a parsley vinaigrette, python, pale and bland like chicken, and crocodile, prepared according to a crab recipe, are in the deep-freeze. Before cooking each animal, M Corcellet reflects and experiments in the kitchen behind his shop.

port and made into a sauce. Bear meat can be made into an excellent pâté. Smoked bear hams taste similar to Parma ham and, like this famous Italian speciality, can be eaten raw. The flavour of the lean meat is beefy. Grizzly bear is best avoided as its meat is coarse by comparison with that of the European brown bear, the polar bear and the American black bear.

The Chinese also favour the distinctive tastes of a fruit-eating wild cat, sharks' fins and birds' nests from which they make soup. Bewildered Westerners, tasting birds' nest soup for the first time, wonder where the twigs have gone. In fact the nests are those of swiftlets, who lay their eggs on a soft bed made from their own saliva. Recipes for making this fine soup begin by advising the cook to remove dust and feathers from the nests. Today, however, in Singapore and Hong Kong, the translucent, noodle-like nests can be bought commercially.

Thousand-year eggs are enjoyed in China, too. The eggs are covered with a mixture of salt, ashes and lime and buried in the ground for months, not years.

Locusts, the destructive insects of Asia and Africa, are said to taste like shrimp and are traditionally eaten with wild honey. According to the Bible, St John the Baptist lived on them when he was wandering in the desert. Today they are fried in butter with a little garlic.

Elephant meat is said to be tough, but the trunk and feet are recommended. M Corcellet sells cooked elephant's trunk in his shop in Paris. The feet should be skinned, boned, chopped into pieces, then cooked for ten hours with a few slices of ham, some onions, spices, garlic, stock, Madeira wine, port and green peppers.

Horsemeat has a rich taste, similar to that of beef when it has been properly hung. In Europe, many people are reluctant to try it, but early man had no such inhibitions. Thousands of bones of wild horses, which were chased over the cliffs, then eaten by Stone Age man, were excavated at Solutré, in France.

For a long time the Germanic inhabitants of the north feasted regularly on horse, and until about the eighth century in England, and later in Scandinavia, it was the sacramental dish for Viking festivals.

To the early Christian missionaries, however, eating horse was a reminder of unpleasant activities, including human sacrifice, at pagan feasts. So strong were the prohibitions from every pulpit that the taboo has outlived the situation.

Horsemeat was not in favour again until the nineteenth century, when, because of the poverty in the growing cities, public-spirited men began to organize banquets in Europe to show how delicious it really was.

By 1850 the Germans, Austrians and Belgians were eating horsemeat. The French turned their culinary talents to the matter, too. In 1868, several Englishmen, who had attended the horse banquets invited French chefs to London, where they prepared a sensational feast which included horse consommé, terrine of horse liver and roast fillet of Pegasus. The piece de resistance was a two hundred and eighty pound baron of horse, preceded by fanfare and carried in on the shoulders of four cooks.

Horsemeat never caught on in England, however, but in France and Belgium horsemeat shops, each with a gold-painted rocking-horse head over the door, are to be found everywhere. The meat is more expensive than pork and almost as expensive as beef.

Beef and Veal

MOST BREEDS OF CATTLE can be traced back to the wild *Bos primigenius*, the cattle that were hunted with such purpose and passion by Stone Age man, and which he painted on the walls of the caves at Lascaux. Judging from these cave paintings, some of the early cattle were spotted and others had a streak of white along their backs. All of them were powerful, yet their descendants include not only the tiny Kerry cows and the white Chillingham cattle of Northumberland, but also the stocky Herefords, Shorthorns, Holsteins and Charolais and the douce, cream-coloured cattle of Normandy.

The wild Lascaux beasts with their curved horns look more like such mythical creatures as the Minotaur of Crete, or the king of bulls, Zeus himself, who took Europa on his back from Tyre to Crete. The bull is a regal animal and beef is considered by many to be the best meat.

For centuries, the finest beef cattle in Europe have been raised in England. Sadly, it is now almost impossible to buy properly hung first-class beef in the shops, for most of it goes to restaurants and hotels, or is exported.

In the United States, however, it is a different story. Perhaps because Americans have always relished their meat, beef, which for years has been their first choice, is well-hung and full of flavour, and the shops offer not just the vast, juicy steaks that astound and overwhelm visitors from abroad, but also many cuts that are not seen in other parts of the world.

Australians also eat more beef than any other meat. Having inherited habits and tastes from their British ancestors, they enjoy roast beef and Yorkshire pudding. Carpetbagger steak, the steak slit and stuffed with oysters, is a more original Australian dish.

Cattle were first brought from Europe to the Argentine in the sixteenth century by the invading Spaniards. Since then, the lush, humid, vast pampas has produced top-quality beef that not only satisfies the home market (the meat-loving Argentinians eat beef several times a day) but also has become the country's most important export.

Unfortunately, many cooks in England and America neglect the offal or variety meats. Few cook tongue, for example, preferring to buy it ready sliced for sandwiches and salad meals, which is the least satisfactory way of using it. Tongue with black cherry sauce or prune and raisin sauce makes a much better meal. Tripe receives an even poorer reception, although in Caen and in Florence it is sensibly elevated to the status of a regional classic.

Britain's long-established claim to being the greatest beef-producing country may today be disputed by farmers in France, America, Japan and Argentina, but it is doubtful whether any of their meat can come up to the standard of Scottish Angus beef when it has been properly hung and lightly cooked. At least it must be recognized that the English word "beefsteak" has firmly niched itself into the languages of the two European countries most famed for their cooking. The Italians have softened the sound to their graceful *bistecca*, and the French have talked about *biftek* at least since the early eighteenth century.

The cow, sheep and pig are the world's major food animals. A country's meat consumption is related to its standard of living, and high meat consumption usually indicates a high per capita income. Religious beliefs, particularly taboos against eating pork, as well as tradition, influence which animals are raised for food, as does the availability of grazing land for cattle. People in countries without sufficient grazing land tend to eat more pork and lamb. This chart is a proportional representation of the beef, lamb and pork consumption in pounds per person per year in various countries. Australia, where each person eats an average of 282 pounds of meat, has the highest overall annual consumption, while India, where only 1.5 pounds of meat are eaten per person yearly, has the lowest.

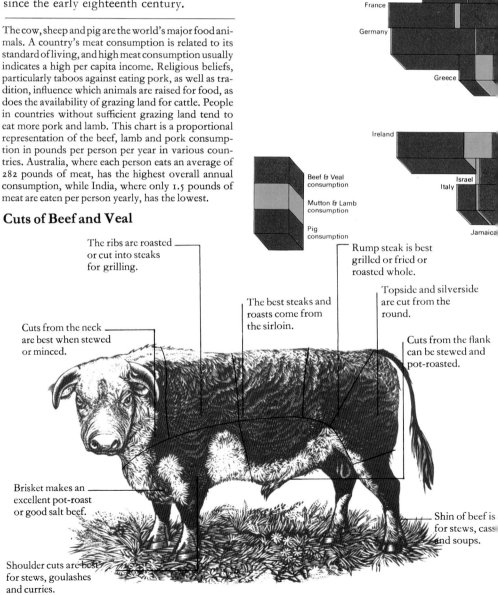

Beef & Veal consumption

Mutton & Lamb consumption

Pig consumption

Cuts of Beef and Veal

The ribs are roasted or cut into steaks for grilling.

Rump steak is best grilled or fried or roasted whole.

The best steaks and roasts come from the sirloin.

Topside and silverside are cut from the round.

Cuts from the neck are best when stewed or minced.

Cuts from the flank can be stewed and pot-roasted.

Brisket makes an excellent pot-roast or good salt beef.

Shin of beef is for stews, cass and soups.

Shoulder cuts are best for stews, goulashes and curries.

Argentina
Australia
Austria
Belgium-Luxembourg
Canada
Caribbean Islands
Central America
Denmark
Finland
France
Germany
Greece
Ireland
Israel
Italy
Jamaica

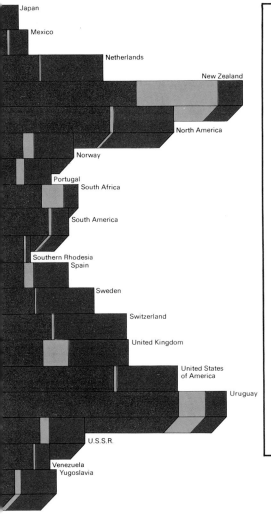

Japan
Mexico
Netherlands
New Zealand
North America
Norway
Portugal
South Africa
South America
Southern Rhodesia
Spain
Sweden
Switzerland
United Kingdom
United States of America
Uruguay
U.S.S.R.
Venezuela
Yugoslavia

Kobe Beef

Until the middle of the nineteenth century, the Japanese, like all strict Buddhists, were vegetarians, although fish was permitted as a concession to human frailty. It is surprising, therefore, that one of the country's most famous dishes should be *sukiyaki*, simmered beef with soy sauce, and that some of the world's finest cattle should be raised at Kobe and Matsuzaka. The animals are fattened with beer and massaged so that the lean meat is marbled with flecks of fat and is, therefore, tastier and more tender.

The oldest recognized breed of beef cattle, as well as the largest and heaviest, is the Italian Chianina. The Tuscans bred them in ancient times for sacrificial animals, and the meat was eaten only by the priests. Bred today for their enormous size, they grow rapidly and are slaughtered at a much younger age than other cattle. The finest French beef comes from the white Charolais cattle, named for the region of Burgundy where the breed originated. Always fed on grass, their meat is unusually lean and much prized for tender *Chateaubriands* and *filets mignons*. Red and white Hereford cattle are the nineteenth-century result of generations of breeding by farmers in Hereford, England. Introduced in the United States, Canada, South America and Australia, Herefords are now a major source of the world's beef supply.

The Tenderest of Meat

VEAL, palest pink and firm, is the meat of milk-fed young calves, killed between two and three months old. The Austrians, Germans, Italians and French are the world's great veal cooks. Italians also eat *vitellone*, which means big veal, young beef which is just past the milk-fed stage.

Veal is a delicacy, an expensive meat. This applies not only to the fine escalopes and cutlets, but also to the liver, sweetbreads and kidneys, which are better flavoured and more tender than those of other animals. Veal has no poor cuts. With the head, the French make a splendidly succulent dish, *tête de veau vinaigrette*. Even the shin, considered a lowly part of the carcass, can be turned into a superb dish like the Milanese *osso buco*, which means hollow bones. Thick slices are cooked upright, so that the marrow does not fall out, in a rich tomato sauce. The dish is sprinkled with chopped lemon peel, parsley and garlic and served with a *risotto* of plump Italian rice.

Veal bones are prized for the jellied stock which can be made from them. Stewing pieces can be turned into a savoury veal *marengo*, or a *blanquette*, its cream sauce flavoured with mushrooms and onions. The Germans and Austrians have even devised an appetizing dish from veal lungs, *kalbs-beuscherl*. But the most popular part of the animal will always be the thin and tender escalopes, called *schnitzel* in Germany and *scaloppini* in Italy.

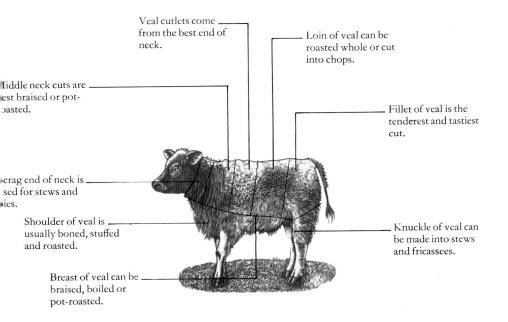

Veal cutlets come from the best end of neck.

Loin of veal can be roasted whole or cut into chops.

Middle neck cuts are best braised or pot-roasted.

Fillet of veal is the tenderest and tastiest cut.

Scrag end of neck is used for stews and pies.

Shoulder of veal is usually boned, stuffed and roasted.

Knuckle of veal can be made into stews and fricassees.

Breast of veal can be braised, boiled or pot-roasted.

Lamb and Mutton

Scrag end of neck can be used for braising or in stews and soups.

Cuts from the middle neck are braised or stewed.

Best end of neck is usually braised or stewed.

Saddle of lamb makes an excellent roast.

Loin of lamb can be cut into chops or roasted whole.

The shoulder can be boned and rolled or roasted whole.

Breast of lamb is usually boned and stuffed before roasting.

Leg of lamb is roasted whole or cut into cubes for kebabs.

THE PEOPLE OF THE MIDDLE EAST have always prized lamb above all other meat. Their methods of cooking lamb were brought across the world by conquering armies and returning crusaders. A Middle Eastern innovation, the cooking or serving of lamb with mint is now a Western tradition.

Throughout the Middle East, lamb is cooked with fruit. Lamb and apricots, for example, is an especially pleasing combination of flavours. The fruit is chopped into a stuffing or made into a sauce which is poured over the meat. Apples, quinces, cherries, cranberries or prunes are included in many Moroccan and Persian lamb dishes.

Shish kebab, pieces of lamb threaded on skewers and cooked over an open fire, is a dish that was brought to the West from Turkey. It is said to have been created during the Ottoman Empire by Turkish soldiers who impaled their meat on their swords and cooked it over open fires. Often, today, to add to the flavour and to ensure that the lamb is tender, it is marinated for several hours in a mixture of lemon juice, herbs and spices before it is cooked.

The *döner kebab* is another popular Middle Eastern method of cooking lamb. In Turkey, a boned and marinated leg is placed on a vertical spit. The heat from the fire roasts the outside of the leg, the spit is stopped, thin slices of meat are carved, then the cooking continues and the operation is repeated until the whole piece of meat has been roasted and served. In other parts of the Middle East, *döner kebab* is made with thin slices of lamb compressed around the vertical spit and cooked and sliced off in the same way.

To the French, lamb is a luxury. They like their roasts to be served delicately pink at the centre. *Navarin printanier*, lamb stewed with early spring vegetables, is a favourite Easter dish. Such a dish needs skilful handling and care, for it can be rendered tasteless. In the hands of a good French chef, however, spring lamb is a delight, particularly the milk-fed lamb from Pauillac. The Romans appreciate suckling lamb, too. They make an Easter dish called *abbacchio*, lamb flavoured with rosemary.

Some of the most delicious-tasting lamb is found on the French Atlantic coast, in Mont Saint Michel, Normandy and, in particular, in Brittany and the Charentes.

Here is the best of *pré-salé* lamb, the finest of lamb, which grazes on the green, sea-tasting grass of the salt-marshes.

This is the lamb which goes so well with laver bread, the Welsh seaweed and oatmeal speciality, or with the oyster, anchovy and crab stuffings of the eighteenth century. In England, the fatter valley lamb was served with mint from the streams. The finer-flavoured mountain lamb or good mutton was set off by redcurrant jelly or a mild onion sauce.

The French consider that beans are the best accompaniment for lamb. They serve the small, truly stringless varieties of green French beans in the summer, pale green flageolets in the later summer and autumn, dried white haricot beans in the winter.

The Chinese have never really taken to lamb, although generations of Mongols, who were great herdsmen, ruled the country from the time of Kublai Khan. Chinese cooks did, however, adapt some of their conquerors' lamb dishes, creating such masterpieces as the famous Peking Mongolian hot-pot. For this dish, delicate slices of lamb are brought to the table with beautifully arranged platters of vegetables and hot, steaming flower rolls. The meat and vegetables are cooked at the table in an elegantly shaped vessel. This civilized ceremony of rinsing the lamb until it is just cooked, is a modern refinement of the robust original as served in Mongol tents of the past. Out of all expectation it has become one of Peking's best and most renowned dishes.

Australia and New Zealand, with extensive grazing lands, are among the world's largest lamb producers.

IN RECENT YEARS, mutton has acquired such a derogatory meaning in England and America that it is unlikely to be on the dining-table of those who pride themselves on serving good food. People have become attuned to buying young lamb, tender but, by comparison, tasteless.

In earlier times, particularly in the nineteenth century, mutton provided some of the best and most famous English dishes—saddle of mutton, boiled leg of mutton with caper sauce and spiced mutton ham. The virtues of the different breeds were understood and preferences were argued.

Although mutton is technically a sheep which is more than fifteen or eighteen months old, it should be between three and four years old, specially bred for the table and properly hung after slaughter.

Crown Roast and Guard of Honour

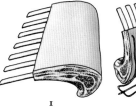 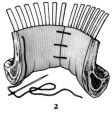 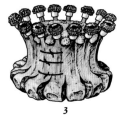 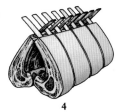

1   2   3   4

Elegant dishes, crown roast and guard of honour are each prepared from two best ends of lamb (1). The thin ends of the bones are first scraped clean of all meat, and most of the fat is carefully trimmed away. To make a crown roast, stand the two best ends on the thick ends, bend them to form a circle and sew them together with a trussing needle and string (2). The cavity may be stuffed with vegetables or forcemeat before roasting (3). A guard of honour, two best ends of lamb tied together with the clean bone ends interlocking, may also be stuffed before roasting (4).

Kebab comes from the Arabic word meaning "on a skewer". *Shish kebab,* meat grilled on a skewer, is said to have first been eaten by Turkish soldiers who cooked chunks of fresh-killed lamb on their swords over open fires. Today, *shish kebab* is much the same—chunks of lamb or other meats and vegetables are marinated, threaded on skewers and grilled over charcoal. *Döner kebab,* also of Middle Eastern origin, is a whole leg of lamb, boned, marinated and roasted on a slowly turning vertical spit. Lamb which has been ground and compressed into a leg of lamb shape is sometime used for *döner kebab.* Slices are cut off the *döner kebab* and served with raw vegetables and *pitta,* round, flat Middle Eastern bread.

GOATS are valued in those countries where there is too little grazing land for sheep, or where goats'-milk cheese is highly prized.

To cook old goat certain measures of desperation are needed. One old recipe says "simmer to rags". Others suggest powerful spices and dried fruits as ingredients of disguise in the true medieval style.

Kid may be cooked in the same way as lamb. In France, young milk-fed kid is roasted, stewed,or pieces are layered in a pot with garlic, chives, seasoning and spices. Cognac, Madeira, white wine or beef stock are added and then the pot is sealed. The dish is gently cooked and, finally, left to cool.

But kid is, above all, a speciality of the Mediterranean. For ceremonial meals it is roasted over charcoal or in an oven dug out beneath a flaming fire. In Saudi Arabia it is cooked whole with a stuffing of saffron rice, chopped onion, raisins and nuts.

Pork and Hams

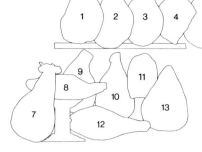

THE PIG is the world's most useful food animal. First domesticated in Turkey in about 7000 BC, it was even then an important source of meat. The fat was used as a preservative as well as a food. Later, dairy farming in the West gave a boost to pig farming, when it was realized that the animals fattened well on skimmed milk and whey.

This type of double farming was never practised in China, where people eat more pork than any other meat, because dairy products have never formed a part of the people's diet. The pig, with its omnivorous tastes, flourishes nevertheless. When the Chinese say "meat", they mean pork. Beef, chicken and lamb are referred to by name. Despite this enthusiasm for pork, and the great variation of fresh pork recipes, few cured products are made in China.

In Germany and France, however, the various parts of the pig are used in countless ways. The reason why this tradition of pork cooking should be so developed in western Europe is not easily explained, apart from lengthy habit. Germanic tribes were enjoying suckling pig before it became a Roman delicacy, and Gaulish hams were prized as a luxury in Ancient Rome. Today, in Germany and France, they make sausages, pies and pâtés, cured hams, shoulders and loins. From the pork belly come such rich products as the thready *rillettes* of Touraine, the large brown cubes of *rillons* and the lightly salted cuts which do so much to improve soups and stews that include *sauerkraut*.

Nothing is wasted. Thin sheets of fat from the back are used for larding and tying around small, lean game birds. Even the *grillons*, the bits left from melting down the fat for lard, are sold as a coarse pâté or are incorporated into bread dough and baked in crusty rings. The veil of caul fat, which encloses the innards, is useful for wrapping around lean roasts of veal, lamb or chicken, and when used to make a little parcel of sausage meat it turns quite a humble dish into something special. Even the pig's ears become a delicacy when they are cooked with the grey-green lentils of Puy de Dôme.

The French use the pig's skin to give a gelatinous, rich texture to beef stews. The English leave it on their roasts, score it into half-inch wide strips and rub it over with oil and salt. In the heat of a roasting oven, the strips cook to rich brown crackling. In America, where pigs were introduced by the early settlers, pork skin is cooked separately and sold as cocktail bits for nibbling with salted nuts and olives.

In Europe the great advance in the breeding of pigs and, consequently, in pork cooking was made about 1760 when Robert Bakewell of Leicestershire crossed the plump, round-faced Chinese pig with the rangier animal of Western farms. The Chinese moon face breeds out quickly, but the sweetness and plumpness remain.

At the beginning of the nineteenth century the British cottagers' pig was enormously fat. The hard manual work of its owner and the hard curing that was necessary if bacon and ham were to keep through the winter, meant that fat was essential from the point of view both of diet and palatability. Today, pigs are much leaner, but entire loss of fat is not to be recommended because meat which is absolutely lean can be tough. Another modern development is the sad disappearance from many butchers' shops of feet, tails, ears, heads and chitterlings and, therefore, the loss of cheap delicacies.

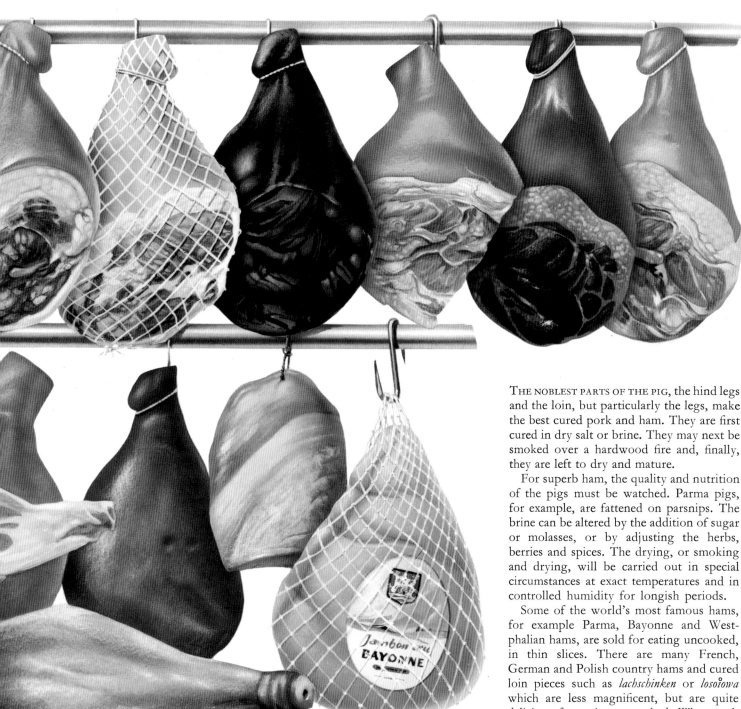

THE NOBLEST PARTS OF THE PIG, the hind legs and the loin, but particularly the legs, make the best cured pork and ham. They are first cured in dry salt or brine. They may next be smoked over a hardwood fire and, finally, they are left to dry and mature.

For superb ham, the quality and nutrition of the pigs must be watched. Parma pigs, for example, are fattened on parsnips. The brine can be altered by the addition of sugar or molasses, or by adjusting the herbs, berries and spices. The drying, or smoking and drying, will be carried out in special circumstances at exact temperatures and in controlled humidity for longish periods.

Some of the world's most famous hams, for example Parma, Bayonne and Westphalian hams, are sold for eating uncooked, in thin slices. There are many French, German and Polish country hams and cured loin pieces such as *lachschinken* or *losołowa* which are less magnificent, but are quite delicious for eating uncooked. When such ham is needed as a flavouring in dishes, Yunnan ham from China, or *prosciutto crudo* from Italy, can be successfully substituted.

Other fine hams, more especially in England and America, are cured and smoked for eventual boiling. The superb York, Bradenham, Smithfield or Virginia ham, or the Norman ham from Burgundy, are far superior to the bland *jambon de Paris* of France, and the unnamed "cooked ham" of most groceries.

Always buy ham on the bone. The kind that has been pressed into shape for convenient cooking and slicing comes from a larger pig, and is often boned before a relatively quick cure and, consequently, has no maturity of flavour.

A Family Tree of Pigs

The domestic pig, descendant of the wild boars of Asia and Europe, was first bred in 2900 BC. Today, there are two basic varieties— the long-backed Chinese pig and the heavier European or Danish pig, which is prized for its large hams, bacon and loin cuts.

Sausages and Pâtés

SAUSAGES were one of civilization's earliest convenience foods. All the small bits and pieces of the pig, or its blood, which were not good for ham-making, were salted and spiced and stuffed into the clean intestine for immediate cooking or for storage. Smoking was also used as a preservative and a flavouring.

The word sausage comes from the Latin *salsicia*, something salted, salted for keeping, like the huge dried sausages which often go under the Italian name of salami, irrespective of the country of origin. To make them, lean raw pork, sometimes with young beef, or horsemeat, is chopped and mixed with pork fat, salt and pepper and stuffed into the cleaned wider pieces of intestine. Such flavourings as paprika, garlic, fennel seeds, red pepper and wine, are varied according to place. The sausages are tied up tightly and then dried. Sometimes they are salted in brine before drying or the drying process is assisted with small smoky fires of wood shavings. As the meat shrinks, it is pushed together to exclude the air and restrung.

Italy, France and Germany are the three great countries of dried sausages and, indeed, of sausages in general. These sausages are usually served in thin slices with bread and wine, occasionally with black olives. Some, *chorizo*, for example, are added in chunks to stews and soups for the sake of their spiced or fiery flavourings.

Other large sausages which have been salted, and then sometimes smoked and sometimes cooked, do not keep as long. They must be stored in the refrigerator. As compensation they have an even greater variety of flavour and texture than salami, although the basic meat is usually pork. Least interesting is Italian *mortadella*—the huge, smooth pink slices studded with bits of fat are often insipidly bland. The succulent *andouille* of France, at its best at Vire in Normandy, is another matter. Long pieces of chitterling are threaded one inside another until a diameter of two or three inches is reached. They are then put into a casing, simmered, often in white wine, and then smoked. When cut, one can see many concentric circles arranged in savoury harmony.

The *blut zungenwurst* of Germany and Eastern Europe is an unusual blood sausage which contains such large pieces of pickled tongue that it slices to a dark mosaic marble of red and purplish black. Several countries make versions of ham-

tasting sausage, often flavoured with garlic. Like the others they are eaten sliced, with bread, but they also make a mildly piquant addition to bean dishes, stews and soups. The liver sausages and *mettwurst*, again from Germany, are soft in consistency.

The simplest of all sausages are the moist-looking, fresh links and huge coils which are sold for cooking at home. Considering the limited ingredients—fresh pork and seasonings—it is surprising how varied fresh sausages can be. Long, coarsely chopped Toulouse sausages are quite different from the coarsely chopped English sausages of Cornwall and Cumberland, and different again from German *bratwurst*. Fresh sausages which have been lightly cured are usually sold for boiling. *Cotechino* and *zampone* from Italy may require several hours, frankfurters five minutes; the thick, long *cervelas* of France and the curled rings of Poland and Germany take forty minutes and can then be eaten with potato salad or haricot beans and some chopped raw onion. The French poached sausage, sometimes flavoured with black bits of truffle, is baked in a brioche dough for special celebrations and Sunday lunch. Most unusual of these boiling sausages is the *zampone*, which has sausage meat stuffed inside a boned pig's foot instead of a gut casing.

The oldest of the "pudding" sausages is the haggis which, since the eighteenth century, has been quite wrongly regarded as a dish originating in Scotland. This excellent pudding is made by stuffing a sheep's stomach with chopped sheep's offal and oatmeal and seasoning. In the recent past it was also made with calf's stomach and offal. The word goes back only to fifteenth-century English, and may have a French origin. The idea must go back to the earliest days of cooking.

Other puddings of the haggis type, which are simmered before being put on sale, are the black and white puddings of Europe. The finest black pudding is made from the blood of the pig mixed with little bits of pork fat, onion and seasoning. The mixture is poured through a funnel into a great length of casing until it swells out into a huge coil which is then poached until the blood has set. White pudding in France is made on the same principle, but with chicken or fine pork, milk, cream, eggs, onion and spices. This type of custard, set with eggs and thickened with pork and bread, also goes back to the Middle Ages

and even to Ancient Rome, although it was not then usually served in sausage skins, but in a shallow dish after being gently cooked over the fire. Although haggis is usually boiled for an hour before being served with buttered turnips (and a glass of good whisky), black and white puddings are grilled or fried.

Indeed, sausages may have started out as a convenience and a saver of scraps, but thanks to the ingenuity of European cooks they have ended up as a pleasure for many occasions and many different kinds of meal.

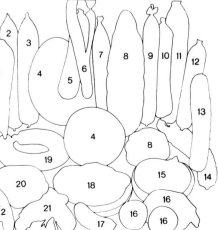

Patés

Patés consist of pork sausage meat or minced liver or both, flavoured with herbs, spices, mushrooms, wine and brandy. Sometimes game and truffles are included, or a whole *foie gras*. Instead of being pushed into casings, the mixture is baked directly in a terrine, or in a terrine lined with pastry. This accounts for the two names terrine and pâté, although today both are used interchangeably without any special significance.

Raised Pies

Raised pies, an English speciality of the Midlands and Yorkshire, are made with a special hot-water dough crust. Water and lard are boiled together and then mixed with flour. (The proportions are 1 scant cup of water, $\frac{3}{4}$ cup lard to 4 cups flour.)

The hot dough is then "raised" by hand up the sides of floured wooden pie moulds. (Jam jars will do instead.) As the dough cools, it firms and takes the shape of the moulds which can easily be removed. The meat is then put inside—a mixture of chopped fat and lean pork with herbs, sometimes with apple, or game and pork, or boned birds packed one inside the other according to size, like a Russian doll. A pastry lid and some decorations are added. Before baking, a piece of paper is tied around the pie to hold it together.

An easier and quicker method is to "raise" the pastry up inside a decorative hinged mould, which is not removed until after baking.

1 Italian zamponia	12 Italian cotechino
2 Polish Krakowska	13 German bratwurst
3 Polish debowiecka	14 German mettwurst
4 Italian mortadella	15 French black pudding
5 German leberwurst	16 Scottish haggis
6 Polish Kabanosy	17 French boudin blanc
7 Italian salami	18 English Cumberland sausage
8 French rosette	19 Polish wiankowa
9 Hungarian salami	20 German blut zugenwurst
10 German cervelat	21 Spanish chorizos
11 Italian crespone	22 German frankfurters

Game Birds and Animals

Black bear

Red deer

Many game birds are protected by law, and there are "close seasons" when they cannot be caught. A large number of frozen game is available, however, throughout the year. In general, turkey, guinea fowl, partridge, pheasant, golden plover, woodcock, young hare, venison leg and loin and mallard duck are best roasted; quail, venison steaks and cutlets are tastiest grilled; and older pigeons and large turkeys are most suitable cooked in casseroles. Very old birds should only be used for stock or soup or for making hash forcemeat and sauces.

Antelope

Moose

Wild turkey

Mallard duck

Mourning dove

Hare

Rabbit

Bustard

Golden plover

Woodcock

Partridge

Grey squirrel

34

The Accompaniments of Game

In the beginning, before man learned to domesticate and breed animals, all the meat that he ate was game meat. He hunted birds and animals to supplement the slender diet of wild berries, roots and grasses on which he otherwise lived. The first game animals included the mammoth elephant and the primeval rabbit, wild pigs and long-horned buffalo, various kinds of deer and fowl, everything to which man, the hunter, could lay an axe, club, spear or stone.

Eating then took more time and energy than it does now. Meat was chewed and consumed raw until the remarkable discovery that fire, which served admirably to keep humans warm, could do wonders with animal flesh. Cooking meat was a revolutionary discovery, one of the most important in the history of mankind. Unlike raw flesh, cooked meat was tender and could be quickly eaten. Suddenly, man, who had devoted most of his energies to finding and eating food, had time on his hands. He could concentrate on such other things as cultivating crops, inventing the wheel and domesticating sheep, goats and oxen to provide a reliable source of meat which was

Today, many game birds and animals are prepared in the same way and are served with the same accompaniments as they were centuries ago. Venison is usually garnished with pears or redcurrant jelly, wild duck is cooked with oranges or cherries, wild goose is stuffed with chestnuts and apples, roast pheasant is served with cranberries and rabbit is stewed with onions and mushrooms. These accompaniments create a perfect blend of flavours. And a glass of fine port will make the perfect complement.

---

not "game", and would not have to be hunted to provide each day's sustenance.

Primitive communities, however, continued to follow the movement of wild herds, sometimes wintering in valleys and summering in the highlands to stay close to their peripatetic food supply. Sometimes they even traversed continents. "Home" was where game happened to be. Even in comparatively recent times, American Indian tribes followed buffalo herds across the western and southwestern United States. Laplanders followed itinerant reindeer across northern Scandinavia until they learned to domesticate them.

Although game animals and birds are also pursued for fur and for sport, their main function, as far as man is concerned, has been to supply sustenance, particularly in unfamiliar, unsettled or uncultivated regions. Deer, rabbit, wild boar, wild turkey and game birds sustained the frontiersmen who, with little more than a rifle and a knife, pressed through the North American wilderness to open up a new continent. Seventeen hundred years earlier, the Roman legions that moved up through England towards Scotland carried some of their own food supplies, but relied heavily on red deer, roebuck, hare, partridge, quail and pheasant along their route of march.

In most regions of the world, game was, and still is in some places, a key constituent of the human diet, whether it was big game, like reindeer (also called caribou), elk and other deer, antelope and bear, or small game, rabbit, hare, squirrel, geese, woodcock and other wild birds. Until recently, armies on the move were expected to "live off the land", which meant hungry soldiers and sometimes military disaster if there wasn't enough game to go around.

Once upon a time, quantities of available game were without limit. Recent recognition, however, of the way in which indiscriminate slaughter has endangered the existence of many species has led to the enactment of conservation laws governing hunting seasons in many countries. In America, seasons vary from state to state, and often from year to year, depending on the toll hunters took the year before. In Britain, August 12th, the "glorious twelfth", is the day when hunters can venture armed and squint-eyed into grouse country. Other dates are applicable for certain other game. Most other countries also have laws to conserve dwindling species. Punishment for violation is generally a fine. Times have changed since William the Second of England decreed that whoever slew a hart or a hind would be blinded.

Game should be "hung" for tenderizing before cooking. Many people like it "high", possibly a vestige of those days when the absence of refrigeration was transformed by necessity into a virtue. Of the game dishes, venison steaks and stews and wild fowl are probably the most popular. In parts of the United States and Canada, roast or braised bear's paw is a speciality. In less affluent mountain regions of America and other countries, an old tradition of squirrel and rabbit stews is maintained. "Humble pie", which has come to mean a humiliation to be tolerated, originally was made in England from the "humble" parts of deer—the tongue, kidneys, liver and heart.

Wild boar

Canadian goose

Pheasant

Wild guinea fowl

Lark

Poultry and Eggs

WHEN children squabble over the chicken wishbone, they are recalling, without knowing it, the first purpose for which these fowl were domesticated. Their importance was for divination and religious use, for cock-fighting and, later, for eggs.

It seems to have been the Greeks who first saw their splendid possibilities for the table, and the Romans who developed the first distinctive breeds. The Middle Ages were a time of lordly chicken-eating. Purées were made of chicken, almonds, eggs and saffron. The birds were roasted with sage or stewed with wine. The poor kept chickens too, but their purpose was eggs—and more chickens. Eventually, the old rooster and hen were simmered for hours with vegetables to make a decidedly simple stew.

Today chicken is the cheapest of all meats and too often tasteless because of its forced and confined rearing. Most animals for the table need proper hanging to develop flavour and the chicken is no exception.

Guinea-fowls are the decorative birds of the farmyard, with a picturesque tendency to hump along the ridge of barns and sheds like relaxed cushions. The Romans were the first to appreciate their delicious flavour, which is slightly gamy, like that of the Cornish game hen. Certainly, roasted like pheasant, with a jacket of fat as permanent basting, they are well worth eating.

When guinea-fowls first came to England from Africa, they were known as turkey-cocks and turkey-hens, because they were brought by "Turkey merchants" engaged in the spice trade with the Near East. Then the name turkey was transferred to a new arrival from Mexico, again brought north by the spice merchants. Guinea-fowls retreated to their other name, given to them by the Portuguese, who had also brought them to Europe, from Guinea in West Africa.

The large new bird was much more satisfactory to cook and eat than the peacocks, swans and herons of the medieval banquet. The turkey rapidly became the festive bird of weddings and Christmas dinners, and later, in America, of Thanksgiving. In time, it ousted the goose, which had been the special bird of the less well-off.

One Yorkshire speciality, fashionable in London as a Christmas delicacy, was the turkey or goose pie, the bird stuffed with birds ever-decreasing in size, all boned beforehand, spiced and seasoned, and baked with pounds of butter in a very thick crust to stand up to the shaking of coaches and, subsequently, of trains, on the journey south. The recipes are in most eighteenth-century cook books, but even in the middle of the nineteenth century the painter Turner was still writing to thank his Yorkshire friend and patron, Mr Fawkes, for his annual goose pie.

In Germany and parts of France, the goose still dominates the festive scene, but a more important reason for rearing geese is *foie gras*, the enormous liver of force-fed birds. Naturally, the rest of the bird is not wasted. The meat is lightly salted, then cooked and potted in its own fat to make *confit d'oie*, a rich, savoury pleasure eaten in *cassoulet*, or with apples, potatoes or beans.

The English seem to have prized goose fat as a chest rub to protect them from colds and bronchitis. The French more wisely made it the basic fat of their cooking in those parts of the country where *foie gras* is a speciality.

Duck, too, has been well taken in hand by the French. There is the Rouen duckling, cooked rare and sauced with juices pressed from the carcass: and Nantes duckling, which is paler and plumper and good with lightly caramelized turnips. Boned duck enclosed in pastry, like a pâté, is a speciality of Amiens. Nevertheless, the prize for duck cooking must go to the Chinese of Peking and Szechwan, who have devised Peking duck and Szechwan aromatic duck, the perfect recipes for bringing out the bird's best qualities.

Quails and squabs are domesticated varieties of game birds. In the United States they also come under the heading of game. In England, however, the only quails available for the table are the specially bred Japanese quails, tiny, plump and delicately flavoured. One of the best recipes for quails comes from northern Italy, where they are pan-fried, braised in wine and served on a buttery *risotto* with Parmesan cheese.

The squab is the pigeon of the dovecot, bred for tenderness and flavour. Under old manorial rights in England and France, these birds belonged to the lord of the manor and had the right to feed on other people's crops. They were a valuable source of winter meat, for a few people at any rate. Today they are an expensive delicacy, usually roasted and served whole.

White Leghorn chicken

Rhode Island Red

Eggs

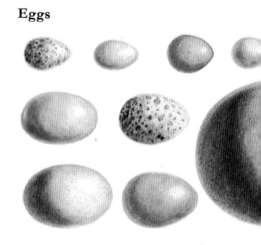

Turkey

Chinese goose

Greylag goose

Quail

Squab

Aylesbury duck

To ancient philosophers the egg was a symbol of the world, of life, of rebirth. Certainly, eggs are one of the most valuable of foods—they are highly nutritious, easily digested and can be used in an infinite variety of ways. Eggs can be boiled, fried, baked or poached. They can be incorporated in numerous dishes. Eggs are used to thicken soups, to emulsify sauces and to bind forcemeats and stuffings. The chicken egg is the most readily available, but the eggs of all birds are edible. The eggs of (*left to right*) quail, pigeon, pheasant, partridge, lapwing, penguin, goose, gull, ostrich, duck, swan, chicken and turkey are all eaten in some part of the world.

The simple egg can become an exotic creation. In Russia, Easter eggs (*left*) painted with wax and dyes are works of art. Unusual Chinese eggs (*centre*) include thousand year eggs, uncooked eggs buried for weeks in clay, which have a gelatinous texture; marbled eggs which are boiled with tea leaves; and red-dyed eggs which are presented as gifts. In the Middle East, *hamine* eggs (*right*) are boiled overnight with onion skins.

The Green Salad

THE IDEA OF EATING uncooked vegetables for health reasons was an early one in the Mediterranean. Greek doctors and herbalists of the first and second centuries AD agreed that lettuce, chicory and rocket were good for the stomach. There were other pleasing effects, too. Rocket "provoked venery" (no one thought it worth mentioning that its slightly bitter leaves make all the difference to a lettuce salad). Lettuce (*Lactuca sativa*) was said to benefit nursing mothers because of its milky sap—hence the name *Lactuca*. Best of all, it soothed people to sleep. In Beatrix Potter's tales the Flopsy Bunnies ate piles of shot lettuce, and fell so sweetly asleep that "they did not awake" when their enemy, Mr MacGregor, poured the grass

shavings on top of them "because the lettuces had been so soporific". The sober and learned authors of one modern book about plants go further than Beatrix Potter. They observe that shot lettuce eaten in quantity can induce a coma.

To the Greeks and Romans, uncooked did not mean untreated. Salad derives from *sal*, meaning salt, for the green leaves were preserved in brine, then in salt and vinegar, and fresh salads were dressed with a vinaigrette dressing.

Then as now, lettuce was the main salad ingredient. Chicory was recommended for wintertime, as was endive. The names of these two plants are confusing. Curly, mopheaded endive (*Cichorium endivia*) and a

related variety *batavia*, with long crisp ragged leaves, are known in France and in the United States as *chicorée* and *escarole* or *batavia*. The blanched shoots of chicory (*Cichorium intybus*; to the French and Americans, *endive*) were first produced in their packed, yellowish-white form in 1850 by the head gardener at the Brussels Botanical Garden.

Watercress, another ancient salad plant, was mainly picked from brooks and springs until the nineteenth century when it was commercially grown.

Two essential virtues of a salad are crunch and bite. The crispness of certain lettuces, of batavia and chicory, can be underlined with celery and Florence fennel. Plants which add zest are sorrel, purslane and mustard and cress. These small, pointed flavours, along with herbs and a variety of oil and wine vinegar dressings, make the daily salad a gastronomic necessity.

Salad Greens

A green salad can be made with a great variety of ingredients. There are many kinds of lettuce, each contributing a different taste and texture. Cabbage lettuce **1** has a mild flavour and a pleasant crispness, cos or Romaine lettuce **4** adds a stronger flavour, while butterhead lettuce **3** is mild and has a buttery texture. Other greens which add variety to a salad include sea kale leaves **2**, chicory **5** and curly endive **8**. These vegetables can be bitter, so the leaves are often blanched and then added to the salad bowl. Fennel **7** and celery **9**, both mild and sweet, add a contrasting crunchiness, as does sliced cucumber **6**. Mustard greens **11** and watercress **12**, too often relegated to the role of garnish, add interest to a salad. And to add a finishing touch of colour—sliced radishes **10**.

Vegetables of the Orient

Unusual Greens

There are literally hundreds of edible greens that can be eaten raw in salads. Some are common, and easily available, like dandelion greens, brooklime, corn salad, salad burnet and the many varieties of cress. These greens can be found in fields and meadows, on hillsides and, often, right in the backyard. They add a strong, fresh, interesting taste to bland cultivated greens and, therefore, are sought out by salad lovers. Raw nasturtium leaves and flowers, sea beet, even young nettles are delicious. Today if you want to taste the more unusual of these salad greens you have to hunt for and pick them yourself. These hardy, wild foods can often be grown in poor soil, and agricultural specialists are beginning to investigate their cultivation. One day marsh samphire may be as common in the supermarket as cabbage. Some unusual greens, well worth including in salads, are dandelion **1**, brooklime **2**, corn salad **3**, salad burnet **4**, watercress **5**, nasturtium **6**, sea beet **7**, nettles **8**, valerian **9**, sorrel **10**, basil **11**, collard greens **12** and beet tops **13**.

THE CHINESE are among the world's best vegetable cooks. They respect texture and fresh flavour and know how to combine meat and fish with vegetables. There are also the refined vegetarian dishes of the Buddhists, whose lively use of vegetables to imitate meat and fish is a world away from the raw cabbage and grated carrots of many Western vegetarian tables.

Some plants from the East, which in the West are enjoyed for their beauty alone, can be useful, too. The buds, for example, of the tiger lily, the oldest of the world's cultivated lilies, are dried to pale orange strips called golden needles, which add a pleasant aromatic flavour to many dishes. From several species of bamboo the Chinese take shoots, which they use as a crisp vegetable.

A widely known, celery-crisp cabbage is the *pe-tsai* or Chinese cabbage (*Brassica pekinensis*). Its long, blanched, sculptured heart, about six inches in diameter, makes a good salad. The leaves can be stir-fried, too, or used in soup. Another cabbage, *bok choi* (*Brassica chinensis*), grows more loosely, with an almost floppy habit. Then there is leaf mustard, or mustard greens, a hot-tasting cabbage which Chinese cooks pickle in salt and vinegar.

Radishes are far more important in the East than in Europe and America. *Daikon*, the large long radish of mild flavour, is used in many Japanese dishes. Another root used as seasoning, *wasabi*, is stronger than horse-radish, and can be bought in tiny tins in powdered form—a beautiful pale green.

Fresh-water vegetables are difficult to come by in the West. The small round corms of a cultivated sedge (*Eleocharis dulcis*) provide water chestnuts, good for their crunchy bite and delicate flavour. The lotus, sacred to the Buddha and Kwan Yin, the Goddess of Mercy, covers many lakes in China. The pierced stem is eaten as a vegetable, the seeds are preserved in syrup and the leaves are wrapped around parcels of food for steaming. The loveliest of all the water vegetables are the many varieties of seaweed of Japan, where they have been cultivated for centuries.

Vegetables of the Old World

No STATUES CAN BE RAISED to the early heroes of vegetable culture. In most cases, scarcely a guess can be hazarded as to when or where they lived. Some vegetables, radishes, for example, became popular so long ago and are known in so many varieties from the Mediterranean to China and Japan, that there is no way of knowing who first decided that their crunchy texture and peppery piquancy made them worth growing. Perhaps it was in Egypt where, as Herodotus records, the slaves who built the Great Pyramid at Giza were kept going on "radishes, onions and leeks"—three of the world's oldest vegetables.

When the wandering tribes began to settle down, to grow wheat and domesticate animals, things moved fast. Like wheat, root vegetables could be sheltered in fields, and develop in size and quality.

Two great needs—storable food and medicine—stimulated vegetable gardening. Roots could be stored in dry sand or earth. Legumes or pulses, in other words, peas and beans, could be dried and kept through the dead season. For medicinal purposes, man depended upon plants, some of which worked—willow and feverfew for headaches, autumn crocus for gout. However, some of the most popular were entirely useless, and not even pleasant to eat. Plants wandered, as it were, between the apothecary and the kitchen. Beetroot was for centuries a medicine. Only the green leaves were cooked as a vegetable—as they still are from such varieties as spinach beetroot, seakale beet and chard. Rhubarb

root was imported into Europe from Asia as a medicine, and it was not until the eighteenth and early nineteenth century that its young stems were forced and blanched, and cooked with sugar in pies and tarts.

Cultivated brassicas, cabbages of one kind and another, have supplied some of the worst and best European vegetables for nearly three thousand years. Cabbage is a convenient shorthand for cabbage-cole, meaning stem or stalk with the big head, from Latin *caput*, head, and *caulis* or *cole*, stalk. Cauliflowers were grown by the Arabs in the Middle Ages. Seeds came, via Cyprus, to Italy, then to France in the sixteenth

1 Wild cabbage
2 Kale
3 Cauliflower   6 Kohlrabi
4 Brussels sprouts   7 Broccoli
5 Spring cabbage   8 Round cabbage
                 9 Red cabbage

century and to England a hundred years later. Brussels sprouts were eaten in Belgium in the early thirteenth century, but were not known in France or England for another five centuries. The wild cabbage is thought to have been developed by the Celts in western Europe.

Vegetables from the East—such as peas and eggplants—came into Europe by way of the Middle East, a continuous movement since Roman times. Later, as the Moslem Empire expanded, the Moors brought vegetables through North Africa to Spain. Spinach from Persia, one of the Moorish imports, which was also taken in the opposite direction, to China, has become the aristocrat of European leaf vegetables.

Following the discovery of America in 1492, the exchange of plants between Europe and America, between America and Africa, America and the Far East, altered the taste of everybody's food. As far as Europe was concerned. Renaissance gardeners had already been busy improving the quality and flavour of vegetables. Italian gardeners had started to blanch celery in the sixteenth century to counteract the bitterness that makes wild celery unpleasant to eat. Other stem vegetables, such as Florence fennel and seakale, also need this attention.

The arrival of new plants added further stimulus. Along with new tomatoes, there were globe artichokes developed from native cardoons. Old, greyish peas of peasant diet and winter storage were transformed into tiny green peas, a luxury for early summer. When *petits pois* were first served at the court of Louis XIV, people who had eaten well at the king's table would retire to their rooms for a surreptitious plate of the new delicacy which became, for a time, a secret vice.

The large seeds of the world's peas and beans, the legumes of the tropics and the temperate regions, of East and West, have provided man with a protein-rich storage food for so long that some of them, peas and chick-peas, for example, are not known in a wild form.

The dried vegetables of the Old World have been reinforced by the beans of the New World, which are now as familiar in Europe as ever they were to pre-Columbian Indians. Yet even without the American bean there would be a rich variety from which to choose.

As the history of vegetables has repeatedly shown, roots and vegetables tend to be discarded when new ones are discovered or developed which do the same job better. Plants such as rampion, alexanders and Good King Henry have all been relegated to the European hedgerow. Others have fallen into disfavour in one part of the world only to become a staple food in another. Taro, for example, which was eaten by the Greeks and Romans, is now an important food in the Pacific and Southwest Asia, but is unknown to most Europeans. Future developments and discoveries are as open to conjecture as the early history of the vegetables that are with us today.

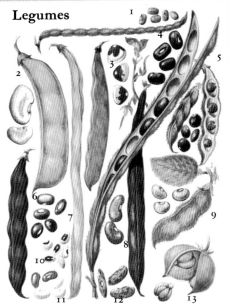

Legumes

Legumes were valued in the past because they could be dried and stored as a source of food for the winter. Modern cultivation and drying methods have so improved the quality of dried vegetables that prolonged soaking and cooking is now rarely necessary. Legumes are an inexpensive and tasty source of protein.
1 Green gram or mung bean **2** Butter bean **3** Pea beans **4** Black gram beans **5** Pigeon peas **6** Lablab beans **7** Black-eyed peas **8** Purple-podded kidney beans **9** Soybeans **10** Brown haricot beans **11** White haricot beans **12** Scarlet runner beans **13** Chick-peas

1 Broccoli	10 Fennel	19 Cauliflower	28 Cabbage
2 Brussels sprouts	11 Celery	20 Rhubarb	29 Kale
3 Seakale	12 Celeriac	21 Onions	30 Spinach
4 Nettles	13 Chard	22 Aubergine	31 Peas
5 Kohlrabi	14 Globe artichoke	23 Chick-peas	32 Cucumber
6 Swede	15 Parsnip	24 Cow peas	33 Lablabs
7 Turnip	16 Salsify	25 Broad beans	34 Chinese cabbage
8 Endive	17 Carrots	26 Radishes	35 Yam
9 Beetroot	18 Asparagus	27 Collard greens	36 Soybeans

Vegetables of the New World

THE sixteenth and seventeenth centuries must have been an exciting period for the gardeners of Europe as explorers returned from the Americas with seeds and plants which were to open the door to a new world of vegetables.

The original home of the edible squashes, the cucurbits—pumpkins, vegetable marrows, summer and winter squashes, and all their varieties—is a matter for argument, but it cannot be denied that they were most exploited and depended upon by the civilizations of South and Central America.

By 1000 BC, squashes had travelled up to North America, and since then many beautiful shapes and flavours have been developed. Some are scalloped, pale and plump, others are warty and gourd-shaped. Some must be eaten as soon as they are ripe. Stored correctly, others will keep for three to four months. Like all the squashes, pumpkins are excellent for savoury gratins and soups, but candied in syrup or turned into pumpkin pie, they are even more delicious.

One cucurbit at least, the *chayote* (*Sechium edule*), is firmly and centrally American. This ridged, bumpy, gourd-shaped fruit may be seasoned with salt or sugar and fried, baked or boiled and mashed. The roots, leaves and shoots are edible, as are the flowers, which, like those of all the squashes, may be stuffed, dipped in batter and fried.

There is no doubt either about the ancestry of such beans as scarlet runners, kidney or French beans, Lima or butter beans, haricot beans, flageolets, and the tribe of string beans and dwarf French beans; all of them came originally from the New World. French beans were probably introduced to Europe by French explorers. The great advantage of beans is that they can be dried for storage and winter food. It was the French and Italians who devised most of the famous bean dishes, and settlers who took them back to North America. A simple dish of dried beans simmered with pickled pork and a bouquet of herbs is the ancestor of both the *cassoulet* of Languedoc and the baked beans of Boston.

Early in the seventeenth century, Jerusalem artichokes were introduced into Europe from Canada. Their flavour reminded

Italian gardeners of the familiar globe artichoke, but to distinguish between them, the new tuber was given the name of its close relative, the sunflower, *girasole*. It seems that the English twisted the word into Jerusalem.

Sweet potatoes (*Ipomoea batatas*), which arrived in Europe much earlier than Jerusalem artichokes or the common potato, have great versatility, which is ignored by most Europeans. While their flavour is too pronounced for them to be a basic food, as an occasional treat they help to vary the diet in a particularly pleasant way.

America's only indigenous cereal, corn, or maize, was introduced into Europe at the beginning of the sixteenth century. The golden cobs, descendants of the wild corn which the Peruvians cultivated over thousands of years, must be cooked fresh, otherwise the sweetness converts to starch and all the fresh, juicy lightness is destroyed.

Although northern Europeans have known about avocados since the end of the seventeenth century, it is only since the Second World War that most of them have seen or eaten one. Once the avocado is ripe it falls quickly to rottenness, so it must be flown to its destination while still firm, to be ripened in the shop or kitchen. Its buttery flesh is best on its own with a good vinaigrette dressing, but in Latin America it is often added to stews or mixed with pickled fish. When used in stews, the avocado should never be cooked, only heated through for the minimum time.

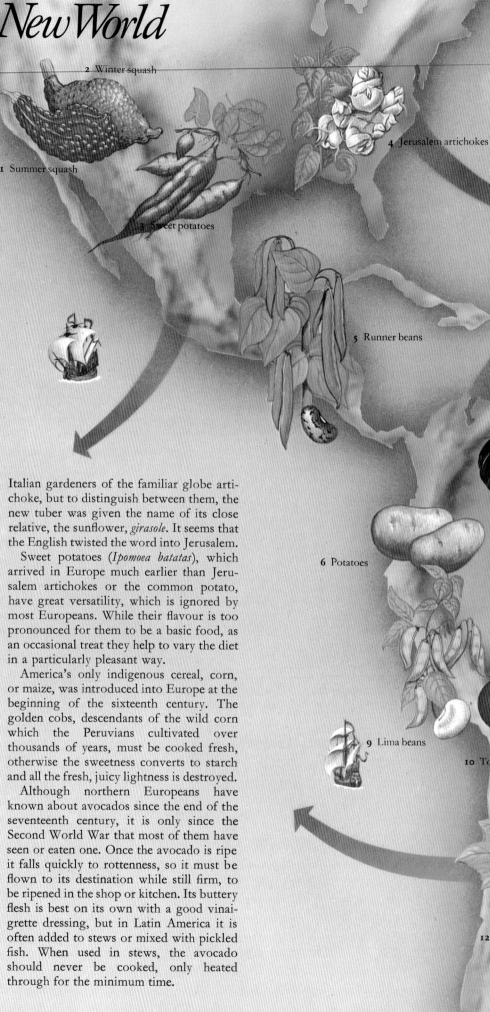

2 Winter squash

1 Summer squash

3 Sweet potatoes

4 Jerusalem artichokes

5 Runner beans

6 Potatoes

9 Lima beans

10 To

12

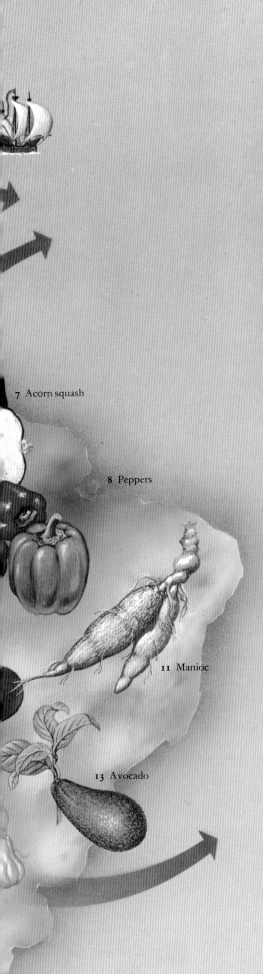

7 Acorn squash

8 Peppers

11 Manioc

13 Avocado

Chilies and Peppers

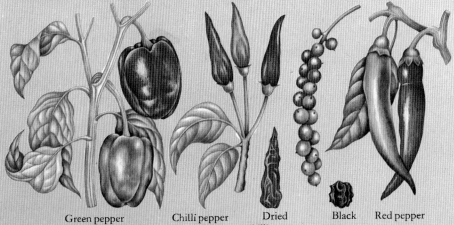

Green pepper   Chilli pepper   Dried   Black   Red pepper
chilli pepper   peppercorn

It would require the wisdom of the ages to disentangle the many varieties of peppers and chillies. Usually, although there are exceptions, the larger the pepper or chilli the milder it will be, the smaller the chilli the hotter. The large roundly-ridged peppers—Bell peppers, capsicums, green peppers which ripen if kept to yellow or red—are all mild with a sweet piquancy. It is these peppers which the Spaniards call *pimiento*, the French *piment doux* and *poivron*, the Italians *pepperone*. The Hungarians have many varieties, some hotter than others, which they use to colourful effect in many dishes. The dark orange-red and the flat taste of paprika are obtained by using peppers in a powdered form.

Chillies are more a seasoning than a food. (Cayenne pepper is powdered chillies.) Their main purpose is to give zest to bland dishes, or dishes which would otherwise be dull.

It is impossible to imagine Mediterranean food without tomatoes. Yet Italian, Spanish and Greek cooks had to wait for Columbus to discover America before travellers could bring tomatoes to Europe from Southern and Central America. The Mexicans called them *tomatl* (the botanical name is *Lycopersicon esculentum*).

On its arrival in Europe, the blazing fruit was blessed by the Italians as *pomo d'oro*, golden apple. The French turned a second name, *pomo dei Mori*, apple of the Moors, to their liking as *pomme d'amour*—a good name at a time when every new luxury was regarded as an aphrodisiac.

The suspicious and puritanical northerners decided that tomatoes were bad, that they caused various illnesses. This opinion was, presumably, shared by North Americans, as they did not begin growing tomatoes on any scale for food until the end of the eighteenth century. And although tomatoes have been widely available in England since the 1880s, they have only become an unremarkable, accepted part of everyone's diet in the last forty years.

Today there are many varieties from which to choose, plum, pear-shaped and egg-shaped tomatoes, striped Tiger Toms and cherry and redcurrant tomatoes growing in miniature clusters. There is also a related tree tomato (*Cyphomandra betacea*), which grows high by comparison, and must have a fairly high altitude to survive. Best of all are the craggy rich tomatoes, which have ripened in the open, under a hot sun.

Tomatoes

Tomatoes are one of the most versatile of vegetables. Delicious when eaten raw, they can also be baked, fried, boiled, puréed or stuffed. A basic ingredient of many jams, sauces, soups and stews, tomatoes are frequently used to enhance a wide range of dishes.

Tree tomatoes

Cherry tomatoes   Common tomato

Mushrooms and Truffles

MUSHROOMS AND OTHER EDIBLE FUNGI are the luxuries, the frivolities, of the kitchen. They have a subtle and deep flavour, a crisp but yielding texture and no real food value. Having said that, it must be added that the difference in taste and texture between the many species of edible fungi is surprising, particularly to anyone who has never been mushroom hunting. This best of pastimes is enjoyed by far too few people.

It is a delightful way to spend a sunny autumn day wandering through woods, the leaves a medley of yellows, oranges and reds. From the camouflage of fallen leaves the moist brown dome of a cèpe is suddenly revealed, or the egg-yolk splash of chanterelles (girolles) against a mossy stump. Later, there is the pleasure of sorting out the basketful and the quiet anticipation of the feast to come.

The dangers of eating wild mushrooms are sometimes exaggerated, but they exist for those who are careless or ill-informed. There are few fatal species, although a number do tend to make people ill. With the aid of good handbooks, the best edible kinds can be learned in an afternoon. Any doubtful sorts should be left growing in peace while the intelligent mushroom hunter enjoys some of the best things the earth provides.

The four best mushrooms, the ones which, along with the truffle, have long been the darlings of the great European chefs, are the cèpe, the chanterelle, the morel and the field mushroom. There are many species of the cèpe (*Boletus edulis*, etc.), all of which have spongy gills. The chanterelle (*Cantherellus cibarius*) has a fluted margin and is smoothly yellow on top, but pleated up the stalk and under the cap like ribs in a fan-vaulted church. The morel (*Morchella esculenta*), a springtime mushroom, resembles a brown sponge and is hollow in the centre. The field mushroom (*Agaricus campestris*), pushing its white cap up through the grass in the morning, pinkish fawn beneath and soft to touch, makes the best of breakfast dishes. Others are the oyster mushroom, the grisette, the rubber brush mushroom, the horn of plenty, certain of the russulas, as well as the blewits, shaggy caps or manes and parasols.

Of the four best mushrooms, the cèpes alone can stand up well to prolonged cooking in stews. They will transform chicken, beef and rabbit dishes. Combined with potatoes in a gratin, or fried with olive

Cèpe

Morel

White truffle

Field Mushroom

oil, garlic, parsley and shallots, they are a dish beyond compare. Chanterelles or morels, fried and moistened with cream, make a luxurious sauce for veal or chicken. If found in quantity, they can be fried in butter and served on toast. Wild fungi will often produce a good deal of liquid that needs to be boiled away. Cultivated mushrooms produce very little moisture and, as a result, they last well. Commercial mushrooms are related to the field mushroom but, unfortunately, they do not have the same exquisite flavour. They are sold young, however, and have the virtues of youth—freshness and a certain bite. Sliced raw and sprinkled with herbs and a vinaigrette dressing, they are delicious. Briefly cooked in butter, with garlic and onion, they improve the mild flavour of white fish and meat.

Today, thanks to modern scientific study, cultivated mushrooms are readily and cheaply available. When mushrooms were first cultivated, at the end of the seventeenth century, in the caves of abandoned quarries around Paris, they were a luxury for the few and remained so until after the Second World War.

The Japanese appreciate the wild mushrooms of the forest as much as people in the West. Pickers scatter over the wooded hillsides in the autumn and the beautiful pine-tree mushrooms, *matsutake*, come to

market, brown and appetizing, in baskets of fern. Unfortunately, they are not dried for export.

The most popular Japanese or Chinese mushroom, the *shiitake*, oak mushroom, is raised on row after row of oak, or *shiia*, logs, propped against fences on the edge of forest clearings. They grow upwards against the tree stump and the caps are often slightly squashed on one side. The brown gills are deeply pleated and the cap has a beautiful patterning of fawn-coloured cracks. *Shiitake* have a delightful juiciness and a taste quite different from any Western mushrooms. *Shiitake* are dried and then exported.

Another less widely used mushroom is the cloud ear. Its name describes the shape of this tree fungus. Dried cloud ears come in a scrubby handful, but in water they swell to a gelatinous and intricate mass which separates into scalloped, ear-shaped clusters. It is a texture mushroom, added to dishes at the last moment for its crunchy bite and delicate flavour. In the West, jew's ears, young and fresh from the tree, make a good substitute.

Many other mushrooms are eaten in Asia, for example the padi straw mushroom, and large quantities of the familiar Western varieties of cultivated mushrooms are grown in Korea and Taiwan for local use and for export.

Shaggy cap

Chanterelle

Parasol

Fairy ring

Black truffle

Giant puffball

Blewit

THE ELUSIVE TRUFFLE is prized for its rarity, flavour and powerful aroma, particularly the black Périgord truffle, *Tuber melanosporum,* and the white Italian truffle, *T. magnatum.* Colette sang the praises of Périgord truffles cooked in dry white wine, flavoured only with fat bacon and eaten in unstinting quantities. This truffle is found in Périgord, elsewhere in France, in Central Italy and other parts of Europe, usually in latitudes between 44° and 46° North. Truffles are the fruit of a fungus which grows as a tuft of whitish threads on the roots of the host tree, often less than a foot below the surface. With luck, truffles can be "cultivated" by planting seedlings from

The Truffle Story

Left A typical truffle ground will be limy soil, with flattish stones below the surface which filter off excess water. This suits plants which go deep for their sustenance, such as truffle oaks, vines and lavender, and also suits juniper, walnut and dogrose, but not foxgloves or chestnuts. The host tree is most often an oak, but may be a beech, hornbeam or hazel.

Top right In Perigord

pigs (usually sows which are more docile and have a keener sense of smell) are trained to hunt truffles. To dissuade them from eating the prize some other reward, like maize or acorns, is given.

Centre Dogs (often mongrels) are used in Piedmont. Unlike pigs they have no desire to eat the truffles.

Bottom Truffles vary considerably in size. This is a good-sized black one.

oaks which have been contaminated with the fungus.

Other black truffles, inferior but still worth looking for, include *T. aestivum,* the summer truffle, and *T. brumale,* the winter truffle, both widespread in Europe, and similar species found in Oregon and California. Such truffles are often used to flavour *pâté de foie gras,* or are canned as surrogates for the "true" black truffle.

The white truffle, about the size of a new potato and putty-coloured, is found mainly around Alba in Piedmont and in the Tusco-Emilian Apennines. It is eaten raw. Often white truffles are thinly sliced to garnish dishes and to perfume them.

Grains, the Staples of Life

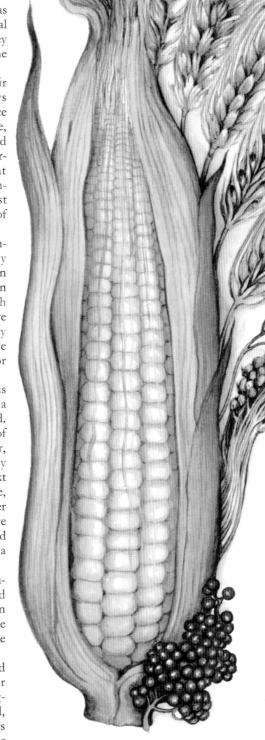

OF THE MANY THREADS that are woven through the fabric of culinary traditions and habits around the world, no strand is as universal and vital as that of the cereal grains. They are the grains of life and they are grown in almost every region of the earth.

With their high energy content and their worldwide availability, grains have always been a basic component of man's diet—rice in Asia, wheat and rye in western Europe, wheat and maize (called corn in the United States and Canada) in the Americas, sorghum and millet in Africa, buckwheat in Russia and eastern Europe and combinations of the different grains almost everywhere. No other single category of food is as important or widespread.

But, despite their prevalence, it is undeniably true that cereal grains are usually only incidental to the planning of an imaginative meal. Such dishes as Italian *risotto* and North African *couscous*, in which grain is the central ingredient, are rare exceptions. Most often grains serve merely as a filler in a meal, or to bring out the flavour of the accompanying meat or fish, or for flour to make bread.

The various grains cultivated in various parts of the globe have, however, played a crucial role in the development of mankind. They were fundamental to the evolution of civilization. Primitive man was a hunter, drifting from place to place, propelled only by his pursuit of animal prey and his next meal. To make his food supply more secure, to cultivate wheat, rice, barley and the other grains, it was necessary for him to observe seasonal requirements for planting and harvesting. He settled down and became a farmer.

The earliest human communities consisted of the first grain farmers, clustered in fertile valleys. The cultivation of grain was the dawn of civilization. With the exception of dwellings, granaries were the first buildings man ever built.

About half of the world's cultivated land is still used to grow grains of one kind or another, indicating that today their significance is only marginally diminished, despite the passage of thousands of years and the mass cultivation of many other kinds of foods. Some contend that the fact that whisky, gin, vodka, sake, beer and other intoxicating beverages are manufactured from fermented grain in so many different countries and cultures is symbolic proof of nature's obvious intention to design the cereal crops as mankind's staple.

There seems to be even more convincing proof. Grains grow under a remarkably wide variety of climatic condions to provide sustenance for people in all parts of the world. There are types of wheat, barley and rye which grow best in temperate regions which have cool winters, such as the Great Plains of the United States, the Canadian prairies and the Ukraine; some types of wheat even flourish in sub-Arctic conditions.

Maize is best cultivated where warm summers combine with adequate rainfall and a clumpy soil, as in Argentina, Brazil and the Corn Belt of the United States. Sorghum and millet are best adapted to subtropical

(*From the top*) maize, barley, oats, rye, wheat, rice, millet and sorghum.

Wheat is the most important grain grown in temperate climates and the United States is the world's leading producer. Reaper-thresher combines like these gather the crops quickly

Wild Rice

WILD RICE is not really rice at all. It is the seed of plume-topped aquatic grass, *zizania aquatica*, which has two conflicting characteristics —it tastes wonderful and it is in short supply, and therefore, very expensive.

The stalk from which wild rice is shaken may reach eight feet or more in height. It grows in swamps or shallow lakes of north-central North America and was once the staple food of some Indian tribes who gathered it by shaking the seeds into their canoes. This primitive but efficient means of harvesting the limited supply of wild rice is still used.

Mixed with mushrooms and onions and flavoured with herbs, wild rice is prepared as a stuffing for poultry or, because of its distinctive flavour, can be served quite plain.

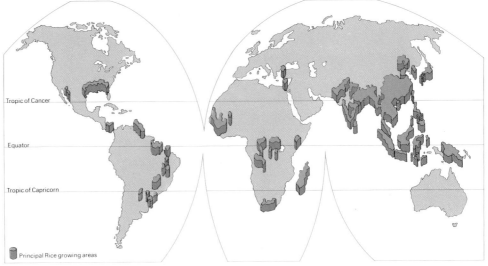

Tropic of Cancer

Equator

Tropic of Capricorn

Principal Rice growing areas

Rice is the staple food of more than half of the world's population. There are three basic varieties of rice—the favoured long-grain type, short, round-grained rice and glutinous rice which becomes sticky when cooked.

The rice plant has a hollow stem which permits oxygen to pass downward and reach the roots, adapting it to growth in flooded paddy fields (*top left*). About 90 per cent of the world's rice is grown in paddy fields. The remainder, upland rice, is grown on dry land like any other cereal grain

(*top right*). The rice plant is indigenous to Asia, and in Asia, particularly in China and India, most of the world's rice supply is grown. The only Asian countries to produce enough rice to export it, however, are Burma and Thailand.

Rice was brought to South Carolina Colony in 1685. American settlers took the plants westward, and rice cultivation began in Louisiana, Texas and California. Mechanized rice farming was introduced in the United States in the late nineteenth century. Today the United States is the leading rice exporter

climates, as in equatorial Africa and India. Most types of rice, upon which hundreds of millions of people in Asia depend, thrive in paddy fields, submerged during the growing season, in deltas and coastal plains.

The cereal grains are the seeds of certain kinds of grasses. Wheat is the most widely grown and the most widely used. Wheat flour, because of its gluten content, is superior for bread-making to flours made from maize, oats, rye or barley. Wheat bread is lighter and more finely textured than other kinds.

Throughout history there has been a remarkable traffic in grain across oceans and continents. Rice, which was first cultivated in Asia more than five thousand years ago, came to Europe during the Middle Ages, brought by invading Saracens who had made its acquaintance while fighting earlier campaigns farther east.

Christopher Columbus and Portuguese explorers found Indian corn in its native habitat in the Americas and brought it back to Europe, from where it quickly spread to Asia and Africa. The other grains were similarly discovered and disseminated by soldiers, explorers and merchants. In whatever new ground the grains were successfully cultivated, they quickly penetrated to the heart of the local cuisine.

Not only are there different kinds of grain, there are different varieties of each kind, thousands of varieties in all. The thirteen major varieties of wheat can, for example, be broken down to many hundreds of different strains grown in different places.

There are more than two hundred different varieties of barley. Barley used for beer brewing and barley used for bread flour or in soup are not the same. Although most wheat, of various varieties, is used for bread baking, a softer variety, one with little gluten, is used to make cake flour. Still other types are processed into cracked wheat, a huge assortment of dry cereals and pasta.

The oats that go into Scottish oatcakes are not the same as those used widely for animal fodder. Rye for pumpernickel bread is different from the grain which ends up as rye whisky. One variety of maize is used for succotash or for eating off the cob, another for *tortillas* and a third for popcorn.

The uses for grains are different in different regions. But one theme keeps recurring—a kind of porridge or mush, grain or grain meal cooked with water, or other liquid to make a nourishing, not unpalatable dish of eminent simplicity and low cost. Frumenty, a thick wheat pudding, has made an appearance at one time or another in the culinary history of Asia, America and Europe. Steamed bread in northern China is probably a descendant of a primitive wheat porridge. The mountain people of Tibet still favour *tsampa*, a barley paste. The Scots are fond of oatmeal. *Polenta*, cornmeal mush, occupies a respected place in the Italian cuisine. In many parts of southern Africa, *mealie*, a porridge of maize or millet, the origin of its name, is the staple food.

Nature has been generous and imaginative with grains, but where Nature has not met continually expanding human requirements, agricultural technology has tried to do the job. Artificial cross-breeding of grains has produced new, prolific varieties of "miracle" wheat, rice, maize and barley. The result has been the "green revolution", with harvest yields as much as tripled in some places. The vastly increased grain supplies have helped feed the world's ever-growing population.

Potatoes and Pasta

No FOOD can mean as much as the potato has to so many people in so many places for so long without being subject to legends and customs well removed from the simple act of eating. The Incas of Ancient Peru, who were among the first to cultivate potatoes, measured units of time by how long it took a potato to cook.

The potato is a peculiar vegetable. It is a tuber, the exposed, swollen protrusion of an underground stem. It thrived in the South American highlands where the climate is bracing and often damp. No wonder it took so well to the soil and elements of Ireland to which Sir Walter Raleigh is said to have brought it from Virginia in the sixteenth century. But the potato's first area of cultivation outside the Americas was Spain and it seems likely that Spanish explorers were, in fact, responsible for originally transplanting it.

Although the potato achieved some following, it took longer to overcome a peculiar revulsion to it felt by many in European countries (but not in America where it had taken a toehold in Virginia and the Carolinas). There was a widespread conviction in Europe that this ungainly lump of mud-brown root with strange eyes was at best a mistake, at worst a curse. Not until a succession of bad grain harvests in northern Europe in the late seventeenth and eighteenth centuries raised the spectre of famine did necessity become the mother of culinary tolerance. The potato had finally arrived. It was widely planted and grew prolifically.

It was so easily cultivated, however, that it presented a temptation to depend on it,

Neither pasta nor potatoes, both staples of Western cuisine, are indigenous to Europe. Italian spaghetti is similar to Chinese noodles, which may have created the popular theory that Marco Polo brought the art of pasta-making from China to Venice in the thirteenth century. Legends also surround the arrival of the potato, with Sir Walter Raleigh, Sir Francis Drake and sixteenth-century Spanish explorers all credited with bringing it from the New World to the Old.

often at the expense of grain crops. The Irish gave up everything for the potato and paid a devastating price. The Irish potato blight and famine of 1845 and 1846 was the greatest disaster in Europe since the Black Death of the fourteenth century. By then, however, potatoes had proved so cheap to grow that even the Irish catastrophe failed to dislodge the once-scorned potato from its place as a basic crop in Germany, England and many other countries, including Ireland. By the turn of the twentieth century, the potato had graduated from being primarily a necessity. It remained among the cheapest of foods, but it had acquired a degree of respectability only the satisfied palate can confer.

In France, the ways to prepare potatoes reach aesthetic heights with *pommes croquettes* and potatoes *Dauphine*. The cold, rich potato soup, *vichyssoise*, is a product of the American cuisine. Swiss *roesti* and German *kartoffelsalat* are many cuts above the reluctantly consumed potatoes of two centuries ago. And new potatoes in the spring and baked potatoes any time—with butter or sour cream or caviar—show exactly how far the potato has come.

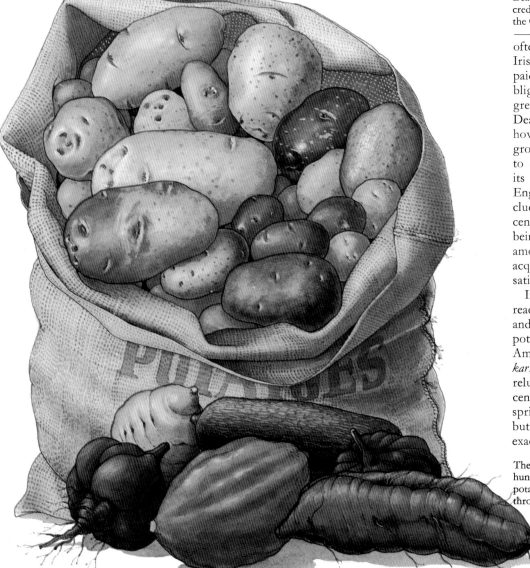

There are several hundred varieties of potatoes grown throughout the world.

White potatoes (*in the sack*) are classified according to their skin colour, size and maturity. Yams and sweet potatoes (*foreground*) are not really potatoes, but similar tuber plants.

ACCORDING TO LEGEND, pasta was one of the unusual exotic things the intrepid Marco Polo brought back to Venice from the mysterious Orient seven hundred years ago. The story has it that while he was in China, Marco Polo also learned the art of making pasta, and that he so impressed the good people of Venice upon his return home that pasta became, and has remained, Italy's most distinctive national food.

According to another story, pasta was brought to Italy in the fifth century by fierce invading Germanic tribes. A handsome Italian soldier is said to have won the love of a tribal chieftain's scullery maid, to have pried the secret of noodle-making from her and to have passed that secret on to his eternally grateful countrymen.

There are other, less romantic accounts of how pasta reached Italy and captured the imagination of the Italian people. But however it happened, it was they who transformed the potentially drab noodle into a culinary art form with a well-deserved international reputation and a wide following. The Italians do not, of course, have a monopoly on pasta.

Noodles still feature with distinction in Chinese and Southeast Asian cooking, and with greater or lesser prominence in the cuisines of Japan, France, the United States, Canada, Greece and other countries. Various noodle dishes are, for example, among the specialities of Alsace. In Central Europe and America they are often served with meat instead of potatoes or rice. But the formidable assortment of Italian pastas and the innumerable ways they are served are incomparable.

There are more than sixty different basic varieties included in the three main categories—tubular forms, such as spaghetti and macaroni; flat, such as *fettuccini* and *lasagne*; and the small, grain-like soup pasta (*pastina*). Tubular and flat pastas come in various lengths and widths, from the thinnest *vermicelli* to sheets of *lasagna*.

Pasta is made from the semolina milled from durum wheat, a hard, flinty wheat, high in gluten and protein, which converts admirably into malleable pasta dough. Sometimes the dough is enriched with eggs or spinach purée is added to enhance its flavour. Pasta is served either boiled and with a sauce, like spaghetti, or boiled and baked, like lasagna. *Ravioli, tortellini* and *cannelloni* are stuffed with meat, cheese or other fillings and usually served either with grated Parmesan cheese or with cheese and tomato sauce.

There may be no truth to the report of a spaghetti factory not far from Rome, six inches high and two miles long, perpetually churning out spaghetti to meet demand. But there is no doubt that the popularity of spaghetti, from the Italian word *spago*, meaning string, knows no borders.

All pasta is made from the same ingredients following a basic method. A flour mixture is prepared from dried durum wheat. This is mixed with boiling water and kneaded vigorously to make a stiff dough. Dried or fresh eggs or spinach purée can then be added although most pasta is a simple flour and water, combination. The pasta dough is forced through perforated cylinders to make it into various shapes. Small pastas like macaroni are cut to size as they emerge from the presses, while longer pastas like noodles and spaghetti are produced at different lengths by the machines. The cut pastas are then taken to drying ovens, the small ones on trays and the long ones draped over special drying racks. The finished products are then ready to be packaged or to be cooked in boiling water and served.

The names for the various types of pasta usually describe their shapes, origins or fillings. *Cannelloni*, for example, are big pipes, *cappelletti*, little hats, *conchiglie*, coach shells *occhi di lupo*, wolves' eyes, *quadrucci*, little squares, *stivaletti*, little boots, *stricchelli*, bows or butterflies and *vermicelli*, little worms. A slight difference in flavour can be distinguished between the shapes.

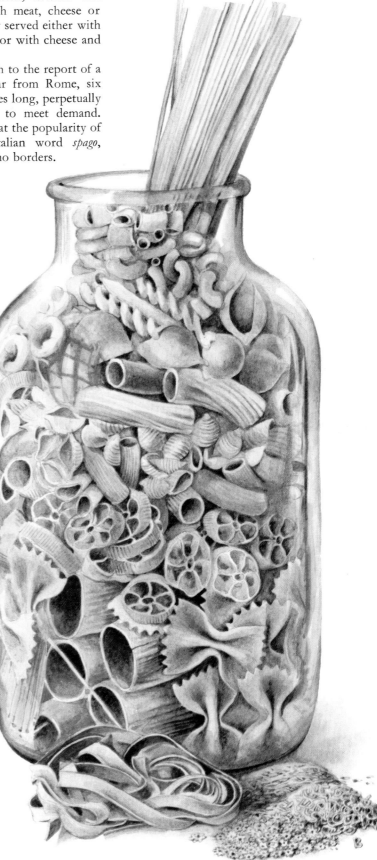

Breads of the World

BREAD has been such a conspicuous feature of so many national cuisines for so long that it tends to be neglected when the art of food preparation is considered.

Bread is, however, the forebear of all prepared foods, the ancestor of the intricate casserole, the antecedent of the succulent stew, the grandfather of the scrumptious soufflé. Indeed, everything that transpires in the kitchen today had its origin in the first loaf of bread, in the grass seeds which an impulsive cave man ground into flour, mixed with water, covered with hot ashes, baked on a hot stone and ate. That is where the process of mixing ingredients for culinary purposes was launched.

Since then, bread has come a long way. It now takes innumerable forms, including white bread, black bread, whole-wheat bread, rye bread, corn bread, barley bread, bread sticks, flatbread, the long, thin French *baguettes*, the round, squat pumpernickel, Caribbean cassava bread, Irish soda bread, Alaskan sourdough bread, raisin bread, Scottish oatcakes, Greek olive bread, malt breads, British crumpets and scones, pancakes all over the world and an endless variety of rolls.

Biblical commentaries call bread "the staff of life". Christians use bread at Holy Communion to symbolize the body of Christ. The Arabic word for bread and life stem from the same origin. In many cultures, the act of "breaking bread together" is a symbol of friendship. Dissatisfaction with the quality of available bread was one of the grievances which touched off the French Revolution. In times of depression, free food has been distributed to poor people who waited on "bread lines". The person who earns a living for the family is still called the "bread winner".

But despite its symbolic significance, despite the many forms it takes and despite modern production methods, bread remains essentially the same thing it was when the cave man first turned his hand to culinary matters. It is simply dough made from flour, moistened with water, usually leavened with yeast or some similar substance, and then baked (although some breads are steamed).

Nutritionally, bread is a relatively inexpensive source of calories, with a respectable offering of proteins as well. New, enriched breads contain an array of vitamins and calcium, too.

Over the centuries, bread has been made from such unlikely ingredients as mashed acorns, ground beans and even crushed tree

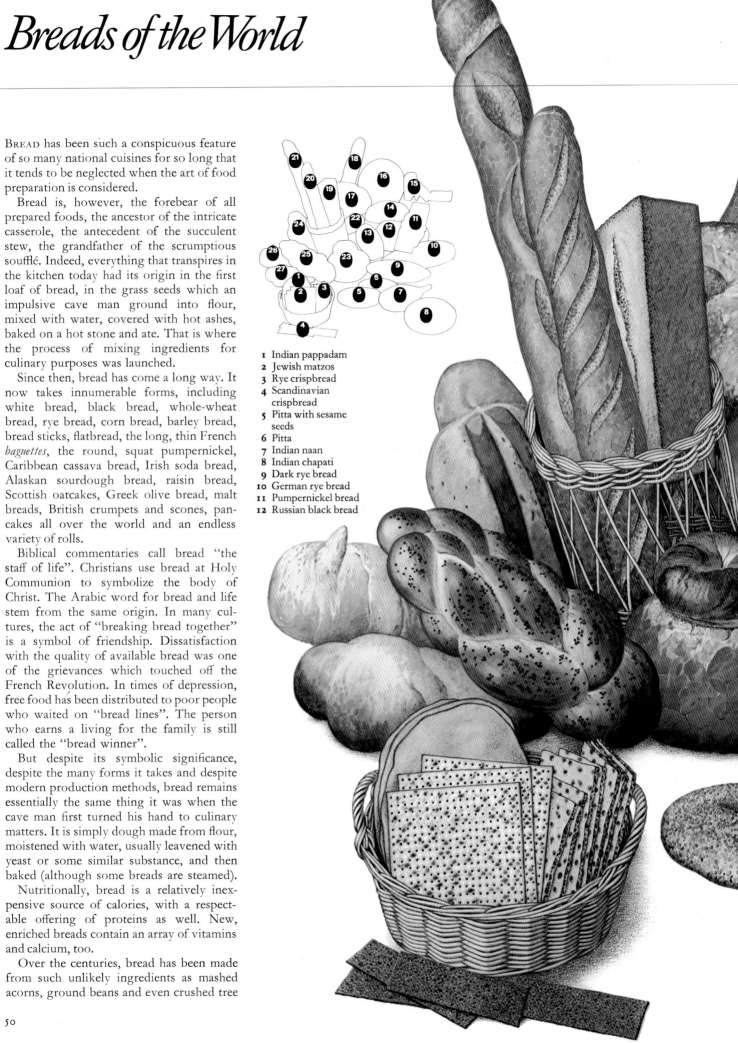

1 Indian pappadam
2 Jewish matzos
3 Rye crispbread
4 Scandinavian crispbread
5 Pitta with sesame seeds
6 Pitta
7 Indian naan
8 Indian chapati
9 Dark rye bread
10 German rye bread
11 Pumpernickel bread
12 Russian black bread

Bread dough is pliable and can be moulded into such shapes as German pretzels, Mexican Christmas-tree figures and the imaginative French breads which are baked for Bastille Day celebrations in Paris.

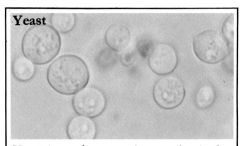

Yeast

Yeast is a plant, a microscopic single-celled fragment of matter with remarkable powers. Combined with water and flour or sugar and subjected to warmth, yeast reproduces, forming the gas carbon dioxide, which makes yeast-leavened dough rise. Commerical yeast is available in two forms—compressed and granular, which can be used interchangeably if proper instructions are followed. Billions of individual yeast cells are contained in a small cake of compressed yeast. In the dough-making process the level of warmth must be carefully controlled or the yeast will reproduce shamelessly and the resulting bread will rise beyond desirable proportions.

bark and nuts. But bread flour is generally made from one of the grains—wheat, rye, maize (corn), barley, oats or millet—finely milled. Wheat flour, because of its gluten, is usually combined with other flours.

The grain which is used depends on availability and taste. But fashions in bread, as in all things, change. For centuries, until recently, white bread at the table in the Western world was a mark of social distinction. Coarse-grained brown bread was considered suitable only for people of lowly rank or untutored taste. In recent years, however, brown breads have gained wide popularity, in part because of an unsubstantiated belief that they are nutritionally superior.

Certain kinds of bread are instruments of cultural continuity, unchanged by fads and fashions. They are the festive breads which have long played a role in religious and seasonal celebrations—north Italian Christmas *panettone*, its rich dough larded with candied fruit and raisins, Mexican Fiesta bread into which ornaments are baked, Jewish *matzoh*, unleavened to mark the hasty departure of the Israelites from slavery in Ancient Egypt, fruit-laden Russian *kulich* for Eastertime and Spanish ringed *cantello* bread, traditionally broken and distributed to the guests at wedding celebrations.

13 Wholemeal loaf	20 French petit Parisien
14 Rye bread with caraway seeds	21 French baguette
15 Danish sourdough bread	22 English bap roll
16 American sourdough bread	23 English cottage loaf
17 Irish soda bread	24 French pain Espagnol
18 French petite baguette	25 Jewish challah
19 American cornbread	26 French Epi de Charente
	27 Croissant

Variation on the Theme

John Montague, the Fourth Earl of Sandwich, a First Lord of the Admiralty, is best known as the British inventor of the sandwich.

ONCE UPON A TIME all bread was flat and unleavened. It was the Ancient Egyptians who first learned that if bread dough was permitted to ferment, it would rise and, when baked, would produce a soft, pulpy loaf. They apparently perfected the process over a long period of time. The Bible tells of a Pharaoh who was offended by his baker and had the unfortunate man hanged, so perhaps some of the early experiments with leavened bread were less than successful.

With modern yeasts, leavening methods today present no problems. Nevertheless, flatbreads—usually made from wheat flour, salt and water—remain popular in many countries. Their preparation is simplicity itself and, for reasons of taste, tradition or climate, many people prefer them to the spongy consistency of risen loaves.

The Scandinavians favour a wide selection of crisp *flatbröds* and pliable *lefsers*. Among India's many variations of flatbreads is the *papadum*, so crisp and thin it is sometimes crumbled and sprinkled over food. India's more substantial but still flat *naan*, similar to Middle Eastern *pitta*, is not to be confused with Russian *non*, which is unleavened onion bread. Mexican *tortillas* are made with maize (corn) flour rather than wheat. Armenian flat *churck* is flavoured with sesame seeds. Slimming fads have popularized a variety of low-calorie flatbreads in many Western countries.

Italian pizza is another kind of flatbread, but it is more than that. Served hot, with its assortment of toppings, including cheese, tomato, sausages, anchovies, olives and mushrooms, pizza enters a new category, the category of bread as a food carrier, one of the major relatively recent revolutions in eating habits.

Pizza is actually an open sandwich. It is related to the much daintier cold Danish *smörbröd*, which also is served with any of a host of different toppings, and to the robust hot beef sandwich doused with gravy.

Remarkably, the open sandwich originated in Europe, with the first stirrings of table etiquette, in the Middle Ages. It was not meant to be a new way of eating. It developed from the concept of a place mat as a way of keeping the dining-table relatively clean during a meal, at a time when only those of highest rank were accustomed to the luxury of a plate for their meat and its drippings. For others, slabs of hard barley or rye flatbread, specially baked for the purpose, were laid at their places and they ate from them. Sometimes these slabs were also consumed at the end of the meal; sometimes they were left to be eaten by the servants or the dogs.

The more sophisticated closed sandwich evolved much later, after the setting of plates for everyone at the table had become more common. In the eighteenth century, the Earl of Sandwich, a compulsive gambler and an indifferent gourmet, had meat placed between two slices of bread and

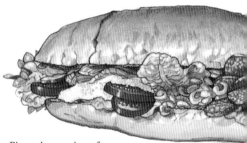

Pizza, the creation of which is credited to Naples, is flat leavened bread covered with a variety of such good things as tomatoes, mozzarella and Parmesan cheeses, mushrooms, anchovies, olives, capers and a profusion of herbs and spices.

served to him at his gaming-table in London to permit him to continue his game undisturbed by anything so pedestrian as a meal. The idea was unconventional, amusing and convenient. It quickly spread through less tradition-bound elements of English high society.

Whatever Lord Sandwich's motives, the food category to which he lent his name has had a profound impact on eating habits. Many millions of people in many countries now have at least one sandwich meal a day. Adults and school-children take sandwiches with them for lunch away from home. (Advances in the design of waxed sandwich

ANOTHER DISTINGUISHED member of the bread family is the pancake. Like most other breads, pancakes are usually made from grain flour. Unlike bread, most pancakes are meant for immediate consumption. Although some kinds of pancakes are strictly utilitarian, the pancake phenomenon injects an element of culinary virtuosity, daring and even playfulness into otherwise largely down-to-earth international bread fashions.

There are sweet pancakes, covered with jam or sprinkled with sugar, and crêpes, topped with creamed chicken or asparagus in onion sauce. There are stuffed pancakes with pâté or melted Gruyère and pancakes drenched in maple syrup or honey.

There are pancakes which are basic national foods, like the *tortilla* and the Indian *chapati*, and national pancake specialities like Scottish dropped scones and American johnnycakes. There are ceremonial pancakes like those served in England on Shrove Tuesday, the eve of Lent. The day was originally chosen for the pancake spree in order to use up butter and eggs which, once Lent began, could not be eaten and which would go bad.

There are superb pancake sandwiches. Bits of Peking duck with plum sauce, cucumber and scallions are wrapped in thin wheat pancakes to make one of the truly great dishes in the world. Equally exalted are Russian *blinis*, which are served with caviar, shreds of smoked salmon or chopped mushrooms and onions.

The sublime *crêpe suzette* was created by accident in the late nineteenth century at Monte Carlo. When the crêpe sauce caught fire, Henri Charpentier, the chef, in despair, tasted it, to discover he had stumbled across what is internationally acclaimed as one of the great pancake concoctions in culinary history.

In recent years *crêperies* offering more modest but still tasty *crêpes* have sprung up all over France, serving pancakes coated or topped with a wide variety of good things.

Dough-encased dumplings are another form of pancake sandwich. They include Chinese eggroll, Polish *piroshki*, Jewish *blintzes*, Italian *ravioli* and various baked, cooked and steamed dumplings whose coatings are made with grain flour.

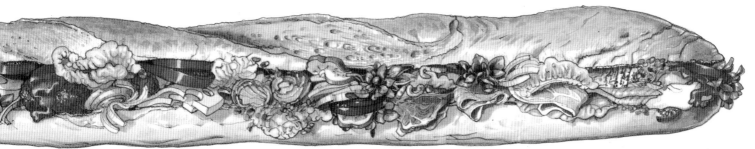

Most foods have at some time been placed between slices of bread and served as a sandwich. Recipes for sandwiches number in the thousands, from the basic cheese sandwich to elaborate concoctions of heroic proportions. It is not difficult to master the true art of sandwich-making. First choose a bread—white, brown, black, rye. Then use a spread which will keep the bread moist. Butter is the most popular, but mayonnaise, mustard, ketchup or jam, if it complements the filling, may be used. Next choose a filling or several fillings. Meat, cheese, fish, salad, fruit, eggs; almost any combination—peanut butter and banana, cream cheese and cucumber, anchovy and egg salad, bacon, lettuce and tomato—is a potential sandwich filling. A delicious hero sandwich can be created from a French loaf filled with such simple ingredients as watercress, scrambled egg, sliced chicken, shrimp, salmon, sliced hard-boiled eggs, hamburgers, raw onions, Emmenthal cheese, tuna fish, sliced beef, bacon, blue cheese and fried egg.

wrapping paper has promoted this practice.) People go to cafeterias, bars and new-styled sandwich supermarkets to have a "quick sandwich" rather than a full meal. Picnickers and other travellers find that sandwiches are a tidy, tasty, inexpensive convenience. And, too, there are those people who consider sandwiches the perfect between-meals kitchen snack.

The once-aristocratic sandwich now comes in a huge assortment of shapes, sizes and categories—the hunk of bread wrapped around a chunk of cheese or sausage, the daintiest canapés, the Norwegian smoked salmon and scrambled egg sandwich, the hamburger smothered in onions, the mashed baked bean sandwich, the Dutch smoked eel sandwich, the chocolate spread sandwich much favoured by many English children.

The various possible sandwich combinations of bread and butter and salad vegetables, meat or fish can provide virtually all the necessary proteins, vitamins and other nutrients. The simple sandwich medley of bread, butter (or another bread spread) and a filling allows for almost an infinity of variations to meet individual requirements and cravings.

A Copenhagen restaurant offers a four-foot-long menu listing more than 250 available sandwiches. The Italian-American hero sandwich can be more than a foot long and stuffed with savoury meatballs, hot sausages, veal *cacciatore* and other tasty fillings.

Along the shores of the eastern Mediterranean, the *pitta* is often cut in half and stuffed with *shish kebab*. The British have managed to reconcile two such opposites as cheese and chutney between slices of bread. The traditional American sandwich can include lettuce, tomatoes, cheese, cold meats, pickles and anything else that happens to be cluttering the refrigerator.

Berries, Wild and Cultivated

Raspberries

Dewberries

Redcurrants

Loganberries

Strawberries

Blue[berries]

Blackc[urrants]

NO BERRY has a history as dramatic as the strawberry. It is the ancient berry which was sacred to Frigg, the northern goddess of love and, later, to the Virgin Mary. It was then only a wild woodland fruit.

The improvement in the size and reliability of strawberries occurred by accident at the end of the eighteenth century. Strawberries from Virginia and from Chile—which had been brought back from opposite ends of the Americas—were pushed off into a corner together in a French market garden. In time they fertilized each other and so produced a new strawberry which combined the good flavour and colour of the one with the size of the other.

The raspberry, with its bloomy clustered fruit of pinkish-red, is a northern plant. It needs long hours of light to ripen, and so the best crops come from areas where summer days are long, temperate and dry. Different varieties and species of raspberries have been developed for other conditions. Many English gardeners grow a yellow raspberry of excellent flavour. In California, two larger, darker fruits have been developed, the loganberry, or phenomenal berry, and the boysenberry, named after Rudolf Boysen, who was responsible for popularizing it there.

The gooseberry, too, likes northern conditions and will grow right up to the Arctic Circle. Large dessert gooseberries should be eaten with a glass of muscat wine. Cream is essential to gooseberries, leading to that most delicious of puddings—the gooseberry fool.

Bilberries, blaeberries, whortleberries, huckleberries and blueberries are all similar species of *Vaccinium*, whether they are gathered on a mountain walk in England, in Ireland, in Scotland, in Sweden, in America, or bought in a supermarket. What is more delicious than blueberry pie?

Cranberries, native to both Europe and America, have a sharp, tangy flavour. They make good pies and puddings, but their best use is with turkey and other poultry as a tasty sauce or jelly. This is true, too, of rowan berries, which, cooked with apples and jellied, provide a tart, agreeable contrast to set off poultry and game.

The mulberry is a sadly neglected fruit which is delicious and rich-flavoured when eaten raw with sugar and cream or turned into jelly and puddings. The related blackberry—the French call them both *mûre*—is a bonus of autumn walks, a small pleasure to help the very young along their way.

The currants, red, white and black, are strictly garden plants for most of us. Although ripe red and white currants are good raw if they are dipped first into plenty of sugar, they are most often used to make beautiful jellies to eat with bread and butter, or with lamb in the winter. A spoonful of redcurrant jelly is used as a finishing touch to French stews of hare and game. In England blackcurrants are the favourite fruit for summer pudding and for jams.

Cranberries

Blackberries

Gooseberries

Fruits of the Orchard

IF PROOF were needed that the world's cradles of civilization were China, Southeast Asia and the Middle East, the history of the orchard would provide it.

Sweet oranges, mandarins and citrons came from the Far East, and the lime is from India. The grapefruit is much later, a hybrid between pomelo and sweet orange which was developed in the New World and not recognized as a species until the first part of the nineteenth century.

Until the seventeenth century, the European orange was the bitter kind. Bitter oranges are still essential to some recipes, the traditional marmalade of the British breakfast table and *sauce bigarade* for duck and game.

The sweet orange was a treat, a luxury. Pepys drank his first glass of sweet orange juice nervously in 1669. This new fruit was known as the China orange. Other debts to China include the apricot and the peach. The persimmon (*Diospyros kaki*), orange-red, very sweet and slightly astringent, originally came from China and Japan. Today persimmons grow in the southern United States, California and France.

The ancestors of gardens and orchards in the West are the gardens and orchards of ancient Middle Eastern civilization. "Orchard" means garden yard, a place set apart especially for growing fruit.

Four thousand years ago, apple and pear trees grew in the orchards of the Hittites. Plums first came from orchards between the Tigris and the Euphrates. The damson has changed little since it left Damascus for Greece and Rome. The cherry conceals its history in its name. It goes back to *karsu*, the Akkadian word used by the Assyrians and Babylonians who first cultivated it.

The golden beauty of the quince was sacred to Aphrodite. Sir Isaac Newton's favourite pudding was not apples, but quinces baked in the oven. Figs, a basic food of the Mediterranean, the medlar, and the pomegranate with its seeds of death and new life, of winter and spring, we owe, too, to those early gardeners who arranged their trees in order, propped up the laden branches and shaped them to increase the next year's harvest.

1 Quince	12 Yellow plum
2 Grapefruit	13 Morello cherry
3 Ugli fruit	14 Starking cherries
4 Crab apples	15 Rainbow-stripe
5 Newton apple	cherries
6 Red Richard apple	16 Conference pear
7 Peach	17 Cyprus lemon
8 Apricot	18 Sweet orange
9 Nectarine	19 Seville orange
10 Cortham pear	20 Clementine
11 Red plum	21 Cyprus lime
	22 Tangerine

Fruits of the Tropics

An Indian fruit merchant prepares his stall for a day of selling. He artistically arranges his display of green and yellow bananas, juicy pineapples, green Benaras mangoes and festoons of fresh, sweet grapes.

The principal tropical fruit-growing areas begin near the Equator and extend into the warmer parts of the temperate zones. Today, modern transportation has made many tropical fruits available and familiar all over the world.

EARLY WESTERN EXPLORERS in the Pacific thought they had found Paradise when they encountered their first palm-fringed tropical island. Further investigation confirmed this belief, for where else had nature bestowed her gifts with such a liberal hand?

The climate—temperatures in the 80s and an annual rainfall measuring as much in inches—is ideal for growing all manner of plants in exotic profusion. What impressed those early travellers, and impresses today's tourists, was the mouth-watering abundance of luscious and succulent fruit. A luxury in the West, these fruits are often a necessity of life in the tropics. The coconut, for example, one of the most versatile of tropical fruits, provides both delectable food and refreshing drink, oil for cooking and flavouring for innumerable dishes, both sweet and savoury, while the sap, tapped and fermented, makes a heady drink called toddy which, when further distilled, becomes a potent spirit.

But for the breadfruit, it is possible that the mutiny of the *Bounty* would never have taken place and Captain Bligh might have died in obscurity. The fruit, as its name suggests, is farinaceous and is a staple food on some Pacific islands. Roasted or baked before it is fully ripe, breadfruit tastes like wheat bread. As it ripens the taste is more like a sweet potato. When fully ripe, its green skin turned to yellow and brown, it is ready to be made into a dessert. The seeds resemble chestnuts in texture and flavour, and can be used as a substitute.

The banana, credited with hiding the serpent in the Garden of Eden and sheltering the sages of Ancient India, produces one of the most important fruit crops in the world and provides an inexpensive staple for millions. Besides the many sweet and subtly flavoured dessert bananas, there are cooking bananas, sometimes called plantains, and one variety grown for the sole purpose of making beer.

Akee Tasting deliciously of scrambled egg, akee, although a fruit, is cooked and served as a vegetable. The size of a peach, it bursts open when ripe to expose three shiny black seeds attached to the base by fleshy cream-coloured arils—the edible portions.

Jack fruit Weighing up to seventy pounds, jack fruit has a warty, dark green skin and an awesome odour when cut. It may be eaten raw as a fruit or cooked as a vegetable. It has a creamy yellow, fleshy pulp with a better flavour than smell.

Sapodilla A Central American fruit, sapodilla has a rough brown skin and sweet, slightly grainy flesh. It is eaten when fully ripe. Its luscious khaki-coloured pulp tastes like slightly astringent brown sugar.

Papaya Sprinkled with lemon juice and sugar, papaya is eaten for breakfast in the tropics. Sometimes called pawpaw, it has sweet, succulent, orange-yellow flesh. The leaves and unripe fruit contain an enzyme, papain, which is used to tenderize meat.

Coconut The coconut is best known in the West in its dry form. The delightful, cool, refreshing water and the soft, white, translucent flesh of an immature coconut are enjoyed only in the tropics.

Rambutan A Southeast Asian fruit native to Malaysia, the rambutan is a close relative of the lychee. The same size as the lychee, it is covered with red and, sometimes, yellow spikes.

Citron A highly fragrant fruit with a thick coruscated rind, thick pith and sour pulp, the citron is mainly used to make candied peel. It was one of the earliest citrus fruits to migrate from the Far East to the Mediterranean, where it now grows extensively.

Custard apple The soft, sweet, creamy, custard-flavoured pulp of the *sweetsop* is the reason this fruit is commonly called a custard apple. Other members of the *Anona* family are often mistakenly called by the same name, perhaps because they all have the same soft creamy pulp.

Mangosteen Soft, white, juicy segmented flesh with a delightful sour-sweet taste encased in a tough, purplish-red skin, the mangosteen is a favourite fruit in Southeast Asia.

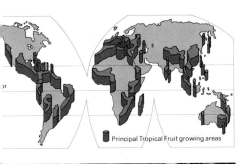

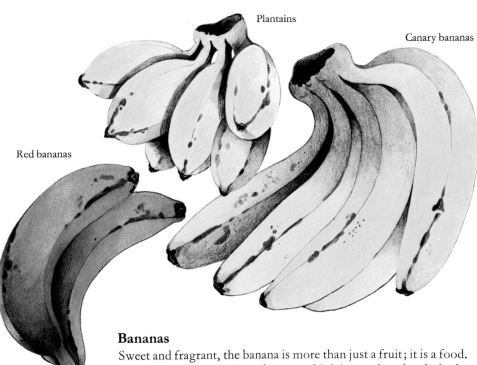

Plantains

Canary bananas

Red bananas

Bananas

Sweet and fragrant, the banana is more than just a fruit; it is a food. They are rich in nutritive substances, high in starch and carbohydrates and easily digested. In the tropics, bananas grow in many sizes, colours and flavours, used variously for eating or for cooking. There are more than one hundred types, and they are available all the year round.

Passion fruit
Passion fruit is a succulent, highly perfumed berry with a delicate flavour. It gets its name from the flower, which symbolizes the passion of Christ— the corona resembling the crown of thorns and the styles bearing the stigmata.

Fig Exquisitely sweet and ambrosial, the fig was one of the earliest cultivated fruits in the world, and is indigenous from eastern Turkey to North India. It was under a wild fig tree that Buddha found enlightenment.

Durian Malodorous but delicious, the durian is a favourite fruit in Southeast Asia. Others find its smell so unpleasant that they are unable to enjoy its sweet, glutinous, creamy-white pulp.

Pomegranate A fruit with many biblical associations, the pomegranate is much loved in Asia. Its rather tart, ruby-red translucent pulp surrounding innumerable seeds is most refreshing to eat. The dark red juice makes a marvellous drink.

Lychee A native of South China, the lychee is the favourite fruit of the Cantonese. It has a brittle, reddish skin and juicy, white, translucent flesh surrounding a single shiny brown seed, and the subtle perfumed flavour of a good grape.

Kumquat Although not a true citrus fruit, the kumquat is very much like a small orange. There are oval and round varieties, the oval being the more common.

Breadfruit The fruit of a handsome, glossy-leaved tree, the breadfruit is native to Malaysia. It spread in prehistoric times to the South Pacific where it is a staple food. There are two varieties, of which the seedless is the most common.

Soursop A close relative of the custard apple, the soursop is a dark green, heart-shaped fruit covered with fleshy spines. It can grow to five pounds or more. The soft sour-sweet pulp is used mostly to make soft drinks and sherbets.

Mango The mango is the king of tropical fruit. Kidney-shaped or oval, long and round, the mango varies in colour from green to gold or rosy red.

Cherimoya The texture and taste of a cherimoya is reminiscent of a creamy ice-cream made from banana and pineapple. No wonder it is such a popular fruit. Native to the tropical highlands of Central and South America, it is related to the custard apple.

Loquat The loquat is an agreeable sour-sweet, yellow fruit with a refreshing flavour. Probably native to China, it has been cultivated in Japan since antiquity.

Borassus palm The borassus or palmyra palm grows wild in South India, Sri Lanka and Burma. In India it is mainly used for making sugar. The sap is also fermented to make toddy. The immature nut provides a refreshing drink and a soft edible kernel.

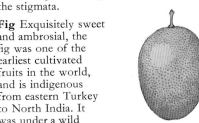

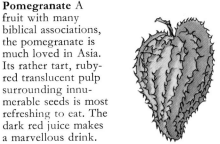

57

Principal Tropical Fruit growing areas

Fruits of the Vine

If Catherine de' Medici survived despite her penchant for melons, it must have been due to her iron constitution. When she complained one day of feeling ill, the Calvinist Queen Jeanne of Navarre, mother of Henry IV, retorted that it was not surprising, considering how many melons she ate.

These would have been a type of muskmelon, the netted, aromatic fruits of opulent colour and shape which are seen in European markets, shaded by striped awnings from the fierce heat of the sun. They exude a sweetness that creeps gently upon the senses, particularly if one has been cut in half to display its orange flesh.

Another favourite is the cantaloupe melon, a dimpled, rough-skinned fruit. It was first grown in Italy in the fifteenth century in the Pope's gardens at Cantalupo, near Tivoli, from seeds brought from Armenia. There are also the small, green-and-white-striped Ogen melons, which take their name from a kibbutz in Israel, and the oval, pale-fleshed honeydews.

An excellent way of eating the smaller, fragrant melons is with Parma, Bayonne or Westphalian ham. Melons also make beautiful ice-creams and sherbets, and chilled summer soups. Pouring port, or similar wines, into melons is a mistake. It does no good whatsoever and only disguises the characteristic flavour.

The watermelon comes from a different genus, but like the muskmelon, it is thought to have originated in tropical Africa. For all its magnificent appearance, dark green skin, red flesh and black seeds, it has a delicate flavour—a natural water-ice.

Grapes have always been the best loved of fruit. Even Pliny, who wrote in the first century AD and was mainly concerned with cataloguing plants and their uses, warmed up when he came to the vine and its cultivation, rejoicing in the early summer when the whole of the country seemed to be scented with the vine's sweet-smelling flowers.

Although wine has come to seem the most important destiny of the grape, it was first prized as a fruit. As food became a matter for discrimination in a Europe without sugar-cane, varieties of grape were cultivated for their sweetness. Grape juice was boiled down to improve its keeping qualities and to concentrate its flavour. Italian dishes of veal or poultry which are fried in butter, then finished in sweet Marsala, are the descendants of dishes flavoured with those concentrates and created by the chefs of the great Romans, Apicius and Lucullus.

The Romans devised techniques to dry the fruit. Ever since those early times, currants, the raisins that take their name from Corinth, have come from a small, seedless variety of grape grown in southern Greece. Smyrna, on the west coast of Turkey, was originally the centre for yellowish brown raisins with quite a different flavour, which in England are called sultanas.

Greece still produces more dried fruit than any other region of the Old World, and more than Australia, although not as much as the United States.

black dessert grapes

white dessert grapes

musk melon

winter melon

balsam pear

ogen melon

cantaloupe melon

watermelon

Nuts

1 Sweet chestnuts
2 Queensland nuts
3 Pecans
4 Pine kernals
5 Walnut
6 Almonds
7 Hazel nuts
8 Cashews
9 Pistachios
10 Brazil nut
11 Butternut
12 Black walnut

Nuts are valued by cooks for their oils, which impart flavour to a great variety of dishes. With the exception of chestnuts, edible nuts contain little starch. Nothing adds a more decorative touch to a table and a fitting epilogue to a meal than a bowl of assorted nuts.

ALMONDS are the world's most sought-after nuts. It is difficult to imagine life without them. How few delicious cakes there would be—no almond tarts, no Florentines, no marzipan or petits fours. A particularly fine variety, the Jordan almond, which despite its name does not come from Palestine but from Malaga in Spain, is a natural partner for the superb Malaga raisins.

Hazelnuts may be tasted at their best at Avellino, a small town behind Vesuvius, which has been famous for them since Roman times. Perhaps the best are the slow-roasted, pale, golden-brown nuts served with the local wine. Cobnuts are a variety of hazelnuts, and filberts are another, their name anglicized from the French *noix de Philibert*, the nut of St Philibert.

The sweet chestnut, *Castanea sativa*, makes the candied *marron glacé* of southern France, one of the world's finest sweetmeats. When fresh chestnuts are not available for cooking, dried nuts, soaked overnight, can be used. Although they lack the subtlety of the fresh nut, a grainy crispness is retained. Apart from the sweet, vanilla-flavoured purée, canned chestnuts are heavy-textured and should be avoided.

After chestnuts, the most important nuts, from the cook's point of view, are pine nuts, which come from the cone of the Roman or stone pine. This ivory-coloured, waxy, bean-shaped nut is much used by Italians in sweet-sour stuffings for sardines, and for rich soups and stews which need bite. In the Middle East, pine nuts are also used a great deal with fish, and to give a contrasting texture in smooth, minced meat dishes.

Another favourite nut of the Mediterranean is the pistachio, a native of the Near East and Central Asia. Its flavour is light but unmistakable. Its pale green colour and the purplish red of its skin make it a happy ingredient in pâtés, sausages and sweet dishes.

The walnut has a pronounced and recognizable flavour which goes marvellously with richness and sweetness: prunes, caramelized sweets, layer cakes and pastry. Fresh walnuts, the first of the harvest dried in the heat of an October sun rather than in kilns, are an autumn treat. In France, they are eaten with hot bread, coarse sea salt, sweet butter and a glass of new wine.

America has many varieties of native walnuts. The black walnut (*Juglans nigra*) is much used in sweet dishes, and the white walnut or butternut (*Juglans cinerea*) has a good flavour and a deeply wrinkled shell. The pecan (*Caya illinoensis*) belongs to the same family, and has a mild walnut taste. It looks like an elongated walnut, too, although the reddish brown shell is smooth. Pecans make better dessert nuts than black walnuts or butternuts, and are much in demand for baking and confectionery.

It often surprises people to see how Brazil nuts grow, nestling in a neatly rounded curl, like orange segments, inside a large, woody shell. To the British, the Brazil nut, a native of the Amazon valley, is the Christmas dessert nut, and for the rest of the year it is eaten in confections made with butter-toffee or chocolate.

The Macadamia or Queensland nut, native to Australia and now widely grown in Hawaii, is soft and delicately sweet when it is fresh. Roasted and salted, it is served with drinks.

Cashew nuts have an unmistakable flavour and texture. Many people enjoy them, but for fineness they cannot compare with almonds, hazelnuts or walnuts.

Peanuts, or groundnuts, are beans rather than true nuts. They come into their own in Far Eastern cooking, where their rich, dominating flavour is balanced in hot spicy sauces. Meeting them in this way will give people a most agreeable shock, if they have only come across them salted with drinks, or misused as a cheap substitute for almonds, or hazelnuts.

The World of Cheese

For thousands of years, since the first seemingly miraculous separation of curds and whey, countless forms of cheese have been developed and carefully tended

1 Provolone
2 Parmesan
3 Samsoe
4 Edam
5 Gouda
6 Mimolette
7 Blue Cheshire
8 Fontina
9 Stilton
10 Gloucester
11 Canadian Cheddar
12 Emmenthal
13 Dunlop
14 Mozzarella
15 Gruyère

16	Danish Blue	23	Feta
17	Cheddar	24	Jack
18	Wensleydale	25	Tomme au Raisin
19	Ricotta	26	Lancashire
20	Bleu de Bresse	27	Caerphilly
21	Caciocavallo	28	Vacherin
22	Leicester	29	Dolcelatte

37 Brie
38 Epoisses
39 Tilsiter
40 Pont l'Evêque
41 Livarot
42 Quargel
43 New England Sage
44 Roquefort
45 Banon
46 St Marcellin
47 Camembert
48 Münster
49 Bel Paese
50 Maroilles

30 Edelpitz
31 Limburger
32 St Nectaire
33 Red Windsor
34 Brick
35 Port-Salut
36 Gorgonzola

61

The Almost Perfect Food

CHEESE, like its traditional companions, bread and wine, is a monument to man's ingenuity and ability to shape the bounty of nature to his needs and tastes. No one can say for certain where and when cheese originated, although this earliest of processed, portable foods has probably existed since about 9000 BC, when milk-yielding animals were domesticated in the Middle East and Europe. Certainly, archaeologists have traced it back to 4000 BC in the records of the Sumerians, to the Egyptians and Chaldeans.

The mysterious quality of milk's spontaneous fermentation gave rise to all manner of beliefs about its curative and strengthening powers, long before it was realized that cheese was a nearly perfect whole food, rich in protein, fat, minerals and vitamin A.

Zoroaster, the Persian mystic, reputedly lived on nothing but cheese for twenty years. The Ancient Greeks fed their Olympic athletes with cheese, believing it to be a divinely sustaining gift from Aristaeus, the son of Apollo. The Romans doted on cheese, making it and importing it. Wherever their empire reached, cheese-making was fostered. Swiss Emmenthal, first made by the Helvetii tribe in the Alpine regions, is one enduring result of this enlightened self-interest.

When the Roman Empire faded, cheese-making passed into the hands of equally dedicated custodians of gastronomy—the monks of the Middle Ages. Until then, cheese had been of three types—soft and fresh, pressed and aged and blue-veined, like the venerable Roquefort and Gorgonzola. With patience and skill, the monks developed cheese with an entirely different character, the soft, ripe, creamily golden Port-Salut and Pont l'Evêque. It is more than likely that they also originated France's most famous soft-ripening cheese, Brie, which Charlemagne sampled in 774 at the priory of Rueil.

While cheese is made in many parts of the world, it reaches its zenith in countries where milk, cream and butter form an integral part of the cuisine. Asia and Africa have little tradition of cheese-making—in the case of China and Japan, none. India is the only major Asian country that regularly eats and cooks with cheese.

Historically, the two most important centres of cheese-making have always been France and Italy. France leads with a staggering four hundred varieties, each subdivided according to the region or town where it is made. In addition to the incomparable sheep's-milk Roquefort, another favourite of Charlemagne, there are *bleus* (the generic name for internally mould-ripened cheeses) from many different provinces; a legion of *chèvres*, the little goats'-milk cheeses, with names like Banon, Chabichou and Saint-Maure; semi-soft, cured cheeses like Reblochon, Port-Salut and Maroilles; the unctuous *double* and *triple crèmes*; semi-hard and hard cheeses such as Comté and Cantal (French equivalents of Gruyère and Cheddar). And a staggering array of soft-ripened cheese of the Brie persuasion has been invented, as well as two thousand different brands of Camembert, although the best still come from Normandy.

The Italians have created Bel Paese, Taleggio and Fontina, Gorgonzola, Provolone and Caciocavallo, the soft, fresh *ricotta* and *mozzarella*, and the formidably hard, grainy, grating cheeses—Parmesan, Pecorino Romano and Pecorino Sardo and Asiago.

Britain has the noble, blue-veined Stilton, and an impressive range of cheeses of the Cheddar family, including Cheshire, Double and Single Gloucester (Double is thicker, heavier and longer aged), Derby, Lancashire, Leicester, the Scottish Dunlop and the Welsh Caerphilly, each with its own characteristic flavour, texture and idiosyncracies. Cheshire, believed to be England's oldest cheese, has a special tang that comes from the salt in the soil of the Cheshire and Shropshire grazing land. Double Gloucester is mellow, with a satin, creamy quality. Caerphilly is white, crumbly, salty and perishable.

Switzerland's reputation rests on Gruyère, Emmenthal and Appenzeller, variations on the many-eyed cheese; the aged, granular Sbrinz and Saaen; Bagnes, melted and scraped for the famous Swiss dish *raclette*, and Schabzieger or Sapsago, a curious, cone-shaped grating cheese.

Holland claims the bland Edam and Gouda and the spiced Leyden. Scandinavia's cheeses range from smooth, bland Jarlsberg, caraway-and-cumin-spiced · Nøkkelost and the strange, brown, sweet, cooked whey cheese, Gjetost, definitely an acquired taste, to a luscious, soft-ripened pair—the richly creamy Hablé Crème Chantilly of Sweden and Denmark's Crema Dania.

Elsewhere the list grows slimmer. Greece brings to mind *feta*, the salted and brine-preserved fresh sheep or goat cheese, and the harder, more pungent *kasseri* and *kefalotyri*. Belgium has strong-smelling Limburger and Herve, Germany and Austria have a variety of types, from smooth and tangy Tilsit and the soft but powerful Romadur and Schlosskäse, which is similar to Limburger, to the mild, firm mountain cheeses, Bergkäse and Alpkäse. Spain is noted for the sheep's-milk Manchego and *queso de cabrales*, a blue-veined cheese from a combination of cow, goat and sheep milk, aged, like Roquefort, in limestone caves.

Portugal offers a bevy of sharp, creamy sheep's-milk cheeses generically known as *quiejo de serra*.

Despite its Spanish heritage, Latin America has, in the past, offered little in the way of local cheeses other than the fresh *queso blanco* and *queso fresco*, and an occasional aged hard cheese. In recent years, however, a taste for cheese, and a talent for cheese-making, have begun to develop and the future may bring some indigenous innovations.

Both Canada and the United States produce cheeses of the Cheddar persuasion, like the US Coon, Colby and Oregon Tillamook. California's Monterey Jack is something between a Cheddar and the blander, softer American version of the Alsatian Münster. The firm Brick and the soft, runny Liederkrantz are native American creations, both strongly pungent. Canada originated Oka, a Port-Salut type of cheese made by Trappist monks, and Quebec's Fromage de l'Ile.

For every original cheese there are imitators by the hundred. Camembert is one of the most copied of the soft-ripening cheeses. Surprisingly good versions of Brie can be found in California and Brazil. Denmark markets its copies of Port-Salut and Emmenthal as Esrom and Samsoe. Even the French are not above purveying an Edam Français or a Gallic version of Cheshire with an un-Gallic name, Chester.

The embryo cheese is born when milk, which may or may not have been heated, is coagulated by the addition of a bacterial starter, or rennet, or both. This separates the curds from the whey. Further steps involve the breaking up and draining of the curd, pressing or moulding, salting, draining and drying, curing and aging.

The simplest and most widespread of all forms of cheese is the fresh, soft, unripened kind. Into this category fall cottage, pot and farmer cheese, the German Glumse, French *fromage blanc*, English Colwick and York, Scottish crowdie, the *queso blanco* or *queso fresco* of Latin America, Italian *ricotta* and *mozzarella*, and cream cheeses of every degree of richness up to the glorious French *double* and *triple crèmes*.

For the very simplest of cheeses, like *fromage blanc*, sour milk is dripped through cheesecloth until all that remains are the curds. For cottage or pot cheese, the curds of skimmed milk are cut into cubes, heated until firm, drained, then salted and sometimes mixed with cream. Cream cheeses are made with milk and cream, or pure cream, and moulded or pressed to velvety smoothness.

The greatest of eating cheeses are the kind known as soft-ripened, where the cheese ripens from the outside to the centre. Brie, Camembert and Coulommiers are called "flowery rind", because the bacterial culture with which they are sprayed or sprinkled grows on the surface, forming a smooth, velvety crust. Cured *double* and *triple crèmes* (as distinct from the fresh) are ripened in the same way, but their butterfat content is much higher.

Next in line come the semi-soft cheeses, such as Reblochon, Münster, Taleggio, Bel Paese, butter-smooth in texture and rather milder in flavour. These are classified as "washed rind" cheeses; they grow no surface mould but are periodically washed with liquid—salt and water, beer, cider, whey or wine—so the rind remains soft and supple, and the interior moist enough to encourage fermentation. The semi-soft blue cheeses, on the other hand, are ripened from within by penicillin mould which induces a spreading network of blue veins.

In a category all their own are the French goats'-milk cheeses. These vary in size and shape (although they are invariably small compared to other cheeses), in flavour from mild and sweet to strong and pungent, and in consistency from soft to very hard. They are an acquired taste, especially in their older and stronger manifestations. According to the great French cheese expert, Pierre Androuet, the best of all are veiled with a thin, bluish film, indicating that they were made on farms and ripened in the traditional manner, on wicker trays in cellars, so forming a natural rind. The commercially made *chèvre*, for which the curds are mixed with penicillin, develops a thick white rind. Cheese made only from goats' milk is labelled *pur chèvre*, while a *mi chèvre* may be only 25 per cent goats' milk and the rest cows' milk.

Finally, at the far end of the cheese spectrum, are the aged, the firm or semi-hard and hard granular types. The majority of the firm cheeses have a low moisture content and improve by being aged anywhere from three months to a year (some special American Cheddars are aged for two years). A fine Cheddar will start out mild, grow mellow in middle age and attain its true stature when old, developing a full, round, pronounced flavour and a firm, smooth, close texture. The degree of sharpness varies according to the country and local taste.

Switzerland's unique contributions in this category are the cheeses with eyes—Emmenthal, Gruyère and Appenzeller. Like Cheddar, Emmenthal is much copied, usually under the generic name of Swiss cheese, but the best is made with the rich milk of the cows that graze in the lush green Emme Valley. The characteristic large spherical eyes are formed by three species of bacteria. The cheese-maker must determine, by thumping and listening to the cheese, when the eyes are of the right size. Then the huge wheels are aged for six to ten months in curing cellars.

Gruyère, a smaller wheel than Emmenthal, with smaller eyes and a brownish rather than a honey-coloured rind, is made in both Switzerland and France, where it is known as Beaufort or Comté. Appenzeller is similar to Gruyère, with a stronger, tangier flavour.

The oldest members of the Swiss family are Sbrinz and Saanen, which age considerably longer (Sbrinz for three years, Saanen for five or six) until they attain the obdurate quality and pungent savour characteristic of the Italian *granas*.

The *granas* (there are two main kinds, Grana Padano and Parmesan, or Parmigiano-Reggiano, as it is officially called) are the most long-lived of all the cheeses. Parmesan, made under strict regulations as to region, milk and season, is considered the superior. Although it can be eaten as a table cheese, it is really designed for grating and flavouring. A Parmesan which has been aged for three years is an awesome and formidable sight, granular, rock-like and yellow, all but impenetrable to the knife. It has a piquant, fruity, sharp flavour that blends magnificently with the blandness of pastas.

Interestingly, the two kinds of cheese that lend themselves best to cooking are the young and the old. The young, fresh cheeses contribute a soft creaminess and a delicate, unassertive flavour, while the more definite taste of the firm and hard cheeses enhances many dishes, melting quickly and combining smoothly with other ingredients.

Europeans serve cheese at the end of a meal, before or instead of a dessert or sweet course. The French firmly bring on the cheese after salad, holding that its role is to erase the sharp acidity of the vinegar and prepare the palate for the sweetness of the dessert, but others choose to eat it with their salad. This is a matter of taste and preference and, of course, the cheese being served.

The same holds true of the butter controversy. While it would be redundant to butter the bread for a sauvely soft and rich Brie or *triple crème*, a touch of unsalted butter can be very appealing with a firm, aged Cheddar. The British like to nibble celery with cheese. Others believe a touch of mustard enhances the flavour of such cheeses as Münster, Tilsit and Gruyère, especially if they are to be eaten with dark breads, for a snack or supper.

Like red wine, cheese should be left at room temperature for an hour or two before serving. Soft cheeses warm up faster than firm ones. A soft-ripening cheese should be bought on the day it is to be eaten.

Salt and Pepper

Pepper is the fruit of the Asian vine *Piper nigrum*. Tiny berries cluster on long, hanging stalks. Black pepper is made by grinding the sun-dried berries. To make white pepper, the dried berries are soaked in water and the outer covering removed before they are ground.

PEPPER has been used since the earliest times of civilization. The word pepper comes from the Sanskrit *pipali*. Pepper was used to make Indian curries spicy and hot until the arrival of chillies from the New World in the sixteenth century. Pepper has long been the world's first spice, in part because peppercorns store well without losing flavour, which is essential to the success of spice trading.

As negotiable as silver, and as common a currency, pepper was of the greatest importance to those people of medieval Europe who needed it and other spices to relieve their dull winter diet of salted and dried foods. Although today the phrase "peppercorn rent" means a nominal sum, in those days a pound of peppercorns was equal to several weeks' wages.

Black peppercorns are the dried berries of *Piper nigrum*, the pepper vine, which is native to Burma and Assam, but is now grown in many of the hottest parts of the world. White peppercorns are the same berries, but the dark outer layer, the scented layer, is removed by soaking, leaving only the fierce peppery centre. Some chefs prefer to use white pepper for pale sauces so that no dark specks will sully their appearance.

Green peppercorns are the fresh berries before they have ripened to redness. From Madagascar they are imported into France where they have recently become a popular flavouring. Green peppercorns are juicy and are much hotter than dried peppercorns. They are delicious when used with sausage meat for stuffing or with purées of dried vegetables to be served with rich meats. Green peppercorns can be bought in cans, and in Paris frozen green peppercorns are available.

The first requirement for good cooking is a pepper mill. The grey dust of commercially ground pepper cannot be compared with the sweet spiciness of freshly ground black peppercorns. It gives an extraordinary lift to the simplest of food, particularly if the pepper is coarsely ground. The aroma, however, disappears with prolonged cooking, leaving only the fiery flavour. Extra pepper should, therefore, be added to food last of all, just before serving. Surprisingly, when pepper is used in quantity, as for steak *au poivre*, or turbot *au poivre*, it does not drown the delicate flavour of the meat or fish, and when a quarter of a teaspoon is sprinkled over pears, for a pear tart, or slices of apples, for fritters, it brings out the flavour of the fruit vividly.

SALT is the first of seasonings. It is essential and is often taken for granted. Certainly the day one first comes across sea salt—grainy salt from Brittany or brilliant crystals from the Mediterranean—can be surprising. To lick a few grains that have that extra flavour of the sea is to have a most ordinary substance become unexpectedly precious and important. Salt is no longer just salty—it has savour.

Salt comes from two sources. There are, first, underground seams of rock salt, which, like coal, must be mined. Salt also comes from salt water, from the sea or from inland brine springs. This water must be heated by the sun or, artificially, by fires before the salt can be won from the evaporating water. The higher the temperature, the finer and whiter and less flavourful the salt. When the water barely bubbles and moves, the salt precipitates into the larger, tastier crystals which make so much difference to cooking.

It seems that man's appetite for salt grew as he settled into farming communities and gave up the nomadic life of the Old Stone Age hunters. He learned that it is easier to preserve surplus food by salting rather than by drying. Where winters were dark and lifeless, the salting down of beef and pork ensured survival through to the next growing season.

By the Iron Age, salt was a large industry in northern Europe. Great centres like Hallstatt, in what is now Austria, traded salt and on the proceeds their societies developed far beyond those of their neighbours.

In England, at Maldon in Essex, sea salt is still produced. In the wide winter fields around the little port there are slightly raised patches of reddish soil which contrast with the surrounding brownness. Imbedded in this soil are sharp, knobbly lumps of brick-like substance, encrusted with smooth areas of an opaque turquoise colour. Here, in Roman times, salt-workers made and stacked earthenware trays to hold the sea water which they took from the inlet a few yards away. Below the trays they lit a fire. The water evaporated, leaving salt to be scraped off the trays. The sand in the water vitrified in the heat to the smooth splashes of turquoise glass. From time to time, the trays broke and were trampled into the ground, causing the red hills of brick dust which many centuries of ploughing have not been able to rub away.

Sea salt is stronger than refined rock salt and less is needed in cooking. Sea salt is the salt to serve with radishes fresh from the garden, with sweet butter and with very young, crisp vegetables. Put it on the table in a salt dish—without a salt mill—so the grains can be crunched between the teeth, savoured and appreciated.

Salt has always been respected as the most important seasoning, and elaborate vessels, like this German seventeenth-century silver salt-cellar, were made to hold it. The salt-cellar was usually placed in the centre of the banquet table. The most revered guests were seated above the salt, towards the head of the table, while those who were less favoured were seated below the salt.

Fruit of the Olive Tree

Green olives are the fruit of the olive tree picked before they ripen. Black olives are those picked when fully ripe. No olives can be eaten fresh off the tree. They must first be soaked and cured.

An olive press extracts oil from cold fresh olives. Second-grade oil is pressed from heated olives. Fermented olive yield lubricating oil.

ATHENA AND POSEIDON once disputed the allegiance of a small settlement on a rock in eastern Greece. A jury of gods agreed to decide in favour of the one who could most benefit the primitive inhabitants. Poseidon, god of the sea, struck a salt spring from the rock. Athena turned and pointed to an olive tree, the first one, which she had caused to grow from the soil. With great perspicacity, the gods decided for Athena, with her gifts of agriculture, against the brash rewards of Poseidon.

In this tale can be read a moving shorthand of history. The olive tree of Athena needs knowledge and the long view; it is not suited to nomadic life. It does not even satisfy an amiable greed, since the owner of an olive orchard cannot saunter among his trees sampling the delicious flavour of his ripe fruit, for the untreated olive is bitter.

How did the first olive farmers acquire their knowledge? Obviously, olives fallen to the ground and trodden on carelessly, would sooner or later, be seen to produce a particularly good oil. But how did someone think of soaking olives first in a lye of water and wood ash, then in brine to palliate their bitterness? How, too, did someone discover the double harvest, that fully grown but still green olives could be prepared for eating just as well as the ones which had ripened to a warm, purplish-black?

Such tales are untold, although it is known that the olive was first cultivated in Syria and Israel six thousand years ago, and that the practice spread slowly westwards, reaching Italy by the sixth century BC. With grapes, figs and wheat, the olive became the basic food of the Mediterranean.

Many varieties of cultivated olive have been produced, accounting for the differences between olives and their oil. There are also many ways of preserving the olive: at one extreme there is the huge, salty green Spanish olive, at the other the small black wrinkled Greek olive with its mildly piquant flavour.

Methods of pressing the olives for oil also vary from place to place. The lovely fruity green oils of Tuscany, Greece and Cyprus are ideal for salads of vegetables straight from the garden, and for the appetizing pastes of anchovies, eggplant and fish roes. The more delicate virgin oil from the first pressing of Provençal olives should be kept for lighter tasting foods, and for making mayonnaise and aioli.

Other Oils

Almond oil is slightly sweet and is used in confectionery and in the making of almond extract.

Coconut oil is widely used in African and Southeast Asian cooking.

Colza or rape oil, made from the seeds of *Brassica napus* is, with olive, the oldest oil of Mediterranean cooking.

Corn oil is completely tasteless and is useful for deep-frying, as it does not begin to smoke until it reaches a high temperature.

Cottonseed oil is used in Indian cooking and to make vegetable fats and margarine.

Grape-seed oil has an agreeable smell and flavour and is an excellent salad oil.

Groundnut or peanut oil arrived in Europe about 1850, when France began to exploit her African territories. Originally it had a pleasant flavour of peanuts, as it still does in Southeast Asia, where it is much used, but modern refining techniques have made it tasteless.

Mustard-seed oil is much used in Indian cooking. In Italy it is used as flavouring for *mostarda di frutta,* fruit pickled in a mustard-flavoured syrup.

Safflower oil is made from the seeds of *Carthamus tinctorius,* the safflower or false saffron, native to Asia. It is a light oil, with a slight nutty flavour.

Sesame-seed oil is much used in Chinese cooking, as a flavouring or to suppress fishy flavours, rather than as a frying fat. It is rich, nutty and full of character.

Sunflower oil is light with a faintly nutty flavour.

Walnut oil is now so expensive that it is kept by cooks for dressing salads for special occasions. In the walnut-producing areas of France, it is used in general cooking.

Mustard and Vinegar

THE MUSTARD SHOP in the centre of the town of Dijon, ancient capital of the Dukes of Burgundy, looks like an old pharmacy, with the beautiful faience jars of all shapes and sizes arranged on the wooden shelves. Some of the jars go back to the seventeenth century when, in the interest of controlled quality, the Dijon mustard industry was put in order. Dijon is now the world's largest mustard centre.

The other main type of French mustard, from Bordeaux, has a sweet-sour taste, and is often flavoured with such aromatics as tarragon. Like the similar German mustard, it is good with sausages, and adds an agreeable tang to French dressing.

French mustard is made from the ground seeds of *Brassica nigra*, *B. juncea* and *B. alba* mixed with grape *must* (in Old French *moust*, later *moût*, and so *moutarde*). *Must* is the incompletely fermented wine, new, cloudy and sharp-tasting, which gives the sharp piquancy and clean flavour still associated with Dijon mustard. Today the brown and less fiery *Brassica juncea* has superseded the black mustard seeds because it is easier to harvest mechanically. The white *Brassica alba* is used primarily for the milder mustards popular in America.

A favourite French mustard, the *moutarde de Meaux*, contains coarsely crushed seeds which give it a speckled appearance and a delicious flavour. It is similar to the medieval mustards which were made by grinding the seeds in small stone querns or a mortar, making a coarse powder.

The move away from this knobbly style occurred at Durham in about 1730, when a Mrs Clements had the idea of milling the seeds to a fine flour, which was then sieved to remove any remnants of the coarse husk. The Hanoverian royal family took it up, and it became the essential partner of the national dish of sirloin of beef. The mustard flour could be kept for a long time without deterioration. When some was needed, a spoonful was mixed with a little water, which released the fiery flavour. There were no palliatives added in the French style to this ferocious paste, which must have put more people in England off mustard than can be imagined. This is also the version of mustard used by the Chinese and it still has many devotees. But the French and German mustards have become increasingly popular and people have come to recognize that mustards flavoured in different ways can enhance a wide variety of foods.

An unusual mustard product is the Italian *mostards di frutta di Cremona,* made from a variety of different-coloured fruits pickled whole, or in large pieces, in syrup flavoured with mustard oil. It was popular in Italy in the sixteenth century—one traveller who enjoyed it was the French philospher and essayist Montaigne—and it can be bought today in Italian stores in the United States and England.

The seeds of *Brassica niger,* black mustard, are the most pungent. They are small, dark and used in most mustards. Like the brown seeds, they also flavour many Eastern curries and pickles.

Juncea, brown mustard, belongs to a smaller plant than black mustard, but the seeds are almost indistinguishable. They are slightly paler and less pungent in flavour.

The mild yellow seeds of *Brassica alba* are the base of most American mustards. The seeds, larger and milder than the two other varieties, are included in English mustard, but never in Dijon mustard.

Moutarde de Meaux, unmistakable in its stout stone jar, is a mild mustard textured with coarsely ground mustard seeds. Its recipe is a closely guarded secret.

Wine vinegars are red or white, depending on the colour of the wine from which they were produced. The best wine vinegar is that which has been allowed to mature slowly. A sprig of tarragon is a popular flavouring for white wine vinegar.

Dijon mustard, one of France's two main varieties, is paler and hotter than its Bordeaux rival. It is made from black seeds, the juice of unripened grapes, white wine, salt and spices.

Powdered mustard, an English speciality, is made from ground black and white mustard seeds and wheat flour. It was perfected in the nineteenth century by Jeremiah Colman. Its powerful flavour only appears after the powder is mixed with cold water or milk and left to stand for 10 to 15 minutes.

ALMOST ANYTHING that can be fermented into an alcoholic liquid can be turned into vinegar, but man has wisely restricted his ingenuity to three or four substances. The word means sour (*aigre*) wine (*vin*) and wine vinegar is the best and finest of all, although the Japanese would argue that their mild, sweetish rice vinegar is just as good. Next in virtue comes cider vinegar. After that, a long way after, come malt and spirit vinegar, which is distilled from wood and diluted with water.

Malt vinegar had become an English vice by the sixteenth century. It was used then as now to ruin salads, cooked vegetables, sauces and fish. The imprudent use of malt vinegar has probably done more to ruin the reputation of English food than any other single thing. It can be used for chutneys, although cider vinegar is better, but should otherwise be kept for removing marks from antique furniture.

Vinegar is a liquid containing three to nine per cent of acetic acid from the oxidation of alcohol. In other words, if wine is left in an unsealed cask, in contact with the air, it will gradually turn to vinegar. Vinegar was the great hazard of the wine trade in the Middle Ages, before the necessity for sealing the cask tightly was understood. At Orléans, the great wine depot for Paris, the hazard was turned to good business and, in the fourteenth century, a guild of vinegar makers was established. Orléans is still the largest vinegar centre in Europe, although now the wine comes from distant countries.

Many modern firms, in France and elsewhere, use a quick method for producing vinegar. The wine or other alcoholic liquid is whirled about by vast turbines, and is ready after several days. There is still one firm, Martin-Pouret, at Orléans, which keeps to the old gentle methods. You can taste the difference.

Behind the long grey façade of one of Orléans's main streets, in huge sheds row upon row of oak barrels, called *vaisseaux*, contain the slowly maturing vinegar. The barrels are never quite emptied, so that there is always ten per cent of mature vinegar in them waiting to greet a new lot of wine and start it on its way. The temperature is kept between 25° and 30° centigrade. The vinegar is cherished for weeks; some of it, the best *Vieille Réserve*, for months. Success has been the norm since 1867, when Pasteur delivered his paper on acetic fermentation at Orléans after his studies there. Before that vinegar-making had been an empirical process, which often went wrong because it was not scientifically understood.

Most vinegar at Martin-Pouret goes into casks for export to Canada, America, Japan and Europe. Some is poured into bottles containing aromatics—tarragon, fresh green peppercorns, garlic, chopped shallots, chillies. This is something that can be done at home with a bottle of red or white wine vinegar. These flavoured vinegars add an exquisite subtlety to a variety of sauces and dressings.

Butter, Cream and Yoghourt

IT IS LIKELY that the man who first tasted butter thousands of years ago was bewildered by it. He had probably set out with milk, to drink when he was thirsty, in a leather bag hung around the neck of his donkey or camel and, later in the day, found that the bag contained instead a strange, oozing, fatty substance. The bobbing of the animal's head had transformed the bag into a churn in which the milk was thoroughly shaken until butter was formed.

That is the way butter is still made; not, of course, with animals prancing about with milk-filled bags, but by churning the cream content of the milk. This process clumps together the cream's butterfat globules. Butter is the result. During butter's earliest days (it is first mentioned in the Old Testament), a much less concentrated, curd-like butter was made from churning whole milk. Today's methods employ mechanically operated centrifugal whirlers to separate the cream from the rest of the milk. The cream is poured into modern churning devices which feed out continuous ribbons of butter for packaging.

Before machines were devised to do the job, milk was placed in shallow pans until the cream rose. The cream was then churned by various contraptions, among the most common of which (sometimes still in use) was a cylindrical container with a manually agitated long-handled piston. An early Arabian camel-skin churn was suspended from a beam or a tree and pummelled with sticks. A nineteenth-century European cradle churn consisted of a box, slung from ropes, which swung back and forth. The task was to agitate the cream, and man, in his infinite wisdom, resorted to a strange catalogue of devices.

Butter has long been used as a spread and a cooking fat, but it has served many other purposes as well in the course of its venerable history. In ancient times, lumps of butter were dropped into springs and ponds to propitiate troubled spirits. The Ancient Greeks and Romans used butter as a hair dressing and a cosmetic ointment. They frowned on what they considered the barbaric habits of butter-eating northern European tribes with whom they came into contact and when they themselves deigned to eat butter, they preferred it rancid, the only way they judged it tolerable for civilized palates. In rural England, it was believed buttering a kitten's paws would keep it from straying from home. Buttered ale and hot buttered rum were considered antidotes for colds and, indeed, when taken in sufficient quantities, can make a person forget all about minor complaints.

Ghee, which is clarified butter, is the most preferred cooking medium in India. It is also used in Hindu religious ceremonies and is a staple food for many yogis who consider it nourishment for both the body and the soul. Old Sanskrit writings suggest the consumption of *ghee* could improve a person's appearance, speaking powers, mental processes and digestion.

In the Western world, cow's milk is virtually the exclusive source of butter. In other countries the milk of sheep, goats and yaks is sometimes used. The taste of butter can be strongly influenced by what the animal grazes on. For example, cows which dine on wild garlic, ragwort or, ironically, buttercups, will produce milk with an unpleasant flavour which will, in turn, be handed on to the butter churned from its cream.

Because butter quickly turns rancid, various methods of preserving it have been devised through the ages. In Ireland, butter casks were once buried in peat bogs. Bog butter, retrieved years later, was said to be still edible, although not overly appetizing. In other places, kegs of butter were sealed with heavy sugar syrup or thick layers of salt. Modern methods include removing harmful bacteria before the cream is churned, refrigerated storage and proper packaging to keep out light and air. Salted butter is likely to stay fresh longer than "sweet" butter.

In recent years, margarine, invented by the French chemist Mège-Mouriés in the nineteenth century, has for reasons of price grown increasingly popular as a butter substitute. Various oils have long been used instead of butter in cooking for the same reason. But if proof is needed that substitutes are not about to relegate the real thing to oblivion, such proof can be found in the inimitable delicacy of Danish pastry made with irreplaceable and generous quantities of butter; in the tenacious popularity of butter straight from the farm, cut from massive loaves in French street markets and *laiteries*; and in the announcement "our eggs cooked in butter only", prominently displayed in so many street-corner diners throughout small-town America.

Butter-making was a laborious process prior to the Industrial Revolution. In the early nineteenth century a dairymaid used a wooden churn to agitate the cream and solidify it (*left*). Part of a dairymaid's work was making cheese, for which a wooden cheese press was used (*right*).

Beurres composés, compound butters, are made by adding various crushed, beaten or puréed ingredients to well-creamed butter. The mixtures are then chilled before being used as sandwich spreads, to baste grilled meat or fish or to flavour sauces. (*Left to right*) lemon butter lends a delicate flavour to canapes; shrimp butter makes a tasty sauce for fish; mustard butter and egg butter are delicious accompaniments to meat.

UNLIKE MANY DELICACIES which have to be laboriously created, cultivated or unearthed, cream is practically a gift of nature. Comparatively light in weight, it rises unbidden from the body of milk and floats on its surface until skimmed off, by hand or mechanically, or shaken back. Cream is the fat of milk, a harsh way of describing something which bestows such great gastronomic pleasures.

Cream for coffee, for cakes, for whipping, for cream sauces, for meat and fish—cream is an embarrassment of riches, capable of converting drab foods into delicacies. It is an instrument for refinement, a lush culinary catalyst.

Lighter creams serve best for pouring, on breakfast cereal and fruit, for example. Heavier creams are heavily homogenized to make them thick enough for dolloping into soups or on to mousses and other desserts. Both light and heavy cream are admirably suited to cooking purposes, depending on the desired effect.

Cream heated over a slow fire in a shallow bowl will clot, producing clotted cream, an outrageously luscious concoction served in England's west country with jam and scones. In the Near East and Asia clotted cream is made from the cream of water buffalo milk and served with honey and cakes.

Cream, commercially soured by the addition of certain cultures, is often used in the preparation of cocktail-party dips, to lend a piquant flavour to meats and to add a touch of elegance to the humble baked potato.

Yoghourt

No FOOD has climbed faster than yoghourt from the fringes of culinary acceptability to the height of culinary fashion. Although part of the everyday diet of people in southeastern Europe, the Near East and Far East for centuries, yoghourt was virtually unknown in America and western Europe as recently as fifty years ago. Today it is a food fad and, fortunately, a healthy one.

Initially a natural food, yoghourt is semi-solid fermented milk. (Milk left standing, particularly in warm climates, curdles quickly.) Today, commercial yoghourt is usually reinforced with additional yoghourt cultures and touched up with flavouring agents and sweeteners. The claim that a yoghourt diet prolongs life has not been proved, although yoghourt does genuinely assist the digestive process. Not without good reason have many people in food-conscious France turned to yoghourt instead of dessert or cheese at the end of hearty meals.

Natural, unflavoured yoghourt is often eaten with other foods, to tone down spiced meat, for example, or to flavour vegetables. Its new popularity has promoted its increased use in the preparation of casseroles, stews, sauces and salads.

To say there are two hundred different flavours of ice-cream is both an underestimate and an absurdity. There are more, as any traveller through America can testify, but that there should be two hundred different flavours of anything seems exorbitantly excessive. Yet ice-cream, which has pleased people and delighted children for centuries, is perhaps worthy of this extraordinary indulgence.

The recent appearance of peanut butter ice-cream, acacia ice-cream, blueberry pie ice-cream and other such exotic flavours makes formerly daring tutti frutti, pistachio and caramel ice-creams seem prosaic. Vanilla, however, is still far and away the most popular flavour in the world.

Ice-cream has its origins in the chilled drink. In ancient Rome, snow was dropped into wine and fruit juices to make them cold. The next logical step was sweetened water ice. It is not known exactly when ice-cream emerged from the combination of snow or ice and cream or milk, sweetened with sugar or honey. But it is known that by the seventeenth century, ice-cream was served at many royal courts in Europe where it was considered delightfully toothsome and where unsuccessful efforts were sometimes made to guard the secret of its preparation. When it finally became accessible to everyone, its delights were quickly and widely appreciated. By the end of the eighteenth century, ice-cream parlours began to appear along America's Atlantic coast.

Today the United States consumes more ice-cream than any other country —seven hundred million gallons a year by a recent survey.

Onions and Garlic

THE ONION FAMILY contributes an impressive range of flavourings which are used, in one form or another, in most of the world's savoury dishes. Onions themselves (*Allium cepa*) are so basic to our civilization that they are not known in a wild form. Some, like the translucently pink Spanish or Bermuda onion, are mild enough to be eaten raw with the greatest of pleasure. They are ideal for salads and for stuffings. The tiny bulbs and stalks of the scallion or spring onion are almost always eaten raw, although they do have quite a hot bite. Other varieties of onion can be quite fiery and strong. They all share a basic sweetness, however, and cooking brings this out.

One kind of onion, the shallot (*Allium ascalonicum*), has achieved culinary independence. It holds an important position in French *haute cuisine* and a reduction of shallots and white wine is the foundation of some of the best French sauces.

The Welsh onion (*Allium fistulosum*) has, apart from the name, no connection with Wales. In old English, welsh means "foreign". Wales is the country of foreigners, walnut, the foreign nut, and Welsh onion, the onion from foreign parts. It came to Europe towards the end of the Middle Ages. Even today, Welsh onions are more popular in Japan and China than in Europe, although many French gardens have a cluster of these elongated onions which can be used for dishes requiring a light onion flavour.

The leek (*Allium porrum*) flourishes in the cold wet of northern Europe. It has become an emblem of Wales, although nobody knows why. Certainly the Welsh, and also the Scots and the French, have kept a regard for the leek. Some of their best dishes depend on its fresh flavouring—Welsh mutton cawl, cockie-leekie, *potage parmentier* and "poor man's asparagus", cold leeks dressed with vinaigrette, parsley and chopped hard-boiled egg.

The mildest of all the onions is the chive (*Allium schoenoprasum*), which grows in dry places in thick, lively tufts of thin, pointed leaves.

Garlic (*Allium sativum*) is the most pungent of this family. There is no more appetizing smell than that of a chopped clove of garlic cooking slowly in butter or good oil. It dissolves into an underlying piquancy, losing its identity as it promotes the success of other ingredients. This is its main role everywhere, although in southern France garlic is sometimes used as a vegetable, too. Forty or fifty cloves—four or five heads—are blanched, then placed under chicken or lamb for pot-roasting. By the end of the cooking time, they disintegrate into a rich purée of appetizing mildness.

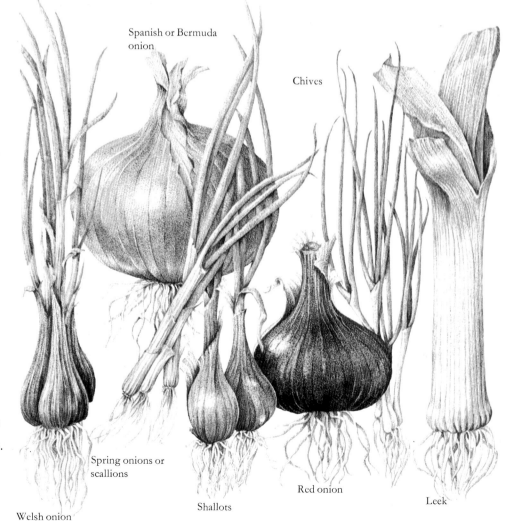

The **Welsh onion** originated in Asia, where it has been cultivated since ancient times. It has a mild flavour and is used as a substitute for spring onions.

The large, reddish-brown **Spanish** or **Bermuda onion** is cultivated throughout the world. Mild and sweet, it can be eaten raw in salads and sandwiches.

Spring onions or **scallions** are always harvested young and are at their best in the spring. The green stalks as well as the bulbs can be used to flavour salads. They are a favourite ingredient in Chinese dishes.

Shallots, a gourmet delight, were once believed to be a distinct species of vegetable. They are, in fact, a particularly tasty variety of onion.

Red onions, small and brightly coloured, have a similar sweet flavour to that of Spanish onions. They grow particularly well in cold climates.

Chives, which add a pleasant onion flavour to many dishes, can be clipped and clipped again, and will only grow the more, like some fairy-tale plant out of the Brothers Grimm.

Leeks are an important crop in Europe, although they are often considered to be "poor man's food". Leeks enhance soups and stews, and when properly prepared are a delicious vegetable.

Spanish or Bermuda onion

Chives

Spring onions or scallions

Red onion

Leek

Shallots

Welsh onion

Seeds for Flavour

Seeds are used to decorate breads and to add a special flavour. Caraway seeds are traditionally sprinkled on rye bread and pumpernickel, poppy seeds on crusty rolls and sesame seeds on breadsticks.

MAN HAS EATEN SEEDS since the dawn of time, and seeds of all kinds—cereals, beans and nuts—are still staple foods. But seeds also have an important role as a flavouring, and they have been used in this way for centuries.

Aniseed is also known as sweet cumin. The liquorice-flavoured seeds were once a common addition to cakes, sweets and breads. Today aniseed is mainly used to make the famous anise-flavoured drinks of the Mediterranean, which include French *pastis*, Greek *ouzo* and Turkish *raki*. Carrots tossed with butter and aniseed are unusually delicious.

Star anise is an essential flavouring in many Chinese dishes. Together with anise-pepper, cassia, cloves and fennel seeds, it makes up the blend known as five-spice powder.

Caraway seeds used to appear frequently on English tea-tables in seedcake, the bane of many an English childhood. They are a favourite flavouring in central Europe. Potato dumplings with caraway seeds is a German speciality, and the seeds add an unusual touch to buttered noodles or a goulash.

Celery seeds, tiny but powerful, are remarkably versatile, the ideal seasoning for vegetable dishes of all kinds, from soups to salads, as well as fish and meat. They also add an interesting accent when sprinkled on bread and dinner rolls.

Dill seeds are used in much the same way as caraway seeds. They have a milder flavour which complements fish and vegetables.

Fennel seeds are good in bread or sprinkled over rolls. They are also used in fish dishes, some sausages, such as the Italian *finocchiana*, and sweets.

Mustard seeds are largely used for the manufacture of the condiment mustard, but the seeds are also added to pickling compounds and are used in Indian cooking.

Poppy seeds feature prominently in the central European cuisines. The tiny blue-black seeds are sprinkled over bread and rolls or ground to a paste which, when mixed with honey or sugar, butter, fruit and nuts, makes a traditional filling for pastries, cakes and strudels.

Sesame seeds, nutty and crunchy, are the most delicious of all the seeds. They are excellent sprinkled over breads, rolls and scones before baking, and are used to garnish creamy soups, or tossed with a green salad, or beaten into puréed potatoes. Indeed, there are few dishes which are not enhanced by a touch of sesame seed—from fish steaks and baked chicken, to a creamy chocolate filling in a sesame-seed pie crust.

Celery seeds from the plant *Apium graveolens dulce*, are often ground and mixed with salt.

Caraway seeds from the herb *Carum carvi* are used to flavour rye breads and cheeses.

Fenugreek, the seeds of the herb *Trigonella foenum-graecum*, is commonly used in curry blends.

Aniseed, the seed of *Pimpinella anisum*, flavours a range of Mediterranean drinks

Dill seeds (*Anethum gravceolens*) may be used in place of caraway when a milder flavour is preferred.

Coriander (*Coriandrum sativum*) adds an exotic touch to home-made marmalade.

Sesame seeds (*Sesamum indicum*) are enjoyed as much for their texture as for their nutty flavour

Cumin, the seed of the herb *Cuminum cuminum*, is an important ingredient of spice blends

l seeds are ted from the herb ulum vulgare and Florence fennel gare dulce) whose us root is served egetable.

Cardamom is the seed pod of *Elettaria cardamomum*, an important spice. A crushed pod adds a delicious flavour to coffee.

Mustard seeds fall into three main categories—black, brown and white and yellow.

Poppy seeds come from the opium poppy, *Papaver somniferum*. The ripe seeds, however, are quite harmless.

Star anise is the star-shaped fruit of a small evergreen tree of the magnolia family, *Illicium verum*.

The Spices of Life

SPICES were once regarded with the same awe and greed as the gold, pearls and silks that were brought with them from the far corners of Asia. Unlike herbs, few of the plants yielding spices, from bark, root or seeds, are native to Europe, and to satisfy their passion for these seasonings, Europeans had to look beyond their own continent.

The history of spices is a saga of triumph and bloodshed. The search for them drove the great explorers over land and sea to every corner of the globe. Their discovery meant not only wealth for the traders, merchants and their cities, but political power which supported vast empires.

Today, the spices that were once more precious than gems are used without a second thought by cooks all over the world.

Allspice, also known as Jamaica pepper, has a flavour reminiscent of clove, nutmeg and cinnamon, with peppery overtones. The berries are used whole or ground, preferably freshly ground, like peppercorns, for flavouring stocks, marinades and pickles, cakes, sweets and spicy puddings. Slices of orange, dipped in a mixture of ground allspice and fried in butter, make an excellent garnish for rich roasts of pork and duck.

Cardamom is used in most cuisines, in particular those of India and the Near East and, surprisingly, Sweden and Finland. The cool, scented flavour, with an undertone of eucalyptus, is equally welcome in a curry blend and in coffee cake or gingerbread.

Cinnamon and **cassia**, which has a stronger, cruder flavour, are used in powder form or in rolled sticks. The sticks can be removed once they have imparted flavour to a dish, in the same way as a vanilla pod. A cinnamon stick may also be used to stir a cup of coffee, giving it a delicate, elusive flavour. An important spice for flavouring meat in the East, in the West cinnamon tends to be used in sweet dishes, with fruit, or in spiced cakes and puddings. It also has a marked affinity for chocolate, and a pinch of ground cinnamon sprinkled over hot chocolate makes a good drink.

Cloves are the most versatile of spices, flavouring all kinds of meat dishes from Indian curries to American glazed hams, Christmas puddings, mincemeats and pickles. Their taste is so distinctive that just two or three are enough for a stew, to spike an onion for stock or to bury among the apples in a pie.

Coriander, warm and fragrant, with a mild flavour which is sweet and citrus-like, is widely used throughout the Mediterranean and the Middle East, and in Indian and Mexican cooking. It adds a delicious touch to soups and vegetables, from sauerkraut to any of the many vegetables which are served *à la grecque,* as well as to spiced cakes and fruit puddings.

Cumin, strong and spicy, has been prized by the people of North Africa and the Near East since the pre-Christian era. It is also used in a large number of Indian dishes and in Mexican cooking. A pinch of cumin adds an unusual touch to bread, to poultry or meat dishes and to rice and vegetables of all kinds.

Fenugreek, an aromatic, bitter-sweet spice, is an essential flavouring in many Indian dishes, and is also used in the cooking of the Mediterranean, particularly in Morocco. Otherwise, its use is restricted to pickles, chutneys and to the manufacture of imitation maple extract.

Ginger was used lavishly by the Romans and in the cooking of the Middle Ages. Today Jamaican ginger is considered to be the best; it is ground to a pale powder with a delicate aroma and a subtle, mild taste. Fresh ginger, peeled and finely chopped or pounded to a pulp, has a richer, sweeter flavour than the dried root or powder. In the Orient, ginger is used to spice dishes of meat and even fish. This is uncommon in the West, but almost every European cuisine has a traditional gingerbread. Many of the elegant silver canisters now used as sugar shakers were originally intended for powdered ginger, and the custom of sprinkling ginger over wedges of fresh melon continues to this day.

Juniper is an evergreen tree, of which there are many species to be found growing in a wide area from the Arctic Circle to North Africa. The blue berries, which take two to three years to ripen, are more strongly flavoured the farther south they are grown. Apart from flavouring gin, juniper berries are used in marinades for game, in some pâtés and pork dishes and for curing hams.

Juniper butter adds an unusual touch to spit-roasted quail or poussin.

Nutmeg and **mace** are parts of the same fruit. Nutmeg is the kernel, and mace the net-like membrane, or aril, which surrounds it. Both go well with eggs, in rich cheese sauces and soufflé mixtures, and for flavouring sweets, puddings and milky drinks. Spinach benefits from a grating of nutmeg and so do mashed potatoes.

Saffron is the most expensive of all spices. It could scarcely be otherwise, for it is made from the dried stamens of the mauve crocus of Asia Minor. It is estimated that between eighty-five thousand and two hundred and fifty thousand stamens are needed to make a pound of saffron, yet each flower produces only three. Good-quality saffron strands should be a deep, red-orange colour, not faded, with a strong pervasive aroma and a warm, bitter-honey flavour. A small pinch of saffron infused in a spoonful or two of warm liquid will release enough colour and flavour for a large dish of Milanese *risotto*, Spanish *paella* or a Mediterranean fish soup or stew such as the classic *bouillabaisse.* Saffron is also used in baking traditional yeast buns, cakes and coffee cakes.

Sassafras, which has a medicinal flavour, is used mainly as a flavouring for liqueurs and soft drinks. It is also made into tea.

Turmeric has a warm, pungent aroma with an exotic flavour that makes it the ideal spice for breakfast kedgeree, a culinary legacy of Britain's colonial past, and adds an interesting touch to a dressing for salad or a simple white sauce. It imparts a brilliant yellow colour to piccalillies, chutneys and mustards and to Indian rice dishes, curries and sweetmeats.

Nutmeg and mace both come from the fruit of the same tropical tree *Myristica fragrans.* The former is the kernel and the latter the net-like membrane, or aril, which surrounds it.

Spices have played an important part in the development of the modern world. The great explorers of the fifteenth and sixteenth centuries were seeking sea routes to the Spice Islands and India in the hope of capturing the spice trade for their countries when they discovered the new world. Today it is difficult to believe that once spices were so important that men were prepared to cross whole continents by camel train (*right*) and even go to war to further this trade. Indian spice merchants (*left*) continue an historic tradition.

Ginger is the rhizome of a tropical plant, *Zingiber officinale*.

Cinnamon, the dried rolled bark of a small evergreen tree, *Cinnamomum zeylanicum*, is native to Ceylon.

...fras is obtained ...the root bark of ...*Sassafras* ...*lis*.

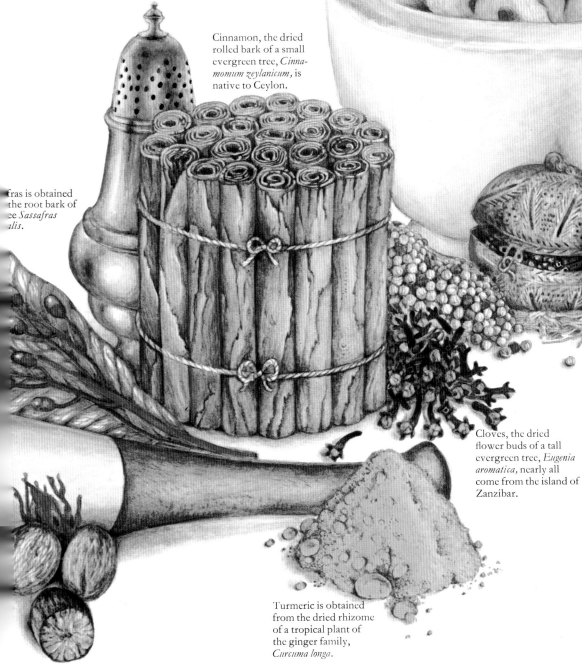

Saffron strands are the dried stamens of *Crocus sativus*, the mauve saffron crocus of Asia Minor.

Allspice is the dried brown berry of *Pimenta dioica*, an evergreen tree that flourishes in tropical America and the West Indies, particularly Jamaica.

Cloves, the dried flower buds of a tall evergreen tree, *Eugenia aromatica*, nearly all come from the island of Zanzibar.

Turmeric is obtained from the dried rhizome of a tropical plant of the ginger family, *Curcuma longa*.

Herbs

Today "herb" is an emotional word, carrying overtones of longing for a past that never existed. It is forgotten that not so long ago a herb garden was simply a vegetable garden. Until recently, in northern England, when women sent children out to the corner shop for "a pennorth of pot-herbs", they did not expect a *bouquet garni*, but vegetables for the basic flavouring of a stew—onion, turnip, carrot and parsnip.

Such herbs as were grown with the other vegetables were not destined only for the kitchen. Often quite ineffectually, they served the important purposes of medicine and perfumery. By the end of the nineteenth century certain affinities of taste which are still enjoyed had been well established, some by way of an illogical logicality—mountain lamb with herbs from springy mountain turf, meadow lamb with mint from valley streams or salt-marsh lamb with oysters. Who first put ham into a parsley and white wine jelly? How rapidly did Italian cooks arrange the perfect marriage of basil from the ancient Mediterranean with tomatoes from the New World?

Out of these ambiguities of medicine and cooking comes one certainty. Fresh herbs give twice the pleasure of dried ones. Parsley, basil and mint deprived of green life are dead beyond recall. Dried herbs may have a *stronger* taste, but the soul has gone, except for sturdier leaves of sage, thyme and dill, which is perhaps why they are the favoured herbs of northern cooking.

Parsley, *Petroselinum crispum,* has been, since classical times, the essential herb of European cooking. Rich in vitamin C, there are both curly and plain-leaved varieties. The parsley stalk is as flavourful as the leaves and should be included in the *bouquet garni* for stew, keeping the leaves for a final garnish. Fresh parsley should always be used.

Basil, *Ocimum basilicum,* is the king of herbs, as its name implies, for *basileus* is Greek for king. This Asian plant is the key flavouring of Provençal and north Italian cooking, particularly for tomato salads and tomato dishes. Basil is not a herb for prolonged cooking. Use the fresh herb, for dried basil loses its special fragrance.

Bay, *Laurus nobilis,* a Mediterranean tree, was sacred to Apollo and provided the laurel crown of poets and victors. The powerful flavour of the sweet bay is essential to beef and to many stews in European cooking, particularly as part of a *bouquet garni.* It makes a good addition, because of its sweetness, to fish soups and chowders.

Chervil, *Anthriscus cerefolium,* is a favourite herb of French cooking. It has a slight resemblance to parsley in flavour, but with a delicate anise note of its own. Chervil should be kept for last-minute additions to salads, soups, sauces and butters, or for lightly cooked egg dishes. Prolonged heat destroys its flavour.

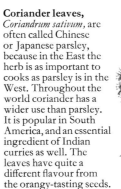

Coriander leaves, *Coriandrum sativum,* are often called Chinese or Japanese parsley, because in the East the herb is as important to cooks as parsley is in the West. Throughout the world coriander has a wider use than parsley. It is popular in South America, and an essential ingredient of Indian curries as well. The leaves have quite a different flavour from the orangy-tasting seeds.

Dill, *Anethum graveolens,* is an easily-grown plant, whose leaves and seeds give a distinctive flavour to dishes of Scandinavia, Germany, Russia and parts of eastern Europe and Turkey. It is used, above all, with pickles and to flavour vinegar. Dill is not a herb for prolonged cooking.

Fennel, *Foeniculum vulgare,* is associated particularly with the fish cooking of Provence. The stalks, leaves and seeds provide a year-long source of delicate liquorice flavouring. Fennel also makes a good seasoning for pork. Chopped fennel leaves, heated slowly in butter and sharpened with lemon juice, make a good sauce for fish.

Wild marjoram, *Origanum vulgare,* usually sold in dried form in northern countries as *oregano,* is related to, although not the same as, sweet marjoram. It has a stronger flavour which stands up to fierce heat and to the piquant dishes of Italian cooking.

Marjoram, *Majorana hortensis,* is highly aromatic . The leaves can be used in salads, or as part of a *fines herbes* mixture.

Camomile, *chamaemelum nobile,* is a herb which grows wild through the world. Camomile tea, an ancient remedy for stomach ailments, is made from the dried flowers. Camomile is also used to flavour vermouths and liqueurs.

Spearmint, *Mentha spicata,* is used by English cooks for mint sauce to go with lamb. It appears far more frequently, however, in Middle Eastern cooking, particularly as a flavouring for yoghourt sauces, which are served with salads and vegetables, as well as with lamb and other meat.

Rosemary, *Rosmarinus officinalis,* with its stiff, greyish leaves and lavender blue flowers, is one of the strongest as well as one of the most decorative of herbs. If it is not used with discretion, its resinous flavour will be too dominant for pleasure, but a few sprigs spiked into lamb, pork or kid, before it is grilled over charcoal, add a most appetizing flavour.

Sage, *Salvia officinalis,* a native of the Mediterranean, has long been a favourite of American and English cooks to counteract the richness of pork, duck and goose. It must be used with restraint. A few leaves put into a chicken before roasting, in the Italian style, gives a light appetizing flavour. It can also be added to sausage meat.

Thyme, *Thymus vulgaris,* a bushy perennial native to southern Europe, is essential to European cooking. It is one of the three basic ingredients of the *bouquet garni,* and in greater quantity is essential to dishes of wild rabbit, hare and game of many kinds, as well as *potage crecy,* carrot soup.

Tarragon, *Artemisia dracunculus,* is the warm, anise herb which, when combined with cream, makes the perfect sauce for chicken in classic French cooking. It is the essential ingredient, the defining ingredient, of *sauce béarnaise.* A bottle of wine vinegar, flavoured with a leafy stalk of tarragon, is an essential item in every kitchen. The mixture of *fines herbes* also requires it.

Celery leaves, *Apium graveolens* var. *dulce,* should never be thrown away. The yellowish-green leaves make a useful seasoning for stews, stock or soups and a pleasant garnish for winter salads.

Summer savory, *Satureja hortensis,* a herb belonging to the mint family, was known to the Romans who relished its fragrant, peppery flavour. It is used today in salads and soups and to flavour roast meats. Winter savory, *S. montana,* has a more resinous flavour. It is the herb for broad beans and peas in German and French cooking.

Sorrel, *Rumex acetosa,* is an aromatic herb with a high oxalic acid content. Cooked sorrel is made into a puree and used as a flavouring for green leaf vegetables and soups. The purée is sometimes used as a garnish for fatty roasts such as goose and pork. Sorrel leaves may be pounded with sugar and vinegar to make a sauce similar to mint sauce.

Fines Herbes

FINES HERBES is a chopping of mixed green herbs which should include chervil, parsley, tarragon, watercress, chives and sweet marjoram. Salad burnet and mushrooms were also once a part of *fines herbes.* Today, *fines herbes* is sadly reduced to parsley and chives. *Fines herbes* is the *bouquet garni* of uncooked or quickly cooked dishes. They may also garnish meat dishes, or be added to them at the end of cooking time so that their freshness is not killed by too much heat. The Italian *gremolata,* a chopping of parsley, lemon rind, garlic and anchovy, is used in a similar way as a garnish and seasoning for *osso buco,* veal shin stewed in tomato, one of the best dishes of Milanese cooking.

Myrtle, *Myrtus communis,* is prized in Corsica, Sardinia and other parts of the Mediterranean for the flavour its leaves impart to lamb and to small birds.

Borrage, *Borago officinalos,* has a cucumber flavour and is best eaten fresh. Traditionally used to flavour punches, it is also added to salads and sauces. Borrage was known to the Moors in Spain who used it as a diuretic. Spaniards, and later the English, flavoured red wine and other beverages with it.

Angelica, *Angelica archangelica,* is a liquorice-flavoured, umbelliferous plant related to celery. Its stems are crystallized with sugar and used in the making of confectionery, cakes and desserts. The roots and seeds are also used in making digestive liqueurs as well as some gins and vermouths.

Salad burnet, *Poterium sanguisorba,* is another herb with a cucumber flavour. It is used fresh to flavour salads and salad dressings. The outer leaves are bitter and, therefore, only the young, tender centre leaves are used.

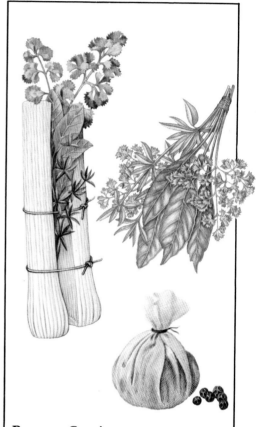

Bouquet Garni

A CLASSIC FLAVOURING, for stocks, stews and casseroles, a *bouquet garni* is composed of a number of aromatic herbs tied together in a faggot. The simplest *bouquet* includes only sprigs of parsley and a more complicated one may include a number of such herbs and vegetables as tarragon, savory, basil, chervil, rosemary, burnet, bay leaf, celery and chives. The most commonly used *bouquet* is composed of parsley, bay leaf and thyme.

For bouquets intended to flavour stock the herbs are tied inside a tube made of celery stalks or they may be sandwiched in a split leek.

If the *bouquet* is made of such dried herbs and flavourings as garlic, peppercorns and dried orange peel (a favourite addition to *bouquets* used in Mediterranean casseroles), they are tied in a small piece of cheesecloth or muslin. All bouquets are removed before the dish is served.

Honey, Sugar and Syrups

THE IRREPRESSIBLE human appetite for sweet-tasting things is totally inexplicable. There is no biological reason to crave sweet rather than bitter foods, or for children to have a passion for sweets instead of, say, spinach. The energy needed by the body, which is derived in substantial amounts from sugar, sugar products, honey and syrup, is readily available in meat, milk and many other foods. Eskimos and other people whose normally traditional diet contained no sweet foods did not suffer nutritionally as a result. Tibetans happily flavour their tea with salt and butter, not sugar.

Nevertheless, most people are so sweet-orientated that the concept of sweet is equated with good, sour with bad. Almost everywhere, a gift of confectionery is a mark of favour and friendship. There is no reason. Human beings like sweet-tasting things because they like them, and that is all there is to it.

Sugar is important, not because of what it is in itself, but because it makes other foods more palatable, more suited to individual tastes. It is the universal sweetener for a vast number of things everyone eats.

Sugar-cane, the source of most of our sugar supplies, was cultivated in India more than two thousand years ago. Considering its enormous appeal, it is remarkable that sugar took so long to reach the Western World, not appearing in European kitchens until medieval times, when the expanding Moorish Empire introduced it to Spain, from where it spread all over Europe.

For hundreds of years, sugar was considered an exotic spice, used only to flavour meat and fish, or to conceal unpleasant tastes, not an unworthy task before the era of food preservation and refrigeration. Most of it was imported from the distant Orient, with the result that sugar was extremely expensive, costing in its time as much then as Beluga caviar does today.

Despite its rarity, the extraordinary capacity of sugar for making unappetizing food taste good and good food taste better was widely recognized and appreciated. Efforts to cultivate sugar-cane in southern Europe met with only little success. But after Christopher Columbus and Spanish colonists ventured into the West Indies, the sugar-cane they planted there took root and flourished. The moist, tropical Caribbean climate was ideal. Enormous plantations sprang up around those first and subsequent cane plantings.

Before long, supplies of sugar were flowing back to Europe. The price fell sharply, but not nearly as dramatically as demand grew. No longer prohibitively expensive, sugar became a household item for the well-to-do and its manufacture was, for a while, the world's largest industry. Its many uses in baking and cooking were discovered. The wealthy, no longer having exclusive access to what once had been "white gold", found novel uses for sugar. Their chefs made plates and goblets of spun sugar, to be consumed at the end of dinner parties. This practice was the origin of the confectioner's art, of the boiled sweets, peppermint sticks, British "rock" candy and the intricate sugar shapes and models still displayed in small, specialized sweet shops in Italy, France, Belgium, Holland and other parts of Europe.

As the demand for sugar continued to soar, slaves were shipped from Africa to the West Indies to harvest expanding cane crops. By the beginning of the nineteenth century, sugar had become an ingredient of virtually every meal for millions of Europeans. When the English blockaded the European continent during the Napoleonic Wars, they cut off supplies from the West Indies and the Europeans sorely felt the loss. To overcome the lack of sweetening, Napoleon ordered the cultivation of sugar-beets, from which sugar had been previously extracted in small amounts and which grows well in temperate regions. (Sugar extracted from cane and beets is identical.) But Napoleon's initiative was short-lived. The beet-sugar extraction process was too cumbersome at the time, and too expensive. When slavery was abolished in the West Indies forty years later, however, the price of cane sugar rose sharply and beet sugar became almost as économical to produce. Today sugar-beets provide about forty per cent of the world's sugar supply.

Orange blossom
Pine
Sage
Eucalyptus
Rosemary
Thistle
White clover
Acacia
Honeysuckle
Lime

Subtle-sweet Flavours

The flavour, aroma and consistency of honey varies according to the type of flower from which it is gathered. Every plant imparts a distinctive flavour to its honey. Favourite single-flower honeys include the aromatic herb honeys—thyme, sage, lavender and rosemary; resinous pine flower honey; strong, dark heather honey; delicate clover honey and pale-coloured orange blossom honey. Most commercial honeys are blends of honey gathered from different kinds of blossoms.

The sugars extracted from sugar-cane and sugar-beets are identical, although the plants themselves are very different. Sugar-cane is a tropical plant which grows in the area between the Tropics of Cancer and Capricorn.

Principal Sugar Beet growing areas

Principal Sugar Cane growing areas

In the Middle Ages sugar was considered a medicine. It may actually have demonstrated restorative powers because of its high energy-producing carbohydrate content.

In many places honey, which is almost pure sugar, is still thought to have medicinal value. It was important to all the peoples of the ancient world—and not only to the Egyptians who used it in embalming. For many it was the only available sweet-tasting food and was used to flavour other foods and drinks. It fermented quickly and palatably to make pleasantly intoxicating beverages.

Honey is one of Nature's wonder foods. More than five hundred bees must gather nectar from more than two million flowers to produce a single pound of honey. And yet millions of pounds are produced every year. The flavour, colour and texture of honey from a given comb depends on the source of the nectar.

Mead — Drink of Antiquity

Mead is among the most agreeable of intoxicating drinks, as one might expect from a mixture of fermented honey and water. It is now, however, largely a thing of the past, a rare beverage, light or rich, sweet or dry, found mostly in quaint jugs in hidden corners of better wine shops—the gift for the person who has drunk everything.

The name comes from the Sanskrit word for honey, *mahdu*, the derivation indicating mead's distant origin. It was a common beverage in ancient and medieval times, particularly in northern countries denied, by climate, the benefits of wine grapes. In England, mead was the most popular alcoholic drink until it was driven into respectable obscurity by beer.

Tapping maple trees for sap to make maple syrup is a winter-time ritual in New England and Canada.

THE WORD SYRUP was once synonymous with the word medicine. Laced with various herbs and roots, syrups were administered by doctors and quacks alike for the treatment of all kinds of pains and fevers. In his play *Othello* Shakespeare refers metaphorically to the "drowsy syrups of the world", equivalent to today's sleeping pills. But the main use for syrups, then and now, is the same as for sugar, to make food taste better.

Three characteristics are common to all syrups—they are sweet, they are liquid and they are sticky. Syrups are used in cake and pastry batters, lending both cohesion and taste; they are poured over cakes, pancakes and ice-cream; they are used for glazing ham and other meats, and they are important ingredients of various sweets and beverages.

Natural syrups, derived from plants, generally require no additional flavouring. Molasses is the syrupy liquid left after most of the water used in processing sugar-cane and sugar-beets has been boiled off.

Long before the Europeans discovered the New World, North American Indians tapped sugar-maple trees in the spring, when the sap was rising, and boiled the sap down into a natural syrup. Maple syrup is now the basis of a thriving industry in the northeastern United States and southeastern Canada. About forty gallons of maple sap yield about one gallon of syrup, now an expensive delicacy.

Artificially manufactured syrups are in more common use around the world, largely because they are cheap to produce. Essentially they consist of sugar boiled with water to a viscous consistency and flavoured according to taste or purpose.

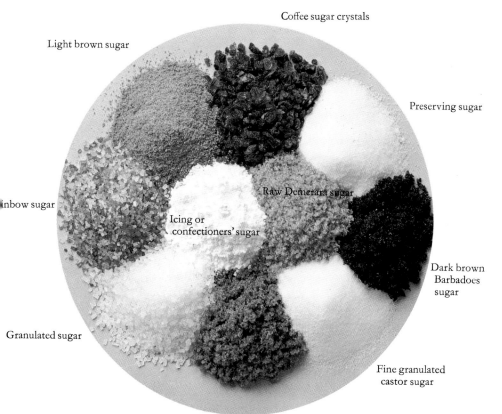

Coffee sugar crystals

Light brown sugar

Preserving sugar

Rainbow sugar

Raw Demerara sugar

Icing or confectioners' sugar

Dark brown Barbadoes sugar

Granulated sugar

Fine granulated castor sugar

Soft brown sugar

Tea

Tea-picking is a delicate task, usually performed by women. A tea-picker is able to gather up to 60 pounds of tea leaves in one day. After processing, 60 pounds of fresh leaves will yield about 15 pounds of tea.

THE ORIGINS OF TEA DRINKING have been lost in antiquity. The earliest written reference is in a Chinese dictionary of AD 350. The tea plant, indigenous to Southeast Asia, was brought to China and Japan by proselytizing Buddhist monks. In the sixteenth century it was brought by the Dutch to Europe and by the mid-eighteenth century tea supplanted coffee as the English drink.

The English East India company held the monopoly for the world trade in tea and played the major role in the introduction of China and India teas into England and colonial America. In an effort to continue this monopoly and to raise taxes, the British Parliament passed the Tea Act of 1773, one of the causes of the American Revolution, and precipitated the Boston Tea Party.

The Cantonese called tea *ch'a*. The Fukienese called it *t'e*. The Cantonese word was used in Japan, India and Russia, and the Fukienese *t'e* was brought by the Dutch to the West. Although early English references were to "chah" and "chai", from their Indian connections, they later changed to "tay", and it stayed that way until late in the eighteenth century when it was finally called "tea".

Tea plants are much the same all over the world. The differences in the tea are due to manufacturing processes and variations in climate and soil. There are fifteen hundred different growths and two thousand different blends.

Tea is divided into three categories: fermented, usually referred to as black; unfermented, or green and semi-fermented, or oolong. For black tea, the leaves are fermented or oxidized until they turn a warm copper colour. Green tea is steamed in cylinders or boilers, and the oolong teas, which have some of the characteristics of both black and green teas, are partially fermented before drying. After the drying processes, the teas are cut, sifted and sorted into four grades: orange pekoe (from the terminal buds and finest leaves); pekoe, pekoe Souchong and congou (from successively coarser leaves); and pekoe dust (fine broken tea) and "dust".

The Chinese produce all three categories of tea. Black China teas include *Lapsang Souchong*, which has a rich, tarry flavour obtained by smoking the leaves over charcoal, and *Keemun,* originally a green tea but now black, with a superior smoky taste and a superb bouquet, which the Chinese consider an excellent tea to serve with food. The most famous of the semi-fermented teas is Formosa Oolong, from the Chinese *wu lung,* meaning "black dragon", a large-leaf tea with the flavour of ripe peaches.

Gunpowder tea, one of the finest of all China teas, is a rare green leaf rolled into small pellets. *Loong Ching* is the best Canton green tea, and jasmine tea is delicately scented with dried jasmine flowers, the last survivor of a variety of flower-scented teas that included gardenia, magnolia and orange blossom.

The teas of India are invariably black. Assam tea from northeast India is a bright, reddish-brown brew, full-bodied, with a strong, malty taste. Darjeeling, grown in the high foothills of the Himalayas, has a rich muscatel and blackcurrant flavour. Tranvancore and Nilgiri, from the uplands of South India, are aromatic teas.

Ceylon teas have blue-black, shiny leaves which produce a bright golden liquor when brewed. Japanese teas are traditionally black.

Coffee and tea are both tropical plants, requiring the hot, damp equatorial climate of the belt between the Tropics of Cancer and Capricorn. The United States imports more than half of the world's coffee supply. Half of all the tea grown is exported to the United Kingdom.

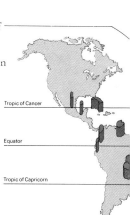

Tropic of Cancer
Equator
Tropic of Capricorn

▮ Principal Coffee growing areas
▮ Principal Tea growing areas

The teapot evolved from the Chinese wine ewer. When tea came to Europe, Chinese teapots came with it. European teapots developed with the perfection of porcelain and bone china in the eighteenth century, and the Oriental tea dish grew into a cup with a handle to protect the fingers from being burned. Silver tea sets became popular in England in the nineteenth century, along with a range of accessories.

Seventeenth-century Chinese teapot

Eighteenth-century European porcelain teapot

Original Chinese teapot

Nineteenth-century English silver tea set

Eighteenth-century European bone china teapots

Eighteenth-century Dutch delft teapots

Traditional Russian samovar

Coffee

As the popularity of coffee drinking grew, the coffee house became a centre of political and cultural life in seventeenth-century London. The House of Commons, however, classified coffee as an "outlandish drink", and an Act of Parliament required all coffee houses to be licensed and imposed a tax on every gallon of coffee sold.

THE AROMA OF ROASTING COFFEE BEANS is one of the most seductive, and holds promise that is all too often unfulfilled. Raw coffee beans have no real flavour. Their flavour is released when they are roasted at carefully controlled temperatures and then there is little that can be done to stabilize it. The escape of the precious volatile oils can be slowed down by cooling the beans as soon as they have been roasted, but with grinding they are again in full flight. Consequently, it is a necessity, not an affectation, to grind coffee beans immediately before the coffee is brewed.

Coffee has come a long way since the day when, well over a thousand years ago, according to legend, an observant goatherd noticed the strange behaviour of his flock after they had fed on the red berries of a small, wild, evergreen tree. He tasted the berries himself and was struck by a feeling of exhilaration. It was produced by caffeine, an alkaloid contained in coffee which acts as a stimulant.

The story stops short of revealing where this incident took place, but it is possible that the original home of the coffee tree was Ethiopia. Coffee gradually spread through the Arab world, although it was regarded with suspicion by religious leaders. Denied the pleasures of alcohol, the Muslim Arabs called it "the wine of Islam". In the middle of the sixteenth century, the first coffee house was opened in Constantinople and reports reached Europe of "coffa, made of a kind of seed called coava; which they drink so hot as possible they can". But it was to be another hundred years before coffee houses came to Europe.

The Arabs retained control of the coffee trade until it was discovered that the tree would grow equally well in other areas. The Dutch took the precious seedlings east to Java and Ceylon; the French planted them in the West Indies, and in 1727 coffee arrived in Brazil. Today, Brazil supplies about half of the world's needs, but coffee grows wherever the climate is suitable, within a band between the Tropics of Cancer and Capricorn.

Connoisseurs of coffee believe that nothing, except perhaps sugar, should be allowed to detract from its flavour. Many additives and adulterants have, however, been used over the years, with varying degrees of success. Milk has long been a favourite, especially at breakfast time. The flavour of the roasted root of the chicory plant, *Chicorium intybus*, originally used as an adulterant, is now enjoyed by many people for its own sake.

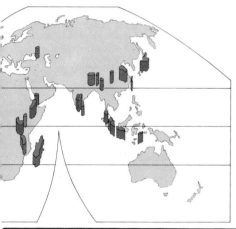

Coffee has a great affinity for spirits and liqueurs, which may be served separately or incorporated into it. The legendary goatherd would have been denied the pleasures of a Café Napoléon, coffee with fine brandy, or Irish coffee, a black brew reinforced with Irish whiskey and sugar and topped with a white blanket of thick cream, or the Café Brulot of New Orleans, a mixture of coffee and brandy or Cointreau and fragrant with orange, lemon and spices. But the refreshing sense of well-being and alertness the goatherd felt when he first tasted the berry of the coffee tree is an experience shared many times each day by people all over the world, from Bedouins in the Arabian desert to city office workers in skyscrapers.

Although there is no way to make coffee other than by adding boiling water to coffee grains, there are numerous ways of accomplishing this. The Turkish method simply boils the coffee and water together. *Cafétieres* and filter methods pour the water through the coffee, then trap the grounds. Vacuums, percolators and espresso machines use pressure to force the water through the coffee.

Filtered

Espresso machine

French cafétiere

Turkish method

Porcelain cafétiere

Boiling coffee grains

Electric percolator

Vacuum method

Chocolate

MANY TALES make up the pot-pourri of fact and legend that surrounds the history of the cocoa tree (*Theobroma cacao*) and its fabulous beans. Indigenous to Central and South America, cocoa was used by the Mayans and Aztecs in religious rites and the beans were used as a form of currency. The Aztecs were probably the first to make the beans into a beverage. Their recipe for a chocolate drink is not recorded in detail, but it is known that the beans were dried in the sun and roasted in earthenware pots before being husked. The kernels were then ground with vanilla, spices and herbs, and the resulting paste was made into small cakes and dried in the shade. When required, the cakes were broken up and whisked with water to make a foamy drink.

Reference was made to cocoa in 1502 in the log of Columbus's last voyage to the New World. Seventeen years later, a follower of Cortes described a banquet given by Montezuma II at which "about fifty great dishes made of 'cacao'" were drunk. Montezuma was probably one of the greatest chocolate enthusiasts in history. Before entering his harem he would drink a golden goblet of the frothing and, as it was then considered, invigorating liquid.

In Europe, the Spaniards jealously guarded the secret of their discovery for a hundred years. They made the beans into a cold drink, often sweetened with sugarcane, which was just being introduced into Europe. Gradually, however, the fame of chocolate spread throughout the Old World. "Chocolate houses" became the rage, and in 1657 the first advertised sale of chocolate at a chocolate house in England was reported.

Nevertheless, chocolate continued to be an expensive luxury until the Industrial Revolution, when machines were invented for grinding the beans and chocolate-making moved into factories.

In 1828, the Dutch firm of Van Houten revolutionized the chocolate industry with a patent for extracting a large proportion of fat—cocoa butter—from the ground beans, leaving a soluble powder. This led to cocoa and drinking chocolate, as well as to eating chocolate, which has a large proportion of cocoa butter. It was not until 1876, however, that a Swiss manufacturer first marketed milk chocolate.

Adventurous cooks have matched chocolate with the most unlikely partners: fish, such poultry dishes as the Mexican *mole poblano de guajolote*, turkey masked with a chilli sauce enriched with bitter chocolate, and game, which the Italians serve with *salsa agrodolce*, a sweet-sour sauce of wine, vinegar, pine nuts, raisins and bitter chocolate.

One of the most fascinating aspects of the history of chocolate is the changing attitude towards it over the years. Montezuma believed it to be an aphrodisiac and a source of great strength, a belief also widely held in Europe in the early years. Today, chocolate is recognized to be one of the most perfect of foods, rich in carbohydrates, vegetable oils, proteins, calcium, iron and phosphorus, an essential part of the soldier's survival kit and the ideal source of quick energy for everyone from boy scouts to astronauts.

The Aztecs were the first to make a drink of the cocoa bean and they introduced it to the conquering Spaniards in the early sixteenth century. Chocolate was taken back to Europe where it eventually became a popular beverage. The Quakers thought that the new drink might be a possible alternative to alcohol, and such companies as Cadbury's were founded by wealthy Quaker families to process cocoa. Today chocolate is the world's favourite confection and it is moulded into every imaginable shape.

The World Atlas of FOOD

A guide to the great regional dishes of the world

Good and delicious things remembered

BRITAIN has been a natural larder for Europe ever since Caesar turned his army towards British grain and oysters. Two thousand years later, foreign buyers, if not conquerors, come increasingly to British markets to buy the good things of these islands.

The best pork, beef, lamb, lobsters and scallops go to France. Three-quarters of Britain's venison goes to Germany. As a result, most women in England would not recognize a haunch of venison if they saw one.

Looking at the map on this page, one might be surprised at the range of food crowded on to so small an area. Yet, it cannot indicate the trout, for the streams are too numerous. Nor can it show the extent of the wide grain fields of East Anglia, where the yield per acre has been the highest in Europe for centuries. How could one begin to indicate the gardens where peaches and grapes ripen on warm brick walls, or the vegetable beds where many gardeners grow globe and Jerusalem artichokes, Britain's own native seakale, the most delicious of vegetables, as well as Chinese cabbage, true French beans, potatoes, sweet-corn, courgettes and even aubergines and peppers?

The standard of much good food in Britain is a private one. It is a standard of quiet satisfaction without drive to public glory. Its celebrations are Sunday lunch for the family, a weekend high tea, or a dinner party with a few close friends. Life at table is very pleasant for a large number of people at home. In public places, food is a matter for shame. The real pleasures of English, Welsh, Irish and Scottish eating are concealed from the sight of strangers beneath a commercial foodscape of monotonous grey.

No part of Britain, which is surrounded by cool and fruitful waters, is more than sixty miles from the sea. Yet it is easier to get a wide variety of fresh fish two hundred miles inland in France than it is thirty miles from a large fish market in Britain. Recently,

an American visitor walked into an inn on the Tweed, one of Britain's best salmon rivers. He nearly fell over a pile of salmon, at least fifty of them, lying on the floor near the reception desk. He rushed to get ready for dinner. He sat down, a bloom of anticipation on his cheeks. "Plaice or scampi, sir?" said the waitress. "But . . . but . . . the *salmon.*" "They are for London, sir. Plaice or scampi?"

Publicly, most Britons do not care. Privately, if they get a salmon, they telephone their dearest friends and make a feast of quality. This, however, is hard on the stranger who has no friends to visit.

To eat good national food in a public place, the visitor can go to the Connaught in London, or drive down to the Horn of Plenty at Gulworthy in Devon. Then there is the fleet of restaurants led so excellently by the Hole in the Wall at Bath, or the Box Tree Cottage in Ilkley, where the food is carefully and deliciously prepared on the standards of honest quality propounded in the books by Elizabeth David, whose criterion of excellence is flavour. All these restaurants have English dishes as well as French dishes on their menus. All of them prove that cooks in England are as skilful as anywhere else, once they can battle through the problems of supply.

It must be recognized that over the last century a continuing development of a strong national cuisine was hindered by a general attitude in Britain that it was better to have cheaper food of lower quality for everyone, rather than to concentrate on producing high quality, more expensive food for the few. Many people were prepared to compromise, if sometimes grudgingly, their own standards of comfort, so that someone else might be a little less ill-fed. This has been fine for civil peace, for the gentle temper of everyday living, but it has done nothing for cooking. The idea of cheap food has become so ingrained that people who could well afford it will not pay for quality. This is one reason why, for example, in a nation of cake and biscuit lovers, there are no pastry cooks in London who come anywhere near their fellows in quite moderate-sized towns of France, Austria, Belgium or Germany. It is not that British pastry cooks are without skill. Their clients refuse to pay for it.

Learning about the good food of Britain becomes an exploration. It means hacking

away the scrub to find the vestiges of civilization below. Gradually one comes to realize that the disgusting meal at the motorway service station was a betrayal of what British food can be.

Puddings, for centuries the national theme, are a good example. Foreign visitors in the seventeenth and eighteenth centuries were enthusiastic about the variety of English puddings. One reads their accounts with astonishment, until one actually goes into the kitchen and makes a steak, kidney and oyster pudding, or the marvellous Sussex Pond pudding, or a really crisp Yorkshire pudding. When proper fresh suet is chopped up, when new-laid eggs and sweet butter go into the pudding basins, British cooks can hold up their heads with anyone in the world.

What could be more delicious than the lovely creams and custards made to eighteenth-century recipes? Is there a better way of ending a dinner than with *crème brûlée* or gooseberry fool, or with an apple pie scented with quince? What about starting with potted crab or shrimp, covered in butter and spiced with mace?

There are many grand set pieces as well—poached salmon with mayonnaise and cucumber, cockie-leekie soup from Scotland, Lancashire's strange and flamboyant dish of chicken stuffed with prunes and coated with lemon sauce, and known as Hindle Wakes. What about roast sirloin of beef, pork with crackling, boiled leg of lamb with caper sauce? Doomed by the gentility of the nineteenth century, cooks have lost, in the south of England at least, the habit of making hearty dishes of tripe, black pudding and cow's heel.

The British never acquired an art of resourceful pork cooking as did the Germans or French. All that remains is the grandeur of certain cures of ham and bacon, or the occasional black pudding that is not too stodgy with cereal for pleasure. The Irish, however, manage better with drisheen, their blood pudding.

It is fun to trace the regional dishes of the British Isles back to their source. Often the results are surprising. One finds that haggis, junket and curd tart have kept quietly on in Scotland, Devonshire and Yorkshire, out of the mainstream of change, although they were once universal dishes and, before that, dishes for the court of Britain's medieval kings. Leek pies, on the menus of good French restaurants, lie forgotten by the rest of the population, although still made in

THE BRITISH ISLES

HAGGIS
Stuffed sheep's stomach

DEER

GROUSE

TROUT

SALMON

SCOTLAND

RIVER SPEY

ROWAN JELLY

• ABERDEEN

HERRINGS

WHITE FISH

PORRIDGE

DUNDEE • DUNDEE CAKE
Fruit cake topped with almonds

SCONES

MARMALADE

RASPBERRIES

EDINBURGH

GLASGOW

PETTICOAT TAILS
Shortbread

RIVER TWEED

BLACK BUN
Fruit cake in pastry

AYR •

BEEF

NORTHUMBERLAND

SINGIN' HINNIES
Griddle cakes

OATCAKES

DURHAM •

DUNLOP CHEESE

CUMBERLAND

RUM BUTTER

TROUT

POTATOES

BELFAST •

GRASMERE •

WENSLEYDALE CHEESE

IRISH STEW

KIPPERS

Gingerbread

HAM

SHRIMP

ROAST BEEF

HAM

ISLE OF MAN

MORECAMBE BAY

YORK •

YORKSHIRE

CARRAGEEN
Edible seaweed

CHAMP
Potatoes with
vegetables and milk

SODA BREAD

PARKIN
Oatmeal and
black treacle cake

LANCASHIRE

HOT POT

YORKSHIRE PUDDING
Savoury batter pudding

IRELAND

GALWAY

RIVER SHANNON

DUBLIN •

DUBLIN BAY
PRAWNS

LIVERPOOL • ENGLAND

WELSH
LAMB

CHESHIRE
CHEESE

BAKEWELL

STEAK AND
KIDNEY
PUDDING

LOBSTER

SALMON

LIMERICK •

HAM

IRISH STEW

SIMNEL
CAKE
Spicy cake

BAKEWELL TARTS
Sweet pastries

PORK PIES

NORFOLK

LEEKS

SHROPSHIRE

MELTON MOWBRAY

GREAT
YARMOUTH

TROUT •

GRIDDLE
CAKES

POULTRY

HERRINGS

STILTON
CHEESE

TROUT

POTATOES

CATTLE

AVON

RIVER BLACKWATER

DRISHEEN
Blood pudding

CORK •

SALMON

WYE

HEREFORD

BANBURY CAKES
Dried-fruit filled pastries

ROAST BEEF

COLCHESTER

WALES

RIVER USK

VALE OF
EVESHAM

RIVER SEVERN

BANBURY •

HAM

CAERPHILLY
CHEESE

FRUIT

BRADENHAM
LONDON •

JELLIED
EELS

OYSTERS

CAERPHILLY •

LAVERBREAD
Boiled edible
seaweed

RIVER THAMES

WHITSTABLE

CARDIFF •

BRISTOL

STEAK AND
KIDNEY
PUDDING

KENTISH
COBS

DOVER •

BRISTOL CHANNEL

BATH •

SOMERSET

BATH BUNS
Sweet buns

BATH OLIVERS
Biscuits

KENT

SOLE

FRUIT

CHEDDAR
CHEESE

SOUTHAMPTON

DEVONSHIRE

CLOTTED
CREAM

CORNISH PASTY
Potato and minces
steak turnover

PLYMOUTH •

• BRIXHAM

SPRATS

MACKEREL

CORNWALL

CRABS

83

Traditional tastes from the British Isles

Cornwall and Wales. The griddle, that source of varied if fattening delights, appears now in folk museums in Wales, Scotland and Ireland and in smart kitchen shops that specialize in supplying the new national enthusiasm for cooking.

Another odd quirk, admitted by Hannah Glasse, the greatest cookery writer of the eighteenth century, was to hang French names on to English dishes. Burnt cream, a standard recipe in books of her day, is now called *crème brulée*. Two other recipes thought of as French, *salmi* and *pain perdu*, have been eaten steadily in Britain since the time of Chaucer, who knew them as *salomene* and *payn pur-dew*.

Unfortunately, the British have often been the victims of their own adaptability and will to progress. The most serious victims were the Irish, who gave up their staple cereals because the potato from Peru was easier to grow. They were dying for this enthusiasm one hundred and fifty years later in the potato famines of the last century.

Less seriously, every child who loathes school custard, and there must be millions of them, should really be complaining about the eagerness shown for Mr Bird's custard powder, which was first produced commercially in the 1840s. How anyone could give up the delicious national sauce—the French called it *crème anglaise*—for such a travesty, it is impossible to understand.

And what about curry, the veil of British leftovers? Surely the civil servants back in Cheltenham from India, and quietly enjoying their kedgeree, could not be held responsible for this. India was Britain's one easily available source of the exotic, and the enthusiasm was overdone.

After the last hundred years, when the government has had to solve the problem of feeding a huge new urban population, a habit is needed of looking backwards critically but lovingly. More people are making a stand against the grey average. Every year more people find pleasure in cultivating their gardens and their cooking skills. It should be remembered that as recently as the 1890s a traveller in France, such as Henry James, brought up in France, speaking perfect French, could not find a decent standard of food outside the main centres of prosperity.

Culinarily, Britain should not be written off dismissively. With a little care, one may soon find the pleasure of many good and delicious things.

Cockie-leekie

This best of Scottish dishes is an old one. A visitor to Scotland described it in 1598—the servants and lower tables had broth with a bit of stewed meat, the "upper messe, insteede . . . had a Pullet with some prunes in the broth". Modern recipes exclude the beef, but this is a pity. Sometimes they even exclude the prunes, which reduces the dish to nothing out of the ordinary.

SERVES 8 TO 10

1 lb prunes
2 lb piece stewing beef
1 boiling fowl
Salt
Pepper
3 lb leeks, half left whole and half chopped

Soak the prunes overnight. Put the beef into a pot large enough to hold both it and the chicken. Cover the beef with plenty of water. Bring to a simmer and skim. Depending on the age of the boiling fowl (an old rooster accounts for the name of the recipe), add it to the pot after 30 minutes or 1 hour, with the salt and pepper and the whole leeks. Cook slowly, only an occasional bubble should appear on the surface of the liquid, until the meat and chicken are tender. The total cooking time should be about 3 hours.

Remove the chicken and beef from the pot. Slice the beef and cut the chicken into pieces and put back into the pot.

About 20 minutes before serving, bring the liquid to a simmer and add the prunes. Finally, add the chopped remaining leeks and give them 5 minutes in the pot. They should remain slightly crisp, and fresh tasting.

To serve, discard the whole leeks, which will be limp and tasteless. Put a slice of beef, a piece of chicken, some prunes, chopped leeks and soup into each bowl. Or, if preferred, serve the soup with some leeks and a few prunes first. Then eat the chicken and meat with the remaining prunes and leeks.

Smoked Finnan-Haddock with Egg Sauce

"Finnan" or, correctly, Findon, is a village near Aberdeen which is famous for its cured haddock. A haddock can be recognized by the "two finger-prints of St Peter", one on each side, at the back of the head. The fish is split along the back, opened, cleaned and salted, before being smoked to a silver tawny colour. Do not be trapped by yellow "golden" fillets—they have been dyed to save money. Proper oak-smoking dries the fish—and gives it the beautiful graduated colour—which means that it loses weight and therefore costs more per pound. Finnan - haddocks usually weigh between one and one and a half pounds, enough for two people.

SERVES 6

3 finnan - haddocks
Milk
Water
1 onion, stuck with 3 cloves
4 long strips of carrot
1 bay leaf
Freshly ground black pepper
Butter
1 heaped tablespoon flour
4 tablespoons double cream
1 tablespoon chopped parsley
3 hard-boiled eggs, shelled
1½ lb boiled potatoes, turned in parsley butter

Place the haddocks, skin side up, in a wide pan. Cover with milk and water, in the proportion of 3 to 1. Add the onion, carrot, bay leaf and pepper. Bring to the boil slowly, then let the liquid judder from time to time. (The fish should never be allowed to boil.) When the flesh can be separated easily from the bone with a fork, remove the haddocks and put them right side up on a serving platter. Using a fork, rub butter over the fish. Cover with foil to keep it warm.

Melt 1 ounce of butter in a pan, stir in the flour and strain in enough haddock liquor to make a sauce which has the consistency of cream. Simmer the sauce for 15 minutes. Stir in the cream and parsley. Correct the seasoning. Crush the eggs with a fork and add to the sauce. Arrange the potatoes around the haddock. Serve the sauce in a separate sauceboat.

Potted Crab

Preserving meat and fish in butter has always been a peculiarly English habit. Other Europeans keep food in fat to prevent deterioration—for example, the French confit d'oie, goose preserved in its own fat, or tuna fish, sardines and anchovies in olive oil—but the English seem to have been the only ones with so much butter at their disposal that they could use it lavishly. This crab dish is one of the best of its kind. Serve it as a first course, with toast, or as a lunch dish to be followed with a green salad.

SERVES 4

2 lb crab, boiled
Black pepper
Mace
Nutmeg
Cayenne
Lemon juice
Salt
About 8 oz unsalted or lightly salted butter
Clarified butter

Preheat the oven to 300°F (Gas Mark 2). Pick the meat from the crab, keeping the firm and

creamy parts separate. Season both with the spices, lemon juice and salt, if necessary. Layer the crab meat into small, heatproof ramekins. Melt the butter and pour it over the crab meat until it is just covered. Place the ramekins in a pan of water, and bake for 25 minutes.

Remove the ramekins from the oven and set aside to cool. When the crab meat is cold, pour a layer of clarified butter over the top. When the clarified butter has firmly set, cover the ramekins with foil, if they are to be kept for a day or two. This will prevent the butter from shrinking away from the sides of the ramekins while they are in the refrigerator.

Salmon in Pastry with Herb Sauce

Every northern country of Europe and America has similar recipes for boiled salmon. Here is something a little more unusual, from one of England's best restaurants, The Hole in the Wall at Bath. There the dish is only made in summer, when fresh salmon from the Wye is available.

SERVES 8

2½ lb centre or tail piece of salmon, skinned and filleted
4 oz lightly salted butter
4 pieces preserved ginger, drained and chopped
1 heaped tablespoon raisins
1 rounded tablespoon chopped, blanched almonds
Shortcrust pastry made with 12 oz flour and 6 oz butter
Beaten egg to glaze
SAUCE
2 shallots, chopped
1 heaped teaspoon chopped parsley
1 teaspoon mixed chervil and tarragon
2 oz butter
1 teaspoon flour
10 fl oz single cream, or half single and half double cream
Salt
Pepper
1 teaspoon Dijon mustard
2 egg yolks, mixed with 2 tablespoons cream from the 10 fl oz cream above
Lemon juice

Preheat the oven to 425°F (Gas Mark 7). Mix together the butter, ginger, raisins and nuts, and sandwich the 2 pieces of salmon together with half the mixture. Spread the remaining mixture on top. Roll out enough shortcrust pastry to enclose the salmon completely. Make a few slashes on top and add a restrained decoration of pastry fish, or some abstract design. (Leaves and roses are kept for meat pies in England.) Brush over with egg glaze. Bake for 35 minutes.

Meanwhile, make the sauce. Cook the shallots and herbs in the butter until softened. Add the flour, then dilute with cream and add the seasonings. Cook for 10 minutes. Finally, beat in the egg yolk mixture and stir over a low heat until thick. Do not allow the sauce to boil or it will curdle. Sharpen slightly with lemon juice. Place the salmon in its pastry on a hot platter. Serve the sauce separately.

Steak, Kidney and Oyster Pudding

Although steak pudding is a classic English dish, the addition of kidneys and oysters was not, it seems, made before the nineteenth century. Today many people are obliged to omit the oysters because of their price, but this is a pity because they add an incomparable flavour to the meat. Traditionally, the meat is cooked for hours inside the suet pastry, however, the result is lighter if the meat filling is pre-cooked, as in this recipe.

SERVES 6

2 lb stewing steak
1 lb veal or ox kidney
2 tablespoons seasoned flour
1 large onion, chopped
3 oz butter
1 pint beef stock, or 10 fl oz each stock and red wine
8 oz mushrooms, sliced
18 to 24 oysters (optional)
SUET PASTRY
8 oz self-raising flour
2 oz breadcrumbs
1 level teaspoon baking powder
½ teaspoon salt
Freshly ground white pepper
5 oz chopped fresh beef suet
Cold water to mix

To make the filling, cut the steak into neat pieces, discarding fat and gristle. Slice the kidneys and cut out the white fatty core. Sprinkle the meat with the flour. Brown the onion lightly in two-thirds of the butter. Push the onion to one side and add the meat, several pieces at a time, to colour rapidly. Transfer the meat with the onion to a casserole.

Pour the stock, or stock and wine into the pan and allow it to boil hard for a few moments, scraping up all the bits and pieces that have stuck to the pan. Pour this over the meat. Cover the casserole and simmer on top of the stove or in the oven at 275°F to 300°F (Gas Mark 1 to 2) for about 1½ hours. Set aside to cool.

To make the pudding, remove any congealed fat from the top of the meat. Fry the mushrooms in the remaining butter and add them with the oysters and their liquor to the steak and kidney. Check the seasoning.

To make the suet crust, mix all the dry ingredients in a bowl and pour in enough water to make a soft dough, which is not too wet and tacky to roll out (the breadcrumbs lighten the suet crust; but you can use a further 2 ounces of flour instead). On a lightly floured surface, roll out the dough into a large circle. Cut a quarter section out of the circle and set it aside, this portion forming the top crust. Grease a 3-pint basin with butter. Drop the three-quarter circle of dough down gently into it, pressing it against the sides and sealing the overlap. The sides of the dough should hang over the rim of the basin. Put the meat, oysters and mushrooms into the dough-lined basin with enough of the sauce to come to just below the top of the filling. Roll out the reserved dough into a circle large enough to cover the pudding. Wet the edges of the dough and press them together to make a firm seal.

Cut aluminium foil to make a circle 2 inches larger than the top of the basin. Fix it in place so that it balloons or pleats above the basin, allowing the pudding a little room to rise. Tie a string firmly around the foil, and make a handle of string over the top so that it can easily be lifted in and out of the boiler. Steam the pudding for 1½ to 2 hours, or slightly longer if this is more convenient (the pudding will not spoil).

When the time is up, lift the basin out of the pan, remove the string and foil, and tie a cloth napkin around the basin. Serve immediately.

Yorkshire Pudding

This delicious crisp batter pudding was invented by frugal housewives in the north of England, who could not bear to see wasted the meat juices which fell into the dripping-pan beneath the spit. This batter was poured into the pan, and received the benefit. Today, the batter is still poured into the roasting pan below the beef 35 minutes before the end of cooking time, although cooking it separately has, sadly, become more common.

SERVES 6

4 oz plain flour
Pinch salt
1 egg
10 fl oz milk or half milk and water

Mix the flour and salt together. Make a well in the middle and put the egg and a little milk in it. Working from the centre, stir the ingredients into a batter, gradually adding the rest of the milk or milk and water.

Make sure that the beef is roasting on a trivet or rack high above the roasting pan, at a temperature of 425°F (Gas Mark 7). Allow 15 minutes to the pound for rare beef. Forty minutes before the end of the roasting time, pour the batter into the pan. It will rise magnificently at the sides, and the centre will be soft and rich with the juices. Serve whole or cut in pieces around the beef.

Sweets to end a proper meal

Sussex Pond Pudding

The English have been famous for their puddings for centuries. This is the best of them all. The exceptional goodness of this recipe comes from the inclusion of a lemon—it adds just the right tart citrus flavour to the butter and sugar sauce, which might otherwise be too sweet. The pudding basin is lined with the dough and covered with foil in the same way as the steak, kidney and oyster pudding.

SERVES 4 to 6

1 teaspoon baking powder
8 oz self-raising flour
4 oz chopped fresh beef suet
Milk and water
4 oz lightly salted butter, cut in pieces
4 oz light brown sugar
1 large ripe lemon

Mix the baking powder, flour, suet, milk and water into a soft dough, which is not too tacky to be rolled out into a large circle. Line a 2½ pint pudding basin in the usual way, setting aside enough dough for a top crust.

Put half the butter and sugar into the dough-lined basin. Prick the lemon all over with a larding needles (so that the juice can slowly escape during the cooking), and put it into the basin. Surround it with the remaining butter and sugar, and cover with the dough. Place aluminium foil on top and boil for 3 to 4 hours.

Remove the cooked pudding from the pan, and remove the foil and string. Ease a thin knife between the pudding and basin, which will part company easily if the basin was properly greased. Put a serving dish on top, invert the whole thing and remove the basin. The golden-brown pudding will be sitting in a pond of richer brown sauce. Make sure that everyone gets a piece of the lemon, as well as a share of the delicious sauce.

Cream-crowdie

This simple, delicious pudding has long been a favourite in Scottish farmhouses. It is important to add enough oatmeal to give flavouring and crunch to the cream, but not so much that the mixture becomes thick and stodgy.

SERVES 4

3 oz coarse oatmeal
10 fl oz double cream
10 fl oz single cream
Up to 2 oz sugar

Toast the oatmeal in a slow oven until it is nicely browned. Whip the creams with sugar to taste. Fold in the oatmeal and serve.

Gooseberry Fool

Many people think that "fool" comes from the French verb, fouler, *to crush, which is what one does to the gooseberries in this recipe. Unfortunately, etymologists insist that it is a humorous name, like trifle, and whim-wham, which also means trifle. Take no notice of fool recipes that advocate the use of milk or custard instead of cream (unless you are prepared to make a custard of the kind required for* crème brulée). *These are the recommendations of meanness which have ruined the British reputation for food. Do not purée the fruit, it makes the mixture too smooth. The volume of gooseberries should be equalled by the volume of cream before it is whipped. Similar puddings can be made with uncooked strawberries or raspberries, with lightly cooked apricots or with cooked dried fruit.*

SERVES 6

1 lb gooseberries, tart green ones preferably
1½ oz butter
Sugar
About 6 oz double cream
About 4 oz single cream

Remove the tops and the tails from the gooseberries. Melt the butter in a pan, add the fruit and 4 heaped tablespoons of sugar. Cover the pan closely and simmer gently until the gooseberries are yellow and soft enough to be crushed. Pour into a measuring jug. Put an equal amount of cream into a bowl and whisk until thick. Mix in the gooseberries and adjust the sweetening to taste. Serve in small bowls with almond biscuits or sponge fingers.

Burnt Cream

The French call custard, crème anglaise, *and this is the queen of custards, the best of lighter English puddings.* Crème brulée *is often credited to Trinity College, Cambridge, at about the turn of the century, but although the college may have popularized it, burnt cream—which is identical—was a standard recipe in a number of eighteenth-century cook books. Here is one from 1769.*

SERVES 6

10 fl oz double cream
10 fl oz single cream
2 curls of lemon peel, shredded
1 stick cinnamon
6 large egg yolks
Granulated sugar

Bring the cream, lemon and cinnamon to the boil and boil it for 1 minute, taking care that it does not spill over the edge of the pan. Meanwhile whisk the eggs in the top of a double boiler, and pour on the boiling cream, whisking it in. Set over simmering water and stir the mixture with a wooden spoon until it thickens a little more. Allow about 10 minutes, and be

THE ENGLISH are not great creators of original drinks like the Americans, who never stop inventing new things to drink and making fortunes in the process. The only original English drink is London gin, which can scarcely be put beside bacon and eggs or Shakespeare as a deathless contribution to Western culture. Aside from the beer which they make no better and no worse than anyone else (or more precisely a little better than the French and a little worse than the Germans), the English gratefully and greedily consume other people's drinks—in some cases (champagne and cognac among them) in greater quantities than any other nation, their native French excepted. London is the world's bazaar for precious drinks, above all for wine.

Scotland and Ireland have both made much greater contributions to gastronomy, respectively with their whisky and stout, which are arguably the best spirit and the best beer, in its broadest sense, made in an imperfect world.

The blended whisky the world knows as Scotch is no better or cheaper in Scotland than anywhere else. What the visitor to Scotland should study are the unblended "single malt" whiskies—the original produce of the hundred or so highland distilleries, grouped chiefly round the river Spey. They are drinks of strong individuality, pungent with malt and smoke, aging to deep complexity and softness like fine old wine.

Ireland. too, has its whiskey, a sweet and smoky kind superficially not unlike a Scotch malt. But Ireland's greatest contribution is Guinness Stout, brewed from barley roasted almost black to be unlike any other drink on earth—a unique blend of bitter and creamy flavours. The taste for Guinness takes some acquiring, but ultimately it is the only brewed drink which can be compared with wine for flavour and texture.

careful not to let the custard become too hot or the yolks will curdle.

Strain the mixture into a shallow, heatproof dish and leave to set in the refrigerator until well chilled.

Cover the custard with an even layer of sugar just under ¼ inch thick. Heat the grill until it is red hot, then slide the dish underneath it. As the sugar turns to a smooth marbled sheet of yellow and brown caramel, move the dish about to make sure of an even effect. Do not let the sugar burn. It should look like "a glass plate put over your cream". Serve when the dish has cooled.

Mincemeat and Pies

To the Countess of Leicester, and to others of her social standing in the thirteenth century, dried fruit was already a necessary luxury as one can see from her steward's household rolls. In time it became a necessity to people living in a climate where, because of the varying humidity, fresh fruit was difficult to store through the winter. This is why mince pies, Eccles cakes and Banbury cakes, and their close relations Cumberland and Hawkeshead cakes, sly cake from Northumberland, and Chorley cakes from Lancashire, remain most popular in the north.

The other important role of dried fruit was to disguise meat, and sometimes fish, which was past its prime. Mincemeat, which even today includes beef suet, although the beef steak has been dropped, is a last relic of this necessity. Almost everybody in England eats mince pies at Christmas, and there are many slight variations in flavour from household to household. The best mincemeat includes hard liquor, as in this recipe from Mrs Beeton's Household Management *of 1856–61, which, apart from the steak, is the one used by most people today.*

Mincemeat

1 lb seedless raisins
1½ lb currants
12 oz lean rump steak, minced (optional, but
   a good idea)
1½ lb chopped beef suet
1 lb soft dark brown sugar
1 oz candied citron peel, chopped
1 oz candied lemon peel, chopped
1 oz candied orange peel, chopped
½ small nutmeg, grated
1½ lb apples, weighed after peeling and
   coring
Grated rind of 1 lemon
Juice of ½ lemon
5 fl oz brandy

Mix all the ingredients in the order given, but chop or grate the apples before adding them.

Press tightly into jars to keep the air out, cover and leave for at least two weeks to allow the flavours to mature.

Mince Pies

Preheat the oven to 425°F (Gas Mark 7). Line tart tins with shortcrust pastry. Put a heaped teaspoon of mincemeat into each one. Add a pastry lid, make a slash in the centre and brush with egg white. Sprinkle with sugar and bake for about 15 minutes. Eat hot, or reheated if this is more convenient, with brandy butter (sometimes called hard sauce). This is also eaten with Christmas pudding. When made with rum and soft brown sugar, a Cumberland speciality, it tastes delicious spread on oatcakes.

Brandy Butter

8 oz unsalted butter, creamed
4 oz icing sugar
4 tablespoons brandy
Squeeze lemon juice
Grated nutmeg to taste

Mix the ingredients together. Chill before serving.

Eccles Cakes

These are instant mince pies, with the filling made when required.
1 oz butter
2 oz sugar
4 oz currants or raisins
1½ oz chopped candied peel
½ teaspoon allspice
½ teaspoon nutmeg

Preheat the oven to 425°F (Gas Mark 7). Melt the butter over low heat, stir in the sugar then add the other ingredients. Stir until the fruit is coated, then remove and cool.

Cut 6 circles, 5 inches in diameter, of shortcrust pastry. Put 1 tablespoon of the fruit mixture in the middle of each one, moisten the edges and draw them together to make a round cake. Cut away surplus pastry. Turn the cakes over and press them lightly with a rolling pin to flatten them. Make a central hole in the top of each cake. Bake for 15 minutes. Sprinkle with sugar and serve warm.

Shortbread

There are a number of recipes for shortbread found all over Britain, but in most people's minds it has now become attached to Scotland. Petticoat tails, Pitcaithly bannock and Ayrshire shortbread are variations of shortbread. Butter, and plenty of it, must be used for the right flavour. Never use margarine. Ground rice flour adds to the sandiness of the close texture. Before it was

baked, shortbread was often stamped with designs from wooden or glazed earthenware moulds.

4 oz butter
2 oz castor sugar
4 oz flour
2 oz ground rice (rice flour)

Preheat the oven to 325°F (Gas Mark 3). Using hands, work butter and sugar together. Mix together the flour and ground rice, and add them gradually. Take care that the mixture does not become oily, so work the dough as little as possible.

Pat out into a circle about ½ to ¾ inch thick on a well-greased baking sheet. Pinch the edges all around, prick the centre part with a fork and, using the back of a knife, mark the shortbread into wedges. Bake for about 1 hour until it is a rich, pale golden colour. Shortbread should not brown.

Brandy Snaps

In the past, crisp, lacy, caramel biscuits were sometimes sold at English fairs, along with gingerbread, eel pies and pickled salmon. They were called fairings—Devizes fairings, for example. The brandy snap is the finest of these recipes and has survived as a universal favourite.

MAKES 20 TO 30

4 oz butter
4 oz golden syrup
4 oz granulated sugar
4 oz plain flour
Pinch salt
2 teaspoons ground ginger
1 teaspoon lemon juice
2 teaspoons brandy
10 fl oz double cream

Preheat the oven to 325°F (Gas Mark 3). Put the butter, syrup and sugar into a pan and stir over a low heat until the mixture has completely dissolved. Allow it to cool to lukewarm, then mix in the flour, salt, ginger, lemon juice and brandy. Drop teaspoons of the mixture on to 2 well-greased baking sheets, allowing a great deal of room between each as they will spread. Six spoonfuls to a sheet is sufficient. Bake them for 8 to 10 minutes.

Remove the first sheet, leaving the other in the oven to keep warm, with the door open so that the brandy snaps do not burn. Quickly loosen one biscuit at a time, still hot and soft, and press each gently around the handle of a wooden spoon to form a cigarette shape. If the biscuits become hard, put them over a gentle heat, or back in the oven for a little while to soften them again.

When cool, store the brandy snaps in an airtight tin. Before serving, whip the cream and pipe it in to fill the biscuits.

The fine art of natural foods

SEVENTEENTH-CENTURY Dutch still life shows the most luscious-looking interrupted meals. Fish, sliced and laid carefully on pewter plates, shining oysters and broken bread have all been left elegantly unfinished, while the soft dim light behind reveals an unfilled goblet or a bowl of huge, velvety peaches.

Close observation of a half-skinned lemon, or the alarming profusion of fallen fruit and game, gives an authentic picture of the traditional Dutch love of food. Even in paintings of family life, in those quiet interiors, there is usually a tempting bowl of fruit or some nuts scattered on the table.

The reputation of Dutch cooking is too often limited either to the unfortunate commercial picture of a coy dairymaid or to the idea, probably strengthened by the fact that the Dutch are longer lived than most other nationalities, that they eat simply to exist and to endure their climate.

The weather in the Netherlands can be harsh, but for people who love the North it has its compensations in rich stews and other sustaining delights. In winter, skaters on the frozen ponds and canals gather at the edge of the ice and sip hot milk flavoured with aniseed or warming *Erwtensoep*, a thick soup made of split green peas, leeks, celery, potatoes and slices of spicy sausages and pork. The generous slices of meat and chunks of vegetables make it quite unlike the usual smooth, sluggish variety of green pea soup.

To make Erwtensoep, *soak 1 pound of split green peas overnight. Drain and put them in a pot with 1 pig's trotter, 6 ounces of smoked pork and 5 pints of water. Bring to a boil, cover and simmer slowly for 3 hours. Add 1 thinly sliced leek and 1 smoked sausage. Chop and add 1 onion, 1 bunch of celery and 1 celeriac. Simmer for 15 minutes. Peel 2 potatoes and grate them into the soup and simmer for 10 minutes more. Remove the pig's* *trotter, bone it and return the meat to the soup. Remove the sausage and smoked pork, slice, and return the sausage slices to the soup, along with 2 tablespoons of chopped parsley. Serve the hot soup with the sliced smoked pork on buttered pumpernickel.*

Such magnificent stews as *hutspot met klapstuck* provide solid winter nourishment and justify Holland's reputation for hearty eating. The English word "hotchpot" comes from *hochepot*, the Belgian name for this stew, because it is made better by all sorts of tasty improvisations besides the basic ingredients of carrots, potatoes, beef and onions.

Curly kale with sausage, sauerkraut with bacon and many other mixed meat and vegetable dishes are all an important part of Dutch home cooking. They are made especially good by the plump fresh vegetables which flourish in the wet climate. The land north of Amsterdam produces excellent cabbages, and little white onions, known for their tender, sweet flavour, are grown in the fine sand along the coast.

Available fresh in May and June, asparagus is a particularly famous Dutch speciality. It is thick and white, like the asparagus in Adrien Coorte's still life, and is cultivated in the south near Bergen op Zoom and Venlo. Fresh vegetables, grown under glass in hothouses, are available all year. Between The Hague and Rotterdam miles of greenhouses look like enormous glass towns.

The large, placid kitchen maid with her milk jug, painted so exquisitely by Vermeer, reminds one of the Holland of "curds and cream". Dutch cheese, butter and milk are famous for their richness. Yoghourt, delivered in bottles each morning, is eaten with fruit and cereal for breakfast. Milk is drunk in vast quantities, besides being used to make the well-known cheeses—the wheel-shaped, yellow Gouda and the round red Edam. The coloured wax is a protective skin, used only for those cheeses that are exported. These cheeses, sold at the markets in Alkmaar and Gouda, are usually "young" and reach their destination abroad with their characteristically mild taste. If they are allowed to mature they begin to harden and to develop a much stronger flavour.

Other Dutch cheeses, less well known than Edam and Gouda, include Leiden, flavoured with cumin seeds, Friesland, spiced with cloves, Bluefort, creamy and blue-veined, and Kernhem, a round, flat cheese.

Cheese is another of the many things eaten by the Dutch for breakfast. It goes well with the creamy butter and the many different types of bread, which include rye bread, black bread and spiced or currant rolls. A *Breakfast Still Life*, painted by Laurens Craens in 1643, shows a crab and a large lobster lying among the goblets and vine leaves. Today, breakfast in Holland, although without shellfish, is still an elaborate meal. The richly buttered rolls and cheeses are accompanied by strong, fragrant coffee, or chocolate, with thick cream, an assortment of jams and marmalades, boiled eggs and slices of cold meat.

Holland's miles of coast make it a fish-loving country. Mussels, large Zeeland oysters and lobsters are mainly restaurant specialities. Eels, particularly good from the Zuyderzee, are smoked in the towns along the water. At the beginning of June, festivals celebrate the arrival of *nieuwe* or "green" herrings, which are sold in the street. They are eaten on the spot, either sliced and mixed with chopped onions, or held by the tail and swallowed in a few mouthfuls.

Sitting in a pastry shop, instead of snatching a herring *en passant*, is another of Holland's pleasures. To go with the coffee there are biscúits and cakes made in all shapes and sizes. Every region has its specialities. Zeeland is famous for treacle cakes, Friesland for sugar cakes and different kinds of gingerbread, and a variety of buns and spiced biscuits is made everywhere.

Speculaas, delicious spiced biscuits in the shapes of windmills and St Nicholas on horseback, are served with tea and coffee all through the winter, although they are an indispensable part of the celebration of the feast of St Nicholas on December 5th. The name is derived from the Latin *speculum*, which means looking-glass, because the biscuits are the reflection of the wooden mould in which they are made. The biscuit dough can also be rolled out and cut into various shapes.

To make speculaas, *mix 7 ounces of flour with ¼ teaspoon salt, 5 ounces brown sugar and 1 teaspoon mixed ground spices (cinnamon, nutmeg, cloves, ginger and cardamon). Cut in 5 ounces of butter. Knead into a dough, adding 3 tablespoons of slivered almonds. Wrap in foil and refrigerate.*

Sprinkle the hollows of the speculaas board with rice flour and press the dough into them. Turn the board on to a greased baking sheet and tap the dough out of the hollows. Bake in a preheated 350°F. (Gas Mark 4) oven for 20 minutes.

THE NETHERLANDS

FRISIAN ISLANDS

LAMB

SUGAR CAKES

PEPERKOEK
Gingerbread · **GRONINGEN**

BUTTER CAKES

F R I E S L A N D

SNEEK

BOKKING
Salted and smoked herring

KRUIDKOEK
Spiced bread

RED CABBAGE

· **ASSEN** CHOCOLATE

LEMMER

IJSSELMEER

ZUURKOOL
Sauerkraut

CABBAGES

URK ·

PLOVERS' EGGS

OLIEBOLLEN
Small doughnuts

EELS

SPECULAAS
Gingerbread

CHEESE · **EDAM**

GEROOKTE PALING
Smoked eel

MONNIKENDAM

· **ZWOLLE**

BLAUWVINGERS
Finger-shaped nut cakes

POFFERTJES
*Hot pastry puffs served
with butter and icing sugar*

EELS

GEROOKTE
PALING
Smoked eel

AMSTERDAM ·

· **HARDERWIJK**

O V E R I J S S E L

CUMIN CHEESE

YOUNG HERRING

KRUIDKOEK
Spiced bread

HAAGSE HOPJES
Coffee and butter sweets

THE HAGUE ·

· **LEIDEN**

HUTSPOT MET
KLAPSTUK
Beef and vegetable stew

BOKKING
*Salted and
smoked herring*

· **DEVENTER**

ASPARAGUS

RIJSTTAFEL
*Dutch-Indonesian
dishes with rice*

PEPERKOEK
Gingerbread

G E L D E R L A N D

POTATOES

ZUURKOOL
Sauerkraut

JUNIPER
BERRIES

GOUDA

STROOP WAFELS
Wafers and syrup

SAUSAGES

SCHIEDAM ·

RIVER LEK

· **ROTTERDAM**

CHEESE

POFFERTJES
*Hot pastry puffs served
with butter and icing sugar*

HAM

HACHEE
*Meat stew served with
potatoes and red cabbage*

LOBSTER

TOMATOES

LETTUCE

RIVER WAAL

CHOCOLATE

CUCUMBERS

POTATOES

WORSTEBROOD
Sausage-stuffed bread

RIVER
MAAS

OLIEBOLLEN
Small doughnuts

KRUIDKOEK
Spiced bread

's-HERTOGENBOSCH ·

MUSSELS

PLOVERS'
EGGS

ASPARAGUS

N O O R D
B R A B A N T

ASPARAGUS

Z E E L A N D

· **BERGEN-OP-ZOOM**

OYSTERS

KORSTJES
Spiced bread sticks

· **EINDHOVEN**

MUSHROOMS

VENLO ·

L I M B U R G

WEERT ·

LIMBURGSE VLAAI
Fruit tart

CHEESE ·

MUSHROOMS

MAASTRICHT ·

· VLAAI
Fruit tart

Dutch chocolate is as famous as its cheese. It is shaped into animals, dolls and flowers. At Christmas, children give each other their names spelled in chocolate letters, and the shop windows are full of such delightful sugar things as marzipan, liquorice and chocolate truffles.

To add to the richness of Dutch food is the amazing *rijsttafel,* or rice table, which was brought to the Netherlands from the Indonesian colonies. A *rijsttafel* is a unique restaurant experience. An enormous bowl of rice is surrounded by as many as twenty-five dishes of eggs, seafood, vegetables and meat in sweet, sour or spicy sauces. Although some of the contrasts and combinations are surprising, it is a precise and balanced meal. As filling as a staunch and simple stew, this complex Eastern banquet is a unique addition to all the natural foods, the asparagus and peaches and oysters, which fill so many of Holland's great paintings.

HOLLAND is another of the sophisticated, eclectic northern trading nations who know their wines well and apparently don't mind paying the going price for them. The Dutch love cockle-warming old amontillado sherry, solid classed-growth claret and burgundy, and the sweet and medium-sweet white wines of Bordeaux. It was largely owing to the Dutch that Bordeaux developed such a big white-wine trade.

The real Dutch speciality, however, is gin, which they make as a virtually un-flavoured spirit, barely distinguishable from vodka. Dutch gin is drunk both new and brisk or old and mellow, at strengths suitable for novices, old hands and everyone in between. *Yong genever* (the word *genever* meaning juniper, is the root of the word "gin", too) is at its very best in spring with the young herrings which are eaten cold and raw (simply cleaned and boned), often off stalls in the streets. The peculiar combination of rich herring and hard spirit is indescribably satisfying.

Foods unusually and excitingly combined

THERE IS A SAYING in Scandinavia that the Norwegians eat to live, the Swedes live to drink and the Danes live to eat. And, unquestionably, in Denmark people not only enjoy eating, but eat very well.

Although the Danes breakfast lightly on coffee or tea, crisp rolls, collected fresh from the baker every morning, and, occasionally, a soft-boiled egg, lunch is usually a selection of the famous open sandwiches which the world has come to know as Danish *smørrebrød*, literally bread and butter.

There are numerous take-away *smørrebrød* shops in Denmark which offer a bewildering selection of sandwiches. These range in complexity, and price, from a modest topping of hard-boiled egg and tomato slices, to as many as three rolls of cold roast pork, with a generous garnish of "Italian" salad (diced cooked vegetables in mayonnaise), and strips of tomato. The base for a *smørrebrød* is always dark rye bread, unless shellfish are included in the topping, in which case soft white bread is used.

Almost every Danish *smørrebrød* has a nickname. The speciality known as the Hans Andersen, for example, is a slice of rye bread liberally spread with butter, then with a good liver pâté and topped with crisp-fried bacon and garnished with slices of tomato and aspic and curls of grated horse-radish. Shrimps in a Traffic Jam consists of a buttered slice of white bread covered with a lettuce leaf and piled so high with shrimp that the bread underneath can neither be seen nor tasted. This is finished off with mayonnaise and a thin slice of lemon.

The main meal of the day—known as *middag*, midday meal, yet served in the evening, as it is throughout Scandinavia—usually consists of two courses, or one course followed by fresh fruit or cakes and coffee.

Soups are great favourites and range from sweet fruit soups thickened with barley or sago, and light summery soups like the pale-green chervil soup which is served garnished with a poached or lightly boiled egg, to cocoa soup, curry soup and *øllebrød*, beer soup made with non-alcoholic beer and day-old rye bread.

In winter, *gule aerter*, a thick, yellow split-pea soup, is always made in sufficient quantity to last the family for two days. The soup is cooked with a variety of vegetables and pieces of lightly salted pork or pigs' trotters. Some of the meat is then served with each portion of soup, to be fished out and eaten from side plates with mustard and coarse, unbuttered rye bread.

As is true in the rest of Scandinavia, fish plays an important part in the Danish cuisine. Wood-smoked herrings from the island of Bornholm in the Baltic are served cold with sliced radishes or rich sour cream as an *hors d'oeuvre*. There are fried herrings, mackerel in parsley sauce and the traditional cod for New Year's, which is boiled whole and served with melted butter and a strong mustard sauce.

Eel parties are popular occasions. Danes will drive miles to visit a country inn reputed to serve the best eels. Coated with seasoned flour and crisp-fried in butter, the fat chunks of eel arrive at the table in a large pan from which the diners help themselves. The eels are eaten with potatoes tossed with dill or in a white sauce, except on the small island of Samsø, where mashed potatoes and unsweetened apple purée are the traditional accompaniments.

Although beef is frequently served, and lamb is gaining in popularity, pork is by far the most popular meat. This is scarcely surprising in a country where the pigs are calculated to outnumber the people by about two to one. Traditionally, the Danes offset the richness of the meat with both sweet and sour flavours. Apples, halved and cored, baked or poached and filled with redcurrant jelly, accompany pork along with sharp pumpkin pickles and sour dill cucumber pickles. And no dish of *flaeskesteg*, roast pork, is complete without sweet and sour red cabbage and caramelized potatoes. Pork, goose and duck are often stuffed with apples and prunes to counteract their richness.

Helstegt mørbrad med svesker og aebler, a pot-roasted pork tenderloin stuffed with fruit served in a creamy sauce, is a favourite Sunday dinner dish.

To make mørbrad *to serve 4, remove the outer membranes and any gristle from 2 pork fillets. Split them lengthwise, without separating the two halves, and pound them out flat. Sprinkle with 1 teaspoon of salt, ½ teaspoon of sugar and a grinding of black pepper. Cover the surface with 2 peeled, cored and thinly sliced cooking apples and 8 to 10 large, plump prunes, soaked, halved and stoned. Roll each fillet up carefully, starting at one of the shorter ends. Tie the rolls securely with string.*

In a heavy, flameproof casserole, gently brown the rolled fillets in 2 ounces of butter. Remove the pork rolls. Add 5 tablespoons of cold water to the casserole and, with a wooden spoon, scrape the bottom of the pan clean. Pour in 5 fluid ounces of single cream. Return the pork rolls to the casserole, cover and simmer over low heat for 30 minutes, or until the pork is tender.

Lift the pork rolls out of the casserole and discard the string. Keep the rolls hot on a serving dish. Thicken the sauce by stirring in tiny pieces of beurre manié, *made by creaming together 2 teaspoons each of butter and flour. Correct the seasoning and flavour to taste with 1 teaspoon of redcurrant jelly. Pour some of the sauce on the pork rolls, which are sliced at the table, and serve the rest separately in a sauceboat.*

THE DANES, even more than the Dutch, are schnapps and beer drinkers. Instead of gin, however, they drink aquavit, clear spirit distilled from potatoes (and sometimes grain) and flavoured with caraway and other seeds. And instead of rather watery beer they drink their famous and excellent lager, either Carlsberg or Tuborg, both names to conjure with in Denmark, being pioneers in social services and labour relations as well as in brewing. Carlsberg is a foundation in which all the profits of trade are used for cultural, educational and scientific purposes.

To Denmark the world's brewing industry owes a good deal of vital technical knowledge. It was Tuborg which introduced the pasteurization of beer, and Carlsberg the pure cultivation of yeast. The difference between lager and beer lies in the yeast used; that for lager sinks to the bottom and acts slowly there at very low temperatures. Although lighter, therefore, lager takes longer to make and is capable of some deep and subtle undertones of flavour. In Carlsberg's Special Brew lager reaches its potent and splendid apogee.

The one famous brand of aquavit is Aalborg, named after the town. Denmark's other internationally known spirit is the sweet cherry liqueur, Cherry Heering.

STEGT DYRERYG
Roast loin of venison

SKIPPERLABSKOVES
Stew with beer, potatoes and chives

AALBORG
AQUAVIT

PLAICE

KATTEGAT

LIM FJORD

OYSTERS

LUMPFISH

MUSSELS
GRUNDLOVSDESSERT
Rhubarb and custard pudding

LUMPFISH ROE

KORVELSUPPE
Chervil soup

FUGLEVILDT POSTEJ
Game pâté

POULTRY

EGGS

DENMARK
JUTLAND

APPLES

RUGBRØD
Rye bread

AARHUS

DAIRY FARMING

BUTTER

CHEESES

RØDGRØD MED FLØDE
Summer fruit pudding

BACON

EELS

COPENHAGEN

LAGER

JULERISENGRØD
Christmas rice porridge

FRIKADELLER
Pork and veal patties

SMØRREBRØD
Open sandwiches

SJAELLAND

KRYDRETAND
Pickled duck

ÆBLESKIVER
Doughnuts

ESBJERG
HERRING

ODENSE

FYN

FRIKADELLER
Pork and veal patties

WIENERBRØD
Danish pastries

HARESTEG MED FLØDE
Casseroled hare in cream sauce

LOLLAND

The potato, the staple Danish vegetable, is served boiled, mashed or sautéed. Small potatoes boiled in their jackets are then peeled and evenly coated in sweet caramel, or dressed with chopped fresh chives, dill, parsley or blanched kale, or served in a thick white sauce.

The Danes are fond of desserts. *Aeblekage,* apple cake, is a popular winter dessert.

To make an aeblekage to serve 4 to 6, peel, core and slice 1½ pounds of cooking apples. Cook them over very low heat with 3 tablespoons of lemon juice and 6 tablespoons of water until they are almost disintegrating. Mash the apples with a fork. Stir in 1 ounce of butter and sugar to taste. Let the mixture cool.

In a heavy pan, melt another 2 ounces of butter. Stir in 4 ounces of dry pumpernickel crumbs and 3 ounces of sugar, and fry them together, stirring constantly, until the crumbs are crisp.

Cool.

Arrange alternate layers of the crumbs and the apple purée in a glass bowl, starting and ending with the crumbs. Cover with 5 fluid ounces of double cream, whipped, and decorate with redcurrant jelly. Serve chilled.

Danish pastries, which the Danes themselves call *Wienerbrød,* Viennese bread, are as popular in Denmark as they are abroad. The rich, buttery pastries filled with marzipan, custard, fruit or raisins, nuts and sugar, are eaten with mid-morning coffee, afternoon coffee, evening coffee and on any other occasion that presents itself, in the numerous little coffee shops and *konditorier,* or pastry shops.

Natural flavours, superb and undisguised

THE NORTHERN RACES are the real spirit-drinkers. No highballs for them. No temporizing with tonic water. The Russians with their vodka, the Swedes with their "snaps", toss back the liquor straight, at deep-freeze temperature.

Swedish snaps can be aquavit, which is drunk with a degree of formality. Someone proposes a *skai* with one or more members of the party. Glasses are raised to the level of the third waistcoat button, the participants bow to each other, and their eyes meet. The aquavit is quaffed, the glasses are lowered to the same waistcoat button level, and again the eyes meet. There follows another slight bow and the glasses are returned to the table.

Norway is equally aquavit-inclined. Finland, on the other hand, drinks more vodka, and specializes in a range of excellent fruit-flavoured spirits.

ROWANBERRY CONSERVE
REINSDYR MARGBEIN
Reindeer marrowbones
GAME
REINDEER
ELK
PTARMIGAN
AQUAVIT
SEAGULLS' EGGS
GJETOST
Goat's milk cheese
COD
SALMON
ROMMEGRØT
Sour-cream porridge
HADDOCK
RAKØRRET
Pickled trout
COALFISH
FENALÅR
Smoked roast leg of lamb
HALIBUT
KABARET
Seafood in aspic
TRONDHEIM
FLØTEVAFLER
Sour-cream waffles
HERRING
PINNEKJØTT
Steamed mutton chops
LUTEFISK
Dried cod speciality
FÅR-I-KÅL
Mutton and cabbage stew
GAMMELOST
Strong cheese
WILD BERRIES
CLOUDBERRIES
JARLSBERG
CHEESE
LEFSER
Potato griddle bread
ROWANBERRIES
LINGONBERRIES
HAMAR
BERGEN
PALESUPPE
Fish soup
FISKEPUDDING
Fish pudding
FLATBRØD
Flat crispbread
MUSSELS IN WHITE WINE
OSLO
SPEKEMAT
Salt-cured meat
RED CURRANTS
SHEEP
STAVANGER
KROTERCAKE
Griddle cake
STOKKFISK
Dried cod
KLIPPFISK
Dried salt cod

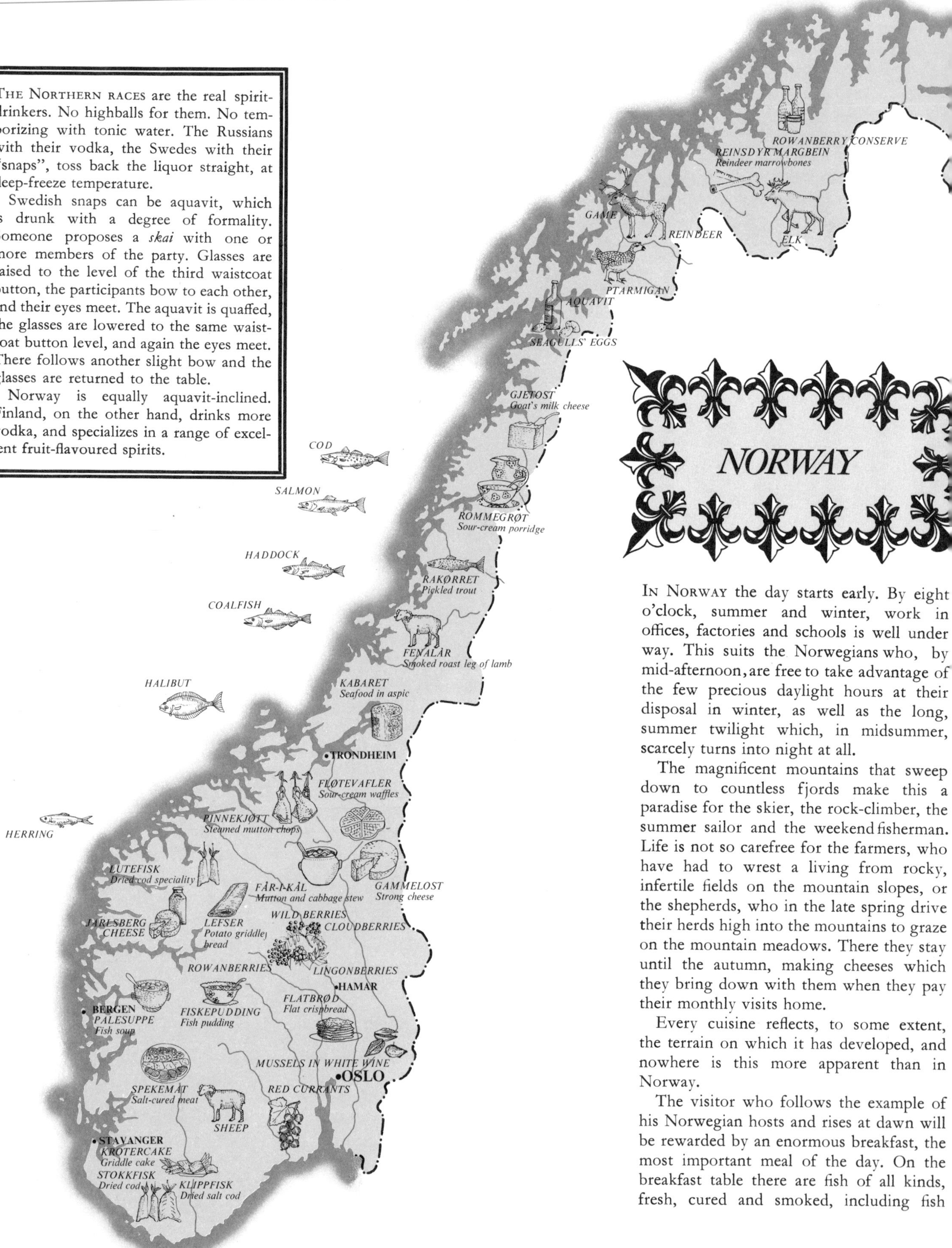

NORWAY

IN NORWAY the day starts early. By eight o'clock, summer and winter, work in offices, factories and schools is well under way. This suits the Norwegians who, by mid-afternoon, are free to take advantage of the few precious daylight hours at their disposal in winter, as well as the long, summer twilight which, in midsummer, scarcely turns into night at all.

The magnificent mountains that sweep down to countless fjords make this a paradise for the skier, the rock-climber, the summer sailor and the weekend fisherman. Life is not so carefree for the farmers, who have had to wrest a living from rocky, infertile fields on the mountain slopes, or the shepherds, who in the late spring drive their herds high into the mountains to graze on the mountain meadows. There they stay until the autumn, making cheeses which they bring down with them when they pay their monthly visits home.

Every cuisine reflects, to some extent, the terrain on which it has developed, and nowhere is this more apparent than in Norway.

The visitor who follows the example of his Norwegian hosts and rises at dawn will be rewarded by an enormous breakfast, the most important meal of the day. On the breakfast table there are fish of all kinds, fresh, cured and smoked, including fish balls, salted herrings in an onion and vinegar marinade and fillets of mackerel in tomato sauce. There are also platters of smoked and cured meat, among them reindeer and mutton salamis, a cheese board, boiled eggs and bowls of delicious sour cream, which is eaten with a sprinkling of coarse sugar. In summer, bowls of wild mountain berries, blueberries, lingonberries, blackberries and cloudberries, as likely as not gathered the same morning, join the other dishes. These are eaten with sour cream.

Crispbreads are popular, as are waffles, which come hot from the iron to be eaten dripping with butter and topped with blueberry jam. The choice of breakfast drinks includes buttermilk, hot chocolate, coffee, occasionally tea and, a comparatively recent innovation, fruit juice.

Having eaten their way through a large breakfast, Norwegians are content with a simple lunch of two or three open sandwiches of bread and butter topped with slices of salami and a few raw onion rings, a slice of cheese or egg and tomato, or some liver pâté. Waffles left over from breakfast are sandwiched with butter and sugar.

The hot meal of the day is rather misleadingly known as *middag*, for although restaurants serve it at midday, at home it is usually eaten in the early evening. *Middag* is a far less elaborate meal than breakfast, usually consisting of only two courses, a soup and a main course. If a sweet fruit soup is served, the order may be reversed.

Soups play an important part in most cold-climate cuisines. In Norway, heavy winter soups made with dried peas and lentils, and such winter vegetables as cabbage and kale, give way to summer vegetable soups like the popular *blomkål-suppe*, cauliflower soup, and soups based on fruit.

As one might expect, fish forms an important part of the Norwegian diet. Fish markets offer the housewife a rich variety to choose from—herring, mackerel, plaice, cod, haddock and halibut, and thick whale-meat steaks, as well as salmon and trout from the mountain streams.

Fresh fish are usually served boiled or baked, not through lack of imagination, but because their supreme freshness is best appreciated with melted butter or a simple parsley sauce and plain boiled potatoes.

Fish are also used to make soup, like the *palesuppe* of Bergen, home of one of Norway's most famous fish markets.

To make palesuppe *to serve 4, clean and fillet about 4 pounds of small haddock, reserving the heads, tails, bones and other trimmings. Cut the fillets into finger-thick slices and rinse them in cold water.*

In a saucepan, combine the fish trimmings with 2 diced celery sticks and ½ turnip, diced, 2 tablespoons of finely chopped onion, 4 peppercorns, 2 cloves and 1 teaspoon of salt. Cover with 2 pints of water. Bring to the boil and simmer gently, covered, for 20 minutes. Strain the stock through a fine strainer.

In another pan, melt ¾ ounce of butter. Blend in ¾ ounce of flour and stir over a low heat for 1 minute to make a pale roux. Gradually add 1½ pints of hot fish stock, followed by ½ pint of milk, stirring vigorously to prevent lumps forming. Bring to the boil, stirring. Add 2 thinly sliced carrots and 6 tablespoons of shredded leek, and simmer gently until the vegetables are soft. Meanwhile, poach the fish strips gently in salted water for 5 minutes, or until tender.

Just before serving, blend 6 tablespoons of sour cream into the soup and taste for seasoning. Add the hot, poached fish strips and serve immediately, garnished with finely chopped parsley or chives.

The poached fish strips are sometimes served after the soup accompanied by boiled potatoes and melted butter.

Mutton and lamb are the most popular meats, usually made into stews. Salt-cured meats, known collectively as *spekemat*, also include leg of mutton, salt-cured and smoked, which must be soaked, like a ham, before it is cooked.

Game is plentiful in Norway—from the majestic elk and herds of reindeer which roam wild in parts of the country, to hare, grouse, woodcock, ptarmigan and waterfowl. Reindeer marrowbones are a particular delicacy, and special picks are provided for extracting the marrow.

Preserves made from wild berries are a favourite accompaniment for game. In summer, families armed with metal canisters set off on berry-picking expeditions. The berries which are not eaten fresh are used to restock the larder with syrups, jams and preserves for the coming year.

Norwegian fields yield little wheat. Breads and crispbreads are usually made with coarse rye flour. But only the best wheaten flour is used for *kringle*, the famous coffee cake. The bakers of Scandinavia hang a gilded image of the cake outside their shops as a symbol of their trade.

To make a kringle, sift 1 pound of plain flour into a large, warmed bowl. Rub in 6 ounces of butter until the mixture resembles fine breadcrumbs. Stir in 4 ounces of castor sugar, 1 teaspoon of ground cardamom and ½ teaspoon of salt, and make a well in the centre.

Cream 2 ounces of fresh yeast with 7 fluid ounces of lukewarm milk. Pour it into the well and put the bowl aside in a warm place for 10 to 15 minutes.

When the yeast liquid is frothy, mix it into the flour, together with 1 lightly beaten egg. Knead to a smooth, springy dough, adding a little more lukewarm milk if necessary. The total amount of liquid will depend on the quality of the flour. Roll the dough into a ball. Cover the bowl with a cloth and leave in a warm place for about 1 hour, or until the dough has doubled in bulk. Meanwhile, cream 5 ounces of butter with 5 ounces of castor sugar.

Turn the risen dough out on to a lightly floured board. Knead it lightly and shape it into a long sausage, then flatten with a rolling pin. Spread it with the creamed butter mixture to within ½ inch of the edges and scatter 2 ounces each of sultanas and candied peel evenly over the surface. (1 ounce of flaked almonds may be included with the fruit.)

Roll up the sausage lengthwise. Lay it on a buttered baking sheet, open edge downwards, and shape it into a kringle *by bringing the two ends round and up to meet in the centre. From the top, the* kringle *will look like a capital B. Cover it with a cloth and leave to prove for 20 minutes. Brush with 1 lightly beaten egg white, sprinkle with crushed sugar lumps and flaked almonds, and bake in a preheated (400°F, Gas Mark 6) oven for 20 minutes, or until the* kringle *is a rich, shiny golden colour. Cool on a wire rack. A* kringle *is best eaten lukewarm, cut in thick slices.*

Superb natural flavour, thanks to the clear sea and the sparkling mountain air, is the theme of much of Norwegian cooking. It is seldom disguised with rich sauces or an overgenerous use of spices or herbs. Like the Norwegians themselves, the food of Norway is wholesome and down-to-earth.

The home of an imaginative buffet

AS FAMOUS AS MIDSUMMER DANCING, the horses of Dalercarlia and Swedish Lapland, is *smörgåsbord*, the best-known aspect of Swedish cuisine. This is scarcely surprising, since the *smörgåsbord*'s impressive selection of dishes promises a feast of unforgettable originality.

There are a number of theories about the origins of the *smörgåsbord*, but it probably began as a kind of rural party to which guests contributed home-made specialities. This pooling of resources was important, particularly in remote country districts where the supply and variety of raw materials were usually restricted.

While the preparation of a full-scale *smörgåsbord* may seem a daunting prospect, it is, nevertheless, an easy way to entertain, since everything is prepared in advance. Guests help themselves, changing plates as they proceed from course to course. First to be eaten are the herrings—cured, smoked pickled and marinated—a tribute to the ingenuity of the Swedish cook. The herrings are followed by other fish dishes which include smoked eel and slices of pink *gravlax*. A famous Scandinavian delicacy, *gravlax* is made with fresh salmon which is halved lengthwise, boned, sandwiched together again with a paste of coarse salt, mustard, fresh dill and brandy, and left under a weighted board for up to a week.

After the cold fish, diners proceed to the *småvarmt*, literally "the small warm dishes", which may include fish balls in sherry sauce, medallions of pork, cutlets, individual *vol-au-vents* filled with diced chicken and asparagus, or fried fish fillets with rémoulade sauce—all scaled down to provide small portions. Then the cold meats and patés are sampled. The feast is rounded off with cheese, often eaten with fruit, and a light dessert such as a fruit compote.

The *smörgåsbord* also includes a selection of salads, which the Swedes like to dress with mayonnaise, dishes of warm vegetables,

and a choice of breads, ranging from large, round *knäckbröd*, crispbreads with a hole in the middle, a reminder of the times when such dry breads were hung on poles and stored near the rafters, to moist, spicy black rye breads which go particularly well with butter and cheese.

Janssons frestelse, or Jansson's temptation, a potato, onion and anchovy casserole, is usually included in the *smörgasbord,* but it may also be served as a first course or as a main-course supper dish.

To make Janssons frestelse *to serve 4, peel 8 potatoes and cut them into thin strips. Slice 2 large onions. Clean and fillet 10 Swedish anchovies or substitute 20 drained canned anchovy fillets.*

In a buttered baking dish arrange layers of potato, anchovy and onion, ending with a layer of potato. Pour ¼ pint of single cream over the top and dot with butter.

Bake in a 400°F (Gas Mark 6) oven for 45 minutes, or until the potatoes are cooked. A few minutes before taking the dish out of the oven, pour another ¼ pint of cream over the top.

With a *smörgåsbord,* ice-cold aquavit is always drunk with a chaser of cold lager. There are more than thirty varieties of aquavit, bearing the names of the town or region that produced them, famous people, or the spices or herbs that have been used as flavourings, including caraway, bitter orange, cumin, wormwood and rowanberry.

Smörgåsbord is not by any means all that the Swedish cuisine has to offer. There is also a whole range of traditional dishes, known as *husmanskost,* developed by generations of country cooks. One of these country-style dishes, which appears at least once a week on Swedish dinner tables, is *pytt i panna,* which means "bits and pieces cooked in the pan". It is made with the meat and vegetables left over from the last two dinners, reinforced if necessary with diced pork or bacon, fried with onions and moistened with any left-over brown gravy. It is served straight from the pan, usually topped with a fried egg or a raw egg yolk.

Festive occasions and regional specialities are sometimes interrelated, as in the traditional *Mårten gås* dinner, the Martinmas goose dinner eaten on November 10th, the eve of St Martin's day. This holiday was originally celebrated in the fertile southern province of Skåne, by the Swedish aristocracy, as the nameday of Martin Luther. By the middle of the seventeenth century, the tradition had spread throughout the country.

On St Martin's Eve, the roast goose is preceded by a traditional black giblet soup made with goose blood. The meal ends with a *spettekaka,* a tall, golden lattice-work of cake made by pouring rich egg batter in a slow, thin stream on to a cone shrouded with buttered white paper and mounted on a rotary spit.

Each of Sweden's twenty-eight provinces has evolved its own specialities. Skåne is also famous for mustard. The best cheesecake is claimed by Småland which, together with Öland, is also famous for *kroppkakor,* potato dumplings stuffed with chopped pork, and served with melted butter or cream and red whortleberry preserve.

As in other Scandinavian countries, fish and shellfish play an important part in the Swedish cuisine. Baltic herrings, star performers in the *smörgåsbord,* and herrings from farther afield, cod, eels, salmon trout, carp, perch and pike, are some of the wide choice available. The *hornfisk,* or garfish, at its best in early summer, is particularly popular with children and finicky fish eaters as its bright green bones are clearly visible. The crayfish season, which begins on August 7th, is celebrated with gay parties at which piles of bright red crayfish garnished with dill heads are eaten.

Delicacies of the nine northern provinces, known collectively as Norrland, include salmon, trout, whitefish and its caviar. Reindeer meat, fresh, frozen or smoked, is sent all over the country. The Lapps make a speciality of lightly smoked reindeer tongue.

Such northern berries as the exquisite Arctic raspberry and the cloudberry are used to make preserves for serving with meat and game, and in light, delicate sweets and cakes like the *hjortrontårta,* or cloudberry tart.

To make a hjortrontårta *to serve 6, first line the bottom of a round, shallow 9-inch cake tin with lightly oiled greaseproof paper.*

Wash 8 ounces of unblanched almonds and dry them thoroughly. Grind them in a blender, and mix them with 8 ounces of castor sugar. Whisk 4 egg whites until stiff but not dry. Fold in the nut mixture lightly but thoroughly.

Spread the mixture evenly in the prepared cake tin and bake in a 350°F (Gas Mark 4) oven for 25 minutes, or until lightly browned and firm at the centre. Carefully turn it out on to a wire rack and peel off the paper. Leave to cool.

Transfer the meringue to a flat serving dish. Cover the base with 12 ounces of drained canned or thawed frozen cloudberries, or raspberries, eserving a few of the best ones for decoration. Pile ½ pint of whipped double cream over the top and decorate with the reserved berries.

Among the many festivals celebrated in Sweden, perhaps the best loved are those associated with Christmas. The celebration of St Lucia's day, December 13th, is a great family occasion. A Swedish Lucia—usually depicted as a beautiful, blonde young girl wearing a white dress and a crown of spruce with seven lighted candles, played by the daughter of the household—wakes her parents with a tray of fragrant saffron buns, known as Lucia cakes, and hot coffee. As this little ceremony often takes place at 5 am, the family usually go back to sleep again until breakfast.

The traditional Christmas Eve supper includes *lutfisk*, lye-cured dried salt cod or ling, served in white sauce with boiled potatoes and peas, and *Julgröt*, the traditional Christmas rice porridge. Buried somewhere in it there is a blanched almond or a tiny coin, and the lucky finder wins a prize or, in the case of a young girl, the prospect of a marriage in the year.

The magnificent *smörgåsbord* served on Christmas Day includes a whole ham garnished with kale, several herring dishes, including a herring salad, platters of brawn, liver pâtés, sausages and spareribs, meatballs, red cabbage and pickled beetroot, and a whole Edam cheese, its red skin matching the bowls of red tulips which traditionally decorate the table. *Pepparkakor*, spiced biscuits, and hot coffee round off the meal.

The Swedish approach to food is neither as frugal as that of the Norwegians, nor as extravagant as that of the Danes. It is, nevertheless, a highly imaginative cuisine, prepared and presented with the same natural good taste as the exquisite glassware and the finely embroidered table linens which have earned the Swedes a world-wide reputation.

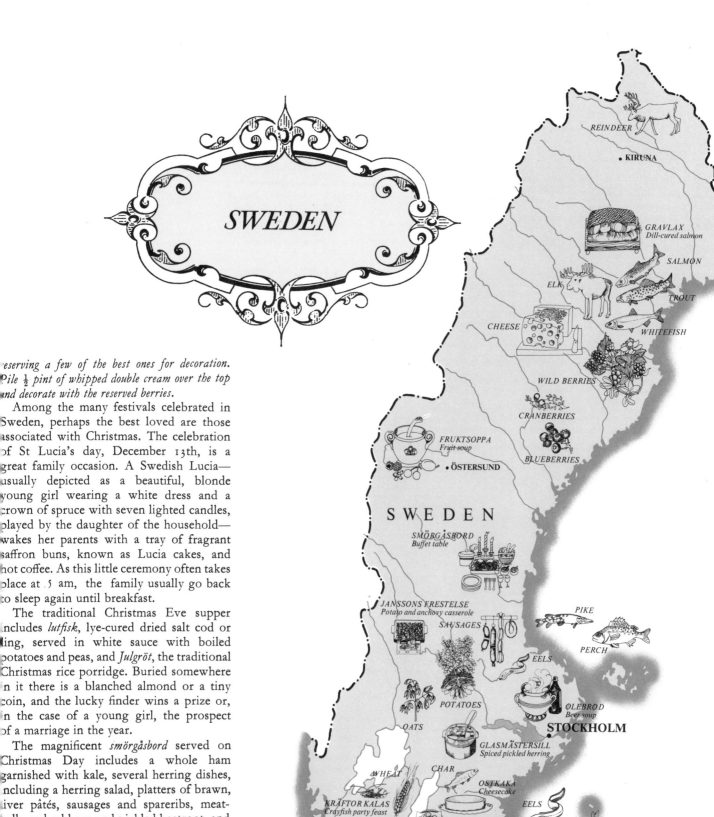

REINDEER

KIRUNA

GRAVLAX
Dill-cured salmon

SALMON

ELK

TROUT

CHEESE

WHITEFISH

WILD BERRIES

CRANBERRIES

FRUKTSOPPA
Fruit soup

BLUEBERRIES

ÖSTERSUND

SWEDEN

SMÖRGÅSBORD
Buffet table

JANSSONS FRESTELSE
Potato and anchovy casserole

PIKE

SAUSAGES

PERCH

EELS

POTATOES

ØLEBRØD
Beer soup

OATS

STOCKHOLM

GLASMÄSTERSILL
Spiced pickled herring

WHEAT

CHAR

OSTKAKA
Cheesecake

EELS

KRÄFTOR KALAS
Crayfish party feast

PEPPARKAKOR
Spiced sweet biscuits

RABBIT

POTATISPLÄTTAR
Potato pancakes

GÖTEBORG
MUSSELS

MUSTARD

LAMB

CRAYFISH

ÖLÄNDSK KROPPKAKOR
Pork-stuffed potato dumplings

LOBSTER

CABBAGE

STEKT
GAS
MED
KATRINPLOMMON
OCH EPLER
Roast goose with
prunes and apples

HARE

SPETTEKAKA
Cake cooked on a spit

GEESE

BALTIC HERRING

ÅLSOPPA
Eel soup

SHRIMP

MALMÖ

EELS

PRAWNS

95

Fine food in a land of lakes and forests

FINLAND, at the northeastern tip of Europe, is thickly forested with dark pine and silver birch, which are interspersed with innumerable lakes and rivers. Until 1917, when Finland achieved independence, her land acted as a buffer between Sweden and Russia and she was permanently under the domination of either one or the other. Both Sweden and Russia have left their mark on the cuisine.

Finnish restaurants serve their own version of the Swedish *smörgåsbord*, which they call *voileipäpöytä*, and the Finns enjoy open sandwiches, *voileipä*, as much as the other Scandinavians. On the other hand, *borsch* and *blini*, the flat Russian buckwheat pancakes are popular, the borsch served with sour cream, just as it would be in Russia, and vodka, not aquavit, is the national drink.

Finnish cuisine is simple and wholesome and served in generous quantities. Breakfast, *aamiainen*, is a simple meal, usually consisting of coffee or milk, and bread or crispbread. Lunch, *lounas*, may be hot soup and a sandwich, or a milky porridge followed by a main course, and dinner, usually eaten in the early evening, will again include soup, followed by a dish of meat or fish and a simple dessert.

Finnish soups are thick and sustaining and rich with meat and game; some, such as *hernekeitto*, the pea soup which is usually served on Thursdays, are made with dried vegetables. Summer brings *kesäkeitto*, made with tender young vegetables, enjoyed all the more because their season is so short, and sweet berry soups. There is also a variety of fish soups, including *lohikeitto*, a magnificent salmon soup.

Some people maintain that the Finnish name for Finland, *Suomi*, and the Finnish word for a fish scale, *suomo*, are derived from the same root. Certainly, the lakes and rivers of Finland and the seas around her island-dotted coast are alive with fish. The Baltic herring, called *silakka*, is as popular here as it is throughout Scandinavia. It is salted or smoked, and used to make a variety of dishes, including salads like *rosolli*, which is gaudy with beetroot and carrots. Salmon is prepared in a variety of memorable ways—poached, barbecued, grilled and served with a savoury butter, or smoked and served cold with a garnish of stewed morels, or encased in pastry with rice and hard-boiled eggs to make one variation of the famous Karelian pastry called *piirakka* or *piiraat*.

Whitefish is either lightly salted or grilled with lemon butter, or smoked and served with scrambled eggs. Trout, pike and pike-perch are also popular, as are smoked or broiled lampreys. In July and August, crayfish feasts are held. The Finnish crayfish, *rapu*, is small and sweet, and piles of them are consumed at a sitting, each crayfish traditionally accompanied by a glass of icy vodka.

The burbot is used in a variety of excellent dishes, including *madekeitto*, a soup garnished with small potatoes, and a rich, allspice-flavoured stew. The liver and roe of the burbot are particular delicacies. Indeed, the Finns consider the golden roe, which they serve with *blini*, sour cream and chives, to be finer than the caviar of the sturgeon.

Beef, veal, pork and mutton all play a part in the Finnish cuisine. In fact, in one famous stew, *karjalanpaisti*, beef, pork and mutton are cooked together. The Finns make excellent sausages, including the reindeer *poromakkara*, and the *saunamakkara*, named after the sauna, or bath-house, because they are usually cooked over an open fire, or on top of the sauna stove, and eaten in the sauna dressing-room where people relax with a beer. The sauna is also a convenient place for hanging hams and legs of mutton to smoke.

In the past, reindeer, besides pulling sledges, also supplied the Lapps with milk, meat and clothing. They are now raised mainly for meat. Dried reindeer meat is still important in the diet of the Lapps. But throughout the country reindeer meat, both fresh and smoked, and smoked reindeer tongues, are delicacies. They are served with Arctic cloudberries, rowanberry jelly or cranberries which are smaller and sharper than those of America and grow wild in many parts of the country.

An unusual aspect of Finnish cuisine is the use of combinations of fish and mea*Kalakukko*, a traditional dish from th province of Savo in east-central Finlanc is a yeast-raised loaf of rye bread baked wit a stuffing which is made up of alterna layers of *muikku*, vendace, small, silver fish related to the salmon, and pieces c fat pork. Another typical meat and fish dis is *forshmak*, a casserole made with salte herrings and chopped lamb or muttor

Some of Finland's finest foods come fro the wild. Apart from a host of wild berrie which are eaten fresh, made into preserve or used to flavour liqueurs, the forest provide a variety of game and mushroom which are hunted with equal determinatio from the moment they begin to appear i late spring. Mushrooms are used in soup casseroles and stuffings. They are pickle and sealed in vats or dried.

During the season *sienisalaatti*, mush rooms in sour cream, is often included o the *voileipäpöytä* table, but it also makes good first course served hot with toast c rye bread.

To make sienisalaatti *to serve 6, trim, was and slice 2 pounds of small mushrooms. In large saucepan, simmer 3 tablespoons of grate onion or 2 thinly sliced medium-sized shallots 4 ounces of butter for 5 minutes, or until soft an golden.*

Add the mushrooms, season with salt, whi pepper and a generous pinch of freshly grate nutmeg and cook over moderate heat, stirrin frequently, for about 15 minutes, or until th mushrooms are lightly coloured and most of th juices they release have evaporated.

Remove the pan from the heat and stir 1½ pints of thick sour cream. Reheat gentl taking care not to allow the cream to boi Garnish with 1 tablespoon of finely choppe parsley. Serve immediately.

Visitors are often surprised to find th importance of dairy produce in this norther country. Vast quantities of fresh milk ar drunk, as well as sour milk, called *piim* Yoghourt is used a great deal, too. *Viili*, smooth, elastic cream, pulls out into lon threads, and is thick enough to eat with spoon.

The Finns also produce a number c cheeses. There is the soft, bland cheese c *Häme*, made with eggs and butter, sma *Turku* cheeses, which are eaten very fresl *Turunmaa*, a hard, strong cheese, and a blu cheese called *Aura*. Flat cakes of *leipäjuust* bread cheese, so named because of thei speckled, golden brown appearance, ar toasted in the embers of the fire before the

FINLAND

are stored, and are sometimes smoked with rosemary.

The Finns also boast a remarkable array of breads, ranging from heavy rye sourdough breads and crispbreads, to delicate white loaves and a sweet, shiny braid called *pulla*.

A dessert or sweet snack made with bread called *rikkaat ritarit*, rich knights, is popular with both children and adults.

To make rikkaat ritarit *to serve 4, trim 12 small slices of white bread. Beat 2 tablespoons of flour and ½ teaspoon of cinnamon with 1 pint of milk and 1 egg until smoothly blended.*

Soak the bread slices in the milk mixture. Then sprinkle them with a mixture of 4 tablespoons of finely chopped almonds and 4 tablespoons of sugar.

Fry the bread slices in plenty of butter until they are crisp and golden on both sides. Serve immediately, accompanied by a berry jam or apple purée.

The bitter cold of the very long Finnish winter has doubtless contributed to the popularity of comforting porridges made from barley, rye, oatmeal, semolina and rice. *Mämmi*, a rye porridge, is served at Easter in a birch bark container, while a rice porridge called *riisipuuro* is a traditional Christmas dish.

The Finns could scarcely be described as an unsophisticated people. Their ultramodern architecture, their glassware, tableware, furniture and textiles have influenced designers all over the world. But the functional good sense which is the keynote of their design also leads them to reject the frivolities of contemporary life. The Finnish approach to living, and the sturdy simplicity of their food will undoubtedly remain as long as their love for the wild, the lakes and the forests, affectionately known as *vihreä kulta*, green gold, which have sustained them in the past and still do today.

ELK

REINDEER

SAVUSTETTUA PORON KIELTA
Smoked reindeer tongues

ROSOLLI

Herring and beetroot salad

WILD BERRIES

FORSHMAK
Meat and salted herring casserole
with baked potatoes

PUMPERNICKEL

PULLA
Plaited coffee bread

DILL

KARJALAN PIIRAAT
Karelian rice-filled pastries

KARJALANPAISTI
Karelian stew

WILD BERRIES

MADEKEITTO
Burbot and potato soup

LAKE OULU

SIENISALAATTI
Fresh mushroom salad

APPLES

ROSOLLI

SUOMOLAINEN LEIPA
Finnish breads

GULF OF BOTHNIA

BUCKLING
Smoked herring

F I N L A N D

• VAASA

CRISPBREAD

CRAYFISH

• KUOPIO

KESAKEITTO
Summer vegetable soup

OATS

MAMMI
Easter rye pudding

POTATOES

KALAKUKKO
Fish turnover

WHITEFISH

PULLA

SAVONLINNA •

BURBOT
ROE

PIKE-PERCH

OHRARYYNIPUURO
Pearl barley porridge

HAME
White cheese

BURBOT

SALMON

LOHIKEITTO
Salmon soup

FRESH-WATER FISH

• TAMPERE

LOHITIIRAS

AURA CHEESE
Blue cheese

Salted salmon
and rice in pastry

WILD
MUSHROOMS

STRAWBERRIES

TURUNMAA CHEESE
Hard strong cheese

• TURKU

HELSINKI •

GULF OF FINLAND

HERRING

97

Wholesome, generous family cooking

THE CLIMATE, the geography, the influence of neighbouring countries and, not least, the fact that Germany did not come into being as a united state until 1871, have all played a part in the creation of German cooking as it is known today. It is wholesome, generous and as full of contrasts as the German landscape, from the flat, sandy plains of the north to the sunny, terraced vineyards in the west, to the forests and mountains of the south.

The cooking of the coastal regions is dominated by the sea. In Hamburg, trawlers come in each day with their hauls of fresh fish destined for the city's elegant restaurants, where plaice, turbot and sole appear frequently on the menus. Excellent shellfish —oysters, mussels and bright-red Heligoland lobsters—and plump, succulent buckling (smoked herrings) are delivered fresh to the shops every day. *Aalsuppe*, a Hamburg speciality, is something of an acquired taste. Chunks of eel, dried fruit and fresh vegetables are cooked in a strong ham stock flavoured with herbs, and frequently garnished with dumplings as well.

From the fertile coastal plain comes some of the finest meat and poultry in Germany. There is excellent veal and beef, fat, force-fed ducks and tender spring chickens called *Stubenküken*, indoor chickens, which are cooked in a *Kürkenragout*, a casserole, and garnished with mussels, calves' sweetbreads, baby peas and asparagus tips.

Most of Germany's great smoked hams and sausages come from the northern and central regions. The peasants of Lüneburg Heath have made a speciality of both, calling them *Katenschinken* and *Katenrauchwurst* after their *Katen*, cottages, in which the smoking is done. Brunswick *Mettwurst*, a smoked, minced pork sausage, and *Leberwurst*, liver sausage, are sold throughout Germany.

The smoked ham of Westphalia is famous all over the world. In eighteenth-century France it was rated more highly than the *jambon de Bayonne*. At a traditional Westphalian *Schinkenmahlzeit*, ham meal, thick, juicy slices, raw and rosy-pink, are eaten with pumpernickel and butter and washed down with ice-cold Steinhäger, a clear juniper brandy.

Broad beans are the Westphalians' other great speciality. Casseroles of broad beans and bacon, flavoured with a touch of savory, are served in summer, as is *Blindhuhn*, which consists of beans, bacon, fresh vegetables, apples and pears.

This taste for sweet and savoury combinations, rare in other European cuisines, continues into the Rhineland with the Rhenish *Sauerbraten*, rolled beef which is first marinated and then pot-roasted and served in a spicy, sweet sauce. The Rhinelanders are a light-hearted people who are blessed with great humour. Cosy taverns nestling in the old quarters of Cologne and Düsseldorf serve dishes with such baffling names as *Himmel und Erde mit Blutwurst*, the "heaven and earth" referring to the bed of mashed potatoes and apple purée on which the slices of *Blutwurst*, blood sausage, are served, and *halber Hahn*, not the half-chicken that its name would suggest, but a rye roll topped with a thick slice of cheese spread with mustard.

The great wines from the vineyards on the banks of the Rhine and its tributaries complement the carp, pike and trout from the same rivers. In the autumn, *Zwiebelkuchen*, yeast tarts heaped with onions in a creamy egg and bacon custard, are baked for the first tasting of the new wine, the *Federweisser*, "featherwhite"—so young that it is cloudy and still fermenting slightly.

The River Main forms a definite culinary frontier between north and south. Even the language of the kitchen changes as northern *Klösse*, dumplings, change into *Knödel*.

Frankfurt stands right on this culinary border. It is the home of the original Frankfurter sausage, and still, as far as the Germans are concerned, the only locality allowed to use the name officially. The taverns serve *Rippchen mit Kraut*, thick pork chops with sauerkraut and mustard, and *Apfelwein*, the astringent local cider. In contrast, the Frankfurt *Grüne Sauce*, a fragrant oil and vinegar sauce mixed with chopped hard-boiled eggs and a variety of herbs, displays a lightness of touch that has little in common with the solid cooking of the north.

Baden, however, is the one region of Germany where the cooking can be ranked as *haute cuisine*. Here, the French influence is unmistakable in the preparation of frogs' legs, snails and carefully seasoned pâtés. Casseroles of lamb, not a popular meat in other parts of the country, have an elegant subtlety.

The fish dishes are magnificent, and Schwetzingen, west of Heidelberg, boasts the finest asparagus in Germany. The fat snow-white stalks are served with melted butter, or accompanied by thin slices of ham and tiny new potatoes. Only *Hopfensprossen*, baby hops dressed with butter or cream, rivals the asparagus in flavour.

Eastern Baden-Württemberg roughly covers the territories once known as Swabia. The Swabians are said to be the most industrious people in Germany, and their housewives live up to this reputation. They spend hours rolling and shaping *Maultaschen*, large ravioli stuffed with meat and spinach, which are cooked in broth or served as a main dish topped with fried onions. The tiniest dumplings in all Germany, *Spätzle*, "little sparrows", are laboriously scraped by hand into boiling water. Most Swabian cooks would not consider using a *Spätzleschwob*, a press. *Spätzle* are served whenever there is a rich gravy to be mopped up—with stews, fricassées or a roast saddle of Black Forest venison served in a sour cream sauce.

The little country inns of the Black Forest offer delicious meals of *Bauernspeck*, country-smoked bacon, with Kirschwasser, a clear, mountain-cherry brandy. Cherries and Kirschwasser are important ingredients, too, in the Black Forest's most famous speciality, the *Schwarzwalder Kirschtorte*, an exquisite creation made of layers of chocolate sponge cake, cherries and Kirsch-flavoured cream, on a base of crisp almond pastry.

To the east of Baden-Württemberg lies Bavaria. No other region exemplifies so perfectly the tourist image of Germany—Wagner in Bayreuth, magnificent Alpine scenery in the south, and, above all, beer.

Not surprisingly, beer dominates the Bavarian kitchen. Every dish seems cleverly calculated to increase one's thirst. *Leberkäse*, a hot meat loaf, fresh Pressack sausages, jellied pig's knuckle, sausage salads, or a dish of pretzels—these are all snacks.

In Munich the old German custom of eating a substantial second breakfast still flourishes. Mid-morning is *Brotzeit*, bread-time, and time to revive oneself with a "snack" of mild *Weisswürste*, white sausages made of veal, brains and sweetbreads, sweet mustard, a rye roll—and the inevitable glass of beer.

Bavarians love pork and transform it into crisp roasts, hams and an endless variety of sausages, most of which are served fresh.

Only the dumplings rival the variety of the sausages. Liver dumplings, bread dumplings, bacon dumplings, dumplings made with yeast dough and cooked in milk instead of water—these are eaten at every opportunity. Large dumplings are served with roast pork, a roast knuckle of veal or a thick meat or mushroom sauce. Small dumplings are used to reinforce a soup. Yeast dumplings are served with fruit or a sweet custard sauce.

Berlin, long a refuge for immigrants, is the most cosmopolitan of German cities. Many of those who came from the East brought with them the dishes they had

GERMANY

FLENSBURG•

RÄUCHERAAL
Smoked eel

KIELER SPROTTEN
Smoked sprats

KIEL

LOBSTER

CATTLE

LABSKAUS
Salted beef mixed
with potatoes
and pickles

RÄUCHERWURST
Smoked sausage

MÖWENEIER
Seagulls' eggs

HOLSTEINER SCHINKEN
Smoked raw ham

EELS

HAMBURG

GEESE

AALSUPPE
Sweet-sour eel,
ham and
vegetable soup

BÜCKLING
Smoked herring

HEIDE HONIG
Heather honey

BERLINER PFANNKUCHEN
Jam-filled yeast fritters

KAHL UND PINKEL
Kale and smoked bacon
and oats sausage

BREMEN

KATENSCHINKEN
Smoked ham

ROLLMÖPSE
Pickled herring with onion

ELBBUDD
Small plaice

•**BERLIN**

WESTFÄLISCHER SCHINKEN
Westphalian ham

•**HANOVER**

WÜRSTE
Sausages

HARZER KÄSE
Soft cheese

EISBEIN
Pickled pigs' hocks

WEST
GERMANY

RIVER WESER

KÖNIGSBERGER KLOSPE
Meatballs in caper sauce

RIVER ELBE

AAL GRÜN
Fresh eel in dill sauce

EAST

HALBER HAHN
Buttered half rye roll
with soft cheese topping

DÜSSELDORF•

PRINTEN
Chocolate-covered gingerbread

LEIPZIGER ALLERLEI
Mixed young vegetables in butter sauce

LEIPZIG•GERMANY

•**DRESDEN**

DRESDNER STOLLEN
Christmas yeast cake
with dried fruit and almonds

•**AACHEN**

•**COLOGNE**

REIBEKUCHEN
Potato pancakes

SAUERBRATEN MIT KARTOFFELKLOSSE
Marinated pot roast with potato dumplings

MUSSELS

*COBURGER
SAFTSCHINKEN*
Mild ham

F R A N K E N

PRESSACK
Fresh sausage

SPEKULATIUS
Small spiced biscuits

HANDKÄSE
Strong cheese

FRANKFURT

COBURG

RIPPCHEN MIT KRAUT
Pickled pork chop with sauerkraut

SPIESSBRATEN
Spit-roasted pork or beef

•**MAINZ**

MAINFISCHLI
Small fish

FRANKFURTER WÜRSTCHEN
Lightly smoked pork sausage

IDAR-OBERSTEIN

*REHRÜCKEN
BADEN-BADEN*
Saddle of venison garnished
with pears and cranberries

•**NUREMBERG**

REGENSBURGER
Small thick sausages

NÜRNBERGER BRATWÜRSTCHEN
Small pork grilling sausages

NÜRNBERGER LEBKUCHEN
Iced gingerbread on thin wafers

•**REGENSBURG**

B A V A R I A

ZWIEBELSUPPE
Onion soup

CHESTNUTS

KNÖDEL
Dumplings

RIVER RHINE

BADEN-BADEN

•**STUTTGART**

STUTTGARTER
ZWIEBELKUCHEN
Onion yeast tart

RIVER DANUBE

GÄNSEBRATEN MIT KARTOFFELKNODELN
Roast goose with potato dumplings

LEBERKÄSE
Hot meat loaf

SPÄTZLE
Dumplings

MUNICH•

SCHWEINSBRATEN
Roast pork

PIKE
FROGS' LEGS
SNAILS

MUSHROOMS

MUSTARD

G'SCHWOLLENE
Skinless sausage

CHIEMSEE

ÄSCHE
Grayling

A L L G Ä U

BODENSEE

KALBSHAXE
Knuckle of veal

SCHWARZWÄLDER KIRSCHTORTE
Chocolate cake with whipped cream and cherries

SALMON TROUT

99

Simple, sustaining and savoury main dishes

cooked in East Prussia and Silesia. *Königsberger Klopse*, poached meatballs in a creamy caper sauce, and *Königsberger Fleck*, thick tripe soup, which originated in the capital of what was once East Prussia, are today typical Berlin dishes. Berliners who share the northerners' love for eels and herrings have also made a speciality of minced meat dishes—*Bouletten*, hamburgers, a meat loaf called *Falsche Hase*, mock hare, and *Hackepeter*, a kind of pork tartare made of highly seasoned raw pork and served as a spread with rolls.

There is one culinary art in which the Germans have few rivals. One need look no farther than the display in the nearest *Konditorei* to realize that the German pastry cook is a master.

The delightful German custom of afternoon coffee is taken as seriously as English tea. Staid matrons sit in the *Konditorein* enjoying featherlight doughnuts, pastries, perhaps a slice of *Sandtorte*, pound cake, *Kirschtorte* or *Frankfurter Kranz*, an extravagant cake even by German standards that is baked in a ring mould, split into layers, sprinkled with rum and reassembled with a delicious butter and egg cream, the whole decorated with flaked almonds and more butter cream.

Most German housewives are themselves skilled bakers. At Christmas, every home is fragrant with honey and spices as the serious baking begins. Each region has its specialities. These are little spiced cakes from Nürnberg, called *Lebkuchen*, and from Lübeck and Königsberg there is marzipan shaped into exquisite miniature fruits, hearts and little Christmas figurines.

The German *Baumkuchen* or Yule Log is a masterpiece claimed by Berlin. A long roll of dough is coated with layer after layer of batter and turned slowly on a spit so that each layer bakes on evenly, resembling the rings in the log. The Christmas *Stollen*, which originated in Dresden, is a long loaf of buttery yeast dough rich with dried fruit, candied peel and almonds. For the children there will be a *Pfefferkuchenhaus*, a gingerbread house, its roof snowy white with icing.

German cooking is wholesome, unpretentious family cooking, revelling in the produce of a fertile soil. Its natural setting is the *Ratskeller* and the country *Gasthöfe*, an *Apfelweinstube* in Frankfurt, a Munich *Bierhalle* or a cosy *gemütliche Kneipe* in Berlin—crowded, warm, friendly inns and taverns where eating is a serious business.

Bavarian Liver Dumpling Soup
BAYERISCHE LEBERKNÖDELSUPPE

Bavarian liver dumplings are almost as large as tennis balls. Two of them make an ample portion, served either in a well-flavoured stock, or as a main course, garnished with fried onion rings and accompanied by mashed potatoes and sauerkraut.

SERVES 4

6 stale crusty rolls, thinly sliced
½ teaspoon salt
10 fl oz lukewarm milk
8 oz ox liver
2 oz beef suet
1 small onion, coarsely chopped
2 eggs, lightly beaten
1 teaspoon dried marjoram
2½ to 3 pints well-flavoured beef stock

Put the sliced rolls in a large bowl. Sprinkle them with salt and pour over the lukewarm milk. Leave them to soak until required.

Trim the liver and put it through a meat mincer together with the suet and onion. Add the soaked bread, the eggs and marjoram, and mix with a wooden spoon until well blended. The mixture will be very soft.

Bring the stock to the boil in a large saucepan. Reduce the heat to low and simmer the stock.

Divide the dumpling mixture into 8 portions. With wet hands, shape a portion at a time into a ball and drop it into the stock. Simmer gently for 25 to 30 minutes, or until the dumplings are cooked through.

Serve two dumplings per person in soup plates, together with some of the stock.

Hamburger Eel Soup
HAMBURGER AALSUPPE

This eel soup is often served as a main course, garnished with flour dumplings that have been boiled separately.

SERVES 4 TO 6

1 meaty smoked ham bone or a 1 lb piece of
  smoked streaky bacon
8 oz prunes, soaked overnight
8 oz dried pears, soaked overnight
1 large onion, thinly sliced
4 carrots, thinly sliced
1 leek, thinly sliced
8 oz shelled green peas
2 to 2½ lb fresh eel
Salt
1 bay leaf
4 black peppercorns
5 fl oz dry white wine
1 tablespoon butter
1 tablespoon plain flour
3 parsley sprigs, finely chopped
2 chervil sprigs, finely chopped

1 marjoram sprig, finely chopped
1 thyme sprig, finely chopped
1 savory sprig, finely chopped
1 tarragon sprig, finely chopped
1 basil sprig, finely chopped
Sugar
Wine vinegar

In a large saucepan, boil the ham bone or bacon in 7 pints of water, partly covered, for 2 hours. Add the fruit and vegetables, and continue to simmer gently until they are soft.

Meanwhile, rub the eel with salt, cut it into chunks and place it in another pan with the bay leaf, peppercorns, wine and enough water to cover. Place the pan over high heat and bring to the boil. Cover the pan, reduce the heat to low and simmer gently until the eel is tender.

Remove the ham bone or bacon from the soup. Cut the meat into chunks and set aside.

Work the butter and flour to a smooth paste. Add it to the soup in tiny pieces, stirring constantly. Simmer for a few minutes longer until the soup is slightly thickened. Stir in the finely chopped herbs. Add the cooked eel together with its cooking liquor and the meat from the ham bone or the bacon.

Taste the soup and correct the seasoning with more salt if necessary, a pinch of sugar and a few drops of wine vinegar.

Baked Pike with Sour Cream Sauce
BADISCHER HECHT

Pike is one of the finest of fresh-water fish. In Baden it is served with a delicate sour-cream sauce.

SERVES 4 TO 6

3 to 3½ lb pike
Salt
Lemon juice
3 oz butter, melted
3 tablespoons grated cheese, a mixture of
  Parmesan and Gruyère or any well-
  flavoured hard cheese
3 tablespoons fine dry breadcrumbs
10 fl oz sour cream
1 tablespoon plain flour
5 fl oz dry white wine
1 to 2 tablespoons finely chopped parsley

Clean, scale and wash the pike. Slit it down the back and remove as many bones as possible. Pat the fish dry with kitchen paper, rub it with salt and lemon juice and put it aside for at least 30 minutes.

Preheat the oven to 350°F (Gas Mark 4). Butter a shallow, oval baking dish. Put the pike in it and sprinkle with the grated cheese and the breadcrumbs. Spoon the remaining melted butter over the pike and pour the sour cream around it.

Bake uncovered for 30 to 40 minutes, or until the flesh comes away from the backbone when lifted gently with a fork. Transfer to a heated serving dish and keep hot while the sauce is finished.

Scrape the contents of the baking dish into a saucepan. Blend the flour smoothly with the wine and stir it into the pan. Bring to the boil, stirring, lower heat and simmer for 5 minutes. Add the parsley and correct the seasoning.

Spoon the sauce over the pike and serve immediately.

Bavarian Roast Knuckle of Veal

GEBRATENE KALBSHAXE
BAYERISCHE ART

In Bavaria a meaty veal knuckle, or heel of round, is served either as a crisp roast or cooked in a vegetable broth. It is usually accompanied by bread dumplings and fresh salad.

SERVES 4

4 lb meaty veal knuckle, cut into 2 pieces
Salt
3 onions
2 celery stalks
1 carrot
1 leek
2 to 3 parsley sprigs
5 black peppercorns
2 bay leaves
2 cloves
Strip of lemon rind
3 oz butter, melted

Bring the veal to the boil in a large pan with 3 pints of salted water. Skim off the scum as it forms on the surface.

Chop the vegetables coarsely and add them to the pan together with the parsley sprigs, peppercorns, bay leaves, cloves and lemon rind. Simmer for 1 hour.

Preheat the oven to 400°F (Gas Mark 6).

Remove the veal from the stock and pat the pieces dry. Place them on a rack in a roasting tin. Brush them with some of the butter and roast, turning occasionally and basting with more butter, for 1 hour, or until the skin is crisp and the meat comes away from the bone.

Meatballs in Caper Sauce

KÖNIGSBERGER KLOPSE

This dish originated in Königsberg, formerly the capital of East Prussia. Berlin adopted it more than a century ago, however, and Berliners have come to regard it as their own.

SERVES 4

8 oz minced beef
8 oz minced pork

1 slice stale bread, trimmed, soaked in water and squeezed dry
3½ tablespoons fine dry breadcrumbs
1 onion, grated
1 egg
2 anchovy fillets, finely chopped
1 tablespoon melted butter
Salt
Freshly ground black pepper
1¼ pints beef stock
1 egg yolk
1 tablespoon capers
Lemon juice or wine vinegar

In a large bowl, combine the minced beef and pork with the bread, ½ tablespoon of the breadcrumbs, the onion, egg, anchovy fillets and melted butter. Season to taste with salt and pepper and mix well. Shape the mixture into 8 large meatballs.

Bring the stock to the boil in a large saucepan. Drop in the meatballs and cook them for 15 to 20 minutes. Lift them out with a slotted spoon and put them aside.

Stir the remaining breadcrumbs into the stock and simmer gently for a few minutes to allow the stock to reduce and to thicken slightly. Remove from the heat.

Beat the egg yolk lightly. Add a few tablespoons of the hot stock and mix well. Stir the mixture back into the pan. Return the pan to low heat and stir until the sauce has thickened. Take care not to let it boil or the egg yolk will curdle.

Add the capers and a few drops of lemon juice or wine vinegar to taste.

Return the meatballs to the sauce and reheat gently, making sure that the sauce does not boil. Serve in a ring of rice, or accompanied by a potato purée.

Marinated Spiced Pot Roast

RHEINISCHER SAUERBRATEN

The Germans love pot roasts. Sauerbraten is the most popular one of all, traditionally served with potato dumplings, puréed apples or stewed dried fruit and often a dish of red cabbage as well.

SERVES 4 TO 6

3 lb topside or silverside of beef
10 fl oz wine vinegar
1 pint water
1 onion, coarsely chopped
1 small carrot, coarsely chopped
2 celery stalks, thickly sliced
1 bay leaf
3 black peppercorns
3 allspice berries
1 clove
Salt
2 oz fat salt pork or bacon
Freshly ground black pepper
2 oz lard or butter

2 tablespoons sultanas
1 slice German spiced honey cake or 2 gingersnaps, crumbled
5 fl oz single cream
1 tablespoon apple jelly

Wipe the meat with a damp cloth and place it in a deep earthenware crock.

Put the wine vinegar and water in a saucepan. Add the onion, carrot, celery, bay leaf, peppercorns, allspice and clove, and bring to the boil. Pour the hot marinade over the beef and leave it in a cool place for 24 to 48 hours, turning it occasionally.

When ready to make the pot roast, remove the beef from the marinade. Strain the marinade and reserve it. Wipe the meat dry and season it with salt. Cut the fat salt pork or bacon into long strips. Roll them in a mixture of salt and pepper, and lard the beef with them.

In a heavy, heatproof casserole which has a tight-fitting lid, brown the meat on all sides in the lard or butter. Measure the marinade and dilute it with an equal quantity of water. Add it to the casserole and bring to the boil. Cover the casserole, reduce the heat to low and cook gently for 2 to 3 hours, or until the beef is very tender.

Remove the beef from the casserole and keep hot while the sauce is finished. Stir in the sultanas, crumbled honey cake or gingersnaps and the cream. Add the apple jelly and salt to taste, and simmer for 10 minutes longer.

Serve the beef in thick slices, coated with the sauce.

GERMAN CAFE-DRINKING is made a double pleasure by the best beer and the best *offener,* open, wine in Europe.

Germany's beer-laws are strict (only barley can be used in the brew) and her local styles of beer still fairly distinct, although even in Germany standardization is tending to make beer taste the same wherever you drink it. Certainly Munich beer remains characteristically dark and soft, and Dortmunder relatively pale and dry. Among luxury beers, Lowenbrau is as good as any in the world.

More of a surprise, perhaps, is the open wine, served in the rotund green-stemmed quarter-litre *pokal,* and sometimes known as *Pokalwein.* In wine-growing areas (which is most of southern Germany) there is often a choice, sometimes of as many as a score of local wines. In many cases an elaborate catalogue lists their qualities. There is always a *kalte aufschnitt,* a plate of mixed cold meats, to be had in the little heavily timbered *stuben* where such lists are found. It is easy to pass days in happy reconnoitring for the best barrel in the neighbourhood.

Appetizing vegetables and luscious desserts

Roast Saddle of Venison Baden-Baden Style
REHRÜCKEN BADEN-BADEN

Germany is rich in game, but even there a roast saddle of venison is an expensive dish. The usual accompaniments are stewed fruit and potato croquettes, but in Baden-Baden they prefer an elegant garnish of pears and maraschino cherries and flour dumplings are served instead of potatoes.

SERVES 6

4½ lb well-hung saddle of venison
4 oz fat salt pork
Salt
Freshly ground black pepper
4 juniper berries, crushed
4 oz butter
5 fl oz game stock
1 tablespoon plain flour
10 fl oz sour cream
1 tablespoon whole-cranberry sauce
2 tablespoons red wine

GARNISH

6 pears, peeled, halved, cored and poached
   in a light syrup
12 maraschino cherries

Preheat the oven to 450°F (Gas Mark 8). Wipe the saddle of venison with a damp cloth. Cut the fat salt pork into long strips about ⅛ inch thick and ⅛ inch wide. Lard the venison with them. Rub the saddle with a mixture of salt, pepper and the crushed juniper berries.

Melt the butter in a large, heavy roasting tin. Brown the venison in it on all sides.

Transfer the roasting tin to the oven. Lower the heat to 375°F (Gas Mark 5), and roast the venison for about 1 hour if you like it slightly pink, longer if you prefer it well done. Baste frequently with the butter remaining in the tin and some of the stock if necessary.

Transfer the meat to a heated serving dish and return it to the turned-off oven to "rest" while preparing the sauce.

In a small bowl, blend the flour smoothly with the sour cream. Place the roasting tin over low heat. Add the remaining stock, stirring and scraping the tin clean with a wooden spoon. Stir in the sour cream mixture. Bring to the boil, stirring, and simmer for 5 minutes. Add the cranberry sauce and the red wine. Taste and correct seasoning.

Reheat the pears in their poaching syrup. Carve the venison and arrange the slices on a dish.

Drain the pear halves thoroughly and arrange them cored side up around the venison. Put a maraschino cherry in each cored cavity. Serve the sauce separately in a heated sauce boat.

Green Beans in Cream Sauce
SCHNITTBOHNEN AUF POMMERSCHE ART

In Pomerania and East Prussia this dish was traditionally served with thick slices of Katen-schinken, the local raw smoked ham, but it also goes well with most roasted or grilled meat dishes.

SERVES 6

1½ lb green beans, trimmed and thinly
   sliced
1 summer savory sprig
Salt
2 slices fat bacon, finely chopped
3 tablespoons plain flour
1 pint milk
Freshly grated nutmeg
2 tablespoons chopped parsley

Boil the beans with the savory sprig in salted water until just tender.

In a saucepan sauté the bacon until the fat runs. Blend in the flour with a wooden spoon and stir over a low heat for 1 or 2 minutes longer to make a pale *roux*.

Gradually add the milk and, stirring constantly, bring to the boil. Simmer gently for 10 minutes, stirring occasionally, until the sauce is thick and smooth. Season with salt and a pinch of nutmeg, and stir in the parsley. Add the cooked beans, reheat gently and serve.

Red Cabbage and Apples
ROTKOHL

This dish is an excellent accompaniment for roasts and sausages.

SERVES 4 TO 6

3 cooking apples, peeled, cored and cut into
   eighths
3 oz lard or butter
2 lb red cabbage, cored and finely shredded
½ onion stuck with 1 clove
2 tablespoons wine vinegar
1 tablespoon sugar
Salt
10 fl oz beef stock
8 tablespoons red or white wine (optional)

In a large saucepan, fry the apples in the lard or butter for a few minutes until lightly coloured. Add the shredded cabbage, onion, wine vinegar and sugar. Season with salt. Mix well and continue to cook over moderate heat, stirring occasionally, for 5 minutes.

Add the stock, cover the pan, reduce the heat and simmer for 1 hour, or until the cabbage is soft.

A few tablespoons of wine are often stirred into the cabbage towards the end of the cooking time.

Summer Fruit Mould
ROTE GRÜTZE

This refreshing summer dessert is equally popular with the North Germans and their Danish neighbours. The Germans serve it with fresh milk or a custard sauce. The Danes prefer cream.

SERVES 4

1 lb redcurrants
8 oz raspberries
10 fl oz water
Small piece vanilla pod
8 oz sugar
2 oz cornflour, mixed with 5 fl oz water

Put the redcurrants and raspberries in an enamelled saucepan with the water. Boil for 10 minutes. Rub the fruit through a fine sieve and return the purée to the pan.

Add the vanilla pod and sugar to taste. Add the cornflour and water to the purée. Bring to the boil and, stirring, cook for 3 minutes.

Remove the vanilla pod. Pour the mixture into a 2-pint mould rinsed out with cold water. Refrigerate for 2 hours, or until quite cold and set, before turning it out.

Chocolate Cream Cake
MÜNCHNER PRINZREGENTENTORTE

This cake will be deliciously moist if it is chilled for 24 hours before serving. The batter is baked in five thin layers, preferably in loose-bottomed cake tins. If only one or two tins are available, the layers may be baked one or two at a time.

7 oz plain flour
⅛ teaspoon baking powder
5 oz butter
8 oz castor sugar
Grated rind of ½ lemon
4 egg yolks
4 egg whites
CHOCOLATE CREAM
8 oz unsalted butter
7 oz icing sugar, sifted
2 egg yolks
1 tablespoon vanilla sugar
3 tablespoons cocoa, sifted
CHOCOLATE ICING
4 oz plain chocolate
2 tablespoons single cream
1 tablespoon rum
6 oz icing sugar, sifted

Preheat the oven to 375°F (Gas Mark 5). Use a 10-inch cake tin with a removable base. Butter it lightly.

Sift the flour with the baking powder. Cream the butter. Add the sugar and continue to beat until light and fluffy. Stir in the lemon rind. Add the egg yolks one at a time, beating well between each addition. Stir in the flour.

Whisk the egg whites until stiff but not dry and fold them lightly into the mixture.

Spread one-fifth of the batter thinly over the base of the prepared cake tin. Bake for 15 minutes, or until golden. Turn out to cool on a wire rack. Repeat with the remaining batter, making 5 layers in all.

To make the chocolate cream, cream the butter until light and fluffy. Gradually add the icing sugar, followed by the egg yolks, vanilla sugar and cocoa, beating vigorously between each addition.

Sandwich the layers of cake with the chocolate cream and press down lightly on the top layer.

To make the chocolate icing, soften the chocolate in the top of a double boiler over simmering water. Beat in the cream and rum, and when well blended, beat in enough icing sugar to give a thick spreading consistency.

Spread the top and sides of the cake with the icing and leave until set before chilling the cake in the refrigerator.

Berlin Doughnuts

BERLINER PFANNKÜCHEN

These doughnuts are traditionally eaten on New Year's Eve and during Carnival—the period between Christmas and Lent. They should be served the day they are made.

MAKES ABOUT 15 DOUGHNUTS

1 lb plain flour
½ teaspoon salt
1 oz fresh yeast or 1 tablespoon dried yeast
About 10 fl oz lukewarm milk
3 egg yolks
2 oz sugar
Grated rind of ½ lemon
1 tablespoon rum
3½ oz butter, melted and cooled
Thick jam or jelly
Vegetable fat or oil for deep frying
Icing sugar, sifted

Sift the flour and salt into a warmed bowl. If using dried yeast, sprinkle it over 6 tablespoons of the lukewarm milk and leave in a warm, draught-free place for 15 minutes or until frothy. (Fresh yeast should be "melted" in a little of the milk just before use.)

Whisk the egg yolks with the sugar until thick and lemon coloured. Add them to the flour together with the dissolved yeast, the grated lemon rind, rum and enough milk to make a moderately firm dough. Knead it until smooth; then gradually knead in the melted butter and continue to knead the dough until it is shiny and pliable, with little bubbles showing just below the surface.

Cover the bowl with a cloth and leave in a warm, draught-free place for 1 to 2 hours, or until the dough has doubled in bulk.

Turn the dough out on to a floured board. Knead it lightly until smooth again and roll it out into a rectangle ¼ inch thick.

Using a glass, the rim of which is about 2¾ inches in diameter, lightly mark circles on one half of the rectangle. Put a teaspoon of jam or jelly in the centre of each circle. Carefully fold the other half of the rectangle over the top. Dip the rim of the glass in flour and stamp out the doughnuts, using the little mounds of jam as a guide. Gather together the trimmings, roll them out and use them to make more doughnuts in the same way.

Arrange the doughnuts upside down on a floured pastry board or cloth. Cover them and leave in a warm, draught-free place to rise again until puffy.

In a large, heavy frying-pan, heat 2 inches of shortening or oil until the temperature registers 375°F on a fat thermometer, or until a cube of bread turns golden brown in 60 seconds.

Fry the doughnuts 3 or 4 at a time. When the underside is a rich golden colour, flip them over and brown the other side. They should be light and well risen, with a pale band around the middle.

Drain the doughnuts thoroughly on kitchen paper and allow them to cool before dusting them with sifted icing sugar.

Black Forest Cherry Gâteau

SCHWARZWÄLDER KIRSCHTORTE

In Germany this magnificent gâteau is always served with afternoon coffee, but it also makes a delicious dessert served chilled from the refrigerator. When fresh cherries are not available a 16-ounce can of stoned cherries in syrup may be used instead. Drain the cherries, boil the syrup with 2 or 3 tablespoons sugar and a squeeze of lemon juice until thickened and pour the syrup over the cherries.

CHERRIES

1½ lb morello cherries, stoned
5 oz castor sugar
PASTRY BASE
4 oz plain flour
2 oz butter
3½ tablespoons castor sugar
1 tablespoon ground almonds
Grated rind of ¼ lemon
1 egg yolk
CHOCOLATE SPONGE CAKE
1½ oz plain flour
1½ oz cornflour
1 teaspoon baking powder
4 egg yolks

4 oz castor sugar
4 egg whites
1½ oz cocoa, sifted
2 oz butter, melted and cooled
FILLING
1 pint double cream
4 tablespoons castor sugar
3 tablespoons Kirsch
3 tablespoons grated plain chocolate

Toss the cherries lightly with the sugar and put them aside.

To make the pastry base, sift the flour into a bowl and rub in the butter until the mixture resembles fine breadcrumbs. Stir in the sugar, ground almonds and grated lemon rind. Add the egg yolk and knead the ingredients to a firm dough. Shape it into a ball, wrap it in foil and leave it in a cool place for at least 30 minutes.

Preheat the oven to 350°F (Gas Mark 4). Lightly butter a 10-inch spring-form tin (or a tin with a removable base).

Roll the dough out thinly and line the base of the prepared tin with it. Bake for 20 minutes. Let the baked pastry rest in the tin for a few minutes before transferring it to a wire rack to cool.

Wipe the cake tin clean and grease it with more butter.

To make the cake, sift the flour, cornflour and baking powder together. Beat the egg yolks with the sugar and 4 tablespoons of hot water until the mixture is thick and foamy. Beat the egg whites until stiff but not dry.

With a large metal spoon, fold the sifted flour, cornflour and baking powder into the egg yolk mixture, followed by the sifted cocoa. Next, fold in the beaten egg whites and, finally, the melted butter.

Pour the batter into the prepared tin. Bake for 35 to 40 minutes, or until the cake is well risen and has shrunk slightly from the sides of the tin. Let the cake stand for a few minutes before turning it out on to a wire rack to cool.

Put the sugared cherries together with their juices in a heavy saucepan. Bring them to the boil over low heat. Drain the cherries, return the juice to the pan and boil vigorously until it is reduced to a thick syrup. Pour this over the cherries and put them aside to cool.

To make the filling, whisk the cream lightly. Add the sugar and Kirsch, and continue to whisk the cream until stiff.

To assemble the *gâteau*, cut the chocolate cake in half horizontally. Place the pastry base on a flat serving dish. Spread it with one-third of the Kirsch cream and spoon half of the cherries and the syrup evenly over the top. Cover with a layer of chocolate cake. Spread it with half of the remaining cream, followed by the remaining cherries and syrup. Put the second layer of chocolate sponge on top. Spread it with the remaining cream and decorate the top with a sprinkling of grated chocolate.

Chill until ready to serve.

Flavours of the sea and French sauces

THE PEOPLE OF BELGIUM are naturally proud of Breughel, the great painter, although the scenes of unparalleled gluttony which he depicted contrast with the magnificence of medieval Flanders and the elegant still lifes of her seventeenth-century masters. With their traditional love of festivities and carnival, the Belgians celebrate this great master of coarse pleasures by re-enacting one of the enormous feasts he loved to satirize. Every other year, the townsfolk of Wingene, in Flanders, dress in sixteenth-century peasant costumes and parade through the street with vast quantities of cheese, beer, salami and country bread. When they reach the market square they set upon the food with true Breughelian zest.

Flanders, in the north, an area particularly rich in history and tradition, has always resisted attempts at engulfment by foreign influences, especially by the southern, Walloon population. The splendour of the thirteenth and fourteenth centuries, when Flanders grew to be one of the richest regions in Europe, can still be seen among the Gothic spires and narrow, cobbled streets of such towns as Ghent and Bruges.

The spires and cities belonging to the past seem part of another world compared to the north coast with its sand dunes and pale, cold light. The close presence of the sea, however, is always apparent in Flemish cooking, pervading its specialities with the freshness of shellfish.

The Flemish are masters of pungent fish soups, the oldest of which, *waterzooi*, originated in Ghent. There are two varieties of *waterzooi*, one of which is light and fragrant, full of fresh fish and flavoured with white wine. Some Belgians prefer *chicken waterzooi*, in which the chicken broth is thickened with egg yolks into a pale, creamy soup.

To make a chicken waterzooi *to serve 4, cut a plump, 3-pound chicken into 8 pieces and season with salt and freshly ground black pepper. Grease the bottom and sides of a large, heavy,* *flameproof casserole with 1½ ounces of butter and cover the bottom with a layer of thinly sliced vegetables—2 carrots, 2 leeks and 2 celery sticks—and 2 tablespoons of chopped parsley. Arrange the pieces of chicken in one layer on top. Cook uncovered, over very low heat, for 15 minutes.*

Pour in about 1 pint of hot chicken stock so that the chicken pieces are barely covered. Bring to simmering. Cover and simmer very gently for 1½ hours. Lift out the pieces of chicken with a slotted spoon and bone them if desired. Keep hot.

Stir 2 tablespoons of fine dry breadcrumbs into the casserole, followed by 2 egg yolks beaten with 1 tablespoon of water. Stir over low heat until the sauce has thickened slightly. Return chicken to the casserole.

Serve the waterzooi *in a soup tureen, garnished with chopped parsley. It is ladled out into soup plates and traditionally accompanied by plain boiled potatoes or bread and butter.*

The Flemish are very fond of eels and have exalted them into a complex dish called *paling in't groen*, eels cooked with pot-herbs. This dish is also enjoyed in the south where it is called *anguilles au vert*. The sliced eels are simmered slowly in butter, white wine and fresh herbs, then egg yolks are added to the green juices to make a rich creamy sauce.

Gratinéed fish, a French contribution to Belgium, is also a favourite dish of the north. Shrimp, still sometimes caught by fishermen trawling from horseback at low tide, are smothered in cream sauce and sprinkled with cheese. Mussels are baked in their shells or cooked with wine and herbs.

A relatively small country, all of Belgium has easy access to fish, game and vegetables. Tended in greenhouses and then transplanted outside, vegetables are carefully hand picked when they are small and sweet. Endive, properly appreciated all over Belgium, is not merely tossed into salads, but is cooked in stews, made into soups or wrapped in ham and bathed in a smooth cheese sauce.

The southern town of Malines grows particularly fine asparagus. They are commonly served with hard-boiled eggs, the yolks crushed in the melted butter with black pepper. Hop shoots are cooked in cream and butter and eaten with boiled eggs and croûtons.

The Fleming version of Holland's *Hotspot met Klapstuck*, which bears the less descriptive name of *hochepot*, is only one of Belgium's repertoire of game and beef stews. These specialities, too good to remain exclusively in one region, cross the culinary border and mix with other traditions. The Walloon casseroles of rabbit and prunes or lamb with chicory or the characteristically Flemish *Vlaamse karbonaden*, beef braised in beer, can be eaten all over the country.

To make Vlaamse karbonaden *to serve 4, cut 1½ pounds of topside of beef or chuck into 1-inch cubes and dust them with seasoned flour. In a heavy pan, fry 2 thinly sliced Spanish onions in 1½ ounces of butter over low heat until the onions are a rich golden colour. Remove the onions with a slotted spoon. Raise the heat and brown the beef in the same fat. Return the onions to the pan. Sprinkle with 1 tablespoon flour and stir over moderate heat to blend it with the pan juices and brown it.*

Gradually stir in 1 pint of dark beer. Add a bouquet garni *made up of 2 parsley sprigs, 1 thyme sprig and a bay leaf, 1 tablespoon of wine vinegar, 2 tablespoons of sugar and salt and pepper to taste. Cover and cook over low heat for 1 hour.*

Trim the crust from a slice of brown bread and spread it with 1 tablespoon of French mustard. Add it to the pan and continue to simmer, covered, for 1 hour longer, or until the beef is meltingly tender. Stir occasionally so that the bread disintegrates and thickens the sauce. Correct the seasoning and serve.

Apart from the ubiquitous waffle, filled and topped with fruit and cream, puddings and pastries change their identity from town to town. Bruges makes its own speciality of nougatine cake and barley sugar cookies, Gand has its aniseed macaroons, while Dinant creates cats, windmills and fishes from hard gingerbread called *couques*. In Brussels, however, spectacular *patisseries* and elegant tea shops display an endless variety of glazed and spiced cookies, round milk breads, *croissants*, chocolate pastries and candied brioches.

Belgium is roughly divided, by a line linking Tournai and Liège, between two landscapes, two languages and the influences of her neighbours, France and Holland. Brussels, situated in the only province without foreign frontiers, is a bilingual city where even street signs are written twice. Elsewhere language differences are fiercely preserved, and the ancient dialects of Flemish in the north and Walloon in the south have been absorbed, respectively, into Dutch and French.

Southern Belgium is a land of châteaux and fortresses among the pastures of Hainaut in the west and the rugged hills of

FLATFISH

SHRIMP

LOBSTERS
OYSTERS

MUSSELS

PALING IN'T GROEN
Eels in a green sauce

FILET D'ANVERS
Smoked prime steak MINERAL WATER

OSTEND
BRUGES

KRAMIEK
Square raisin loaf

ANTWERP

HAM WATERZOOI
Fish or chicken soup

NŒUDS
Sugar biscuits

KLETSKOPPEN
Nougatine cakes

GHENT

ASPARAGUS

MALINES COUCOUS
Chickens

BEER

JUNIPER

HASSELT

MOKKES
Cinnamon or aniseed macaroons

CARBONADES A LA FLAMANDE
Braised beef in beer

MASTELLES
Macaroons

CHŒSELS
Offal stew

CAFE LIEGEOIS
Mocha cream dessert

PEPERBOLLEN
Dice-shaped cakes

BRUSSELS

CRAMIQUES
Brioche bread with raisins

COURTRAI

HOCHEPOT
Meat and vegetable stew

CRAQUELINS
Crisp cakes

FRUIT TARTS

LIEGE

ROGNONS DE VEAU
A LA LIEGEOISE
Sautéed veal kidneys

HERVE
Soft cheese

VERVIERS

MANONS
Cream-filled chocolates

GRIVES A LA LIEGEOISE
Larks with juniper berry butter

HUY

POTKES
Cheese

SPA

MINERAL
WATER

B E L G I U M

MACAROONS

BEAUMONT

ENDIVE

DINANT

COUQUES
Hard gingerbread

ESCAVECHE
Fried fish in marinade

DEER

CHARCUTERIE

CHIMAY

TROUT

HAM

GAME BIRDS

BELGIUM

the Ardennes in the east. A beautiful hunting ground, with rivers full of trout and forests bristling with game, the Ardennes also produces fine *charcuterie* and the famous ham smoked in the mountains.

The history of medieval civilization has also been preserved in towns like Tournai, one of the oldest in the country, and Liège, the capital of Walloon Belgium. It is a town with a marked history for the love of food and the creation of great culinary specialities.

Famous for juniper berries, Liège has used their savour in three classic Walloon dishes, *Civet du pays de Liège,* a mélange of brandy, prunes, hare, hare's blood and red burgundy, sharpened with the flavour of the berries, *grives a la Liègeoise,* a casserole of thrushes stuffed with juniper-berry butter, and *rognons de veau a la Liègeoise,* a tribute to

veal kidneys in which the berries are crushed in a gin sauce.

Liège is also a town for sweet things, including *marrons glacés,* sugared nuts and the world-famous Godiva chocolates. The Belgians have perfected chocolate making, not only with luxurious fillings, but also in the care and attention given to the various shapes and images of the chocolates.

Belgian coffee, which is always strong and never bitter, is used to flavour many sauces and essences, but none so tempting as *Café Liègeois,* in which coffee-flavoured syrup is poured over mocha ice-cream and crowned with *crème Chantilly.*

Liège, where stews, sauces and puddings are tempered with French discretion reveals the other side of divided Belgium's double-edged cuisine, the counterpart of the bracing air and fresh flavours of Ostend.

BELGIUM keeps an impressive record as a wine-importer, shipping, despite her small size, more red Bordeaux than any other country, including Britain and the United States. The nearest thing she has to her own wines are the little-known Moselles of Luxembourg, featherweight and characteristically sharp wines of no great account. What makes her wine-enthusiasm the more remarkable is that Flemish-speaking Belgians are almost non-participants; the French-speaking population drink four times as much wine per head. Despite this, Belgium drinks far more wine per head than any other non-wine-growing country.

Beer plays a large part in Belgian life, but is more remarkable for quantity than quality. Stella Artois is the best-known brand, also well established in the north of France.

Sumptuous produce skilfully prepared

As a result of France's geographical position in Europe, it is perfectly placed to have the best of all worlds. To the south, the heat of the Mediterranean adds flavour and richness to fruit, to the olive and peach, and to vegetables and herbs, including the aromatic delights of basil and garlic which are, above all, the flavours of the sun. In the east, southwest and centre, mountain massifs dictate a tougher, more solid peasant fare, based on chestnuts, cabbages and hard cheeses which can be stored through the winter, with grace-notes of trout, crayfish and woodland mushrooms.

In the north there is the finest of fish, oysters, lobsters, which are cooked to perfection in the fine cream and butter of a colder climate. The great navigable rivers, the Rhône, the Seine, the Loire and the Gironde, have brought produce and ideas from the rest of the world right into the heart of France to influence the local resources and to stimulate the skill of chefs. Duck with orange, red mullet *provençal* with tomato sauce, aniseed-flavoured mussel dishes of La Rochelle, the combination of corn dumplings and bread with meat stews in southwestern France, all reflect this marriage of world trade and native resources which, over the last three centuries, has made French cooking the finest in Europe, if not the finest in the world.

France has great climatic variation and, consequently, French cooking has two groups of basic ingredients. First, there are the fats—olive oil, goose fat and butter. Second are the basic flavourings of garlic, shallot and onion. The regions where olive oil is used are most firmly determined by climate. To the west it overlaps with goose fat in the great *foie gras* regions. To the north it overlaps with butter as one goes up the Rhône into the Lyonnais and Burgundy. To a certain extent, garlic matches olive oil because the finest garlic, the pink *ail Lautrec* of the south, grows to abundant ripeness in the warmth of the Mediterranean, and can also be grown successfully in the area of the Loire and in the northerly areas around Paris. The shallot is the great flavouring of Bordeaux, but with the wine trade it made its way around the coast and up the Seine to Paris where it had long been an important part of *haute cuisine*. The onion, the most widely used of the family of culinary lilies, has pervaded France from its great centre of cultivation in the north.

On these foundations the different regions have built up their cuisine with astonishing diversity. When it is remembered, however, that the final boundaries of France were not fixed until the middle of the last century, this is not so surprising. The familiar pentagon was built up slowly from a central Parisian core.

Although Louis XIV kept the noblemen of the provinces firmly under his eye and Napoleon split the provinces into departments, most Frenchmen still think of themselves as belonging to the old areas. They say that they come from the Vendômois or Berry rather than Lôir-et-Cher, from Touraine rather than from Indre-et-Loire, from the Béarn rather than the Basses-Pyrénées.

This provincialism is splendid fun for the traveller. Picnics every day will be different. From town to town, even from village to village, local feeling and tastes will ensure a variation of cheeses, wine, *charcuterie*, cakes and even of bread. At small roadside cafés the menu will vary according to what is locally available. There may be eel or crayfish if the proprietor was out by the stream the night before. There may be cèpes in autumn if the children had a school holiday and went into the woods. A tiny inn in the Orléanais might serve the most simple yet exquisite meal of radishes, crisp and juicy with excellent butter, loin of salt pork, tender and spicy in a light tomato sauce, strawberries and fresh cheese of paradisal

fragrance. Yet the proprietor's wife, when praised, might apologize, saying that it had all come from the garden or village, but at the weekend, she might cook some fish from the river.

This is what food in France is really all about. Even the skill of a three-star chef is exercised on local supplies, or on specialities which come to the region by long established routes.

In another sense, this provincial cooking of France is only fifty years old. It was discovered and recorded in the 1920s, after the First World War had so dramatically changed European life. French cooking writers looked back to the open-minded Montaigne who, in the sixteenth century, travelled in his own country and through Switzerland, Germany and Italy to record the things he ate as well as the things he saw and experienced. He, too, lived in a time of great change under the superior influence of the Italian Renaissance. Montaigne said that if ever he was interested by something he saw on a journey he would make certain of going back there to study it properly as soon as he could. In the same way, twentieth-century French writers exhorted people to leave Paris, get out on the road and travel, certainly, but also to know when and where to stop.

The following sections about the food of France are a kind of journey. The stopping places, which make it worthwhile, have been marked, and the differences and the delights of the provinces have been indicated. To travel through this small country is a gastronomic adventure.

This French farmer harvests his grain without the help of sophisticated modern machinery. He works in much the same way as did his thirteenth-century forefathers, shown in this stone carving on the facade of Chartres Cathedral. Such care and simplicity is part of the tradition which has made French food famous.

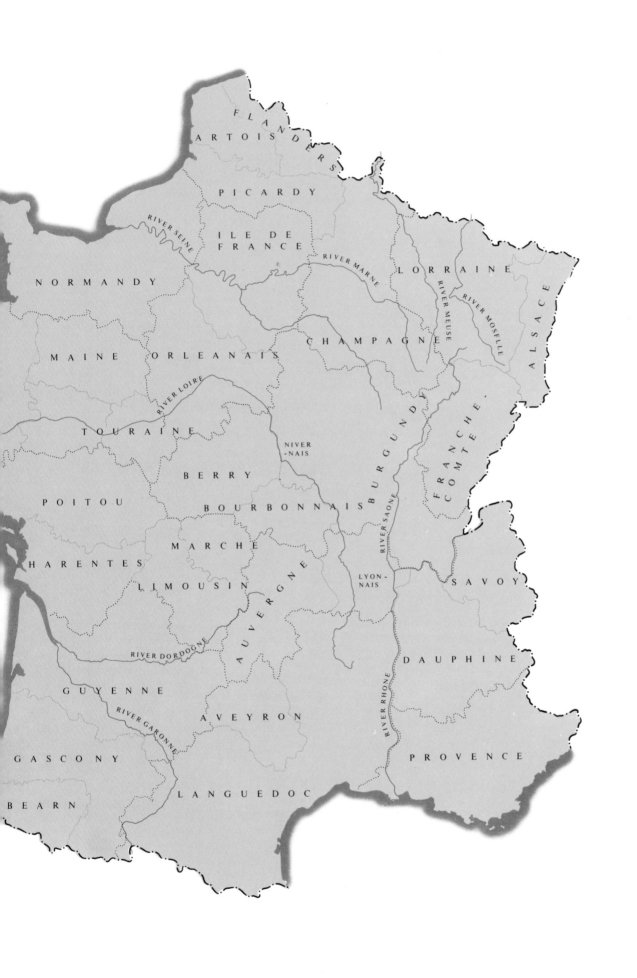

FLANDERS

ARTOIS

PICARDY

ILE DE
FRANCE

RIVER SEINE

NORMANDY

LORRAINE

RIVER MARNE

ALSACE

RIVER MEUSE

RIVER MOSELLE

MAINE   ORLEANAIS

CHAMPAGNE

RIVER LOIRE

TOURAINE

BURGUNDY

FRANCHE-
COMTHE-

NIVER
-NAIS

BERRY

POITOU

BOURBONNAIS

RIVER SAONE

MARCHE

HARENTES

LIMOUSIN

LYON-
NAIS

SAVOY

AUVERGNE

RIVER DORDOGNE

DAUPHINE

GUYENNE

RIVER RHONE

RIVER GARONNE

AVEYRON

GASCONY

PROVENCE

BEARN

LANGUEDOC

CORSICA

Where natural flavours are respected

THE BEACH of the Morbihan is long and windy, blue and gold. Standing there, it is pleasant to think contentedly of picnicking on buckwheat pancakes and sausage, and of the langoustines to be eaten at La Trinité in the evening. It's almost impossible to believe how new the calm prosperity of Brittany is, or how brief a tradition the excellent menus of each small hotel represent.

Even as late as the 1820s, inns between the centres of Rennes and Nantes were "abominable holes". A dirty bed and a hen coop were pushed beside the fireplace where the food was cooked. A slushy pool occupied the centre of the earthen floor—a paradise for ducks.

With so long a background of neglect, it is not surprising that Brittany has never developed a rich, elegant cuisine which can be compared, say, with the skills of Burgundy or Normandy. Instead there is a sturdy goodness of ingredients, deliciously and respectfully used.

From Plougastel come fine strawberries. Roscoff is famous for its artichokes and onions. Turnips, leeks, carrots, lettuces have a bursting look of health. Beef, veal and tripe are magnificent, especially when enriched with prunes. Peppery, spiced *andouillettes*, tripe sausages, are a speciality. Most famous of all is the salt-marsh lamb from the green muddy edges of the Bay of Mont St Michel.

The smallest towns have at least one *crêperie*. The peasant buckwheat *crêpes* of the north taste good when wrapped round grilled sardines or sausages, or just a finger of salted Breton butter. In Basse-Bretagne *crêpes* are huge and made of wheat flour. The most delicate of all, the sweet *crêpes dentelles*, come best from Quimper.

Above all, Brittany is for fish. Oysters, lobsters and *langoustines* are expensive, but spider crabs and clams, mussels and scallops, made into *piquant gratins*, are so abundant that no one need go without shellfish.

Other fish to look for are mackerel in white wine marinade, sweet firm anglerfish *à l'américaine* (here pronounced *à l'amoricaine* after the ancient name of Brittany), fresh sardines grilled over charcoal, sole and cod in perfection. In many dishes, a Breton flavour is given by using cider instead of dry white wine.

Lastly, remember with thankfulness the grey sea salt of Brittany. Its production goes back to neolithic times, and its full flavour enhances the cooking of much of northwestern France.

Touraine, Anjou and Maine

Touraine and Anjou form an extended garden; the countryside is immersed in peace and civilization. People driving through the woods and orchards of Maine might think of the sixteenth-century poet du Bellay, who returned, happy like Ulysses, to his amiable homeland, and of his famous friend Ronsard, who loved the cheeses, fish and ivy-bearded caves of the Loir.

The village and market gardener produce fat asparagus, strawberries and the juiciest garlic. Every year for more than one hundred and fifty years, Tours has held a garlic and basil festival on St Anne's day, July 26. Vegetables, chosen when small and perfectly flavoured, fill the markets, and from the orchards come Golden Delicious and Reinette apples.

The *batons*, or sticks, of goat cheese from St Maure are rightly famous, but many soft cheeses are produced in village dairies or on the farms. The best known of these is the *Petit Trôo*, once made of goats' milk, but now mainly a cow's milk cheese. If you want to eat kid, a number of villages have *Pot de Biquet* festivals in April, when the herds are culled.

Visit the *charcuteries* and *pâtisseries*. If you ask an assistant what is in this or that cake, she will smilingly produce her singsong litany: *pâte d'amandes, pâte noisette, crème*

OYSTERS

COD BAY OF MONT
ST MALO ST MICHEL
CANCALE

ONIONS

APPLES

PANCAKES

GIGOT DE PRE-SALE A LA BRETONNE
Roast leg of lamb with haricot beans

CATTLE

GORRON

ANDOUILLETTES
Tripe sausages

PORT SALUT
Cheese

RILLETTES
Potted pork

POULTRY

MINGAUX
Cream cheese

RENNES

ENTRAMMES

LE MANS

MAINE

WILD BOAR

SNAILS

JANZE

RILLETTES D'OIE
Potted goose

SABLES
Shortbread

SABLE

GOAT S'
CHEESE

TROO

CHESTNUTS

MELONS

CRAON

APPLES

PEARS

CHICKENS

RIVER LOIR

MONTOIRE

CROQUETS
Sweet almond fingers

CARP

LA FLECHE

CRAQUELINS
Crunchy griddle cakes

CHICKENS

GATEAUX CRAONNAIS
AUX AMANDES
Sweet cakes with almonds

RILLETTES
Potted pork

COINTREAU

RILLONS
Cubes of browned pork

PRUNEAUX FOURRES
Stuffed prunes

FAR
Batter cake

A N J O U

GALETTES
Griddle cakes

CREMETS
Fresh cream cheeses

ANGERS

RILLETTES
Potted pork

TOURS

MACAROONS

ALOSE A L'OSEILLE
Shad with sorrel sauce

CORMERY

PETIT-BEURRE
BISCUITS

SALMON

RIVER LOIRE

BOUILLETURE AUX
PRUNEAUX
Eel stew with prunes

SAUMUR

TOURAINE

CROISIC

DUCK

BROCHET AU BEURRE BLANC
Pike in white butter sauce

NANTES

CAILLEBOTTE A LA CHARDONETTE
Curd cheese

CHINON

STE MAURE

LOCHES

LARD
Pork braised in white wine

LERNE

CHEESE

RIVER INDRE

PORNIC
BOURRIDE
Monkfish stew

CHOLET

LANGUES DE BOEUF EN GELEE
Ox tongues in aspic

MATELOTE D'ANGUILLES
Eel stew

FOUACES
Griddle cakes

CORDES
Braided biscuits

pralinée, parfumé au kirsch . . . au rhum . . . au café, enrobé au chocolat. At the pork shop vigorous gestures analyse the *pieds de porc truffés*, pigs' feet wrapped in fine pork force-meat with bits of truffle which show through the white netted caul fat.

In these parts of France, the damp harshness of the north is tempered by the south. The two meet here and combine in that harmonious sweetness typified by the vineyards, orchards, gardens and carefully tended forests. The sun turns everything to gold, but

does not scorch too much. The gastronome Curnonsky, who was born at Angers, where his fine taste for food was formed, said the quality of the area was *la mésure*-moderation, a sense of the fitness of things. Here, he said, things taste of what they are.

Delicious dishes from the Breton coast

Eel Stew

MATELOTE OR BOUILLETURE D'ANGUILLES

This is one of the best dishes of the Loire, and of the Loir as well, where eels lurk behind the sluices of disused mill leats. Recipes vary, but here is a basic method.

SERVES 4

2 eels, skinned and cut in pieces
3 tablespoons brandy
3 tablespoons olive oil
Salt
Freshly ground pepper
8 oz prunes, stoned
1 bottle red or white Loire wine: Bourgueil, Vouvray, Jasniéres, etc.
4 shallots, chopped
2 garlic cloves, chopped
1 leek (white part only), sliced
1 small carrot, halved
Bouquet garni
1 tablespoon butter and 1 tablespoon flour
or
2 egg yolks beaten with 6 tablespoons double cream
Chopped parsley, to garnish

Toss the eel pieces with brandy, olive oil and seasoning. Leave to marinate for several hours. At the same time, soak the prunes in tea or some of the wine.

Simmer the wine, shallots, garlic, leek, carrot and *bouquet garni* together for 45 minutes. Strain into the pan in which the stew is to be made. Add the eels and prunes and simmer for 20 minutes, or until the eel flesh parts easily from the bone. Do not overcook.

Transfer the eels and prunes to a deep serving dish and keep hot while the sauce is being finished.

If red wine is being used, thicken the sauce with a *beurre manié* made by mashing the butter and flour to a smooth paste. Add the *beurre manié* to the simmering sauce in small pieces and stir until they have dissolved and thickened the sauce. If white wine is being used, stir the egg yolk and cream mixture into the sauce off the heat. Return the pan to a low heat and stir until the sauce has thickened, taking great care to keep it below the boiling point.

Check the seasoning. Pour the sauce over the eels and prunes and sprinkle with chopped parsley.

Serve the stew with triangular croûtons fried in butter, mushrooms and diced bacon fried in butter and glazed onions.

White Butter Sauce

BEURRE BLANC

This rich butter sauce is claimed by both Brittany and Anjou. It is really a Loire sauce to be served with such fresh-water fish as pike and shad, but

The fine yellow onions grown in the Roscoff area of Brittany are sold by pedlars who travel all over Europe. They even cross the Channel by ferry and their bicycles, festooned with strings of onions, are a familiar sight in Britain as well.

try it with turbot, sole, John Dory or whiting.

In most Breton restaurants the fish will be poached in a white wine court-bouillon. *Sometimes it will be stuffed with a mixture of shallots, sorrel, spinach, cream and hard-boiled eggs before it is baked in the oven. Sorrel is a favourite seasoning in this region—its juicy sharpness invigorates pale food.*

ENOUGH FOR 2 TO 3 POUND FISH

3 shallots, finely chopped
3 tablespoons white wine
3 tablespoons white wine vinegar
12 oz unsalted butter, at room temperature
Salt
Freshly ground pepper

In a heavy, medium-sized pan, simmer the shallots in the wine and vinegar until they are reduced to a concentrated purée. This is the flavouring essence and can be prepared a little in advance, making it possible to cook the fish and keep it hot on its serving dish while the sauce is being finished.

Whisk the butter, a little bit at a time, into the warm shallot mixture over the lowest possible heat. The butter should cream without turning oily.

Lift the pan off the stove from time to time to check any tendency to overheat. As an added precaution, have a bowl of ice cubes at hand, ready to cool the base of the pan the moment the butter looks as if it is melting rather than creaming. Then, once the sauce has solidified, return the pan to a low heat and finish it with the remaining butter.

Season to taste.

Pork with Prunes

PORC AUX PRUNEAUX DE TOURS

In this fine dish, the author Henry James would certainly recognize his "good-humoured and succulent Touraine". It is rich with cream and prunes, slightly sharp with wine and redcurrant jelly and altogether delicious.

SERVES 8

8 boneless pork chops
Seasoned flour
2 oz butter
1 lb stoned prunes soaked in ½ bottle Vouvray wine
1 tablespoon redcurrant jelly
15 fl oz double cream
Salt
Freshly ground pepper
Lemon juice

Turn the pork chops in seasoned flour. Using a pan into which they will all fit in one layer, fry the chops in the butter until they are golden brown on both sides. Reduce the heat, cover the pan and cook gently for about 20 minutes, or until the chops are tender. Meanwhile, simmer the prunes in the wine until they are soft.

Arrange the chops and prunes on a hot serving dish. Keep hot while the sauce is being finished.

Pour the prune juice into the frying-pan and boil it down to a syrupy essence, frequently stirring and scraping the bottom of the pan with a wooden spoon. Add the redcurrant jelly. When the jelly has dissoved, stir in the cream. Boil hard until the sauce is thick and smooth and almost honey coloured. Season to taste with salt, pepper and a dash of lemon juice.

Pour the sauce over the pork and prunes and serve very hot with a few boiled potatoes. No other vegetables are necessary.

Potted Pork

RILLETTES

Rillettes, *a kind of potted pork, appear in* charcuteries *all over France these days—and are also available in cans at the* épiceries. *But to eat* rillettes *at their finest one must go to Anjou, Tourains, the Sarthe or to Mamers, in*

e north of this region, where they hold a competi-
on every year for the best maker of rillettes.
lsewhere, rillettes are too dense. Often they are
ound rather than shredded and mixed with too
uch lard. Only in this chosen region of France
n they be relied upon to be rich but light, a
lectable thready mass.

The best rillettes of all are made on the farm
hen a pig is killed. The huge iron pot, set over a
re, is stirred for four or five hours with a long
ooden spoon. Everyone who is tall enough takes
turn stirring, until the bits and pieces soften
d consolidate to a meaty porridge. Finally it is
dled into unlipped jugs or small stoneware
ts.

illettes are simple to make. Cut up all kinds of
ork bits, but mainly pork belly, into 1-to 2-
ch squares. Put enough water or melted lard
to a heavy pot to cover the bottom by ¼ inch.
dd the pork, and seasoning, and cook gently
r 5 hours. Unless you want to stir for hours,
ver the pot. The meat should not stick or
own: it should dissolve slowly.

Crush the pork down with a meat mallet, then
rn the contents of the pot into a colander set
ver a large bowl. Remove any bones. Using
o forks, shred the meat or pulverize it with
electric beater. Check the seasoning. Moisten
ith a little of the cooking juices and turn the
ixture into ramekins. Cover with ½ inch of
rd and store in the refrigerator with a lid
f foil. They will keep for several weeks. *Rillettes*
re best eaten hot with diced apples fried in
utter, and with mashed potatoes, but they are
sually eaten cold with mustard.

---

he menu card of the Barrier restaurant shows the
atue of Réne Descartes, the seventeenth-century
hilosopher from Tours. The restaurant is famous
r its fine Touraine dishes.

CHARLES BARRIER
TOURS

Tours.

VUE DU PORT ET LA STATUE DE DESCARTES.

THE PROVINCES bordering on the Loire are happily self-sufficient for their drinking. Brittany not only has her traditional cider (and claims that that at Fouesnant, at least, it is the world's best), but she has in Muscadet precisely the dry white wine she needs to wash down her abundant fish and shellfish. Muscadet is a surprisingly ripe and unacidic wine for such a northern vineyard (at least in a good vintage). The same area around Nantes also produces the sharper, less refined and cheaper Gros Plant. It is worth trying, but not with a grand dinner.

Anjou and Touraine are the old drinking-ground of that son of excess, Rabelais. It is odd that such a one should come from the land of *la mesure* in all things. His favourite "taffeta wine" was a white from what is now one of the Loire's few red-wine areas—Chinon. Chinon, Bourgueil, St Nicolas de Bourgueil and the rather humbler Saumur-Champigny are all

light reds made from Bordeaux grapes and are capable of near-Médoc distinction. The same grapes make the admirable Anjou rosé de Cabernet. On the whole, however, it is white-wine land, with the emphasis on medium-sweet, or not wholly dry, clean and fruity wines in a sometimes quasi-German style.

In the best vintages fully sweet and luscious golden wines are made from the same vineyards which give sharp dry wine in lesser years. Much of the sharp wine is made by the champagne method into the very next best thing to champagne—sparkling Vouvray and Saumur. In Anjou the names to watch out for are Coteaux du Layon (and better Quarts de Chaume, La Roche aux Moines or Coulée de Serrant). In Touraine, Vouvray is usually better than Montlouis. Sauvignon de Touraine is often a bargain: the same sort of flinty fruity wine as Pouilly Fumé at half the price.

Crémets

Often in the dairies of Anjou, there will be white trays of metal pots, each one lined with muslin and filled with a creamy mixture. These are crémets, *delicious mixtures of cream and curd or cream cheese, lightened with egg white. They are eaten with sugar and cream, alone or with the early fruits of summer, strawberries and raspberries in particular. Here is one recipe.*

SERVES 4

½ pint double cream
¼ pint sour cream
2 egg whites
Pinch salt
6 oz curd cheese or cream cheese
Milk

Whisk the double cream and the sour cream together until thick. Whisk the egg whites with salt until they are stiff. Mix the cheese with just enough milk to soften it to a consistency which can be stirred. If a rather wet cream cheese is used no milk is required. Mix the cream mixture, the egg whites and the cheese together lightly but thoroughly. Line small heart-shaped moulds (or pierced cream cartons) with muslin. Ladle in the mixture.

Leave to drain, standing on a plate, until required.

Griddle Cakes
FOUACES

Fouaces have been made all over France for centuries. At first they were a kind of griddle cake, baked under cinders on the hearth. Rabelais called them "a celestial food to eat for breakfast . . . with grapes, especially the frail clusters, the great red grapes". Here is a modern Touraine recipe.

SERVES 8

10 oz plain flour
2 teaspoons salt
¼ teaspoon sugar
6 oz butter
2 eggs, lightly beaten
Milk
Extra butter

Sift the dry ingredients into a bowl. Rub in the butter with fingertips. Make a well in the centre and drop in the eggs and enough milk to make a soft dough. Leave for 2 hours.

Preheat the oven to 325°F (Gas Mark 3).

Roll out the dough less than ½ inch thick and cut into 2 large rounds. Put them on baking sheets. With fingertips dipped in flour, make dents all over the surfaces of the cakes and put a little piece of butter into each dent.

Bake for 45 minutes, or a little longer if the cakes are on the thick side. Eat hot with more butter and, to be Rabelaisian, with grapes.

A cool and placid land of plenty

FOR THE ENGLISH, on a motor holiday, Normandy is usually the first sight of France—and the last. They eat the food it generously offers with joy after the hard winter's work, and with sad thankfulness at the end of summer.

In Cherbourg in the spring, pale-coloured cows graze in the small fields of the Cotentin. The fields are enclosed by hedges and Cornish elms and the tufty banks are starred with primroses. The last camellias, pink and formal on dark green shrubs, decorate the front gardens of grey-shuttered, grey stone houses.

The evening meal may be at Valognes, where guests go through a fine old kitchen, all copper pans and ordered bustle, to the dining-room to eat first-class beef and veal. People who go to Bayeux to look at the tapestry may eat sole with *crêpes* and an exquisite local cheese from the village of Ranchy.

Farther on is Caen, with its famous tripe in a spicy, gelatinous sauce to be settled with a glass of Calvados. The western road down the peninsula leads to Avranches. Mont St Michel offers seafood, the Mère Poulard's omelette and salt-marsh lamb.

Near Le Havre, under the limestone cliffs of the Seine, there is an inn right under the Pont Tancarville which drops its red Japanese-looking curve down to the low southern bank of the river. Diners watch the Seine barges come and go beneath the framing arch, and eat *éclairs*, unsweetened pastry puffs, filled with a delicious ham mixture, followed by duck.

Those who feel extravagant drive to the valley town of Pont-Audener, to the ancient wood and daub tannery which is now the Auberge du Vieux Puits. To the courtyard, the owner has added a giant wellhead from Ry, on the other side of Rouen. This was the village of Madame Bovary, the famous heroine of Gustave Flaubert's novel.

Flaubert, a mid-nineteenth century Realist, wrote with microscopic detail of Madame Bovary's wedding feast, of the four sirloins of beef and six chicken fricassees set out on tables in the cartshed of her father's farm, and of the yellow custards which trembled at the least shake of the table, and had the initials of bride and groom picked out on the surface "in arabesques of nonpareil".

Normandy's rich abundance has the attractive flavour and quality which comes from production on a small scale. Most things seem to come from little farms and market gardens, little trout farms, little fishing ports, small co-operative dairies and unassuming orchards.

This element of success has developed steadily since the Middle Ages. Normandy benefited much earlier than almost all the rest of France by the possession of a single legal code, which was first set out in the thirteenth century. No wonder that in those days the fields of Caux and lower Normandy were the richest in all France, and that agriculture there had attained what has been described as "peak of perfection".

The food enterprises of Normandy today are small by the standards of America and even of England. But they are on an ideal human scale—small enough to combine quality with a reasonable profit. It seems as if the high traditions of the food there (and in other parts of France, such as Burgundy) are so strongly established that they have not yet been overthrown by the giants of the international food trade.

Some years ago, France was criticized for its lack of supermarkets and for a situation where French housewives were forced to shop every day for fresh food instead of replenishing their freezers once a month. Yet it hardly seems that the new hypermarkets built in the past fifteen years have spoiled public demand in France for good food.

Certainly in the Normandy towns which draw in much of the produce of the countryside, there remains the same vitality of individual care. Stocks are not yet reduced to rows and cabinets of plastic-wrapped boxes. At the bakeries, bread, rolls, *croissants* and *brioches* shine with a golden-brown glaze. *Charcuteries* are piled with *boudins*, black and white puddings (a competition is held every year at Mortagne in the Perche for the best *boudin* maker); the pâtés are in white bowls or enclosed in pastry; the jellied pigs' ears, *tripe à la mode de Caen* and various kinds of savoury tarts are bought for reheating at home. (French housewives are very pampered.)

Fishmongers offer sole, anglerfish an whiting full of freshness. Small oyster stal appear on the corners of the streets of Roue in the autumn. People stop for a little ligh refreshment before going on to *La Couronn* in the market-place to eat duck or some mor fish. Vegetables and fruit shine with vigour sometimes they include a basket of *cèpes* c *chanterelles* or *morilles* in the spring.

Best of all are the dairy shops. Cream often sold from huge stoneware pots with greyish glaze, and there are many cheeses the well-flavoured Livarot, Camembert an Pont-l'Eveque from the Vallée d'Auge, nea Lisieux, and the less famous but equall delicious triple cream cheeses and *peti suisses* of the Bray valley in the windy chal downland of north Normandy. The Bra cheeses many people prefer are the salt white-crusted cheeses made in Neufchate which are shaped like logs and hearts.

Of all the products of country and se after the game and mushrooms from th woods, after the cider and Calvados, it is th sole which has most stimulated the lyric skills of France's chefs. Mussels are pleasure of Normandy, particularly aroun

In Normandy the sheep graze on the marsh grass the salt flats along the coast. As a result, the lamb this region is incomparably tender and has a dele able flavour. Restaurants like Mouton Blanc spec lize in roast salt-marsh lamb.

Dieppe. So are the queen scallops and
demoiselles or tiny lobsters of Cherbourg. St
Vaast has its oysters—but the sole is supreme.

In one of his books, Escoffier gave eighty-
four recipes for sole—fifty is the usual number in comprehensive books of cooking.
Only chicken in its various forms has received anything like the same attention. In
many of these classic sole recipes, the other
ingredients are best provided by Normandy:
Isigny butter, cream, shallots, onions and
herbs from the gardens, cider and Calvados,
mushrooms, both wild and cultivated, and
shellfish for a final embellishment, including
the grey shrimp and the pink prawn known
poetically as *bouquet rose*.

One of Normandy's writers, André Gide,
went to North Africa in search of the earthly
paradise. Anyone who enjoys food might
well prefer the one he left behind.

SOLE DIEPPOISE
Sole poached in onion sauce

MUSSELS

MACKEREL • DIEPPE

• FÉCAMP
SALADE CAUCHOISE
Potato, celery and ham salad

CHEESE
• NEUFCHATEL-EN-BRAY

DUCKLING

BÉNÉDICTINE • YVETOT

TARTE AUX CERISES
Cherry tart

PETIT SUISSE CHEESE

BISCUITS ANISES
Aniseed biscuits

• DUCLAIR

• GOURNAY-EN-BRAY

CANETON A LA ROUENNAISE
Pressed duck

TURBOT

• HONFLEUR

ROUEN

LANGOUSTES
spiny lobsters

SCALLOPS

SHRIMPS

LOBSTERS
• BARFLEUR

• CHERBOURG

• ST VAAST-LA-HOUGUE
OYSTERS

CREAM

BUTTER

CATTLE

• ISIGNY   GIANT MUSSELS   OYSTERS

SOLE

• DEAUVILLE

• COURSEULLES

• BAYEUX

BERLINGOTS
Burnt sugar sweets

TRIPE

• CAEN

PONT-L'ÉVÊQUE

PONT-L'EVEQUE
CHEESE

• LA BOUILLE

MIRLITONS DE ROUEN
Puff cakes

DOUBLE CREAM CHEESE

CEPES
Boletus mushrooms

SHAD

TERREGOULE
Rice pudding

RIVER SEINE

SABLES DE CAEN
Shortbread

VALLEE
D'AUGE

APPLES

CIDER

DUCHESSES DE NORMANDIE
Almond petit fours

JAMBON AU CIDRE
Ham with cider

• COUTANCES

CHEESE
• LIVAROT

N O R M A N D Y

ANDOUILLE FUMÉ
smoked tripe sausage

CALVADOS
Apple brandy

• VIMOUTIERS
CAMEMBERT CHEESE

A GRANVILLOISE
...hed with shrimp

• GRANVILLE

• VIRE

TROUT

BOURDELOTS
baked apple dumplings

TRIPE

BOUDIN BLANC
White Pudding

• ARGENTAN

BOUDINS
black and white puddings

• AVRANCHES

PIEDS DE PORC GRILLES
grilled pigs' trotters

• MORTAGNE

• MONT-SAINT-MICHEL

BOUDIN
black pudding

• LA FERTÉ-MACÉ
TRIPE

PHEASANT

DOMFRONT

SANGUETTE
black pudding with rabbit's blood

HONEY

OMELETTE POULARD

• ALENÇON

AGNEAU DES PRES-SALES
salt-marsh lamb

• BELLÊME

Specialities from the good Norman table

Sole Deauville Style
SOLE A LA DEAUVILLAISE

Normans are fond of onions and in this dish they are used to flavour their favourite fish, sole.

SERVES 6

12 fillets of sole
6 oz butter
6 oz onion, chopped
8 fl oz double cream
4 fl oz single cream
Salt
Pepper
Nutmeg
Puff pastry, diamonds or croûtons fried in butter

Season the sole fillets with salt and pepper. Heat one-third of the butter in a large saucepan. Add the onion and cook to a golden purée. Add the creams, salt, pepper and nutmeg to taste and another one-third of the butter. Poach the sole fillets in this sauce. When the fillets are cooked, transfer them to a heated serving dish.

Strain the sauce into a clean pan and bring to the boil. Remove the pan from the heat and whisk in the remaining butter. Pour the sauce over the fish. Garnish with the pastry diamonds or croûtons.

Fillets of Sole Normandy Style
FILETS DE SOLES A LA NORMANDE

Although this dish is served in many restaurants in Normandy, it was originally created in Paris.

SERVES 6

12 fillets of sole
Butter
Salt
Pepper
White wine
SAUCE

15 fl oz fish stock, made with cider
6 oz unsalted butter
2 oz plain flour
2 to 4 fl oz oyster or mussel juice
2 to 4 fl oz juice from cooking mushrooms
3 egg yolks
6 fl oz double cream
Salt
Pepper
Lemon juice
GARNISH

Shrimp, cooked and peeled
Oysters or mussels, shelled and poached
Mushrooms, sliced and cooked in butter
Black truffle, sliced (optional)

First make the sauce. Strain and heat the fish stock. Melt one-third of the butter in a saucepan. Stir in the flour and cook for 2 minutes over low heat without browning. Add the fish stock, stirring constantly, until the sauce is thick and creamy. Beat the shellfish and mushroom juices together with the egg yolks and two-thirds of the cream. Add it to the sauce with half the remaining butter and heat, without boiling, until the sauce is very thick, stirring constantly. Mix in the remaining cream and butter. Season with salt, pepper and lemon juice to taste.

Preheat the oven to 375°F (Gas Mark 5).

Place the sole fillets in a large buttered baking dish. Season with salt and pepper and cover with a mixture of half wine and half water. Bake for 10 minutes, or until the fillets are cooked. Transfer the fillets to a heated serving dish and keep warm.

Boil the juices in the pan until they are reduced to a concentrated essence and add to the hot sauce.

Pour the sauce over the fillets. Garnish with the peeled shrimp, oysters or mussels, mushrooms and the sliced truffle if it is being used.

Normandy Pheasant
FAISAN A LA NORMANDE

This is the best way to cook pheasant, which can be a dry bird. If Calvados is not available, whisky is the best substitute.

SERVES 2 TO 3

1 large oven-ready pheasant
4 oz butter
Salt
Freshly ground black pepper
2 lb Reinette or Cox's apples, peeled, cored and sliced
8 fl oz double cream
¼ cup Calvados

Preheat the oven to 350°F (Gas Mark 4).

Melt half the butter in a large frying-pan. Add the pheasant, season with salt and pepper, and brown it all over. Melt the remaining butter in another frying-pan. Add the apple slices and cook them until golden.

Put a layer of the apple slices in a deep casserole in which the pheasant will fit closely. Place the bird on top of the apple slices, breast down, and pack it around with the rest of the apple.

Pour in one-third of the cream. Roast, covered, for 1 hour, or until the pheasant is cooked, turning the bird over after 30 minutes.

Remove the casserole from the oven and increase the heat to 450°F (Gas Mark 8). Pour the remaining cream and then the Calvados over the pheasant.

Adjust the seasoning, cover the casserole and return it to the oven for 5 minutes.

Serve from the casserole.

Fluffy Omelette
OMELETTE POULARD

La Mère Poulard was only a Norman by marriage. She came from the Nivernais at the end of the nineteenth century and rapidly became the most famous cook on Mont St Michel. The secret of her omelette is very simple—fresh eggs of the highest quality, and their prolonged beating.

Allow two eggs per person, season them and then beat them until they double in volume. Put a good piece of butter into an omelette pan over the heat. When it stops "singing" tip in the foamy mixture. Allow it to cook to firmness underneath, but do not stir or tip the pan about as one does when making a classic omelette. The top should remain mousse-like and creamy. Flip the omelette over to fold it in half, and slide in on to a serving dish.

Chicken with Cream and Calvados
CHICKEN VALLEE D'AUGE

Every hotel in Normandy seems to have a different method of preparing this famous dish. Here is a basic recipe, with suggested variations.

SERVES 4

4 lb chicken, cut into serving pieces
Seasoned flour
5 oz unsalted butter
15 fl oz double cream
3 fl oz Calvados
Salt
Pepper
Lemon juice

Turn the chicken pieces in the seasoned flour. Melt the butter in a large pan. Add the chicken pieces and cook them gently for 30 to 40 minutes, or until they are tender. The pieces should be stewed not browned in the butter. If they seem to be cooking too fast, reduce the heat to low and cover the pan.

When the chicken pieces are cooked pour on the Calvados and set it alight. Allow the juices to bubble hard for a few minutes. Stir in the cream and cook for another 5 minutes.

Transfer the chicken pieces to a heated serving dish. Reduce the sauce by boiling until it is thick. Add salt, pepper and lemon juice to taste. Pour the sauce over the chicken.
VARIATIONS

1. Thicken the sauce with half the cream and 2 egg yolks. Stir over a low heat to thicken without boiling.

2. To the recipe add 4 ounces of mushrooms and 12 tiny onions, cooked in butter, at the last moment.

3. To the recipe, add 4 ounces of mushrooms cooked in butter when the sauce is thick. Decorate the dish with little heaps of diced apple cooked in butter.

Tripe and Cream
TRIPES A LA CREME

The most famous Normandy dish of tripes à la mode de Caen *has to be baked in such a large quantity, with ox and calf's feet and all-night cooking, that it is not suitable for making at home. This rather different tripe recipe, however, is an ideal family dish.*

SERVES 6

2½ lb cooked tripe
Beef or veal stock
2 large onions, sliced
Salt
Freshly ground black pepper
8 fl oz double cream
2 oz butter, cut into pieces

Put the tripe and enough stock to cover in a large saucepan and bring to the boil. Reduce the heat, cover the pan and simmer for 1½ hours.

Remove the pan from the heat and drain the tripe. When it is cool enough to handle cut it into finger-length strips. Put the strips in a generously buttered pan with the onions, salt and pepper to taste, and the cream. Cover the pan and simmer over low heat until the onions are cooked through. Stir in the butter and serve.

Duck with Orange Sauce
CANARD A LA BIGARADE

Ducks are a speciality of Rouen and Duclair. The most famous way of cooking them, à la rouennaise, is a restaurant dish because a special press is needed for squeezing the last delicious juices from the carcass, and so are skilled hands to complete the final presentation. Duck with orange, a favourite dish in Normandy as well, can be made much more successfully at home.

One warning, underplay the sweetness of the fruit. Acidity is what matters, acidity softened by the flavour of the fruit but no more. The bigarade *or* bitter orange *(which the English call Seville) was Europe's first orange, until the sweet China orange arrived in the seventeenth century. Sweet oranges doused with lemon juice are an acceptable substitute, but frozen orange juice is not. A glass of orange liqueur, such as Curaçao, Cointreau or Grand Marnier, is often added.*

SERVES 4

1 duck, dressed weight 5 to 6 lb
Salt
Pepper
SAUCE BIGARADE
1½ oz butter
1 heaped tablespoon flour
15 fl oz stock, made from the duck giblets
but not the liver
5 fl oz dry white wine
3 bitter oranges or 2 sweet oranges and
1 lemon
4 teaspoons sugar
Salt
Freshly ground black pepper
A few slices of orange for garnish

Preheat the oven to 400 to 425°F (Gas Mark 6 to 7).

Pierce the duck skin firmly with the tines of a fork, all over. This enables the fat to run out more freely. Season it with salt and pepper, rubbing them into the skin, and place breast up on the rack in a roasting tin. Roast the duck for 15 minutes a pound. No basting is necessary. When the duck is ready, place it on a serving dish and keep it warm. Carefully pour off the fat in the roasting tin and add the remaining meat juices to the sauce below.

If the brown essences have stuck to the pan, deglaze it with a little stock or liqueur, and add this concentrated liquid to the *bigarade* sauce.

While the duck is cooking make the sauce.

In a saucepan, melt the butter. Cook it until it just begins to turn golden brown—it should smell nutty. Stir in the flour and cook for a few minutes, stirring constantly, to make a pale brown *roux*. Stir in the hot stock gradually, then the white wine. Simmer the sauce until it is much reduced, skimming off the foam as it rises. The longer this sauce is simmered, up to 2 hours, the richer it will taste.

Meanwhile, using a vegetable parer, remove the orange rind in strips. Cut the strips into matchstick shreds. Blanch them in boiling water for 5 minutes and drain. Refresh under cold running water. Twenty minutes before the sauce is required add the orange rind to the sauce with the juice of the oranges and the lemon juice, if it is used. Stir in the sugar and the salt and pepper to taste. Sometimes a dash of wine vinegar improves the flavour of sweet oranges; or use brown sugar instead of white. Finally add the juices from the roasting tin.

Serve the duck on a dish with a discreet garnish of orange slices. Pour a very little sauce over it with some of the shredded peel. Serve the rest of the sauce in a sauceboat.

Rouen Puff Cakes
MIRLITONS

Mirlitons, *a speciality of Rouen, are best eaten hot or warm while they are still puffed up and light.*

MAKES 18 TARTS

¾ lb weight puff pastry dough
1 vanilla pod
2 oz castor sugar
4 egg yolks
4 oz butter
½ tablespoon orange-flower water (optional)
Extra sugar

Preheat the oven to 425°F (Gas Mark 7). Roll out the dough and line 18 individual tartlet tins with it.

Scrape the seeds and pulp of the vanilla pod into a bowl. Add the sugar and egg yolks and beat to a thick creamy mousse.

In a small saucepan, cook the butter until it turns golden brown and smells nutty. Remove the pan from the heat, cool the butter slightly and beat it into the egg mixture.

Pour the mixture into the pastry cases until they are two-thirds full. Sprinkle with sugar and bake for 10 minutes, or until the filling is puffed up and brown.

THE NORMANS have no vineyards of their own, but like the British they make a virtue of necessity by being excellent judges of the wine of the rest of France. As Byron said, "The very best of vineyards is the cellar." It is customary to quote cider as the principal Norman drink. In fact the traveller may very well never see any cider at all. It is deprecated by good restaurants as inimical to rich and subtle cooking—either in the dish or in the glass. French law decrees that cider must be at least three and a half per cent alcohol, which makes it stronger and drier than the English variety. It can be bought *bouché* (in a corked bottle, slightly fizzy and relatively clear) or not (cheaper, flat and usually cloudy). No one can deny that its sharpness is thirst-quenching beween meals.

Calvados, the spirit distilled from cider, is another matter. It is not only a vital ingredient of a number of Norman dishes; it has a special role in the composition of the meal itself. A small glass of it between courses, slugged back like vodka in Russia, makes the *trou normand* or "Norman hole" (into which more rich food can be fitted). The Pays d'Auge (in the *département* of Calvados) is the Appellation Contrôlée of the best quality—and also the clue on a menu that there is Calvados in a sauce. The best commercial Calvados is aged for two or three years in oak, coloured with caramel but not sweetened as brandy is. It remains a very dry spirit, uniquely and marvellously evocative of fresh scented apples.

Bénédictine is made at Fécamp (no longer by monks), but can scarcely be called a local speciality. The ingredients— brandy, sugar and herbs—come from far and near, and the result is enjoyed as much in New York as in Normandy.

A tradition of fine old-fashioned fare

FAMILIAR WARTIME NAMES, from Armentières to Dunkirk, abound like Flanders poppies in this part of France. In Le Crotoy, centuries before British and American armies battled here in two world wars, Joan of Arc was handed over for execution. In the long, deserted field of Agincourt, enclosed and punctuated by trees, starving, naked Welsh archers won the day for Henry V.

In between wars, Flemish France, once part of the dukedom of Burgundy, has drawn great prosperity from wool and cloth. Think of the many Victorian heroines who wore cambric, originally from Cambrai, and Valenciennes lace. The food, copious and straightforward, matches this comfortable trade. People living here have kept a tradition of good, old-fashioned fare. It is the kind of food that demands quality as well—and this it has.

Boulogne provides fine-tasting fish from northern waters: mussels and herring which in the pickled disguise of *hareng saur* is one of the best dishes of Europe. In Le Crotoy one may eat first-class shellfish, gurnard, mackerel and sole.

All over France, pork is brilliantly utilized. Here it appears with cheerful sturdiness in dishes like *potée* (a soup stew with cabbage, of a kind still popular in the southwest), or *hochepot*, a mixed boiling of beef, mutton, veal, pork and vegetables. The grilled chops of Avesnes-sur-Helpes are a more elegant dish. They are spread with a rarebit of cheese, cream and mustard, and grilled again until they bubble with a golden-brown crust.

Vegetables are decidedly northern, but of great flavour, and offer the opportunity truly to judge the cooking of the area. Here a tart, a *flamiche* of leeks and cream, can be so good that it is difficult to imagine anything better. In the *soubise picarde*, onions are stewed to a purée in butter and lard, then spiced with a

dash of wine vinegar and served with grilled or roast meat.

The people of Artois and Picardy do not shrink from positive flavours: try the orange-crusted cheese of Mariolles or *fromage fort*, the strong cheese of Béthune. Like the Bretons, they have never seen why they should give up such medieval combinations as meat and prunes just because fashions change. The development of the sugar-beet industry in the area early in the nineteenth century reinforced their taste for sweet things and stimulated the skill of pastry cooks and confectioners.

With this kind of food, and beer as the main drink, visitors from England and North America can feel very much at home.

Champagne

A description of food in Champagne must start with Victor Hugo. In July 1839, he visited the kitchen of the Hôtel de Metz in Sainte-Menehould and later he wrote about it, and of his travels in and around the Rhineland, in *Le Rhin*.

It was a real kitchen: a great fire in the enormous chimney threw brilliant flecks of light on to a battery of cooking implements and cast shadows on to the smoke-blackened beams of the ceiling, which were hung with baskets, lamps and sides of bacon.

The walls were hung with copper pans and blue and white earthenware. People and animals bustled about. Huge pots clucked on the pot hook, the spit creaked and the dripping pan underneath it chirruped with falling fat. "This kitchen is a world and the fire its sun."

Victor Hugo did not mention what he ate in Sainte-Menehould. It must have been good and amiable, or he would not have liked the kitchen so well. Certainly the food of Champagne is still like this. Fish from the rivers, game, wild boar and venison from the mountains of the Ardennes, with pork, hams and thrush pâtés, are used appreciatively, but without dazzling combinations.

There is plenty of enjoyable food. At Reims, there is a ham pastry made with the lightest of puff pastry crusts, into which Madeira sauce is poured just before serving. At a less elegant level, there is a salad of dandelion leaves which has an unusual hot dressing. Little cubes of pork belly are cooked in their own fat and then poured sizzling over the greenish-white leaves. A spoonful of vinegar is swished round the pan and added to the bowl for piquancy.

The district around Troyes, almost into

Burgundy, is famous for its smoked sheep's tongues and *andouillettes*, tripe sausages which burst with spiced, peppery knobbliness as a fork is pushed into them.

Dom Pérignon, who perfected the champagne process, was born in Sainte-Menehould. It might be expected that the wine would stimulate the cooks to brilliance, but it didn't. Perhaps it is because champagne is a wine for sending elsewhere. It is a wine for other people's formal or glamorous celebrations.

When champagne is used in cooking, it replaces the dry white wine of other districts in recipes which are a commonplace of good cooking in France, such as chicken *fricassée* or sole in a cream sauce. The great and grand dishes depend on other wines.

The following map labels appear:

CANNED FISH
• CALAIS
MUSSELS
HARENGS SAURS
Smoked salt herring
PA
• BOULOGNE
MACKEREL
VEGETABLES
CHIQUES
Boiled sweets
• MONTREUIL
BEC
Woo
PA
• BERCK
CHAUDIERE
Fish soup
ANGUILLES A LA GELEE
Jellied eels
LE CROTOY
• ABBEVILLE
PATE
Duck p
AGNEAU DES PRES SALES
Salt-marsh lamb
CAQHUSE
Cold braised pork
FLAMICHE A
POIREAUX
Leek tart

E

OTS
oked
t leaves

KOKE-BOTEROM
Sweet buns

ANDOUILLETTES
Tripe sausages

IERES

● **LILLE**

N D E R S

CRAQUELINS
Crunchy cakes

ETHUNE

GE FORT
eese

LANGUES FUMEES
Smoked tongues

*MAROILLES
CHEESE*

● **ARRAS**

● **VALENCIENNES**

● **MAUBEUGE**

*MATELOTE
DU SAMBRE*
Fish stew

D'ARRAS
aped sweets

TARTE DE CAMBRAI
Fruit and batter pudding

TROUT

C A R D

● **CAMBRAI**

D

Y

AVESNES-SUR-HELPE

C

BETISES
Mint flavoured
sweets

SOUBISE PICARDE
Creamy onion sauce

*BOULETTE
D'AVESNES*
Cheese

PATE DE GRIVES
Thrush pâté

TE DE CANETON
ckling pâté

● **ST QUENTIN**

CRAYFISH

● **ROCROI**

T H I E R A C H E

A R D E N N E S

RIVER SOMME

SABLES
Shortbread

● **CHARLEVILLE-MEZIERES**

● **SEDAN**

TIRON

SMOKED HAM

BOUDIN BLANC
White pudding

CHOCOLATE

GAME

OIE A LA FLAMANDE
Braised goose

● **RETHEL**

TROUT

BISCUITS DE REIMS
Macaroons

HAM

PIEDS DE MOUTON FARCIS
Stuffed sheep's trotters

● **REIMS**

PEARS

PIKE

PAIN D'EPICES
Spiced honey cake

● **STE-MENEHOULD**

● **EPERNAY**

PIEDS DE PORC A LA SAINTE MENEHOULD
Pigs' trotters cooked in breadcrumbs

C H A M P A G N E

● **CHALONS-SUR-MARNE**

POCHOUSE
Fresh-water fish stew

DRAGEES
Sugar-coated almonds

MATELOTE
Fresh water fish stew

FILETS DE SOLE AU CHAMPAGNE
Fillets of sole poached in champagne

RIVER MARNE

MUSHROOMS

CARP

PIKE

SNAILS

CAISSES
Meringues with almonds

*CAILLES SOUS
LA CENDRE*
Quail cooked
in embers

LANGUES DE MOUTON FUMEES
Smoked sheep's tongues

SHEEP

● **JOINVILLE**

● **TROYES**

ANDOUILLETTES
Tripe sausages

TROUT

CHAOURCE CHEESE

● **BAR-SUR-SEINE**

● **CHAUMONT**

CHAOURCE ●

GOUGERE
Cheese pastry

SALADE DE PISSENLIT AU LARD
Dandelion leaves and bacon salad

● **LANGRES**

CHEESE

PICARDY
FLANDERS
ARTOIS
CHAMPAGNE

PICARDY is as eclectic as Normandy in its drinking habits. In place of Norman cider it makes use of the very tolerable beer of Lille, Pelican (which is now swallowed up in the giant Pelforth group). Increasingly called for are "le Watney's Red" or "le Whitbread" as these Britannic specialities begin their continental invasion. But at table, turned to without prejudice is Muscadet for a wine to match the *moules marinières,* Alsace for a glass of Gewürztraminer to go with the *flamiche,* Beaujolais or St-Emilion for a bottle for the cheese. If there is a vinous speciality it is very properly the wine of the nearest vineyard—Champagne. Some of the very best fish restaurants between Dieppe and Dunkirk make a point of keeping Champagne Nature—unprocessed, unfizzy champagne of a sharpness and delicacy that goes magically well with fish in creamy sauces. Champagne officially discourages the export of its wine in this state, on the grounds that it is a poor traveller. It is no hardship to meet it halfway if the rendezvous is a *turbot sauce hollandaise* at Wimereux or Le Crotoy.

Champagne's delicacies with Flemish touches

Amiens Duck Pâté
PATE DE CANETON D'AMIENS

Amiens duck pâté is made with a partially cooked, unboned duck, in the old style, or with a boned duck in a terrine. The latter method makes for easier serving, but whichever method is used the duck should be young.

SERVES 6 TO 8

1 boned duck, bones and giblets reserved
Salt
Freshly ground black pepper
Shortcrust pastry made with 1 lb plain flour and 8 oz butter
Pork fat, cut into thin strips to line the terrine

FARCE

3 oz butter
4 oz mushrooms, chopped
4 oz foie gras or chicken livers
1 duck liver
1 truffle
4 oz boned rabbit, cut into pieces
12 oz boned pork belly, diced
4 oz lean pork, cut into pieces
4 fl oz brandy
4 fl oz meat jelly or good stock
4 fl oz Madeira
2 medium-sized eggs
Salt
Freshly ground black pepper
Dried thyme
1 bay leaf
A little beaten egg
Jellied stock

First make the jellied stock. Put the duck bones and giblets and any pork skin left from trimming the pork into a large pan. Cover generously with water and bring to the boil. Cover the pan and boil hard for 1 hour. Remove the pan from the heat and strain the liquid into a clean pan. Boil the strained liquid down to 10 fluid ounces. It should have a good, strong flavour, but do not add any salt yet.

Put the stock in the refrigerator. If it does not set to a good jelly, return it to the heat and reduce it further.

Add a dash of Madeira and seasonings to taste. Set aside.

Season the duck inside and out with the salt and pepper. Set aside. Line a terrine, large enough to hold the duck comfortably, with two-thirds of the dough. Arrange the strips of pork fat around the sides.

Next make the *farce*. Melt one-third of the butter in a small pan. Add the mushrooms and cook them until the juices have evaporated.

In another pan, melt the remaining butter. Add the *foie gras* or chicken livers, the duck liver, truffle, rabbit and both pork meats and

brown well. Pour over half the brandy and set it alight. Remove the pan from the heat and set aside to cool. When cool, grind the meats finely or purée in a blender. Put the mixture into a bowl and beat in the remaining brandy, meat jelly or stock, Madeira and eggs. Season with salt, pepper, thyme and crumbled bay leaf to taste.

Spread a quarter of the meat mixture on the bottom of the dough-lined terrine. Stuff the duck with half the mixture and fold it into shape. Put the duck into the terrine and spread the remaining quarter of *farce* mixture on top. Roll out the remaining dough to make a lid and seal it in place. Make a hole in the centre and brush over with the beaten egg. Bake for 1½ hours. If the crust browns too quickly, protect it with foil.

Reheat the jellied stock and while the pâté is still warm, pour it through a funnel placed in the central hole of the lid. Pour slowly so that the stock has a chance to sink right down. Stop when the pâté is full.

Leave the pâté in a cold place or in the refrigerator for at least 12 hours, or preferably 24 hours, before serving.

Boulogne Mussel Salad
SALADE AUX MOULES A LA BOULONNAISE

Delicious fish salads are a speciality of Boulogne. Here is a tasty mussel and potato salad.

SERVES 6

3½ quarts mussels, scraped, washed and bearded
4 fl oz dry white wine
4 shallots, chopped
1 thyme sprig
6 parsley sprigs
Freshly ground black pepper
2 lb waxy potatoes, scrubbed, boiled, peeled and sliced
4 fl oz vinaigrette sauce
Chopped parsley
Chopped chives

Put the mussels, wine, shallots, thyme, parsley sprigs and plenty of black pepper into a large pan. Cook rapidly over high heat for about 8 minutes, or until the mussels open. Lift out the mussels as they open, remove them from the shells. Set the mussels aside. Discard the shells.

Put the potato slices into a bowl. Strain the boiling mussel liquor over the potatoes and set aside to cool.

To assemble the salad, drain the potato slices and arrange them on a serving dish. Put the mussels on top and pour over the *vinaigrette*. Sprinkle with the chopped parsley and chives. Serve well chilled.

Flemish Leek Pie
FLAMICHE AUX POIREAUX

Leek pie or tart is a favourite dish in Burgundy and Berry, as well as across the Channel in Cornwall and Wales. There are local variations, such as the inclusion of bacon or the use of a shortcrust rather than a puff pastry, but basically the recipes are the same. The refinements of cooks in this part of France, however, give their version the edge over the others. This is a dish of simple perfection.

SERVES 4

FILLING

4 oz butter
1 medium-sized onion, sliced
1 lb leeks, sliced
4 fl oz double cream
1 teaspoon flour
Salt
Freshly ground black pepper

PASTRY

1 lb weight puff pastry
Beaten egg to glaze

Melt half the butter in a large frying-pan. Add the onion and cook it gently until it is soft but not brown. Add the leeks and the remaining butter and cook slowly, uncovered, until the vegetables soften to a moist but not liquid mass. If there is any risk of the vegetables sticking to the pan, add a little water. Mix the cream with the flour and stir it into the vegetables. Cook for a moment to thicken the mixture slightly. Season well with the salt and pepper.

Preheat the oven to 450°F (Gas Mark 8).

Roll out the pastry and cut it into 2 large circles. Place one on a baking sheet. Spread the leek mixture in the centre, leaving a 1-inch rim. Brush the rim with the beaten egg. Lay the second circle on top, pressing it well down to seal the pie.

Brush the top with beaten egg. Nick a pattern around the edge and trace a pattern of diamonds over the top with a pointed knife, being careful not to go through to the filling. Make a hole in the centre. Bake for 15 minutes. Reduce the heat to 350°F (Gas Mark 4) and bake for a further 20 minutes, or until the pie is well risen and a golden brown.

Poached Fillets of Sole with Champagne
FILETS DE SOLES AU CHAMPAGNE

A good, dry white wine may be used instead of the champagne in this excellent recipe.

SERVES 6

12 fillets of sole
Salt

Pepper
12 evenly matched mushrooms
8 oz mushrooms, chopped
6 shallots, finely chopped
2 oz butter
Juice of $\frac{1}{2}$ lemon
8 fl oz dry champagne
4 fl oz double cream
2 tablespoons brandy
2 egg yolks
Chopped parsley

Season the fillets with the salt and pepper and roll them up skin side inside. Remove and chop the stems of the evenly matched mushrooms and put them in a bowl with the chopped mushrooms and shallots.

Melt half the butter in a small frying-pan. Add the 12 mushroom caps and cook them gently. Remove the pan from the heat and keep the mushrooms warm.

Grease a shallow pan with the remaining butter and spread the chopped mushrooms and shallots evenly over the bottom. Sprinkle with the lemon juice and arrange the rolled fillets on top.

Pour in the champagne and, over low heat, bring to simmering point. Cover the pan and cook gently until the fillets are just cooked. Carefully transfer the fillets to a heated serving dish.

Boil the juices in the pan for a few moments to reduce them a little and to concentrate the flavour.

In a small bowl, combine the cream, brandy and egg yolks. Stir in a little of the pan juices and pour the mixture into the pan. Cook over very low heat, stirring constantly until the sauce thickens. Correct the seasoning. Pour the sauce over the sole fillets. Garnish with the chopped parsley and the 12 mushroom caps and serve immediately.

Lambs' Kidneys with Champagne
ROGNONS DE MOUTON SAUTES AU CHAMPAGNE

In this recipe champagne nature, *still champagne, is used. Other dry white wines, however, can be substituted.*

SERVES 6

4 oz butter
8 oz mushrooms, sliced
12 lambs' kidneys, thinly sliced
Salt
Freshly ground black pepper
Nutmeg
1 heaped teaspoon chopped parsley
1 tablespoon flour
Generous 4 fl oz champagne nature or other dry white wine

3 tablespoons meat jelly or stock
Lemon juice
12 bread triangles fried in butter

Melt a quarter of the butter in a small pan. Add the mushrooms and cook them lightly. Melt half the butter in another pan and fry the kidney slices quickly, until they are lightly browned on both sides. Season with salt and pepper to taste, a pinch of grated nutmeg and the parsley. Sprinkle with the flour. Stir in the wine, meat jelly or stock and the mushrooms. Cook gently for 5 minutes. Correct the seasoning, add lemon juice to taste and mix in the remaining butter.

Turn the kidneys on to a heated serving dish, tuck the bread triangles around the edge and serve immediately.

Venison (or Veal) Chops in the Ardennes Style
COTELETTES DE CHEVREUIL (COTES DE VEAU)

Smoked ham and juniper berries, the two most evocative flavours of the Ardennes Forest, go most appropriately with venison. This is a good recipe, too, for veal.

SERVES 4

12 juniper berries, crushed
1 teaspoon dried marjoram or thyme
Salt
Freshly ground black pepper
8 venison cutlets or 4 thick loin chops
Lemon juice
4 oz butter
1 small onion, chopped
2 carrots, diced
4 fl oz dry white wine or vermouth
4 fl oz water
4 tablespoons chopped, cooked, smoked ham
2 oz fresh breadcrumbs
2 tablespoons chopped parsley
1 tablespoon redcurrant jelly
Juice of $\frac{1}{2}$ orange, preferably bitter orange

Mix the juniper berries with the marjoram or thyme, salt and pepper. Brush the meat all over with the lemon juice and rub in the herb mixture. Set aside for 2 hours.

Preheat the oven to 300°F (Gas Mark 2).

Melt 3 ounces of the butter in a large frying-pan. Add the onion and carrots and fry until lightly browned. Push them to one side of the pan and add the meat. Brown the chops or cutlets on both sides.

Add the wine or vermouth, boil hard for a few moments to reduce it and then add the water.

Transfer the contents of the pan to a large ovenproof dish which is suitable for serving from and in which the chops fit in a single layer. Place equal portions of the chopped ham on each chop. Mix the breadcrumbs with the parsley and sprinkle a layer on top. Cut the remaining butter into small pieces and put on top of the chops. Bake, uncovered, for about $1\frac{1}{2}$ hours, or until the meat is tender. The cooking time varies according to the thickness of the chops or cutlets.

When the meat is ready, pour off the juices into a wide pan. Cover the meat and return it to a low oven to keep warm. Skim the fat off the top of the cooking juices, then boil them down to concentrate the flavour. Stir in the redcurrant jelly and the orange juice. When the sauce is smooth, correct the seasoning and pour over the chops and serve.

Cambrai Tart
TARTE DE CAMBRAI

Wherever people live in the damp, cold parts of Europe, you will find them taking comfort in fruit and batter cakes or puddings like this one.

SERVES 6 TO 8

BATTER

10 tablespoons plain flour
1 teaspoon baking powder
6 tablespoons vanilla sugar
$\frac{1}{8}$ teaspoon salt
2 large eggs
8 tablespoons milk
4 tablespoons corn oil

FRUIT

4 ripe pears or dessert apples
Lemon juice
2 oz butter, cut into small pieces
Sugar

Preheat the oven to 400°F (Gas Mark 6). Butter 1 large or 2 medium-sized tart tins.

To make the batter, sift the dry ingredients into a bowl. Hollow out a well in the middle with the back of a spoon and put the liquid ingredients into it. Stirring the liquid ingredients, slowly incorporate the flour mixture until they form a smooth, thick batter. Pour the batter into the prepared tart tins or tin.

Peel, core and slice the fruit. Sprinkle with lemon juice. Arrange the fruit slices decoratively on top of the batter—the slices will sink a little, but this does not matter. Dot the butter over the top, sprinkle evenly with sugar. Place the tart in the oven for 30 to 40 minutes, or until it is puffed up and golden.

Serve warm with cream or, if preferred, cold as a cake.

The favoured city of the epicure

A VISIT to the best provision shops of Paris, to Fauchon, Hédiard or Paul Corcellet, recalls allegorical paintings in which personifications of Africa, India and the Orient come to lay their finest fruits at a conquering ruler's feet. They might make the visitor think that the world exists for the benefit of this one city.

The spectacle of food in Paris amazes the eye and the mind, even if reason insists that, with jet planes and refrigerated ships, most of the big centres of the prosperous world are equally well, if less dramatically, supplied.

In the past, at least until the development of trade in the nineteenth century, a French city depended mainly on the surrounding countryside for its food supplies. Unless it was well placed for the necessary imports, a bad season meant famine. Neighbouring areas were unwilling to sell what stores they might have for fear of suffering, too.

As well as a fertile, temperate countryside, Paris had two great rivers for survival: its own Seine (Napoleon observed that Paris, Rouen and Le Havre were one city, the Seine their one street) and the Loire, which at Orléans was only seventy-odd miles away.

Barges sailed upstream from Nantes, downstream from as far south as Roanne, to bring the surpluses of France to Orléans. Local products went to Paris, too: Gâtinais honeys, cotignac, a delicate quince paste, cheeses and mutton and lamb from Berry.

The main trade, however, was wine, and its important by-product, wine vinegar. Even today the wines of the Loire do not travel well. In the past many wines suffered so much on the journey that the lowest innkeeper in Paris would not touch them. Consequently, the wine merchants turned it into vinegar, an important ingredient in cooking and food preservation.

A major problem, the bread supply, hardly existed for Paris, because the huge plain of the Beauce, centred on Chartres and ringed with towns, has been a vast granary since Roman times.

The cathedral of Notre Dame, the queen of this unending Beauce, was built on grain. Its windows shine with luminous cornflower blue, poppy red, corn-cockle purples and pinks, corn marigold yellow. They were paid for by the prosperous traders of the town: the bakers provided four, the butchers two, fishmongers, watercarriers and grocers one each. Their vigorous craft pride is shown in detailed scenes. The baker kneads his dough, the butcher swings an axe, the grocer sells his spices, the wine merchant drives a cart loaded with barrels. The good food of Chartres was much prized in Paris, in particular the game pâtés.

To the north and east of Paris many farms provide root vegetables, including sugarbeet, as well as grain in the pays de Brie and beans at Soissons. Arpajon, to the south of Paris, is another bean centre. From Brie, too, come the huge wheels of cheese on their straw mats and the smaller Coulommiers.

Fresh curd cheeses and cream from Chantilly or Fontainebleau were once particularly prized. (To the French, whipped cream is always crème Chantilly.) The abundant forests provided game and wild mushrooms. Mushrooms were first cultivated late in the seventeenth century, in the disused quarries from which Paris had been built, hence champignons de Paris.

Orchards nearer the city provided exquisite fruit. Montreuil is still not too engulfed to have some peach trees left; the fruit trees between Groslay and Montmorency run to hundreds of acres. (Montmorency cherries are tart and ideal for cooking with duck.) The walled enclosures of Thomery, near Fontainebleau, still produce Chasselas dessert grapes.

The memory of this intensive cultivation lingers mainly in the menus of classical French cooking. They are a history in shorthand of the capital, and of France itself; economic, social, political, literary history called up by the names of people and places, a moving piety towards the past which it is hoped will never be relinquished in favour of time and tourism.

The establishment of high-class restaurants, which made Paris the world capital of good eating, was stimulated by the Revolution. When aristocratic heads began to roll, many chefs were out of work, at least temporarily. Some of the best managed to remain in private employment or went to the grand families of England, Austria and Russia. Others started restaurants where people might meet for pleasure and conversation, assisted by elegant surroundings and the best food and wine.

Cooking was taken as seriously by the new clients as it had been by the nobility of the court in the seventeenth and eighteenth centuries. A writer like Dumas did not think it beneath his talents to write a majestic grand dictionnaire de cuisine.

At the end of the nineteenth century, it might seem that restaurants were more famous for royalty, actresses and professional beauties, but food remained a serious matter of skill and intelligence. That is the reason it survived the reality of the First World War. Although higher prices were increasingly demanded for provisions and labour, restaurateurs adapted themselves adroitly to changing ways.

There are still about half a dozen restaurants in Paris which provide the best food in the world and the necessary high standard to stimulate all the restaurateurs in France.

The break in tradition and the social changes brought about by the Second World War, however, gave other types of restaurants a chance. Paris has enclaves of people from all over France, and from many parts of the world. Bars and simple eating places in these colonies provide a sympathetic atmosphere for nostalgic Auvergnats or Lyonnais to meet and exchange news from home. Because of the general interest in food from the provinces, people from outside Paris have come to the capital with increasing confidence to provide the best of the food they know best for a wider clientele.

Today one can eat stuffed goose neck, truffled dishes and foie gras from ducks as well as geese in Périgordian or Béarnaise restaurants. There are bouillabaisse and red mullet with fennel in Provençal restaurants, and perhaps best of all snails, chicken simmered in red wine, fresh-water fish and eggs in Burgundian establishments. Even Berry, one of the least famous of provinces, has its restaurant, the Quincy, named after one of its best wines.

Speciality restaurants flourish. Drouant's and Prunier's have been supplying superb fish since they were founded in 1872 and 1888 respectively. Androuet's, which started as a cheese shop, has provided cheese dishes since the Second World War: the menu lists nearly four hundred.

Nowhere in the world can one eat as well as one still does in Paris.

ILE DE FRANCE
PARIS
ORLEANAIS

ROGNONS SAUTES
Sauteed kidneys

CONFITS
Fruit paste sweets

● BEAUVAIS

ARTICHOKES

● LAON

HURE
Boar's head

HARICOT BEANS

GATEAU DE COMPIEGNE
Round brioche cake

● COMPIEGNE

● SOISSONS

TERRINE DE GARENNES
Coarse wild rabbit pâté

● VILLERS-COTTERETS

TRUITE AU POIVRE BOUILLI
Trout in pepper sauce

PATE DE CERF
Venison pâté

CHANTILLY

● SENLIS

● VIARMES

CREAM

PAINS ANISES
Aniseed rolls

● FERE-EN-TARDENOIS

WILD MUSHROOMS

MUSTARD

● MEAUX

SAUCE BERCY
White wine and shallot sauce

BOEUF A LA MODE
Beef braised in wine

PARIS ●

● CRECY

POTAGE CRECY
Carrot soup

CHICKENS
● HOUDAN

● VERSAILLES

BRIOCHE

● COULOMMIERS

GAME
WILD STRAWBERRIES

CHEESE

WHEAT

● RAMBOUILLET

RIVER SEINE

PAIN D'EPICES
Spiced honey cake

BRIE DE MELUN
Cheese

● MELUN

PATE D'ALOUETTES
Lark pâté

● CHARTRES

● ETAMPES

GAME

● FONTAINEBLEAU

● THOMERY

PATES DE GIBIER
Game pâtés

GATEAU DE PITHIVIERS
Almond and puff pastry cake

GRAPES

WHEAT

B E A U C E
CULOTTE DE BOEUF BEAUCERONNE
Rump of beef with potatoes, onions and bacon

● PITHIVIERS

G A T I N A I S

WINE
VINEGAR

GIGOT A L'EAU
Boiled leg of mutton

HONEY

MATELOTE D'ANGUILLES
Eel stew

COTIGNAC
Quince paste

● MONTARGIS

SAFFRON

FROMAGE CENDRE
Cheese rolled in ashes

ORLEANS ●

● JARGEAU

ANDOUILLES
Large tripe sausages

● VENDOME

S O L O G N E

● BEAUGENCY

LIQUORICE SWEETS

CARP

● GIEN

CHOCOLATE

GAME

RILLETTES
Potted pork

● BLOIS

LAMOTTE BEUVRON

PATE DE GRIVES
Thrush pâté

RIVER LOIRE

TARTE DES DEMOISELLES TATIN
Caramelized apple tart

ASPARAGUS

LAPEREAU A LA SOLOGNOTTE
Stuffed young wild rabbit

● ROMORANTIN

POULTRY

GOATS' CHEESE

● SELLES-SUR-CHER

Traditional recipes from the great chefs

Carrot Soup
POTAGE CRECY

In northern France there are two small towns called Crécy—Crécy-en-Ponthieu, in Picardy, and Crécy-en-Brie in the cheese country to the east of Paris. Both claim this soup, but as it has become such a part of classical French cookery it is best linked to Paris.

SERVES 2

3 oz butter
8 oz carrots, sliced
1 medium-sized onion, chopped
2 oz rice
1½ pints chicken or veal stock
1 thyme sprig
Salt
Pepper
Bread croûtons, fried in butter

Melt two-thirds of the butter in a saucepan. Add the carrots and onion, cover the pan and simmer for 5 minutes. Add the rice, stock, thyme and salt and pepper to taste and cook, covered, for 30 minutes, or until the carrot is soft.

Remove and discard the thyme sprig. Purée the soup in a blender or a food mill, adding more stock if the consistency is too thick.

Return the soup to a clean pan and reheat it. Stir in the remaining butter just before serving. Serve the *croûtons* in a separate bowl.

Lobster with Tomato Sauce
HOMARD A L'AMERICAINE

There has been much culinary argument about this dish. Should it perhaps be à l'armoricaine, which means in Breton style? The facts of the matter, and the determining ingredients of the sauce, seem to indicate that it was by origin a dish of southern France, in particular from Nice. It was improved upon in Paris, in the restaurant Bonnefoy, by the chef Constance Guillot in the 1860s. The proprietor of another restaurant, Pierre Fraisse, who had spent some time in Chicago, altered the name, but not the recipe, to flatter some American clients.

SERVES 2

3½ fl oz olive oil
4 oz butter
2 shallots, chopped
1 garlic clove, crushed
1½ to 2 lb live lobster, cut in pieces (reserving the coral and liver)
2 fl oz brandy
8 fl oz dry white wine
6 fl oz fish stock
1 tablespoon meat glaze or jelly
3 medium-sized tomatoes, blanched, peeled and chopped

Parsley
Cayenne pepper
Salt
Freshly ground black pepper

Heat the oil and 1 ounce of the butter in a large, heavy frying-pan. Add the shallots and the garlic and fry until soft but not coloured. Add the lobster and flame it with the brandy. When the lobster turns bright red, add the wine, stock, meat glaze or jelly, tomatoes, a little parsley, a pinch of cayenne and salt and pepper to taste. Simmer, covered, for 15 to 20 minutes, or until the lobster is cooked. Transfer the lobster pieces to a serving dish, remove and discard the shell, keep the lobster warm.

Boil the juices in the pan until there are only 8 fluid ounces left. Mix in the coral and liver and a pat of butter. Strain the sauce into a clean pan and reheat to just below boiling point. Whisk in the remaining butter, correct the seasoning and pour the sauce over the lobster. Sprinkle with parsley and serve very hot.

Steaks with Foie Gras and Truffles
TOURNEDOS ROSSINI

Tournedos Rossini, one of the great simplicities of French cooking, was devised in the late 1850s by the composer Rossini and Modeste Magny, the owner of the Restaurant Magny in the rue Mazet. Apart from the exquisite food, Magny's was famous for the literary dinners held there between 1862 and 1872. The Goncourt brothers, Sainte-Beuve and Flaubert met there twice a month, with Turgenev, George Sand, Taine, Renan, Théophile Gautier and their friends.

SERVES 4

4 round thick fillet steaks
4 croûtons of bread, the same size as the steaks, fried in butter
1 tablespoon butter
1 tablespoon oil
4 slices of foie gras, each a little smaller than the steaks (about 3 oz in all)
4 slices of truffle, preferably fresh
Salt
Freshly ground black pepper

Prepare the *croûtons* first and keep them very hot. Fry the steaks in the butter and oil on each side. They should be kept rare, so allow about 6 minutes in all. Quickly place the steak on the *croûtons*, the *foie gras* on the steak and the truffle on the *foie gras*. Serve immediately, with a discreet garnish of watercress.

The heat of the steak melts the *foie gras* slightly, and the delicious juices are soaked up by the *croûtons*. Some restaurants serve a *sauce périgueux* (a Madeira sauce, finished with truffle essence and chopped truffle) with *tournedos Rossini*, but this is excessive.

Hollandaise Sauce and Béarnaise Sauce
SAUCES HOLLANDAISE ET BEARNAISE

French cooking is famous, above all, for its sauces. While it might be argued that sauces were invented to disguise food, for meat which had been over-salted, for example, or which had started to go off by the eighteenth century in France, however improved gardening and farming, marketing and the use of ice houses meant that chefs were increasingly free to devise sauces for pleasure and to enhance and vary the excellent provisions at their command.

To see how these sauces were developed, one must turn to the Art de la Cuisine Française du Dix-neuvième Siècle, by Antonin Carême, perhaps the greatest of French chefs, who cooked for Talleyrand, the French foreign minister, for Napoleon, for the Prince Regent, and for the Tsar of Russia. He stands at the central moment of French cooking. Behind him were the laborious methods of the past. As assistant to one sauce chef he had to get up at three in the morning on the day of a banquet, to set the grandes sauces on the fire, so that by the time his master arrived the basic stocks would be reduced, thickened and skimmed. In the future, he could see a diminution of drudgery, and he sought to improve cooking in this direction, without the loss of quality.

Here is his recipe for the most versatile of the petites sauces, hollandaise. It can be served with vegetables, poached fish, chicken and, in the later béarnaise variation, with steak and lamb.

SAUCE HOLLANDAISE

"Put 5 fresh egg yolks in a pan with a little butter, salt, pepper and grated nutmeg. Stand it in another pan of simmering water and stir. As soon as the sauce begins to thicken, start adding Isigny butter. When just over half a pound of butter has been used, finish the sauce with a spoonful of ordinary wine vinegar. Your sauce should now be velvety, with a well-seasoned flavour." Be careful not to overheat the sauce, or the eggs will scramble.

SAUCE BEARNAISE

Before starting the sauce, make a strong flavouring essence by boiling together

1 tablespoon chopped shallots
2 tablespoons chopped tarragon and chervil
4 tablespoons tarragon vinegar
4 tablespoons dry white wine
Black pepper

When they are reduced to about 2 tablespoons of liquid, set aside and leave to cool. Strain into a bowl, add the egg yolks and continue as for *hollandaise*, omitting the vinegar at the end. The final seasoning should be salt, cayenne pepper and a good chopping of tarragon which adds an aromatic flavour to the sauce.

Fillet of Veal Laguipière
GRENADINS DE VEAU LAGUIPIERE

This dish, served at the Hostellerie du Château, *Fère-en-Tardenois, commemorates Laguipière, the chef Carême's honoured master, to whose "illustrious shade" he dedicated his enormous book. The style of the dedication may be a little grand for these cautious days, but the love and passion with which Carême recalled his debt, and lamented the old man's appalling death from frostbite during the retreat from Moscow, is moving.*

Veal grenadins *are thick slices cut from the fillet, usually weighing about 5 ounces. They must be larded with pork or bacon fat.*

SERVES 4

4 grenadins of veal, larded
salt
freshly ground black pepper
2 oz butter
4 fl oz port or Madeira
4 fl oz veal stock or gravy
1 tablespoon sliced truffle
½ oz very cold butter

GARNISH

4 artichoke hearts, finished in butter and seasoned with salt, pepper and lemon juice
16 cooked asparagus tips

First prepare the garnish and keep it warm.

Season the *grenadins* with salt and pepper. In a large, heavy frying-pan, heat the butter. Add the *grenadins* and cook over moderate heat, turning them once, for 10 to 12 minutes. Remove the *grenadins* from the pan and keep them warm while the sauce is made.

Pour the wine into the juices in the pan and boil hard for a few moments, scraping the pan to mix in all the delicious brown essences. Add the stock or gravy and boil hard again until the mixture is reduced and concentrated in flavour. Season to taste and add the truffle.

Remove the pan from the heat and whisk in the very cold butter, which should melt but not boil. Put the veal back into the pan and reheat over low heat for 5 minutes.

To serve, arrange the veal *grenadins* on a heated serving platter, pour the sauce over the veal and garnish with the artichoke hearts and asparagus tips.

Sologne Asparagus Blois Style
ASPERGES DE SOLOGNE A LA BLESOISE

Every garden in this part of France seems to grow asparagus. But the best asparagus comes from the Sologne, where it flourishes in the steely furrows of drained meres. It is not green all over like asparagus in England, nor is it as fat and yellow as Bassano asparagus in Italy, but somewhere in between. The stems are plump and pale, the tips purple and green. It is wonderful asparagus.

SERVES 4

2 lb asparagus, stems scraped
Rind of 1 lemon, cut into matchstick strips
Rind of 1 orange, cut into matchstick strips
2 fl oz Grand Marnier
6 fl oz double cream
8 fl oz hollandaise sauce (see p. 122)

Boil the asparagus in the usual way, preferably in an asparagus pan.

Meanwhile make the sauce. Put the lemon and orange rind and the Grand Marnier in a small saucepan and simmer, covered, for 3 to 4 minutes. Whip the cream in a small bowl.

Just before serving, mix the cream, the lemon and orange rind with the cooking liquid into the *hollandaise* sauce. The asparagus should be warm rather than boiling hot.

Pears with Hot Chocolate Sauce
POIRES BELLE HELENE

The superb restaurants created by César Ritz and the great chef Escoffier during the last part of the nineteenth century made an elegant and, at last, respectable setting for women dining out in public. The new clientele was cosseted by Escoffier, who invented an exquisite collection of desserts in their honour. They in turn rewarded him. "My success," Escoffier once said, "comes from the fact that my best dishes were created for ladies." He excelled at light, simple but unexpected combinations of flavours—peaches on vanilla ice with a fresh raspberry purée (pêches Melba, after the singer), peaches with wild strawberries and a zabaglione sauce (pêches Eugénie, in honour of the Empress Eugénie), strawberries with pine-apple and Curaçao mousse (fraises Sarah Bern-hardt, for the actress)—and this most famous and most travestied of all, poires Hélène (now usually called poires belle Hélène),

Here is Escoffier's simple recipe, which conceals that to be made perfectly the ice-cream should be made of egg yolks and cream as well as milk, and that the chocolate sauce should not be muddied with cocoa and similar powders. Nor is it a recipe for canned pears.

Pears
Vanilla-flavoured syrup
Ice-cream
Crystallized violets

Poach the pears in the syrup and leave to cool. When ready to serve, dish them on a bed of vanilla ice-cream and scatter with crystallized violets. Serve a hot chocolate sauce separately.

Apple Upside-down Tart
TARTE DES DEMOISELLES TATIN

A speciality of Lamotte-Beuvron, where the Tatin hotel, in the rue Vierzon, may still be found, although not, quite probably, the demoiselles. The original tart was cooked on charcoal with a metal oven placed over it. The strong heat from below caramelized the sugared and buttered apples, so that when the tart was inverted on to a serving dish, the neatly arranged slices had turned an appetizing tawny brown. To get the same effect with modern stoves, one must cheat. Either the butter and sugar can be caramelized in the tart tin before the apple is arranged in it, or the tart can be turned out and sprinkled with sugar, and placed under the grill, or a separate, small amount of sugar can be caramelized and poured over the apples before serving.

Use a sharp dessert apple which will keep its shape; Cox's or Sturmers, Golden Delicious or Reinette varieties are best.

PASTRY

8 oz plain flour
1 tablespoon castor sugar
⅛ teaspoon salt
5 oz unsalted butter, softened
1 egg
1 tablespoon iced water

FILLING

2 oz butter
Up to 3 lb apples, peeled, cored and sliced
4 tablespoons sugar

Spread the flour in a circle on a board or working surface. Make a well in the centre and put in the sugar, salt, butter and egg. Using fingertips, mix all the ingredients except the flour together to make a paste. Slowly incorporate the flour to make dough, using the water if necessary. Pat the dough into a ball. Put the ball into a bowl, cover and leave it in a cold place or in the refrigerator for an hour or two.

Preheat the oven to 400°F (Gas Mark 6). Grease a 9- or 10-inch tart tin with a quarter of the butter and sprinkle 1 tablespoon of sugar over it. Pick out the best apple slices and arrange them elegantly in the tart tin. Make a second layer of apples and fill in the gaps with the remaining slices. Cut the remaining butter into pieces and dot the top of the pie with them. Sprinkle with the remaining sugar.

Roll out the dough thinly. Cut out a circle to fit inside the tart tin. Prick it all over with a fork and set it in place. Bake for 30 minutes. Remove the tart from the oven, put a serving dish on top and turn upside down. Place under a hot grill for a few minutes for the top to caramelize, or make a caramel with 3 tablespoons of sugar and 1 tablespoon of water and pour it over the top.

Where German and French tastes blend

COUNTRIES with long histories are often thought to have always had the same boundaries. Talk about the Gauls, about the Gallic chief Vercingetorix and his battles with Caesar, and the familiar pentagonal shape of modern France comes to mind.

France, however, has not had such precise frontiers for very long. The pentagon began in the ninth century with Francia, the kingdom of the Franks, and the present-day Ile de France and Orléanais. It was not complete until Nice and Mentone were handed over to France in 1860 and 1861.

Alsace and the Franche-Comté were acquired by Louis XIV in the seventeenth century, but Lorraine hung on in a dependent independence until the death in 1766 of Stanislaus Leszczyński, the deposed king of Poland who became the father-in-law of Louis XV and duc de Lorraine.

Thanks to his taste and intelligence, Nancy, which is now the centre of a heavy industrial area, can console itself with the exquisite Place Stanislaus, where the buildings of Emmanuel Héré and the wrought-iron work of Jean Lamour combine in an exceptional grace.

Certain items of food are, rightly or wrongly, attached to Stanislaus's name: for example, the rum baba and the shell-shaped madeleines of Commercy. His daughter, Marie, is the queen of *bouchées à la reine*, pastry puffs filled with creamed chicken, sweetbreads and mushrooms.

Noticeable of these provinces is the resourceful style of pastry cooks and confectioners. Macaroons, spiced and anise-flavoured cakes, small gingerbreads known as *nonnettes* (little nuns) and the impudently named *pets de nonne* (choux pastry fritters), tiny biscuits in great jars, rich dark chocolate cake, sugar-coated almonds, glacé fruit, *kugelhopf*, and the savarins and babas have a rococo air of the eighteenth century. Preserves are another delight; the most famous centre is Bar-le-Duc.

The central plains of the provinces are separated by the Vosges mountains. Because of the vicissitudes of history, including the German occupations of 1872 and 1918 and the Second World War, they developed a resolute stoicism which may seem harsh.

The Germanic influence is strong. Many dishes are like those across the Rhine: *choucroute*, sauerkraut, saddle of hare baked in cream and served with noodles, cakes, such as *kugelhopf*, and *baeckeoffe*, a braised hotpot of beef, lamb and pork.

For wine, Alsace is supreme, and this has stimulated the skills of chefs and cooks at different levels of society. The delicious and hearty tarts, in which Lorraine also excels, seem to belong most appropriately to the farms. There are also the stewed dishes of *bourgeois* cooking, the game (venison, wild boar, hare, partridge), delicate trifles such as frogs' legs, and the supreme luxury of *foie gras*, the fat liver of geese.

This costly speciality, which goes back to Roman times, is the result of a cruel inhumanity: factory farming methods are reinforced by the prison technique of forced feeding. Alexandre Dumas said in his dictionary of cooking that the geese were often blinded and nailed by their webbed feet to planks so that they could not move. That was in the nineteenth century. Although a battery cage must cope far more efficiently these days, the geese still have a maize porridge poured down their throats by means of a special funnel until their livers swell enormously. The best *foie gras* will weigh about one and a half pounds.

The poultry-keepers raise excellent chickens, turkeys and ducks. Hotel menus are full of *fricassées*, *terrines*, *salmis*, *coq au vin de Riesling* with morel mushrooms. Turkeys nestle among chestnuts.

The most popular, most utilized meat is pork. The best pork cooks in the world are French and German, and the people of these provinces have lived for centuries beneath their joint influence. As a result their *charcuterie* combines a robust directness with refinement. There are smoked joints and sausages which partner the acid *choucroute*, the pickled, slightly fermented cabbage which was brought across the Rhine into Alsace and Lorraine centuries ago. The sausages, too, show the combination of influences. The Strasbourg sausage, for example, much resembles the frankfurter, and the use of cumin, anise and fennel also comes from Germany.

The pâtés look to France, particularly the Chartres style, in which the *foie gras* or fille of the best game are cradled in a layer finely flavoured forcemeat and then bake in a decorated and golden pastry case.

The two great cheeses of the area are th strongly flavoured *Munster* and *Géromé*, ofte underscored with cumin and aniseed. Tw smaller white-coated cheeses, like a cream camembert in texture, are the *Carré de l'es* which is also made in Champagne, and th *Récollet*.

One great product of the Vosges kirschwasser, the *eau-de-vie*, white brand made from cherries required in so man French and German recipes. The real thin is now very expensive, but makes all th difference to puddings and *soufflés glacé*. Kirschwasser has its other uses, for example in cheese *fondue*.

The Franche-Comté

The Franche-Comté is separated from th Vosges and Alsace by a huge rift of a valle known as the Trouée of Belfort. For cen turies, to the discomfort of the people livin there, it has been a handy passageway fro the Rhineland to the Rhône.

When the visitor arrives, the Franche Comté encloses him in the familiarity of th painter Courbet, particularly in the are around Ornans where he was born. The gre brows and crags of rock shown on so man well-known canvases come into sight, th green fields shine with that deep luminou clarity of colour. Forests and full-grow streams suggest the excellent food whic will be found in the inns and restaurants game, trout and crayfish.

The long, wood-panelled dining-room o the hotel at Ornans cannot have change much since Courbet's day. One enters by door from the central carriageway by whic coaches went through to the stable yard. A the table, local specialities are presented wit a friendly aplomb.

The Franche-Comté has its own smoke hams, sausages spiced with cumin and plump, rather red sausage picturesquel known as the *Jésus* of Morteau. At Besanço long, four-sided, reddy-brown sausage known as *gendarmes* can be bought. The mai cheeses are on the Swiss model: hug Gruyère and Emmenthal cheeses and th local Comté are ideal for *gratins*.

For many people, the mushrooms are th best thing in the Franche-Comté. Few pleasures can compare with mushroom hunting and mushroom eating afterwards and for this the Franche-Comté is a paradise

VENISON

OEUFS A L'ESCARGOT
Eggs with snails

THIONVILLE

...ES AUX QUETSCHES ET AUX MIRABELLES
...tarts

OIE EN DAUBE
Braised goose

POCHOUSE
Fresh-water fish stew

VERDUN

BOULAY

CHEVREUIL AU PUREE DE MARRONS
Venison with chestnut purée

QUETSCHES
MIRABELLES

FRAISES DE METZ
Crystallized strawberries

METZ

DRAGEES
Sugar-coated almonds

CHOUCROUTE
Sauerkraut

CHOUX ROUGES AUX MARRONS
Red cabbage with chestnuts

RED CURRANT JELLY

RABLE DE LIEVRE A LA CREME
Saddle of hare in cream sauce

CRAYFISH

TRUITES A LA CREME
Trout in cream sauce

GRENOUILLES AU GRATIN
Frogs' legs in cheese sauce

ESCARGOTS EN CHOUCROUTE
Snails in sauerkraut

MADELEINES
Shell-shaped cakes

QUICHE LORRAINE
Bacon and cream tart

BAECKEOFFE
Mutton baked with pork and potatoes

BAR-LE-DUC

COMMERCY

BOUDIN
Black pudding

OIE FARCI
Stuffed goose

PERDRIX AUX CHOUX A LA LORRAINE
Partridge with cabbage

NANCY

STRASBOURG

GRAS DOUBLE LORRAINE
Tripe

PORCELET EN GELEE
Suckling pig in aspic

ZEWELEWAI
Onion tart

SAUCISSON DE STRASBOURG
Strasbourg sausage

BERGAMOTTES
Boiled sweets

BILBERRIES

PATE DE FOIE GRAS TRUFFE
Truffled pâté de foie gras

PATES DE FOIE GRAS

POULARDE A LA CREME
Chicken in cream sauce

VOSGES

POCHOUSE
Fresh-water fish stew

GEROME CHEESE

SELESTAT

CONTREXEVILLE

EPINAL

ORBEY

BROCHET BARDE ET TRUFFE
Barded and truffled pike

GERARDMER

COLMAR

ANDOUILLETTES
Tripe sausages

REMIREMONT

KIRSCH

FOUGEROLLES

CONFIT D'OIE
Preserved goose

LUXEUIL

NONNETTES
Iced gingerbread

KUGELHOPF
Sweet yeast cake

SMOKED HAM

POULET AUX MORILLES
Chicken with morels

MULHOUSE

GAME

SOUPE AUX GRENOUILLES
Frogs'-legs soup

VESOUL

BELFORT

ALTKIRCH

OMELETTE AU SANG
Blood omelette

TRUITE AU BLEU
Blue trout

QUENELLES DE BROCHET
Pike dumplings

MONTBELIARD

MONTBOZON

SAUCISSE AU CUMIN
Cumin-spiced sausage

CANCOILLOTTE
Cheese spread

LANGUES FOURREES
Stuffed tongues

PAIN D'EPICES
Spiced honey cake

COMTE CHEESE

BESANCON

VERCEL

GOUMOIS

"JESUS"
Morteau sausage

DOLE

MORTEAU

GAME

CRAYFISH

TROUT

PONTARLIER

ARBOIS

POLIGNY

PATE DE GIBIER
Game pâté

CHAMPAGNOLE

TIMBALE DE MORILLES
Moulded morels

LONS-LE-SAUNIER

PATE CHAUD AUX PIGEONS
Hot pigeon pâté

FROMAGE BLEU
Blue cheese

ST AMOUR

GALETTE DE GOUMEAU
Open tart

SEPTMONCEL

ALSACE LORRAINE FRANCHE-COMTE

125

Substantial stews and delicate confections

Foie Gras Cooked in Brioche Pastry
BRIOCHE DE FOIE GRAS FRAIS

When the Maréchal de Contades was made military governor of Alsace in 1762, he wanted to avoid a change of diet, so he arrived at Strasbourg with his head-chef, Josèphe Close, who was a Norman. The geese of Alsace furnished him with the idea and material for a new dish. He surrounded the smoothly rich and firm foie gras with a farce of minced, seasoned veal, and baked the whole thing in pastry. A little later, he added the fine-flavoured truffles of Périgord to his dish.

This recipe, from the Auberge de l'Ill at Illhausern, surrounds the foie gras with a more delicate wrapping of brioche mousseline.

SERVES 12

1 fresh foie gras, about 1½ lb weight
Salt
Freshly ground black pepper
Quatre-épices
8 fl oz brandy
3 truffles
BRIOCHE DOUGH
½ oz yeast
4 tablespoons tepid water
1 lb plain flour
⅛ teaspoon salt
6 eggs
13 oz butter, softened
Beaten egg to glaze
JELLY
1 pint aspic jelly, flavoured with port

Carefully cut away all the thready and greenish parts of the liver and remove the skin. Put it in a bowl. Season it with salt, pepper and a pinch of *quatre-épices*. Pour on the brandy, cover the dish and leave it overnight.

First thing next day, make the brioche dough. Cream the yeast with the water. Add one-third of the flour gradually, plus the salt—there should be just enough to make a soft ball of dough. Put the dough in a bowl, cover with a cloth and leave it to rise in a warm, draught-free place for 2 hours. This is the *levain*, the raising dough. In another bowl, put the remaining flour. Clear a well in the centre and break in the eggs. Add the soft butter. With the hands, mix into a dough. With the palm of the hand, spread the dough on a floured board. In the middle put the risen *levain* and mix the two doughs together, kneading with both hands.

Roll out the dough and with it line a loaf tin, large enough to contain the *foie gras* comfortably; cut away the surplus dough. Drain the *foie gras*. Make three cuts in it and put the truffles into them, and lay it in the dough-lined tin. Make a lid with the surplus dough. Fix it in place, pressing the edges firmly together and using the beaten egg to seal. Leave to rise for 30 minutes. Brush over with beaten egg.

Preheat the oven to 375°F (Gas Mark 5). Bake for 40 minutes. This may not seem long, but Strasbourg *foie gras* should always be cooked pink. If it is subjected to the heat for too long, it will dissolve into delicious, but very expensive, fat.

When the brioche is cool, make a small hole in the centre and pour in the cool but liquid aspic jelly to fill up the gap which inevitably develops between the *foie gras* and the risen brioche. (Any leftover aspic should be left to set; it can then be chopped and served round the brioche.) Leave the whole thing in a cool place (not the refrigerator—too much cold spoils the flavour) for several hours. Cut it into slices just before serving.

Bacon Tart
QUICHE LORRAINE

Quiche lorraine must be one of the world's most popular and most traduced dishes. But there are a number of other good open tarts made in this part of France, both savoury and sweet.

To make quiche, begin with a pastry-lined pie tin, preferably with a removable base. Do not use porcelain or china—metal conducts the heat more quickly. A shortcrust pastry, made with 8 ounces of flour and 4 ounces of butter, is the thing: add 1 tablespoon of sugar if it is for a sweet tart, and bind it with egg instead of water.

Choose the filling, and bake the tart for 45 minutes at 350°F (Gas Mark 4).

SERVES 4 TO 6

4 oz bacon, diced
9-inch tart tin lined with shortcrust dough
4 oz cooked ham, diced
3 eggs
5 fl oz single cream
5 fl oz double cream
5 fl oz milk
Salt
Pepper
Nutmeg

Preheat the oven to 350°F (Gas Mark 4).
In a small frying-pan, fry the bacon in its own fat for a few minutes. Spread the bacon over the base of the tart, with the diced ham. In a bowl, beat the eggs with the single and double cream and milk. Season with salt, pepper and nutmeg and pour over the bacon and ham. Bake in the oven for 45 minutes, or until the top is puffed and golden.

Carp in the Jewish Style
CARPE A LA JUIVE

This dish is an unusual sweet and sour descendant of those medieval dishes in which meat or fish was combined with a number of sweet and spicy ingredients. Carp, a plump, firm fish, takes this kind of treatment very well; and it turns its juices to the most excellent jelly.

SERVES 10

4 to 5 lb carp, 1 large or 2 small fish, cleaned and washed
10 fl oz olive oil
2 large onions, chopped
4 shallots, chopped
2 tablespoons flour
1 tablespoon sugar
Water or light fish stock
1 tablespoon vinegar
Bouquet garni
3 oz raisins
4 oz blanched, split almonds
Salt
Freshly ground black pepper

If the fish is large, cut it into thick slices; if small, leave whole. Put the fish on the perforated tray in a fish kettle or steamer.

Heat the oil in a saucepan. Add the onions and shallots and fry lightly, stirring, until they begin to turn golden. Stir in the flour, sugar and 3 pints water or stock. Add the vinegar, bouquet garni, raisins, almonds and salt and pepper to taste. Bring the mixture to the boil and pour it over the fish. If the sauce does not cover the fish, add more water or stock. Cover the kettle or steamer and simmer the fish for 25 minutes, or until it is cooked. Transfer the fish carefully to a deep, close-fitting dish.

Increase the heat and boil the sauce until it has a good, strong flavour. Correct the seasoning with salt, pepper and sugar if necessary. Pour the sauce over the carp and set aside to cool. Serve chilled.

Chicken with Vinegar Sauce
LE POULET AU VINAIGRE

The sauce in this dish is mildly piquant, very good and fresh tasting. Courgettes go well with it. Blanch them in water and finish them in butter over a low heat.

SERVES 6

4 to 5 lb chicken, cut into serving pieces
Seasoned flour
4 oz butter
4 garlic cloves, finely chopped
1 onion, chopped
4 fl oz white wine vinegar, preferably tarragon vinegar
4 fl oz dry white wine
1 tablespoon tomato purée
Salt
Freshly ground black pepper
Veal or beef stock
1 tablespoon Dijon mustard (moutarde forte)

urn the chicken pieces in the flour and shake off the surplus. In a deep frying-pan, melt half the butter. Add the chicken pieces and, turning them frequently, brown them lightly. Add the garlic, onion, vinegar, wine, tomato purée and seasonings.

The liquid must barely cover the chicken; if it does not, add a little stock. Bring the mixture to the boil. Cover the pan, reduce the heat and simmer, turning the pieces occasionally, for 30 minutes, or until the chicken is cooked. Transfer the chicken pieces to a serving dish.

Skim the fat from the cooking liquid. If the flavour is weak, increase the heat and boil the sauce to concentrate the flavour. Add more tomato purée if necessary. Remove the pan from the heat and whisk in the remaining butter and the mustard to taste. Strain the sauce over the chicken pieces and serve.

Chicken Franche-Comté Style
POULET A LA COMTOISE

The Comté, Gruyère and Emmenthal cheeses of France are all made after Swiss originals, but they are good and close in flavour. With Parmesan from Italy, these are the great cheeses for cooking, in particular for dishes which need a crusty but mellow finish.

SERVES 4

4 to 5 lb farm chicken
Salt
Freshly ground black pepper
3 oz butter
White part of 2 leeks, sliced
2 medium-sized carrots, sliced
3 stalks from the heart of celery, sliced
1½ pints boiling water or chicken stock
3 oz button mushrooms
1 tablespoon flour
1 egg yolk
3 fl oz double cream
Juice of ½ lemon
Nutmeg
4 oz Comté, Gruyère or Emmenthal cheese, grated

Rub the chicken inside and out with the salt and pepper. In a deep casserole, melt one-third of the butter. Add the chicken and brown it all over. Remove the chicken and set it aside on a plate. Add the leeks, carrots and celery to the butter in the casserole and fry until lightly browned. The butter must not be allowed to burn or the flavour will be spoiled. Return the chicken to the pan, pour in the boiling water or stock and season lightly. Cover the pan and simmer the chicken for 1 hour, or until it is cooked. Transfer the chicken to a serving dish and keep warm in the oven. The chicken can be carved into serving pieces or left whole for more dramatic effect.

Increase the heat and boil the stock down to 15 fluid ounces. Strain the stock, return it to a clean pan and place it over low heat. Meanwhile, melt half the remaining butter in a frying-pan. Add the mushrooms and fry them until they are cooked. Arrange the mushrooms around the chicken.

To finish the sauce, mash the flour with the remaining butter to make a *beurre manié*. Add the *beurre manié* a small piece at a time to the sauce, stirring constantly. In a small bowl, whisk together the egg yolk and cream and stir it into the sauce as a further enrichment. The sauce must not be allowed to boil and it must be stirred constantly. Season with lemon juice, nutmeg and more salt and pepper if necessary.

Preheat the oven to 450°F (Gas Mark 8). Sprinkle the chicken with half the cheese, pressing it down a little into the skin. Pour on the sauce slowly so that it coats the bird without dislodging too much of the cheese. Pour any extra sauce over the mushrooms. Sprinkle the chicken with the remaining cheese and put it into the oven for 5 to 10 minutes to brown or, if the chicken has been cut up, place it under a preheated grill.

Chocolate Cake

This is an unusual cake which is crisp outside and moist and rich inside. It is best when sliced into two layers and spread with apricot jam and served with whipped cream, but it is also good with a chocolate icing.

ONE 8-INCH CAKE

4 oz plain chocolate, preferably French, Belgian or Swiss
4 oz unsalted butter
4 eggs, separated
4 oz vanilla sugar
1 heaped tablespoon flour
2 oz almonds, grated
ICING
4 oz plain chocolate
5 teaspoons sugar
2 tablespoons water
1 oz unsalted butter

Preheat the oven to 350°F (Gas Mark 4). Butter a round 8-inch cake tin with a removable base.

Melt the chocolate in a double boiler or in a bowl placed over a pan of simmering water. Remove from the heat and cool to tepid. Meanwhile, in another bowl, cream the butter until light and fluffy. Beat in the tepid chocolate. Add the egg yolks, one at a time, beating constantly. Beat in the sugar and when the mixture is smooth, fold in the flour and grated almonds. Whisk the egg whites in a bowl until stiff. Fold them carefully into the egg mixture with a large metal spoon. Pour the mixture into the prepared cake tin. Bake the cake for 1 hour, or

until it is cooked. Test by inserting a skewer into the centre of the cake. If it comes out clean the cake is done.

When the cake is cool prepare the icing. Melt the chocolate and the sugar in the water in a double boiler. Add the butter and beat to a smooth consistency. Pour the icing over the cake and spread it evenly with a palette knife, dipped in hot water and then dried.

Madeleines

A plain, but delightful, little shell of a cake with its curved and fluted sides set the writer Marcel Proust off on his majestic novel, A la Recherche du Temps Perdu. He came home one day in winter, weary and depressed. "My mother, seeing that I was cold, offered me some tea . . . she sent out for one of those plump little cakes called petites madeleines, *which look as though they had been moulded in the fluted scallop of a pilgrim's shell. And soon, mechanically . . . I raised to my lips a spoonful of the tea in which I had soaked a morsel of the cake. . . . And suddenly the memory returns. The taste was that of the little crumb of* madeleine *which on Sunday mornings at Combray (because on those mornings I did not go out before church-time), when I went to say goodday to her in her bedroom, my aunt Leonie used to give me, dipping it first in her own cup of tea or of lime-flower tea. . . ."*

Just as Combray, in fact the small town of Illiers near Chartres, was the home of the early part of the novel, so Commercy is the home of madeleines. It is said that Stanislas Leczynski, Duke of Lorraine, made them popular in France. Now one can buy them everywhere, even in plastic bags. There are many recipes, but avoid the ones which begin by whisking eggs and sugar together; the mixture becomes too foamy and the cakes do not develop their characteristic little hump on top.

MAKES ABOUT 24 MADELEINES

3 oz butter
4 oz castor sugar
3 large eggs
Scant 4 oz plain flour
Rounded ½ teaspoon baking powder
1 tablespoon eau de vie or brandy
¼ teaspoon vanilla essence

Preheat the oven to 425°F (Gas Mark 7). Lightly butter 24 shell cake tins and dust with flour.

Cream the butter in a bowl. Add the sugar and beat until light and fluffy. Beat in the eggs one at a time. Sift the flour and baking powder together and fold them into the cake mixture along with the *eau de vie* or brandy and the vanilla essence. Fill the prepared cake tins with the mixture. Bake for 15 minutes, or until the cakes are golden brown and risen in the centre.

Great ingredients married to great skill

BURGUNDY SEEMS almost unfairly blessed with the fruits of the earth and of man's skill. The Charollais provides the best beef in France; the Morvan, some of the best ham, together with honey, game in the forests and goat cheeses.

In the Nivernais, dishes of ham are served with a piquant wine and cream sauce. Veal and beef are garnished *à la Nivernaise*, with small glazed carrots and onions. In the Bresse, they produce the best chickens in France, and the small, creamy, blue-veined cheese, the *bleu de Bresse*.

Near Chablis and south from Dijon, vines cover the low hills in ordered rows. In the vineyards there are huge snails: the *gros Bourgogne* and *Helix pomatia*, which has a beautiful two-inch fawn and white shell. In Dijon, one can choose mustard in an elegant museum of a shop or buy slabs of *pain d'épice*, which looks like gingerbread although the main flavouring is honey. The Burgundian blackcurrant liqueur, *crème de cassis*, transforms water ices and pears cooked in red wine.

In mountain streams and rivers, anglers may catch trout or entice crayfish into bundles of wood tied round a piece of sheep's head, which they find irresistible. Coarse fish are used to make delicious wine stews called *meurettes* and *pochouses*.

As to human skill, think of the Dukes of Burgundy, and their farsighted Chancellor Rolin, who, in the fifteenth century, bought paintings from Van Eyck and Rogier van der Weyden. He built the Hôtel-Dieu at Beaune and insisted on such exigent standards of production that the wines of Burgundy have been famous ever since.

The monks of Cluny, the civilizing centre of medieval northern Europe, could feed kings and their retinue without flurry. In more modern times, Brillat-Savarin, the amiable magistrate and theorist of gastronomy, was another witness to the civilization of Burgundy, as was Colette, who knew better than anyone how to describe the ripeness of a pear or a cheese.

The intertwining in Burgundy of spiritual and material joy is evident in the small church of Montréal, not far from Avallon. The two brothers who carved the wooden stalls are depicted on a bench end, not in attitudes of prayer, but raising their tankards at either end of a table with food on it.

In that part of Burgundy, the best things are the rich cheeses—the orange-coloured Soumaintrains and Epoisses, the Saint-Florentins and Chaources—and the *gougères*, rings of puff pastry flavoured with Gruyère cheese.

The reputation of Burgundy's food does not rest simply on the high quality of the ingredients: there is the matter of skill. For that, one should go to the Côte d'Or at Saulieu. The atmosphere of the dining-room, with its large round tables, is friendly and quite without pretentiousness. There one can choose oysters with a champagne and hollandaise sauce, or delicious little chicken liver gâteaux served with a crayfish sauce, or pike marinated in brandy and Madeira and sauced with Meursault and cream, or Morvan ham in a cream sauce with mushrooms.

Saulieu does not have the social air of a Paris restaurant, where people go to be seen as well as to eat fine food, nor the opulence of businessmen's restaurants in a great commercial town. It has something better: the classless simplicity of many French restaurants where everything combines to stimulate warmth and the pleasures of conversation, a true civilization of ease and *savoir-faire* in which everyone can feel at home.

Berry and the Bourbonnais

Across the Loire to the west, over the high moulded landscape of Sancerre and into the Bourbonnais, the food belongs very much to the farms—prosperous food with an extra touch of skill. Berry, after all, was the centre of a civilized court, although not for as long as Burgundy.

In the cathedral of Bourges, one can walk up to the kneeling statue of Jean, duc de Berry, and smile back at the cheerful, round-faced man who obviously sustained his mind and spirit with the pleasures of the table. He was a generous, endearing prince in times when princes were rarely lovable.

When the brothers Limbourg painted the *Très Riches Heures* for him, they put in plenty of food: pigs fattening for slaughter in the woods, hounds chasing wild boar and peasants reaping corn or working in the vineyards.

This piquant cheerfulness is exemplified by the *piquenchagnes*, the peppered pear tarts of Berry and the Bourbonnais. The fruit is sugared, then peppered before being cooked in a round pastry. Finally thick cream is poured in as a caudle and the pastry has another five minutes in the oven. But the pepper is the thing. It gives the pears a point of flavour that lingers on the tongue. In this region they are very good at pies and tarts.

In the south at Vichy, the cooking is more elegant, as befits a spa. Charollais beef and fine dishes of chicken with cream and tarragon sauce appear on the menus. Here they discovered the best way to cook carrots: glazed, with a spicing of lemon and parsley. This was the home of Louis Diat, head chef of New York's Ritz-Carlton, who sixty years ago invented *crème vichyssoise glacé*, based on his mother's leek and potato soup.

VALENÇAY
GOATS' CHEESE

LEVROUX
GOATS' CHEESE

GAME

TENC

CHATE

LE BLANC

TERRINE
BERRICHONNE
Rabbit in aspic

TÊTE DE VEAU
Calf's head

CARPES FARCIES
Stuffed carp

BURGUNDY
NIVERNAIS
BERRY
BOURBONNAIS

MATELOTE
Fresh-water fish stew

SENS

SOUMAINTRAIN

FROMAGE A PATE MOLLE
Cheese

JOIGNY

MERINGUES

TONNERRE

B

SNAILS

CHABLIS

AUXERRE

ST BRIS

ANDOUILLETTES
Tripe Sausages

GOUGERE
Cheese pastry

U

SNAILS

MEURETTE
Fresh-water fish stew

CHERRIES

CHEESE

EPOISSES

MUSTARD

CASSIS
Black currant liqueur

E AUX TRUCHES
tatoes

GROTTINS
Goats' cheeses

VEZELAY

**OREILLER
DE LA
BELLE
AURORE**
Game pâté

ANISEED

FLAVIGNY

R

**PATE CHAUD
DE BECASSES**
Hot woodcock pie

DIJON

CHAVIGNOL

GOATS' CHEESE

SANCERRE

WALNUTS

SAULIEU

CRAYFISH

JAMBON PERSILLE
Ham and parsley in aspic

PAIN D'EPICES
Spiced honey cake

**ROGNONS
DE MOUTON**
Sheep's kidneys

ANDOUILLES
Large tripe sausages

BOURGES

ARNAY-LE-DUC

GAME

PORK

BEAUNE

G

**ESSES
CHONNES**
paste sweets

NOUGATINES
Small nougat sweets

SAUCE MEURETTE
Red wine sauce with onions, carrots and garlic

VERDUN-SUR-LE-DOUBS

TARTE BOURBONNAISE
Country cheesecake

NEVERS

CATTLE

POCHOUSE
Fresh-water fish stew

GRENADINS DE VEAU A LA NIVERNAISE
Veal steaks with glazed carrots and onions

DECIZE

RIVER SAONE

ST. AMAND MONTROND

RIVER LOIRE

LIEVRE A LA DUCHAMBAIS
Hare stuffed with calves' liver

SAUPIQUET
Ham in cream sauce

**ONIONS
CARROTS**

PORK PRODUCTS

LOUHANS

wine sauce

CHICKENS

U

MOULINS

PRALINES
Sugared almonds

BEEF

OYONNADE
Jugged goose

POMPE AUX GRATTONS
Savoury brioche bread

CHAROLLES

BLEU DE BRESSE
Small, Gorgonzola-like cheese

**LANGUES DE MOUTON
AUX NAVETS**
Sheep's tongues with turnips

PIKE

Z

MONTLUCON

VERITES
Coffee and chocolate flavoured sweets

BOEUF A LA BOURGUIGNONNE
Beef in red wine with onions and mushrooms

MACON

QUENELLES DE BROCHET NANTUA
Pike dumplings in creamy sauce

E AU FOUR
carp

LA PALISSE

COQ AU VIN

BOURG-EN-BRESSE

BRIOCHE DE GANNAT
Cheese brioche

VICHY

TOURTE A LA VIANDE ET A LA VOLAILLE
Meat and chicken pie

CHICKENS

NANTUA

GANNAT

POULET VICHY
Braised stuffed chicken in cream sauce

ECREVISSES A LA NANTUA
Crayfish in creamy sauce

PATE AUX FRUITS
Fruit paste

CAROTTES A LA VICHY
Glazed carrots cooked in Vichy water

WOODCOCK

CRAYFISH

FROGS' LEGS

TROUT

BELLEY

A sampling of a historic cuisine

Easter Pie from Berry
PATE DE PAQUES

As might be expected with the wheatfields of the Beauce so near, the people of Berry are as skilful at making pâté encased in pastry as are the Orléanais. Being farther from the capital, one does not find such elaborations, such fine mixtures as the exquisite lark pâtés of Chartres and Pithiviers, but they are very good and suitable for making at home. This recipe in particular is excellent. The eggs in the filling and the coffin shape are in reference to Easter, but there is no reason why it should not be made at any time of the year.

SERVES 6

1½ lb weight short crust pastry
Beaten egg, for glazing
FILLING

12 oz lean veal
12 oz lean pork
4 fl oz dry white wine
2 tablespoons eau de vie or Madeira
2 tablespoons chopped parsley
Salt
Freshly ground black pepper
1 medium-sized onion, finely chopped
2 oz butter
6 oz mushrooms, sliced
Grated nutmeg
Ground cloves
6 hard-boiled eggs, cut in half lengthways

To make the filling, cut the veal and pork into small pieces, put in a bowl, cover with the white wine and *eau de vie* or Madeira and refrigerate overnight.

The next day, mince the meat. Add the parsley and salt and pepper to taste.

In a small saucepan, cook the onion in the butter over low heat until it is soft but not brown. Add the mushrooms and cook for 5 minutes. Season with the nutmeg, cloves, salt and pepper to taste.

Preheat the oven to 350°F (Gas Mark 4).

Roll out two-thirds of the dough into a large rectangle and put it on a baking sheet. Leaving a 2- to 3-inch margin all around, spread half the mixture in the middle. Spread half the onion and mushroom mixture over the meat. Arrange the egg halves in a double row on top and put the remaining onion and mushroom mixture in between them. Cover with the remaining meat mixture.

Cut out an arrow-head shape at each corner of the dough rectangle. Brush the edges with the beaten egg and bend them up, pinching the edges together so that the pastry forms a coffin around the filling.

Roll out the remaining dough to the shape of a lid. Lay it on top of the pie and pinch the edges together to make a close seal.

Slash the top, decorate with two lines of pastry leaves and brush all over with beaten egg.

Bake for 1½ hours. Serve cold or just warm with a green salad.

Beef Stewed in the Burgundy Style
BOEUF A LA BOURGUIGNONNE

This best of all stews can be made with meat other than beef, venison or ox tail, for example. When the recipe involves chicken, it is known as coq au vin. *The method is to marinate and cook the meat in a red wine sauce, and to serve it with the Burgundy garnish of button mushrooms fried in butter, glazed onions and triangles of bread fried in butter.*

SERVES 6

3 lb chuck, topside or stewing steak, cut in 1½-inch cubes
MARINADE

1¼ pints red burgundy
4 fl oz brandy
1 large onion, sliced
Bouquet garni
Rosemary sprig (optional)
12 peppercorns
1 teaspoon salt
SAUCE

2 oz beef dripping or butter
8 oz streaky bacon, cut in strips
2 large onions, chopped
2 large carrots, diced
3 garlic cloves, crushed
1 heaped tablespoon flour
Beef stock
Bouquet garni
Salt
Freshly ground black pepper
1 tablespoon sugar (optional)
GARNISH

1½ lb small or pickling onions
1 tablespoon castor sugar
4 oz butter
Salt
Freshly ground black pepper
12 oz tiny button mushrooms
6 slices of white bread, cut into triangles
1 tablespoon oil
Chopped parsley

Put the meat into a large bowl. Mix all the ingredients for the marinade and pour it over the beef. Cover the bowl and set it aside for at least 6 hours.

Remove the meat from the marinade and dry on absorbent paper. Strain the marinade. Melt the dripping or butter in a large, heavy frying-pan. Add the bacon strips and fry until lightly browned. Transfer the bacon to a large casserole. Brown the meat next, then the onions, carrots and garlic. Add them to the casserole in their turn. Stir the flour into the pan juices, cook for 2 minutes, then add the strained marinade to make a smooth sauce. Pour the sauce into the casserole with enough stock to cover the meat and bring to a boil. Add the *bouquet garni* and salt and pepper to taste. If the wine used in the marinade was a substitute for the burgundy, add the sugar as well. Reduce the heat to low, cover and simmer on top of the stove or in a 350°F (Gas Mark 4) oven for 2 to 3 hours, or until the meat is tender.

Meanwhile prepare the garnish. Put the onions in a single layer in a large pan. Add the sugar, 1 ounce of the butter, a little salt and pepper, enough water to cover and bring to the boil. Boil hard until the water is reduced to a syrupy brown juice and the onions are cooked. Shake the pan occasionally so that the onions are coated and become an appetizing brown, but be careful not to let them burn. Cook the mushrooms in another 1 ounce of the butter. Fry the bread in the remaining butter and the oil. Keep the garnish warm.

When the meat is cooked, remove the pieces with a slotted spoon and put them in a large shallow dish—an oval *gratin* dish is ideal—and distribute the garnish over and around the meat in a decorative way. Reduce the sauce by boiling it down a little so that the flavour is rich and concentrated. Pour some of the sauce over the meat, sprinkle with the parsley and serve. The remaining sauce can be served separately in a sauceboat.

Roast Pork with Red Cabbage and Chestnuts
ROTI DE PORC A LA BOURBONNAISE

Food in the Bourbonnais, as in Berry, is substantial rather than brilliant. It belongs to farm and prosperous merchants' homes, the food of well-provided family life.

SERVES 6

3 lb boned loin of pork
Salt
Freshly ground black pepper
1 heaped teaspoon castor sugar
1 large garlic clove, slivered
2 lb chestnuts, nicked, blanched and peeled
6 fl oz veal or light beef stock
GARNISH

1 red cabbage
8 oz smoked streaky bacon, cut into small strips
2 oz butter
6 fl oz red wine
Salt
Freshly ground black pepper
1 bay leaf
Brown sugar

The day before this dish is to be served, spread out the pork, fat side down, and sprinkle with salt, pepper and the sugar. Make cuts in the meat and insert the garlic slivers. Roll the pork and

tie it. Cover the meat and refrigerate it until it is required.

Meanwhile make the garnish. Slice the red cabbage and blanch for 5 minutes in boiling salted water. Drain in a colander. In a large saucepan, brown the bacon lightly in the butter. Add the cabbage and stir well. Pour in the wine, season with salt and pepper and add the bay leaf. Cover the pan and simmer for 1 hour, or until the cabbage is cooked. Taste and adjust the seasoning, adding brown sugar if desired.

The next day, roast the pork in the usual way in a 375°F oven (Gas Mark 5), allowing 30 minutes per pound. Add the chestnuts and stock to the roasting tin halfway through the cooking time.

To serve, remove the pork from the tin and place it on a heated platter. Remove the chestnuts from the tin and mix them with the reheated red cabbage. Arrange the cabbage and chestnut mixture around the pork. Taste the juices in the roasting tin and adjust the seasoning or boil down to concentrate the flavour. Pour enough of the sauce over the pork so that the dish is moist but not soggy and wet.

Ham with Cream Sauce
JAMBON A LA CREME

A favourite dish in Burgundy and the Nivernais consists of slices of ham spread out on a dish, covered with a cream sauce and browned under the grill or in a hot oven. This simple formula always delights people out of all proportion to the time and trouble involved in preparing it. The one important thing is to make sure that the sauce is worthy of the ham.

SERVES 4

8 slices of cooked ham
SAUPIQUET DES AMOGNES
4 shallots, finely chopped
3 juniper berries, crushed
6 tablespoons white wine vinegar
1 oz butter
2 tablespoons flour
8 fl oz good beef stock, heated
8 tablespoons dry white wine
Salt
Pepper
7 fl oz double cream
Extra pat of butter
Breadcrumbs

Arrange the ham slices in a shallow baking dish. In a small saucepan cook the shallots and juniper berries in the wine vinegar until all the liquid has evaporated.

Meanwhile, melt the butter in another pan. Stir in the flour and cook gently until the *roux* is a pale coffee colour. Pour in the heated beef stock gradually, stirring constantly. Add the wine, the shallot mixture, salt and pepper to taste and, stirring occasionally, cook over low heat for 30 minutes.

Preheat the oven to 425°F (Gas Mark 7).

Bring the cream to boiling point in a small pan. Stir the cream into the sauce. Remove the pan from the heat and stir in the extra butter. Pour the sauce over the ham, sprinkle a few breadcrumbs over the top and place in the oven for 20 minutes, or until the top is lightly browned.

Chicken Derby
POULARDE DERBY

Although the English had started their peaceful invasion of the Côte d'Azur as early as the 1830s, the real signal for the desecration of this quiet coast was the opening of the Casino at Monte Carlo in 1861. At first it was all very smart. Kings and princes went there to enjoy the winter sun, to gamble at the Casino—and to eat the exquisite food provided by Escoffier at the Grand Hotel. There, in 1881, he served to the Prince of Wales, poularde Derby, a new dish he had invented in his honour. This is a royally simple dish.

SERVES 4 TO 6

5 oz long-grain rice, boiled
1 fat roasting chicken
1 chicken liver, chopped
7 truffles, washed and scrubbed
Salt
Freshly ground black pepper
3 oz butter
6 fl oz hot water
6 fl oz champagne
6 slices bread, fried in butter
4 oz foie gras

Take as much of the rice as will fill the cavity of the chicken loosely and mix it with the chicken liver and 1 chopped truffle. Season well with salt and pepper and stuff the bird.

Melt the butter in a deep, flameproof casserole and brown the chicken all over, but not too fast or the butter will burn. Add salt, pepper and the hot water. Cover the casserole and cook gently, turning the bird over twice, for 1 to 1½ hours, or until it is cooked. If necessary, replenish the water so that the juices do not burn.

Meanwhile simmer the truffles in the champagne for 10 minutes. Season with salt and pepper.

When the chicken is cooked, remove it from the pan and cut it into 6 pieces. Arrange the chicken pieces around the stuffing on a heated serving dish. Spread the *croûtons* of bread with the *foie gras* and arrange them alternately with the chicken pieces. Place the whole truffles on top of the *foie gras*. Add the truffle juices to the chicken juices and boil them over high heat. Pour the juices over the chicken and serve.

Cherry Batter Cake
CLAFOUTIS AUX CERISES NOIRES

Clafoutis is a fruit dessert much eaten in central France, particularly when the black cherries are sweet and ripe. Other fruit can be used instead.

SERVES 6

2 oz butter
4 eggs
4 oz castor sugar
4 oz plain flour
2 tablespoons melted butter
10 fl oz milk
2 tablespoons kirsch
⅛ teaspoon salt
1 lb ripe, black cherries, stoned

Preheat the oven to 425°F (Gas Mark 7). Using half the butter, grease an oblong baking tin, measuring about 7 x 11 x 1¼ inches.

In a large bowl, whisk the eggs and sugar together until they become thick and foamy. Still whisking, add the flour slowly, then the melted butter, milk, kirsch and salt. Pour a ¼-inch layer of the batter into the prepared baking tin. Bake for 5 minutes, or until the batter just sets. Cover with the cherries and pour the remaining batter over the top. Dot the remaining butter over the top and bake for a further 30 minutes. If the top begins to brown too much, cover with aluminium foil.

Sprinkle with sugar and serve warm or cold.

IN THIS WORLD HEADQUARTERS of food and drink, it is hard to know where to start and harder still to know when to stop. There is a choice of three great styles of dry white wine. From the Côte d'Or around Beaune there are the classic white wines—Meursault, Corton-Charlemagne and the Montrachets—and their near-relations, the white Mâcon wines (Pouilly-Fuissé, Mâcon-Viré, Mâcon and St-Véran) from further south. There is the highly individual, pungent, stony Chablis from the north. And there are the more perfumed whites of the upper Loire—Sancerre, Pouilly-Fumé and Quincy from Berry.

Burgundian cooking expects, and indeed needs, to be appreciated with burgundian wine. Red burgundy is the most sumptuously savoury of all red wines, varying in depth and concentration of flavour from the intense and massive Chambertin, the northernmost of the reds, to the fruity but ephemeral Beaujolais of the south. Prestige and demand have made the great burgundies great luxuries today. They seem to cost even more in Beaune, the wine capital, than abroad. Nonetheless, a bottle of a great vintage (the vintage matters almost more than the vineyard) is something no one should deny himself in Burgundy.

Hearty food in the mountains

Although the Auvergne is the solid mountain centre of France—the great Massif Central—it is a land of lumps and bumps and unexpected dips rather than a land of mountainous drama like the Alps. The name comes from the Arverni, the Gallic tribe whose young leader, Vercingetorix, won a victory over Caesar in 52 BC. The area's cooking, however, cannot lay claim to such spectacular fame. In general, the local dishes can be best described as comforting and solid.

Like other mountainous parts of France, the Auvergne is famous for ham. It is also well known for dishes which include the hard Cantal cheese; *soupe de Cantal*, an onion soup so thickened with slices of toasted bread and cheese that it will hold a spoon upright; eggs in the Cantal style, baked in the oven with yolks set in the stiffly beaten whites and covered with cheese and cream; and *truffade*, a potato and cheese cake cooked until brown and crisp in the frying-pan.

One great speciality is the succulent *tripoux*—packages of sheep's tripe stuffed with smoked fat bacon, ham, chitterlings, parsley, garlic and spices—which are cooked for hours in white wine.

The finest "vale of beautiful verdure" is the Limagne, near Clermont-Ferrand and Riom, one of France's great grain-growing areas. Vines cover the slopes at the edge of the valley and there are orchards everywhere. Here is grown the soft fruit for the glacé-fruit industry of Clermont-Ferrand and Riom, which provides the angelica and delicious candied apricots and strawberries that brighten Christmas.

The Lyonnais and the Bas-Dauphine
It is easy to see how the Rhône makes a natural pathway into France, and how in the past a combination of the rivers Rhône, Saône, Loire and Seine linked people in the north with the Mediterranean centre of civilization. Before the railways, many people made the journey in *coches d'eau*, river boats which made regular stops for food and sleep along the banks. This chain of river ports still dominates the fine cooking of the area.

This part of France has the best of everything. From the north come wine from Burgundy, chickens from Bresse and beef from Charollais; from the south, a dazzling abundance of fruit and vegetables is supplied.

The way in which women have always ruled the restaurants of the Lyonnais contradicts the tradition of French cooking. The most famous woman restaurateur was Mère Fillioux, who made a speciality of *volaille truffée demi-deuil* (truffled chicken in half-mourning). Discs of black truffle were slipped under the transparent skin of the bird before it was poached in an aromatic stock with vegetables, which accounts for the name of the dish, as well as for the reputation of her restaurant.

The menu and tradition were carried on by Mère Brazier, once cook at the Fillioux establishments, at two restaurants, one in Lyon itself, the other thirteen miles outside the town at Col de la Luère. Other names on the list of restaurants recall this strong feminine tradition, in particular the elegant restaurant of *La Mère Guy*. To the north of Lyon at Mionnay is the *chez la Mère Charles*, which has the same rich choice of dishes: hot eel pie, lobster and truffle salad and chickens boiled in a bladder along with such delicious delicacies as truffles and *foie gras*, brandy and white wine.

After these feasts, nothing is nicer than a *bonne bouche* of nougat. Few sweets are as good as soft nougat bought in the main street of Montélimar, and made from local almonds and honey from Provence and the Alps.

The Savoie and the Dauphiné Alps
This Alpine country forms France's massive and busy frontier with Italy. Its very names have a noble and impressive sound: from the Dauphiné, the heirs of French kings, the Dauphins took their title. Here, amid the jagged mountains and deep valleys, the famous winter sports centres and spas, is regal and impressive food. Excellent cooking abounds in Aix-les-bains, Evian, Albertville and Chamonix, while Sassenage and Tailloires are places of sheer gourmet delight. Even in tourist-ridden La Chambotte, poised over the Lac du Bourget, ther is good food.

Freshness of flavour is the keynote Piquant crayfish are set off in a rich sauce Trout and local varieties of char and white fish come to the table at their best, straigh from the lakes and mountain streams Creamy, cheese-flavoured *gratins* of potatoe with onion and a hint of garlic, or *matefaim* a crisp and puffy pancake (something like Yorkshire pudding), accompany the excel lent lamb and beef of the Alpine pastures The taste of chicken becomes more mem

orable because of the *cèpes* or *girolles* mush rooms and the tiny, crisp slivers of salt pork or bacon which surround it.

Freshness and elegant skill are found a their best in the *Père Bise* restaurant at Tal loires. Over a dish of chicken with tarrago cream sauce, visitors may recover from the appalling traffic which encircles the lake Walking down to the lake afterwards through the garden, is to be back in the peaceful days when Cézanne painted hi majestic view from Talloires, looking acros to the wooded headland of Duingt.

LYONNAIS SAVOY AUVERGNE DAUPHINE

TIMBALE DE FOIES DE LOTTE
Moulded turbot livers

FERA
Fresh-water fish

THONON
EVIAN

FISH SOUP
ABONDANCE

LONGEOLE
Country sausage

VACHERIN
Cheese

HAM

EELS
ANNEMASSE

SIXT

ONIONS

TANINGES
TOME
Cheese

CHARLIEU
ANDOUILLES
Large tripe sausages

MUSHROOMS

CERVELLE DE CANUT
White cheese with herbs

OMBLE CHEVALIER
Char

TROUT
CHAMONIX

ROANNE

FONDS D'ARTICHAUTS AU FOIE GRAS
Artichoke hearts with foie gras

CIVET DE LIEVRE
Jugged hare

PEACHES

ANNECY

SABLES
Shortbread
NOIRETABLE

CERVELAS TRUFFE
Truffled pork sausage

POTEE SAVOYARDE
Pork and vegetable soup

TROUT

BEAUFORT CHEESE

FARCON
Creamed potatoes with cheese and eggs

BEAUFORT

FEURS
ROSETTES
Lyonnais pure pork sausages

LYON
GRAS DOUBLE
Tripe

AIX-LES-BAINS
ALBERTVILLE

SALMON

POULET CELESTINE
Chicken sautéed with tomatoes, wine and cream

ONIONS
ST. GENIS

VERMOUTH

NOUILLES
AUX OEUFS
Egg noodles

AIGUEBLANCHE

AMBER
FOURME
Cheese

RIGOTTES
Small round cheeses

GATEAU DE SAVOIE
Sponge cake

CHAMBERY

ESCARGOTS EN BROCHETTE
Snails on skewers

ST-ANTHEME

VIENNE
CONDRIEU

GRATIN SAVOYARD
Potato baked with cheese

WILD MUSHROOMS

ST-ETIENNE

DAUBE A LA VIENNOISE
Beef braised in wine

GRATIN DE MORILLES
Morels in cheese sauce

MATELOTE
Fresh-water fish stew

CATIGOT
Eel and carp stewed in wine

CHEESE

PIKE

OMBLE CHEVALIER
Char

QUENELLES DE BROCHETS
Pike dumplings

POGNES
Sweet brioche rings

SASSENAGE
GRENOBLE

RED-LEGGED PARTRIDGE

ST-MARCELLIN

WALNUTS

HAZEL GROUSE

TOMME
Cheese

GRATIN DAUPHINOIS
Thinly sliced potatoes baked with cream

ROMANS

WOODCOCK

MERINGUES

VALENCE

CHABEUIL

CAILLETTES
Faggots

BRIANCON

PATE DE GRIVES DES ALPES
Alpine thrush pâté

TROUT

FRITURE DE GOUJONS
Deep-fried gudgeon

GAME

CREST

GRATIN DE QUEUES D'ECREVISSES
Baked crayfish tails in cream sauce

PORK

DEFARDE
Lamb's trotters and tripe casserole

NOUGAT
MONTELIMAR

GRATIN DE MACARONI
Macaroni baked in cheese

LAMB

GAP

TOURONS AU MIEL
Honey nougat cakes

PEACHES

APRICOTS

GRATIN DE CEPES
Mushrooms baked in cheese sauce

GRAS-DOUBLE DAUPHINOIS
Tripe baked in cheese sauce

GRAPES

NYONS

TRUFFLES

133

Unusual recipes from the French Alps

Cream Cheese with Herbs
CERVELLE DE CANUT

This refreshing mixture of cream cheese and herbs is the best version of a dish which is eaten all over France, either during the cheese course or as a snack with drinks. The traditional mould for this sort of cheese in France is called a faiselle. An alternative is to use a plastic pot and make holes in it with a heated skewer.

8 oz curd cheese
1 shallot, finely chopped
1 heaped tablespoon finely chopped fresh
  parsley
1 heaped tablespoon finely chopped chervil
1 heaped tablespoon finely chopped chives
8 fl oz double cream, whipped
3 tablespoons oil
3 tablespoons wine vinegar
Salt
Freshly ground black pepper

Mix the cheese, shallot and herbs together in a bowl. Fold in the whipped cream, then the oil and vinegar. Season to taste. Line a pierced mould with muslin and put the cheese into it to drain for two or three hours or longer.

Turn out the cheese on to a dish and surround it with such salad vegetables as radishes, carrot sticks and celery. Serve with rye bread and butter.

Veal and Pork Pate in Crust
PATE PANTIN FERDINAND WERNERT

Pâtés cooked in a pastry crust look special even if the mixture inside is quite simple. This recipe comes from the famous restaurant of Paul Bocuse, just outside Lyons at Collonges-au-Mont d'Or. It can be enriched with strips of chicken and game —or with truffles and foie gras. Spiced salt (sel épicé) is salt seasoned with white pepper and mixed spices and used to season forcemeats.

SERVES 6 TO 8

PASTRY
1 lb plain flour
3 teaspoons salt
6 oz butter
2 oz lard
1 egg
Cold water
FILLING
1 lb veal fillet
2 thin sheets pork back fat measuring 12 × 8
  inches plus extra back fat to bring total
  weight to 1 lb
8 oz lean raw ham
4 fl oz brandy
2 to 3 teaspoons spiced salt
Freshly ground black pepper
Dried thyme

Crumbled bay leaf
8 oz pork fillet
2 eggs
Beaten egg for glazing

First make the pastry. Sift the dry ingredients into a large bowl. Add the fats and cut them into the flour with a knife. Crumble the fat into the flour until the mixture resembles fine breadcrumbs. Make a well in the centre and drop in the egg. Mix it in with enough cold water to make a smooth dough. Shape the dough into a ball, cover it and place it in the refrigerator for 30 minutes.

Meanwhile, from the veal cut off 8 strips 6 inches long and just under ¼ inch thick. Do the same with the extra pork fat and the ham. Put the meat and fat strips in a bowl. Combine the brandy, salt, pepper and a pinch of thyme and bay leaf and pour over the meat and fat strips. Set aside to marinate.

Mince the remaining veal, fat and ham with the pork fillet and put in a bowl. Mix in the eggs and season to taste with the salt, pepper, thyme and bay leaf.

Preheat the oven to 350°F (Gas Mark 4). Remove the meat and fat strips from the marinade.

Remove the dough from the refrigerator, break off three quarters of it and roll it out into a rectangle measuring 14 × 10 inches. Place a sheet of fat in the centre of the dough rectangle. On it layer the minced meat mixture and the meat and fat strips alternately, beginning and ending with the minced meat. Lay the second piece of fat on top. Bring up the long sides of the dough, then the short sides so that the paté is enclosed. Dampen the dough to make the edges join well. Roll out the remaining dough to form the lid and fit it on, joining it firmly to the dough sides. Brush with the beaten egg to glaze and decorate with lightly scored lines and pastry leaves. Make a hole in the centre of the lid.

Bake for 1½ hours, protecting the top of the paté with foil when it is nicely browned. Serve warm or cold.

Braised Beef in Jelly
PIECE DE BOEUF A LA ROYALE

Boeuf a la Mode, beef larded and braised with carrots and wine, is one of the best dishes of French bourgeois cooking. Here is an elegant version, which came originally from Marius Guillot, who had a restaurant in Lyons, and was a close friend of Fernand Point, the proprietor of the Pyramide at Vienne, where this noble dish is still served. If a calf's foot is not available use 2 pig's trotters.

SERVES 12

6 lb piece beef rump
7 strips pork fat, seasoned
6 strips uncooked ham, seasoned
2½ oz butter
1 tablespoon olive oil
3 large carrots, halved
2 large onions, halved
8 fl oz cognac
1 bottle dry champagne
Strong beef stock
1 calf's foot, split, blanched
  and rinsed
8 oz pork fat, blanched and rinsed in cold
  water
8 medium-sized tomatoes, blanched, peeled,
  seeded and chopped
6 garlic cloves
1 small celery stick
Bouquet garni of parsley, chervil, thyme
  and tarragon
2 tablespoons peppercorns
Salt

Preheat the oven to 350°F (Gas Mark 4).

Lard the beef with the pork and ham strips and tie it up. In a large, deep casserole, heat the butter and the oil. Add the beef and brown it together with the carrots and onions. Pour the cognac over the beef and light it. Turn the meat in the flames and pour over the champagne and enough stock to cover. Add the calf's foot or pig's trotters, the fat, tomatoes, garlic and celery. Bring to the boil and add the *bouquet*

LYON is a city on three rivers, the local saying goes, the Rhône, the Saône and the Beaujolais. Beaujolais in uncountable little half-litre *pots* is the recommended lubricant for almost every Lyonnais dish. A great deal of it is drunk *en primeur*, fresh and new, in the winter following the vintage. When the vintage is a good one the Beaujolais Nouveau is at the same time richly plummy and almost gauzily light. It is no good sipping it—it goes down naturally in uninhibited swallows.

With the exception of the Rhône's very finest vineyards, the red Côte Rôtie and the white Château Grillet, at Condrieu just south of Lyon, the mountainous terrain of the rest of these regions from the Massif Central to Savoie gives light wines, of no consequence outside their districts but often irresistibly fresh and lively with the local cooking.

The main red grape, both in Savoie and the Auvergne, is the Gamay of Beaujolais. The Auvergnat Chanturgues is perhaps its best-known product in these lesser regions.

Chambéry in Savoie makes what many consider the world's best vermouth in the pale and hereby French style. Better still is a version which is flavoured and rose-tinted with wild strawberries.

garni and peppercorns. Cover the pan and place it in the oven for 2½ hours.

Remove the beef and put it in another large pan. Strain the stock and skim off the fat. Pour the strained stock over the beef and bring to the boil.

Reduce the heat to low, cover the pan and simmer the beef for 1½ hours, or until it is tender, turning it from time to time.

When the beef is tender, put it into a terrine which fits it closely. Taste the stock and add salt if necessary. Strain the stock over the beef, which it should cover. Cover the terrine with foil and refrigerate for 24 hours. Unmould the beef on to a plate or leave it in the terrine, cutting it down into slices. Serve with a green salad.

Braised Chicken with Tarragon Cream Sauce
POULARDE BRAISEE A LA CREME D'ESTRAGON

The word "classic" can be defined as meaning "the best of its kind". Chicken with tarragon cream sauce is truly a classic of French cooking. There are many versions, although all involve chicken, tarragon and cream. This recipe is from the Auberge du Père Bise, on the shore of Lake Annecy. Because herbs increase in flavour with the sun, northern tarragon may have to be used in greater quantity to achieve the same effect. Fresh, not dried, tarragon must be used.

SERVES 4

4 lb fat chicken with giblets
Salt
Freshly ground black pepper
1 bunch fresh tarragon
1 oz butter
5 tablespoons chicken stock
6 tablespoons double cream
Chopped tarragon

Season the inside of the chicken with salt and pepper and tuck the bunch of tarragon in the cavity.

Melt the butter in a deep, flameproof casserole and brown the chicken gently until it is a light golden colour. Slip the giblets underneath the bird, add the stock and cover the pan. Simmer on slow heat for 40 minutes, or until the chicken is cooked. Because of the gentle heat the cooking juices should be a pale colour, neither brown nor burned. Remove the tarragon from the chicken and discard it. Leave the chicken for another few minutes before cutting it up and placing it on a heated serving dish.

Stir the cream into the pan juices, correct the seasoning, and heat the sauce thoroughly. Pour the sauce through a strainer over the chicken. Add a small sprinkling of chopped tarragon and serve very hot.

Gratins of Savoy
GRATINS SAVOYARD

The gratins of Savoie, Dauphiné and Auvergne, the mountain districts of the south, have become the best loved dishes of French cookery. This is, in part, because they are simple to make at home. But the inspired, irresistible point of any gratin is the way in which the food is spread out so that there is a maximum of golden-brown crustiness on top.

The general principle in making a gratin is always the same. First choose a large, shallow, round or oval dish about 12 inches in diameter. Butter it more or less lavishly according to the sticking powers of the main ingredient. Layer the main ingredient with the flavourings, pour over cream or a creamy sauce, and dot the top with butter or butter and cheese. Leave in a fairly hot oven (425°F, Gas Mark 8) for a short time if the main ingredient is already cooked, or in a slow oven (325°F, Gas Mark 3) for 1½ hours.

SERVES 4 TO 6

Butter
2 lb potatoes, peeled and thinly sliced
4 oz Gruyère cheese, grated
1 garlic clove, finely chopped
10 fl oz milk *or* beef stock *or* water
Salt
Pepper
TOPPING
2 tablespoons grated Gruyère cheese
1½ oz butter, cut into small pieces

Preheat the oven to 325°F (Gas Mark 3). Generously grease a *gratin* dish with butter.

Layer the potatoes, cheese, garlic and seasonings in the dish, ending with the potatoes. Pour over the milk, stock or water. Sprinkle over the 2 tablespoons Gruyère cheese and dot the top with the butter. Bake for 1½ hours, or until the potatoes are cooked through. If the top is not brown enough put the dish under a hot grill for 1 or 2 minutes.

Gratin with Mushrooms
GRATIN AUX CEPES

This is the best gratin of all because cèpes have such a perfect affinity with potatoes. Even ordinary cultivated mushrooms give quite a good result. It can be served on its own, or with lamb, chicken or beef.

SERVES 6

Butter
2 lb potatoes, peeled and thinly sliced
1½ lb cèpes, sliced
4 tablespoons finely chopped onion
4 tablespoons finely chopped parsley
6 tablespoons Gruyère cheese

1 garlic clove, finely chopped
Salt
Pepper
10 fl oz double cream
2 fl oz water
TOPPING
1 oz butter, cut into pieces
3 tablespoons grated Gruyère cheese

Generously grease a *gratin* dish with butter. Preheat the oven to 325°F (Gas Mark 3).

Layer the potatoes and *cèpes* in the dish, sprinkling each layer with the onion, parsley, cheese, garlic and seasoning. Combine the cream and water in a small saucepan and bring to just under boiling point. Pour over the dish. Sprinkle the butter and cheese over the top. Bake for 1½ hours, or until the potatoes are cooked through.

Apple and Apricot Tart
TARTE PANACHÉE MIRLTON

The river Loire rises in the volcanic mountains of the Velay and comes down through gorges to its first valley, the plain of Forez. Here on the Loire itself is Montrond les Bains, where this recipe comes from.

SERVES 6

12 oz weight sweet shortcrust pastry
FILLING
4 oz butter
1½ lb crisp dessert apples, peeled, cored and sliced
5 oz castor sugar
4 tablespoons rum
6 fresh apricots, halved and stoned
MIRLETON CREAM
2 large eggs
2½ oz icing sugar
2½ oz ground almonds
8 fl oz double cream

Preheat the oven to 425°F (Gas Mark 7). Roll out the dough and line a 10-inch tart tin with a removable base.

Melt the butter in a large frying-pan. Add the apples and the sugar. Cook, turning the slices over, until they are golden-brown and the juice is slightly caramelized. Flame with the rum. Remove the pan from the heat and set aside to cool slightly. Arrange the apple slices in an even layer in the lined tart tin. Put the apricots on top, cut side down. Bake the tart for 20 minutes, or until the pastry is nicely browned. Remove from the oven and set aside to cool.

Reset the oven to 350°F (Gas Mark 4). In a small bowl, beat the eggs, sugar, ground almonds and cream together. Pour the cream mixture over the tart and bake for 20 to 25 minutes, or until the cream is set and the fruit heated through. Serve the tart warm.

From oyster beds to the vineyards of Cognac

The Charentes coastline is a strange area of sand dunes and pines, of rocks and occasional cliffs and flat, silted or reclaimed bays. The tides and winds of the Atlantic have worked continually, eating away the softer rock, leaving the resistant parts to form offshore islands like the Isles de Noirmoutier, d'Yeu, de Ré and d'Oléron. Around the Marais of the River Sèvre Niortaise are inland cliffs which were once washed by the sea.

The gentle sloping of land into sea makes this area ideal for mussel and oyster farming. Mussel farming is said to have started here in the 1250s by an Irishman who was shipwrecked to the north of La Rochelle. He kept alive by netting birds on the shallow coast. One day he noticed that colonies of mussels had grouped themselves tightly around his net supports. He gave up birds for mussels and in time the beaches began to bristle with rows of posts known as *bouchots*. At low tide, mussel farmers punt themselves along these lines of posts in flat-bottomed boats called *accons*, which are also claimed as an invention of the resourceful Irishman.

The big centres for mussels, the tiny, sweet ones labelled *bouchots* in the markets, are Fouras and Aiguillon. Mussel stews, *mouclades*, made with white wine, cream and different seasonings, such as saffron or aniseed, are favourite dishes in the Aunis, the district centred on La Rochelle.

There are two main types of oyster in Europe: the round, flat *Ostrea edulis*, the finest for flavour, and the longer, knobbly-shelled *Crassostrea angulata*, or Portuguese oyster, a more resistant type grown predominantly in the area of Marennes and La Tremblade. The beautiful green colour and the particularly good flavour of oysters from Marennes are caused by algae called the *navicule bleu*.

Huge trawlers go out from La Rochelle after tuna—and sometimes return with a catch of swordfish instead. Down at Royan, a popular seaside resort at the mouth of the Gironde, sardines are plentiful. More precious from a financial point of view are the salmon and shad of the Gironde, and the sturgeon which provides caviar. La Cotinière, on the Isle d'Oléron, is the biggest French port for shrimp.

In the spring, there is the fishing for elvers, the tiny, thready inch-long creatures which have swum from the Sargasso Sea to mature in the fresh waters of Europe. Here they are called *piballe*, at the mouth of the Liore *civelle*.

The other water speciality of the Charentes maritime is frogs' legs, although the local population of frogs has long since disappeared and huge quantities are imported.

This strange country of the Marais, which runs inland from the bay of Aiguillon, has been created, structured and reclaimed by man—as well as by the tides—since the eleventh century. On the coast there are dams and polders which should make a Dutchman feel at home, particularly since in Henri IV's day it was an engineer from Berg-op-Zoom who supervised construction of the drainage canal now known as the *Ceinture des Hollandais*.

In the drier Marais near the sea, cereal crops are grown. This is good land for cattle, and sheep feed on the salt marshes as they do farther north in Brittany and near Mont St Michel.

Near Niort, the local people fish from boats for fine fat eels, crayfish, perch, gudgeon, carp and tench. Boats are used, too, to carry market produce: milk and dairy items, artichokes, garlic (a pronounced feature of local recipes), beans of various kinds, courgettes and the exquisite Charentais melons, with their aromatic flavour and greenish, segmented skins.

Coming farther into the country, into the centre of Poitou, the landscape flattens into extensive farms, cut by great river valleys. The towns specialize in delicious cream cheese tarts, macaroons, croquets, sweets of many kinds and biscuits. The *charcutiers* sell hams from the Vendée and *pâté de foie gras* or *confits* from local ducks, as well as the wide range of cooked and cured pork available in France.

Continuing the tradition of goat cheeses south of the Loire, Poitou makes and exports *Pyramide de Poitou*, truncated pyramids of cheese, little cylindrical *chabichous*, and *bûcherons*, great logs of cheese about a foot long and four inches in diameter, which proudly display two brown chestnut leaves on either side of the label. These last two cheeses are made in the neighbourhood of Civray, from which *foie gras* also comes.

In the east of the region, edging up on to the Massif Central, roads twist and wind. This part of France is wet and cold, but with good dinners of beef or goose, and crisp pies, finishing up with *clafoutis*, cherry pastry, even a rough climate is bearable.

One of the loveliest sights in this area, on the way towards Brive, are the silver-trunked walnut trees. Usually they grow in orchards of vivid grass, surrounded by walls of dark grey stone covered with lichen. Specialities of Brive are salads dressed with

LOBSTER
ILE D'YEU

CROQUETS DE MILLET
Millet biscuits

CHAUDREE
Fish soup

SARDINES

LES SABLES D

MUSSELS

FIGS
ILE DE RE

WINKLES

HAKE

ILE D'OLERO

LE CHATEAU D'O

OYSTER

LA TR

SARD

CHARENTES POITOU LIMOUSIN MARCHE

POITOU

A LA POITEVINE

ESCARGOTS AU VIN
Snails in wine

WALNUT OIL ● CHATELLERAULT

CENNE

CHABICHOU
Goats' cheese

AGERS

BOUILLETURE D'ANGUILLES
Eel stew

NOUGATINES
Nougat sweets

CHEESE ● PARTHENAY
● LA MOTTE ST HERAY ● POITIERS

ENOUILLES
gs' legs

MELUSINES
Mermaid-shaped cakes

● LUSIGNAN

LAMB
● MONTMORILLON

M A R C H E

MACAROONS

CARPE AU VIN BLANC
Carp in white wine

CHESTNUTS

CAULIFLOWERS ARTICHOKES
● NIORT

CONFIT D'OIE
Preserved goose

● LE DORAT

● GUERET

ANGELICA

HARICOTS BLANCS
White haricot beans

● BELLAC

PATE CREUSOIS AUX
POMMES DE TERRE
Potato pie

HELLE

LAMB

LADE
soup
ELAILLON

● COURCON D'AUNIS

● CIVRAY

PATE DE FOIE GRAS

BREJAUDE
Cabbage and bacon soup

GAME

● CHEF-BOUTONNE

● AUBUSSON

AS
E

GALANTINE DE BECASSES
Woodcock in aspic

● RUFFEC

WALNUTS

PATE DE FOIE GRAS
ET DE PERDREAUX TRUFFES
Goose liver and partridge
pâté with truffles

LIEVRE A LA ROYALE
Stuffed hare braised in wine

● FELLETIN

NOISETTINES
Hazelnut cakes

NNES

● ST JEAN D'ANGELY

COUP DE JARNAC
Meringue-topped
sponge cake

● LIMOGES

BALLOTTINE DE DINDE AUX CEPES
Boned stuffed turkey with boletus mushrooms

● EYMOUTIERS

CEPES AU VIN BLANC
Boletus mushrooms in white wine

OAD BEANS

SNAILS
SAINTES

COGNAC

LA ROCHEFOUCAULD

CLAFOUTIS
Black cherry cake

● COGNAC
JARNAC

TROUT

YAN

● ANGOULEME

CIVET DE LIEVRE
A LA GELEE DE GROSEILLES
Hare casserole with red currant jelly

L I M O U S I N

TRUITE A LA D'USSEL
Poached trout baked in breadcrumbs

● USSEL

MELONS

HUITRES AUX SAUCISSES
Oysters with sausages

CHICKENS ● BARBEZIEUX

BOUDIN AUX CHATAIGNES
Black pudding with chestnuts

GIRONDE

● JONZAC

MERINGUES ● UZERCHE

CROQUANTS
Crunchy petits fours

● BORT-
LES-ORGUES

VEAUX DE LAIT
Milk-fed calves

TOURTONS
Buckwheat pancakes

URGEON

C H A R E N T E S

● CHALAIS

● TULLE

BROCCANA
Meat pies

● BRIVE-LA-GAILLARDE

CONFIT D'OIE
Preserved goose

BUTTER

walnut oil and black puddings and sausages
which include little knobs of chestnuts.

This part of France includes Cognac. The
fine or best brandy comes from wine produced in the districts known as La Grande
Champagne and La Petite Champagne. This
most celebrated product influences the
whole of French cooking.

The fine fare of fishermen and shepherds

La Rochelle Fish Chowder
LA CHAUDRÉE

The white wine for this dish ideally should come from the Ile d'Oléron or the Ile de Ré, and the chaudron, or cauldron, in which it is cooked should be buried in a fire of vine prunings from the islands' vineyards, which are fertilized with seaweed. Even without these ideal conditions, however, chaudrée is a delicious soup, a meal in itself. Incidentally, the American word "chowder", and the recipe, derives from this chaudrée of western France, which was taken to North America by the men who fished off the Newfoundland coast.

SERVES 6

3 lb assorted sea fish, such as small sole, plaice, cod or gurnard, filleted
1 lb eel, skinned and cut into 3-inch chunks
Salt
Pepper
12 onions, quartered
2 large garlic cloves
Bouquet garni
12 peppercorns
4 cloves
4 oz butter, cut into pieces
6 medium-sized potatoes, scrubbed
2 pints dry white wine
or
1 pint wine and 1 pint water

Sort out the fish. Put the firmest fish on one plate, the less firm on another and the thinnest and softest on a third plate. Cut the fillets into chunks and season with salt and pepper.

Into a large pot, from which the fish can be served as well as cooked, put the onions, garlic, *bouquet garni*, peppercorns and cloves. Scatter the pieces of butter over them and place the potatoes on top. Finally arrange the fish on the potatoes—first the firm pieces, then the medium pieces and, finally, the thinnest pieces. Pour the wine, or wine and water, over the fish. Bring the mixture to the boil and simmer for about 30 minutes, or until the potatoes are cooked.

Remove the fish and the potatoes. Raise the heat and reduce the liquid by about half. Correct the seasoning. Put back the fish and potatoes, which will reheat in the very hot soup, and serve immediately.

Mussel Stew from Esnandes
MOUCLADE D'ESNANDES

Esnandes, a small village on the Anse d'Aiguillon, is famous for its mussel farming. There, on poles placed in long lines in the shallow water of the bay, the mussels cling and grow. They are harvested at low water, when the fishermen skim from pole to pole in flat-bottomed boats known as accons.

The trade is said to go back to the thirteenth century. Mouclade, which means a stew made of mussels, or moules, *is the local version of* moules marinière.

SERVES 6 AS A FIRST COURSE

4 to 6 lb mussels, preferably small ones
8 fl oz dry white wine
6 oz shallots, finely chopped
3 garlic cloves, finely chopped
2 oz butter
1 tablespoon flour
15 fl oz milk
1 tablespoon pastis Ricard or other anise-flavoured liqueur
2 egg yolks
3 fl oz double cream
Salt
Pepper

Scrub and scrape the mussels. Discard any which are broken, or which remain open when tapped sharply. Put the mussels in a large pan with the wine. Cover the pan and set it over high heat for 5 minutes. Remove the opened mussels, and throw away one half shell from each if they are large. Put the mussels into a serving bowl or a soup tureen and keep them warm. Strain and reserve the liquor.

Cook the shallots and garlic in the butter over a low heat, until they are soft and golden. Stir in the flour to make a *roux*, then add the mussel liquor and the milk to produce a slightly thickened sauce. Add the *pastis*, and reduce the sauce slightly by boiling it down.

In a small bowl, beat the egg yolks and the cream together. Mix in a little sauce. Pour the mixture into the pan and stir over low heat without boiling for 5 minutes. Correct the seasoning, adding a little more *pastis* to taste—the anise flavour should be just noticeable, very delicate and fragrant. Pour the sauce over the mussels and serve.

Shepherd's Pie in the Correze Manner
HACHIS PARMENTIER

Boiled beef is a standard dish in French families. Inevitably, there is the problem of the leftovers which are sometimes later used up in a miroton *(slices of meat reheated with a covering of onions and breadcrumbs) or in this dish which has become familiar to most people of European descent. Like many other simple dishes it is terrible if it is badly made, but delicious if the cook has skill and generosity. Good mashed potatoes are the secret of success. Choose a fine-flavoured variety with a floury texture.*

This is a patient dish, and could be cooked for longer at a lower temperature.

SERVES 4 TO 6

3 onions, chopped
4 oz butter
1 lb cold boiled beef (or cold roast beef)
4 oz pork belly, fat salt pork or unsmoked bacon
2 heaped tablespoons chopped parsley
Salt
Pepper
Milk
1 oz breadcrumbs
2 tablespoons beaten egg
2½ to 3 lb potatoes
1 tablespoon grated Gruyère
1 tablespoon grated Parmesan

Cook the onion gently in half the butter. Meanwhile, mince the beef together with the uncooked pork or bacon. Add the parsley and season the mixture. Add just enough milk to the breadcrumbs to make a thick paste and beat it into the minced meat. Add the mixture to the pan of softened onions and stir for a few moments over the heat. Remove the pan from the heat and when the meat mixture has cooled a little, stir in the beaten egg. Grease a shallow ovenproof dish with a little butter and spread the meat mixture over it.

Preheat the oven to 400°F (Gas Mark 6).

Boil, peel and mash the potatoes with the remaining butter and enough milk to make them creamy. Spread the mashed potato over the meat. Sprinkle the grated cheeses on top. Bake for 30 to 40 minutes.

Frogs' Legs Marais Style
CUISSES DE GRENOUILLES A LA MARAICHINE

In France, frogs' legs are usually sold by the dozen on wooden skewers. Where they can be bought frozen, they are remarkably cheap considering how good they taste. Most general books of French cooking give the recipe for frogs legs with a sauce poulette. *Here is a recipe from the Marais district, near Luçon, where frogs' legs are big business. They now import them from Russia, and Eastern Europe generally, as well as from Egypt and Turkey.*

SERVES 6

4 to 6 dozen frogs' legs, depending on size
4 fl oz vinegar
Seasoned flour
5 to 6 oz butter
5 large garlic cloves, chopped
8 fl oz double cream
Salt
Pepper
Lemon juice
2 tablespoons chopped parsley
1 lemon, sliced

Rinse the frogs' legs quickly. Drain them and put them into a bowl. Pour the vinegar over them, plus an equal quantity of water. Leave for hour. Dry them on a clean tea towel and turn them in seasoned flour.

Melt about 2 ounces of the butter in a large frying-pan. Add the frogs' legs and cook them, not too fast, turning them frequently, for 20 minutes, or until they turn an appetizing golden colour. Arrange them on a dish.

Meanwhile, make the sauce. Melt the remaining butter in a small frying-pan, add the garlic and cook gently until the butter turns a golden brown. Stir in the cream and simmer for a few minutes until it thickens. Season with salt and pepper and a dash of lemon juice.

Pour the sauce over the frogs' legs, sprinkle them with parsley and arrange the slices of lemon around the edge. Serve very hot.

Onion Sauce for Roast Ribs of Beef

Charentes produces excellent beef, particularly to the east of the River Vienne. Roast beef is always cooked rare, or saignant, and in the neighbourhood of Bellac it is sometimes served with this piquant sauce.

SERVES 4

1 large onion, sliced
Oil
5 fl oz dry white wine
3 fl oz beef stock
Salt
Pepper
1 heaped teaspoon French mustard

Cook the onion gently in a little oil, allowing it to brown slowly without burning or becoming dark brown at the edges. The mixture should end up a rich chestnut colour. Add the wine and stock. Simmer for about 10 minutes. Add the seasoning and stir in the mustard gradually to taste. Do not boil any more or the flavour of the mustard will decrease. Pour around the sliced beef and serve immediately.

Potato Pie Limoges Style

GATEAU LIMOUSIN DE POMMES DE TERRE

This delicious potato pie of Limoges is shared by the Bourbonnais district. So excellent are the recipes the French have devised for potatoes, it is odd that the potato did not become popular until the beginning of the nineteenth century. Then the potato gained popularity due mostly to the persistence of one man, Antoine Parmentier, who even presented a bouquet of potato flowers to Louis XVI in an effort to publicize potatoes. Marie Antoinette wore one of the flowers in her hair, which will not surprise any gardener, who will know how beautiful they can be. Today in French cookery Parmentier means potatoes.

SERVES 6

1 lb puff pastry, or enough for a double-crust, 10-inch pie
1½ lb new potatoes, scraped
1 medium-sized onion, finely chopped
3 to 4 garlic cloves, finely chopped
Salt
Nutmeg
Freshly ground black pepper
2 oz butter, cut into pieces
3 fl oz single cream
3 fl oz double cream
1 egg
Finely chopped parsley, chives, chervil

Roll out slightly over half the pastry, and line a 10-inch flan tin with a removable base. Using either the cucumber blade of a grater, or a mandolin, slice the potatoes paper thin into a bowl of cold water to prevent discoloration. Blanch the potatoes for 2 minutes in boiling salted water. Drain in a colander.

Preheat the oven to 450°F (Gas Mark 8).

Put a layer of potatoes into the pastry case, sprinkle them with the onion, garlic and seasoning. Repeat until all the potatoes have been used up. Dot the butter over the top. Mix the creams together and pour half over the potatoes.

WHETHER OR NOT THE CHARENTAIS actually drink more cognac than the French of other regions, they must certainly imbibe a good deal through their pores. For more cognac evaporates in the warehouses of the Charentes, it is said, than France manages to consume.

Cognac and Jarnac are the twin centres of the enormous cognac industry. They are small towns with nothing grand or gastronomic to reflect their wealth and fame. Distillers entertain at home.

Vineyards stretch from Angoulême to the sea, even on to the island of Oléron. But there is no local wine to be had. It all goes to the distilleries where its characteristic sharpness is seen as a virtue—indeed a necessity for producing brandy with the distinctive cognac flavour. It takes ten barrels of wine to make one of cognac.

The other necessity is providentially also supplied by the region—the fine white oak from the forests of the Limousin.

Cognac is the world's drink, but one local speciality is rarely seen outside the region. That is Pineau des Charentes, a cordial made by adding cognac to unfermented grape juice. Like the very similar ratafia in Champagne, it is one of France's quiet pleasures, an aperitif you are most likely to meet in the home of a friend.

Roll out the remaining pastry and cover the pie. Make a hole in the centre and score the pastry lightly with a modest decoration, being careful to press the edges of the pastry together to seal the pie. Beat the egg into the remaining cream. Use a little of this mixture to brush over the top of the pastry. Place the pie in the oven and bake for 30 minutes. Protect the top with a piece of buttered paper or foil, if the pastry browns too quickly.

Meanwhile, add the chopped herbs to the remaining cream mixture. When the pie is baked, pour the cream mixture into the centre hole using a kitchen funnel. Do this with caution as there may not be enough room for all the mixture. Return the pie to the oven for 5 minutes, then serve immediately.

Walnut Oil Salad

At one time every painter in Europe used walnut oil to mix "white and other delicate colours, also for gold size and varnish", but today they must use something a little cheaper. Walnut oil is expensive, even in France, but it is worth the extra money because of its exquisite flavour. Good grocers sometimes stock it.

SERVES 4 TO 6

1 large crisp lettuce

DRESSING

1 tablespoon white wine vinegar
4 tablespoons walnut oil
1 small garlic clove, crushed
Salt
Pepper
Pinch of sugar
Chopped parsley
Chopped tarragon
Chopped chervil

CHAPONS

4 slices white bread about ½ inch thick
2 garlic cloves, cut in half
Walnut oil

Pull the lettuce apart, wash it and drain it well.

In a salad bowl, mix all the dressing ingredients together, adjusting them to taste. Cross the salad servers over the dressing to make a platform for the lettuce.

Just before the meal, remove and discard the crusts from the bread to make the *chapons*. Rub the bread all over with the cut side of the garlic and divide it into cubes. Chop the garlic and fry it with the bread in the walnut oil. Drain the *chapons*, and allow them to cool to tepid or cold. Sprinkle them on the lettuce.

After the meat course, at the table, turn the whole thing over gently to mix the lettuce, dressing and *chapons* together. Eat immediately, while the lettuce and *chapons* are still crisp. There is no better salad than this.

A feast from the streams and fields

IN THIS CORNER OF FRANCE, more than in almost any other part of Europe, the discovery of America has had an obvious effect on the food. From the early sixteenth century, when they were first introduced, maize, pumpkins, tomatoes and peppers have gradually taken over a large part of the best dishes of daily life.

Maize replaced millet in the old diet of the peasants. *Milhas*, for example, which as its name suggests was once a thick porridge made of *mil* or millet, is now made from maize and resembles the *polenta* of northern Italy. There are cakes of maize flour, too, again replacing millet, and known as *milhassou*. *Méture* and *talos* are maize breads raised with yeast. Soups and stews are made more filling by the hearty maize dumplings called *farcidure* and *mique*.

Some people point out, perhaps undiplomatically, that the pumpkin recipes of southern France are far more resourceful and varied than those of North America. As well as pumpkin pie, there are *gratins*, pumpkin cakes and breads and dishes in which pumpkin is given body by maize flour.

It is difficult to find any European diet which does not include tomatoes, but in Southwest France tomato dishes are made more piquant with the addition of peppers and chillies, particularly in *pipérade*, where they are combined with scrambled eggs.

In some of the prune and walnut delicacies made in Gascony and in Guyenne there are reminders of another foreign influence—the Arabs who, in the Dark Ages, invaded France right up to the gates of Poitiers. Recipes for such dishes are often identical with those used in the Middle East.

The elegant food of the area is more recent. *Foie gras* is produced in Gers and in Les Landes, that long strip of uncertain, shifting coast that is now tethered in place by a wide band of pine forest. In Gers, too, truffles are cherished in semi-cultivation,

using methods which were developed in the nineteenth century. The oyster farming of the coast is also done in accordance with methods developed more than one hundred years ago.

Apart from the old *civets* and *ragoûts* of lamb, more delicate dishes with *sauce béarnaise* and *sauce paloise* have been developed since the middle of the nineteenth century, when *sauce béarnaise* was invented at St-Germain-en-Laye, near Paris, at the Pavillon Henri IV. It was soon taken to Henri's native country of the Béarn, and chefs at Pau, the capital, began to use mint, instead of tarragon, to flavour it. They named it *sauce paloise* and served it with the local herb-flavoured mountain lamb.

This part of France is rich in game as well. Game of all kinds abound, but especially the wild doves, the *palombres*, and ortolans. They are caught as they fly south to winter in the warm climates of the Mediterranean. Ortolans, as anyone who has read Colette's *Gigi* will know, are delicate little birds that are to be eaten bones and all.

This, too, is one of the great lands of garlic. Garlic in quantity is, for example, mashed with goose fat to make *beurre de Gascogne*. And goose fat (without the garlic) is used in much of the cooking, even in the cakes, in place of butter.

Another typical flavour of the region is provided by the excellent hams of Les Landes, of which the Bayonne ham, which, in fact, is cured at Orthez nearby, is one of the finest. This ham lends a special flavour to some of the fish cooking, as does the garlic which, with onions, is used to prepare fish *à la basquaise*.

One of the best of Basque dishes is stuffed squid. The finest of the fresh-water fish is the trout, called *gaves*, from the swift mountain torrents. They are served bathed in sauces of *cèpes* and tomatoes, or in cream which is flavoured with anise pastis.

It is not surprising that everyone loves Guyenne. Its monuments, its villages and its small towns and, above all, its food, seem to have their standards set by the great wines of Bordeaux. Farmers, *charcutiers*, pastry cooks and fishermen set out to match the great wine-growers with their *foie gras* and *confits* of goose and duck, salted and laid up in rich-flavoured fat; their maize-fed turkey, chicken and guinea fowl; their salt-marsh lamb from Pauillac on the Gironde; their exquisite prunes from Agen and little macaroons from St Emilion; their beef for steak *à la bordelaise*; their pork for pâtés

GREY MULLET

EN
Grille
LAMPROIE

AR
O

TUNA

GUIN

ORTOL

SARDINES

LEON
ANG
Eels w

FOIE GRAS

CHIPIRONES
Squid

CHOCOLATE

BAYONNE

BIARRITZ

HENDAYE
MATELOTE
D'ANGUILLES
Eel stew

ST JEAN-DE-LUZ
TTORO
Fish stew with onions

CEPES A LA BORDELAISE
Boletus mushrooms in oil with garlic and parsley
●NONTRON

●BRANTOME

BALLOTTINES DE PERDREAU ET DE DINDE
Boned and rolled partridge and turkey

PATE DE BECASSES
Woodcock pâté

●PERIGUEUX   TRUFFLES

CEPES FARCIS
Stuffed boletus mushrooms

CONFIT D'OIE
Preserved goose

STRAWBERRIES

PERDREAUX FARCIS ET TRUFFES
Stuffed and truffled partridge
LIBOURNE

OMELETTE AUX TRUFFES
Truffle omelette

SARLAT   ●

ROGNONADE
Loin of veal with kidney
●SOUILLAC

●ST EMILION   MACAROONS

BORDEAUX

●BERGERAC   ●ST CERE

BALLOTTINE DE DINDE A LA GELEE
Boned turkey in aspic

TROUT

MARIE BRIZARD
Anisette liqueur

TOURIN
Onion soup

LANGON   PALOMBES EN SALMIS
Wood pigeons in rich sauce

COU D'OIE FARCI
Stuffed neck of goose

●BAZAS   SOUPE A L'ALOSE
Shad soup   CHESTNUTS

●CAHORS

GARONNE RIVER

●VILLENEUVE-SUR-LOT

TOURIN
Onion soup

BECASSES
Woodcock purée

BREZOLLES DE VEAU
Slices of veal in white wine

OIE FARCIE AUX PRUNEAUX
Goose stuffed with prunes
PLUMS   ●AGEN

TURKEYS

●NERAC

DAUBE DE CEPES
Boletus mushrooms stewed in wine
●CONDOM

●MOISSAC

CHASSELAS GRAPES

CONFIT DE CANARD
Preserved duck

CONFIT D'OIE
Preserved goose

●VILLENEUVE-DE-MARSAN

WILD MUSHROOMS

BALLOTTINE DE DINDE
Boned and rolled turkey

●AUCH

ESTOUFFAT DE PORC
Stewed pork   ARMAGNAC

OIE SALEE
leg

●MASSEUBE

POULE AU POT
cooked in broth

SAUCISSON
Sausage

GASCONY

●PAU

●TARBES

RON   TROUT

THRUSHES

WOODCOCK

CRAYFISH

PIPERADE
Sweet peppers and tomatoes mixed with eggs

IAT
soup

---

and the spicy sausages to be eaten with oysters from Arcachon; their fine onions for *tourin* soup; and their shallots, the great *bordelaise* flavouring, which are the most piquant and lively of the onion family.

Marmande has given its name to one of the best varieties of tomato. Rivers offer up the finest trout, lampreys, eels, pike and shad. The forests yield fleshy, dark-headed *cèpes*, acres of chestnut trees and some of the best truffles in France.

There is no pleasure greater than a holiday spent visiting the painted caves around Les Eyziers and Cahors. Visitors can sit beneath a great rounded brow of grey limestone, streaked with black, which has sheltered human beings for well over twenty thousand years, and picnic on pâté, strawberries and goat cheese. At the tiny inn at Cabrerets they can lunch on trout from the River Célé, which runs by the tables, and recall the horses and mammoths of the cave of Pech-Merle nearby. As sauce to the food, there is the sound of orioles calling gently from the poplars, and the brilliant light of reflections in the clear river.

GUYENNE GASCONY BEARN

Where elegant food matches fine wines

Goose or Duck Liver with Grapes
FOIE GRAS AUX RAISINS

In its perfection, this dish should be eaten in Les Landes, where it can be made from fresh duck or goose liver. However, it tastes so good when made with canned foie gras *(look for* en bloc au naturel, *or* sous vide, *on the labels), or even with chicken or duck livers, that the recipe is worth trying.*

FOR EACH PERSON

Butter
1 slice foie gras or 3 chicken livers
1 slice bread, larger than the foie gras, fried in butter
8 large grapes, preferably Muscat, peeled and pipped
1 tablespoon Muscatel wine, such as Frontignan, or Madeira
Salt
Freshly ground black pepper

Heat a little butter in a frying-pan. Add the *foie gras*, and fry lightly on both sides over low heat so that the butter retains a good flavour. If using chicken livers, add them to the butter and fry lightly until they are brown outside and just pink in the centre. Put the *foie gras* or chicken livers on the bread and keep warm.

Add the grapes to the pan and heat them gently. When they are hot arrange them around the *foie gras* or chicken livers.

Add the wine to the pan and bring to the boil scraping the bottom of the pan with a wooden spoon. Add salt and pepper to taste and pour the sauce over the liver. Serve immediately.

Boiled Chicken Bearn Style
POULE AU POT

Whether or not Henri IV really said that he would like all his subjects to be able to afford a poule au pot *on Sundays, the dish has become part of his reputation as France's most popular king. It is a splendid dish, simple to make and as delicious as its cousin, the Scottish cockie-leekie. Do not omit the beef—it makes all the difference to the flavour of the soup and is good to eat with the chicken.*

SERVES 8

1 fine boiling fowl
Salt
Freshly ground black pepper
1 firm cabbage
8 potatoes, scrubbed but not peeled
STUFFING
6 oz Bayonne ham or lean smoked gammon, chopped
8 oz lean veal, chopped

8 oz pork belly, chopped
3 chicken livers, chopped
2 oz butter
2 large onions, chopped
2 large garlic cloves, finely chopped
1 oz fresh white breadcrumbs
Single cream
3 tablespoons Armagnac or brandy
Salt
Freshly ground black pepper
Grated nutmeg
Ground cinnamon
Ground cloves
1 large egg yolk
STOCK
8 oz chicken giblets
1 beef marrow bone
2 lb flank of beef
3 large carrots
1 large onion, stuck with 3 cloves
1 medium-sized turnip
1 celery stick
1 small parsnip
2 garlic cloves, peeled but left whole
Salt
Freshly ground black pepper

Rub the inside of the chicken with the salt and pepper. Set it aside. Next make the stuffing. Put the chopped ham, veal, pork and chicken livers in a large bowl. Heat the butter in a frying-pan. Add the onions and garlic, cover the pan and cook gently until the onions are soft and golden. Add the onion mixture to the chopped meat.

In a small bowl, mix the breadcrumbs with just enough cream to make a soft paste. Add the paste to the chopped meats. Add the salt, pepper, nutmeg, cinnamon and cloves to taste. Mix the ingredients together well. Stuff the chicken with half the stuffing and reserve the rest.

In a large saucepan or casserole, combine all the ingredients for the stock. Add 7 pints of water and bring to the boil. Add the chicken, cover the pan, reduce the heat to low and barely simmer for 3 hours. The liquid should raise an occasional bubble, but should never boil.

Meanwhile, blanch the cabbage in boiling water for 10 minutes. Cut off the largest leaves, refresh them under cold running water, then spread them out on a clean cloth. On to each leaf put a spoonful of the remaining stuffing. Roll up the leaf neatly, tucking in the sides, and tie with strong thread. Quarter the remaining cabbage.

After the chicken has cooked for 2¼ hours, put the potatoes in the pan. After a further 15 minutes, put in the cabbage quarters and the stuffed cabbage leaves and cook for 30 minutes. Remove the potatoes and peel them.

To serve, remove the chicken, beef, cabbage and stuffed cabbage leaves and any of the stock vegetables which still look presentable and taste good. Keep them warm. Strain the stock into a clean saucepan. Skim off the fat and correct

THE GREAT WINES OF BORDEAUX, the world's biggest fine-wine region, belong to gastronomy on the international plane. They are not so intimately linked with the regional food as those of Burgundy. There are certain classic combinations which the Bordelais manage to build into every banquet. Sauternes with fresh *foie gras* is one of the most delectable. It is natural and right to drink a young white Graves or Entre-Deux-Mers with Arcachon oysters. But, thereafter, names you rarely see on wine-lists abroad, up-country wines without the great prestige of the Médoc and St-Emilion, are happily accepted as normal drinking.

Most middle-class families have their favourite *petit fournisseur*—a grower who furnishes them with the cases of each vintage they need. They take trips by car over the river to Bourg or Fronsac or up the Dordogne to Castillon or Bergerac to fill up. In doing so they are repeating history, for the vineyards of the "right bank" (that is, the east of the Garonne and the Gironde) are much older than

the celebrated modern growths. Some of those of the hinterland—notably Cahors and Gaillac—go back to pre-Christian times. Bordeaux started as *entrepôt* for wine rather than producer.

All the red wines of Gascony are cast into the same sort of mould. They are all in the lighter and more astringent style which has been known in English for five hundred years at least as "claret". What distinguishes good claret from bad, better from good and best from better is increasing depth and warmth of flavour, which in turn is determined by a combination of soil and weather. The permanence of the soil factor is reflected in the remarkable validity, even today, of classifications of estates made as long ago as two hundred years. As for the weather, on the Atlantic coast anything can happen. Bordeaux, like most wine centres, maintains a thriving distillery industry on the wine of regrettable vintages. Vieille Curé, Cordial Médoc and a whole range of liqueurs from the firm of Marie Brizard, founded in the eighteenth century, are the consolation prizes.

he seasoning. Serve the soup as a first course with plenty of bread.

For the main course, put the chicken and beef on a large serving platter surrounded with the potatoes, cabbage quarters, stuffed cabbage leaves and vegetables. Serve with mustard, coarse sea salt and pickled gherkins and onions.

Leg of Lamb with a Crown of Garlic from Périgord

GIGOT PERIGOURDIN A LA COURONNE D'AIL

This wonderful dish appears in various parts of France under different names. The long slow cooking removes any slight bitterness from the garlic and it becomes a vegetable—tender, golden brown nuts of delicate flavour. It is a dish for midsummer, when the young garlic is still tender and juicy, its fat stalk coloured with green and purple streaks, its skin silky.

SERVES 8

4 to 5 lb leg of lamb
Salted water
1½ oz goose fat or butter
50 garlic cloves, peeled
3 tablespoons Armagnac or brandy
8 fl oz Sauternes or Montbazillac or other sweet white wine
Salt
Freshly ground black pepper

Blanch the lamb by putting it in boiling, salted water for 15 minutes. Drain the leg and dry it well with absorbent paper or a clean cloth.

Melt the fat in a large, deep casserole. Add the lamb and brown it all over. Put the garlic cloves around the lamb. Pour over the Armagnac or brandy and set it alight. When the flames die down, add the wine and season with salt and pepper to taste. Cover the casserole tightly, using foil to make a perfect seal. Cook over very low heat for 5 or 6 hours, turning the meat over every 2 hours.

Serve the lamb on a large dish with its cooking juices and place the garlic around it in a circle. This dish is traditionally served with puréed haricot or broad beans or a dandelion salad.

Beans with Garlic and Parsley Butter

HARICOTS BLANCS AU BEURRE DE GASCOGNE

The butter of Gascony is really the fat from geese and ducks which have been force-fed to produce foie gras. Goose fat gives a special flavour to many dishes of this area of France and is most successful with potatoes or dried vegetables. Naturally, the fat from roasting any variety of

goose or duck will do, as well as the butter left from cooking a good turkey or chicken. Lard is another alternative, so long as it has not been refined to the nullity of vegetable cooking fats.

SERVES 4

1 lb haricot beans, soaked overnight
6 oz piece salt pork belly or green streaky bacon
Freshly ground black pepper
Salt
BEURRE DE GASCOGNE
8 large garlic cloves, unpeeled
6 tablespoons goose, duck or pork fat
2 heaped tablespoons chopped parsley

Drain the beans. Put them in a large casserole with the pork or bacon and cover with water. Season with plenty of freshly ground black pepper, but do not add salt as it will harden the beans. Bring the mixture to the boil. Cover the pan, reduce the heat to low and simmer for 1 to 2 hours, or until the beans are cooked. Remove the pork or bacon from the pan and slice it. Drain the beans and add salt to taste.

Meanwhile, in a small saucepan, blanch the garlic in salted, boiling water for 5 minutes. Drain the garlic cloves and peel them. Put the warm garlic cloves in an electric blender with the fat and blend to a paste. Mix in the parsley.

Spoon the beans on to a heated serving dish. Arrange the slices of meat around them. Mix half the *beurre de Gascogne* into the beans. Serve the remaining butter separately.

Dax Almond and Hazelnut Cake

DACQUOISE

This cake from Dax, the spa town near Bayonne, has conquered France to become part of the national culinary repertoire.

SERVES 6

8 egg whites
⅛ teaspoon salt
⅛ teaspoon cream of tartar
8 oz castor or icing sugar
5 oz ground almonds
3 oz hazelnuts, grated
BUTTER CREAM
4 large egg yolks
4 oz castor sugar
12 fl oz milk
5 oz unsalted butter
2 oz almond brittle, powdered
3 oz roasted hazelnuts, grated
DECORATION
Icing sugar
Blanched, toasted almond slivers

Preheat the oven to 275°F (Gas Mark 1). Line a large baking sheet with Bakewell parchment paper.

In a large bowl, whisk the egg whites and the salt until the whites are stiff. Fold in the cream of tartar and 1 teaspoon of sugar then whisk in the remaining sugar until the mixture is satiny and voluminous. Fold in the ground almonds and grated hazelnuts. Spread the meringue mixture in 2 large discs on the prepared baking sheet. Bake for about 1 hour, or until the meringue is slightly browned. When the paper can be peeled away without sticking, the cakes are done. They will be slightly chewy.

To make the butter cream, put the egg yolks in a bowl. Bring the milk to the boil in a saucepan and pour it on to the eggs, beating thoroughly. Pour the mixture into a clean pan and, stirring constantly, thicken the custard over low heat without allowing it to boil. Remove the pan from the heat and set aside to cool to tepid. When the custard is tepid, beat in the butter and the nuts and leave to become cold.

Sandwich the cakes with the butter cream. Sprinkle the top with icing sugar and the toasted almond slivers.

Perigueux Chocolate Truffles

TRUFFES AU CACAO

French confectioners love to imitate natural objects, and they do it beautifully. Whatever the local speciality may be—sardines, mussels, oysters, snails, finely marked and shaped pebbles, hazelnuts with their green frilled collars, smooth chestnuts, red and black blackberries—delectable sweet copies can be found in the local confectioners' shops. Naturally, at Périgueux there are truffles —round, unevenly shaped, rolled in dark cocoa for the right matt surface and presented in little baskets like the real truffles in the market-place.

MAKES 36 SMALL OR 18 LARGE TRUFFLES

8 oz good plain chocolate (Menier, Velma, Suchard or Cote d'or)
4 egg yolks
2 oz unsalted butter
2 teaspoons single cream
2 teaspoons rum
cocoa

Break the chocolate into pieces and put them in the top of a double boiler over hot but not boiling water. Keep it over a low heat, stirring until the chocolate melts. Whisk in the egg yolks one by one—the warmth will help to thicken them slightly. When everything is well mixed and very thick, remove the top of the double boiler, add the butter, cream and rum, beating them in thoroughly. The chocolate should not be so hot that the butter turns to oil before it is incorporated. Leave the mixture to cool and harden before rolling it into unevenly shaped balls—36 small ones, or 18 large ones. Turn them in cocoa powder, and arrange in little frilled paper cases in a small basket.

Bubbling cassoulets and ripening Roquefort

GASTRONOMIC KNOWLEDGE OF LANGUEDOC goes back, in part at least, to the Middle Stone Age. At the huge cavern of Mas d'Azil in the Pyrenees, pierced now by a wide road as well as by the River Arize, post-Magdalenian man left huge deposits of shells from snails.

In the small town of Mas d'Azil, under the plane trees in the small square, one may still eat snails, excellent snails, as well as trout from the river, and veal, local cheese and peaches. It is food full of life and delicate flavour.

In the market at St Girons, fifteen miles away, gypsies often sell young goats' cheeses dripping with moisture. The long swaddling bands of brown chestnut leaves have to be unwound before you arrive at the most succulent cheese, milky, creamy and soft. These small mountain cheeses are superb, but the best cheeses of Languedoc are found at Roquefort in the Aveyron.

There, on the edge of the *causses*, those chalky, pot-holed uplands, herds of sheep have for centuries been taken to graze on the thyme-scented grass. From the milk of these sheep, large cheeses are made and sent to ripen and develop their blue veins in the crypt-like caverns of Roquefort. Sheep's cheeses now come there from as far away as Corsica. Only cheese which has spent its maturing weeks in the ideal conditions of those caves has the right to be labelled Roquefort.

It is in this part of France that one becomes aware of the division of the country into people who say, or said, *oc*, instead of *oui*. The strange-sounding names of the food disturb the confidence of visitors who think they know French quite well. Even a much-relied-upon dictionary will be of little help.

There is, for example, *alicuit*, a giblet and salsify stew, thickened with a paste made from garlic and poultry liver, and *la rouzole*,

a pancake with fat and lean ham, flavoured with mint and thickened with breadcrumbs, which is served with soup. *Mourtayrol*, a saffron-flavoured bread sauce eaten with chicken and beef, is an unfamiliar dish, as are *catigot*, a fresh-water fish stew, and *cargolade*, a particularly piquant preparation of snails and chilli peppers.

In the *charcuterie* a speciality is *melsat*, a black pudding containing chopped pork and chopped pork spleen. There are surprises, too, in the *pâtisseries*. At Limoux, there are little pepper cakes, made with freshly ground black pepper. And in Montpellier a speciality is aniseed, almond and pine nut biscuits called *gals*.

Some of the strange-sounding dishes of Languedoc, such as *cassoulet*, have become famous outside France. To eat a *cassoulet* at Castelnaudary or Carcassonne or Toulouse is to delight in the rich possibilities of the humble baked bean. The grey lentils of Puy, another humble food, are unexpectedly delicious after the yellow and orange lentils of the north, which, because they collapse so easily into a mush, can only be used for soup. The other famous dish of Languedoc is *brandade*, a rich blend of puréed dried salt cod, garlic, olive oil and cream.

The coastal strip of Languedoc also provides good fresh fish, such as sardines, tuna, monkfish, mackerel and squid. From Collioure, around the curving line to the Rhône, pickled anchovies may be added to the salty delight of olives. The salt itself is likely to come from the moonscape of the salt marshes around the golden-walled medieval town of Aigues Mortes, where pink flamingos pick their way carefully through the shallows of the Camargue's brackish waters.

Two dishes of this province have their place in grand French cooking. One, *langouste à la sètoise*, crawfish in the style of Sète, has a family resemblance to *lobster à l'americaine*. It was a chef from Sète, Pierre Fraisse, who popularized this dish in Paris in the last century.

Then there is the famous green herb-butter from Montpellier, which was often served with salmon in the days when kitchen maids and scullions were at hand to pound the ingredients to a smooth paste. As the maids and scullions disappeared, the green herb-butter waned in popularity, to reappear in its old vigour when electric mixers and blenders took their place.

The sun of the Mediterranean influences other fruit, besides the olive, in this part of

France. Luscious cherries, apricots, peaches and, of course, dessert grapes, as well as fine pears and apples, are grown on the flat land towards the sea and up the valleys of the Rhône and its tributaries. Peaches are fine of all in the valley of Eyrieux, near the chestnut town of Privas.

The aspect of much of modern Languedoc would astonish Michelet, the French historian who, in the middle of the nineteenth century, remarked that the south, in spite of its beauty, was a land of ruins compared with the north. He described the stony landscape of Languedoc, where people subsisted on chestnuts, and where the hills were only sparsely covered with olive trees. He commented on the lack of navigable rivers, and observed that the ponds, even the soil itself, were bitter with salt. Much has happened in recent years and the old robust dishes of peasant life are now partnered with the sweetness of modern cultivation and skill.

MONGETADO
Casserole of haric[ot]
● ST G[A]
GARONNE

PETERAM
Offal and potato
● LUCHON

LENTILLES VERTES
Green lentils • LE PUY

RABLE DE LIEVRE AUX MURES
Saddle of hare with blackberries

• ST AGREVE

PORK PRODUCTS

GRIVES AU GENIEVRE
Thrushes with juniper
• LANGOGNE

PRIVAS

CHESTNUTS

• AUBENAS

• MUR DE BARREZ

PICOUSSEL
Buckwheat flan
with plums

TRIPOUX
Little parcels of sheep's tripe
• ESPALION

• JOYEUSE

POUYTROLLE
Chopped pork and vegetables
in pig's bladder

• MARCILLAC-VALLON

OMELETTE AUX TRUFFES
Truffle omelette

• VILLEFRANCHE
DE ROUERGUE

• RODEZ

MOURTAYROL
Chicken broth with saffron

AIGO BOULLIDO
Garlic soup

PELARDON
Goats' cheese

TRIPES A L'ALESIENNE
Tripe

CHESTNUTS

TRIPES AU SAFRAN
Tripe flavoured with saffron

• ALES

SAUSAGES • ANDUZE

TRUFFLES

• UZES

• VALENCE D'ALBIGEOIS

• ROQUEFORT

• LE VIGAN

ORONGES FARCIES
Stuffed mushrooms

BOEUF GARDIANE
Beef in tomato and
wine sauce with olives

GIGOT AU GENIEVRE • ALBI
Leg of mutton flavoured with juniper

ALICUIT
Chicken or turkey giblet stew

ROQUEFORT
CHEESE

• NIMES

AUBERGINES AUX CEPES
Aubergines with boletus mushrooms

BRANDADE DE MORUE
Creamed salt cod

PORK PRODUCTS

CANDIED
VIOLETS

PATE DE BECASSES
Woodcock pâté

• LACAUNE

GRAPES

BEURRE DE MONTPELLIER
Herb butter with mustard and anchovies

• TOULOUSE

CLERMONT - L'HERAULT •

• MONTPELLIER

• CASTRES

CASSOULET
Pork and haricot
bean casserole

• DOURGNE

MELSAT
Black pudding

PALAVAS •

GIGOT DE MER
Monkfish, ratatouille,
white wine and cream

• PEZENAS

PATES A LA VIANDE SUCREE
Sweet meat pies

SETE •

LANGOUSTE A LA SETOISE
Spiny lobster in tomato and wine sauce

CANARD AUX RAISINS • CASTELNAUDARY
Duck with grapes

BEZIERS • • BOUZIGUES

HAMS

• CARCASSONNE

NARBONNE • EELS

CASSOULET
Pork and haricot bean casserole

SOUPE DE POISSON
• LIMOUX   Fish soup with garlic

• FOIX

OEUFS A LA CAUSALADE
Eggs and bacon

FOIES DE CANARDS
EN PATE TRUFFES
Truffled duck livers in pastry

HONEY

GAME

• FORMIGUERES

TROUT

PERDREAUX A LA CATALANE
Partridge in orange and wine sauce

PERPIGNAN •

• PRADES

APRICOTS

BRAOU BUFFAT
Cabbage and rice soup

COLLIOURE

CARGOLADE
Snails cooked in wine

CERBERE •

RIVER RHONE

AVEYRON

LANGUEDOC

LANGUEDOC

145

Dishes to satisfy the heartiest appetites

Chicken, Beef and Bacon Soup with Saffron
LE MOURTAYROL

The thick, potées *and garbures of the southwest of France are well known. Less familiar are* ouillade, *a bean soup, and the* mourtayrol *of Languedoc with its unusual saffron-flavoured bread sauce which accompanies the clear soup and gives the dish its name. The meat and vegetables of the dish are eaten afterwards as the main course.*

SERVES 10

3 lb beef silverside
1 fat boiling fowl
1½ lb gammon
Salt
Freshly ground black pepper
4 whole carrots
4 whole leeks
2 small whole turnips
3 whole onions

MOURTAYROL

⅛ teaspoon saffron
1 loaf French bread
2 tablespoons olive oil

Put the silverside, chicken and gammon into a large pot. Cover generously with water. Add a little salt, but not too much as the gammon is salty, and plenty of pepper. Bring slowly to the boil. Skim off the scum and add the vegetables. Reduce the heat, partly cover the pot and gently simmer, with just the occasional bubble bursting on the surface, for 4 hours.

After 2½ hours remove 1 pint of stock from the pot, add the saffron to it and leave it to infuse for 20 minutes. Meanwhile, cut the bread into slices, toast them lightly and arrange them in a stoneware pot or in a heavy casserole. Pour on the stock and saffron, cover the pot and cook gently for 1 hour either on top of the stove, using an asbestos mat, or in a moderately low oven. Stir occasionally so that the bread dissolves into a creamy yellow paste. If it becomes too dry, add a little more stock from the pot. Finally stir in the oil.

Remove the meats and the vegetables from the soup to serve later as the main course. Strain the soup and ladle it into individual soup bowls. Add a large spoonful of the *mourtayrol* to each bowl and serve.

Creamed Salt Cod
BRANDADE DE MORUE

It is difficult to believe that anything which looks as unappetizing as the grey, kite-shaped boards of salt cod could be turned into this rich and creamy purée. Brandade *comes from Languedoc, but there is much argument as to whether Béziers or Nîmes was its original home. It is eaten on*

Fridays, above all on Good Friday. The name, according to the man who "discovered" the dish in the late eighteenth century and made it popular all over France, comes from brandir, *which means to stir, shake and crush with energy. It is an appropriate name.*

SERVES 6

2 lb piece salt cod
1 garlic clove, crushed
1 pint olive oil
10 fl oz single cream
Salt
Pepper
Nutmeg
Lemon juice
2 tablespoons chopped parsley
16 triangles of bread, fried in olive oil

Put the cod in a bowl and cover it with cold water. Leave it to soak for 48 hours changing the water 2 or 3 times.

Drain the cod and cut it into pieces. Put the pieces in a saucepan, cover with water and bring very slowly to just below boiling point. Simmer until the large flakes of cod part easily from the bones. Remove and discard the bones. Drain the fish. Break up the fish without skinning it and put the pieces and the garlic into a heavy stoneware pot or heavy casserole.

In a small saucepan, warm the olive oil over low heat until it is tepid. In another saucepan, heat the cream until it is tepid. Keep both pans over very low heat so that they do not cool.

Put the stoneware pot or casserole over a low heat. (Use an asbestos mat under the stoneware pot.) Using a wooden spoon, start stirring and crushing the cod. Pour in a little warm oil and work it in. Then do the same with the warm cream. Repeat until all the oil and cream are used and the cod is a rich, white, thready mass. Add the seasonings and the lemon juice to taste.

Spoon the *brandade* on to a heated serving dish and keep warm. Spread the parsley on a plate. Dip a corner of the fried bread triangles in the *brandade*, then into the parsley before tucking it into the edge of the *brandade*, parsley side up.

Bean and Meat Stew
CASSOULET

This is the best of all the baked bean dishes of the European tradition. Three places claim it, all of them in Languedoc—Castelnaudary, which is really cassoulet's *ancestral home, Toulouse and Carcassonne. At Toulouse, extra pork and a pig's trotter are added. At Carcassonne, a boned and braised leg of lamb, well studded with garlic, is included. The three basic ingredients, however, are the beans, the* confits d'oie *and a good meaty sausage. Tomatoes are added as flavouring and the top should be brown and crusty.*

Instead of making the confits d'oie, *it ca be bought in tins at fine food stores.*

SERVES 8 TO 10

1½ lb haricot beans, soaked for 6 hours a drained
Large piece of pork skin, cut into squares
1 lb salted pork belly or unsmoked strea bacon, cut into pieces
1 knuckle or hock of pork
1 large onion, stuck with 4 cloves
1 carrot, sliced
4 garlic cloves, chopped
Bouquet garni
Thigh and wing of confits d'oie with the fat (see p. 147)
1 lb garlic sausage
1 lb meaty sausage

RAGOUT (OPTIONAL)

Goose fat or lard
3 large onions, chopped
1 lb boned shoulder of pork, cut into piece
1 lb boned shoulder of lamb, cut into piece
4 garlic cloves, chopped
4 large tomatoes, blanched and peeled
2 tablespoons tomato paste
2 pints water
Salt
Freshly ground black pepper
Fresh white breadcrumbs
Chopped parsley

Put the haricot beans, pork skin and pork bel or bacon, knuckle or hock of pork, onio carrot, garlic and *bouquet garni* in a large cass role. Cover with water and bring to the boi Reduce the heat, cover the pan and simmer fc 1½ hours, or until the beans are cooked but n splitting.

Meanwhile, heat the goose fat or lard in large frying-pan. Add the thigh and wing c *confits d'oie* and the sausages, a few at a tim and brown them lightly. As they brown ad them to the beans cooking in the casserole.

If the ragoût is included, heat the goose fa in a large saucepan. Add the onions and fry ov low heat. Add the meats, increase the heat an brown the meat lightly. Add the garlic, toma toes, tomato paste, water and seasoning an bring to the boil. Reduce the heat and simme uncovered for 30 minutes. The liquid should b much reduced by the end of the cooking tim

Preheat the oven to 325°F (Gas Mark 3).

Add the ragoût to the beans just as they ar cooked. Spread the top with a ½-inch layer c breadcrumbs and sprinkle it with a little melte goose fat or lard.

Put the casserole into the oven and cook fc 1½ hours. The crust will turn a beautiful golde colour. Traditionally, the crust is pushed dow into the *cassoulet* with a spoon 7 times, so tha it can re-form with a rich brown colour. If th is done, add a thin sprinkling of fresh whi crumbs each time.

Nut and Garlic Mayonnaise
AILLADE

Aillade is a good mayonnaise for cold fish of all kinds. In Languedoc, it is eaten with snails cooked in a herb-flavoured stock with potatoes.

3 oz shelled walnuts
2 oz shelled, toasted hazelnuts
3 oz peeled garlic cloves
1 large egg yolk
8 fl oz olive oil
Salt
Pepper

Pour boiling water over the walnuts and remove their fine skins. Rub the skins from the hazelnuts.

Crush the nuts and garlic in a mortar with a little salt. Add the egg yolk, then beat in the oil drop by drop as in making a mayonnaise. Season with salt and pepper to taste.

Preserved Goose or Duck
CONFITS D'OIE OU DE CANARD

When the fattened geese and ducks have had the valuable foie gras removed, the carcasses are not wasted. They are made into a valuable household preserve, and used to add flavour to soups, such lean dishes as cassoulet, and to make a meal on their own with fried potatoes or apples. Of course these birds have developed a great deal of fat on their bodies, as well as in their livers. To make confits with an ordinary goose or duck, a lot of lard will be needed to make up the weight.

Cut up the duck or goose (or part of a goose) into pieces. Reserve the fat. Weigh the duck or goose pieces.

For every 2 pounds, mix together:

3 tablespoons sea salt
1 teaspoon saltpetre
1 teaspoon dried thyme
1 bay leaf, crumbled
1 teaspoon freshly ground black pepper
Lard

Mix together the salt, saltpetre, thyme, bay leaf and black pepper. Rub the goose or duck pieces with this mixture. Put them in a bowl, cover and set aside for 24 hours, turning the pieces once.

The next day, rub off the salt and dry the pieces with a clean cloth or kitchen paper.

Weigh the goose or duck fat and add enough lard so that the combined weight is half that of the salted meat. In a large, heavy casserole melt the fats. When the fat is hot add the goose or duck pieces—the fat should cover them—and simmer very gently for 1¼ hours. Test the meat by piercing a piece with a larding needle. If juices still run out of it, cook for a little longer. The meat will remain pink because of the saltpetre.

Wash several small, wide-mouthed bottling jars with soda water, rinse them and dry them upside down in a warm oven. Pour a little lard from the casserole into each jar. Put the jars into the refrigerator until the fat sets. Pack in the goose or duck pieces, not too tightly, leaving 1 inch at the top. Fill the jars with fat from the casserole. If there is not enough fat, melt some more lard. When the meat and fat are cold, put a piece of aluminium foil over the surface of the fat. Cover the jars with air-tight covers and store in a cool place.

To use the *confits*, stand the opened jar in hot water over a very low heat until the fat melts and the pieces of meat can be taken out. For this reason, it is wise to pot the meat in a number of small jars rather than in one large one as most French women do. The fat will be delicious and can be used for pastry, frying potatoes, making *beurre de Gascogne*, as well as a good *cassoulet*.

THE LANGUEDOC will take a long time to live down its reputation for mediocre wine. Somewhere in France there has to be a production line for the red tide of *vin de consommation courante*. The coastal plain from Montpellier to Narbonne is just that. It is not the place for stopping for a bottle of the *vin du pays*, for the *vin du pays* is on its way to Paris by tanker-train to be blended with something a little redder and stronger and labelled *Vin Rouge, onze degrés*.

The wines to look for in the Languedoc are the ones from the foothills rising from the plain to north, west and southwest—the areas of *Vin Délimité de Qualité Supérieure* or VDQS. Four or five of the red-wine areas in this category are heading determinedly for the rank of Appellation Contrôlée, using every modern wine-making dodge to make better and better wine. St-Chinian, Minervois, Corbières and Roussillon already fetch premium prices as wines with vigour and distinction of their own. Since few are exported at the moment there is every reason to conduct your own on-the-spot research.

The Languedoc has VDQS white wines (*clairettes*) too, but they cannot compare with the red. If there is an exception it is the peculiar sun-tanned strong dry white of La Clape, the eccentric seaside massif near Narbonne. Strangely, the Languedoc does have a good white sparkling wine, Blanquette de Limoux from the hill-country south of Carcassonne. Down towards the Spanish border the specialities are *vin vert*, a passably fresh dry white wine compared with the dull *clairettes* of the plain, and the heavy sweet port-like *vin doux naturel* of Banyuls.

St Clément's Charlotte

The St Clément of the title of this dessert was the name-saint of Monsieur Clément Faugier, of Privas in the Ardèche. When the silk trade slumped in his town in the nineteenth century, he helped to save the people from unemployment by producing marrons glacés, a local delicacy, on a commercial scale. It is likely to be his firm's chestnut purée, both natural and sweetened, that is found on grocery shelves today, as well as his marrons glacés, all made from the fine, abundant chestnuts of this part of France.

SERVES 6 TO 8

Boudoir (sponge finger) biscuits
24 sugar cubes
3 tablespoons water
3 oz unsalted butter
1 lb canned sweetened chestnut purée
5 tablespoons rum
2 tablespoons castor sugar
10 fl oz double cream
Marrons glacé

Use a 1½-pint charlotte mould or cake tin. Trim the boudoir biscuits to the right height for the mould. Reserve the trimmings.

Dissolve the sugar cubes in a tablespoon of water over a low heat. When the sugar has dissolved, increase the heat and boil until the syrup is golden brown. Use the caramel to hold the boudoir biscuits together. Place one boudoir biscuit in the mould, curved side against the mould and cut edge up. Dip the long side of another biscuit in the caramel and put it against the first biscuit. Always have the caramel on the inside of the boudoir biscuits as they must only stick to each other and not to the mould. Arrange the trimmings and any left-over biscuits decoratively in the base of the mould using a little caramel to keep them in place.

In a bowl, beat the butter to a cream. Beat in the chestnut purée and 3 tablespoons of the rum. Pour the mixture into the mould which it will half fill.

In a small saucepan, over low heat, dissolve the 2 tablespoons of sugar in the remaining rum and water. Increase the heat and bring the mixture to the boil. Remove the pan from the heat. Moisten the ends of the boudoir biscuits with a little of the hot syrup.

If there is any caramel left, remelt it and mix it in with the rum syrup. In a small bowl whip the cream. Whip in the rum syrup and then pour the mixture on top of the chestnut and butter cream filling in the mould. Reserve a little of the whipped cream mixture.

Cover the charlotte with foil and leave it in the refrigerator for at least 5 hours, but preferably overnight. To serve, ease the charlotte with a thin knife and turn it out on to a serving plate. Decorate the charlotte with the reserved cream and pieces of *marrons glacé*.

Mediterranean fragrances and flavours

Map labels:

ALMONDS

VEGETABLES — FRUIT

ARTICHAUTS BARIGOULE
Stuffed artichokes

CARPENTRAS

TRUFFLES

BANON — CHEESE

• DIGNE

PISTOU
Vegetable soup with basil and cheese

• AVIGNON
MELONS
JAMS

POULET A L'AIL
Chicken cooked with garlic
ASPARAGUS

• APT

THRUSHES

LAVENDER HONEY

RATATOUILLE
Vegetable stew

CAVAILLON

CRYSTALLIZED
FRUIT

TAPENADE
Caper paste

PISSALADIERE
Onions, anchovies and black olive open pie

• ST REMY

"POIVRE D'ANE"
CHEESE

• LAURIS

SALADE NICOISE
Salad with anchovies, olives and

PETITS GRIS
Snails

• PERTUIS

GRILLADES AU FENOUIL
Fish grilled over fennel

NICE •

ARLES

SAUCISSON
Large sausage

LAMB

ASPARAGUS

GRASSE

SOU FASSUM
Stuffed cabbage

RICE

ORANGES

• AIX-EN-PROVENCE

OLIVES

DRAGUIGNAN

ANCHOIADE
Anchovy hors d'oeuvre

GURNARD

CATIGAU
Eel stewed with garlic and red wine

DAUBES
Meat stewed in wine

ECHAUDES
Little doughnuts

ST RAPHAEL •

POUTARGUE
Grey mullet roe

MARTIGUES

AIGO-BOUIDO
Garlic soup

PAN BAGNA
Olive-oil soaked bread
topped with anchovy
and capers

MARSEILLE

STOFICADO
Stewed salt cod

SEA BASS

BOUILLABAISSE
Fish stew with saffron

BOURRIDE
Fish stew

RASCASSE
Scorpion fish

AIOLI
Garlic mayonnaise

• TOULON

SARDINES

SEA BREAM

ESQUINADO
Crabs cooked in
vinegar and water

THE IMAGE OF PROVENCE, its light, its exuberant glory, remains magical. It is from Provence that the Central Mediterranean core of civilization branched towards the chilling north, by way of the pathway of the Rhône.

The terrestrial abundance of Provence is the glory of every small market town. The profusion of the basic flavourings of garlic and olive dazzles the visitor. The fish may not have the flavour of northern seas, but they flaunt their colours unabashed by such comparison. Here is the red and spiky *rescasse*, scorpion-fish, essential to *bouillabaisse*, the brilliant shimmer of the *daurade*,

sea bream, the red mullet, which the Romans prized for its liver, the coral gurnards and the silver sardines ready for grilling over charcoal.

Piquant and vigorous preparations of fish are used as seasoning for bland salads of haricot beans or chick-peas. The fish used in this way are usually anchovies, salted, canned in oil or rolled around capers. *Poutargue* is also used. A speciality of Marrigues, this is grey mullet roe compressed to rich, grainy dryness. It is also served in thin slices on its own with drinks, and has been produced in the Mediterranean since classical times.

Another dish from Marrigues, traditionally eaten on Christmas Eve, consists of eel baked on a layer of chopped leeks, moistened with white wine and flavoured with parsley, garlic, bay leaves and black olives. Apart from *bouillabaisse*, the most famous dish of the coast is *pissaladière* from Nice. Its name comes from *pissalat*, a pungent preparation of anchovies with

which it is flavoured, not after the Italian *pizza*, meaning pie, which it resembles.

Rice comes from the Camargue, where paddy fields produce large, oblong grain that swell to tender succulence when cooked. As might be expected, it resembles Italian rice, and it is made into such Italian style dishes as *risotto* and pilaf of chicken and shellfish.

Northern Italy has its influence, too, on soups and salads flavoured with basil, the king of herbs. (Its name comes from the Greek *basileus*, which means king.) It is easy to understand how it got its royal name when one eats the superb tomatoes of Provence sprinkled with chopped fresh basil and olive oil vinaigrette.

To a northerner, it seems that tomatoes only become fit to eat in Provence, where they grow to rich, sweet firmness, out of doors, in the sun. Up in Touraine, people wait eagerly for the day in spring when the tasteless tomatoes of Dutch glasshouses disappear before the first enormous and craggy

PROVENCE AND CORSICA

CORSICA

BASTIA
FIADONE
White-cheese tart

CALVI
BROCCIO
CHEESE

BLACKBIRDS

COPPA
Salami

CALACUCCIA
NIOLO CHEESE

CORTE

VIZZAVONA
TROUT

LONZO
Smoked fillet of pork

FIGATELLI
Pork-liver sausages

PATE DE MERLES
Blackbird pâté

AJACCIO

BOUILLABAISSE
Fish stew

CHESTNUTS

MYRTLE

OURSINS
Sea urchins

WOOD
PIGEONS

MULLET

BONIFACIO
MURENE AUX RAISINS SECS
Moray eel with raisins

tomatoes from the south. In May, too, the Provence peaches come to Paris like the first swallows of summer. In July and August, orange-fleshed melons from Cavaillon, kept cool beneath a blue and white striped market awning, mark the holidays more firmly than any calendar.

The novelist Stendhal, who was born in Grenoble, which is not far from Provence, nevertheless sighed as a child for the "real" south of Provence, where orange trees grow in the ground and not in movable tubs. The word orange goes back to pre-Aryan India, to a word which means "perfume within". The Arabs pronounced it as *naranj*. The Italians turned *naranj* into *arancia,* and the French of the Middle Ages slipped into *orange,* because the town of Orange was the big centre for growing the fruit. From the waxy blossoms comes the fragrance of orange-flower water, which adds a musky depth of flavour to certain *provençal* dishes. At Grasse, the perfume town which is surrounded by fields of lavender, orange flowers are candied into aromatic sweets.

Besides oranges, other luxuries of Vaucluse are the glacé fruits of Apt, and the asparagus of Lauris, which were so appreciated by Escoffier. Then there is Carpentras, which is a truffle town.

The first successful method of cultivating truffles was discovered by a peasant, Joseph Talon of Vaucluse, in 1810. He had planted a piece of rough, flinty ground with acorns. A few years later he found truffles growing beneath the young oak trees. Quietly, he bought patch after patch of flint ground, and sowed them all with acorns from those first trees. A friend, a truffle merchant, sent the first cultivated truffles to Paris in 1855, and publicized the Talon method. Dishes using cultivated as well as wild truffles increased in *haute cuisine*: in 1890 four million pounds of truffles were produced from one or the other source.

It was about the same time that the Mediterranean coast became increasingly popular as a winter holiday place. People had been wintering there since the Old Stone Age Aurignacians made the journey to what is now the French-Italian border (and left their bones and necklaces in a burial cave to prove it). However, the arrival of Lord Brougham, thousands of years later, at Cannes in 1934, made the coast really popular with the rich and the grand.

The development of the Casino at Monte Carlo in 1862 set the seal on what many would regard as the Riviera's doom. By 1884, the luxurious express trains brought royal and famous persons to spend a restorative season at Nice or Cannes or Monte Carlo. Their comfort was soon assured by César Ritz, the Swiss hotelier, and his friend and working partner, Auguste Escoffier, who realized that a fine hotel needed the extra attraction of fine food.

Corsica

Corsica, happily, has never been fashionable. There the visitor can still find solitude on lonely beaches of great beauty. The blue air is fragrant with the sweet-smelling bushes which form the *maquis,* on the lower slopes of the mountains. Blackbirds fatten on the berries, and are caught by the hundred to be made into Corsica's best-known speciality, *pâté de merles*. They are a browner and plumper blackbird than the northern variety. Their rich flavour is underlined by the use in their preparation of juniper berries and a myrtle-flavoured spirit, products again of the *maquis*.

The general Corsican style of cooking fish and meat is Provençal-Italian—tomatoes, peppers, garlic, olive oil and fennel bring out the flavours of squid, crawfish and red mullet. The *charcuterie* is dominated by the Italian style of *coppa* and *lonzo,* which are preparations of smoked pork in a long sausage shape.

Many of the sheep's milk cheeses of the island go to the Roquefort caves, in Languedoc, to mature. But in the spring, summer and autumn there are the soft cheeses, *nioli* and *broccio*. Some are dried for winter eating, but when they are fresh they are eaten with fruit, or used in omelettes and sweet curd tarts. Corsicans also have a variety of small cakes made from chestnut flour, which are baked in the oven on chestnut leaves. Indeed, the food of Corsica has a note entirely of its own, in spite of the obvious Italian and French influences.

Dishes rich with herbs and garlic

Fish Soup with Aïoli
BOURRIDE

It is impossible to make a proper bouillabaisse *away from the Mediterranean, because one cannot get the right fish elsewhere, but here is a recipe for another excellent Provençal soup,* la bourride.

SERVES 6

3 to 4 lb firm white fish or squid, cleaned
2 large onions, chopped
1 leek, chopped
2 large tomatoes, blanched, peeled and chopped
1 lb potatoes, peeled and thinly sliced
4 garlic cloves
2 to 3 strips of thinly pared orange peel
Bouquet of thyme, fennel, parsley, bay leaf
Salt
Pepper
1 recipe Aïoli
12 slices French bread, toasted lightly then rubbed with garlic and fried in olive oil

Cut the fish into large slices. Put all the vegetables and the garlic into a large pot. Place the fish on top with the orange peel and bouquet of herbs. Season discreetly because the stock will later be reduced. Pour in 2½ to 3½ pints of water. Bring to the simmer and cook for 10 minutes or longer depending on the fish.

When the fish is cooked transfer it to a warm serving dish with the potatoes. Boil the ingredients left in the pot until there is about 1 pint of liquid left. Correct the seasoning and strain the liquid.

Put half the *aïoli* into a large bowl (the other half goes into a serving bowl for the table). Slowly pour in the hot liquid using a wooden spoon to mix it with the *aïoli*. Tip into a clean pan and stir over a low heat until the liquid thickens slightly—be careful not to let it boil, or the egg will curdle. Put the bread into a tureen, pour the soup over it and serve with the dish of potatoes and fish, and the bowl of *aïoli* as an extra seasoning. If preferred, the potatoes can be cooked separately; if so do not slice them.

Garlic Mayonnaise
AÏOLI

Aïoli *is not only used for the magnificent spread of cold food,* aïoli garni *to which it has given its name, but also for enriching such soups as* bourride. *The amount of garlic put into the sauce depends on individual taste, but there should be plenty of it.*

4 to 8 garlic cloves
Salt
2 large egg yolks
15 fl oz olive oil
Pepper
Lemon juice

Crush the garlic with a little salt in a mortar. Beat in the egg yolks, then the olive oil drop by drop, just as if making a mayonnaise. When the sauce becomes really thick, beat a little faster. Season with pepper and lemon juice.

Aïoli garni is usually served on a huge dish. There should be salt cod, soaked, simmered and boned, poached squid, monkfish or mullet, or some fresh-water fish. Surround them with potatoes boiled in their jackets, and lightly cooked cauliflower, carrots, green beans, peas, chick-peas, white haricot beans, snails and hard-boiled eggs. Cold beef or lamb can be served on a separate dish.

Basil Soup
SOUPE AU PISTOU

This is really a minestrone soup, flavoured with a Niçois version of the Genoese pesto, *a pommade of basil, garlic, pine kernels, pecorino or Parmesan cheese and olive oil. It shows the influence of Italy on this part of the French Mediterranean coast. (At the Pyrenean side, by Collioure, Spain has influenced a number of dishes* à la catalane.)

SERVES 6

1 onion, sliced
Olive oil
8 oz tomatoes, blanched, peeled and chopped
8 oz French beans, sliced
4 oz cooked haricot beans
8 oz courgettes, sliced
8 oz potatoes, peeled and diced
8 oz carrots, peeled and diced
Water
Salt
Pepper
2 handfuls vermicelli
PISTOU
3 large garlic cloves
Good bunch of basil
Salt
3 tablespoons olive oil
3 heaped tablespoons grated Gruyère
Bowl of grated Gruyère or Parmesan

Cook the onion gently in a very little olive oil until it just begins to brown. Put all the vegetables into the pan and add enough water to cover them by 2 to 3 inches. The proportions of the vegetables can be varied, but they should always include French beans, tomatoes and potatoes. Season with the salt and pepper. Simmer for 10 minutes, then add the vermicelli and cook for a further 15 minutes.

Make the *pistou* while the soup cools. Pound the garlic and basil with a little salt in a mortar, or mix in a blender. Pour in the oil drop by drop, then add the grated Gruyère.

Pour the soup into a tureen, mix in the *pistou* and serve immediately with the bowl of grated cheese.

Beef Stew Provençal Style
BOEUF EN DAUBE

In the past, braised beef stews of this kind were cooked in a daubière, *a pot with a saucer-shaped lid. It was buried in the red-hot cinders at the edge of the fire on the hearth and more cinders were put on top. The modern enamelled cast-iron pot roaster or* daubière, *often called a* doufeu, *placed over a low heat instead of ashes, and water is poured into the lid. This increases the condensation of steam inside the pot, keeping the contents moist during the long, slow cooking. There are many versions of this recipe, which can be made with lamb instead of beef.*

A beef daube *of this kind is served with boiled macaroni. Put the drained macaroni in layers in a well-oiled pot and sprinkle each layer with grated Gruyère cheese. Pour on some of the sauce from the* daube, *and brown it in the oven until the top layer of cheese is crusty and golden. Macaroni cooked this way is known as* macaronade.

SERVES 6 TO 8

3 to 4 lb beef for braising
½ calf's heel or 2 pig's trotters
Olive oil
8 oz salt belly of pork or unsmoked streaky bacon, cut in strips
Black olives *or* capers *or* a mixture of chopped garlic and parsley
MARINADE
2 onions, quartered, each piece stuck with clove
3 carrots, halved
2 whole garlic cloves
1 garlic clove, crushed with a knife
2 strips of orange peel
½ celery stick, left whole
½ teaspoon juniper berries
Bouquet garni
2 pints red wine
2 tablespoons olive oil
4 tablespoons red wine vinegar
Salt
12 peppercorns

Cut the beef into large pieces. Put them in a large bowl with the calf's heel or pig's trotters. Add all the ingredients for the marinade. Cover and leave for 6 hours, turning everything from time to time. At the end of this time, remove the onion and carrot pieces, and the beef, and leave them to drain in a large strainer over the bowl.

In the *daubière*, or in a flameproof casserole, heat 4 tablespoons of the olive oil and brown the pork or bacon. Next put in the marinated pieces of onion and carrot. When they are limp, add the meat. Once the meat is completely browned, pour the marinade and all its ingredients into the pot. Bring it to the boil, cover tightly and lower the heat so that the liquid barely simmers. By tradition, a *daube* is left to

ook for 6 hours, so the longer it simmers the etter. If it is more convenient, the pot can be ut into an oven, set at a temperature between 50° and 275°F (Gas Mark ¼ to ½). Make sure hat the lid is wedged tightly, so that no steam scapes.

Be careful to skim the fat from the top. Black lives are often added when the stew is re-eated, or capers or a savoury chopping of arlic and parsley can be added just before erving.

It is also important to check the seasoning nd the consistency of the sauce, which should e slightly syrupy with the gelatine from the eal or pork bones. If it lacks a concentrated avour, strain it off and reduce it.

Chicken Corsican Style
POULET A LA CORSOISE

his is a simple and piquant recipe. Do not add ny salt until the end of the cooking, as the olives nd pork or bacon will provide seasoning.

ERVES 4

lb roasting chicken
Olive oil
oz salt belly of pork, or unsmoked streaky
  bacon, cut into strips ¼ inch thick
oz button mushrooms left whole
oz stoned olives
lb tomatoes, blanched, peeled and
  chopped
fl oz brandy
lb new potatoes
ugar
epper
alt

Brown the chicken in the oil in a deep flame-proof pot, along with the strips of pork or acon and the mushrooms. Add the olives ogether with the tomatoes and the brandy. Cover tightly and leave to simmer for 1 hour, r until the chicken is cooked.

Meanwhile, in a frying-pan, brown the new

When Providence set out to make the earthly paradise it left Provence lacking in only one thing—wine worthy of all its other pleasures. Provençal wine does not rise to great heights. It is easy to forgive it, and concentrate on the setting sun in the rim of the glass. But the fact must be recorded. With the rarest exceptions, notably the red wine of Bandol and the white of Cassis, Provence wine is generally rosé—which means, almost by definition, one cut above ordinary and no more.

Of the little white there is, someone made the remark, "tarpaulin edged with lace". Perhaps the red of the hills around Aix, resin-and-thyme-scented, comes the closest to being worthy of its setting.

potatoes lightly in olive oil. Add them to the pot halfway through the cooking time.

When the chicken is cooked, transfer it to a serving dish together with the potatoes. Taste the sauce. Add a little sugar, pepper and salt if necessary. Pour the sauce around the chicken and serve.

Vegetable Stew Nice Style
RATATOUILLE A LA NICOISE

There are many versions of this famous dish of southern France. The word ratatouille means a stew, and it derives in part from the old verb touiller, to stir up. Vary the proportions of aubergines, courgettes and peppers but avoid wateriness at all costs.

SERVES 6

1 lb courgettes, sliced
1 lb aubergines, sliced
Salt
3 sweet peppers, if possible 1 red, 1 yellow
  and 1 green
4 tablespoons olive oil
2 to 3 large onions, sliced
2 large garlic cloves, chopped
2 anchovy fillets, chopped (optional)
1 lb tomatoes, blanched, peeled and
  chopped
Black pepper
Sugar or tomato concentrate
Chopped fresh basil or parsley

Arrange the courgette and aubergine slices in 2 colanders and sprinkle them with salt. Leave for 1 hour, then blot them dry with kitchen paper. Remove the stalks and seeds from the peppers and cut them into strips.

In a wide pan, heat the olive oil. Add the onions, garlic and anchovies and cook gently until the onions are soft and very lightly browned. Add the aubergines, courgettes, peppers and tomatoes. Season with plenty of black pepper. Cook steadily, uncovered, until the vegetables are reduced to a thick stew. Apart from the tomatoes and onions, the other vegetables should retain an identifiable shape. Correct the seasoning, adding sugar or tomato concentrate if the flavour is not sufficiently piquant. Sprinkle with the basil preferably, or parsley; these herbs should be fresh, not dried.

Serve hot or cold as a first or vegetable course, or hot with veal, lamb, steak or pork chops.

Crêpes Suzette

The chef Henri Charpentier claimed to have invented Crêpes Suzette. In the middle of the 1890s he was working at the Café de Paris in Monte Carlo. One day, the Prince of Wales brought several friends to lunch, all gentlemen except for one little girl called Suzette. Henri

Charpentier had made a special sauce for the occasion, based on a simpler dish which had often been made by his peasant foster-mother. As he stood near the Prince's table, nervously reheating the pancakes in his new sauce, the whole thing caught fire. He tasted it apprehensively, and found that the sauce had become far more delicious.

The Prince ate the pancakes with his fork in the polite way, then spooned up the sauce and asked the name of the pudding. "Crêpes Princesse," replied the astute young chef. The Prince realized that the name was ruled by the feminine gender of the word crêpes, and that the compliment was intended for him, but "he protested with mock ferocity that there was a lady present. She . . . rose to her feet and holding out her little skirt wide with her hands she made him a curtsey. 'Will you change Crêpes Princesse to Crêpes Suzette?' he asked."

If you want to make the pancakes in advance, use the recipe for fouaces under Brittany. There is such a high proportion of egg in this recipe that the pancakes become tough with keeping, so do not make them in advance. The batter is best kept for several hours before using.

SERVES 4
PANCAKES
3 eggs
2 rounded tablespoons plain flour
1 tablespoon water
1 tablespoon milk
Pinch salt
SAUCE
1 heaped tablespoon vanilla sugar
1-inch square orange peel
1-inch square lemon peel
4 oz unsalted butter
6 tablespoons Maraschino
6 tablespoons Kirschwasser
8 tablespoons Curaçao

Beat the pancake ingredients together to make a smooth batter. Cook them in an 8-inch omelette pan in the usual way. When each pancake is done, fold it in half, then again to make a pocket-handkerchief triangle. There is enough batter to make 8 pancakes. Make them shortly before the meal.

For the sauce, liquidize the sugar and peels in a blender. Put the butter, cut in pieces, on a small plate. Mix the liqueurs and put them into a small pitcher. When ready to serve the pancakes, melt the butter over a table burner in a chafing dish. When the butter bubbles, pour just over half the liqueur mixture into it and allow it to catch fire in the burner flame. When the flames die away, put in the pancakes and the sugar mixture. Turn the pancakes over so that they are reheated and bathed in the sauce. Finally pour in the remaining liqueur and allow it to catch fire again. Serve immediately the flames have died down.

Three small cuisines, simple and excellent

TUCKED INTO THE ALPS and surrounded by powerful neighbours, Switzerland is divided into three linguistic regions that are further subdivided into twenty-five self-governing cantons. Not surprisingly, the linguistic borders are also culinary borders.

The largest of the three regions that form the Swiss Confederation is known as the Deutsch-Schweiz. It stretches from the Austrian and German borders across to Bern, the capital, and includes Zurich, Basle and Lucerne. German is the official language, but in the eastern cantons there are small pockets where Romansch, an ancient Latin dialect, is spoken. The French-speaking region, known as the Suisse-Romande, covers the area around Geneva and Lausanne. The Ticino, the canton which includes Lugarno and Locarno, comprises the Italian-speaking region.

The German-speaking part of Switzerland is the home of some of the country's most famous dishes. A national dish, for example, is Zurich's *Geschnetzeltes Kalbfleisch*, thin strips of carefully sautéed veal in a cream and wine sauce which is also made in the Suisse-Romande, where it is called *émincé de veau*. Sometimes calves' liver is substituted for veal and the dish is then called *Lebergeschnetzeltes*. When chicken is used it is called *émincé de volaille*.

To make Geschnetzeltes *to serve 4, slice 1 pound of veal, fillet or top of leg, across the grain as thinly as possible. Cut the slices into small squares. Melt 2 ounces of butter in a large, heavy frying-pan. Add the veal and 1 finely chopped Spanish onion. Sauté over high heat, stirring constantly, until the veal begins to brown.*

Lower the heat, add 6 tablespoons of dry white wine and 8 tablespoons of double cream. Season to taste with salt and freshly ground black pepper. Bring to the simmering point, stirring and scraping the bottom of the pan clean with a wooden spoon. Serve immediately.

Nothing goes better with a dish of *Geschnetzeltes* than *Rösti*, a crisp, brown potato cake which also appears frequently as a breakfast or supper dish in Swiss homes. *Rösti* can be made with boiled or raw potatoes. Sometimes a few tablespoons of grated cheese are mixed with the potatoes before they are fried, or they are flavoured with bacon or onion.

To make Rösti *to serve 4, boil 2 pounds of potatoes in their jackets and drain them. When the potatoes are completely cold, peel them and grate them coarsely. Cut 4 slices of bacon into small pieces. In a large, heavy frying-pan sauté the bacon until the fat is transparent. Add the potatoes. Season them with salt and freshly ground black pepper and fry over a moderate heat, turning the potatoes constantly with a spatula so that the bottom of the pan remains clean.*

With the spatula pat the potatoes into a firm cake. Melt 2 ounces of butter around the sides of the pan. Cover, and fry the potato cake gently for a further 10 to 15 minutes, or until a golden crust forms on the bottom. Shake the pan from time to time to prevent the potato cake from sticking. Invert the Rösti *on to a heated serving dish and serve immediately.*

Throughout the German-speaking region there are excellent sausages, with names like *Schublige, Wienerli, Emmentalerli* and *Pantli*, which are boiled, fried or served cold. Small, freshly cooked hams, known as *Schufeli* or *Schinkli*, which are served hot in thick slices, are another speciality of the area.

The most famous preserved meat of all, *Bündnerfleisch*, takes its name from the canton of Graubünden in eastern Switzerland. It is salted beef which is hung to dry in the cold mountain air. Shaved into the thinnest of slices, it is served with a grinding of black pepper as an appetizer.

Graubünden is also the home of the Engadin pastry cooks, who are famous throughout Switzerland. The *Engadiner Nusstorte*, made according to jealously guarded family recipes, is a closed tart of rich pastry filled with coarsely ground hazelnuts or walnuts, cream and honey. Every canton has its favourite cake. *Ruebli-torte*, made with grated carrots and blanched almonds and decorated with tiny marzipan carrots, is a speciality of Aargu. *Zuger Kirschtorte* is flavoured with kirsch distilled from the cherries that grow in great orchards around Zug. Glarus is famous for its *Birnbrot*, pear bread, a long, golden brown loaf filled with a rich, dark filling of dried pears, nuts and raisins and fragrant with spices and kirsch.

A strong French influence is evident in the cooking of the Suisse-Romande. The best restaurants equal those of France and standards are also high in the little bistros, or *pintes*.

The speciality of the Valais is *raclette*, the very special cheese dish which was immortalized in *Heidi*, the classic children's novel. *Raclette* is traditionally made with Gomser cheese from the Val de Bagne. The cheese is cut in half and while it is melting at an open wood fire, or in a Raclette oven, a hot potato is peeled and then placed in a little basket. As the surface of the cheese melts it is scraped off and spread over the potato. Baby gherkins, pickled onions and red wine are served with this wonderfully simple and aromatic dish.

The border between the Deutsch-Schweiz and the Suisse-Romand regions is not always immediately apparent, and menus offering *émincé de güggeli*, chicken in cream sauce, suggest that the Swiss themselves have not quite made up their minds. But there is no mistaking the dramatic change that greets the eyes as one emerges from the St Gotthard tunnel into the Ticino. Here the Alps are softened with lush greenery, the air is warmer and the people are unmistakably Italian. The cooking, too, has an unmistakably Italian flavour.

Minestrone replaces the substantial, cold-weather soups of the north. *Risotto* is cooked the Italian way, the liquid stirred in little by little rather than all at once as it is in the other parts of Switzerland. *Polenta* and pasta appear on menus, together with *piccata*, thin slices of veal baked with egg and cheese, and *stufato*, a pot roast of beef that is a speciality in Lombardy. In the Ticino the *Lamm-Gigot* of the northern cantons is called *coscia di agnello*, and is generously flavoured with garlic.

Switzerland's international culinary reputation rests largely on cheese. Two of these, Emmenthal, with its large-sized holes, and Gruyère, which has smaller holes and a piquant, nutty flavour, are exported all over the world. Sbrinz, which takes its name from the town of Brienz in the Bernese Oberland, is a hard, matured cheese which can be used for grating and is eaten fresh. Appenzeller is another traditional cheese that has acquired an international reputation.

Every canton has its traditional cheese dishes—soups, fritters, tarts, cakes and puddings, both savoury and sweet. But the

SWITZERLAND

BASLE
BASLER LECKERLI
Spiced Christmas biscuits

AARGAU

GESCHNETZELTES (EMINCE DE VEAU)
Veal strips in wine and cream sauce

APPENZELLER RÄSSKÄSE
Strong cheese
APPENZELL

RÜEBLITORTE
Sweet carrot and almond cake

ZÜRICH

ZÜRCHER LEBERSPIESSCHEN
Skewered calves' liver with bacon and sage

ZUGER
KIRSCHTORTE
Cherry cake

BERNER PLATTE
Mixed boiled meats
with French beans
or sauerkraut

BIRCHERMÜESLI
Dried fruit and oats

ZUGER SEE

NEUENBURGER FONDUE
Melted cheese with bread cubes
NEUCHATEL

LUCERNE

RÖSTI
Fried potato cake
BERNE

SBRINZ CHEESE

BIRNBROT
Pear bread

WHITEFISH

VAUD

EMMENTALER CHEESE

BÜNDNERFLEISCH
Air-dried beef

BURE-BROT
Country bread

LAKE NEUCHATEL • **FRIBOURG**

DAIRY CATTLE

GRAUBÜNDEN

ILET DE PERCHE
X AMANDES
h almonds

LAKE TROUT

VACHERIN MONT D'OR CHEESE

BÜNDNER KÄSESUPPE
Cheese soup

FRIBOURG FONDUE
Melted cheese with bread cubes

EMMENTALERLI
Sausages

ENGADINER NUSSTORTE
Honey and hazelnut tart

SWITZERLAND

OMBLE CHEVALIER
Char

STUFATO ALLA TICINESE
Pot roast of beef with wine

WILD CHERRIES

LAKE GENEVA

GRUYERE CHEESE

TICINO

PICCATA ALLA TICINESE
Breadcrumbed pork slices

VALAIS

GENEVA

FONDUE
BOURGUIGNONNE
Meat chunks dipped
in boiling oil

RACLETTE
Melted cheese with baked potato

LAKE LUGANO

KALBSCHNITZEL
CORDON BLEU
Breaded veal cutlet
filled with cheese and ham

FRUIT

SHAD

most famous of all is *fondue*, an inspired combination of Swiss cheese, Swiss wine and Swiss kirsch.

A Swiss fondue is a meal and a party game. Everyone sits round the earthenware *caquelon*, the fondue dish, in which the creamy cheese mixture bubbles slowly, kept hot over a small spirit heater. Each guest has a long fork and a plate. A basket of fresh bread cubes is placed on the table, and the trick is to spear a bread cube on to one's fork, dip it into the cheese and transfer it to one's mouth without dripping. Anyone who loses his bread in the sauce must pay a forfeit, traditionally a round of drinks—although an attractive woman may settle her debts with a kiss.

Fondue recipes vary from region to region. For *Fondue Neuchâtel* equal parts of Gruyère and Emmenthal are used; *Fondue Fribourg* is made with a mature Vacherin cheese; the Vandois begin by sautéing a

clove of garlic in butter before adding the cheese; and in Geneva, where the French influence is strongest, mushrooms are included.

In spite of its French name, *fondue bourguignonne* is neither French nor a fondue, although the procedure is similar. Each person dips a cube of steak into a pan of sizzling oil and holds it there until it is cooked to his taste. The meat is then transferred to an ordinary fork—the fondue fork would be too hot to eat from—and dipped into one of the little bowls of *tartare*, *rémoulade*, *béarnaise* or tomato sauce.

The three mini-cuisines of Switzerland may not add up to a great culinary tradition. However, excellent meals in the best French, German or Italian tradition are prepared by Swiss chefs in the cities' great restaurants, and the cooking of the cantons is unsurpassed for people who like to eat simply and very well.

THE DRINK-PROFILE OF SWITZERLAND can be compared with that of Alsace. In both, vineyards and orchards alternate on the hills, the vineyards giving principally white wine, and the orchards the distilling material for a range of potent white spirits.

Although Switzerland's vineyards are scattered through the three language-divisions of the country, it is the French-speaking zone that has the most and the best—above all the Rhône valley almost from its beginning down to Lake Geneva. Rather yeasty white wines of varying degrees of crispness are its speciality. The Vaud (the north shore of Lake Geneva) in addition is planting more and more red-wine grapes. The region of Neuchâtel also makes an important contribution. None of this, however, discourages the Swiss from buying vast quantities of burgundy, and their special love, Beaujolais.

Kirsch, which they distil from cherries, is the Swiss national spirit, and one of the most useful of spirits in the kitchen.

Over two thousand years of culinary artistry

VAL D'AOSTA
TROUT
RIVER ADIGE
APPLES
HARICOT BEANS
PEARS
SHAD
TRENTINO-
ALTO
ADIGE
GAME
FRIULI-
VENEZIA
GIULIA
ORCHARD FRUIT
LAKE
MAGGIORE
LAKE
COMO
SNAILS
LOMBARDY
LAKE
GARDA
MAIZE
TREVISO
RADICCHIO
ROSSO
Wild chicory
VENICE
PERCH
IVREA
CIPOLLINE
Small onions
VERCELLI
RICE
MILAN
WHEAT
VENETO
LARGE
PRAWNS
TURIN
GRAPES
PIEDMONT
RIVER PO
ROVIGO
DUCKS
WHEAT
ALBA
MUSHROOMS
PARMA
CATTLE
COMACCHIO
EELS
SQUID
CUNEO
CHESTNUTS
WHITE
TRUFFLES
EMILIA-ROMAGNA
TOMATOES
OLIVES
LIGURIA
GENOA
BASIL
OLIVES
PIGS
FRUIT
BOLOGNA
SOLE
SHELLFISH
SARDINES
ANCHOVIES
LUCCA
CHESTNUTS
FLORENCE
RIVER ARNO
CHICKENS
THE MARCHES
VEGETABLES
INKFISH
MONKFISH
SQUID
HARICOT
BEANS
TUSCANY
CATTLE
RIVER TIBER
TROUT
BLACK
TRUFFLES
PIGS
WILD
PIGEONS
BABY CLAMS
GAME
UMBRIA
NORCIA
SAFFRON
SEA BREAM
PEAS
SHEEP
KID
LAZIO
LAMB
CHILLIES
L'AQUILA
RED MULLET
OCTOPUS
ROME
NEMI
WILD
STRAWBERRIES
ARTICHOKES
ABRUZZO-
MOLISE
SWEET
PEPPERS
TROUT
SHEEP
SPINY LOBSTER
GREY MULLET
VEGETABLES
TOMATOES
WHEAT
APULIA
BARI
LAMPREYS
BABY CLAMS
MUSSELS
CAMPANIA
NAPLES
GRAPES
ALMONDS
CRABS
SASSARI
OLIVES
MYRTLE
CITRUS
FRUIT
BROCCOLI
BASILICATA
FIGS
OLIVES
TARANTO
OYSTERS
OCTOPUS
FRUIT
CHILLIES
SHEEP
GOATS
GAME
RED MULLET
LARGE PRAWNS
SWEET
PEPPERS
SARDINIA
CITRUS FRUIT
S
SALT
CAGLIARI
DOGFISH
ANCHOVIES
GARFISH
TUNA
SARDINES
ANCHOVIES
SWORDFISH
CALABRIA
AUBERGINES
PALERMO
CITRUS
FRUIT
MESSINA
DURUM
WHEAT
GRAPES
SICILY
TOMATOES
FENNEL
PISTACHIO NUTS
ALMONDS

ITALIAN CUISINE is one of the world's best and reflects the colour and vitality of the country and the imagination of its people. It is a culinary tradition which goes back over two thousand years. When people in other parts of Europe were still living on a staple diet of millet gruel and oatmeal porridge, in Sicily the Greek conquerors were feasting lavishly and Plato, the Greek philosopher, wrote with disgust about Sicilian gluttony.

A few centuries later, Petronius described a typical Roman feast which began with peahen's eggs, truffles, oysters, asparagus, lobsters, fried sausages, olives and Syrian plums, followed by the main course—vast platters piled high with stuffed geese, chickens and pigs, stewed flamingos' tongues and peacocks' brains, goose-liver pâté and game.

The art of cooking declined with the fall of the Roman Empire, and it was not until the fifteenth century that it revived in the merchant cities of Genoa, Venice, Pisa and Florence. While France is generally considered to possess the greatest of all cuisines, Catherine De' Medici, on her marriage in 1533 to the future Henri II of France, took Florentine cooks with her and introduced the French to the skills of cooking. The French were more than apt pupils, but the original credit must go to the Italians, who also brought with them artichokes, haricot beans, peas and other vegetables not previously known outside Italy.

Italy has been united for barely a hundred years. Before that there was a tradition of small city-states. Each was independent of the next, even at war with it, although separated by only a few miles, and each had its own individual way of cooking and its specialities. There is, therefore, no Italian cuisine as such, but rather many regional cuisines.

Due to modern methods of transportation and food distribution, however, good things have spread from one region to another. Pasta, originally from the south, is today eaten everywhere, even in the traditional maize- and rice-eating north. *Pesto*, the Genoese basil sauce, can be found in restaurants in any large Italian town. Bolognese meat sauce has its imitators everywhere. *Grissini*, bread sticks, from Turin and *panettone*, rich yeast cake, from Milan, are commercially made and sold all over the world, as is the most famous of all, the Neapolitan pizza. The best Italian food is, as a rule, still eaten in its own region—beef in Tuscany, artichokes in Rome, peas in the Lazio and the Marches, rice in the north, fish in the port where it has just been landed.

Every Italian loves food and insists on it being cooked with care. Pasta must be just the right texture—*al dente*, still slightly firm. Italians expect to wait twenty minutes in a restaurant while the spaghetti is prepared, and at home, the cook will call out that she is about to *bùttar giu*—throw in—the pasta so that no one has any excuse for arriving late to eat it.

An Italian meal usually begins with *antipasti*, which may include, besides the expected salami and Parma ham (often served with melon or fresh figs), sardines, a seafood salad, stuffed tomatoes and such vegetables as artichoke hearts or mushrooms. The next course will be *minestra*, soup, possibly *minestrone*, thick vegetable soup, *pasta in brodo*, small pasta shapes in broth, or *past'asciutta*, which literally means dry pasta, served with a sauce or cheese rather than in broth. The variations of *past'asciutta* are legion.

Spaghetti are found everywhere. Ribbon noodles, called *fettuccine, tagliatelle* or *pappardelle*, are popular in Central Italy, and the larger tubes (*ziti, rigatoni* and *penne*), made of wheat flour and water, in the south. Then there are *lasagne*, wide strips of pasta; *vermicelli*, fine spaghetti, although the word is used generally for spaghetti in the south, *tonnarelli* and *tonnellini*, match-like noodles; *bucatini*, spaghetti tubes; and *maccheroni*, which can mean short, curved tubes of pasta or any of the many shapes of pasta in general. There are all the stuffed pastas made with fresh dough from the *ravioli* and *agnolotti*, usually square, to the semicircular *anolini* of Parma and the navel-shaped *tortellini* of Bologna. Fillings vary from meat to spinach with cheese. In Bologna spinach is mixed into pasta dough to make *lasagne verdi* or *tagliatelle verdi*, green pasta or noodles. Pasta can be made with eggs (*pasta all'uovo*), as is usual in Central Italy, or simply with flour and water; in a factory (*pasta secca*, dried pasta) or at home (*pasta fatta in casa*). Freshly made egg pasta really does taste different from the commercial product, and is not difficult to make, although it does take a little time.

The main course is meat, fish or poultry. Meat is often roasted, sometimes on a spit. Chicken may be cut in pieces and served in a sauce. Fish, too, is often served roasted or baked. Salad, either plain or a mixture of lettuce, sweet ripe tomatoes, tender green beans and other vegetables, can be dressed by each person, who helps himself to the olive oil, red wine vinegar, salt and pepper which are nearly always on the table. Spinach, green beans or cauliflower are often cooked, allowed to cool and served as a salad with an oil and vinegar dressing.

The desserts are usually simple—ice-cream, and especially water ices, are found all over Italy. Fresh fruit is often preferred by Italians themselves. The luscious peaches and cherries and the delicate little wild strawberries are often eaten simply with a little orange or lemon juice or even a drop or two of vinegar to enhance their flavour, but never with cream, which is not much used in Italy.

Many Italian cheeses are famous—strong Gorgonzola, creamy Bel Paese, piquant Parmesan—but these, too, it is often best to eat in the region from which they come: buttery Fontina in Piedmont, fresh *ricotta*, creamy cottage cheese, in Rome, or in Naples the little *mozzarella* cheeses, kept moist in their own buttermilk. *Provolone* or *pecorino*, both piquant cheeses, leave a lovely taste in the mouth at the end of a meal.

Eastern Italy, north of the Po River, is collectively called *le tre Venezie*, the "three Venetias". These are Venezia Euganea, the modern-day Veneto with Venice as its capital, Venezia Tridentina, now shortened to Trentino and with the Alto Adige added, and the Venezia Giulia, together with the Friuli. Although they share a certain geographical unity, their culinary traditions are quite distinct.

Venice itself, despite long Austro-Hungarian occupation, has remained true to her tradition of the "cuisine of the Doges". Under the Doges, men of foresight and learning, such artists as Bellini and Tintoretto flourished. Burano still produces the exquisite lace that once adorned the rich silk and velvet robes. Delicate blown glass from the factories of Murano, still in operation, graced the Doges' tables. This same subtlety and craftsmanship inform the cuisine of Venice today. It is not peasant cooking. Many dishes must be prepared with care, watched until the exact moment of perfection is reached. Typical of such dishes are the *risotto* (*risoto* in dialect) which in Venice must always be served *all'onda*, rippling, a reference to its liquid consistency, and singularly appropriate to this city of the sea.

Delicate delights and sober simplicity

A dish of which the Venetians are rightly proud is *fegato alla veneziana*, paper-thin slices of calf's liver, cooked with onions. It is meltingly tender and delicately flavoured. Dried salt cod, *baccalà*, although not a product of the region, is widely eaten. In Venice it is beaten with olive oil and a seasoning of salt, pepper, parsley and garlic until white and creamy. In Vicenza it is baked with onions and traditionally served with *polenta*.

The Adriatic is the richest of all Italy's seas. Granceole, spider crabs, with a taste somewhere between lobster and crab, are a delicacy, as are *moleche*, soft-shell crabs. Shellfish of every kind appear on restaurant menus, as well as the famous scampi, sardines and the small Adriatic sole. A typical way of preparing sole is *in saor*: first fried, then marinated in olive oil and wine vinegar with onions, raisins and pine nuts—a legacy from the days of trade with Byzantium. Another delicious fish is the angler-fish or monkfish, here known as a *rospo*, toad, because of its hideous appearance. For this reason its head is invariably removed before it is served.

Excellent wild mushrooms are found in the Veneto, and there are some fine vegetables, such as the famous asparagus from Bassano del Grappa, often eaten cold with mayonnaise, and the even better-known *radicchio rosso*, red chicory. This grows only in a very small area, around Castelfranco Veneto, where it looks not unlike a pink cabbage rose, and in nearby Treviso, where it grows dark purple-red and torpedo-shaped. Even those who do not appreciate its rather bitter taste willingly buy it for the attractive appearance it gives to any fresh salad.

Austrian influence is still strong in the remaining two Venetias. Although the Veneto was reclaimed from Austria in 1866, the Alto Aldige was ceded only in 1919. Trieste, its port built as the principal sea outlet of the Austro-Hungarian empire in the second half of the nineteenth century, came most recently to Italy in 1954 after a time as a free territory.

The cooking of the Trentino, while leaning a little to neighbouring Lombardy, is basically Austrian. Much of the food keeps its original name: *Speck*, bacon; *Crauti*, sauerkraut; and *Apfelstrudel*, the origin of which is unmistakable although, perhaps, the pastry is not quite so thin as in Vienna. Apples and pears abound—the area is one of the great apple orchards of Europe.

Smoked meats of every kind—beef and pork, goose, even donkey and horsemeat—are stored against the long mountain winters. Rye bread, pickled cucumbers and goulash are common, although they would not be considered typical Italian food. Tripe soup, *polenta* and dried salt cod are, however, shared with the Veneto. The Dolomites provide abundant game and fresh-water fish.

The cuisine of the Alto Adige is almost completely Tyrolean. Semolina dumplings are known as *Griessnockerln*, and ravioli stuffed with sauerkraut and cheese are called *Schluzkrapfen*. One of the most popular Christmas treats, almond-shaped sweet yeast cakes with dried fruit, candied peel and nuts, a speciality of Bolzano, are called *Zelten*.

The Friuli-Venezia Giulia is a simple, even primitive region. Its cooking is without delicacies and flights of fancy, unlike the subtle flavours and delicate dishes of the neighbouring Veneto. It shares the Adriatic coastline, and seafood stews are particularly good in Grado and Trieste. Here, too, the original names are retained. Goulash, *Wiener Schnitzel* and *Kugelhupf* appear on menus. Nourishing soups are a speciality. The most traditional is *iota*, a hearty peasant soup stew of pork, dried white haricot beans, pickled turnips and potatoes.

The hearth is an important part of even modern Friulian houses. A spit turns in the wide chimney, roasting beef, lamb, poultry or the universal pig. Beans are a mainstay of soups and stews. Desserts are substantial, often stuffed with dried fruit and nuts as in the *gubana*, a pastry spiral, or *putizza*, a Trieste sweetmeat of Slavic origin, or the similar *strucolo*.

In contrast to so much basic fare, there is one renowned speciality which can hardly be too much praised—the tender pink air-dried ham from San Daniele, which compares in quality with Parma ham.

South of the Po, across the river's great plain, the land rises to the base of the Apennines and to Bologna, capital of Emilia and for centuries the gastronomic centre of Italy. Cream, almost unknown elsewhere in Italy, is used lavishly in sauces. Excellent black and white truffles are found locally and garnish poultry, sauces and pasta.

Each Emilian town has its own jealously guarded recipe for pasta, plain or stuffed. Bologna has the famous *tortellini* as well as *lasagne verdi*, wide bands of pasta coloured green with spinach and baked with a rich and delicious meat sauce, and *tagliatelle* ribbon noodles, also often made with spinach in the Emilian manner. Parma has its *anolini*, little stuffed semicircles of pasta; Ferrara its *cappellacci* stuffed with pumpkin and Parmesan cheese; Reggio Emilia, Ravenna and Forlì make *cappelletti*, little hats, which can be stuffed with turkey, chicken, pork or brains, with egg and Parmesan cheese. In Bologna, Reggio Emilia and Ferrara as well as in the Romagna, there are variations of *pasticcio*, pastry filled with *tortellini* and sauce, which can be a most exquisite dish.

Cattle graze in the fertile plain of the Po. Rice and sugar-beet flourish, and vines grow up through mulberry trees planted in lines across the fields. Poultry is of excellent quality.

Parma has given its name to two of the most famous products in the whole of Italy—ham and cheese. Parma ham, *prosciutto di Parma*, is air-dried in the hills around Parma, especially Langhirano, the climate of which is uniquely favourable. Hams are sent from all over Emilia and Lombardy to hang for months maturing in the gentle breeze which wafts over pine and chestnut forests to the high windows, which are opened and shut at certain hours of the day to make the best use of the air currents, essential for a successful curing. Tender, wafer-thin slices are served as an *antipasto*, often with melon or figs.

No part of the pig is wasted. Every town has its own particular sausage or salami. The most famous must be Bologna's *mortadella*, pink and bland and studded with pistachio nuts. Equally esteemed are Modena's specialities: *zampone*, literally trotter, the skin of a pig's foot stuffed with minced pork and spiced with nutmeg, cloves and cinnamon and *cotechino*, a large salami made of the same mixture.

Parmesan cheese is the other glory of the region. Its full name is *Grana Parmigiano-Reggiano*, from Parma and Reggio Emilia. Because of its granular appearance it is often

NORTH EAST ITALY

TRENTINO-ALTO ADIGE

SPECK
Smoked bacon

KNÖDEL
Dumplings

•MERANO

•BOLZANO

GOULASH

MINESTRA DI TRIPPA
Pickled tripe soup

•TRENTO

CHEESE

BIGOLI CO L'ANARA
Spaghetti in duck sauce

•ASIAGO

FRIULI-VENEZIA GIULIA

CARNI AFFUMICATE CON CRAUTI
Smoked meats with sauerkraut

PASTA E FASIOI
Pasta and haricot beans

ZUPPA DI FAGIOLI
Bean soup

HAM

•SAN DANIELE

RISI E LUGANEGHE
Rice with pork sausage

•UDINE

GUBANA
Easter fruit-filled pastry

GORIZIA

TRIESTE

GRADO

BRODETTO DI PESCE
Fish stew

VENETO

PANDORO
Sweet Christmas bread

TREVISO

•VICENZA

VERONA

PADUA

RISI E BISI
Rice with peas

•VENICE

FEGATO ALLA VENEZIANA
Calves' liver fried with onions

SARDELLE IN SAOR
Fried sardines with onions and vinegar

BACCALA ALLA VICENTINA
Dried salt cod with onions and cheese

POLENTA
Cornmeal

•CHIOGGIA

PANPEPATO
Spiced bread

BRODETTO DI SEPPIOLINE
Cuttlefish soup

RISOTO A LA CIOSOTA
Rice in fish broth

EMILIA-ROMAGNA

•PIACENZA

PARMESAN CHEESE

HAMS

PARMA

CAPPELLACCI CON LA ZUCCA
Pumpkin-filled pasta

•FERRARA

DI ERBETTE
stuffed ravioli

MODENA•

MORTADELLA
Salami

•BOLOGNA

TAGLIATELLE AL RAGU
Ribbon noodles with rich meat sauce

AGNELLO ALLA ROMAGNOLA
Lamb with green peas

•RAVENNA

COTECHINO
Salami

ZAMPONE
Salami

TORTELLINI
Small stuffed pasta rings

BRIGIDINI
Small aniseed wafers

LASAGNE VERDI AL FORNO
Pasta baked with meat sauce

ACETO BALSAMICO
White wine vinegar with herbs

CIECHE ALLA PISANA
Tiny eels cooked with sage and garlic

•PISTOIA

ARISTA DI MAIALE
Roast saddle of pork

CENCI
Deep-fried pastry strips

•RIMINI

BRODETTO
Fish stew

BRODETTO
Fish stew

•PESARO

CONIGLIO IN PORCHETTA
Rabbit stewed in white wine with fennel

TUSCANY

PISA

CACCIUCCO
Fish stew

LIVORNO•

•FLORENCE

BISTECCA ALLA FIORENTINA
Grilled rib steak

PAPPARDELLE CON LA LEPRE
Ribbon noodles with hare sauce

•URBINO

•ANCONA
PORTO RECANATI

PASSATELLI
Tiny veal and spinach dumplings in broth

BRODETTO ALLO ZAFFERANO
Saffron-flavoured fish stew

•AREZZO

MACERATA•

TRIGLIE ALLA LIVORNESE
Fried red mullet

SIENA•

THE MARCHES

PAPPA COL POMODORO
Bread and tomato soup

PANFORTE
Spiced honey cake

CHOCOLATES

PERUGIA

VINCISGRASSI
Pasta with chicken liver and mushroom sauce

ACQUACOTTA
Vegetable broth

•ASSISI

ELBA

GROSSETO

UMBRIA

COLOMBACCE ALLA GHIOTTA
Spit-roasted pigeons

•NORCIA

•ASCOLI PICENO

PORCHETTA
Roast suckling pig

SBURRITA
Fish soup

POLLO ALL'ARRABBIATA
Chicken with chilli sauce

SPOLETO

PORK PRODUCTS

SPAGHETTI ALLA SPOLETINA
Spaghetti with black truffles

---

referred to simply as *grana*. After maturing for two to four years it becomes an excellent grating cheese. Freshly grated and fluffy, it is used in every soup and pasta dish.

Across the Apennines in Tuscany, the style of cooking changes. It becomes less opulent, more sober, simple and natural. There is less pasta and fewer creamy sauces, more plain roasts and charcoal-grilled meat. Much of Tuscany is mountainous. It is not one of Italy's most fertile regions, but what its produce lacks in quantity it makes up for in quality. The olive oil is excellent—that from Lucca is reputedly the best in Italy—and much used for frying, which is a favourite Tuscan method of cooking.

The beef from the Val di Chiana is celebrated. It is used for the *bistecca alla fiorentina*, a large tender steak, grilled and sprinkled with olive oil and salt before serving. The famous Leghorn breed of chickens is rivalled only by those from the Arno valley. They can be charcoal-grilled or roasted, like the *arista fiorentina*, loin of pork roasted with garlic, rosemary and cloves and served cold. A similar version is found in Perugia, in Umbria, using fennel instead of rosemary.

Kidney beans have been popular in Tuscany since their introduction from America in the sixteenth century. There are many bean soups, and *minestroni*, vegetable soups, with beans added. In Arezzo they are cooked with garlic and tomato and in Livorno with sage and cloves. Served cold with tuna fish and onion rings, they make a refreshing summer luncheon dish. They are cooked *all'uccelletto*, with sage, or even *nel fiasco*, in an empty wine flask with oil, garlic and water. The narrow neck of the flask prevents too rapid evaporation and loss of flavour.

Herbs are much used in Tuscan cooking, the common Italian ones—thyme, oregano, mint, basil, parsley—and also tarragon around Siena, which is the only place in Italy where it grows. Fennel seeds, cloves and cinnamon are popular and garlic and lots of pepper give taste to the simplest dish.

One of Florence's specialities is *risotto nero*, rice with cuttlefish and its ink, unexpected for a city which neither grows rice nor relies overmuch on the sea. Siena, whose citizens were castigated by Dante as greedy, is renowned for its bread soup, *pappa col pomodoro*, and its *ricciarelli*, marzipan sweetmeats, which have been made there for centuries.

Although the Tuscan coastline stretches from Viareggio to Orbetello, fish is not as

Robust food flavoured with truffles

widely eaten as might be expected. At Livorno there is a famous seafood stew, the *cacciucco*, made with at least five varieties of fish, wine, and tomatoes. The best-known speciality of Pisa is *cèe*, meaning blind in local dialect, the tiny still-blind elvers that are caught in quantity at the mouth of the Arno and cooked in oil with sage and pepper.

The heath-like countryside offers good hunting, and all over the hills and forests of Central Italy can be found such small game as hare, which makes a delicious sauce for *pappardelle*, wide ribbon noodles (one of the few traditional Tuscan pasta dishes; they are great bread eaters), and wild boar is still common around Orbetello and Grosseto. To the east of Tuscany, both Umbria and the Marches are famous for their wild pigeons, often spit-roasted in the time-honoured way. *Porchetta*, roast suckling pig, which originated here but is now a favourite ceremonial dish all over Central Italy, is stuffed with wild fennel, other herbs and garlic before it is roasted.

Pork is particularly good in Umbria and the Marches, especially the acorn-fed pigs of Norcia—the word *norcino* has come to mean pork-butcher throughout Italy. The true *norcini*, natives of Norcia, are fortunate, for besides their hams and sausages they have at hand one of the great delicacies of Italy, the black truffle, *tartufo nero*. Found in quantity around Norcia and Spoleto, and indeed all over Central Italy, it was prized by the Ancient Romans. Black truffles are cooked with eggs to make the most superior of omelettes, or sliced and baked with cheese on toast for *crostini di tartufi*, or, most frequently, chopped finely and served with spaghetti—a princely dish.

The other towns have their specialities. Perugia is famous for its chocolates, Trevi for its celery, Ascoli Piceno for its large juicy olives, which are stuffed, coated with breadcrumbs and deep-fried. Almost every town on the Adriatic coast has its *brodetto*, or fish stew. That of Porto Recanati is distinguished by its use of saffron, from the nearby Abruzzi.

In North Italy the staple diet is traditionally rice and *polenta*, cornmeal or maize porridge. Maize (corn), is widely grown, tall fields of it stretching away on either side of the road in summer. Although pasta is now also popular in the north, *polenta* is still eaten, often combined with butter and cheese to make a rich and filling dish, or with small

birds, *polenta e uccelli*, grilled on a skewer and stuck into the thick *polenta*.

Rice is cultivated in the valley of the Po, especially around Vercelli and Novara in Piedmont, in the Lomellina region south of Milan, and in the Rovigo province in the Po delta. *Risottos*, made with the round-grain Italian rice, are of quite a different texture from dishes made with the more familiar long-grain rice. To make a *risotto*, the rice is first gently fried in butter. When the butter is absorbed, hot stock or water is added, and, sometimes, also white wine. The result should be very moist, even soggy. Italian rice is never dry and fluffy.

Risotto is almost always served as a first course and usually contains other ingredients: frogs' legs or fresh kidney beans in Lombardy, *scampi* in Venice, *lugànega*, home-made pork sausage, in Treviso; or chicken livers, spring vegetables, *risotto primavera*; or little cuttlefish whose ink turns the rice black, *risotto nero*; or simply plenty of butter and cheese, a popular way in Piedmont and Lombardy.

One native pasta dish of northern Italy is Piedmontese *agnolotti*, little square ravioli stuffed with meat or spinach. An alternative to pasta are *gnocchi*, little dumplings which can be made of potatoes, semolina or just flour and water.

The origin of potato *gnocchi* is claimed by Emilia, the Lazio, the Friuli and Verona, but no Piedmontese would ever admit they came from anywhere else. Shaped like little shells, they are often served with a meat and tomato sauce and grated Parmesan cheese, but the typical Piedmontese way is *alla bava*, alternate layers of cooked *gnocchi* and thin slices of the local Fontina cheese, sprinkled with butter and put into a hot oven for a few minutes to melt the cheese.

The glory of Piedmont is the white truffle, *tartufo bianco*. It is found mainly in the forests of the Langhe region, south of Alba, bordering on Liguria. During the

short season those who can afford them ea truffles with almost everything. Whether o not they are superior to black truffles i entirely a question of taste; the two do no resemble each other. White truffles have strong earthy smell and a flavour unlike anything else. They are eaten raw, thinly sliced, with *risotto*, *polenta*, or *agnolotti*; with Parmesan cheese, for which they have special affinity; and with one of the specialities of Piedmont, the *fonduta*, fondue, made from melted Fontina cheese, milk and egg yolks, and served in individual bowls, with the truffle slices scattered on top just before serving.

Piedmontese cooking is robust, wholesome, sparing of frills, typical of a mountainous region where the beef, poultry, game and vegetables are excellent. The famous red Barolo wine is equally robust and marries well with the food in such dishes as *capriolo alla valdostana*, roast venison, *carbonata*, beef stew, *bue brasato*, braised beef, *lepre in civet*, jugged hare, and even *camoscio al Barolo*, chamois, which can still be eaten in the Val d'Aosta during the shooting season.

A typically simple but excellent dish of this area is *bollito misto*, mixed boiled meats, full of flavour and set off by the sharp sauces that accompany it. It consists of several large cuts of different meats including beef, tongue, pigs' trotters, chicken, a boiling sausage and oxtail, and is accompanied by *bagnet verd*, a green sauce of parsley, garlic and anchovies, *bagnet ross*, a red sauce of tomatoes, onions, garlic and chilli; *sottaceti*, mixed pickles, or *mostarda di frutta*, an unusual but excellent sweet pickle of assorted fruit in a mustard-flavoured syrup.

When something tastes good in its natural state, the Piedmontese see no point in cooking it. Mushrooms, as well as truffles, are often eaten raw, and there is an *insalata di carne cruda*, raw fillet of beef cut paper-thin. Most famous of all is the *bagna cauda*, a hot, spicy garlic and anchovy dip which is eaten with such raw vegetables as cauliflower, Jerusalem artichokes, sweet peppers and the local cardoons, a kind of thistle, closely related to the artichoke, with stems which look a little like celery, and are particularly tender and sweet in the Monferrato area.

Lake Maggiore has excellent perch, but is better known for the interesting speciality it makes of its shad. The fish is salted and sun-dried, then packed into cans with bay leaves. It is grilled, then marinated in wine vinegar for an hour or so before being served on *polenta*.

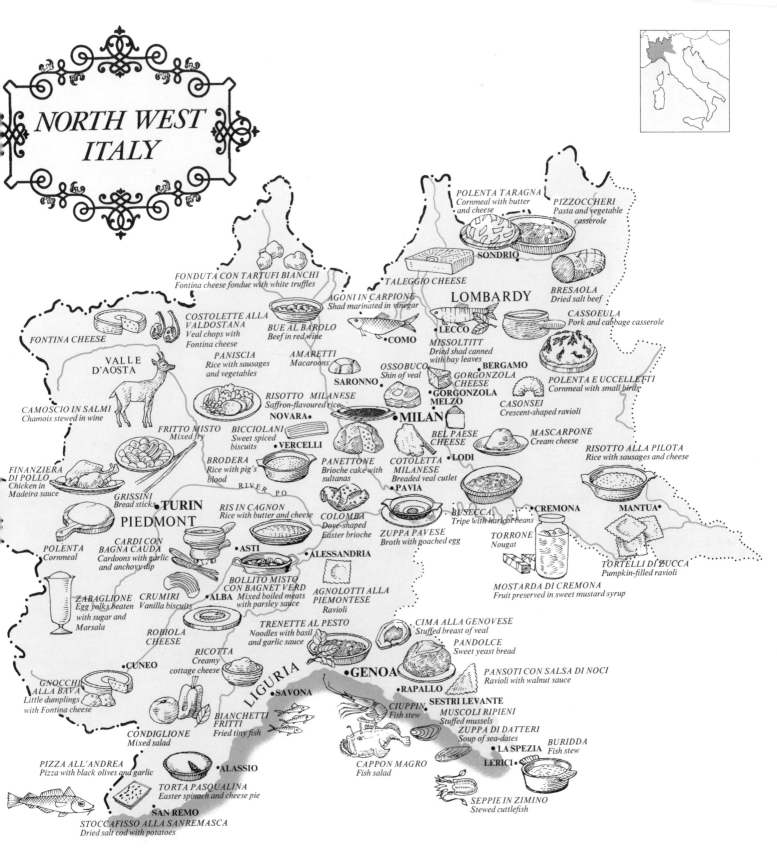

NORTH WEST ITALY

POLENTA TARAGNA
Cornmeal with butter and cheese

PIZZOCCHERI
Pasta and vegetable casserole

SONDRIO

FONDUTA CON TARTUFI BIANCHI
Fontina cheese fondue with white truffles

AGONI IN CARPIONE
Shad marinated in vinegar

TALEGGIO CHEESE

BRESAOLA
Dried salt beef

LOMBARDY

COSTOLETTE ALLA VALDOSTANA
Veal chops with Fontina cheese

BUE AL BAROLO
Beef in red wine

LECCO

COMO

CASSOEULA
Pork and cabbage casserole

FONTINA CHEESE

MISSOLTITT
Dried shad canned with bay leaves

BERGAMO

VALLE D'AOSTA

PANISCIA
Rice with sausages and vegetables

AMARETTI
Macaroons

SARONNO

OSSOBUCO
Shin of veal

GORGONZOLA CHEESE

GORGONZOLA

POLENTA E UCCELLETTI
Cornmeal with small birds

MELZO

CASONSEI
Crescent-shaped ravioli

RISOTTO MILANESE
Saffron-flavoured rice

CAMOSCIO IN SALMI
Chamois stewed in wine

NOVARA

MILAN

MASCARPONE
Cream cheese

RISOTTO ALLA PILOTA
Rice with sausages and cheese

FRITTO MISTO
Mixed fry

BICCIOLANI
Sweet spiced biscuits

BEL PAESE CHEESE

VERCELLI

PANETTONE
Brioche cake with sultanas

COTOLETTA MILANESE
Breaded veal cutlet

LODI

FINANZIERA DI POLLO
Chicken in Madeira sauce

BRODERA
Rice with pig's blood

RIVER PO

PAVIA

CREMONA

MANTUA

GRISSINI
Bread sticks

TURIN

RIS IN CAGNON
Rice with butter and cheese

COLOMBA
Dove-shaped Easter brioche

BUSECCA
Tripe with haricot beans

PIEDMONT

ZUPPA PAVESE
Broth with poached egg

TORRONE
Nougat

POLENTA
Cornmeal

CARDI CON BAGNA CAUDA
Cardoons with garlic and anchovy dip

ASTI

ALESSANDRIA

TORTELLI DI ZUCCA
Pumpkin-filled ravioli

ZABAGLIONE
Egg yolks beaten with sugar and Marsala

CRUMIRI
Vanilla biscuits

ALBA

BOLLITO MISTO CON BAGNET VERD
Mixed boiled meats with parsley sauce

AGNOLOTTI ALLA PIEMONTESE
Ravioli

MOSTARDA DI CREMONA
Fruit preserved in sweet mustard syrup

ROBIOLA CHEESE

TRENETTE AL PESTO
Noodles with basil and garlic sauce

CIMA ALLA GENOVESE
Stuffed breast of veal

PANDOLCE
Sweet yeast bread

RICOTTA
Creamy cottage cheese

CUNEO

PANSOTI CON SALSA DI NOCI
Ravioli with walnut sauce

LIGURIA

SAVONA

GENOA

RAPALLO

SESTRI LEVANTE

GNOCCHI ALLA BAVA
Little dumplings with Fontina cheese

CIUPPIN
Fish stew

MUSCOLI RIPIENI
Stuffed mussels

ZUPPA DI DATTERI
Soup of sea-dates

BIANCHETTI FRITTI
Fried tiny fish

BURIDDA
Fish stew

CONDIGLIONE
Mixed salad

LA SPEZIA

LERICI

PIZZA ALL'ANDREA
Pizza with black olives and garlic

ALASSIO

CAPPON MAGRO
Fish salad

TORTA PASQUALINA
Easter spinach and cheese pie

SAN REMO

SEPPIE IN ZIMINO
Stewed cuttlefish

STOCCAFISSO ALLA SANREMASCA
Dried salt cod with potatoes

Some northern dishes are to be found all over Italy. The Milanese, for example, have documents to prove that *costoletta alla milanese*, breaded veal cutlet, is the fore-runner of the *Wiener Schnitzel*. Other dishes that originated in this region are *zuppa pavese*, from Pavia, broth with a poached egg, fried bread and cheese, and *zabaglione*, a fluffy egg custard with Marsala, which is served warm. A *fritto misto*, mixed fry, is popular everywhere. Turin has a famous one

which may include sweetbreads, brains, baby lamb cutlets, cocks' combs, chicken croquettes, semolina croquettes, macaroons, slices of aubergine and zucchini, marrow flowers, mushrooms, frogs' legs, all coated in batter and deep-fried until crisp. In the *fritto misto* of Milan, each ingredient is coated with beaten egg and breadcrumbs rather than batter. A *fritto misto di mare,* of the sea, is unavoidable in almost any seaside town and will generally include shrimp,

squid, cuttlefish and, perhaps, small red mullet.

Liguria curves in a south-facing crescent, protected by high mountains from extremes of cold. In their shelter are cultivated the flowers for which this coast is famous, as well as delicate crops, including citrus fruit, which are not seen again until as far south as Naples. It is a land of garlic, olives and basil. The climate is ideally suited to the olive, and in every household sweet basil,

A profusion of pasta and pizzas

the indispensable herb in Ligurian cooking, is grown in pots. The famous Genoese sauce, *pesto,* combines all three ingredients—basil, garlic and olive oil—pounded to a paste with *pecorino,* ewes' milk cheese, Parmesan cheese and pine nuts. It goes marvellously with pasta, traditionally made here in the form of *trenette,* ribbon egg noodles, but is also added to the local *minestrone,* the thick vegetable and pasta soup.

From the twelfth to the fifteenth century, Genoa was a powerful maritime state with a flourishing fleet. Today it is still Italy's largest seaport, and like all ports boasts a famous fish stew, *buridda,* similar to the French *bourride.* From the sea Liguria gets all kinds of shellfish, from mussels and baby clams, here called *arselle* but in other parts of Italy known as *vongole,* to the less-known sea-dates, and sea-truffles. There are cuttle-fish, red mullet, *moscardini* (small octopus) and anchovies, which are filleted and marinated in lemon juice for twenty-four hours before serving, which gives them an exquisite, almost smoked, flavour.

Liguria is steep and mountainous and not rich in grazing land. As a consequence meat is not plentiful. There is, however, the Genoese *cima di vitello,* stuffed breast of veal, and the famous *stecchi* or little skewers. Each *stecco* has threaded on it such small delicacies as chicken livers, sweetbreads, pieces of cheese, bone marrow, cocks' combs, mushrooms and artichokes, and is then coated with a very thick white sauce, dipped in beaten egg white and breadcrumbs and deep fried.

The olive oil which is so characteristic of Liguria is used in almost every dish, even in some of its sweet foods, although not in one of the best known, the Christmas *pandolce,* a rich spiced loaf with raisins, nuts and candied peel.

Two Ligurian specialities which are

popular far beyond its boundaries are the *pizza all'Andrea,* a pizza with black olives, tomatoes and anchovies, and *torta pasqualina,* Easter pie, filled with a mixture of *ricotta,* eggs and spinach or artichoke hearts. The flour and water dough for it is rolled out wafer-thin. Traditionally, thirty-three sheets of dough were used, one for each year of Christ's life.

There are countless little *trattorie* and *osterie* in Rome, especially in the old quarter of Trastevere. In these unpretentious eating-places true Roman cooking, in a tradition which goes back for two thousand years, can still be found.

Many dishes are quite unlike those of other regions. Among these specialities are *coda alla vaccinara,* oxtail stewed with tomatoes, herbs, raisins, pine nuts, bitter chocolate and celery, a favourite vegetable in Rome, and *manzo garofolato,* beef braised with cloves, a very Roman spice, the rich and thick sauce of which can be served with spaghetti or with tripe. Tripe is also flavoured with mint, another particular Roman favourite, in *trippa alla romana.* Roman artichokes are famous. *Carciofi alla romana* are artichokes stuffed with finely chopped mint, parsley and garlic.

Almost every Roman menu features *stracciatella,* broth with grated cheese and egg beaten into it until the egg forms a mass of fine strands, and *saltimbocca alla romana,* thin slices of veal and prosciutto with sage leaves. In season there is the famous *abbacchio,* milk-fed lamb. This is a great delicacy at Easter, as is *capretto,* kid, both often roasted and well flavoured with rosemary, which also perfumes *porchetta,* suckling pig stuffed with herbs and spit-roasted, which is sold everywhere in the streets on festive occasions.

From the Alban Hills come the exquisite tiny wild strawberries. Particularly famous are the strawberries which grow in profusion in the woods around Nemi, a small village on the steep slopes of its mysterious volcanic Lake Nemi, called the Mirror of Diana by the Ancient Romans.

Good cooking, of whatever origin, has always been appreciated in Rome, and many dishes originating in other parts of Italy have been appropriated and are now regarded as Roman. *Saltimbocca,* which originally came from Lombardy, is one example. *Piselli al prosciutto,* peas with ham, probably came from Emilia, although the use of the sweet, tender little Roman peas is

undoubtedly an improvement. Equally tender raw young broad beans, fava beans are eaten with sharp ewes' milk cheese and white wine from the Alban Hills, in a dish called *fave pecorino e vino bianco,* another custom that may have had its origins in Emilia. Broad beans are also delicious cooked with bacon in *fave al guanciale,* a popular and truly Roman dish.

Roman vegetables have always been renowned for their exceptional sweetness and flavour, and now that the surrounding marshes have finally been successfully drained, much of the land has been cultivated and turned into fertile market gardens.

The Abruzzi, to the east of Latium, have produced many famous cooks. The home-made pasta of this region, especially *maccheroni alla chitarra,* is among the best in Italy. The dough is pressed through the wires of a special instrument called the *chitarra,* literally guitar. It is often eaten with a sauce of lamb and sweet peppers, or with tomato sauce spiced with fiery little chillies. A typical dish of the Abruzzi is *agnello all'arrabbiata,* lamb pieces sautéed with chilli and rosemary—a favourite herb here, too. Lamb is the most common meat in this traditionally sheep-rearing region.

While there is a surprising lack of fish dishes in the Lazio, on the opposite Adriatic, coast there is a wealth of ways of cooking both salt-water and fresh-water fish. Trout abound in the rocky mountain streams of the Abruzzi and the Molise, and every town along the coast has its fish stew. A speciality of Vasto is *scapece,* thick slices of fish fried and then marinated in saffron vinegar. This is the only local dish to use saffron.

Teramo is a town famous for its cooking. Here can be found *le virtu,* a rich soup with many kinds of vegetables, dried legumes, pork, herbs and pasta, and *scrippelle,* pancakes which can be served with broth poured over them or baked in layers in the oven, in the manner of *lasagne.*

Aquila is famous for its celery, and also provides the excellent mountain hams of the region, as well as trout and the local *scamorza,* a soft cows' milk cheese, often smoked or grilled on a spit. In the Molise, lamb and kid are much eaten, and there is an unusual speciality, a nettle soup made with only the stems of the plant.

From Naples southward is the true pasta country. Both Neapolitans and Sicilians have been nicknamed *mangiamaccheroni,* macaroni-eaters. But an enormous amount of pasta is

SOUTHERN ITALY

MARITOZZI
Sweet buns with pine nuts and candied peel

VITERBO.

RIETI.

•TERAMO

AMATRICE.
BUCATINI ALL'AMATRICIANA
Spaghetti with bacon, tomato and chilli sauce

SCRIPPELLE 'MBUSSE
Thin pancakes in broth

PECORINO
Ewes' milk cheese

L'AQUILA.

•PESCARA

BRODETTO
Fish stew

GUANCIALE
with bacon

RICOTTA
Curd cheese

PARROZZO
Chocolate-covered almond cake

ABBACCHIO AL FORNO
Roast baby lamb

ABRUZZI

SCAMORZA
CHEESE

•VASTO

SCAPECE
Fried fish preserved in vinegar

CARCIOFI ALLA GIUDIA
Fried whole young artichokes

MACCHERONI
ALLA CHITARRA
Home-made pasta

MOLISE

POLPI IN PURGATORIO
Octopus with chillies

ROME.

SPAGHETTI AGLIO
OLIO E PEPERONCINO
Spaghetti with garlic, olive oil and chillies

LAMPASCIULI
AL FORNO
Baked bitter wild onions

SALTIMBOCCA
ALLA ROMANA
Veal slices with ham and sage

PORCHETTA
Roast suckling pig

CAPRETTO ALLO SPIEDO
Spit-roasted kid

SPAGHETTI ALLA ZAPPATORA
Spaghetti with oil, garlic and chillies

SPAGHETTI ALLA CARBONARA
Spaghetti with eggs, cheese and bacon sauce

•CAMPOBASSO

BISTECCA ALLA PIZZAIOLA
Beef with tomato and garlic sauce

•FOGGIA

PROVOLONE CHEESE
Cows' milk cheese

STRACCIATELLA
Broth with beaten egg and cheese

STRUFFOLI
Small honeyed puffs

ZEPPOLE DI SAN GIUSEPPE
Sweet fritters

PIZZA

SFOGLIATELLE
Filled sweet pastries

BARI.

MOZZARELLA IN CARROZZA
Deep-fried mozzarella cheese sandwich

PEPERONATA ALLA CARNE
Sweet peppers and pork

CARTEDDATE
Sweet Christmas pastries

CONIGLIO ALL'ISCHITANA
Rabbit cooked in white wine with herbs

NAPLES.

PASTIERA
Curd cheese tart

CANNELLONI
ALLA NAPOLETANA
Cannelloni with tomato sauce

ZUPPA DI PESCE
Fish stew

•MATERA

CACIOCAVALLO
CHEESE

•BRINDISI

SPAGHETTI AI TOTANI
Spaghetti with squid

ISCHIA

SALERNO.

AMALFI.

MOZZARELLA
CHEESE

•POTENZA

ORECCHIETTI
AL RAGU
Pasta with meat sauce

ALICI
CRUDE
Anchovies in oil and lemon juice

CAPRI

•TARANTO

SCATTIATA
Sweet pepper salad

•LECCE

TARALLI
Sweet biscuits

POLPI ALLA LUCIANA
Octopus with chillies and tomatoes

FUSILLI
Corkscrew spaghetti

GNIUMERIEDDI
Lamb offal on skewers

SPAGHETTI AL POMODORO
Spaghetti with tomato sauce

LUCANICHE
Pork sausages

VERMICELLI ALLE VONGOLE
Spaghetti with baby clam sauce

MELANZANE
ALLA PARMIGIANA
Aubergines with Parmesan cheese

BUTIRRI
Butter-filled cheese

SALAMI

•COSENZA

CALABRIA

PECORINO
Ewes' milk cheese

CROTONE•

SAGNE CHINE
Stuffed pasta

•CATANZARO

MURSEDDU CON PITTA
Flat bread with pork filling

MUSTICA
Preserved sardines

SORIANO•

MOSTACCIOLI
Honey and aniseed sweets

PEPERONI ALLA CALABRESE
Sweet peppers and tomatoes

REGGIO CALABRIA•

MELANZANE SOTT'OLIO
Aubergines preserved in oil

---

also eaten in Apulia where, made simply with flour and water, it appears in countless shapes and sizes with an infinite variety of names.

Besides the ordinary spaghetti and *lasagne*, there are *orecchietti*, little ears, *laganelle*, small rectangles, *ricci di donna*, ladies' curls, *fusilli*, pulled-out spirals, *strascinati*, little rectangles with one side ribbed, and *maccheroni ai ferri*, made by shaping the dough around an iron instrument like a knitting needle. Factories produce the larger, tubular kinds of pasta such as *penne, ziti, rigatoni* and *cannelloni*, which are cooked in Naples with a sauce worthy to rival the Emilian meat sauces.

The vegetables which grow in the southern sun are particularly fine. The incredibly sweet tomatoes are used in sauces, or stuffed with a mixture of capers, olives, breadcrumbs and herbs, and baked.

Produced abundantly in the south are fresh cheeses, such as *mozzarella* and the *scamorza,* as well as *Provolone* and *caciocavallo* cheeses made from cows' milk. *Caciocavallo* cheeses come in pairs, as if strung astride a horse (*cavallo* means horse). Very good *Provolone* comes from Apulia, and the smaller *provole*, pear-shaped cheeses, are found all

161

Islands scented with myrtle

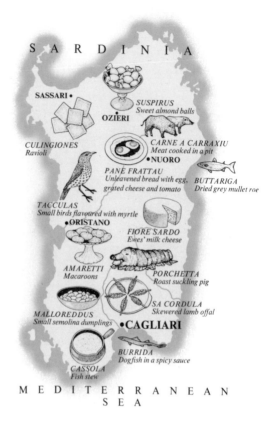

over the south. Little *butirri*, cheeses filled with butter, are popular everywhere, as are *ricotta* and *pecorino*.

Two of Campania's most typical products, *mozzarella* cheese and tomatoes, are combined in Naples' best-known food, the pizza. There are hundreds of versions, including the *pizza Margherita*, named in honour of the first queen of United Italy. The *pizzaiolo*, pizza-maker, gives his name to a concentrated tomato sauce strongly flavoured with garlic and oregano, often served to disguise the toughness of a local steak.

Fish are part of the Neapolitans' way of life. Specialities are octopus *alla luciana*, with tomatoes and chillies, anchovies and sardines, *cecenielli*, larval anchovies no bigger than tiny chick-peas, moray eels, fish stews from Pozzuoli and Ischia, *fritto misto del golfo*, mixed fried seafood, and, of course, *spaghetti con le vongole* with baby clams.

Neapolitan pastry cooks are famous. Savoury *calzoni* and *sfogliate* are turnovers stuffed with *mozzarella, ricotta*, salami or ham. *Sfogliatelle* are puff-pastry versions with sweet fillings. *Pastiera*, a curd-cheese tart flavoured with cinnamon, orange-flower water, lemon, candied peel and vanilla, is eaten from Twelfth Night until Easter. *Zeppole* are sweet fritters eaten at Carnival time.

Southern Italy is much poorer than the north, and meat is not so commonly eaten. Cattle are kept for working and for providing milk and cheese. The main sheep-rearing region is Apulia, although some of the traditional grazing-grounds have now been irrigated and given over to growing wheat and vegetables.

Wheat is needed for making the indispensable pasta. It is eaten with meat sauces, fish sauces and vegetable sauces, which may be made with a mixture of wild herbs and garden herbs, or with broccoli, aubergine or peppers. Calabria has perhaps the greatest number of recipes for aubergines of any region: it is stuffed, marinated, pre-

pared *alla parmigiana* (baked in layers with Parmesan cheese), fried or baked, served as a salad with mint, and preserved with salt or in olive oil. The hot little *peperoncini*, chillies, are eaten with almost everything in Basilicata, where they are called simply *forte*, strong.

Bread, with pasta, forms the backbone of the diet of this area of little meat and much wheat. In Apulia a ring-shaped bread called *frisedda* is soaked in water, wrung out and eaten with olive oil, salt and pepper. Tomatoes and onions are sometimes added to make it a more substantial dish.

With the longest coastline of any Italian region, it is not surprising that Apulia is rich in fish. Especially famous are the oysters of Taranto which are cultivated in lagoons where fresh and salt water mix. Swordfish, caught off the Calabrian coast and off Sicily, are excellent. In Apulia, sardines are fried and marinated in oil and vinegar with mint, and are cooked with oregano in Calabria. There are notable fish stews in Bari, Brindisi and Taranto, and the squid, scampi, sole and red mullet from the Adriatic and the Gulf of Taranto are excellent. Sweetmeats are similar throughout the south, and many show their Arab origin, such as the *mostaccioli*, hard little cookies in various fancy shapes—hearts, fish and sea-horses.

The Italian islands, Sicily and Sardinia, preserve simple, traditional ways of cooking. The sea around them yields tuna, sardines, which take their name from Sardinia, anchovies, excellent red mullet and lobster.

Although Sicily is smaller than Sardinia, it has better harbours and nearly twice as many seaside settlements, and Sicilians are traditionally great sailors and fishermen. Messina is famous for its *pescespada a ghiotta*, swordfish cooked in onion and tomato sauce with potatoes, olives, capers and celery. It is sometimes enclosed in pastry and baked. Tuna is cooked in various ways in Trapani, where the roe is made into a delicacy called *bottarga*. *Sarde a beccaficu* are sardines marinated in vinegar, stuffed and deep fried.

Sardinia does, however, have one unusual fish speciality, the *burrida* (not to be confused with the Genoese fish stew of the same name). This is a large fish, usually dog-fish, boiled, then left to cool in a sauce of oil, pine nuts, garlic and vinegar.

In Sicily, figs, prickly pears, almonds, pistachio nuts and citrus fruit grow in abundance, especially citrus fruit. The lemon groves covering the volcanic slopes of Mount Etna and the profusion of almond blossoms in early spring belie the poverty of much of the land. Bread, pasta, tomatoes, cheese, olives and olive oil are the staple

iet. The greatest part of Italy's durum wheat for the manufacture of pasta is grown here. In Sicily, pasta is eaten at least once every day. Two famous ways of preparing it are *con le sarde*, with raisins, pine nuts, saffron, wild fennel and sardines, and *con le melanzane*, with tomato sauce and aubergine. In Catania this is known as *pasta alla Norma*, after the best-known opera of Catania's famous son, the composer Vincenzo Bellini.

Sicily has been invaded at various times by Greeks, Romans, barbarians, Saracens and Normans, of whom the Saracens have left most mark on the cooking. This influence can be seen in the number of dishes which use dried fruit, nuts and spices. Messina's cuisine has a strong Arab influence. *Pescestocco alla messinese* is salt cod Messina style, cooked with tomatoes, potatoes, capers, pine nuts, olives, celery,

raisins and pears. Trapani has its *cuscusu*, a fish stew cooked with steamed semolina on the same principle as the Arabic *couscous*.

The Arab influence is evident, too, in the sweets. Marzipan is used for making colourful fruit, *frutti della Martorana*. A paste of sugar and sweet almonds, flavoured with cloves, is also used for making fruit and animal shapes. Other shapes are known as *minni di virgini*, virgins' breasts, and *sospiri di monaca*, nuns' sighs. The word *cassata* comes from the Arabic *qas'at*, a large round-bottomed bowl, like the mould which is still used for shaping the *cassata gelata*, an ice-cream dessert. Sicily's candied fruit is world famous, as are Sicilian ices, which range from exquisite water ices to the elaborate *cassata* and ice-cream bombes.

The Arabs did not stay in Sardinia long enough to make much impression on the

food, although there is a saffron-flavoured soup called *fregula* which is made with semolina prepared in the same way as *couscous*. More important to Sardinian cuisine were the Phoenicians, who probably introduced saffron, still commonly used.

Sardinia remains a land of shepherds, with much of its cooking still dictated by the life the shepherds lead, away from home for months at a time. Wild boar, kid, lamb and suckling pigs are roasted on hand-carved spits over aromatic fires of juniper wood and myrtle. This method is called *a furria furria*, meaning to turn and turn again. *Porceddu*, suckling pig, is cooked on a spit or in an oven with herbs and myrtle leaves.

In Sardinia bread is a symbol of family unity. There are crisp paper-thin rounds, *pane carasau* or *carta da musica*, literally sheet music, which will keep for a long time and are carried by the shepherds, to be softened in hot water and eaten with their roasted meat or perhaps with *sa cordula*, plaited lamb's entrails roasted on skewers. With the addition of egg, tomato and grated *pecorino* it becomes known as *pane frattau*. Sardinian *pecorino*, also known as *fiore sardo* or simply *sardo*, is highly esteemed.

The women who stay at home while the shepherds are away with their flocks have evolved different methods of cooking which require more time and equipment. *Malloreddus* are tiny saffron-flavoured *gnocchi* made of flour and water. *Culingiones* are *ravioli* filled with meat or cheese or, in Cagliari, with potatoes. *Impanadas*, pies of stewed meat or eels, and *fabbada*, a bean, pork and cabbage soup, show the Spanish influence.

Sweets are made as they have been for centuries, flavoured with almonds, orange or lemon peel, raisins, walnuts, aniseed, cocoa and cinnamon. Macaroons are popular, especially those from Oristano. They are often crushed, mixed with *ricotta* and made into fritters. *Suspirus*, sighs, are similar to macaroons. *Pabassinas* are little nut and raisin cakes, traditionally made for All Saints' Day, Christmas and Easter. *Aranciata*, a speciality of Nuoro, is an orange-flavoured nougat.

Indeed, it is surprising how so much of this cuisine, from the shepherds' spit-roasts and pit-cooking to the ancient honey and almond confections, has hardly changed for centuries. Much of what is eaten today on these islands is not so far removed from the way the shepherds and their families prepared it in the time of Augustus.

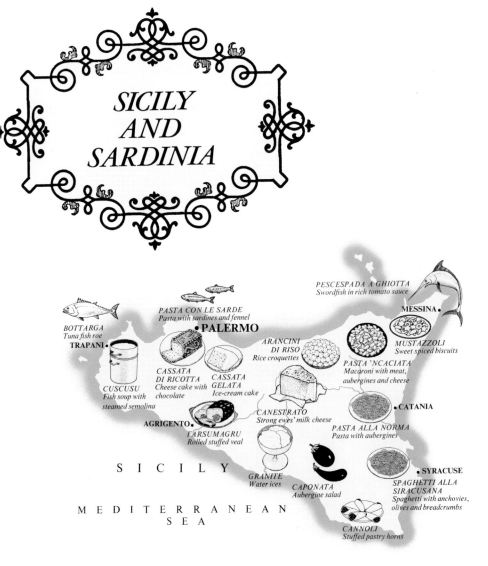

SICILY AND SARDINIA

PESCESPADA A GHIOTTA
Swordfish in rich tomato sauce

MESSINA•

PASTA CON LE SARDE
Pasta with sardines and fennel

•PALERMO

BOTTARGA
Tuna fish roe
TRAPANI•

ARANCINI
DI RISO
Rice croquettes

MUSTAZZOLI
Sweet spiced biscuits

PASTA 'NCACIATA
Macaroni with meat,
aubergines and cheese

CASSATA
DI RICOTTA
Cheese cake with
chocolate

CASSATA
GELATA
Ice-cream cake

CUSCUSU
Fish soup with
steamed semolina

•CATANIA

CANESTRATO
Strong ewes' milk cheese

AGRIGENTO•

FARSUMAGRU
Rolled stuffed veal

PASTA ALLA NORMA
Pasta with aubergines

S I C I L Y

GRANITE
Water ices

•SYRACUSE

CAPONATA
Aubergine salad

SPAGHETTI ALLA
SIRACUSANA
Spaghetti with anchovies,
olives and breadcrumbs

M E D I T E R R A N E A N
S E A

CANNOLI
Stuffed pastry horns

Savoury soups and spicy spaghetti

Consomme with Egg and Cheese
ZUPPA ALLA PAVESE

This elegant soup, which is named after the city of Pavia in Lombardy, has become a favourite all over Italy. The secret of a good zuppa pavese *lies in having the consommé boiling hot when it is poured over the raw eggs so that the whites set lightly, leaving the yolks very soft.*

SERVES 4

4 thick slices white bread
Butter for frying
4 fresh eggs
Salt
4 tablespoons freshly grated Parmesan cheese
About 2½ pints boiling chicken or beef consomme

Fry the slices of bread quickly in butter until crisp and golden brown on both sides. The bread should remain soft in the centre. Drain on paper towels.

Put the fried bread slices in each of 4 pre-heated soup bowls. Carefully slide a raw egg on to each slice. Be sure the eggs are fresh and have firm whites. Season each egg with a pinch of salt and sprinkle 1 tablespoon of Parmesan cheese on top.

Ladle the boiling consommé carefully into each bowl, pouring it around, rather than over, the eggs to avoid breaking them. Serve immediately.

White Bean and Noodle Soup
PASTA CON I FAGIOLI

This is a hearty, cold-weather peasant soup from the Veneto and Friuli, where it is called pasta e fasioi.

SERVES 4 TO 6

8 oz dried white beans, soaked overnight and drained
8 oz fresh pork belly with skin
1 onion, finely chopped
1 carrot, finely chopped
1 celery stalk, finely chopped
1 garlic clove, finely chopped
3 parsley sprigs, finely chopped
1 sage sprig, finely chopped
1 bay leaf
Salt
6 oz spaghetti or ribbon noodles
2 tablespoons fruity olive oil
Freshly ground black pepper

Put the beans in a pan with the pork, the onion, carrot, celery, garlic, parsley, sage and bay leaf and water to cover. Bring to the boil, reduce the heat, cover the pan and simmer gently for 2 hours, or until the beans are soft.

Put 1 cup of beans through a food mill or rub them through a sieve. Stir the bean purée back into the soup. Season to taste with salt and pepper and bring to the boil again.

Add the spaghetti or ribbon noodles and boil for about 12 minutes, or until they are cooked through, but are still firm to the bite.

Remove the piece of pork belly and cut it into thin strips.

Just before serving, dribble the olive oil into the soup and add with a grinding of black pepper. Serve the soup warm rather than hot, accompanied by the strips of pork on a separate plate.

Fried Mozzarella Cheese Sandwiches
MOZZARELLA IN CARROZZA

The Neapolitan name of these sandwiches is literally Mozzarella in a coach. To be at their best, they should be served crisp and hot from the frying-pan. Anchovy fillets are sometimes added to the sandwiches.

SERVES 4

8 large slices white bread
4 thick slices Mozzarella cheese
2 eggs
2 tablespoons milk
Salt
Flour
Olive oil for frying

Trim the crust from the bread slices and make sandwiches with the Mozzarella cheese. Dip the edges of the bread in cold water for a moment and press them together to seal in the cheese.

Whisk the eggs with milk and a pinch of salt until foamy.

Dust the cheese sandwiches with flour. Soak them thoroughly in the beaten egg mixture and fry them in 2 inches of hot oil, 2 at a time, until golden.

Drain the sandwiches on paper towels and serve immediately.

Noodles with Baby Clams
VERMICELLI CON LE VONGOLE IN BIANCO

The Gulf of Naples is rich in shellfish of all kinds, including baby clams and mussels, oysters, razor shells and sea urchins. Vongole are baby clams, but in recipes of this kind mussels can be substituted.

SERVES 4

2 quarts baby clams
8 tablespoons olive oil
2 garlic cloves
½ small hot chilli
3 anchovy fillets, finely chopped

1 lb vermicelli noodles or spaghetti
Salt
1 tablespoon finely chopped parsley or fresh basil
Freshly ground black pepper

Scrub the clams thoroughly under cold running water.

Put 1 tablespoon of olive oil in a large pan. Add the clams. Cover the pan tightly and cook over high heat until the clams open.

Shell the clams over the pan to catch the liquor. Discard any which have not opened. Strain the liquor through a sieve lined with muslin to trap any grains of sand.

In another pan, fry the garlic cloves in the remaining oil until they are lightly coloured. Add the chilli and the chopped anchovies, and fry for 2 minutes. Pour in the clam liquor and simmer gently to reduce it slightly.

Boil the noodles in a large pan of salted water until they are cooked, but still firm.

Remove and discard the garlic cloves and the piece of chilli from the simmering sauce. Add the clams and reheat them. Stir in the parsley or basil and season to taste with salt and pepper.

Drain the cooked pasta in a colander. Divide it between 4 heated plates. Spoon the sauce over the top and serve immediately.

Stuffed Pasta Rolls in Tomato Sauce
CANNELLONI ALLA NAPOLETANA

The filling for cannelloni *may be varied according to the ingredients available. It is an excellent way to use up leftover roast meat.*

SERVES 6

PASTA DOUGH
14 oz plain flour
½ teaspoon salt
4 eggs

FILLING
8 oz leftover roast veal, sliced
4 oz cooked ham (prosciutto cotto), sliced
2 oz raw smoked ham (prosciutto crudo), sliced
1½ oz butter
1½ oz plain flour
10 fl oz milk
3 tablespoons meat gravy
Freshly ground black pepper
Freshly grated nutmeg
1 egg yolk
1 small can mushrooms, drained and chopped

TOMATO SAUCE
1 onion, finely chopped
2 slices streaky bacon, diced
1 lb ripe, fresh tomatoes, blanched, peeled, seeded and chopped

tablespoons olive oil
teaspoon dried oregano
alt
reshly ground black pepper

O FINISH DISH

Butter
oz Parmesan cheese, freshly grated

o make the pasta dough, sift the flour and salt
Into a bowl and make a well in the centre. Add
he eggs and work the ingredients to a dough.
.nead vigorously until the dough is smooth
nd pliable, and little blisters appear just under
he surface. Roll the dough into a ball, return
o the bowl, cover and leave for 20 minutes.

To make the filling, put the veal, the cooked
am and the raw ham twice through the fine
lade of a meat mincer.

In a heavy pan, melt the butter until it is
oaming but not coloured. Blend in the flour
vith a wooden spoon and stir over low heat for
minutes to make a pale *roux*. Remove the pan
om the heat. Stirring vigorously, gradually add
he milk. Stir in the meat gravy. Bring to the
oil, stirring. Reduce the heat and simmer for
o minutes, stirring occasionally, to make a
mooth, thick sauce. Season to taste with salt,
epper and nutmeg.

Remove the pan from the heat. Beat in the
gg yolk. Then stir in the minced meat mixture
nd the chopped mushrooms. Set aside.

To shape the pasta, on a lightly floured board,
oll the dough out as thinly as possible. Cut the
heet of dough into 4-inch squares.

Fill a large saucepan with salted water and
ring to the boil. Have ready a large bowl of
old water mixed with 1 tablespoon of olive oil.
When the water boils, drop in the pasta squares,
or 4 at a time, and boil them for 7 or 8
ninutes, or until they are tender but still firm.
Lift them out with a slotted spoon and drop
hem into the bowl of cold water to cool. The
il will prevent the squares from sticking
ogether.

To make the tomato sauce, fry the onion and
acon together in the oil until the onion is
ightly coloured. Add the tomatoes and oregano,
nd simmer gently, uncovered, until the
omatoes are reduced to a thick sauce. Season to
aste with salt and pepper.

Preheat the oven to 425°F (Gas Mark 7).
Generously butter a large ovenproof baking
lish and spread a layer of tomato sauce over the
oottom.

Pat the pasta squares dry with absorbent
aper. Spread one end of each square with the
tuffing. Roll them up and lay them in the
aking dish, seam side down, in a single layer.

Spoon over the remaining tomato sauce. Dot
vith about 1 ounce of butter cut in small pieces
nd sprinkle with the grated cheese. Bake the
annelloni for 12 to 15 minutes, or until the
urface is bubbling and golden brown.

Spaghetti with Bacon and Egg Sauce
SPAGHETTI ALLA CARBONARA

Any noodles may be served alla carbonara—
thick, ribbed rigatoni, *macaroni, ribbon noodles
or spaghetti—and there are also many versions
of the sauce. Sometimes a clove of garlic is sautéed
in the oil and removed before frying the bacon, and
often a combination of Parmesan and Pecorino
cheese is used. The dish is said to have been created
by the* carbonaii, *charcoal-burners, who worked in
the woods outside Rome.*

SERVES 4

1 lb spaghetti
Salt
4 oz streaky bacon, diced
1 tablespoon olive oil
4 eggs
2 tablespoons single cream
3 oz freshly grated Parmesan or 2 oz grated
  Pecorino cheese
Freshly ground pepper

Boil the spaghetti in a large pan of salted water
until it is cooked through but still firm to the
bite.

Meanwhile, fry the bacon gently in the oil
until the fat is translucent.

In a large tureen or serving bowl, beat the
eggs with the cream, the grated cheese, salt and
pepper, to taste.

Drain the cooked spaghetti thoroughly and
immediately toss it with the egg and cheese
mixture so that the heat of the pasta "cooks" the
sauce. Add the hot bacon. Toss again and serve
immediately, accompanied by a bowl of grated
cheese.

Spaghetti with Garlic, Oil and Chilli Pepper Dressing
SPAGHETTI AGLIO OLIO E PEPERONCINO

*This marvellously spicy spaghetti dish, which
comes from the Abruzzo, can be made hotter still
by chopping both the chilli and the garlic finely,
and leaving them in the sauce. No cheese is served
with this dish.*

SERVES 4

1 lb spaghetti
Salt
4 garlic cloves
1 small hot chilli, cut into 3 pieces
4–6 tablespoons olive oil
1 tablespoon finely chopped parsley

Boil the spaghetti in a large pan of salted water
until it is tender but still firm to the bite.

Meanwhile, prepare the sauce. Cook the
whole garlic cloves and the pieces of chilli in
olive oil over moderate heat until the garlic is
golden but not brown. Using a slotted spoon,
remove and discard the garlic and chilli.

Drain the spaghetti and put it in a heated
serving bowl. Pour over the sizzling oil, add the
parsley and toss until well mixed.

IN FRANCE WINE AND FOOD are seen as equal
partners in their gastronomic marriage. In
Italy wine plays second fiddle. What matters
first and foremost is the bountiful spread of
good things to eat. There has always been
an ocean of adequate wine to wash it down
with. What more could anyone want?

The answer, which only dawned on Italy
a decade or so ago, is an export trade.
Italian wine has always in the past been dog-
ged by a well-merited reputation for un-
reliability that has made foreign buyers
steer clear of all except a few famous names.
Excellent wines as a result were being un-
justly neglected. The government decided
to act, and in 1963 produced the laws of
Denominazione di Origine Controllata,
based on the practice of scattered local
consorzi of more-than-usually conscientious
growers. In the years since, exports have
multiplied, prices have soared, and Italian
wine has taken on a completely new look

At present a wine can carry either a
Denominazione Semplice, which is in practice
no more than an assertion as to where it
comes from, or a DOC label which carries
guarantees both of origin and quality.
Most wine regions of distinctive character
are now eligible for DOC labels. By using
them, growers put themselves not only
within the law, but also into a higher price
bracket. The public has proved eager to
pay more to know what it is buying.

Authenticity is not everything, however.
There are authentically bad wines as well as
authentically good ones. The sensible thing
in Italy is always to try the local wine—but
after stringent enquiries as to where it is
best. Start by trying the wine of the local
growers' cooperative, *cantina sociale*—it will
give you a fair average standard for the
region on which to base your assessments.
Nothing a book can tell you about such a
passionately individualistic animal as the
Italian wine-maker is any substitute for
personal research.

Fish and meat in the Italian style

Bolognese Meat Sauce
SALSA (RAGU) BOLOGNESE

Spaghetti with Bolognese sauce is world famous. The hot drained pasta may be dotted with flakes of butter before the sauce is ladled over the top, for an extra touch of richness. When truffles are in season they are sometimes used instead of dried mushrooms.

SERVES 4

2 oz salt pork fat or streaky bacon, diced
2 oz butter
1 onion, finely chopped
1 carrot, diced
1 celery stick, diced
4 oz minced lean pork
4 oz minced lean beef
4 oz minced raw smoked ham (prosciutto crudo)
2 tablespoons dried mushrooms, soaked and chopped
1 tablespoon tomato purée
½ teaspoon dried oregano (optional)
5 fl oz beef stock
5 fl oz red wine
4 tablespoons hot cream or milk
Salt
Freshly ground black pepper

Melt the butter in a large, heavy pan, add the diced salt pork fat or bacon and simmer, stirring, until the fat is transparent. Add the onion, carrot and celery, and cook over a moderately low heat, stirring frequently, for 5 minutes. Add the minced meats. Raise the heat to moderate and sauté briskly, stirring, until the meats are lightly browned.

Stir in the chopped mushrooms, the tomato purée, oregano if used, stock and wine and bring to the boil. Lower the heat, cover the pan and simmer gently for 40 minutes, stirring occasionally.

Add the hot cream or milk. Season to taste with salt and pepper. Bring the sauce to the boil again and cook for a few minutes longer, stirring, until the cream has blended with the other ingredients.

Basil, Garlic and Pine-Nut Sauce
PESTO ALLA GENOVESE

The Genoese boast that the basil they grow is the finest in all Italy. Almost every house has a pot of it growing on the windowsill. Although basil is used a great deal in all Italian cooking, there is nothing to compare with the pesto *of Genoa, a thick green sauce which is served with thin* trenette *noodles or* gnocchi. *A few tablespoons may also be stirred into vegetable soup to enrich the flavour.*

In most Italian kitchens the mortar and pestle is essential equipment and many Genoese cooks insist that pesto *should be pounded by hand in a marble mortar. But an electric blender makes a good substitute, provided it is turned to its lowest speed to preserve the aroma of the basil. If using a blender, add the olive oil first.*

MAKES ABOUT 5 FLUID OUNCES

5 garlic cloves
1 tablespoon pine nuts
1 bunch fresh basil (30 to 40 large leaves)
½ teaspoon cooking salt
1 tablespoon crumbled pecorino cheese
1 tablespoon coarsely grated Parmesan cheese
8 tablespoons best-quality olive oil

Chop the garlic and pine nuts coarsely. Put them in a mortar and crush them finely. With scissors snip the basil leaves into shreds. Add them to the mortar together with the cooking salt and pound them to a paste with the garlic and pine nuts. Add the cheeses and continue to pound until the mixture is reduced to a smooth purée.

Add the olive oil a little at a time, beating vigorously with a wooden spoon to create a creamy emulsion.

If serving the *pesto* as a dressing for noodles, thin it down slightly with 2 or 3 tablespoons of the water in which the noodles have been cooked.

Swordfish Palermo Style
PESCE SPADA ALLA PALERMITAN

During the season elegant metallic-blue swordfish can be found in all the Sicilian markets. It is a firm, fat fish with a fine flavour and has inspired many excellent recipes.

SERVES 4

4 swordfish steaks, about 8 oz each
Salt
Flour
2 garlic cloves
8 tablespoons olive oil
4 anchovy fillets, finely chopped
1 onion, finely chopped
4 medium-sized tomatoes, blanched, peeled, seeded and chopped or a 14-oz can Italian peeled tomatoes
1 tablespoon finely chopped parsley
⅛ teaspoon dried rosemary, crumbled
12 green olives, stoned and sliced
1 tablespoon capers
Freshly ground black pepper

Wash the swordfish steaks and pat them dry with kitchen paper. Sprinkle them with salt and dust them with flour.

In a large, deep frying-pan, fry the whole garlic cloves in the olive oil over a low heat until golden. Remove and discard the garlic.

In the same oil, brown the swordfish steaks on both sides over moderate heat. Remove them from the pan with a slotted spoon.

To the oil remaining in the pan, add the chopped anchovy fillets and onion, and fry gently until the onion is translucent and the anchovies are reduced to a purée.

Add the tomatoes to the pan, together with the parsley and rosemary. Mix well and simmer gently, uncovered, for 30 minutes, or until the tomatoes are reduced to a thick sauce. Add the olives and capers to the tomato sauce. Season to taste with pepper, and a little salt if necessary and mix well.

Return the swordfish steaks to the pan. Spoon the sauce over them and simmer gently for a few minutes longer until the fish is hot and cooked through.

Stuffed Veal Rolls Milanese Style
MESSICANI ALLA MILANESE

Even though these veal rolls are called messicani *or Mexicans, they are a typical Milanese dish.*

SERVES 4 TO 6

12 small, thin slices of veal
2 oz raw smoked ham (prosciutto crudo) finely chopped
1 chicken liver, finely chopped
3 tablespoons fine, dry breadcrumbs
2 tablespoons freshly grated Parmesan cheese
1 teaspoon finely chopped parsley
1 egg, lightly beaten
Salt
Freshly ground pepper
¼ teaspoon freshly grated nutmeg
6 fresh sage leaves
2 slices streaky bacon, each cut into 3 pieces
Butter for frying
4 tablespoons Marsala
4 tablespoons dry white wine

Beat the slices of veal out flat. Mix the finely chopped ham and chicken liver with the breadcrumbs, Parmesan cheese and parsley. Bind with the lightly beaten egg and season to taste with salt, pepper and grated nutmeg.

Put a little of the meat mixture on each slice of veal and roll it up. Thread 2 veal rolls on to each of 6 short skewers or wooden cocktail sticks, together with a sage leaf and a piece of bacon.

Fry in butter, turning the skewers so the veal browns evenly on all sides. Remove from the pan and keep hot.

Add the Marsala and wine to the buttery pan juices and bring to the boil, scraping the bottom of the pan clean with a wooden spoon. Simmer the sauce briefly to reduce it slightly. Pour over the veal rolls and serve immediately.

Calves' Liver Venetian Style
FEGATO ALLA VENEZIANA

This famous Venetian recipe lifts a simple dish of liver and onions into the gourmet class. The secret lies in slicing the liver as thinly as possible

SERVES 4

6 tablespoons olive oil
1 tablespoon butter
4 medium-sized onions, thinly sliced
2 tablespoons finely chopped parsley
4 tablespoons light stock
1 tablespoon wine vinegar
1¼ lb calves' liver, thinly sliced
Salt
Freshly ground black pepper

In a large frying-pan, heat the oil and butter together. Add the onions and parsley, mix well and simmer over very low heat, stirring occasionally, for 40 minutes, or until the onions are soft and translucent but not coloured.

At the first sign of browning, add the stock and vinegar. Increase the heat. Add the liver and sauté briskly for 4 to 5 minutes, or until the slices are browned on both sides.

Season with salt and pepper. Turn out on to a heated dish and serve immediately.

Veal Escalopes Bologna Style
SCALLOPINE DE VITELLO ALLA BOLOGNESE

Both Parma ham and Parmesan cheese come from Emilia, and meat, ham and cheese are frequently combined in dishes of this region.

SERVES 4

8 small veal escalopes, about 3 oz each
Salt
Flour
3 oz butter
8 thin slices raw smoked ham (prosciutto crudo)
8 thin slices Gruyère or Emmenthal cheese
3 tablespoons light stock
3 tablespoons Marsala

Beat the escalopes lightly. Sprinkle them with salt and coat them with flour.

Preheat the oven to 450°F (Gas Mark 8), or the grill to high.

In a large frying-pan, brown the escalopes on both sides in foaming butter. Arrange them side by side in a buttered ovenproof dish. Cover each escalope with a slice of ham, and top with a slice of cheese. Keep hot.

Add the stock and Marsala to the butter remaining in the frying-pan. Bring to the boil, scraping the bottom of the pan clean with a wooden spoon. Pour the sauce over the escalopes.

Transfer the baking dish to the oven (or put it under the grill) until the cheese has melted.

Veal Escalopes with Parma Ham and Sage
SALTIMBOCCA ALLA ROMANA

These delicate little escalopes cooked with fresh sage and Parma ham are a gourmet's delight. Their name, translated literally, means "jump in the mouth".

SERVES 4

8 small veal escalopes, about 2 oz each
4 large or 8 small paper-thin slices of raw smoked ham (prosciutto crudo)
Salt
8 fresh sage leaves
Butter
4 tablespoons dry white wine or Marsala

Beat the escalopes out thinly. Trim the slices of ham to about the same size as the escalopes.

Sprinkle each escalope with a small pinch of salt. Lay a sage leaf on it and cover with a slice of ham. Secure each little "sandwich" with a short wooden cocktail pick. These escalopes are never rolled up.

Heat about 1½ ounces of butter in a large frying-pan until foaming, and sauté the escalopes briskly on both sides for 6 to 8 minutes, or until they are cooked through and golden. Transfer the escalopes to a heated serving platter. Keep hot.

Add the dry white wine or Marsala to the buttery juices remaining in the frying-pan and bring to the boil, scraping the bottom of the pan clean with a wooden spoon. Stir in 1 ounce of butter and spoon the bubbling sauce over the escalopes. Serve immediately.

Baked Lamb Roman Style
ABBACCHIO ALLA ROMANA

The abbacchio which is served in Italy at Easter time is milk-fed baby lamb, so young and small that a leg will serve no more than four people. Baby lamb is almost impossible to find in Britain or the United States, but this method can be used to cook older lamb with excellent results.

SERVES 4

3 to 3½ lb leg of young lamb
2 rosemary sprigs
Salt
Freshly ground black pepper
2 oz butter or lard
4 large potatoes, peeled and cut into chunks
4 tablespoons dry white wine (optional)

Preheat the oven to 450°F (Gas Mark 8).

Sprinkle the lamb with rosemary leaves, or make small incisions all over the meat and push a few rosemary leaves into each one. Season with salt and pepper.

In a heavy, heatproof casserole, brown the lamb on all sides in the butter or lard. Surround it with the potatoes.

Bake for about 1 hour, or until tender. Turn the lamb and the potatoes occasionally so that they brown evenly. If necessary baste the lamb with a little white wine to prevent it browning too quickly.

Transfer the lamb to a heated serving dish and surround it with the potatoes.

Braised Shin of Veal
OSSO BUCO ALLA MILANESE

Osso buco is traditionally served with a risotto alla milanese. Narrow forks are sometimes provided to scoop out the bone marrow, but one can also use the tip of a knife.

SERVES 4

1 onion, finely chopped
4 oz butter
Meaty shin of veal, sawed into 4 slices, about 2½ inches thick
Flour
1 carrot, thinly sliced
1 celery stick, thinly sliced
3 tomatoes, blanched, peeled, seeded and chopped
Salt
Freshly ground pepper
¼ teaspoon dried sage (optional)
5 fl oz dry white wine

GREMOLATA

2 tablespoons finely chopped parsley
1 garlic clove, finely chopped
2 anchovy fillets, finely chopped
Finely grated rind of ½ lemon

In a wide, shallow pan, fry the onion in half the butter until golden. Dust the slices of veal with flour and fry them in the same pan until golden brown on all sides. Stand them on their sides to prevent the marrow in the bones slipping out during cooking.

Add the carrot, celery and tomatoes. Season with salt, freshly ground pepper and the sage, if it is being used.

Add the wine. Cover the pan and simmer for 1 hour, or until the veal is tender. A few tablespoons of water may be added to the pan if the sauce evaporates too quickly.

While the veal is cooking, prepare the *gremolata* by mixing all the ingredients together.

Five minutes before serving, spread each piece of veal with some of the *gremolata*.

When the veal is tender, transfer to a heated serving dish. Add a few tablespoons of water to the pan juices and bring to the boil, scraping the bottom of the pan clean. Simmer until slightly reduced. Stir in the remaining butter and when it has melted, pour the sauce over the veal.

167

Dishes from a food-loving people

Veal Chops with Cheese
COSTOLETTE ALLA VALDOSTANA

An authentic costolette alla valdostana *is made with Fontina cheese from the Val d'Aosta —the word* valdostana *means "from the Val d'Aosta"—but a good, fat, melting cheese like Gruyère can be substituted.*

In some versions of this dish a pocket is slit in each chop and stuffed with a slice of cheese. The chops are then coated with a mixture of flour, egg and breadcrumbs and fried gently in butter until golden brown on both sides.

SERVES 4

4 veal chops
Seasoned flour
1 egg, lightly beaten
Fine, dry breadcrumbs
Butter for frying
4 slices (about 4 oz) Fontina cheese

Beat the chops out thinly to about twice their original size without separating them from the bone. Dust them with seasoned flour, dip them in the lightly beaten egg, allowing the excess to drain off, and coat them with fine, dry bread-crumbs.

Fry the chops in foaming butter until they are cooked through and golden brown on both sides.

Meanwhile, preheat the grill to high. Put the chops on a hot, heatproof serving dish. Cover them with slices of cheese and place them under the grill just long enough to melt the cheese without letting it colour. Serve immediately.

Sardinian Stuffed Pork Rolls
INVOLTINI DI MAIALE ALLA SARDA

In Sardinia, meats are grilled over an aromatic wood fire which imparts a unique flavour. These pork rolls are also delicious when baked in the oven.

SERVES 4

8 thin slices boned loin of pork
½ stale, crusty roll
4 oz pig's liver
3 oz fresh or salt pork fat
1 garlic clove, finely chopped
4 sage leaves, crumbled
1 egg yolk
Salt
Freshly ground black pepper
French bread sliced ⅓ inch thick
Olive oil

Preheat the oven to 375°F (Gas Mark 5).

Beat the pork slices as thin as possible with a mallet. Soak the half roll in cold water and squeeze it dry.

Put the liver, pork fat and soaked roll through a meat mincer. Add the garlic, sage leaves, egg yolk, salt and pepper, and mix well.

Divide the liver mixture between the slices of pork, and roll them up. Grease 4 short skewers with olive oil. Thread the bread slices and pork rolls alternately on to the skewers, starting and ending with a slice of bread. Brush the bread and pork liberally with olive oil and sprinkle with salt and pepper.

Place the skewers in a baking pan. Bake, turning the skewers occasionally, for 30 minutes, or until the meat rolls are cooked through and evenly brown and the slices of bread are crisp and golden.

Baked Aubergines with Cheese
PARMIGIANA DI MELANZANE

Every little restaurant in southern Italy has a dish of parmigiana di melanzane *to serve as a first or a main course. It is equally delicious hot, warm or cold.*

SERVES 4

3 lb round aubergines
Salt
1 medium-sized onion, finely chopped
Olive oil
2 lb ripe tomatoes, blanched, peeled, seeded and chopped
3 fresh basil sprigs, chopped, or 2 teaspoons dried basil
Freshly ground black pepper
Flour
5 oz Parmesan cheese, freshly grated
½ lb mozzarella cheese, thinly sliced
2 hard-boiled eggs, thinly sliced

Trim the stems from the aubergines and slice them lengthwise. Sprinkle each slice with salt. Put them in a colander and cover with a plate. Weight the plate down and leave the aubergines to drain for 30 minutes.

In a heavy pan, fry the onion in 4 tablespoons of olive oil until golden. Add the tomatoes and basil, mix well and simmer gently, uncovered, until the tomatoes are reduced to a thick sauce. Season to taste with salt and pepper.

Preheat the oven to 400°F (Gas Mark 6). Oil a large, shallow ovenproof dish.

Rinse the aubergines slices in cold water. Pat them dry and dust them with flour. Fry them in hot olive oil until soft and golden brown on both sides, and drain them on kitchen paper.

Cover the bottom of the baking dish with a layer of aubergines. Sprinkle with Parmesan cheese and cover with slices of mozzarella cheese and a few slices of hard-boiled egg. Spoon some of the tomato sauce over the top. Repeat these layers until the ingredients are used up, ending with tomato sauce. Bake for 30 minutes.

Stuffed Rice Croquettes
SUPPLI ALLA ROMANA

The Romans have nicknamed these rice croquettes suppli al telefono, *or telephone wire croquettes, because the cubes of mozzarella cheese in the filling pull out into long thin strands like telephone wires when bitten into.*

Many Italian recipes call for meat gravy. Italians use the rich gravy left over from braised beef, which is strained and saved for dishes of this kind, but the jellied juices left over from a roast can be substituted.

SERVES 4 TO 6

RICE MIXTURE

5 fl oz meat gravy
3 medium-sized tomatoes, blanched, peeled, seeded and chopped
2 oz butter
1 lb Italian rice
6 tablespoons freshly grated Parmesan cheese
3 eggs, lightly beaten
Salt
Freshly ground black pepper
MEAT FILLING
1 oz dried mushrooms, soaked in warm water
2 slices raw smoked ham (prosciutto crudo) shredded
1 small onion, finely chopped
2 oz butter
4 oz veal, chopped
2 medium-sized tomatoes, blanched, peeled, seeded and chopped
4 oz chicken livers, chopped
Salt
Pepper
4 oz mozzarella cheese, cut into small cubes
Fine dry breadcrumbs
Oil or lard for deep frying

Bring 1 pint of water to the boil in a large pan. Stir in the meat, gravy, tomatoes and butter. Pour in the rice. Mix well and simmer over a low heat for 15 minutes, or until the rice is cooked but still firm to the bite. Stir the rice occasionally to prevent it sticking and add more boiling water if it dries out too quickly.

Remove from the heat. Stir in the grated cheese and the eggs, and season to taste with salt and pepper. Turn the rice mixture out into a bowl and leave it to cool.

To make the meat filling, drain the mush-rooms and chop them finely. In a heavy pan, cook the ham and onion in the butter until the onion is soft and golden. Add the chopped veal and mushrooms, and continue to cook until the veal is lightly browned. Add the tomatoes and simmer, stirring frequently, until the mixture is reduced to a thick concentrated sauce. Add the chicken livers and cook just until they change colour. Season to taste with

salt and pepper. The mixture should be very thick. Set aside to cool.

To shape the *suppli*, put a rounded tablespoon of rice in the palm of one hand. Make a depression in the centre and fill it with some of the meat mixture and 2 cubes of cheese. Close the rice carefully over the filling and shape it into a ball. Coat with breadcrumbs. The finished *suppli* should be the size of a large apricot.

Deep-fry the *suppli* in hot oil or lard, a few at a time, until golden brown. Drain on absorbent kitchen paper and serve immediately.

Saffron Risotto Milanese Style
RISOTTO ALLA MILANESE

Risotto alla milanese *is deliciously buttery and golden with saffron. It is best to use the fat, round Italian rice which takes better to this unusual method of cooking than ordinary long-grain rice. If you use saffron threads, presoak them in 3 tablespoons of boiling water, then mash the strands against the sides of the bowl with the back of a spoon to release as much colour as possible. Then stir them in together with the water. Do not add the saffron until halfway through the cooking time as prolonged cooking tends to lessen its delicate, unusual flavour.*

SERVES 6 TO 8

1 lb Italian rice, preferably Vialone
3 oz butter
2 oz fresh beef marrow, finely chopped
1 small onion, finely chopped
About 2 pints boiling stock
⅛ teaspoon powdered saffron or saffron threads
Freshly grated Parmesan cheese

Wipe the rice with a cloth if necessary to remove any powder on the surface of the grains. Heat 1 ounce of the butter with the beef marrow. (If marrow is not available use another ounce of butter instead.) Add the onion and fry gently until it is soft but not coloured. Add the rice and stir over a moderately low heat until the grains begin to turn translucent round the edges.

Stir in a ladleful of boiling stock and simmer gently until it has been absorbed. Continue adding stock in this manner, stirring more frequently as the cooking proceeds, until the rice is cooked through with a firm core running through the grain. This will take 15 to 20 minutes, depending on the quality of the rice. Halfway through the cooking time, stir in the saffron.

When the rice is ready, gently mix in the remaining butter and 6 tablespoons of Parmesan cheese.

Serve the risotto with a separate bowl of grated cheese to sprinkle over the top.

THE NORTHEAST gives Italy her most sumptuous red wines and her most inspiring sparkling white ones. But its most characteristic contribution to the Italian feast is its aperitifs, of which Turin is surely the world capital. Campari, Carpano, Cinzano, Martini, are household words where not a single Italian wine has ever penetrated.

Essentially there are two kinds of aperitifs in the Italian curriculum—those in which wine plays a leading role, and those based on a spirit, flavoured, coloured and diluted with water. Martini (sweet and dry), the classic example of the first, is known as vermouth from the wormwood (*vermuth*) which lends it bitterness. Campari is the classic spirit "bitters". Almost every nuance of the bittersweet principle is explored in the range of both, covering a whole wall in every café in the northeast.

Café-life in Turin and Milan is made fragrant, moreover, with the richest and best coffee in the world, spurting from the hell's-kitchen of Espresso machines. There seems no time, in these gloriously gossipy cities, when either an aperitif or a cup of coffee, and half an hour at a café table, does not seem the perfect answer.

Sicilian Cheesecake
CASSATA ALLA SICILIANA

A traditional Sicilian cassata *is not a layered ice-cream dessert, but fresh* ricotta *mixed with candied fruit and sandwiched between layers of light sponge cake which is flavoured with Maraschino. Whipped cream can also be used to decorate the* cassata, *and the candied fruits in the cheese mixture are sometimes supplemented with chopped nuts.*

SPONGE CAKE

Butter
3 egg yolks
4 oz castor sugar
Finely grated rind of ½ lemon
4 oz plain flour
1 teaspoon baking powder
3 egg whites
FILLING
12 oz castor sugar
1½ lb fresh ricotta cheese
1 lb mixed crystallized fruit
⅛ teaspoon ground cinnamon
3 oz dark chocolate, chopped in small pieces
8 tablespoons Maraschino liqueur

To make the sponge cake, preheat the oven to 375°F (Gas Mark 5). Butter a 10-inch springform cake tin.

Whisk the egg yolks with the sugar, grated lemon rind and 3 tablespoons hot water until light and foamy.

Sift the flour and baking powder together, and fold it into the egg yolk mixture.

Whisk the egg whites until stiff, but not dry. With a large metal spoon, fold them into the cake mixture.

Pour the mixture into the prepared cake tin and bake for 15 to 20 minutes, or until the cake is a rich golden colour and springs back when pressed lightly. Turn out and cool on a wire rack.

For the filling, dissolve the sugar in 3 tablespoons of water over low heat. Beat the sugar syrup with the *ricotta* cheese until it is smoothly blended. Put aside about half of the best pieces of candied fruit to decorate the *cassata*. Chop the remainder coarsely.

Add the cinnamon to the sweetened *ricotta* and beat until smooth and creamy. Put aside a few tablespoons of the mixture for decoration. Combine the remainder with the chopped fruit and chocolate.

Line the bottom of the cake tin with greaseproof paper.

Cut the sponge cake in half horizontally. Put one layer on the bottom of the cake tin, cut side up, and sprinkle it with half of the Maraschino. Spread with half of the cheese mixture. Place the second layer of sponge, cut side down on top and sprinkle with the remaining Maraschino. Spread with the remaining cheese mixture. Fit the ring of the cake tin in position and chill the cake for several hours.

When ready to serve, remove the cake from the tin and place it on a large, flat serving dish. Coat the top and sides with the reserved cheese cream and decorate with the reserved crystallized fruit.

Whipped Wine Custard
ZABAGLIONE

Zabaglione *is always freshly made and is usually served hot. To serve it cold, continue beating the mixture, off the heat, until it has cooled down completely.*

SERVES 4

4 egg yolks
5 tablespoons sugar
8 tablespoons Marsala or dry white wine

Put all the ingredients in the top of a double-boiler or in a bowl set over—not in—a pan of gently simmering water. Beat with a wire whisk or a hand-held electric mixer until the *zabaglione* is thick, light and hot. Pour into 4 tall glasses and serve immediately.

Flamboyant dishes from basic ingredients

THE IBERIAN PENINSULA was described by Strabo, the Greek geographer, as lying "outstretched like a bull's hide between East and West", and it has, in the course of history, taken its culture from both the East and the West to produce a unique blend of the exotic and the very simple. It is this that makes Iberian cuisine so different from that of the rest of Europe.

The occupation of Iberia by the Moors for seven hundred years had a great influence on the cultural and culinary development of both Spain and Portugal. The Moors were a cultured and sophisticated people who brought a new way of life to the Iberians and to the Roman colonists who inhabited the peninsula at that time.

Experts at irrigation, the Moors introduced the cultivation of rice, now a staple food, and brought with them figs and citrus fruits, peaches and bananas and many of the Eastern spices, including cumin and aniseed, which are used so much in Iberian cooking today. They used almonds a great deal in the cooking of both savoury and sweet dishes. The huge groves of almond trees along the Levante coast and in the Algarve were originally planted by the Moors.

Today, in all the areas of the peninsula where the Moors once ruled, rich and varied rice dishes, little cakes and confections made from eggs and almonds, cinnamon, butter and honey, as well as crystallized fruit and the special *turrones*, sweet nougats, are part of the Iberian legacy from the East.

Although Spain and Portugal shared a common early history, they are two very different countries. Portugal became a nation in her own right in 1143 and after the expulsion of the Moors in the thirteenth century, she struggled to extend her boundaries and to retain her newly found independence. A nation of natural navigators, Portugal founded a huge empire in the fifteenth century which, for nearly two hundred years, was one of the most powerful in the world. Today, there is a touch of

exoticism in the cooking of Portugal—a reminder of the years of colonial rule in India, Africa, China and South America.

Also in the fifteenth century the Spanish began their conquest of the New World, and with it not only such riches as silver and gold, but such gastronomic treasures as sweet and hot peppers, chocolate and tomatoes came to Iberia.

While travellers and armies spread the culinary influence of Spain and Portugal throughout Europe, Europe in turn influenced Spain through Catalonia, from the 1130s part of Aragon, an independent kingdom whose influence reached across the Pyrenees into what is now Provence. Many Catalan dishes have a recognizably provençal touch, and many of the dishes of Provence were clearly influenced by Catalan cooking.

Spanish and Portuguese cooking is simple, sober and conservative. The natural flavours of the ingredients are undisguised by sauces or dressings. Basically a peasant cuisine, it relies on the simple excellence of the natural produce in the most favoured regions and on the ingenuity required in creating interesting dishes where the raw materials are sparse or of poor quality.

The Castillian peasants, hard put to eke out a living from the arid land, have originated some of Spain's simplest and most delicious dishes. *Migas*, for example, which literally means crumbs, is a dish of lightly fried pieces of stale bread mixed with bits of meat, fish and vegetables.

Such ingenuity is apparent, too, in the surprising number of variations on a single theme. In Portugal alone there are said to be as many ways of cooking *bacalhau*, dried salt cod, as there are days in the year. And in Spain every province has its own imaginative *cocido*, stew. Into the pot go tasty combinations of game and poultry or pork, veal and mutton, together with sausages and every kind of vegetable, dried or fresh, that can be persuaded to grow.

Around the central plateau, where the climate runs to extremes and the bare bones of the land seem to show through the sparse vegetation, *cocidos* have been developed to a fine degree. The *cocido madrileño*, for example, is served in three separate courses. First the broth, followed by the vegetables and then the meats—a simple but fine meal from a single pot.

The Spanish pig, lean, blackish and long of leg, is a versatile and economical animal used for a great variety of *chacinas*, pork products. *Chorizo*, a rich ruddy brown

sausage, with a warmly spiced and smoky flavour, is the essence of Spanish cooking. To a certain extent its counterpart, the *chouriço*, plays as important a part in the cuisine of Portugal. Raw hams, expertly cured in the cold, sunny mountain air of the Sierra Morena, are another delicacy, as is *lomo*, fillet of cured pork which is thinly sliced and eaten as an *hors d'oeuvre*. Equally delicious are *butifarras* and *sobresadas*, sausages from Catalonia and the Balearic Islands.

The huge olive groves of Andalusia, famous even in Roman times, produce the strong-flavoured, aromatic olive oil which is the basis of so many Spanish dishes. Portuguese olive oil, although equally pure, has, for some people, a slightly rancid taste. This is because it is made by a somewhat different process and not because the quality of the oil is anything but excellent.

Andalusia, the region which for most people epitomizes the romantic bravado of Spain, is also known for *gazpacho*, a cold, tomato-based soup which has been described as a soupy salad or a salady soup. *Gazpacho*, like the *paella* of the Levante, can change with the taste and ingenuity of each cook.

Rice flavoured with saffron, the basis of every *paella*, is cooked in wide pans, or *paelleras*, with a variety of ingredients. The classic finished dish is a colourful, fragrant mélange of saffron-tinted rice, lobster, shrimp, chicken, clams or mussels and vegetables.

Butter and lard are more common in northern Spain. The lush pastures of the Pyrenees foothills, a complete contrast to the stark plains of the south, produce superb beef, dairy products, fruit and vegetables, while the Catalan coast is rich in fish and shellfish. The northern provinces of Spain are the regions for light, pungent sauces. Some made from the cooking juices of one ingredient are used to cook another. For example, *chilindrón*, a piquant sauce from Aragon, is obtained from the cooking juices of game, pot-roasted with onions and tomatoes. Chicken cooked in this sauce is one of the best-known dishes of this region. The Basque delicacy *kokotxas*, hake's throat, is casseroled in a traditional *salsa verde*, green sauce made from parsley, green peas and garlic. *Angulas*, baby eels, are cooked in bubbling oil flavoured with chillies, and squid cooked in its own ink is another typical recipe of the Basque country.

Bacalao is also a feature of many Basque recipes, but it is also common in the north-

BACALAO A LA VIZCAINA
Salt cod with onions and peppers

GALICIA

ASTURIAS

BILBAO •

BASQUE PROVINCES

VIEIRAS
Scallops baked in their shells

QUESO DE CABRALES
Cheese wrapped in vine leaves

CENTOLLA A LA BILBAINA
Spider crab baked in the shell

LACON CON GRELOS
Hand of pork with turnip tops

FABADA ASTURIANA
Bean, salt meat and blood sausage stew

CHIPIRONES EN SU TINTA
Squid cooked in their ink

CHORIZO DE PAMPLONA
Spicy sausage

NAVARRE

BUTIFARRA
Cinnamon-spiced sausage

MORCILLA
Blood sausage

PULSES

CATALONIA

ALI-OLI
Garlic mayonnaise

RIVER DUERO

LEON

TERNASCO
Roast lamb

SOPA DE AJO
Garlic soup

BARCELONA •

OLD

MPREYS

TRIPE

OPORTO •

SMOKED PORK LOIN

CASTILE

CORDERO ASADO
Roast lamb

COCHINILLO ASADO
Roast suckling pig

ARAGON

RIVER EBRO

CUTTLEFISH

HAKE

HAM

GRAPES

TORTILLA DE PATATAS
Potato omelette

GOATS

ANCHOVIES

PRAWNS

CORDERO ASADO
Roast lamb

CHURROS Y CHOCOLATE
Finger-shaped doughnuts dipped in chocolate

HAKE

CALDO VERDE
Kale and potato soup

MADRID •

SQUID

PORTUGAL

ARROZ DOCE
Rice pudding

RIVER TAGUS

COCIDO MADRILEÑO
Vermicelli, chick-pea, carrot and potato soup

BACALAO
Salt cod

SPINY LOBSTER

PAELLA A LA VALENCIANA
Classic paella

ET

AS A PORTUGUESA
d thinly sliced liver

PORK

CHORIZO
Spicy sausage

PISTO MANCHEGO
Stewed peppers, tomatoes and onions

TURRON
Nougat

VALENCIA •

BALEARIC

LISBON •

ELVAS PLUMS

SWEET ORANGES

ISLANDS

RIVER GUADIANA

NEWCASTILE

SOPA DE AJO
Garlic soup

ASPARAGUS

CALDEIRADA
Fish stew

MANCHEGO CHEESE

LEMONS

EXTREMADURA

FLAM
Caramel custard

AÇORDA
Bread soup

SPAIN

MURCIA

MEDITERRANEAN

GAZPACHO ANDALUZ
Cold vegetable soup

RIVER GUADALQUIVIR

SEA

SEVILLE •

GARLIC

BACALHAU A GOMES DE SA
Salt cod casserole

OLIVES

JAMON SERRANO
Mountain-cured ham

SEVILLE ORANGES

ANDALUSIA

COD

ZARZUELA DE MARISCOS
Shellfish stew

western regions, Asturias and Galicia, where fish dishes rival in number and variety those of Catalonia and the Basque country. These cold, damp provinces have inspired warming dishes like *fabada asturiana*, the famous bean stew, and corn bread eaten with Asturian blood sausage. Galicia, a wet, fertile region to the north of Portugal, also favours heavy foods and excels in baking pies called *empanadas*.

In the cold northern provinces of Portugal, soups are filling and warming, like the *caldo verde*, the cabbage or kale soup of Minho province, *canja*, the chicken gruel of the Beira region. *Acordas*, bread broths of the Alentejo, which is wheat country, are almost as thick as stews. The Algarve, in the far south, welcomes the traveller with light shellfish soups, stews and vegetables. Vegetables are steamed together with fish, shellfish or *chourico* in a *cataplana*, a covered pan in which the flavours are sealed until seconds before the dish is eaten.

Although Spain is changing more rapidly than Portugal, the pursuit of progress has not destroyed the traditional pleasure of long, reflective meals. In a country where to be thin was once a sign of poverty, meals are enormous. Dinner, which never begins before ten-thirty, can be prolonged far into the night, and the conversation and drinking often continues in a street café.

Strong, vibrant colour first attracts the visitor to an Iberian table. Red and green peppers, saffron-yellow *paellas* and the pink and white flesh of fish increase anticipation of the flavours which await, for as the discerning Iberians say, "Half the eating is in the eye."

Colourful combinations of a peasant cuisine

Andalusian Iced Soup
GAZPACHO

Experts have failed to agree on the origin of the word gazpacho, *but one theory suggests that it is derived from a pre-Roman word "caspa", meaning remains or bits and pieces. The suffix "acho" has a derogatory meaning probably attached to the word by those who could afford better food. This humble peasant salad-soup has, however, risen to the ranks of international cuisine. It should be served ice-cold and is often accompanied by small bowls of finely chopped salad vegetables.*

SERVES 4

2 tablespoons stale breadcrumbs
2 garlic cloves, crushed
1 tablespoon wine vinegar
1 tablespoon olive oil
1 green pepper, seeded and chopped
1 onion, chopped
4 tomatoes, blanched, peeled, seeded and chopped
½ cucumber, peeled and chopped
8 almonds, blanched, peeled and crushed
Freshly ground black pepper
Salt

In a small bowl, soak the breadcrumbs and garlic in the vinegar and olive oil for 1 hour. Put the vegetables, together with the soaked breadcrumbs, in a blender or food mill and reduce to a smooth purée. Add the crushed almonds, season with pepper and salt and dilute with cold water to the required amount. Chill for several hours before serving.

Spanish Omelette
TORTILLA A LA ESPANOLA

The Spanish omelette bears little resemblance to its French cousin, although perhaps as much skill is needed to cook it properly. It should be thick and cake-like, golden brown and crusty on the outside, and soft and succulent on the inside. It is eaten all over Spain, hot or cold, and may have peas, spinach, sliced mushrooms, garlic and parsley, chopped ham, anchovies or pieces of chorizo *sausage added.*

SERVES 4

3 tablespoons olive oil
2 large potatoes, peeled and cut into ¼-inch cubes
2 large onions, coarsely chopped
Salt
6 eggs

In a medium-sized frying-pan, gently heat the olive oil. Add the potatoes and onions and season with salt. Cover the pan and cook the vegetables over low heat, stirring frequently, for 15 to 20 minutes without browning. Add more oil if necessary.

Break the eggs into a bowl and beat them together with a fork just enough to blend the yolks and whites thoroughly. When the vegetables are tender, carefully remove them from the pan with a slotted spoon, draining as much oil as possible, and stir them quickly into the eggs. Pour most of the oil out of the frying-pan, allowing only a thin film to remain. Increase the heat and when the oil is hot, pour in the egg mixture, smoothing it down with a fork to fill the entire pan. Cook for about 5 minutes, shaking the pan occasionally to prevent the mixture from sticking.

Place a large heatproof plate over the pan. Invert the omelette on to the plate and slide it back into the pan and brown the reverse side. Alternatively, place the frying-pan under a grill until the egg is set and the top brown.

Paella from Valencia
PAELLA A LA VALENCIANA

There are innumerable recipes for paella; *some including both meat and seafood, others using only seafood and still others using only vegetables. The methods of preparation also differ. One school of thought has it that the rice should be fried first, others say that it should be added after the liquid and simply boiled. One rule, however, must always be followed: the liquid used must be double the volume of rice. Usually 3 ounces of rice should be allowed per person.*

SERVES 4

2 fl oz olive oil
3 garlic cloves, cut in halves
1 medium-sized onion, chopped
3 medium-sized tomatoes, blanched, peeled and chopped
1 sweet red pepper, seeded and sliced
1 chicken, cut into serving pieces
1 teaspoon paprika
12 oz rice
¼ teaspoon powdered saffron
1½ pints chicken stock, well seasoned
1 lb peas, podded
½ lb cooked, shelled shrimp
½ quart mussels, scrubbed and bearded

Heat the oil in an iron *paellera* or a large, deep frying-pan. Add the garlic and cook for a few minutes to flavour the oil. Remove and discard the garlic.

Add the onion, tomatoes, red pepper and chicken pieces. Reduce the heat and add the paprika Cook for 10 minutes, stirring frequently.

Spread the rice evenly in the pan and cook for 2 to 3 minutes more, stirring constantly. Remove the pan from the heat and add the saffron. Pour in the stock, stir thoroughly and bring to the boil. Add the peas and shrimp and cook over low heat for 15 minutes, or until almost all the liquid has been absorbed. Put the well-scrubbed mussels on top of the rice, cover the pan and cook for 6 or 8 minutes, or until the mussels open. Discard any that remain shut. Serve hot.

Madrid Stew
COCIDO MADRILENO

Cocidos are traditional Spanish stews which combine a mixture of dried and fresh vegetables or a selection of different meats. This cocido from Madrid is a mixture of garbanzos (chick-peas) *and beef, chicken, bacon and sausage.*

SERVES 4

8 oz garbanzos (chick-peas), soaked overnight
Salt
1 chicken
½ lb bacon, in 1 piece
Stock
2 onions, sliced
2 leeks, sliced
2 carrots, sliced
2 tomatoes, quartered
1 lb small potatoes
1 chorizo (garlic sausage), sliced
MEATBALLS
½ lb minced beef
1 egg yolk
2 tablespoons breadcrumbs
1 tablespoon chopped parsley
Salt
Freshly ground black pepper
Oil

Put the *garbanzos* in a saucepan. Cover generously with water and bring to the boil. Add salt to taste, partly cover, reduce the heat and simmer for 2½ hours.

Meanwhile, make the meatballs. In a bowl, combine the minced meat, egg yolk, breadcrumbs, parsley and salt and pepper to taste. Mix the ingredients well together and shape into small balls. Heat some oil in a frying-pan, add the meatballs and fry until they are brown all over. Drain and set aside.

Put the chicken and the bacon in a large pan. Cover with stock and bring to the boil. Reduce the heat, cover the pan and simmer for 30 minutes. Add the onions, leeks, carrots and tomatoes and continue cooking for 20 minutes. Add the potatoes and cook for another 20 minutes. Add the *garbanzos*, *chorizo* and the meatballs and cook for a final 10 minutes.

Lift out the chicken and the bacon. Strain the remaining contents of the pan. The strained stock is served as soup. Slice the bacon, cut the chicken into pieces and arrange in the centre of a large serving dish with the meatballs and sliced *chorizo*. Surround the meat with the *garbanzos*. Arrange the vegetables around the *garbanzos* and serve.

Rice and Lemon Caramel Custard
FLAN DE ARROZ AL LIMON

The Spanish prefer to end a meal with fruit and, consequently, there are not many recipes for desserts. In southern Spain the most common dessert is flan, *a caramel custard. This recipe is a pleasant variation.*

SERVES 4 TO 6

15 fl oz milk
15 fl oz single cream
4 tablespoons rice
Finely pared rind of 1 lemon
4 oz castor sugar
6 egg yolks

Put the milk, cream, rice and lemon rind in a saucepan. Bring to the boil over low heat. Simmer gently for 1 hour, stirring occasionally.

Meanwhile, put three-quarters of the sugar in a saucepan over moderate heat. Shake the pan occasionally until the sugar begins to melt. Stirring, cook the syrup until it is a rich brown, being careful not to let it burn. Remove the pan from the heat and pour the caramel into a 2½-pint heatproof bowl. Turn the bowl around quickly so that the caramel coats the sides evenly. Set aside.

Preheat the oven to 300°F (Gas Mark 2). In another bowl, beat the remaining sugar with the egg yolks. Remove the pan from the heat. Remove and discard the lemon rind. Stirring constantly, gradually add the beaten egg yolks to the milk and rice. Pour the mixture into the caramel-lined bowl. Put the bowl in a baking tin filled with boiling water and bake for 30 minutes.

Cool then chill the pudding in the refrigerator. When thoroughly chilled, turn out on to a serving dish.

Cabbage and Potato Soup
CALDO VERDE

Caldo verde *is the soup most commonly served in Portugal. The cabbage cooks for a very short time so it must be very finely shredded.*

SERVES 4

2 pints water
4 medium-sized potatoes
Salt
½ small cabbage, coarse veins and leaves discarded and finely shredded
2 tablespoons olive oil
Freshly ground black pepper

Bring the water to the boil in a large saucepan. Add the potatoes and salt to taste. Cover the pan, reduce the heat and cook the potatoes until they are tender. Remove the potatoes and mash them. Return the mashed potatoes to the pan and stir to mix. Add the shredded cabbage, olive oil and pepper to taste. Bring the mixture to the boil and cook, uncovered, for 5 minutes. Adjust the seasoning and serve.

Dried Cod with Potatoes and Olives
BACALHAU GOMES DE SA

Bacalhau *is eaten far more in Portugal than it is in Spain, and there are literally hundreds of recipes and regional variations. It is often combined with potatoes, as in this popular dish.*

SERVES 4

1½ lb dried salt cod
2 lb potatoes, peeled and thickly sliced
8 fl oz olive oil

4 medium-sized onions, sliced
1 garlic clove, crushed
White pepper
12 black olives, stoned
4 hard-boiled eggs, sliced
1 tablespoon chopped parsley

Soak the cod for 24 hours, changing the water once. Put the cod in a saucepan. Add just enough water to cover and bring to the boil. Reduce the heat and simmer for 30 minutes. Add the potatoes and simmer for 20 minutes, or until they are tender and the fish is cooked. Lift out the fish. Remove and discard the skin and bones and flake the flesh into 1-inch pieces.

Meanwhile, heat the oil in a large casserole. Add the onions and garlic and fry until the onions are soft. Season with a little pepper and stir in the olives, fish and potatoes with their liquid. Cook gently for about 5 minutes. Arrange the egg slices on top of the dish, sprinkle with parsley and serve hot.

Lisbon Liver
ISCAS A LISBOA

The Portuguese have a way of cooking liver which is quite delicious. It should be cut into small wafer-thin slices and marinated for several hours or, better still, overnight, in a mixture of dry white wine and a little wine vinegar. A bay leaf, a few cloves and peppercorns, a crushed clove of garlic and a little salt added to the marinade give the liver its subtle flavour. This dish is a speciality of Lisbon.

SERVES 4

10 fl oz dry white wine
2 tablespoons wine vinegar
1 bay leaf
1 garlic clove, crushed
4 peppercorns
2 cloves
½ teaspoon salt
1½ lb pig's or lamb's liver, thinly sliced
2 tablespoons olive oil
4 oz smoked bacon, diced

Combine the wine, vinegar, bay leaf, garlic, peppercorns, cloves and salt in a bowl. Add the liver slices and turn them in the marinade. Cover the bowl and put it in the refrigerator to marinate overnight.

Remove the liver slices and dry them on kitchen paper. Reserve the marinade. Heat the oil in a large frying-pan. Add the bacon and fry gently for 3 minutes, stirring constantly. Add the liver and cook for 3 minutes on each side. Transfer the liver and bacon to a heated serving dish. Strain the marinade into the pan and boil quickly to reduce it, to concentrate the flavour and thicken the sauce. Pour the sauce over the liver and serve with sliced fried potatoes.

THE SPANISH ATTITUDE to wine is almost biblically simple and undemanding, with the result that most Spanish wine is disappointingly dull. The high points are well sign-posted: sherry for aperitifs; Rioja for excellent table wines; Catalonia for good sparkling wines (and a rather higher standard than the rest of Spain in everything else). Between them there are some Alice-in-Wonderland experiences like Chacoli, the Basque near-wine of legendary acidity, but much more that is neither good nor spectacularly bad.

Portugal is just the opposite. There is no Rioja with old traditions and sophisticated standards. Instead there is a remarkably high general level of wine-making, so that the jug wine in any country inn may well be excellent. The Atlantic climate of most of Portugal gives its wine an affinity with that of France. With the few obvious commercial exceptions this great potential remains excitingly unexplored.

Northern Portugal shares with Spanish Galicia a style of wine of its own: green wine, or *vinho verde*, made fresh and fizzy, often cloudy, generally sharp, utterly hit-and-miss, but in lucky moments exquisite. The Douro valley is the source of port, which is all handled by the merchants of Oporto in their "lodges". It is also the source of some excellent red and white wines which rarely get further than those same Oporto lodges' dining-room tables.

Every part of Portugal, except the Alentejo, has its vineyards. Often it is unclear, from the label, where a wine comes from. But with good wine so cheap, and cheap wine so good, it hardly matters.

Culinary traditions shaped by invaders

FROM BAGHDAD in AD 788, leading his army of horsemen, came King Idriss I and in the name of Allah he planted the flag of Islam in North African soil. The inhabitants, all Christians, but a conglomeration of many races, were forced to listen to this triumphant prophet of Allah, who claimed to have brought them a highly civilized culture with a long tradition that governed everything from etiquette to the culinary arts.

The people of the Maghreb, the North African Coast that includes Morocco, Algeria and Tunisia, were soon converted to Islam. Today they are called Arabs, but although they have absorbed the Arab culture, it is perhaps more accurate simply to call them North Africans, for their own culture and history goes far back to the earliest days of recorded history.

It was here that the Phoenicians spent their wealth, the Romans posted their tired garrisons and Moors and Berbers intermarried. Much later French sophistication and self-sufficiency also had their influence and have been absorbed into the essence of the Maghreb.

Algeria, occupied by France for longer than Tunisia or Morocco, has accepted much of its culture. Middle-class Algerians speak French in preference to Arabic, and housewives buy French-style loaves, called *baguettes*, rather than *kesra*, the Arab bread. The Sahara desert, however, which covers a large area of Algeria, has kept its own traditions. Here, ancient rituals of eating, rather than being neglected, have been kept alive by nomadic tribes. Feasts, at which *mechoui*, spitted baby lamb, is the main dish, are enjoyed by the Bedouins in the course of their long journeys. This dish has been adapted in the cities where the lamb is halved or quartered and roasted over a brazier.

Couscous, the national dish of the Maghreb, was introduced by the Berbers, whose influence, above all others, has shaped the culinary tradition of North Africa. Today *couscous* is eaten throughout the Arab world, as well as in Europe. A type of fine semolina made from wheat grain, *couscous* is steamed over a lamb or chicken and vegetable stew or broth. The vegetables vary from region to region and even from home to home, but chick-peas, onions, carrots, turnips, courgettes, peppers, aubergines, leeks, celery and raisins are always included.

The vegetables are cut into large pieces, put into the bottom part of the *couscousier*, seasoned and covered with water, to which a little oil is added. They are then simmered, until tender, while the steam cooks the semolina which has been placed in the top part of the *couscousier*. The dish can be served with *harissa*, a hot and pungent Tunisian sauce.

The seasoning and ingredients of *couscous* depend on individual tastes but also reflect the general tastes of each country. A Moroccan *couscous*, for example, is generally distinguished by the subtle aroma of saffron, echoing the richness of their cuisine. The Algerians prefer a broth thickened and flavoured with tomato purée. The Tunisians, whose preference is for fiery food, spice their sauce with ginger and chilli pepper.

In the Moroccan city of Fez, with its *medina*, ancient Arab quarter, *tajine*, another speciality of the Maghreb is cooked to perfection. *Tajine* is an exotic stew, varied in flavour, spiced or sweet, which includes honey, almonds, raisins, dates and prunes, cooked with meat, fish or poultry.

The cooks of Fez are also known for their skill in producing the famous Moroccan pigeon pie, *bstilla*. This dish requires as many as fifty paper-thin circles of *malsouqua* pastry, a Tunisian dough made of semolina. These are peeled quickly from the underside of a heated pan and laid over a succession of exotic fillings. Finally the pie, stuffed in layers with spices, sugar and pigeon meat, is fried on both sides, slid out of the pan and sprinkled with cinnamon and sugar.

Cooking a Tunisian *brik*, or meat turnover, is based on only one round of pastry, but it requires the same virtuosity. A mixture of minced lamb and cheese is put on to the pastry circle, an egg is broken on top and the pastry is folded over and sealed. It is then fried in oil so that the egg yolk remains intact, the filling is cooked and the pastry is crisp and golden.

In a middle-class North African home meals are served with formal elegance. The walls of the dining-room are ornately decorated with bright mosaics which harmonize with the richly woven carpets. The Baroque silverware, hand-carved chairs and serving tables shine in the brilliant desert sunlight. In the midst of this abundance the host and his guests sit around a low table. In silence perfumed water is passed around. Each person in turn dips three fingers into the bowl. Then the food is served.

The meal begins with *bstilla*, juicy and crisp, sour and sweet. Next comes chicken cooked with prunes and honey. This is followed by *couscous*, which is rolled into small pellets and eaten with three fingers. There is little conversation and no wine. A glass of cold milk is served with a semolina dessert made of raisins, currants and chopped, blanched almonds gently cooked in milk or fruit juice. The meal ends with mint tea. Then the table is taken away and again hands are washed with warm, fragrant water.

Outside, in the *medina* and *kasbahs*, the potters create colourful, conical-shaped dishes for *couscous* and high-lipped soup tureens. Traces of different civilizations can be seen in the pottery, in the shapes of the roofs, the archways and the open yards with clear blue fronts. Donkeys bray as they wend their way through the winding streets. In dark and narrow shops, men cook fish kebabs. Spice shops display every known spice. More than any other people, the North Africans have adopted every spice that has come their way en route to Europe.

In the tea houses, old men sip mint tea. Mint tea has become associated with Morocco, and yet it was introduced there only in 1854, when, during the Crimean War, British merchants were obliged to seek new markets for their wares. They disposed of large quantities of tea in Tangiers and Mogador. The North Africans took it, adapted it and made it their own, as they have done so successfully with many other dishes.

Bstilla, for example, was brought from Andalusia and introduced by the Moors. *Salata meshwiya* is a Tunisian salad much like *salad niçoise*. *Chakchouka*, similar to the Turkish *menemen*, is a tasty Tunisian egg, pepper and tomato dish. *Ossa bil mergas* is a version of the Persian *kuku* omelettes. The Moroccan preparation of stuffed shad is very much like that cooked in Iraq, but far more exciting for the dish includes rice, sugar, cinnamon, ginger and onions.

North African desserts, works of art in their own right, are less sweet but more colourful than those of the rest of the Arab world. *Rghaifs*, pancakes, are fried in butter, topped with honey or stuffed with almonds. Honey, almonds and sesame seeds are used in many other sweetmeats, such as *briovats au miel et aux amandes*, little almond-stuffed pastries, *criouch*, honey and sesame-seed covered cakes and the well-known *sellou* which is prepared during Ramadan and for

very special occasions from fine flour, sesame seeds, almonds, powdered sugar and gum Arabic.

Among the splendours of a sweet shop, with its special aromas and colours, can be seen the golden red of *briovats*, the dark red of *criouch*, the deep brown of *haloua chebbakia* and almond-coloured *choribas*. *Kaabs*, shell-shaped and orange in colour, lie next to the *sellou*, which are sand-coloured, piled high and scattered with almonds.

The narrow streets conceal little court-yards decorated with perfumed flowers and

trickling fountains. Stark exteriors of stone and mud belie the dazzling mosaics within the houses, whose charm is echoed in a rich and colourful approach to food.

Disguised by convenient cosmopolitan hotels in Alger, Tunis or Casablanca, the essence of the Maghreb becomes no more than a cliché of foreign expectations. Only by sauntering through the pages of history, through the dark, sunless alleys, the *souks* and the *kasbahs*, can the people, their way of life and their superb cuisine be truly appreciated.

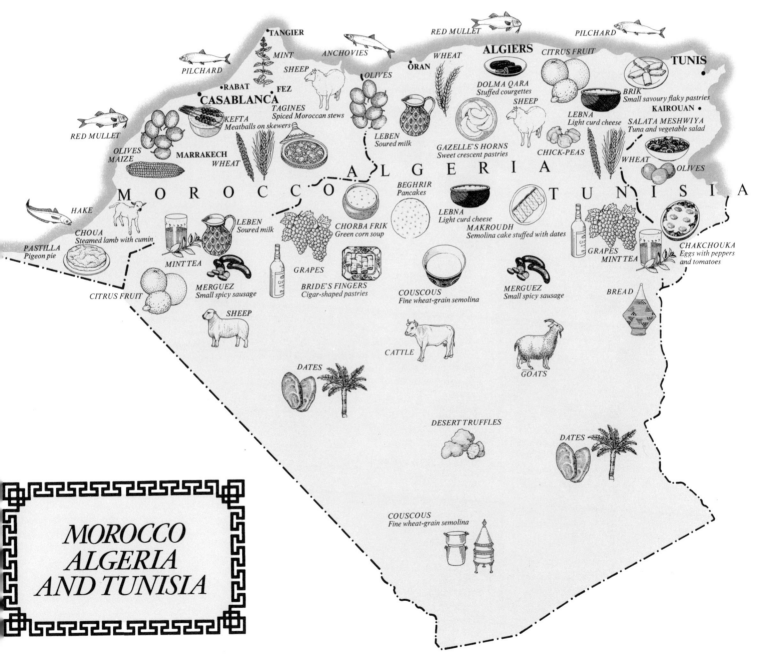

MOROCCO
ALGERIA
AND TUNISIA

A rich and tasty approach to food

Lamb and Chicken Soup
HARIRA SOUIRIA

This rich Moroccan soup, especially prepared and eaten during Ramadan, *is usually served accompanied by dates.*

SERVES 8 TO 10

4 oz lean lamb, cut into ½-inch cubes
1 oz butter
1 medium-sized onion, chopped
1 tablespoon chopped parsley
2 teaspoons sweet paprika
1 teaspoon powdered saffron
Salt
Freshly ground black pepper
6 pints water
2 oz chick-peas, soaked overnight
2 oz brown lentils
1½ lb tomatoes, blanched, peeled and finely
    chopped or puréed
6 tablespoons lemon juice
2 oz rice
2 oz flour
1 egg

Put the meat into a large saucepan with the butter, onion, parsley, paprika, saffron and salt and pepper to taste. Cook gently, stirring frequently, for 5 minutes.

Add the water, chick-peas, lentils, tomatoes and lemon juice.

Cover the pan and cook for 1½ hours. Add the rice and cook for 15 to 20 minutes, or until the rice is cooked.

Meanwhile, put the flour into a bowl and slowly add cold water until you have a thin paste the consistency of single cream. Stir the flour mixture into the pan and cook for a further 15 minutes. Break open one end of the egg, hold it above the soup and let it drop slowly into the soup, stirring constantly. Pour the soup into a heated tureen and serve immediately.

Tuna Fish Salad
SALATA MESHWIYA

This fresh vegetable and tuna fish salad is a Tunisian speciality, but similar salads are common all along the North African coast.

SERVES 2

2 green peppers, halved and seeded
4 tomatoes, blanched and peeled
6 spring onions
1 dried chilli
4 oz can tuna fish
2 hard-boiled eggs, sliced
1 tablespoon capers
2 tablespoons chopped parsley

DRESSING

3 tablespoons olive oil
1 tablespoon lemon juice
Freshly ground black pepper
Salt
Chopped parsley

Place the peppers, cut side down, under a hot grill until soft. Skin the pepper halves and cut into thin strips.

Slice off the tops of the tomatoes and scoop out the seeds. Cut them into rings. Chop the spring onions and chilli finely.

Put all the vegetables into a bowl. Drain and crumble the fish and add to the salad. Arrange the sliced eggs on the top and sprinkle with the capers.

Mix all the ingredients for the dressing and pour over the salad. Garnish with the parsley.

Cooked Vegetable Salad
SALADE DE ZAALOUK

A spicy cooked salad from Tunisia, Salade de Zaalouk, *will keep for 2 to 3 days if it is well covered and kept in the refrigerator.*

SERVES 4 TO 6

2 aubergines, cubed
4 courgettes, sliced
8 tablespoons vegetable oil
½ to 1 teaspoon cayenne pepper
2 garlic cloves, crushed
Salt
4 green or red peppers, seeded and sliced

4 medium-sized tomatoes, blanched, peele[d]
    and chopped
2 chillies, seeded and chopped

Place the aubergines, courgettes, oil, cayenn[e] garlic and salt to taste in a large saucepan. Po[ur] in enough water to cover the vegetables an[d] bring to the boil. Cover the pan, reduce the he[at] to low and simmer for 10 minutes.

Add the peppers, tomatoes and chillies an[d] cook, uncovered, stirring occasionally, until a[ll] the water has evaporated. Taste and adjust t[he] seasoning.

Remove the pan from the heat and let th[e] salad cool. Serve cold with crusty bread.

Marinated Fish Cooked in Olive O[il]
POISSON EN TAJIN MQUALLI

A tajin *is the name given to a shallow dish whi[ch] can be used either on top of the stove or the ove[n.] Any fish such as halibut, whiting, grey mullet [or] cod can be used for this Moroccan dish. If the fis[h] is small, remove the head and tail but leave th[e] rest of the body whole.*

SERVES 4

MARINADE

15 fl oz water
2 tablespoons olive oil
1 teaspoon cayenne pepper
1 teaspoon ground cumin
1 teaspoon ground coriander
2 garlic cloves, crushed
2 teaspoons salt

TAJIN

8 fl oz olive oil
2 lb halibut steaks, each steak boned and cu[t]
    in four
⅛ teaspoon of powdered saffron
1 teaspoon ground ginger
1 lemon, quartered
12 black olives, stoned

Mix all the marinade ingredients in a shallo[w] bowl. Add the fish pieces and set aside for [4] hours, turning the pieces over occasionally.

Preheat the oven to 375°F (Gas Mark 5).

Remove the fish from the marinade and pat i[t] dry on kitchen paper. Reserve 1 tablespoon o[f] the marinade.

Heat a little of the oil in a flameproo[f] casserole. Arrange the fish pieces in one laye[r] in the casserole. Mix the remaining olive oi[l] with the saffron, ginger and 1 tablespoon of th[e] marinade and pour it over the fish. Cover th[e] casserole and simmer over very low heat for [5] minutes.

Place the casserole in the oven for 30 minutes[,] or until the fish is tender. Transfer the fis[h] to a heated platter.

Thicken the sauce, if it is too thin, by simmer[-] ing it, uncovered, for a few minutes. Pour th[e]

ITALIAN, FRENCH AND SPANISH influences have come and gone in North Africa. The underlying Islamic culture has remained. Islam prohibits alcohol, how effectively no one ever seems quite sure, but certainly the enormous wine industries built up in Tunisia, Morocco and, above all, Algeria by the colonists began to dwindle when they departed. In theory there is no home market for its products any more.

In practice North African wine still exists, and is still as good as ever it was, which is better than its rather sleazy reputation. There is no white wine worth having, but adequate rosé, especially the very pale *vin gris* of Boulaouane in Morocco, and more than adequate red. That it is no better is the fault of the common, high-yielding grape varieties the colonists planted.

Wine apart, the North African drink is mint tea, an infusion containing more mint than tea and more sugar than either, served in tall glasses in relentless succession on any social occasion.

...uce over the fish. Garnish with the lemon quarters and the black olives and serve immediately.

Chicken with Prunes and Honey
TAJINE DE POULET AUX PRUNEAUX ET MIEL

This Moroccan dish is typical of the ancient North African tradition of cooking meat and fruit together.

SERVES 4

1 large roasting chicken, jointed
salt
black pepper
½ teaspoon powdered saffron
1 stick cinnamon
1 medium-sized onion, chopped
2 oz butter
8 oz prunes
1 teaspoon powdered cinnamon
4 tablespoons clear brown honey

GARNISH
2 oz almonds, blanched and fried in butter until golden
1 tablespoon sesame seeds, toasted

Put the chicken pieces into a large saucepan with salt and pepper to taste, saffron, cinnamon stick, onion and butter. Pour in enough water to cover the chicken and bring to the boil. Cover the pan, reduce the heat to low and simmer for 1 hour, or until the chicken is tender. Transfer the chicken pieces to a plate and set aside. Remove the cinnamon stick.

Add the prunes to the pan and cook gently for 15 minutes. Stir in the powdered cinnamon and the honey. Simmer, uncovered, stirring occasionally, until the sauce is thick and syrupy.

Return the chicken pieces to the pan, taking care to keep the prunes whole. Continue cooking for a further 10 minutes, or until the chicken is heated through.

To serve, place the chicken on a heated platter. Pour the sauce and prunes over the top. Garnish with the almonds and toasted sesame seeds.

Semolina and Meat Stew
COUSCOUS

Couscous is the national dish of all the North African countries. The dish gets its name from a fine semolina made from wheat grain. The correct way to cook couscous is in a couscousier, but it is possible to improvise with a steamer or with a metal strainer which fits well over a large saucepan. This recipe is for an Algerian couscous which includes tomato purée. Tunisians usually prefer a much spicier sauce with plenty of

cayenne and chillies and the Moroccan couscous *is distinguished by the use of saffron. Couscous is often served with a sauce prepared from garlic, chillies, a concentrated red pimento sauce called* harissa *and a little of the broth from the* couscous.

SERVES 6

2 oz chick-peas, soaked overnight
½ teaspoon bicarbonate of soda
1 lb couscous
2 lb lean lamb, cut into 1-inch cubes
2 carrots, cut into large pieces
1 onion, quartered
3 bay leaves
4 tablespoons tomato purée
3 teaspoons salt
1½ teaspoons chilli powder
1 teaspoon ground ginger
2 teaspoons ground cumin
4 tablespoons olive oil
8 celery sticks, cut into large pieces
2 turnips, peeled and cut into large pieces
2 courgettes, cut into large pieces
2 leeks, white parts only, cut into large pieces
2 green peppers, cut in half and seeded
2 aubergines, cut into large pieces
2 oz raisins
1 oz butter

Put the chick-peas in a saucepan. Cover well with water and add the bicarbonate of soda. Boil for 1½ hours, or until almost tender.

Meanwhile pour the *couscous* on to a tray or baking sheet. Sprinkle with warm salted water. Work lightly between the fingers so that each grain is separate, moistened and beginning to swell. Let the *couscous* rest for 15 minutes. Repeat this process 3 times.

Drain the chick-peas and place them in the bottom of the *couscousier* with the lamb, carrots and onions. Pour in enough water to cover and bring to the boil. Reduce the heat, cover the pan and simmer for 30 minutes. Add the bay leaves, tomato purée, salt, chilli powder, ginger, cumin, oil, celery, turnips and courgettes. Put the *couscous* in the upper pan of the *couscousier* and place it on top of the lower pan. Make sure that the liquid in the lower pan cannot enter the upper pan or the *couscous* will become lumpy.

Cover the *couscousier* and place it over the heat. Simmer for 15 to 20 minutes, or until the vegetables are half cooked. Add the leeks, peppers, aubergines and raisins to the stew and add the butter to the *couscous*. Continue cooking for a further 15 to 20 minutes, or until the meat and vegetables are tender. Do not overcook or the vegetables will disintegrate.

Stir the *couscous* with a fork to ensure an even distribution of the butter. To serve, pile the *couscous* on to a large, heated platter, make a well in the centre and spoon the vegetables and meat and some of the sauce into it.

Almond Crescents
SESAME CORNES DE GAZELLES

These little Moroccan almond crescents may be served with tea or coffee.

MAKES ABOUT 20 CRESCENTS

8 oz blanched almonds
4 oz castor sugar
6 tablespoons rose water
⅛ teaspoon ground cinnamon
2 eggs, beaten
6 tablespoons sesame seeds

Put the almonds into a small saucepan. Cover with water and simmer for 30 minutes. Drain the almonds and reduce them to a paste in an electric blender, adding a little of the cooking water if necessary.

Preheat the oven to 375°F (Gas Mark 5).

Put the almond paste into a bowl and add the sugar, rose water and cinnamon. Knead well together. Divide the mixture into walnut-sized balls. Roll each ball between the palms of the hands until they form "cigars" 2½ inches long and thicker in the middle than at the ends.

Place the beaten egg on one plate and spread the sesame seeds on another. Dip the almond "cigars" first into the egg and then into the sesame seeds. Shape them into crescents and arrange them on a buttered baking sheet.

Bake on the centre shelf of the oven for 45 minutes to 1 hour, or until the crescents are golden. Cool on a rack before serving.

Plain Light Pastries
GHORIBA SABLEE AU BEURRE

These Tunisian pastries are very light and melt in the mouth. They are also made in the shape of bangles or balls.

MAKES ABOUT 60 GHORIBA

1 lb 10 oz plain flour
9 oz icing sugar
1 lb unsalted butter, melted

Sift the flour and sugar into a large mixing bowl. Make a well in the centre. Pour in the melted butter. Gradually blend the butter with the dry ingredients to make a dough. Shape the dough into a ball and set aside for several hours.

Preheat the oven to moderate, 350°F (Gas Mark 4). Lightly butter a large baking sheet.

Turn the dough out on to a lightly floured surface and knead until it becomes soft. Pinch off a large walnut-sized piece of the dough and shape it into a ball. Press the ball between the palms until the dough is very soft and flattened in shape. Put it on the prepared baking sheet. Continue until all the dough has been used up.

Bake for 10 to 15 minutes, or until the *ghoriba* are golden brown. When they are cold dust with icing sugar.

Spicy flavours and sweet delights

"ONE'S EATING SHOWS ONE'S LOVE." Only an Arab could think in this way, hastening to add, "The poor woman killed herself with work, yet the feast lasted only one day." But what a day and what a feast!

In the Arabian desert the most gracious compliment a Bedouin can pay is an invitation to a *mansaf*, a formal feast. The food is simple, consisting of boiled lamb and rice covered with a seasoned butter sauce and piled on layers of *shrak*, thin whole-wheat bread baked on a domed, cast-iron griddle. No cutlery is used. Each person uses his right hand to tear off a piece of lamb, makes a bolus of it with a little rice and neatly flicks it into his mouth.

For centuries the Arabs of the desert have eaten this way. It is the simple food of simple people, a contrast to the lavish meals served in the cosmopolitan restaurants of modern Cairo, Beirut and Damascus.

The Bedouin with their trains of camels, zig-zagging around the dunes, across the vastness of Jordan and Saudi-Arabia, carrying spices, silks and carpets, are shadows from a distant past, separated from modern life by over a thousand years which witnessed the rise and fall of brilliant empires. As the warrior tribes of Arabia moved relentlessly upwards from the dese basins, they occupied vast territories fro the green forests and valleys of Lebanor Syria, Iraq and Persia, up to the Caucasus and westwards through Spain and Portug to the shores of the Atlantic. As a result, great cuisine was born in which the contr butions of conquerors and conquered, Christians, Moslems and Jews, can scarcel be disentangled.

The obligations of hospitality enjoine by Islam have become second nature to th Arab. No effort is spared in the attempt t please one's guests. Hours will be spen stuffing vegetables, fish, meatballs, and the the results will be modestly decried.

The Arab takes an instinctive delight i colour and pattern and this finds its expres sion in the presentation of even the simples dish of *hummus*, chick-peas pounded wit sesame-seed paste, which will be decorate with a pattern of red pepper, brown cumi and green parsley. Dishes are coloured gol with saffron as a mark of joy. Jars of *torshi* pickled turnips, onions, peppers, eggplants and cucumbers, some of them tinged pink with slices of beet, shine like jewels in the windows of restaurants. Spices and herb play an important part in Arab cuisine and sweets are perfumed with orange-flowe water and rose water.

The coastline of the eastern Mediter ranean is teeming with magnificent fish, the Sultan Ibrahim, or red mullet, grey mullet, sea bream and sea bass, turbot, swordfish, cod and sardines. These are grilled over charcoal, baked or poached.

Large fish are served coated with *tarator*, a creamy sauce of pine nuts, almonds, wal nuts or sesame seeds pounded with lemon juice and garlic. The great Iraqi speciality, *maragut*, is made with *shabait*, a kind of trout, caught in the Tigris, which is smoked over charcoal and served in riverside restaurants.

Lamb, which dominates the cuisine, is grilled over charcoal, baked, used with vegetables in robust stews and made into a variety of meatballs and kebabs. For *kofta wa kebab*, an unusual speciality, chunks of whole lamb alternate with lumps of minced meat which are shaped around the skewer and grilled.

Although the whole of the Arab world shares an approach to food, there are also regional and national specialities. Many of the traditional dishes of Egypt, for example, are as old as the windswept stones of the pyramids. *Ful medames*, a dish of brown beans flavoured with garlic, dressed with

THE ARAB WORLD

BURGHUL *Cracked wheat*

WALNUTS

BAKLAVA *Honey and nut pastries*

ALEPPO
BRIDE'S FINGERS *Cigar-shaped pastries*

KIBBEH NAYE *Pounded raw lamb and burghul*

WHEAT

MAIZE

MA'MOUNIA *Semolina and syrup dessert*

BABA GHANOUSH *Aubergines with sesame paste*

SHEEP

S Y R I A

SWORDFISH

OLIVES

SAMAK TARATOR *Fish with sesame-seed sauce*

TABBOULEH *Cracked wheat salad*

TOMATOES

DESERT TRUFFLES

YOGHOURT

L E B A N O N

TRIPOLI

PEPPERS

TAHINA *Sesame-seed paste*

MA'AMOUL *Small filled pastries*

SESAME

KIBBEH *Pounded meat and cracked wheat*

BEIRUT

SHAWARMA *Lamb roasted on a vertical spit*

HALVA *Sesame and nut confection*

KONAFA *Shredded dough pastries*

DAMASCUS

DRIED APRICOTS IN SYRUP

HAKE

HUMMUS *Chick-pea and sesame-oil dip*

ICE-CREAM

JERUSALEM ARTICHOKES

PINE NUTS

J O R D A N   R I V E R

CITRUS FRUIT

AMMAN

DATES

JERUSALEM

MENSAF *Lamb with rice and yoghourt*

DEAD SEA

YOGHOURT

VEGETABLES

J O R D A N

CAMEL

BLACK CARROTS

MAQLOUBA *Meat and vegetables with steamed rice*

oil and lemon juice, is served for breakfast, lunch and supper in many Egyptian homes and is said to have been eaten in the days of the pharaohs.

The aroma of *melokhia* soup, dark green and glutinous, made with the leaves of a spinach-like herb and garnished with *taklia*, a sauce of fried garlic and coriander, perfumes the houses of rich and poor alike. It, too, goes back to the ancient past. Indeed, some scholars claim that the chopping of the *melokhia* leaves is portrayed in pharaonic tomb paintings.

The ancient Egyptians were said to favour roast goose. Poultry and game birds are still popular. Chickens and delicately flavoured baby pigeons are spit-roasted or stuffed with rice and pine nuts, or whole-wheat, and baked in an earthenware casserole. Quail are marinated in oil with cumin and coriander and grilled over charcoal, or embedded in a rice pilaf.

The full richness and subtlety of which the Arab cuisine is capable can be most appreciated in Syria and Lebanon. Here the traditional dishes of the nomadic Arabs have been replaced by a highly sophisticated cuisine which owes much to the Turks, Armenians and, particularly in Lebanon, the French. It is perhaps this mixture of diverse influences that has produced one of the most classic of Arab cuisines, that of Aleppo, in Syria. Here the kebabs are richer, more varied, spicier. And the cafés and pastry shops exhibit a bewildering variety of exquisite sweets and pastries, piled in high, golden mountains.

Burghul, cracked wheat, plays an important role in the cuisine of both Syria and Lebanon, reflecting the Greek, Assyrian and Armenian origins of the people who inhabited this region before the arrival of the Semitic Arabs. It is an integral part of *kibbeh*, the national dish of both the Syrians and the Lebanese. Basically a pounded mixture of raw meat and *burghul* flavoured

with onion, *kibbeh* is eaten with crisp lettuce leaves or shaped into round cakes and grilled or fried, or baked, or shaped into small ovals or balls, hollowed out, stuffed with meat and deep-fried in oil.

The sweets of the Arab world are famous throughout the world. Pastries like *baklava* and the shredded *konafa* (*kadayif* to the Turks) need no introduction. There are also *ma'amoul*, delicate pastries stuffed with dates or nuts and coated with powdered sugar, or bathed in a brilliant white cream; *ataif*, pancakes drenched in syrup and served with chopped pistachio nuts or almonds and thick clotted cream; the great Aleppan speciality, *ma'mounia*, made with semolina and sugar syrup, and *muhallabia*, a milk

pudding fragrant with orange-flower water.

Throughout the Arab world the bazaars thrive, despite growing competition from brash supermarkets. And in the spice streets of every town one can still buy a great variety of exquisite spices, including cinnamon, cumin, ginger, coriander, allspice and hot peppers. The vendors scoop them out of large bags on to squares of newspaper which they twist into cones. It is in these bazaars, in Aleppo, Damascus, Baghdad and Cairo, that the essence of the Arab world is still preserved.

In a changing world, this great culinary heritage, time-consuming and laborious, but delightfully exciting and an integral part of the Arab past, is to be cherished.

Unusual dishes as cooked for the caliphs

Cracked Wheat Salad
TABOULEH

This refreshing salad of burghul *(bulgar wheat) and finely chopped vegetables is served as part of the* mezze, *or hors d'oeuvre in most Middle Eastern countries. This salad is traditionally served on individual plates lined with lettuce leaves, or boiled cabbage or vine leaves.*

SERVES 4

3 oz burghul
1 cucumber, peeled and finely diced
4 tomatoes, chopped
2 green peppers, seeded and finely chopped
4 tablespoons chopped parsley
1½ tablespoons chopped fresh mint
½ onion, finely chopped
2 tablespoons olive oil
Lemon juice
Salt
1 cos lettuce

Wash the *burghul* under cold running water until the water runs clear. Drain and squeeze out the excess water. Put the *burghul* in a bowl with the cucumber, tomatoes, peppers, parsley, mint and onion. In a small bowl, mix the oil with the lemon juice and salt to taste. Pour the dressing over the *burghul* and vegetables and toss well to mix.

Line individual plates with the lettuce leaves and pile the *tabouleh* in the middle.

Egyptian Herb Soup
MELOKHIA

Melokhia is a soup made from an Egyptian herb similar to spinach. It is one of the national dishes of Egypt. Melokhia leaves are available dried from Greek shops, and occasionally the fresh leaves are available in some markets.

SERVES 6

4 oz dried melokhia leaves or 2 lb fresh leaves
3 pints strong stock made from chicken or knuckle of beef or veal
Salt
Freshly ground black pepper
1 oz butter
3 garlic cloves, crushed
1 tablespoon ground coriander
¼ teaspoon cayenne pepper

Crush the dried *melokhia* leaves. Put them in a bowl and moisten with a little hot water. Set aside until they swell and double in bulk. If the leaves are not brittle enough to crumble, dry them out in a warm oven for a few minutes. If fresh leaves are being used, wash them thoroughly and cut off the stalks. Spread the leaves out on a clean cloth to dry. Chop them finely.

Put the stock in a large saucepan. Season with salt and pepper and bring to the boil. Add the chopped or crumbled leaves and simmer for 10 minutes if the leaves are fresh and for 30 minutes if dry.

Meanwhile, prepare the *taklia* or garlic sauce. Melt the butter in a small frying-pan. Add the garlic and fry, stirring, until it is golden brown. Add the coriander and cayenne and cook, stirring, for 2 minutes. Add the garlic mixture to the soup, cover the pan and simmer for 3 minutes, stirring occasionally. Adjust the seasoning and serve.

Chicken Balls
KOFTIT FERAKH

These chicken balls may be served as appetizers or added to chicken stock and served as soup, or simmered in a tomato sauce and served as a main dish with potatoes.

SERVES 4

1 lb cooked boned chicken breast, minced
1 thick slice white bread, crusts trimmed
1 egg
2 tablespoons chopped parsley
¼ teaspoon turmeric
Salt
Freshly ground black pepper
4 tablespoons oil
Lemon juice

Put the chicken into a bowl. Soak the bread in a little water, squeeze it dry and add it to the chicken, with the egg, parsley, turmeric and salt and pepper to taste. Mix and knead the ingredients well together and shape into small marble-sized balls.

Heat the oil in a large frying-pan. Add the chicken balls and fry, turning them frequently, until they are golden brown. Drain on kitchen paper. Arrange the chicken balls on a serving plate, sprinkle with lemon juice and serve.

Aubergine Salad
ABOU GANOUSH

Aubergines are almost a staple food in the Middle East. There are innumerable varieties different in shape, size and colour—round and long, small and large and from white through mauve to deep, blackish purple. This salad is a favourite in Aleppo.

SERVES 4

4 medium-sized aubergines
4 medium-sized tomatoes, sliced
1 green pepper, seeded and sliced
1 small onion, chopped
4 tablespoons olive oil
2 heaped teaspoons ground cumin
2 garlic cloves, crushed
½ teaspoon red pepper
Salt
Lemon juice
Chopped parsley

Preheat the oven to 375°F (Gas Mark 5). Pu the whole, unpeeled aubergines in a shallow baking dish and bake for about 45 minutes, o until they are very soft to the touch. Remov from the oven and when the aubergines are coo enough to handle, peel them. Chop the auber gines and put them into a bowl with th tomatoes, pepper and onion.

In a small bowl, mix together the olive oil cumin, garlic, red pepper, salt and lemon juice to taste. Pour the dressing over the vegetable and mix well. Sprinkle with chopped parsley and serve.

Baked Fish with Walnut Stuffing
SAMAK HARRAH

In the Middle East, one large fish, a sea bass, re mullet or shad, is usually used for this dish an then divided into individual portions after cooking It is just as satisfactory to use 1 fish per person such as trout.

SERVES 4

4 trout, gutted, washed, with heads and tails left on
4 tablespoons olive oil
1 onion, chopped
1 green pepper, seeded and sliced
4 oz walnuts, crushed
2 tablespoons chopped parsley
3 tablespoons fresh pomegranate seeds (optional)
Salt
Freshly ground black pepper
Lemon slices
MARINADE
4 tablespoons olive oil
Salt
Black pepper
Juice of 2 lemons
1 garlic clove, crushed

In a shallow dish, mix together the ingredients for the marinade. Put in the fish, turn several times and set aside for 4 hours.

Preheat the oven to 400°F (Gas Mark 6). Lightly oil a baking dish large enough to take the fish in a single layer.

Heat the olive oil in a frying-pan. Add the onions and fry them until they are soft and beginning to brown. Add the green pepper and the walnuts and cook, stirring, for 5 minutes, or until the pepper is soft. Remove the pan from the heat and stir in 1½ tablespoons of the parsley, 1½ tablespoons of the pomegranate seeds and salt and pepper to taste. Fill each of the fish with the stuffing. Secure the openings with small skewers. Put the fish in the prepared baking dish. Bake for 20 to 30 minutes, or until the

sh parts easily from the bone. Do not over-
ok. Baste the fish occasionally with the
arinade to prevent them drying out.
Arrange the fish on a serving dish. Remove
e skewers. Garnish with lemon slices and
rinkle with the remaining parsley and pome-
anate seeds.

Lamb and Okra Stew
BAMIA

n Egyptian speciality, bamia *is an easy*
d tasty stew to make. If canned or frozen
kra is used, add it at the end of the cooking
me.

ERVES 4

lb okra
oz butter
onions, finely chopped
large garlic cloves, chopped
lb boned lean lamb, cut into 1-inch cubes
medium-sized ripe tomatoes, sliced
tablespoons tomato purée, mixed with 4
 tablespoons water
alt
reshly ground black pepper

ash the okra and cut off stems. If they are
rge, cut into pieces. Melt the butter in a
rge saucepan. Add the onions and garlic and
y, stirring, until the onions are soft but not
rown. Add the lamb pieces and brown them
l over. If fresh okra is being used, add them to
e pan and fry, stirring, for 2 to 3 minutes. Add
e tomatoes, tomato purée and salt and pepper
 taste. Add enough water to cover the meat
d vegetables and bring to the boil. Reduce the
eat, cover the pan and simmer for 1½ hours, or
ntil the meat is tender and the sauce is rich.

Brown Beans
FUL MESDAMES

he national dish of Egypt, ful mesdames *is a*
easant dish which is eaten by rich and poor. The
ans can be bought in Greek shops. Traditionally,
e eggs are cooked overnight. Called hamine *eggs,*
ey are simmered with onion skins until the
hites become beige in colour.

ERVES 4

lb brown Egyptian beans, soaked
 overnight
garlic cloves, crushed
alt
reshly ground black pepper
hard-boiled eggs, shelled
hopped parsley
emon quarters

rain the beans. Put them in a large saucepan.
over with water and bring to the boil. Reduce

the heat, partly cover the pan and simmer for 2
to 2½ hours, or until the beans are tender.
Remove the pan from the heat and drain the
beans. Return the beans to the pan and stir in
the garlic and salt and pepper to taste.
  Spoon the *ful mesdames* into individual soup
bowls, put a hard-boiled egg in the middle,
sprinkle the parsley on top and serve with
lemon quarters.

Egyptian Omelette with Aubergine
EGGEH BI BETINGAN

An Egyptian omelette is a firm egg cake full of
vegetables, meat, noodles or chicken. It may be
served hot or cold, turned out of the pan on to a
plate and cut into wedges. It may be served in
small pieces as an hors d'oeuvre, *in larger*
pieces as a first course or, if it is made with meat
or chicken, as a main dish.

SERVES 4

2 aubergines, cubed
Salt
1 oz butter
1 medium-sized onion, finely chopped
1 garlic clove, crushed
8 eggs, lightly beaten
Freshly ground black pepper

Put the aubergine cubes in a colander. Sprinkle
with salt and set aside for 1 hour. Rinse the
aubergines and dry on kitchen paper.
  In a large frying-pan, melt the butter. Add
the onion and garlic and fry, stirring, until the
onion is soft. Add the aubergine cubes and cook
until tender. Pour in the eggs, season with salt
and pepper to taste and stir to mix. Reduce the
heat to low, cover and cook the omelette for
20 to 25 minutes, or until the bottom is set.
  Preheat the grill. Place the frying-pan beneath
the heat and grill until the egg is cooked through
and the top is lightly browned. Alternatively,
invert the omelette on to a plate and then slide it
back into the pan and cook the other side.

Aleppo Semolina Pudding
MA' MOUNIA

It is said that this dessert was invented for a
ninth-century Caliph of Baghdad called Ma'moun.
Today, there are many variations and it is eaten in
many parts of the Middle East. This is a Syrian
recipe.

SERVES 4

1 lb sugar
1¼ pints water
1 teaspoon lemon juice

4 oz unsalted butter
6 oz semolina
Whipped or clotted cream
1 teaspoon ground cinnamon

In a large saucepan, dissolve the sugar in the
water, stirring constantly, over low heat. Add
the lemon juice and bring the syrup to the boil.
Reduce the heat and simmer the syrup for about
10 minutes, or until it thickens slightly.
  Meanwhile, melt the butter in a large saucepan. Add the semolina and fry gently, stirring,
for 5 minutes. Stirring constantly, pour in the
syrup. Simmer for 2 minutes. Remove the pan
from the heat and set aside for 20 minutes.
  To serve, spoon the *Ma'mounia* into individual
serving bowls. Place a spoonful of cream on top
and sprinkle with a little cinnamon.

Bride's Fingers
ASABEH EL ARDUS

These cigar-shaped sweets are made with paper-
thin pastry stuffed with an almond filling and
dipped in syrup. Although they have much the
same ingredients as the more celebrated baklava,
they are simpler to make and lighter to eat.

MAKES ABOUT 36 PASTRIES

About 4 oz butter, melted
8 oz phyllo pastry
8 oz ground almonds
2 tablespoons castor sugar
2 heaped teaspoons ground cinnamon
SYRUP
12 oz sugar
8 fl oz water
Juice of 1 lemon
2 tablespoons rose water

First make the syrup. In a saucepan, dissolve
the sugar in the water over low heat, stirring
constantly. Add the lemon juice. Raise the heat
and boil until the syrup thickens and coats the
back of a spoon. Stir in the rose water and set
aside to cool. When cool, refrigerate until
required.
  Preheat the oven to 375°F (Gas Mark 5).
Brush melted butter all over a large baking
sheet.
  Cut the *phyllo* sheets into rectangles about 5
by 10 inches. Brush each rectangle with the
melted butter. Mix together the almonds, sugar
and cinnamon. Spread 1 teaspoon of filling
along the short side of the rectangle. Fold the
long sides inwards and then roll up the pastry
to make a cigar. Place the cigars on the baking
sheet and bake for 15 to 20 minutes, or until
they are golden brown.
  While the pastries are still hot, dip them in the
cold syrup. Drain the pastries and arrange them
on a serving dish.

Exotic influences on a thrifty tradition

NOTHING IS SO TRULY EVOCATIVE of a country, nothing so precisely draws together and distils all its history, its culture, its geography and its religions, as the sights and smells and tastes of its food. And of no country is this more true than of South Africa. To talk to any South African of *meilies* or *sosaties*, of *biltong* or pawpaws, is to evoke at once subtle memories and associations of childhood and the folk-history of the country.

South Africa is a large country with a wide variety of climatic conditions, and its recorded history, although short, starting as it does in the early seventeenth century, is rich and was subject to many influences, all of which have had their effect on the pattern of its cuisine.

The Cape is where the recorded history of South Africa began. Although the Portuguese were the first to see the famous Table Mountain, it was the Dutch who, finding that the Cape had one of the most blessed climates in the world, long hot summers followed by short, rain-filled winters, decided to establish a station there. This station would be a halfway house between Europe and the East, where the sailing vessels could find fresh meat and vegetables on their way eastward.

They found that almost everything they planted flourished. They began to keep sheep, cows, pigs and chickens. The great tradition of hospitality that exists all over South Africa must have started then, when the visits of the ships were so eagerly looked forward to and their sailors were so warmly entertained.

The earliest food traditions were laid down by those first settlers, the Dutch. From them present-day South Africa has inherited not only many individual recipes, like *melk tert*, custard tart, and *soetkoekies*, spiced biscuits, but a whole attitude to the kitchen that makes being a housewife and running a well-ordered, thrifty kitchen, a source of pride and honour.

Soon other, more exotic influences began to be grafted on to the culinary traditions of the Dutch. As they began to build homes, the Dutch needed more labour to help farm the land. From the Far East, from Java, Sumatra and Malaya, they brought slaves and with them came strange new ways with food. These Malays (as they commonly, but inaccurately, came to be called) were the first gardeners, fishermen, labourers and domestic help. They, more than any other racial group in South Africa, seem to have preserved their culture, their religion and their language almost completely intact and their influence has been permanent and profound.

The Malay culinary traditions could be adapted perfectly for South African needs. The rather tough meat that they got from the stringy cattle, bred from animals bought from the Hottentots, could be rendered tender and succulent when turned into a *bredie*.

A *bredie* is to South Africa what Irish stew is to Ireland, goulash is to the Hungarians and Lancashire hotpot is to the English. Thinly sliced onions are browned in mutton fat, and the meat, or fish, is then itself gently browned. Finally, the chosen vegetable, tomatoes, beans, carrots, peas or even pumpkin, is placed over the meat. Chillies and other seasonings—green ginger, cinnamon sticks, cloves, garlic—are added and the whole dish is gently braised until the meat is so tender it falls from the bone.

Curries and spices could usefully be used to disguise meat that had gone slightly off in the great heat. *Bobotie* is the most famous dish of this kind.

To make a bobotie to serve 4, fry 2 coarsely chopped, medium-sized onions and 2 crushed garlic cloves in 3 tablespoons of butter. When the onions are golden brown transfer them to a large mixing-bowl. Add 2 tablespoons curry powder, 2 ounces flaked almonds, 3 ounces raisins, 1 teaspoon mixed herbs, the juice of ½ lemon, 1 teaspoon salt, 1 tablespoon sugar, 1 tablespoon vinegar, ⅛ teaspoon black pepper and 2 pounds of minced beef or lamb. Mix together.

Soak 3 thick slices of white bread in 10 fluid ounces of milk. Squeeze out the bread, reserving the milk. Mix the bread and 1 egg into the meat mixture. Put into a well-buttered pie dish. Beat the remaining milk, about 6 fluid ounces, with 1 egg and pour over the meat. Bake in a 350°F (Gas Mark 4) oven for 1 hour, or until the mixture is set and the top is lightly browned.

Sosaties are very like the *shashliks* of the Middle East. Cubes of mutton or lamb are marinated in a mixture of finely chopped onions, curry powder, chillies, garlic and tamarind water. They are then skewered with pieces of mutton fat between each piece of meat, and either roasted on an open fire, broiled or fried. The marinade is heated and reduced to make a sauce and then served with the traditional rice, which is flavoured and coloured yellow with turmeric and saffron.

The Malays also knew how to preserve fish, whether they came from the icy waters of the Atlantic and the Antarctic or from the peaceful, warmer waters of the Indian Ocean. By pickling, salting and drying fish they could provide the sailors of the Dutch East India Company with enough food to last them for the rest of their long journeys. Pickled or curried fish, served cold, made delicious dishes to eat on a hot day, and both can be kept for several days even in hot weather.

For curried fish, fillet a fleshy fish and fry the usual way. For each piece of fish take 1 large onion and cut in slices about ⅛ inch thick. Put the onion slices into a saucepan with enough mild vinegar to cover them well. If the vinegar is very strong a little water may be added. Add to the onions and vinegar 1 teaspoon of curry powder, 1 teaspoon of turmeric, a little salt and 1 or 2 tablespoons of sugar. Bring this to the boil and boil for 5 minutes. The onions must be kept crisp. Place the fish in an earthenware bowl and pour the mixture over. Allow to marinate for hours before serving.

The Huguenots, who fled from France from 1685 onwards, came to South Africa after the Malays. It is astonishing how little impact their great culinary traditions made on the South African kitchen. The influence is there, primarily in the growth of the wine industry, which South Africa owes to them, but it by no means swamped the existing Dutch and Malay traditions. Wine was added to sauces and marinades, thus helping to enrich the sauces and to tenderise tough meat. Chicken stuffed with the delectable Hanepoot grapes and pot-roasted with a little wine is a dish that clearly owes much to the French.

With the Scots came another sturdy thrifty tradition. Fruit cakes, desserts, steamed puddings, marmalade—all the warming economical dishes that the Scots had learned in Scotland they brought to South Africa with them. To these they allied the uniquely South African fruits so that there are few things more evocative to South Africans than mulberries, loquats

SOUTH AFRICA

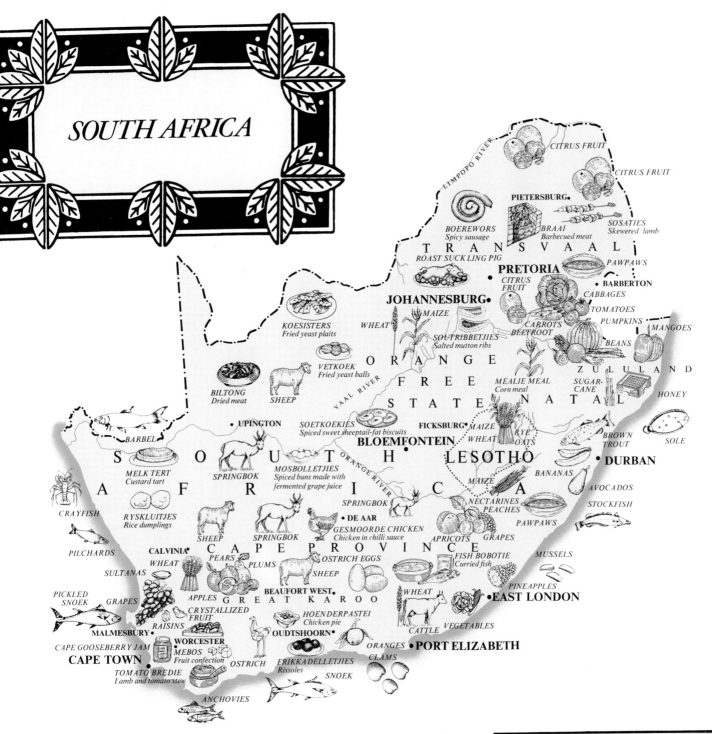

CITRUS FRUIT

CITRUS FRUIT

LIMPOPO RIVER

PIETERSBURG•

BOEREWORS
Spicy sausage

BRAAI
Barbecued meat

SOSATIES
Skewered lamb

T R A N S V A A L

ROAST SUCKLING PIG

PAWPAWS

PRETORIA

CITRUS FRUIT

• BARBERTON

JOHANNESBURG•

CABBAGES

TOMATOES

PUMPKINS

MANGOES

KOESISTERS
Fried yeast plaits

WHEAT

MAIZE

SOUTRIBBETJIES
Salted mutton ribs

CARROTS
BEETROOT

BEANS

O R A N G E

Z U L U L A N D

VETKOEK
Fried yeast balls

F R E E

MEALIE MEAL
Corn meal

SUGAR-
CANE

N A T A L

HONEY

BILTONG
Dried meat

SHEEP

VAAL RIVER

S T A T E

• UPINGTON

SOETKOEKIES
Spiced sweet sheeptail-fat biscuits

FICKSBURG•

MAIZE

RYE

BROWN
TROUT

SOLE

BLOEMFONTEIN•

WHEAT

OATS

BARBEL

S O U T H

LESOTHO•

• **DURBAN**

MELK TERT
Custard tart

SPRINGBOK

MOSBOLLETJIES
Spiced buns made with
fermented grape juice

ORANGE RIVER

MAIZE

BANANAS

CRAYFISH

A F R I C A

RYSKLUITJIES
Rice dumplings

SPRINGBOK

AVOCADOS

• DE AAR

NECTARINES
PEACHES

STOCKFISH

GESMOORDE CHICKEN
Chicken in chilli sauce

PAWPAWS

PILCHARDS

SHEEP

SPRINGBOK

OSTRICH EGGS

APRICOTS

GRAPES

FISH BOBOTIE
Curried fish

MUSSELS

CALVINIA•

C A P E   P R O V I N C E

PEARS

WHEAT

PLUMS

SHEEP

PINEAPPLES

SULTANAS

WHEAT

•**EAST LONDON**

PICKLED
SNOEK

GRAPES

APPLES

BEAUFORT WEST•

GREAT KAROO

HOENDERPASTEI
Chicken pie

WHEAT

CRYSTALLIZED
FRUIT

CATTLE

VEGETABLES

RAISINS

MALMESBURY•

WORCESTER

OUDTSHOORN•

ORANGES

•**PORT ELIZABETH**

CAPE GOOSEBERRY JAM

MEBOS
Fruit confection

OSTRICH

FRIKKADELLETJIES
Rissoles

CLAMS

CAPE TOWN

TOMATO BREDIE
Lamb and tomato stew

SNOEK

ANCHOVIES

---

peaches, apricots, figs and Cape gooseberries, all preserved and bottled in orderly
rows. These were essential to the rigorous
life of the *binneland*, the interior, where the
long, dry, hot summers were followed by
bitter winters when nothing fresh was to be
had.

From the Africans themselves, the indigenous people of the land, the white South
Africans learned how to use millet or
"Kaffir corn". They pounded it and turned
it into porridge, into bread and into beer.
Maize was then imported from America and
widely planted. There can be no South
African child who does not passionately
love *mielies*, corn-on-the-cob. On the farms
of the Orange Free State and the Transvaal
freshly made *mielie* bread, eaten hot with lots
of butter, is a great delicacy.

From the great treks through the Karoo
and the Orange Free State came the methods
of drying, spicing and preserving meats.
When an animal was killed only a small
portion could be eaten fresh but the rest of
the carcass could not be wasted. Sausages,
the famous *Boerwors*, were made and pigs
were killed at the same time as oxen so that
the casing for the sausages could be provided.

Biltong is the South African version of
jerky or *Bündnerfleisch*, although it must
be said, a less delicious version.

While trekking inland the Boers had no
time to set up elaborate ovens, and the food
was usually cooked simply over open fires.
As a result the *braaivleis*, barbecue, became a
great South African tradition and all over
the country parties are held this way.

THE WINE SOUTH AFRICA makes so well has
been unaccountably neglected by the South
Africans. As a people they have preferred
brandy, or in Natal, where the sugar-cane
grows, rum. Only in very recent years have
the good, and very low-priced, wines of the
Cape started to find appreciation at home.

The one international winner South
Africa has had up to now has been her
sherry, the closest approximation to real
Spanish sherry of any of its many imitators.
But meanwhile the standards of her table
wines have caught up. In white wines her
Steen and Riesling and in red her Hermi-
tage, Cabernet and Pinotage (a South
African special, a cross between Pinot and
Hermitage) are all beginning to be very
good. All they lack now is a broad and dis-
criminating market.

The exciting foods of a multitude of cultures

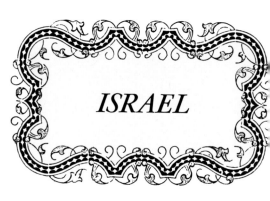

ISRAEL

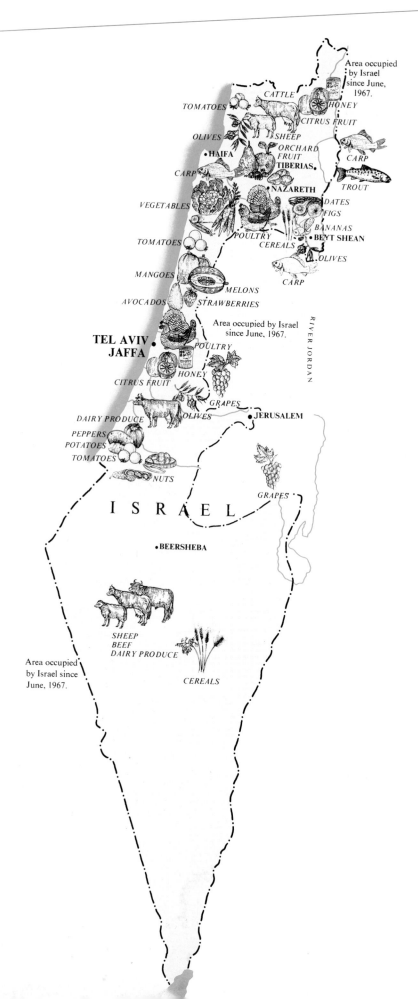

SOME GASTRONOMICALLY ill-used visitors to Israel might only need one word to describe the food. But the cuisine of many countries has often been similarly misjudged by those who have eaten the wrong things at the wrong places. There is a lot of indifferent cooking in Israel, but this is changing—although it was never less than good, and often very exciting, if one knew where to look.

As might be expected, the worst food is ersatz American or English; the best, the traditional food of the multitude of nationalities which make up the Israeli population. Yemenite *steak im pitta,* thin slices of charcoal-broiled steak served in an envelope of Arab bread, together with crunchy raw vegetables, sesame-seed cream and a dash of hot chilli sauce, has, for example, acquired the status of a national dish. The Levantines make good use of lamb, a meat severely underrated among Ashkenazi, central European, Jews, but justly appreciated by the Oriental community, who either bake succulent pieces of it in a slow oven, or toast a cone of herby lamb on an outdoor perpendicular spit.

The North Africans specialize in varied salads and hot "hashes", all brilliantly coloured, highly spiced and delicious.

nions and liver in many savoury guises. In Haifa there is a Moroccan dockside café where all these colourful salads and savoury, highly seasoned delicacies are set out in shallow tin pans to choose from, and various cuts of meat are grilled to order while the *hors d'oeuvre* are sampled.

In the European and South American communities, many dishes are those familiar to Jewish homes all over the Western world. The meat basis is poultry; the raising of chickens, ducks and, especially, turkeys, is now a major industry in Israel. It is possible, too, to buy a great variety of cuts of turkey; sliced breast for *schnitzel*, chopped turkey pieces for stewing, whole breasts rolled for roasting and, of course, livers for frying, chopping or making into pâté. The one thing that has to be specially ordered is a whole bird and there are many young Israelis who have never seen a whole roast turkey.

Mention must be made of the ubiquitous carp. The Israelis devote much time to the production of this bony and tasteless fish, which is fried or made into *gefilte* fish, highly seasoned fish balls. But *bourri,* grey mullet, an insignificant-looking little white fish, is full of flavour although it is considered a mere makeweight in the fish ponds. It is superb stuffed with tomatoes, sprinkled with fresh lemon juice and baked in foil.

It is worth remembering that the Oriental and Western cuisines of both Jews and Arabs were created by basically poor people who could not afford luxury food and had to make the very best of cheap local products. Chicken was a luxury in the European ghettoes and every edible morsel had to be made palatable. Out of this necessity came such delicious improvisations as *helzel,* the neck-skin stuffed with seasoned breadcrumbs or flour mixed with onion, baked and served in slices, *knadlach,* a dumpling made of matzo-meal, egg and chicken fat, dropped into chicken broth, *gribbenes,* the chopped-up skin of a boiled chicken fried into crispy nibbles, and *kourkeven,* or *puplichlach,* now a popular kibbutz stand-by—the gizzards, long and gently stewed in well-seasoned gravy.

The indigenous citrus fruit, grapes, melons, figs, dates and almonds of Israel have inspired many cooks to create exquisite desserts and also main courses. Among these is turkey pieces, dredged with flour and browned and then stewed with peas and mushrooms in pure orange juice. Among the lesser-known citrus fruits,

the crown goes to pomelo, a sort of king grapefruit, as easy to peel and depith as a tangerine, with refreshing pink flesh. The rind and thick white pith, when stewed for hours in syrup, makes a divine conserve.

As Israeli agriculture expands and new crops are tried out, it appears there is little that will *not* grow in a land of such varied climatic and soil conditions. Today, Israel grows not only most of the fruit and vegetables familiar in Europe, but also such exotic fruits as pomelo, uglifruit (which weigh the branches to the ground), quinces, loquats, clementines, pomegranates, guavas, custard apples—unbelievably good for breakfast, chilled and eaten with a teaspoon like a boiled egg—and pitango cherries, with their "serrated edges" and sharp, thirst-quenching tang. No imagination is needed to concoct the most mouthwatering fruit salads out of all this, but the Moroccans prefer theirs hot, and serve glorious fruit fry-ups.

Tourists will naturally want to sample the food which is sold by street vendors. The universal favourite is *felafel,* fried chick-pea balls, garnished with a choice of sharp salads and sauces, stuffed into Arab bread. There is hot sweet-corn in season, *shashlik* and *shish kebab* any time, and sabra-fruit, taken straight off a block of ice and its prickles stripped away just before you eat it. In Jerusalem, crunchy, tart, unripe almonds are sold in the same way. Green, fuzzy and damp from the ice, they are eaten shell and all. In the *souks,* the street markets, they sell *baklava* and other very sweet cakes made of shredded wheat, semolina, honey and almonds, decorated with the unrivalled pistachio nut, and baked in enormous round trays. To wash all this down, there is freshly squeezed fruit juice including pomegranate juice and carrot juice, which is almost the best.

Israeli breakfasts are delicious and enormous. Set out buffet-style the choice ranges through hard-boiled or scrambled eggs, various cheeses, including cream cheese, strong rubbery ewes' milk cheese and bland yellow cheese; herrings prepared in many different ways, sardines and tuna; peppers, tomatoes, cucumber; black and green olives and coarse dark bread and wonderful fresh rolls, butter and jam.

The breakfasts eaten by kibbutz fieldworkers are even heartier and also include fried garlic sausage full of whole peppercorns, freshly made salad, fried potatoes, pickles, halva, fresh fruit and strong tea.

The best place to eat lunch or dinner in Israel is in a private home, Oriental restaurants or even a culinarily despised *kibbutz* where the following chicken dish would be a typical main course:

To serve 4, arrange 8 chicken pieces in one layer in a shallow baking dish, season well with salt and pepper and sprinkle with 1 tablespoon of flour. Coarsely chop 1 red and 2 green peppers, 3 medium-sized onions, 6 blanched and peeled garlic cloves and 4 ounces of blanched almonds, and spread over the chicken pieces. Add 8 fluid ounces of tomato juice. Bake in a 350°F (Gas Mark 4) oven for 1½ hours, or until the chicken is tender.

There are many excellent Israeli aubergine dishes. This is one of the best.

To serve 4 people, use two medium-sized aubergines. Wash and slice them thickly, without peeling. Dip each slice in lemon juice and then seasoned flour. Fry in very hot vegetable oil, not too fast, until they are crisp on both sides, then drain well on absorbent paper. Meanwhile fry together 3 finely chopped, medium-sized onions and 2 crushed garlic cloves. Drain well. In a greased, deep baking dish arrange the aubergine slices alternately with layers of onion and garlic, and 2 ounces of grated Cheddar cheese. Pour in 8 fluid ounces of well-seasoned tomato sauce. Cover with a thick layer of cheese, and bake in a 375°F (Gas Mark 5) oven for 30 minutes, or until the top is crisp and bubbling.

For dessert, fresh fruit is unbeatable in Israel. A richer favourite is chocolate biscuits dipped into hot, very strong coffee, and arranged in layers with whipped cream flavoured with Sabra liquor. It is chilled well and served cut like cake.

Israeli wines are improving every year, but on the whole Israelis don't drink much. They prefer the sweet, syrupy festival wine which they drink from tiny, beautifully ornate silver goblets. Taken thus, it would not intoxicate a baby and, in fact, most babies are given a few sips every Sabbath eve and seem to thrive on it.

A refined fusion of flavours

THE FOOD OF IRAN is little known outside its homeland, yet of all the Middle Eastern cuisines it is, undoubtedly, the most refined. Every home has its own individual tradition of preparing imaginative and highly sophisticated dishes that have been handed down from mother to daughter. Like the Persian carpet-makers, the cooks of Iran have been weaving the same patterns, colours and flavours since the days of Darius the Great.

There have, of course, also been outside influences on the cuisine. In the south of Iran, curry dishes appear and disappear with the mountain ranges. In the west and south-west, around the periphery of the Persian Gulf, Arab-style rice dishes, salads and sweets are widespread, while in the north, which borders Turkey, and in Persian Azerbaijan, there is a persistent tradition of Turkish cuisine.

Tabriz, the administrative centre of this region, is famous for *kufteh tabrizi*, meatballs, which can be as large as footballs. They are stuffed with a mixture of fried onions and currants, chopped walnuts and hard-boiled eggs; or a whole cooked chicken, itself stuffed, may be enclosed in a casing of meat pounded with cooked yellow peas.

Around the fertile green coast of the Caspian Sea, fish is the most popular dish. The seaside towns of Pahlavi and Resht are famous for their fish kebabs, soups and sauces. The majestic sturgeon of the Caspian have provided the Iranians with a flourishing caviar industry, second only to that of the Soviet Union. Yet few Iranians have developed a taste for this delicacy and in the past fishermen threw away the precious roes.

The Iranians are, above all, connoisseurs of rice. It, too, is cultivated on the Caspian coast. Several types of rice are grown of which the finest and rarest is *domsiah*, black-tailed rice, so called because of the tiny black speck at one end of the grain.

In Iran, rice appears in generous quantities at practically every meal. Nowhere in the world is such care devoted to the preparation of a simple dish of boiled rice, known in Iran as *chelo*. First, the fine long grains are washed and left to soak for several hours in a bowl of salted water. The rice is then boiled quickly until almost tender, rinsed and thoroughly drained. A few tablespoons of melted butter or oil are poured into the pan. The rice is returned to the pan and more butter is spooned over the top. The pan is then covered tightly, with a cloth stretched under the lid, and left to steam gently over low heat until the grains are tender, fluffy and separate, and a rich, golden crust has formed on the bottom. This crust, called *tah dig*, the bottom of the pot, is carefully scraped out and used as a garnish for the rice dish.

Iran's greatest national dish is *chelo kebab*. The kebab itself is of lamb, which dominates Iranian cuisine as it does all the cuisines in this part of the world. The pieces of meat are marinated in a mixture of lemon juice and grated onion, then grilled over charcoal. The rice, or *chelo*, which accompanies the kebab is served topped with a pat of butter, each portion garnished with a raw egg yolk which has been left in a half shell. Other classic accompaniments include little bowls of chopped herbs, raw onions and *sumac*, a sour, wood-scented spice, with which each person flavours the rice to his own taste. The egg yolk is dropped on to the rice and mixed in with a fork, transforming it into a creamy, golden dressing.

Chelo also serves as a backdrop for a glorious variety of *khoresh*, thick sauces or stews which are subtle combinations of meat or poultry with vegetables, fruit, both fresh and dried, nuts, herbs and spices. Long before the West discovered the exciting harmonies that could be created by combining savoury flavours with sweet, the Iranians were combining meat and poultry with apples, quinces, bitter cherries, peaches, apricots and pomegranates, the choice dictated by the seasons and by the cook's imagination.

One of the great classic *khoreshes* is *fesenjan*, duck or chicken in a sauce thickened with ground walnuts and flavoured with sweetened pomegranate and lemon juice.

To make fesenjan *to serve 4, cut a large duck or chicken into 8 pieces. Grind 1 pound of shelled walnuts in a blender, reserving a few nuts for decoration.*

In a frying-pan, fry 1 thickly sliced onion, with

½ *teaspoon turmeric, in 3 to 4 tablespoons olive oil until the onion is soft and golden brown. With a slotted spoon transfer the onion to a large heavy casserole. Add the ground walnuts and 2 pints of chicken stock to the casserole. Season to taste with salt and freshly ground black pepper. Bring to the boil and simmer for 20 minutes, stirring occasionally.*

Add more olive oil to the frying-pan and brown the duck or chicken pieces in it. Transfer them to the casserole and mix to coat them with the walnut sauce. Cover and cook gently over very low heat, stirring occasionally, for 1 hour, or until the chicken or duck pieces are tender.

Mix ¼ pint of fresh pomegranate juice (or 2 tablespoons of concentrated pomegranate juice) with the juice of 2 lemons and 2 ounces of sugar. Skim the casserole of excess fat. Stir in the sweetened juice and simmer for a further 20 minutes. Correct the seasoning.

Arrange the duck or chicken on a bed of rice. Spoon some of the sauce over the top and garnish with the reserved walnuts, coarsely chopped. Serve the remaining sauce separately.

When rice is cooked with other ingredients it becomes a *polo*, a relative of the Turkish *pilav* and the Indian *pilau*. In this dish, too, sweet, sour and savoury are subtly matched, as in this favourite combination of lamb with apricots.

To make a lamb and apricot polo to serve 4, clean and wash 14 ounces of basmati rice until the water runs clear. Put the washed rice in a large bowl and cover with plenty of cold water mixed with 2 tablespoons of salt. Leave it to soak for at least 2 hours.

Meanwhile, in a large pan fry 1 finely chopped onion in 2 ounces of butter until golden. Add 1 pound of lean lamb, cubed, and continue to fry until it is browned. Stir in six ounces of dried apricots, halved, 2 ounces of raisins and a pinch of saffron. Season to taste with salt and freshly ground black pepper, and continue to stir over moderate heat for a few minutes longer. Add water to cover. Bring to simmering point. Cover the pan and cook gently for 1½ hours, or until the lamb is very tender.

While the lamb is cooking, bring 2½ pints of water to the boil in another pan. Drain the rice and stir it in gradually so that the water remains on the boil. Cover the pan, boil briskly for 5 minutes and drain the rice well in a sieve.

When the lamb is cooked, melt 2 ounces of butter in another heavy pan. Add half of the par-boiled rice, smoothing it to make an even layer. Spoon the lamb, fruit and sauce over the top and cover with the remaining rice. Stretch a clean folded cloth over the top of the pan. Clamp on the lid and steam gently for about 30 minutes.

CASPIAN SEA

CHELO KEBAB
Grilled marinated lamb with rice
TABRIZ RICE
KUFTEH TABRIZI
Large meatballs
BANDAR-E-PAHLAVI
STURGEON
RASHT
CAVIARE
PISTACHIO NUTS
WHEAT
SHEEP
LIMES
HAMADAN SUMAC
LEMONS
PEACHES
POMEGRANATES QUINCES
CANTALOUPE MELONS
ISFAHAN
NANÉ SANGAK
Bread cooked on pebbles
ABADAN
HALVA KHORMA KUKU SABZI
Date dessert Thick vegetable omelette
MAST-VA-KHIAR
Yoghourt with cucumber and mint
SHIRAZ LAUSE BADAM
Almond squares
KHORESH BADEMJAN
Braised lamb and aubergines
HAVIJ POLO
Rice with carrots

WATERMELON
KUFTEH SABZI
Meatballs
ABGOOSHT
Thick meat soup
TEHERAN
FESENJAN
Duck with walnut and pomegranate sauce
TAH CHIN
Meat with steamed rice and yoghourt
SAFFRON
NANÉ BARBARI
Thin bread
CHELO KHORESH
Stew with rice
ALOO-BALOO POLO
Steamed rice with black cherries and chicken
DUGH
Yoghourt drink
SHARBATE RIVAS
Rhubarb drink
YOGHOURT
PANIR
Goat's milk cheese
ASH MAST
Yoghourt soup
BLACK CHERRIES
GORMEH SABZI
Braised lamb with kidney beans
BORANI
Cold spinach and yoghourt salad
BAGHLA POLO
Lamb with rice, dill and kidney beans
DIZI
Lamb, chick-pea and bean casserole
CURRY DISHES

Serve the polo *on a large, heated platter, carefully mixing the meat and fruit with the rice. The crust at the bottom of the pan should be scraped out and arranged in small pieces around the* polo.

Not all of Iran's traditional cuisine is based on rice. The famous *kuku*, a thick flat omelette, which appears as an appetizer, as a first course and as a side dish, served cut in wedges, hot or cold, displays the same versatility as many other dishes. Most popular of all is the *kuku sabzi*, an omelette fragrant with a profusion of chopped green vegetables and herbs. Iranians love herbs. Street vendors sell them tied in bunches, ready mixed for *kuku*. Bowls of herbs are served as an appetizer, and handfuls of chopped fresh herbs are mixed with rice to make a brilliant green *chelo*.

As in all Middle Eastern countries, yoghourt plays an important part in the cuisine of Iran. In one early medieval manuscript it is referred to as "Persian milk". Today *mast*, or yoghourt, is used to make hot and cold soups, and is whisked with water and mint to make a refreshing drink.

Most desserts are made of fresh fruit. Iran grows some of the finest fruits in the Middle East—peaches, pomegranates, apricots, apples, quinces and pears, dates, grapes, watermelons and the world-famous Persian melons. Fruit is sliced or grated, sweetened, perfumed with orange-flower water or rose water, and served with crushed ice, or is made into beautifully coloured sherbets.

Many of the pastries and sweetmeats of the Middle East are also to be found in Iran, including the *halvas* and *baklava*, made with *phyllo* pastry, but much smaller, and far less sweet than their Turkish or Syrian counterparts.

Coffee plays a far less important role in Iranian life than it does among the Turks and Arabs. Its place is taken by tea, served clear in small glasses. Even in the *khavekhane*, coffee houses, simple mud buildings by the roadside where travellers can stop for refreshment, tea is more likely to be offered than coffee.

Few restaurants in Iran serve classic Iranian food, and those which do tend to specialize in one type of dish. Iranian *chelo* restaurants are rather like Italian pizza houses. Restaurants in the big cities concentrate on foreign cuisine prepared to a high standard.

Traditional Iranian cooking is reserved for the home. The gourmet from abroad who has the good fortune to eat in an Iranian home will recognize in it an ancient and aristocratic tradition that bears comparison with the best in the world.

An extravagant cuisine created by patient skill

THE SURRENDER OF CONSTANTINOPLE to the Ottoman Turks in 1453 marked the end of the glory that was Byzantium, and the unique way of life evolved over many centuries by Romans, Greeks, Armenians and Jews. But the influence of these civilizations and these peoples lived on in the traditions and in the cuisine of the country. The cooking of modern Turkey is richly varied, exotic and frequently extravagant. It is not purely Turkish, nor Greek, nor Arab, nor Armenian, but an amalgam of all. It is a sensual cuisine which likens a meatball dish to ladies' thighs and sweet pastries to ladies' fingers, lips and navels.

Although it is difficult to regionalize the cooking of Turkey, the country can be roughly divided into three major "spheres of influence". Western Turkey, the area stretching inland as far as Ankara, the capital, has an obvious affinity with neighbouring Greece, the Balkans and western Europe, especially France, whose cuisine found favour with the middle-class Greeks, Armenians and Jews in the nineteenth century.

The seas that surround the region on three sides provide an abundance of magnificent fish and shellfish. Restaurants built on floating platforms along the Bosphorus and the Golden Horn serve grilled red mullet, swordfish steaks and kebabs, cold mackerel, which has simmered with diced vegetables in a rich court-bouillon, and superb lobster and shrimp.

The central south covers an area as far east as Elazig and Urfa. Here the staple cereal is *burghul*, cracked wheat. *Bulgur pilâv* is the national dish of the Armenians who, until the First World War, made up a large part of the population and greatly influenced Turkish cuisine. The other major influence, perhaps the most important of all, is that of the Arabs who for centuries ruled over this part of the country. There is a marked affinity here with the food of Syria,

particularly the great cuisine of Aleppo.

The food of eastern Turkey, which borders on Armenia and Iran, although similar to the neighbouring regions, also has certain individual characteristics. A strong central Asian influence is obvious in the wide use of yoghourt in such dishes as *yoğurtlu çorba*, yoghourt soup, *yoğurtlu köfte*, meatballs in yoghourt sauce, and the classic *çaçik*, slices of cucumber in a yoghourt sauce flavoured with mint.

In Turkey, sights, sounds and aromas seem to conspire to make one think of food. From early morning, the street vendors, a chorus of monotones, can be heard. The cries of the vegetable man, the milk vendor and the fish seller, as he comes down the street escorted by a column of wary cats, mingle with calls of *Semit!* from the bakers' boys, who carry long poles on to which are threaded the *semit*, crisp bracelets of bread sprinkled with sesame seeds.

Restaurants, spotlessly clean however modest they may be, tempt the appetite with trays of stuffed peppers and tomatoes, or a majestic *döner kebab*, a pillar of lamb turning slowly on a vertical spit.

The Turks adore snacks and throughout the day nibble on pumpkin seeds, nuts and *leblebi*, toasted chick-peas. *Mezze*, the Middle Eastern equivalent of *hors d'oeuvre*, is a long, relaxed overture to a meal, a miniature feast of nuts, olives, vine leaves stuffed with the favourite Turkish combination of rice, pine nuts, currants and parsley, diced poached brains dressed with oil and vinegar, cubes of salty white cheese, liver, tiny meatballs, creamy *tarama salata*, mussels stuffed with rice or dipped in batter and deep-fried, *lakerda*, or smoked bonito, smoked sword-fish, vegetable salads and purées, and thin slices of *pastirma*, dried spiced beef. Little *börek*, packets of paper-thin pastry known as *yufka*, are folded around fillings of cheese, meat or spinach, baked or fried and served hot and crisp.

Lamb is the most important meat in the Turkish cuisine and every part of the animal is used. Beef tends to be tough and pork is forbidden on religious grounds.

Turkey's most famous meat dish is *şiş kebab*, cubes of tender young lamb soaked for several hours in a marinade of olive oil, lemon juice and slices of raw onion, then threaded on to skewers and grilled over charcoal so that the meat remains slightly pink inside. Served with a salad of sliced tomatoes and rice, or bread, this is simple cooking at its best.

The Turks share their neighbours' enthusiasm for stuffed vegetables. Hours are spent wrapping vine leaves around fillings of rice and nuts or meat, stuffing peppers, tomatoes and courgettes. Aubergines, okra, beans, both fresh and dried, and artichokes are simmered in oil and served lukewarm or cold; stewed with meat; turned into salads and purées; or sliced and deep-fried in olive oil and served with yoghourt. The classic aubergine dish, *Imam bayildi*, which, as its name suggests, made the priest faint, calls for so much oil that it is uncertain whether he was overcome by the excellence of the dish, or by his wife's extravagance.

Another pillar of Turkish cuisine is rice pilaf, or *pilâv*, "the king of dishes", served plain as a side dish, or mixed with pine nuts and currants, or flavoured with tomatoes. It also appears as a course in its own right cooked with vegetables, lamb, chicken or liver.

TURKEY

SARDINES

HERRING

BLACK SEA

MULLET

TEA

KARS KEBAB
Meat skewered on swords

MPS

CITRUS FRUIT

TREBIZOND •

• RIZE

KARS

FRUIT

OLIVES

HAZELNUTS

ORANGES

VEAL

CHERRIES

CULLUK KIZARTMAZI
Woodcock in olive and wine sauce

MOUNT ARARAT

KADAIF
Shredded dough pastries
ANKARA •

DOLMA
Stuffed vegetables

WATERMELON

ERZURUM •

LAMB

WHEAT

SUT KUKUSI BASI
Lamb's head cooked in a casing

• SIVAS

SHISH KEBAB
Meat on skewers

KAYMAK
Clotted cream

BLACK BARLEY BREAD

T U R K E Y

BÖREK
Filled pastries

AYRAN
Yoghourt drink

PEACHES

LAKE VAN

URGHUL PILAV
teamed cracked wheat

RICE

IMAM BAYILDI
Stuffed aubergines

BASTURMA
Dried salt beef

KAYMAK
Clotted cream

• DIYARBAKIR

BURGHUL
Cracked wheat

IMAM BAYILDI
Stuffed aubergines

PILAVS
Rice-based dishes

KONYA •

OLIVES

KADAIF
Shredded dough pastries

SESAME
CUMIN

PINE NUTS

YOGHOURT

PISTACHIO NUTS

T AURUS MOUNTAINS

• ADANA

BANANAS

CHEESE

• **GAZIANTEP**

ULLET ROE

The Turkish sweet tooth is legendary. Many pastries and sweetmeats—the great *baklava, kadayif*, pastries soaked in syrup, and *tel kadayif*, the famous "shredded wheat" dough of the Middle East, and *halva*, known as *helva* in Turkish—are popular throughout the eastern Mediterranean.

The imaginatively named *kadin göbeği*, ladies' navels, are little balls of short pastry complete with a dimple in the centre, baked, soaked in syrup and served with *kaymak*, a rich clotted cream. *Hanim parmaği*, ladies' fingers, are finger-shaped pastries deep-fried and drenched with syrup.

The fruit of Turkey is in a class of its own. Peaches, apricots, grapes and apples are often presented in a brilliant green basket made of a watermelon shell. Earlier in the season, there are purple figs and huge black cherries, and before that strawberries. Fruits are eaten fresh or lightly poached to make a *kompostosu*, compote. They are made into luscious jams and preserves. Frequently, with coffee, a bowl of jam is passed around. Each person takes just one spoonful, and savours it with sips of coffee or water.

The most famous of all the Turkish sweetmeats is surely *rahat lokum*, Turkish delight, the dark gold of the grape jelly contrasting with the powdery white coating of sugar and the bright green pistachio nuts which are often hidden inside. Real *rahat lokum* bears no resemblance to the shocking pink synthetic jellies that often pass as Turkish delight in the West.

Turkish coffee is synonymous with hot summer afternoons when ladies sit gossiping in their drawing-rooms, the shutters drawn to keep out the blazing sun, and sultry nights when it is too hot to sleep and men sit in the open-air cafés playing *trictrac*, backgammon, until dawn.

Since sugar is added to the coffee before it is heated, each person is asked how he prefers it. *Sade* is without sugar, *orta* is medium and *şekerli* or *tatli*, is sweet. The coffee beans are ground to a powder in a long, tubular mill, and then mixed with water and sugar in a small brass pot and heated until the coffee foams up to the brim. This is repeated three times. The coffee is then deftly poured into tiny cups in such a way that each cup receives a little of the foam. In Turkey, the coffee is frequently accompanied by a glass of cold water which should be drunk first, to cleanse the palate, but in practice is usually sipped alternately with the strong black brew.

Turkish cooking requires patience and hard work. There is, however, an unhurried rhythm about it—whether stringing beans under a tree, rolling vine leaves or grinding coffee beans—and an unerring balance in the composition of each dish and each menu that makes it one of the world's most pleasing cuisines.

Food from a Sultan's banquet

Turkish Savoury Pastries
BÖREK

These pastries are made all over the Middle East with a variety of doughs, from the fine Strudel-like phyllo *or* yufka *to puff pastry and short pastry. Fillings include cheese, spinach and minced meat, and the pastries are baked or deep-fried in oil. They are at their best served hot from the oven, as part of a buffet, as an* hors d'oeuvre *or with salad as a main course.*

If phyllo *pastry is available, cut the sheets into long strips 3 inches wide. Brush each strip with melted butter. Put a small heap of filling at one end of the strip; fold the bottom edge of the strip up over it to make a triangle, then fold the triangle over on itself, and so on, until the whole strip has been folded. Tuck in the end.*

Arrange the little packets on greased baking sheets and brush the tops with more melted butter.

Bake them in a moderately hot oven, 400°F (Gas Mark 6), for 20 minutes, or until they are crisp and golden. Alternatively, the little packets may be deep-fried in hot oil and drained thoroughly on absorbent paper before serving.

MAKES ABOUT 30 BÖREK

Butter
12 oz weight puff pastry
2 small eggs, lightly beaten
8 oz cheese, feta, Heloumi, Cheddar or Edam, grated
2 tablespoons finely chopped parsley
Freshly grated nutmeg
Freshly ground black pepper
1 egg yolk, beaten with 2 tablespoons water

Preheat the oven to 450°F (Gas Mark 8). Lightly butter 2 large baking sheets.

Roll out the dough very thinly and cut it into 3-inch squares, or circles 3 inches in diameter.

In a small bowl, beat the eggs into the grated cheese with the parsley, and season to taste with nutmeg and pepper—no salt should be necessary.

Put a small heap of the cheese mixture in the centre of each dough square or circle. Dampen the edges lightly with water and fold the pastry in half, making triangles out of the squares and half-moon shapes out of the circles. Seal the edges carefully. With the back of a fork, decorate the edges of the *börek*.

Arrange the pastries on the prepared baking sheets. Brush the tops with the beaten egg yolk and water.

Bake for 15 minutes, or until the pastries are crisp and golden.

Stuffed Aubergines in Olive Oil
IMAM BAYILDI

This is probably the most famous of Turkey's many aubergine dishes, a splendid first course to serve at a summer dinner party.

SERVES 4

4 medium-sized aubergines, stalks removed
Salt
Olive oil
2 onions, thinly sliced
2 green peppers, seeded and thinly sliced
2 garlic cloves, coarsely chopped
2 ripe tomatoes, blanched, peeled and thinly sliced
3 tablespoons concentrated tomato purée
$\frac{1}{2}$ teaspoon sweet paprika
$\frac{1}{8}$ teaspoon allspice
Finely chopped parsley.

Wash and dry the aubergines. Leaving an inch at each end make a deep slit lengthways down each aubergine. Then, using a potato peeler, peel off long thin strips of skin lengthwise, leaving stripes of shiny skin. Rub salt into the incision and into the peeled flesh and put the aubergines aside for 1 hour.

Meanwhile, in a frying-pan, heat the olive oil.

Add the onions, peppers and garlic and fry unt the onion is soft but not coloured. Stir in th tomatoes and the tomato purée. Add th paprika, allspice and salt to taste. Simme gently for 5 minutes longer. Stir in 4 table spoons finely chopped parsley and remove th pan from the heat.

Preheat the oven to 375°F (Gas Mark 5).

Rinse the aubergines thoroughly and pat ther dry. In a large frying-pan, heat plenty of oliv oil.

Add the aubergine and fry gently until th flesh begins to soften, turning them once o twice taking great care not to spoil their shape Arrange the aubergines in an ovenproof dish slits uppermost.

Prize open the slits and spoon some of th fried vegetable mixture into each one. Mix an remaining mixture with 1 pint of water an pour it into the dish. Bake for 45 minutes, o until the aubergines are very soft.

Serve cold, sprinkled with finely choppe parsley.

Stuffed Vine Leaves
DOLMAS

In Turkey fresh vine leaves are used for this dis in the summer, but in the winter when they ar not available either canned vine leaves or fres cabbage leaves are used. Fresh leaves, either vin or cabbage, must be blanched in boiling water fo a few minutes to soften them.

SERVES 6 TO 8

4 oz long-grain rice, thoroughly washed an drained
1 lb lean lamb, minced
1 medium-sized onion, finely chopped
2 tablespoons finely chopped parsley
2 tablespoons finely chopped dill
Salt
Freshly ground black pepper
Lemon juice
Vine or cabbage leaves, blanched
4 tablespoons olive oil

First cook the rice. Half fill a saucepan with water, add $\frac{1}{4}$ teaspoon salt and bring to the boil Pour in the rice and boil for 3 minutes. Remove the pan from the heat and drain.

When the rice is cool put it into a bowl with the minced lamb, onion, parsley, dill, salt pepper and lemon juice to taste. Mix and knea the ingredients well together.

Spread out the leaves and, according to size put either a teaspoon or tablespoon of filling or to the leaf. Fold the leaf to make a small parce Place the leaf parcels side by side in a large par so that they do not open out. Put a plate on top of the *dolmas* to hold them in place. Mi together 1 pint of water, the olive oil and pinch of salt. Pour this over the *dolmas* and bring to the boil. Cover the pan, reduce the heat to low

---

TURKEY must be one of the few countries where the government has actively tried to get the people to drink alcohol, Western-style, and where the people have resisted. Kemal Atatürk, the great Turkish leader, knowing how healthful and profitable wine can be, went so far as to start a winery himself. But, like their ancestors, most Turks still insist on eating grapes and drinking coffee. Only three per cent of Turkey's huge grape crop, one of the world's largest, is fermented.

Most Turkish wine is made by the State Monopoly in Thrace, on the Aegean coast and in Anatolia. Actually, the word monopoly gives a false impression for there are a number of private firms in the business as well. Doluca and Kavaklidere are names particularly worth remembering. On the whole the red wines are more successful than the white. Trakya and Buzbag, respectively lighter and heavier reds from the State enterprise, are Turkey's best-known brands.

In most places the visitor is likely to go, at least in western Turkey, there is a range of half a dozen reds and whites of remarkably even and satisfactory quality. The whites are heavy, and, on a hot day, benefit from a lump of ice and a dash of soda. But the only wine to avoid on principle is the rosé.

Turkish beer is admirable, and Turkish mineral water leaves nothing to be desired.

d simmer for 1 hour. Remove the *dolmas* from
ne pan and serve hot or cold.

Skewered Lamb
SHISH KEBAB

This famous Turkish dish is popular throughout
ne Middle East, its preparation varying from
*gion to region. The red wine in this recipe is an
Armenian touch. Turks would substitute the
*ice of 1 lemon or a crushed onion. Kebabs are
*equently served without sauce, but in eastern
*urkey and neighbouring Syria they are eaten
ith a rich, spicy tomato sauce.

*Serve the kebabs in a pocket of flat Turkish or
*reek bread, garnished with chopped tomato and
aw onion, or with a rice or burghul *pilav.*

ERVES 4

½ lb boned, lean leg of lamb, cut into 1-inch
   cubes
 large onion
ARINADE
 tablespoons olive oil
 tablespoons red wine
 teaspoons salt
 teaspoon freshly ground black pepper
 teaspoon ground allspice
AUCE
 tablespoons olive oil
 onion, finely chopped
 green pepper, seeded and chopped
 ripe tomatoes, blanched, peeled and
   chopped
 tablespoons concentrated tomato purée
   diluted with 4 tablespoons water
 Salt
 Sweet paprika

Combine the marinade ingredients in a large
bowl. Add the lamb cubes. Turn them to mix
thoroughly with the marinade. Set aside to
marinate overnight.

 Prepare the sauce before cooking the kebabs.
n a saucepan, heat the olive oil. Add the onion
and pepper and fry until the onion is soft. Add
he tomatoes and cook for 5 minutes. Stir in the
omato purée. Season to taste with salt and a
generous pinch of paprika, and cook gently,
covered, for a further 15 minutes. Keep hot.

 When ready to cook the kebabs, slice the
onion in four from stem to root. Then cut each
segment in half horizontally. Separate the onion
"leaves".

 Thread the marinated lamb on to 4 long
bayonet skewers, alternating each chunk with
a piece of onion. Grill the skewers over charcoal, or under a preheated grill turning them
frequently and basting them with the remaining
marinade, for 7 to 10 minutes. The lamb cubes
should be richly browned on the outside, but
still slightly pink in the centre.

 Serve with the tomato sauce.

Roast Lamb with Tomatoes and Potatoes
KUZU KAPAMA

Kuzu Kapama *is a traditional dish eaten all
over Turkey. Because few homes in the small
towns and villages have ovens the dish is prepared
in the morning, taken to the local bakery to be
cooked and collected in the evening in time for
dinner.*

SERVES 6

Olive oil
2 medium-sized onions, finely chopped
3 garlic cloves, finely chopped
6 large firm tomatoes, sliced
6 large potatoes, peeled and sliced
4 parsley sprigs, finely chopped
Salt
Freshly ground black pepper
5 lb leg of lamb
Light stock

Preheat the oven to 450°F (Gas Mark 8).
Liberally grease a large roasting pan with olive
oil.

 Mix together the chopped onions and two-
thirds of the garlic. Sprinkle half the mixture
over the bottom of the roasting pan. Arrange the
tomato and potato slices in an overlapping layer
in the pan. Sprinkle generously with the
chopped parsley and salt and pepper to taste.
Sprinkle the remaining onion and garlic mixture
over the top and pour over 4 tablespoons of
stock.

 Rub the leg of lamb with the remaining garlic,
salt and pepper. Place the lamb on the bed of
vegetables and put it in the oven. Immediately
reduce the heat to 350°F (Gas Mark 4) and roast
the lamb for about 2 hours (25 minutes to the
pound), basting it occasionally with the stock.

Burghul Pilav

Burghul (bulgur *in Turkish) makes a pleasant
and unusual alternative to rice pilav.*

SERVES 4

8 oz burghul (cracked wheat)
4 oz butter
1 small onion, finely chopped
Salt

Wash the *burghul* in several changes of cold
water until the water runs clear. Drain
thoroughly.

 Melt the butter in a heavy pan. Add the onion
and fry until it is soft and golden. Add the
burghul and cook over high heat for 5 minutes,
stirring constantly.

 Add 1 pint of hot water. Season to taste with
salt and boil vigorously for 5 minutes. Reduce
the heat and simmer gently uncovered, for 6 to 8

minutes longer, or until all the water has been
absorbed.

 Turn off the heat. Cover the top of the pan
with a clean folded tea towel. Clamp on the lid
and leave the *burghul* to "rest" for 15 to 20
minutes before serving.

Syrup-soaked Pastries
BAKLAVA

Baklava *is very easy to make, provided the sheets
of paper-thin dough which are usually sold under
their Greek name* phyllo *are available. The
secret of a crisp baklava lies in having the syrup
ice-cold and to pour it over the hot pastry as soon
as it comes out of the oven.*

MAKES ABOUT 36 PASTRIES

6 oz unsalted butter
8 oz phyllo sheets
6 oz walnuts, almonds or pistachio nuts,
   coarsely chopped
4 tablespoons castor sugar
1 teaspoon ground cinnamon
SYRUP
8 oz sugar
1 tablespoon lemon juice
1 tablespoon orange-flower water

First prepare the syrup. In a saucepan, dissolve
the sugar in 5 fluid ounces of water, over low
heat, stirring constantly. When the sugar has
completely dissolved, stir in the lemon juice and
bring to the boil. Reduce the heat and simmer
until the syrup thickens and is reduced to about
10 fluid ounces. Stir in the orange-flower water
and simmer for 2 to 3 minutes longer. Pour the
syrup into a pitcher and set aside to cool. When
cool, refrigerate the syrup until required.

 Preheat the oven to 350°F (Gas Mark 4). Melt
the butter in a saucepan without letting it sizzle.
Brush a 10-inch × 12-inch baking tin with some
of the melted butter. Put half of the *phyllo* sheets
in the baking tin brushing each one with melted
butter. Trim the edges. Do not worry if the
sheets tear, only the top one need be perfect.

 Mix the nuts, sugar and cinnamon together,
and spread the mixture over the top. Cover with
the remaining sheets of dough, brushing each
with melted butter as before, including the top
one.

 With a sharp knife, cut right through all the
layers of dough lengthwise into 1-inch strips.
Then cut across diagonally to make rectangles
2½ inches long.

 Bake the *baklava* for 30 minutes. Then increase
the heat to 425°F (Gas Mark 7) and bake for 10
to 15 minutes longer, or until the pastry is crisp
and a rich golden colour.

 Remove the *baklava* from the oven and
quickly pour the cold syrup over the entire
surface. Leave it to cool before cutting along the
original lines to separate the rectangles.

191

The evocative fragrance of herbs and lemons

THE GREEKS were cooking fine food five hundred years before the birth of Christ. One of the world's first cook books was the work of Hesiod of the Epicureans. Greek civilization and cuisine, the two inextricably bound together, spread throughout the Mediterranean. It was the Greeks who taught the Romans to eat and live well. But with the occupation of Greece by various invaders, Greek civilization declined and with it, the culinary arts.

Today much of the delight of Greek food lies in its simplicity and in the surroundings in which it is eaten. What could be more enchanting than eating a midday meal on an island in the Aegean, surrounded by the shimmering blue sea, the colour echoed by the opaque blue of glass worry beads and the painted eyes—said to ward off evil—on the fishing boats?

The boats, moored by the jetty, red or brown sails furled, unload the morning's catch of red mullet, crawfish, cuttlefish and octopus, one of which will probably provide the main course at lunch.

The market stalls are a patchwork quilt of scarlet tomatoes, green peppers, white cauliflowers, wine-dark aubergines and the sharply coloured and scented lemons.

The meal will begin with appetizers called *mesethakia,* with which a glass or two of *ouzo,* the anise-flavoured Greek national aperitif, will be drunk. The *mezze* may be simple, possibly little squares of *feta,* goats' milk cheese, sliced tomatoes, pickled peppers, a few olives or, from the morning's catch, baby squid or octopus, fried until crisp. There may be a rich, smooth fish-roe pâté called *tarama salata, dolmathes,* stuffed vine leaves, *melitzanes salata,* an aubergine salad, or *keftethakia,* tiny, spicy meatballs.

Probably the main course will be fish grilled over an open fire, brushed with olive oil, flavoured with wild *rigani,* oregano, and served with lemon slices. Possibly *retsina,* the best-known, resin-

flavoured, Greek wine, will be served. The meal will end with fruit and Greek coffee which, like Turkish coffee, is dark and strong.

The olive grows everywhere in Greece and its flavour dominates Greek food. The ancient Greeks knew the olive well and used its oil medicinally as well as in their food. Greek olive oil is fruity, thick and green and is more flavourful than the more refined olive oils of western Europe.

Greek cheeses, although not exceptional, are pleasant, particularly *feta,* a slightly salty, soft, crumbly, white goats' milk cheese. *Feta* is most commonly served, cut into small cubes, as an appetizer. It is also used as an ingredient in meat and fish dishes and in the salad which accompanies almost every meal.

To make a Greek salad to serve 4, first rub a salad bowl with garlic. Put into the bowl 4 ounces of cubed feta *cheese, 4 large tomatoes cut in pieces, 1 sliced green pepper, 12 large, stoned black olives and 4 finely chopped spring onions. Pour in a dressing made with 3 tablespoons of olive oil, 1 tablespoon lemon juice, salt, pepper and a pinch of dried oregano or 1 teaspoon of dried mint. Toss the salad well.*

Kefalotiri and *kasseri,* hard cheeses made from ewes' milk, are somewhat like Parmesan although less flavourful. They are sometimes cut into thick slices, dusted with flour, fried in olive oil, seasoned with a little lemon juice and served as appetizers. *Mizithra,* an unsalted cottage cheese, mixed with honey and eggs and baked in *phyllo* pastry, makes a delicious cheesecake.

The scent of lemons is everywhere in Greece. The lemons are large and juicy and essential to Greek cooking. Lemon juice is combined with egg to make *avgolemono,* one of the most popular of Greek sauces which is served with fish and vegetables and used to flavour stews and soups.

To make avgolemono, *melt 1 ounce of butter in the top of a double boiler. Stir in 2 tablespoons of flour and cook for 1 minute. Gradually pour in 10 fluid ounces of hot fish or chicken stock, stirring constantly, and bring to just under the boiling point. Keep the sauce hot. Beat 2 egg yolks with 3 tablespoons of lemon juice and 1 tablespoon of cold water. Add the hot sauce to the egg mixture, a spoonful at a time, stirring constantly. Return the mixture to the double boiler and cook, stirring, over simmering water, until the sauce is thick and smooth. Stir in some chopped parsley if desired.*

Romans, Venetians and Turks occupied Greece for hundreds of years and it is, therefore, not surprising that modern Greek

food includes dishes of Italian and Turkish origin. The Italian influence can be seen in the large number of pasta dishes on menu all over the country. Kebabs, such rich sweet pastries as *baklava,* the coffee and the thick and delicious yoghourt, were introduced by the Turks.

Greek honey is famous and is used to sweeten desserts, cakes and pastries. The ancient Greeks learned about honey and bee keeping from the Egyptians. Aristotle wrote about the different kinds of Greek honey in the second century BC. Then, as now, it was used to make honey cakes—the ancients thought them a fit offering for the gods and modern Greeks celebrate the New Year with *melomacarons,* little honey cakes.

Greeks are fond of sweets and there are sweet shops in every town and village. Some shops which sell only *rahat lokum,* Turkish delight, positively glow with the pink and yellow confections. Other shops sell pastries many of which are made from *phyllo,* paper-thin pastry which is prepared commercially and sold in sheets to those who prefer to do their own baking. This pastry is difficult to make and most Greek housewives buy it from the local baker.

Phyllo is made of flour and water. It is worked for a long time by an expert pastry cook who throws it from one hand to the other until, in some mysterious fashion which seems to deny all laws of physics, it turns into a wafer-thin transparent sheet. It is then used in many different ways to make sweet and savoury pastries and pies. Such pastries as *baklava* are made from layers of *phyllo* liberally brushed with butter, filled with nuts and sugar, baked until crisp and golden and then drenched in a honey syrup. Another favourite is *galat oboureko* in which the pastry is layered with a rich semolina custard.

The *tavernas* of Athens are famous for good food and entertainment. Dinner is served late and the entertainment goes on until dawn. The staccato notes of the *bazouki* accompany the animated conversations and the air is filled with an aroma of grilling meat and wild oregano.

The kitchens are taken up with huge charcoal grills and cooking ranges and often form part of the main dining-room. The clientele spills out on to the pavement particularly in the hot weather. There are few women in the *tavernas,* but the men eat or drink there two or three nights a week sitting for hours over their *ouzos* and *mezze* before the meal itself is served.

GREECE

The diners are welcomed into the kitchen to inspect the food, selecting their favourite dishes from the big pans filled with stuffed peppers, tomatoes, aubergines and marrows, *moskhari psito*, pot-roasted veal, and *moussaka*, baked minced meat with aubergines and béchamel sauce, the best known of all Greek dishes.

To make a traditional moussaka *to serve 4, slice 3 large aubergines, put the slices in a colander, sprinkle with salt and leave them to drain for 30 minutes, then rinse and dry well. Fry the aubergine slices in hot olive oil, a few at a time, until they are well browned. Drain them on absorbent paper and set aside.*

Heat 1½ ounces of butter in another frying-pan and fry 1 finely chopped medium-sized onion and 2 crushed garlic cloves until the onion is golden. Add 2 pounds of minced veal or lamb and fry, stirring constantly, for 10 minutes. Blanch, peel and chop 2 medium-sized tomatoes and add them to the meat, along with 1 teaspoon dried oregano, 1 tablespoon chopped parsley, ¼ teaspoon ground nutmeg and salt and pepper to taste. Stir in 3 fluid ounces of red wine and simmer, uncovered, for 25 minutes.

Meanwhile, make 1¼ pints of béchamel sauce. Stir 3 tablespoons of the sauce into the meat mixture. Lightly butter a deep baking dish and, beginning and ending with the fried aubergine slices, make layers with the meat mixture. Sprinkle the layers with 3 ounces of grated Parmesan or kefalotiri cheese. Lightly beat 3 eggs and mix them into the béchamel sauce. Pour the sauce over the meat and aubergines, sprinkle with 1 ounce of grated Parmesan or kefalotiri and bake in a 375°F (Gas Mark 5) oven for 45 minutes, or until the top is golden brown.

The hour is late and the meal eaten. The talk dies down and the *bazouki* takes over. Later there is time for a cup of strong, sweet coffee and a piece of *baklava* or *loukoumades*, little dough puffs, dusted with cinnamon and dripping with honey. Then home, an hour or two before dawn, to sleep.

193

Spicy, satisfying peasant fare

TAKE SOME DACIANS, Illyrians and Slavs; add Romans, Greeks, Goths and Bulgars; lace liberally with Venetians, Austrians, Hungarians and Turks; spice with two alphabets, three religions and five or six languages. Simmer for a thousand years with subjugation, insurrections and wars, and top with modified Marxism. The result is the Balkans—Yugoslavia, Romania and Bulgaria.

These three countries make up an area of 233,259 square miles—thirty-four thousand square miles smaller than Texas—that mingles the toughness of the Slav with the indolence of the Turk and the gaiety of the Hungarian, the desires of a capitalist past with the needs of a socialist future. It is an area dotted with Orthodox domes, Muslim minarets, Catholic spires and Red Stars.

The food of the three countries reflects all these influences. It reflects, too, the tastes of a people basically peasant in origin and the limitations of a supply system which is predominantly seasonal. *Burek*, minced meat wrapped in *Strudel* pastry, is eaten for breakfast as far north as Belgrade; but the Slav alternative, designed to get the day off to a good start at six o'clock, can be pork chops, the local hot peppers and a few glasses of strengthening *slivovica*, plum brandy. There are, too, the shortages that follow from economies so keen for foreign exchange, and relatively so new, that there are days when there is no meat to be had. The market system largely depends upon a fresh daily supply from the hinterland. The food undoubtedly tastes better than its deep-frozen supermarket equivalent, but that flavour is not won without sacrifice. Even in the cities, many Balkan housewives rise at five or six o'clock in the morning to get the best of the day's produce and then spend long hours in their kitchens. Their efforts are usually rewarded: in the Balkans "divine" and "fantastic" are words more commonly applied to food than to anything else.

The Balkan housewife, unlike her Western counterpart, cooks only once a day. If the main meal is eaten at lunchtime, as it often is, then the evening meal consists of the same dish served cold or reheated. Some dishes, like the ever-popular *čorba*, a soup thick with vegetables and meat or fish, tastes even better the second time around.

Čorba is often eaten after a cold *hors d'oeuvre* of ham, cheese, salami or hard, spiced sausage, peppers (raw, cooked or pickled), olives and tomatoes. In summer, the soup is followed by grilled fish or meat—usually pork or lamb—accompanied by a salad. *Srpski salata*, a Serbian salad of tomatoes, raw onions, chillies, goat cheese and baked peppers, is a dish typical of the region.

Hungarian-style goulashes and meat and vegetable stews, generously flavoured with garlic, like the Romanian *stufat de miel,* lamb stew with spring onions and spring garlic, provide variety.

To make stufat de miel *to serve 4, cut 30 spring onions into small pieces and finely chop 4 peeled garlic cloves or 30 spring garlic bulbs. Put the spring onions and garlic in a small saucepan, add just enough water to cover and bring it to the boil. Simmer for 5 minutes. Drain and reserve the water.*

Cut 2 pounds of lean lamb into 2-inch cubes. Heat 2 tablespoons of vegetable oil in a large saucepan. Add the lamb cubes and brown well, stirring constantly. Add the spring onions and garlic, 2 tablespoons of concentrated tomato purée, 8 fluid ounces of water and black pepper to taste. Mix well, cover and cook over low heat for 1½ hours, or until the lamb is tender.

Blend 1 tablespoon of flour with 3 tablespoons of the reserved onion and garlic water. Stir it into the stew. Bring to the boil and simmer, uncovered, for about 5 minutes, or until the sauce thickens. Add 1 tablespoon of wine vinegar. Correct the seasoning and serve garnished with finely chopped parsley.

Each country has its version of minced meat rolled into rissoles and cooked over charcoal. They are called *ćevapčići* in Yugoslavia, *kebabche* in Bulgaria and *mititei* in Romania. The meats differ, too. Beef, lamb or pork are used in Yugoslavia, mixed veal and pork in Bulgaria and beef in Romania. Chopped raw onion is a favourite side dish in Yugoslavia and Bulgaria. The Romanians prefer peppers in oil.

Fish, except on the Adriatic and Black Sea coasts, are fine-boned river fish. Romanians, born to the method, eat the smaller varieties, bones and all, starting from the head, and

derive much amusement from the visitor who follows suit.

Bread is to the Balkans what the potato is to Ireland. Today, there are dozens of varieties of bread. The staple food of the Romanian peasant is *mamaliga*, a cornmeal porridge like the Italian *polenta*, that is allowed to cool and become firm. Bulgarian specialities are breads made with butter, cheese and yoghourt. Apparently unique to that country is a taste for bread dipped in *cuibritsa*, a mixture of powdered spices. The main ingredient is similar to tarragon.

In the Balkans people eat what is available. A food that is eaten out of season is eaten pickled or preserved. Such dishes as minced meat wrapped in pickled cabbage leaves—*sarma* in Yugoslavia, *sarmale* in Romania and *sarmi* in Bulgaria—form the heart of a typical winter meal.

The cabbages are put down in autumn, stacked whole in a barrel of heavily salted water, which is changed twice a week for a month. In Bulgaria the meat used is veal and the dish is served with egg sauce. In Yugoslavia beef or lamb is used. The Romanians serve *sarmale* with *mamaliga*.

An important addition to many dishes in the Balkans is yoghourt. The Bulgarian variety is said to be the best in the world and the longevity of the country's inhabitants, especially those who live in the mountains, is attributed to it. All three of the Balkan countries use it in cucumber salads, on vine-leaf *sarma*, stuffed marrows and French beans. It is the basis of Bulgarian *tarator* soup.

To make tarator *soup to serve 6, pound 4 ounces of shelled walnuts in a mortar with 5 peeled garlic cloves. Add 5 teaspoons of olive oil, a few drops at a time, stirring constantly, until smooth.*

In a bowl, beat 2 pints of yoghourt until it is smooth. Blend in the walnut and garlic mixture and 4 fluid ounces of cold water. Add 1 medium-sized cucumber, peeled and diced. Season to taste with salt.

Chill in the refrigerator. Serve cold, sprinkled with finely chopped parsley or dill.

Historical influences on the cuisine of the Balkans are most obvious in the desserts. In the old Austro-Hungarian areas—Slovenia, Croatia and Transylvania—sweets are similar to those of Vienna. Elsewhere they are Turkish—*baklava, halva, cataif.* Between the two extremes are modified *tortes*—cakes of which the main ingredients are puréed walnuts, hazelnuts or chestnuts, or fresh fruit.

YUGOSLAVIA ROMANIA AND BULGARIA

This chestnut cake which requires no baking, is a Yugoslavian speciality. To make it for 8, purée 2 pounds of shelled, boiled chestnuts (3 pounds in their shells) in a blender or in a meat mincer. Put the purée into a bowl and beat in 5 ounces of sugar and 5 ounces of unsalted butter. Beat until the mixture is smooth. Shape the mixture into a roll and then roll it out like dough into an oblong. This is best done on a sheet of cellophane paper.

In the top of a double boiler melt 7 ounces of plain chocolate with 4 ounces of unsalted butter over simmering water. Stir until the mixture is smooth. Remove the pan from the heat and let the mixture cool and thicken.

Spread half the chocolate mixture over the rolled out chestnut purée. Roll the chestnut purée, Swiss-roll style and then pat it gently into a loaf shape. Reheat the remaining chocolate mixture until it is thin enough to spread and ice the cake with it. When the cake is cool, serve it in slices with whipped cream. This cake can be kept for up to one week, in foil, in the refrigerator.

Years of deprivation and a wholesome respect for the landmarks of life have combined in the Balkans to produce a great fondness for feasts. The centrepiece is often a whole lamb or suckling pig, roasted over charcoal in the open air or cooked in the oven of the nearest bakery. The ears of the pig are regarded as a great delicacy.

For many people, Balkan food is an acquired taste. The fierceness of the spices and peppers, the strength of the garlic, the seeming rawness of the aperitifs are, at first, often disenchanting to a foreign palate. But, as in any developed cuisine, the flavours blend with and complement each other. The real danger in the Balkans is that the need to placate tourists will destroy the restaurateur's inventiveness and replace it with the standard pallid diet of all European holiday resorts.

In Romania the wine industry is old; in Yugoslavia it is ancient; in Bulgaria it is new. Yet all three make highly creditable wine. Europe's Balkan corner has little to learn from the West in terms of up-to-date winemanship.

Yugoslav Riesling is the best-known single wine, but Romania makes a Riesling as good (that of Tirnave) and Bulgaria makes a Chardonnay maybe better. Yugoslavia has excellent Traminer, too, and a local grape, the Zilavka, which makes admirable wine touched, it seems, with apricots.

None of the reds is as good as these whites, but the Cabernet and Merlot wines of Yugoslavia are very sound, and everyday wine made from the Hungarian Kadarka grape almost everywhere is worth drinking.

The Balkan spirit is plum brandy, slivovitz or slivova according to where you are. Few spirits make a better aperitif, or digestif. Distillation standards are high, even if the spirit is usually sold too young.

The glory of paprika, pancakes and pastries

"IF THE HABSBURG EMPIRE had not existed, it would have been necessary to invent it." These words were spoken in 1848. Seventy years later the empire lay in ruins. The rule of the Habsburgs had lasted for over 600 years and over the centuries the fortunes of the empire had ebbed and flowed. It had, at times, controlled territories as diverse as Spain, the Netherlands and, for one brief period, Mexico. It had, too, fought for its very existence against the Turks, who twice laid siege to its capital, Vienna.

But war was not to the Austrians' taste. They preferred to extend spheres of influence by astute marriages and diplomacy and to fight battles in the law courts over a chocolate cake. The "seven years' war" that raged between the Hotel Sacher and Demel's, a café and pastry shop, two rival Viennese establishments, over the right to sell *the* original *Sachertorte*, must be unique in the annals of culinary, if not legal, history.

At the end of the nineteenth century the Austro-Hungarian Empire, of which Austria, Hungary and Czechoslovakia were part, stretched from southern Poland to the Adriatic. Its capital, Vienna, was one of the gayest, most sophisticated cities in Europe. Powerful and cultured, it was the home of one of the most elegant cuisines ever created.

Vienna is no longer the capital of a great empire. All that remains of its vast territories are a handful of provinces, but nevertheless it still retains its place in the world of gastronomy.

Viennese food is like a Strauss waltz—light, subtle and bewitchingly appealing. Beneath the charm, however, the master touch can be detected. There are the butchers who can produce forty cuts from a carcass of beef; the cooks who know how to deal with every one of these cuts, from the fillet to the last scrap, and the *Konditors,*

pastry cooks, whose ability to pull a sheet of *Strudel* out so thinly that a newspaper can be read through it, is little short of a miracle.

Viennese cooking is not for anyone who favours quick snacks and light work. Time and effort are needed to prepare the nourishing soups, the appetizing main dishes and the tantalizing cakes and pastries.

Although the glory of the Empire died long ago, the Viennese still cultivate the art of good living and good eating. Having disposed of an early breakfast of rolls and coffee, followed by a *Gabelfrühstück*, a second "fork" breakfast—a few slices of cold sausage, or, perhaps, a *Frühstückgulasch*, breakfast goulash—the Viennese usually eat the main meal of the day at lunchtime.

The meal generally begins with soup, often a rich beef broth made with the stock in which the meat for the main course has been cooked. What makes the soup exceptional is the garnish. No other European cuisine has devised such a variety of garnishes—some light and elegant and others surprisingly substantial. There are little light *Schöberln*, dumplings made with egg, meat and potato or other vegetables; *Nockerln*, light pasta made of semolina, breadcrumbs and meat; *Knöderln*, made with cream, puff pastry, eggs and breadcrumbs; *Frittatten,* pancakes which have been rolled up and cut into thin slices; *Strudel* stuffed with meat. The list is as long as a recital of Italian pastas. If the soup is served without garnish, it is quite likely to have been thickened with a *roux* so that it is, nevertheless, a filling first course.

The most popular Viennese meat dish is *Tafelspitz*. Full of flavour, this tender boiled beef is cut into thick slices and accompanied by sautéed potatoes and a piquant sauce. The Viennese are connoisseurs of boiled beef. The names of restaurants and *Beiseln*, little inns, serving the best *Tafelspitz* are passed around in confidence like stock-exchange tips.

The secret of a good *Tafelspitz* lies in the surgical precision with which the butcher cuts the meat and the meticulous care with which the pot is supervised so that it simmers and no more, with only the occasional bubble breaking the surface. On Sundays, kitchens throughout Austria echo to the pounding of *Schnitzel. Wiener Schnitzel* as it is prepared in Austria is an example of culinary perfection. The veal escalope must be cut just right, at a slight bias, so that it can be pounded paper-thin without shredding. From beginning to end,

its preparation is carried out in one uninterrupted operation so that it comes straight from the pan to the table—crisp, dry and golden.

No Austrian meal is complete without sweet. Austrian cook books devote long chapters to *Mehlspeisen*, flour dishes, a term used to cover anything from *Palatschinken* pancakes stuffed with creamy, curd cheese nuts or jam, and *Zwetschgenknödel*, delicious little fruit dumplings which conceal a plum and a sugar lump, a fresh apricot or a few cherries, to the cakes and pastries that are the crowning glory of Viennese cuisine.

The beautiful coffee houses and superb pastry shops of Austria are legion and they still play an important part in the life of every Austrian town. The twentieth century has swept away the brilliant society of merry widows and handsome hussars who danced and flirted in these coffee houses. In their place, elderly gentlemen sit huddled over chessboards or read the newspapers, which are threaded on to long batons to leave one hand free for the coffee cup. They are joined at the afternoon *Jause*, the coffee break, by attractive women, well-dressed businessmen and solemn children who choose from the bewildering assortment of Viennese cakes.

There is oven-warm *Strudel* filled with apples, cherries or cream cheese, the thin fragile pastry introduced originally, as was coffee, by the Turks. *Sachertorte*, the queen of chocolate cakes with its thin layer of apricot jam under the chocolate icing, is another favourite. Popular, too, are *Dobostorte*, its top shiny as glass with caramel, and *Esterhazytorte*, a nutty meringue and buttercream confection, whose names testify to their Hungarian origin. In the same way, the only reminder that Austria's marvellous yeast cakes are of Czechoslovakian origin is their names, for example, *Topfenkolatschen,* made with curd cheese; *Pressburger Nussbeugel*, the crisp, nut-filled crescents from Bratislava, and *Dalken*, heavy, yeast doughnuts of Bohemia. The Viennese, however, can lay claim to *Gugelhupf*, the coffee cake traditionally baked in a large, fluted, ring mould.

Viennese cuisine dominates Austrian cooking and there are few regional specialities. Carinthia and Styria have always been a source of good fresh-water fish and game. Styria also has *Sterz*, a dish similar to Italian *polenta*, made with cornmeal or buckwheat flour, and served with pork crackling. *Speckknödel*, bacon dumplings, and liver in

AUSTRIA HUNGARY AND CZECHOSLOVAKIA

CZECHOSLOVAKIA

KARLOVY VARY
HAM
PRAGUE
PLUMS
SAUSAGES
GAME
WILD MUSHROOMS
ČESKÉ KOLÁČE
Sweet buns
BOHEMIA
BRNO
LIPTAUER CHEESE
BRAMBOROVÁ POLÉVKA
Potato soup
LIPTOVSKÝ SV. MIKULÁŠ
CARP
GHERKINS
FRUIT
VEPŘOVÁ PEČENĚ
Pork roast
PEČENÁ HUSA SE ZELÍM
Roast goose with sauerkraut
HUCHEN
Danube salmon
PIKE-PERCH
WIENER SCHNITZEL
Breaded veal escalopes
MAKOVÝ ZÁVIN
Poppy seed roll
KNEDLÍKY
Dumplings
PÖRKÖLT
Veal and onion stew
LINZ
SACHERTORTE
Chocolate cake with apricot jam
VIENNA
BRATISLAVA
GHERKINS
SZÉKELY GULYÁS
Pork stew with sauerkraut
LINZERTORTE
Jam tart
APFELSTRUDEL
Apple strudel
ZNOJMO
OŘECHOVÉ ROHLÍKY
Pastry with nuts
DOBOS TORTA
Layer cake topped with caramel

AUSTRIA

SALZBURG
SALZBURGER NOCKERLN
Sweet soufflé
FISH
VANILLEKIPFERLN
Sweet crescent biscuits
NEUSIEDLER SEE
FATTENED GOOSE LIVER
DEBRECEN
SMOKED PAPRIKA SAUSAGE
WHITEFISH
REGENZ
HONEY
GAME
RÉTES
Hungarian strudel
BUDAPEST
BOGRÁCS GULYÁS
Hungarian goulash
FRUIT
INNSBRUCK
GRÖSTEL
Meat fried with potatoes
KRAPFEN
Doughnuts
KRAUTFLECKERLN
Noodles with stewed cabbage
GRAZ
SCHMARRN
Shredded pancake
BAKONY FOREST
CABBAGE
SMOKED SAUSAGE
GYULA
KALBSLEBER TIROLER ART
Calves' liver in sour-cream sauce
FRUIT
LAKE BALATON
SALAMI
SZEGEDI HALÁSZLÉ
Piquant fish soup
FOGAS
Pike-perch
CARP
SZEGED
ONIONS
PAPRIKAS
Paprika stew with cream
MAKÓ
STERLET
RIVER DANUBE

HUNGARY

sour-cream sauce are typical of Innsbruck and the South Tyrol, where there is also a marked Italian influence. But Salzburg's sweet soufflé *Nockerln*, and the *Linztorte*, or "Linz tart", a crumbly nut pastry filled with jam and decorated with a lattice of pastry strips, are as popular in Vienna as they are in the regions where they originated.

Just as Vienna dominates the cuisine of Austria, so, until the Second World War, many Viennese kitchens were ruled by Bohemian cooks. These ladies would arrive from Czechoslovakia armed with a seemingly endless repertoire of recipes for roasts, dumplings, sweets and pastries.

Today evidence of such culinary talent is rarely found in Czechoslovakia's state-run restaurants. Prague hams, praised in classic gastronomic encyclopedias may be difficult to find in Prague. Roast goose or roast pork, flavoured with caraway seeds and garlic, accompanied by *Ceske Knedliky*, Bohemian dumplings, may also be absent from restaur-

ant menus. But the juicy fresh sausages called *parký*, pairs, because they are always served two at a time, are as good as ever, as are the dumplings, pancakes and *kolače*, yeast pastries filled with sweet curd cheese, nuts, poppy seeds or jam.

Hungarian cuisine differs from that of her neighbours by the generous use of paprika, which can be hot, medium or mild. The names of the different dishes imply the way they are prepared. A *paprikas* is a meat, poultry or fish dish that is made with paprika and cream.

In Hungary, a *gulyás* is everything a goulash should be. Rich and hot, it is made with large cubes of beef and potatoes, onions, paprika and, occasionally, a little garlic or tomato. *Székely gulyás*, is an exception, made with pork instead of beef, sauerkraut and cream. The favourite accompaniment are *csipetke*, little dumplings, or *tarhónya*, tiny grains of dried pasta boiled and then browned with chopped onions.

Hungarians share their neighbours' love of dumplings, pancakes and elegant *Torten*, and they cannot resist mentioning that it was their wheat that produced the fine, strong flour necessary for a good *Strudel*, that they call *rétes*.

In the markets, the fruit and vegetable stalls are a kaleidoscope of colour. There are rows of plump geese, ducks and chickens and beef and pork of the finest quality. Displayed, too, are some of the best freshwater fish in Europe, including carp, crayfish and *fogos*, the pike-perch of Lake Balaton.

Few Eastern European cuisines have withstood the traumatic upheavals of this century as well as that of Hungary. The coffee houses of Budapest, which once rivalled those of Vienna, are a bit shabbier now, but they are as popular as ever. Little inns still ring to the haunting music of gypsy violins and serve food which is as delicious as it was in bygone days.

197

Dishes from the Habsburg Empire

Viennese Boiled Beef
WIENER TAFELSPITZ

Tafelspitz *is nothing more or less than boiled beef. The Viennese, however, can transform this simple dish into a culinary delight. The secret is to use a good cut of beef and to cook it very, very slowly. Serve* tafelspitz *with potatoes that have been boiled, cooled, cut into chunks and fried in butter, spinach and grated horseradish mixed with whipped cream or grated apples.*

SERVES 4

1 lb beef bones
Salt
2 to 2½ lb topside or silverside of beef, tied into a good shape
1 large leek, halved
1 large carrot, halved
2 celery sticks, sliced
1 onion, sliced
4 parsley sprigs
6 black peppercorns

In a large saucepan, cover the beef bones with 3½ pints of salted water. Bring to the boil slowly, skimming off the scum as it rises to the surface. Add the beef and the remaining ingredients. Slowly bring to the boil again. Lower the heat so that the liquid barely simmers. Partly cover the pan and cook for 2½ to 3 hours, or until the beef is very tender.

To serve, cut the beef into thick slices and arrange them on a warm platter.

Viennese Veal Escalopes
WIENER SCHNITZEL

The true *Wienerschnitzel is large, round and paper thin. Served straight from the frying-pan in which it is cooked, it comes to the table crisp and dry. The classic accompaniment is a mixed salad.*

SERVES 4

4 large thin slices veal
Flour
1 egg
1 tablespoon oil
1 tablespoon water
Fine, dry breadcrumbs
Salt
Lard or butter for frying
Lemon slices
Parsley sprigs

Have the slices of veal cut at a slight angle across the grain from the top of the leg. Beat the slices out thinly between two sheets of grease-proof paper.

Put the flour, the egg, beaten with the oil and water, and the fine, dry breadcrumbs on separate plates.

Season the veal with salt. Dip each slice into the flour, then into the egg mixture, allowing the excess to drain off, and finally coat it with breadcrumbs, pressing them in firmly.

Using two frying-pans, if possible, heat about 2 ounces lard or butter in each pan. When the fat is hot, fry the veal until crisp and golden brown, allowing 3 to 4 minutes on each side. Drain thoroughly.

Garnish with lemon slices and parsley sprigs

Salzburg Soufflé
SALZBURGER NOCKERLN

This light, fragile dessert is said to have been created two hundred and fifty years ago by a chef in the Hohensalzburg, the Archbishop's palace in Salzburg.

SERVES 4

2 oz butter, softened
6 egg yolks
7 egg whites
4 oz castor sugar
2 tablespoons plain flour
5 fl oz milk
1 tablespoon vanilla sugar

Preheat the oven to 400°F (Gas Mark 6). Lightly butter a 12-inch rectangular or oval baking dish.

In a large bowl, cream the butter until it is fluffy. Beating continuously, add the egg yolks one at a time and continue to beat the mixture until it is very light.

Whisk the egg whites until they form soft peaks. Add the sugar gradually, whisking vigorously, to make a stiff, shiny meringue.

Fold first the flour and then the meringue into the egg yolk mixture.

Pour the milk into a small saucepan and add the vanilla sugar. Bring the milk to the boil. Pour it into the baking dish. Spoon the meringue mixture on top in large dollops.

Bake for about 18 minutes, or until well risen, but still creamy inside. Serve hot.

Sacher's Chocolate Cake
SACHERTORTE

Sachertorte *was created almost one hundred and fifty years ago by Franz Sacher, pastry cook to Prince Klemens von Metternich. When the Sacher family opened their own hotel the cake became an immediate success with the Viennese. But another great Viennese bakery, Demel's, produced their own version of the cake, and the* Sachertorte *became the object of a lawsuit which was to last for seven years. Both establishments claimed that theirs was the original* Sachertorte. *The main difference between the two cakes was that Demel's was simply coated with apricot jam and chocolate icing, while Sacher's also had a layer of apricot jam spread through the centre. The court finally decided that both were permissible and to this day* Sachertorten *are served in both establishments and exported all over the world.*

5 oz unsalted butter
5 oz plain chocolate, melted
5 oz castor sugar
6 eggs, separated
4 oz plain flour, sifted
Apricot jam
CHOCOLATE ICING
7 oz plain chocolate
8 oz castor sugar
5 fl oz water
Butter

Preheat the oven to 350°F (Gas Mark 4). Lightly butter a deep, 9-inch cake tin and line the bottom with buttered greaseproof paper.

Cream the butter and beat in the cooled melted chocolate 1 tablespoon at a time. Add the sugar and egg yolks alternately, beating well after each addition. Mix in the flour.

Whisk the egg whites until stiff but not dry and fold them into the chocolate mixture.

Pour the mixture into the prepared cake tin and bake for 1 hour, or until the cake is well risen and has shrunk slightly from the sides of the tin.

Remove the cake from the oven and let it stand for 5 minutes before turning it out on to a wire rack to cool.

When the cake is quite cold, either spread the top and sides with warmed, strained apricot jam, or split it in half horizontally, spread the strained jam between the layers and put it together again before spreading the top and sides with more jam.

To make the chocolate icing, melt the chocolate in the top of a double boiler. In another pan dissolve the sugar in the water over low heat. When the sugar has dissolved increase the heat and bring to the boil. Simmer for 5 minutes.

Beat the chocolate until smooth; then gradually beat in enough hot sugar syrup to make the icing the consistency of thick cream. Finally, beat in a small piece of butter.

Pour the hot icing over the top of the cake and let it run down the sides. Quickly smooth the icing round the sides of the cake with a spatula. The less the icing is touched, the shinier it will be. Set the cake aside until the glaze is quite hard and dry.

Hungarian Stuffed Cabbage Rolls
TÖLTÖTT KAPOSZTA

Stuffed cabbage rolls can be made with fresh cabbage leaves and cooked on a bed of sauerkraut. The traditional Hungarian method, however, using a head of cabbage that has been specially soured both for the cabbage rolls and for lining the

ooking pot, is fun to try, although it means
planning a week ahead.

SERVES 4

1 large white cabbage
1 small slice rye bread
Salt
8 oz long-grain rice
1 lb minced pork
2 onions, finely chopped
2 slices bacon, finely chopped
1 garlic clove, crushed
2 eggs
1 teaspoon dried dill
Sweet paprika
1 thick slice smoked fat pork
15 fl oz meat stock
1½ oz lard or butter
2 tablespoons plain flour
10 fl oz sour cream
1 teaspoon finely chopped fresh dill
(optional)

Wash the cabbage thoroughly and, with an apple corer, hollow out the end of the stalk. Place the cabbage in a deep earthenware jar and add the rye bread. Dissolve 2 tablespoons of salt in 3½ pints of water. Pour this over the cabbage. Put a plate on top and weight it down so that the cabbage is submerged. Cover the top of the jar with a cloth and leave it in a cool place for 6 to 8 days.

To make the cabbage rolls, drain the cabbage thoroughly. Place it in a large bowl and pour boiling water over it. As soon as the cabbage cools, separate the leaves, taking care not to tear them. Trim the stem end of each leaf. Put the leaves aside.

To make the stuffing, boil the rice for 8 minutes in salted water. Drain well and combine with the minced pork, onions, bacon, garlic, eggs and dried dill. Season with 1 tablespoon of paprika and salt to taste. Mix well.

Using the large cabbage leaves, place 2 tablespoons of the meat mixture at the stem end of each leaf. Fold the two sides in and roll the leaves up tightly.

Finely shred the remaining cabbage leaves. Put the slice of fat pork on the bottom of a large, heavy casserole, and arrange the shredded cabbage over it in an even layer. Put the stuffed cabbage rolls on top. Pour in the stock and bring to the boil over moderate heat.

Cover the casserole, lower the heat and simmer gently for about 1½ hours.

To finish the sauce, melt the lard or butter in a saucepan. Blend in the flour with a wooden spoon and stir over low heat for 2 to 3 minutes, or until the mixture is lightly coloured. Drain the cooking juices from the casserole and, stirring constantly, add slowly to the flour mixture. Still stirring, add the sour cream. Bring to the boil, stirring, and simmer until the sauce is thick and smooth. Season to taste with salt, a generous pinch of paprika and fresh dill.

Pour the sauce over the cabbage rolls. Cook over a low heat for 10 minutes before serving.

Hungarian Goulash Soup
BOGRÁCS GULYÁS

The shepherds of the puszta, *the vast Hungarian plain, are called* gulya. Gulyás, *which can be either a soup or a stew, has become one of Hungary's most famous national dishes. It was originally cooked by the shepherds over an open fire in a pot called a* bogrács.

SERVES 4

1 oz butter or 2 tablespoons cooking oil
8 oz onions, chopped
1 tablespoon sweet paprika
Salt
Freshly ground black pepper
1 tablespoon tomato purée
1 lb stewing steak, cut in 1-inch cubes
1 large carrot, sliced
1 garlic clove, crushed
½ teaspoon dried marjoram
¼ teaspoon caraway seeds
3 large potatoes
2 pints light beef stock

CSIPETKE DUMPLINGS
3½ oz plain flour
¼ teaspoon salt
1 egg

In a large saucepan, melt the butter or heat the oil. Add the onions and fry until transparent and golden. Remove the saucepan from the heat, stir in the paprika, salt and freshly ground pepper to taste, and the tomato purée diluted in 1 tablespoon water. Add the beef, carrot, garlic, marjoram and caraway seeds. Mix well, cover and simmer over low heat for 1¼ hours.

Peel the potatoes and cut them into large cubes. Put them in the pan and pour in the stock. Partly cover and simmer gently for 30 minutes, or until the meat is tender and the potatoes are cooked.

Meanwhile, prepare the *csipetke* dough. Sift the flour and salt into a bowl, make a well in the

centre, drop in the egg and work the ingredients to a firm dough. Knead it vigorously until the dough is smooth and pliable. A few drops of water may be necessary, but the dough should remain firm.

About 10 minutes before the soup is ready, flatten the dough out, pull off bean-sized pieces, roll them smoothly between fingers and drop them into the simmering soup.

Baked Ham in Bread Crust
PRAŽSKÁ ŠUNKA

Prague hams are difficult to buy, but this method of cooking ham keeps the meat moist and flavourful and is well worth adapting to any uncooked ham.

5 to 6 lb uncooked ham
About 2 lb bread dough
1 egg yolk, lightly beaten

Soak the ham overnight in cold water. The following day, put it in a large saucepan, cover with fresh cold water and slowly bring to simmering point. Cook gently for 1 hour.

Cool the ham in the liquid. As soon as it is cool enough to handle, lift it out and carefully peel off the skin. If the ham is very fat, remove some of the fat with a sharp knife.

Preheat the oven to 400°F (Gas Mark 6). Liberally butter a large baking dish.

Roll out the bread dough. Carefully wrap the ham in it, taking care to seal the dough so that none of the juices can escape. Reserve a small ball of dough for repairing the crust should it split open during baking.

Put the wrapped ham in the buttered baking dish. Brush the top and sides with the egg yolk. If using a meat thermometer, wrap a small ball of dough around the point before pushing it into the joint to reinforce the casing around it.

Bake for 30 minutes, then reduce the oven to 325°F (Gas Mark 3) and continue to bake for 1½ hours longer, or until the ham is cooked

Serve warm in slices.

AUSTRIA AND HUNGARY share a taste for the creamy and spicy things of life which extends to their wine as well as their cooking. The ideal wine of either country is golden-white and powerfully grape-flavoured with a distinct touch of fiery strength. It reaches its apotheosis in Hungary's Tokay, which is as rich and sweet as butterscotch. Hungarian wine is almost always good of its kind. White is in the majority; the best vineyards are around Lake Balaton and at Mor and Somlo. But red from Eger ("Bull's Blood") and Vilanyi is remarkable value.

Austria's best wine is all white. Vienna itself and the Sudbahn, southern railway, are famous for their *heurige*, new wine served in taverns run by the growers. Better wine, on the other hand, comes from the Wachau on the Danube to the west. The firm of Lenz-Moser is the name to conjure with here.

Hungary's national spirit, *barack palinka*, could be described as slivovitz made from apricots instead of plums, and correspondingly sunnier in flavour.

Wine is made in Czechoslovakia, too, but it is beer for which the country is famous. Pilsen is the original home of a style which is imitated wherever the word Pils appears on a label.

The self-sufficient cooking of the country

POLAND LIES AT THE VERY HEART of Europe on the great fertile plain that rolls uninterrupted from the Netherlands to the Urals. In the sixteenth century, Polish kings ruled over a vast empire that stretched from the Baltic to the Black Sea, yet the history of the last two hundred years has been one of partition, oppression and war. In 1814 the Congress of Vienna wiped the name of Poland off the map, and for the next hundred years the nation fought to preserve its identity and its traditions. Polish cuisine is as much a product of her history as is every other aspect of Polish life—intensely national and fiercely traditional.

Early in the sixteenth century, a Milanese princess, the young bride of the King of Poland, introduced the court to such vegetables as tomatoes, artichokes, cauliflower and leeks. The Polish names of these vegetables still echo their Italian origin. She also introduced the Poles to pasta, to which they added their own touch. *Łazanki*, small squares of pasta, baked with ham or cabbage and mushrooms, or sweetened poppy seeds, is a Polish adaptation of *lasagne*.

Polish cooking is essentially country cooking, based on the self-sufficiency of the *szlachta*, the country gentry, who, much more than the aristocracy, were the backbone of the nation. Until the upheavals of two world wars, barrels of cabbage were salted down for the winter; fruits were carefully stored on racks, dried or made into preserves, jams or liqueurs. In the poultry yard, speckled guinea fowl mingled with chickens and turkeys, and flocks of geese were marched out each morning to feed in the meadows. Once or twice a year, the butcher would arrive from the nearest town to kill a pig and supervise its transformation into puddings, sausages and hams, some of which would be eaten fresh, while the remainder were cured or smoked for later use.

In winter, partridge, pheasant, wild duck and hare, as well as such big game as deer and wild boar, would be shot. *Bigos myśliwski*, hunter's stew, a steaming cauldron of sauerkraut rich with meat, game and chunks of sausage, has become one of Poland's most famous national dishes.

Polish winters are cold, and substantial soups like *krupnik*, a creamy barley and potato soup, and *grochówka*, a purée of dried peas flavoured with a smoked ham bone, are served in steaming tureens.

The Poles are great meat eaters. Pork dominates the menu. Roasts are flavoured with a touch of caraway seed and served with red cabbage, sauerkraut or pickled cucumbers. Chops are breaded and fried. *Golonka*, a lightly pickled pork hock, is boiled and served with sauerkraut and mashed potatoes. Beef is pot-roasted to buttery tenderness

Rivers, lakes and ponds provide a great variety of fish, which are prepared with delicacy and skill. Carp are fried, poached or served in a sweet wine sauce darkened with caramelized sugar, thickened with crumbled honey cake and finished with raisins and shredded almonds. *Karasie*, crucian, small fish related to carp, which look rather like goldfish, are fried or baked in cream.

Sea fish have never played an important part in the Polish cuisine, with the exception of herrings which are salted and prepared in a variety of ways. They are pounded with butter and hard-boiled egg yolks to make *masło śledziowe*, herring butter, a delicious spread for canapés, or they are filleted and served with a mustard vinaigrette. *Śledzie w śmietanie*, salted herrings in sour-cream sauce, are the best of all. Accompanied by rye bread and butter and small glasses of ice-cold vodka this dish makes an excellent appetizer.

To make śledzie w śmietanie *to serve 4, soak 3 plump salted herrings in several changes of cold water for 24 hours. Fillet the herrings and cut the fillets into bite-sized pieces. Put them in a shallow serving dish.*

Mix 5 fluid ounces of sour cream with 2 tablespoons of finely chopped onion, 6 tablespoons of coarsely chopped apple, the juice of ½ lemon, 2 teaspoons of sugar and a grinding of black pepper. Pour over the herrings and chill for at least 2 hours. Garnish with chopped chives or parsley.

Honey plays an important part in traditional Polish cooking. The city of Toruń, the birthplace of Copernicus, has been famous for its honey cakes since medieval times. Little *katarzynki*, Catherine cakes, are coated with chocolate, and *pierniki*, fragrant with spices, are baked in moulds stamped with pictures of knights in armour, birds, animals and even of Copernicus himself.

The traditional celebrations of Christmas and Easter, kept alive with loving and meticulous attention to detail in Polish homes all over the world, have given rise to some of the finest of Polish dishes.

Christmas Eve is a meatless day and only fish is served. Tradition decrees that there should be twelve courses in the Christmas supper. The number symbolizes the apostles and the dishes themselves represent the fields, forests, orchards and lakes which provided the Slavic tribes with their food. Today, most families would find it difficult to produce, or to eat, twelve courses, but honour is satisfied by including bread, butter, even the salt if necessary, in the total count. First the cold dishes are served. These include herring salads, stuffed pike or tench in aspic. They are followed by a hot soup. Most families serve the traditional *barszcz z uszkami*, a brilliant clear red beetroot soup garnished with tiny, ear-shaped dumplings which are stuffed with a mixture of chopped dried mushrooms, onion and breadcrumbs. Next come the hot dishes, fish baked or fried or cooked in a sauce, and there may also be a meatless sauerkraut or cabbage-stuffed dumplings.

Christmas sweets traditionally include poppy seeds in some form. *Kluski z makiem* are noodles tossed with sweetened ground poppy seeds. People from the east of Poland serve *kutia*, boiled whole-wheat kernels mixed with poppy seeds and honey. The traditional cakes are *strucla z makiem*, sweet yeast dough shaped into a long roll with a filling of poppy seeds, nuts and raisins, and honey cakes.

From Twelfth Night until the beginning of Lent is the doughnut season. Polish doughnuts, *pączki*, are soft and light, with a teaspoon of rose petal jam or *powidła*, thick plum preserve, hidden in the centre. Another Carnival speciality are the delicate deep-fried pastries known as *chrust* or *faworki*.

To make faworki, *sift 8 ounces of plain flour into a large mixing bowl with 1 tablespoon of sugar and the grated rind of ½ lemon. Make a well in the centre. Add 4 egg yolks, 4 tablespoons of single cream and 1 tablespoon of rum. Work the ingredients to a stiff dough, using a little more cream if necessary. Knead the dough until it is smooth and pliable. Roll it into a ball and leave it for 30 minutes, covered with a cloth.*

Roll the dough out very thinly and cut it into

POLAND

Map labels (clockwise/as placed):

COD — SPRATS — HERRING — BRISLING — MACKEREL — FLATFISH

KISZONE OGÓRKI *Dill pickles*

BALTIC SEA

SALT HERRINGS

KRUPNIK *Barley potato soup*

MIZERIA *Fresh cucumber and sour cream salad*

TEAL — WILD DUCK

CHŁODNIK *Cold sour cream and beetroot soup*

KOŁDUNY LITEWSKIE *Mutton-stuffed dumplings*

GAME

KURCZĘTA PO POLSKU *Roast spring chickens with dill and breadcrumb stuffing*

PIERNIKI TORUŃSKIE *Spiced honey cakes*

EELS

TROUT

PIKE-PERCH

VENISON

SZCZECIN

KARASIE W ŚMIETANIE *Crucian baked in cream*

MAZURKI *Small fruit and nut pastries*

FLAKI PO WARSZAWSKU *Tripe in cream sauce*

BIAŁYSTOK

WILD BOAR

KAPUŚNIAK *Sauerkraut soup*

LENIWE PIEROGI *Potato cheese dumplings*

TORUŃ

PORK

BABKI *Yeast coffee cakes*

PĄCZKI *Doughnuts*

WILD MUSHROOMS

TORTY *Layer cakes*

RIVER WARTA

PIEROGI *Stuffed dumplings*

KASZA GRYCZANA *Buckwheat groats*

WILD STRAWBERRIES

RYE

POTATOES

POZNAŃ

GOLONKA Z KAPUSTĄ *Pickled pork hocks with sauerkraut*

SAUERKRAUT

WĘDLINY *Sausages and cured meats*

WARSAW

BILBERRIES

ZIELONA GÓRA

GRAPES

ZRAZY ZAWIJANE *Stuffed beef rolls*

PIECZEŃ PO HUZARSKU *Stuffed pot-roasted beef*

BLACKBERRIES

KUTIA *Whole wheat, honey and poppy-seed pudding*

STRUCLA Z MAKIEM *Rolled poppy-seed cake*

KLUSKI Z MAKIEM *Sweet noodles with poppy seeds*

WILD RASPBERRIES

KARTOFLANKA *Potato soup*

SZCZUPAK PO ŻYDOWSKU *Pike stuffed in the Jewish style*

BIGOS *Sauerkraut and mixed meat stew*

GOŁĄBKI *Stuffed cabbage leaves*

LUBLIN

PLACKI OWOCOWE *Open fruit pastries*

KISIEL OWOCOWY *Summer fruit pudding*

BARLEY

SUGAR BEET

WOODCOCK

KASZANKA *Black pudding*

KARP W SZARYM SOSIE *Carp in sweet sauce*

SERNIKI *Cheese cakes*

POWIDŁA *Thick plum preserve*

SANDOMIERZ

ORCHARD FRUIT

CAPERCAILLIE

PYZY *Yeast dumplings*

ŻUR *Sour rye soup*

CATTLE

RIVER VISTULA

OATS

SHEATFISH

KACZKA PIECZONA Z JABŁKAMI *Roast duck with apples*

KRAKÓW

KASZKA KRAKOWSKA *Fine groats*

SHEEP

BRYNDZA *Sheep's milk cheese*

CRAYFISH

WILD MUSHROOMS

POLAND

RIVER

---

trips 1 inch wide and 3 inches long. Make a slit down the centre of each strip and pull one end of the strip through so that it resembles a knotted bow. Deep-fry, 3 or 4 at a time, in lard heated to 375°F. The strips will puff up as soon as they are in the fat. When they are a rich golden colour on one side, flip them over and fry until the other side colours. Drain on absorbent paper. When the faworki *cool, dust with icing sugar.*

The Carnival revels culminate with dancing on Shrove Tuesday. At midnight, a symbolic herring is brought in, the music stops and Lent has begun.

Good Friday comes and goes in a fever of cooking and baking. Lunch on Easter Sunday, *święcone*, the blessed meal, is a magnificent cold buffet. In the centre of the table stands a little Easter lamb made of sugar or sculpted from butter. Surrounding

it are platters of cold baked ham, roast veal and turkey, quivering moulds of jellied pigs' trotters, garlands of fresh and smoked pork sausages, vegetable salads, pickled mushrooms, mayonnaise, mustard and *ćwikła*, a grated horseradish and beetroot sauce. Easter cakes are extravagant. Tall, feathery *babki*, golden with egg yolks and saffron, cheesecakes and rich layer cakes are surrounded by plates of traditional Polish *mazurki*, small rectangular pastries topped with nuts, dried fruit, chocolate or marzipan.

The Polish housewife prepares a simple supper or an elaborate feast as her mother and grandmother did. She prides herself on her skill as a cook and is reluctant to compromise with modern shortcuts that might change the character of this generous and satisfying cuisine.

According to the Polish story, on the rare occasions when a shipment of Polish vodka gets to Russia people wait for hours in the snow to snap up a bottle. The Poles consider theirs is the *grand cru* of vodkas, and not without reason. They make it not only penny plain but twopence, threepence and indeed tenpence coloured in countless permutations of age, strength and flavouring matter. The trays of glasses at a reception sparkle like junk jewellery—diamond-white, ruby, amber and soft grassy green.

Most original and best is the grassy one, Zubrowka, flavoured with the reed-like grass "beloved" so the label says, "by the European bison" which inhabits the Pripet marshes in eastern Poland. Zubrowka is acknowledged the luxury liquor of the Communist world. Polish Plain Spirit is their strongest vodka, and at ninety-eight proof it is the strongest drink on earth.

Borshch, black bread, blinis and caviar

THE SOVIET UNION straddles two continents and covers more than one-sixth of the earth's surface. Her fifteen republics are made up of many nationalities, all of which, while they now speak Russian, proudly preserve their own mother tongues and traditions. The climate ranges from the permafrost of the Siberian tundra to the subtropics of Transcaucasia. All these factors make any attempt at defining a "Soviet" cuisine as impossible as trying to cover simultaneously the cooking of one country in South America and another in Central Europe.

The majority of the Soviet peoples are, however, Slavs—Russians proper, Byelorussians and Ukrainians, and it is largely their culinary traditions that have come to represent Russian cooking to the world.

Before the Revolution in 1917, the life of the peasants was harsh. According to an old Russian saying, *shchi da kasha pishcha nasha*—"cabbage soup (*shchi*) and groats or porridge (*kasha*), those are our food".

At the other end of the scale was the aristocracy, people often of untold wealth. They lived largely cut off from the outside world until the eighteenth century whe[n] Peter the Great, impressed by what he ha[d] seen on his travels in western Europe[,] ordered his court to adopt Western customs[.] Although reluctant and ill at ease at first, b[y] the nineteenth century Russian aristocra[ts] were travelling to the playgrounds o[f] western Europe, hiring foreign tutors an[d] nannies for their children and importin[g] French chefs.

Few new dishes, however, were in[-]troduced. The aristocrats who returned t[o] their country houses in summer remaine[d] true to beetroot *borshch* and black brea[d,] and even royal menus might include [a] peasant *shchi* or a traditional, althoug[h] majestic, *koulebiaka*.

Koulebiaka is one of a glorious family o[f] pies and pasties, generally known as *piro[g]* when they are large, *pirozhki* when the[y]

are small. The word *pirog* comes from the Russian word *pir,* meaning feast. They may be made with a rich, sweetish yeast dough, short or puff pastry, and stuffings range from meat, mushrooms or cabbage and hard-boiled eggs, to the salmon and rice used in a classic *koulebiaka.* Hot *pirozhki* are served with soup or as appetizers.

The country house gave birth to the famous Russian *zakuski,* or appetizers. In many grand houses, the table of *zakuski* was a permanent feature, always in readiness to revive guests after a long journey. Gentlemen would be invited to sample such delicacies as caviar, smoked salmon, fish in aspic, sliced cold meats, patés, and salads of all kinds. And while the gentlemen regaled themselves with *zakuski* and vodka, the ladies would be offered tea from the

E UNION
OF
SOCIALIST
PUBLICS

samovar, and an array of small savouries and cakes. *Zakuski* remain an important feature of the Russian cuisine, usually served before guests sit down to dinner.

Soups, the staple of peasants in cold countries all over the world, still dominate the Russian kitchen. Specialities include *shchi* and the famous *borshch,* which can be anything from a sparkling clear consommé, ruby red with beetroot, to the Ukrainian version, a sturdy soup thick with vegetables. Other favourites include *solianka,* made with meat or fish and salted cucumbers, *rassolnik,* a mixture of sorrel, cucumber and other vegetables and garnished with chopped kidneys, and *ouha,* a clear fish consommé garnished with pieces of fish. In summer there are refreshing soups soured with *kvas,* a fermented mixed cereal or rye bread liquor, and sweet fruit soups enriched with sour cream.

In the past, meat was eaten regularly only by the well-to-do. Such classics as Chicken Kiev, chicken breast stuffed with butter, breaded and deep-fried; *shashlik,* cubes of marinated lamb grilled on a spit; or Beef Stroganov, a dish which has become a highlight of international cuisine, would not have appeared on a peasant's table.

To make Beef Stroganov to serve 4, cut 2 pounds of fillet or rump of beef into slices ¼-inch thick and then into 2-inch strips.

In a large heavy frying-pan, simmer 2 thinly sliced medium-sized onions in 2 ounces of butter until soft. Add ½ pound of trimmed and sliced button mushrooms, and stir over moderate heat for 3 to 4 minutes longer, until their juices have evaporated, adding a little more butter if necessary. Remove the onions and mushrooms with a slotted spoon.

Melt another 1 ounce of butter in the pan and brown the beef strips over a high heat, stirring constantly, for 4 to 5 minutes. The strips should not be well done.

Return the onions and mushrooms to the pan. Season to taste with salt and freshly ground black pepper, and cook, stirring, for 1 minute longer. Remove the pan from the heat. Add 10 fluid ounces sour cream mixed with 2 teaspoons mild French mustard. Stir over low heat for 1 minute, just long enough to reheat the sauce without letting it come to the boil. Serve immediately.

In Russia, vegetables have always been eaten according to season. In the winter there is sauerkraut, pickled cucumbers and marinated and dried mushrooms. Potatoes and cereals, however, are staple foods, eaten all year round. *Kasha,* the Russian

word that has been adopted in English as the word for buckwheat groats, has a much wider meaning in Russian. It is a blanket term for any cooked cereal, including buckwheat, barley and semolina. Buckwheat, a staple cereal of the northwest, is called *grechnevaya kasha.* It is served plain, as an addition to soups, as a side dish with meat dishes or baked with curd cheese, cream and sugar to make a pudding.

Some of Russia's most famous dishes originally had a religious significance. *Blini,* buckwheat pancakes which are served with caviar or smoked fish, butter and sour cream, were traditionally eaten during *Maslenitsa,* butter week, the last days of Carnival before the austerities of Lent. And Easter was celebrated with beautifully decorated eggs and *kulich,* a tall, golden yeast cake, eaten with *paskha,* which must surely be the king of cheesecakes.

While the majority of people in modern Russia eat better than ever before, they will never lose their taste for the dishes of the past, be they peasant or aristocratic in origin.

THE RUSSIANS drink much too much vodka —or so their government thinks. Since the 1950s there has been an official campaign to promote wine-drinking at the expense of vodka. In practice the two co-exist very happily. Wine consumption goes up—vodka stays put.

Good vodka is the nearest thing to plain alcohol that the distiller can produce. He may start with grain, or potatoes, or even wood shavings, but his object is to remove, by distilling and filtering, every vestige of anything but alcohol and water. The result is a drink which is more like an injection. It seems absurd to claim that in some way this clear spirit is delicious. But so it is— ice-cold, snorted back a glassful at a time with richly oily tidbits. This is the classic beginning to a Russian meal. Nothing can replace it.

Russia's vineyards cluster around the Black Sea. A few are old. The Ancient Greeks planted the first vines in the Crimea and Armenia and there was a lively wine industry on private estates around the Crimean resorts in late Imperial days. Most are new. Two and a half million acres have been brought into production in the past twenty years.

The Russian sweet tooth is very much in evidence, whether in the syrupy *champanski* produced in the valley of the Don or the muscats and port, sherry and madeira-types made in the Crimea, the Russian Republic and Moldavia.

Where hospitality is more than a social formalit

PAKISTAN came into existence on August 15th, 1947. Until the secession of its eastern wing (now Bangladesh) in 1971, it covered those areas of the Indian subcontinent where the population was predominantly Muslim. Present-day Pakistan borders on Iran and Afghanistan in the west and north and reaches the shores of the Arabian Sea in the south. India lies to the east.

Pakistan is a land of contrasts. In the northern areas is the "Roof of the World", where the Hindu Kush, the Karakoram, the Kunlun and the Himalayas converge. Between the mountains and the fierce desert lie green valleys and fertile plains watered by the Indus and its four tributaries.

The climate of Pakistan encompasses the full range from extreme heat to cold. This ensures the availability of a wide range of foodstuffs all the year round. A bread-eating country, because the staple grain is wheat, Pakistan also grows some of the finest long-grain rice and a considerable amount of corn.

Although Pakistan as a nation is only twenty-six years old, the area has a known history of more than five thousand years. From time immemorial, successive invaders poured through the passes that breached the forbidding high wall of mountains. Beginning with the Aryans, there came the Babylonians, Persians, Greeks, Huns, Mongols, Arabs, Turks and Afghans. In recent history there was the powerful impact of European culture, habits and customs—especially those of the British, who ruled for almost two centuries.

The result was a mingling of races, religions, languages and cultures unparalleled in its complexity. This cultural and racial kaleidoscope has subjected the area to many influences. Not the least of these is a legacy of widely varied culinary and eating habits which are, even today, discernible in the typical dishes of the main regions of Pakistan.

The majority of Pakistanis live in villages and it is among these people that the traditional values are most apparent. The foremost of these values is hospitality, and it is common to all, urban and rural, rich and poor. In a social pattern where "family" means an extended rather than a nuclear family, where friends—and friends of friends—are thought of as relatives, hospitality also has an extended meaning. All of life's important occasions, religious or secular, are excuses for feasts to which as many friends and relatives as possible are invited. The giving and sharing of food—of hospitality—is more than a social formality.

In the major cities, particularly where European influences are strong, the manner of serving food and eating it are much the same as in the West. Where tradition forms the pattern of living, however, food is cooked, served and eaten in simpler ways. Although food is served with a spoon, it is eaten with the right hand. Hands are carefully washed before and after a meal, and the mouth is rinsed thoroughly.

A basic Pakistani meal will include a meat dish, a vegetable dish, bread, rice, accompanying pickles and fruit and dessert. Pakistanis eat a great deal of meat, but like all Muslims they are forbidden to eat pork, which is religiously considered unclean. To drink alcoholic beverages, also religiously forbidden, is not considered such an abomination.

The main regions of Pakistan are the North-West Frontier, Baluchistan, Punjab and Sind, with overtones from Kashmir.

The North-West Frontier, with the rugged, barren and mountainous terrain of the Khyber Pass, is famous for its fierce Pathan tribes and its peaceful, fertile valleys. Here are magnificent orchards that yield abundant crops of peaches, apricots, almonds and apples. Mushrooms grown in the valley of Swat are exported all over the world.

Based on meat—mainly mutton, beef and chicken—the food here is simple but varied. It lacks the spiciness of the food of the Indo-Gangetic Plain, but it appeals to the most sophisticated palate. There are such dishes as *shashlik*—known here as *tikka kebabs*, small pieces of meat cooked on skewers and basted with the fat of *doombas*, fat-tailed sheep—and *burra*, roast baby lamb, stuffed with rice, nuts and raisins.

An unusual dish, evoking Mediterranean cooking, although entirely indigenous, is *aash*, which is eaten by the Persian-speakin people of this area. The dish include cottage cheese, meat sauce, shredded chillie lemon juice and noodles.

The bread eaten with all these dishes *naan*. Flat and leavened, it is cooked in th earthenware *tandoors*, or ovens, which are i every home. Goats' milk cheese is made home, and yoghourt is eaten at almost ever meal.

Baluchistan borders on Iran and Baluch live on both sides of the border. It is large a pastoral area and, therefore, the food simple, mainly barbecues and roasts. Man of the people are nomadic, and most dishe are cooked over an open fire as well as in tandoor. One of the best of these dishes *sajji*, the main ingredient of which is a new born lamb or a sheep, roasted whole.

Another favourite dish is *aloo bukhar gosht*, meat cooked with plums, almonds raisins, onions and green chillies. In thi area, too, *naan* is the bread which is usuall eaten.

The Punjab has always been known as th granary of the subcontinent. Watered b five rivers, the land is fertile and there is a abundance of raw material for food and industry. The rivers provide fish and th land provides, among other things, wheat corn, cotton and pastureland. Sugar-cane i plentiful and there are many varieties o fruit and vegetables.

To Punjabis, rice is a delicacy. They ea all kinds of bread, not only those made in *tandoor*, but also many kinds of *parathas* fried, unleavened bread, corn bread and corn cakes. They use milk in many forms in their dishes.

Yoghourt is beaten with milk and wate and a little salt to make *lassi*, a refreshing drink particularly welcome in the long, ho summer months. In winter, *kanji*, a semi-fermented drink, is made from black carrots.

Mustard greens, *sarson ka sag*, is a favourite vegetable in the Punjab. It is traditionall eaten with *makai ki roti*, a corn bread.

Sind is the home of the Indus Valley civilization. Here there is not only game and meat, but also fish and shellfish, including sole, crab, mussels, oysters, crayfish and pomfret. There are many interesting Sindh dishes. One of the simplest and best is made from *palla*, a local fresh-water fish which has a unique flavour. Rubbed with turmeric, the fish is roasted over an open fire.

Chicken cooked with coriander seeds and tamarind sauce is a delicious change from the usual curry. Another Sindhi speciality is

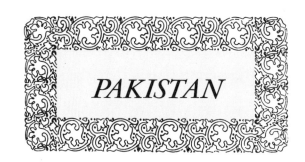

PAKISTAN

kori gosht, saddle of mutton marinated in a mixture of salt, tamarind and yoghourt and roasted slowly over a low flame. Here, too, food is accompanied by *naan*, or *chapatis*, unleavened wholemeal bread.

It is in this area that the famous *Basmati* rice is grown, together with red rice, an indigenous variety which is rich in minerals and vitamins.

In Karachi, Pakistan's major seaport, many cultures meet. The Sind Club, bastion of the old British colonial régime, boasts both a Western and an Oriental menu and offers excellent food. The Boat Club is reminiscent of a prototype on the Thames and provides excellent seafood. Lobster thermidor is a great favourite. It is served with a chilli sauce, which provides a touch of Oriental piquancy. In clubs such as these, in spite of what Rudyard Kipling said, "the twain" have met.

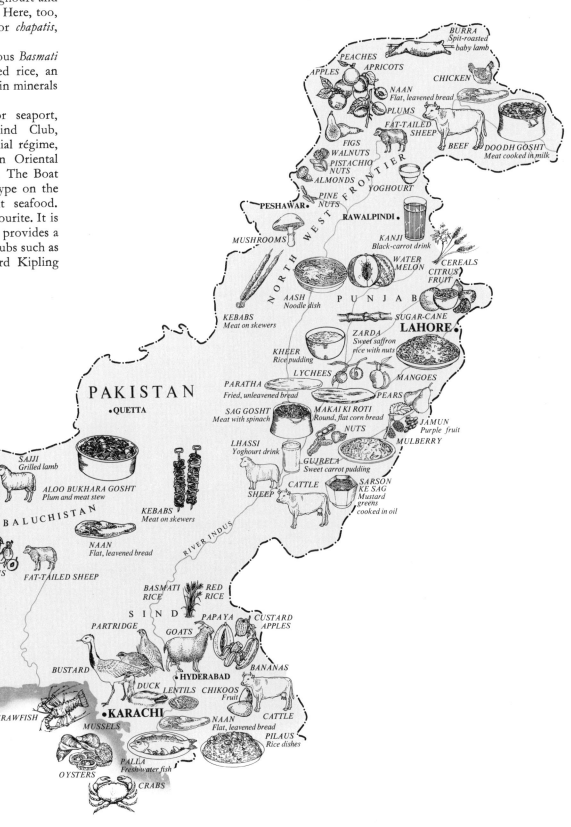

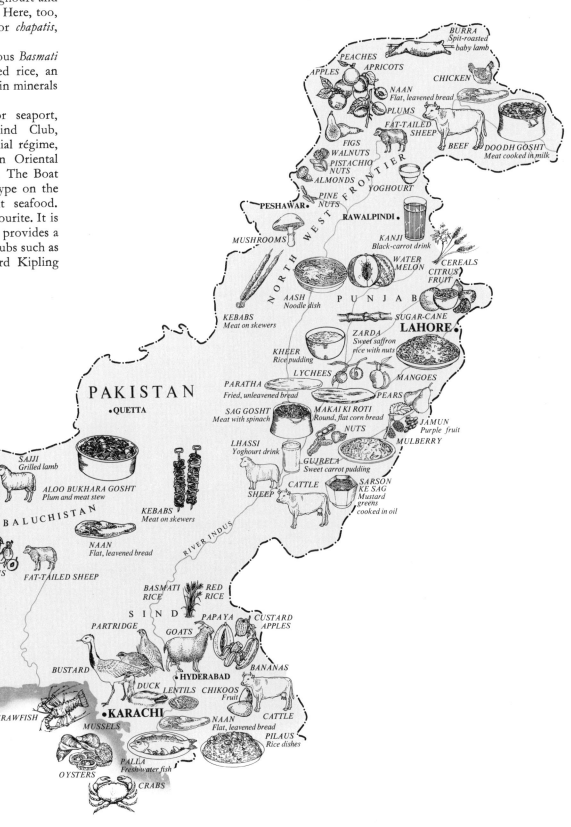

BURRA
Spit-roasted baby lamb

PEACHES
APPLES   APRICOTS
CHICKEN
NAAN
Flat, leavened bread
PLUMS
FAT-TAILED SHEEP
FIGS
WALNUTS   BEEF   DOODH GOSHT
PISTACHIO NUTS   Meat cooked in milk
ALMONDS
PINE NUTS   YOGHOURT
NORTH WEST FRONTIER
PESHAWAR•
RAWALPINDI•
MUSHROOMS
KANJI
Black-carrot drink
WATER MELON   CEREALS
CITRUS FRUIT
AASH
Noodle dish   PUNJAB
KEBABS
Meat on skewers
ZARDA
Sweet saffron rice with nuts
SUGAR-CANE
LAHORE•
KHEER
Rice pudding
LYCHEES   MANGOES
PARATHA
Fried, unleavened bread   PEARS
SAG GOSHT   MAKAI KI ROTI
Meat with spinach   Round, flat corn bread
NUTS   JAMUN
Purple fruit
MULBERRY
LHASSI
Yoghourt drink
GUJRELA
Sweet carrot pudding
CATTLE
SHEEP   SARSON KE SAG
Mustard greens cooked in oil

PAKISTAN
•QUETTA

GRAPES
MELONS
PEACHES
APPLES   BALUCHISTAN
CHERRIES
PLUMS   FAT-TAILED SHEEP
SAJJI
Grilled lamb
ALOO BUKHARA GOSHT
Plum and meat stew
KEBABS
Meat on skewers
NAAN
Flat, leavened bread
RIVER INDUS

BASMATI RICE   RED RICE
SIND   PAPAYA   CUSTARD APPLES
PARTRIDGE   GOATS
BUSTARD   BANANAS
DUCK   LENTILS   CHIKOOS
•HYDERABAD   Fruit
CRAWFISH   •KARACHI   CATTLE
MUSSELS   NAAN
Flat, leavened bread
PALLA   PILAUS
OYSTERS   Fresh-water fish   Rice dishes
CRABS

205

A long tradition of savoury dishes

Chicken Pilaff
MURGH BIRYANI

Biryani *is a dish of Central Asian origin and was a speciality of the North-West Frontier. Today it is a favourite dish all over Pakistan. The secret of a good* biryani *is that both the chicken and the rice are partially cooked before being combined and cooked further.*

SERVES 4 TO 6

RICE

12 oz basmati or other long-grain rice, washed, soaked in cold water for 1 hour and drained
1 oz ghee or melted butter
1 teaspoon salt

CHICKEN

1 large chicken cut into 8 serving pieces *or* 2 small chickens, each cut into 6 serving pieces
5 fl oz yoghourt
1 teaspoon grated onion
1 teaspoon salt
2 medium-sized onions, chopped
2 garlic cloves
2-inch piece fresh root ginger, peeled and chopped
1-inch stick cinnamon
4 cloves
6 whole cardamom pods
½ teaspoon ground mace
1 mint sprig
1 sprig coriander leaves
1 green chilli
3½ oz ghee or melted butter
15 fl oz boiling chicken stock
½ teaspoon saffron threads soaked in .2 tablespoons of boiling water

GARNISH

2 onions, sliced and fried
1 oz shredded almonds, fried until brown
2 hard-boiled eggs, quartered

First parboil the rice. Place the rice, *ghee* or melted butter and salt in a pan with 10 fluid ounces of water and bring to the boil. Reduce the heat to low, cover the pan and cook for 5 minutes. Remove the pan from the heat and set aside.

Place the chicken pieces in a bowl. Mix the yoghourt, grated onion and salt together. Rub the mixture into the chicken pieces and set aside to marinate for 2 hours.

Meanwhile, put the onions, garlic, ginger, cinnamon, cloves, cardamom, mace, mint, coriander leaves and the green chilli into an electric blender. Add 2 or 3 tablespoons of water and blend to a smooth purée.

Heat 1½ ounces of the *ghee* or melted butter in a small frying-pan. Add the spice purée and fry, stirring, for 5 minutes. Remove the pan from the heat and let the mixture cool. When it is cool, stir it into the chicken marinade.

Heat a further 1 ounce of the *ghee* or melted

butter in a large saucepan over high heat. When it is very hot add the chicken and the marinade all at once and fry, stirring constantly, for 20 minutes or until the chicken is half cooked.

Preheat the oven to 350°F (Gas Mark 4). Grease a large casserole with the remaining 1 ounce of *ghee* or melted butter. Beginning and ending with the rice, make layers of the rice and chicken mixture in the casserole. Pour over 8 fluid ounces of the boiling stock. Cover the pan and place it in the oven for 20 minutes. Reduce the heat to 250°F (Gas Mark ½) and continue cooking for 20 minutes. Remove the casserole from the oven. Mix the saffron with the remaining stock and trickle it, through a funnel, into different parts of the *biryani*.

Return the casserole to the oven and continue cooking for a further 20 minutes, or until the ingredients are cooked and all the liquid has been absorbed.

Heap the *biryani* on to a serving platter or silver tray. Garnish with the fried onions, almonds and hard-boiled eggs.

Curried Lamb with Yoghourt
ROGHAN JOSH

This is a Kashmiri dish especially popular in the Punjab and on the Frontier.

SERVES 4

4 oz ghee or melted butter
1 medium-sized onion, finely chopped
2 lb boned lean lamb, cut into ½ × 2-inch pieces
8 fl oz yoghourt
½ teaspoon saffron threads soaked in 2 tablespoons of boiling water for 20 minutes
2 oz slivered almonds, lightly fried

MASALA (SPICE PASTE)

1 large onion, chopped
3 garlic cloves
3-inch piece fresh root ginger, peeled and chopped
1 sprig coriander leaves
1 mint sprig
2 green chillies
½ teaspoon turmeric
1 tablespoon whole coriander seeds
2 teaspoons white poppy seeds
1 teaspoon whole black cumin seeds
4 cloves
½-inch piece cinnamon
Seeds of 6 cardamom pods
24 blanched almonds
1 teaspoon salt

Heat half the *ghee* or melted butter in a large saucepan. Add the onion and fry, stirring occasionally, for 8 minutes, or until it is golden brown. Add the meat and the yoghourt and stir to mix. Cover the pan, reduce the heat to low and simmer the lamb for 20 minutes.

Preheat the oven to 350°F (Gas Mark 4).

Meanwhile prepare the spices. Put all the ingredients for the spice paste into an electric blender. Add 2 tablespoons or more of water or yoghourt and blend until the mixture forms a purée.

Heat the remaining *ghee* or melted butter in a flameproof casserole. Add the spice paste and fry, stirring constantly, for 5 minutes. Add a spoonful of water and stir until the butter is separated from the spices. Add another spoonful of water and fry for a minute. Add the meat and yoghourt mixture and stir to mix. When the mixture comes to the boil cover the pan tightly and place it in the oven. Reduce the heat to 275°F (Gas Mark 1) and cook for 1 hour.

Remove the casserole from the oven. Stir in the saffron and the soaking water and the slivered almonds. Increase the heat of the oven to 300°F (Gas Mark 2) and return the casserole, uncovered, for 30 minutes, or until the lamb is tender. Served hot.

Spicy Meat Patties
CHAPLI KABAB

Another speciality from the northern areas, these kebabs are fried. Serve with naan.

SERVES 2 TO 3

1 lb finely minced meat
1 egg
4 oz bone marrow
2 teaspoons dried pomegranate seeds soaked in 2 tablespoons of boiling water for 20 minutes
1 teaspoon whole coriander seeds
Seeds of 3 cardamom pods
½ teaspoon whole cumin seeds
2 cloves
¼ teaspoon grated nutmeg
6 peppercorns
1 green chilli
Juice of ½ lemon
1 tablespoon melted butter
1 teaspoon salt
2 oz ghee or vegetable oil

GARNISH

1 onion, thinly sliced
½ tablespoon chopped coriander leaves

Combine the meat, egg and bone marrow in a bowl. Pound the pomegranate seeds in a mortar. Place the pounded seeds and the soaking water with all the remaining ingredients except the *ghee* or oil, in an electric blender. Blend at high speed until the mixture forms a purée. Add the spice purée to the meat mixture and mix them well together. Divide the mixture into 6 equal portions. Shape each portion into a pear-shaped patty ¼ inch thick.

Heat the *ghee* or oil in a large frying-pan. Add the patties and fry them, turning them over once or twice, for 10 minutes, or until they are cooked through and nicely browned.

Serve on a heated dish garnished with onion slices and chopped coriander leaves.

Lamb cooked with Yoghourt
MOGHLAI KORMA

Of Moghul origin, this dish is a favourite in most Pakistani homes. Serve with naan, chapatis *or* rice.

SERVES 4

1½ oz ghee or melted butter
3 medium-sized onions, finely sliced
2 lb boned lamb, cut into 2-inch cubes
5 fl oz yoghourt
20 almonds
3 garlic cloves
2-inch piece fresh root ginger, peeled and chopped
1 mint sprig
1 sprig coriander leaves
6 whole cardamom pods
1-inch cinnamon stick
6 peppercorns
1 teaspoon black cumin seeds
½ teaspoon chilli powder
2 teaspoons salt
1 teaspoon sugar
Juice of 1 lemon

Preheat the oven to 350°F (Gas Mark 4).

Heat the *ghee* or butter in a casserole. Add the onions and fry, stirring occasionally, for 8 minutes, or until golden brown. Add the lamb and the yoghourt and cook for 5 minutes.

Meanwhile, put all the remaining ingredients in a blender and blend until the mixture forms a purée. Add the purée to the lamb mixture and cook, stirring, for 5 minutes. Cover the casserole tightly and place it in the oven for 1 hour, or until the lamb is tender.

Spinach and Meat
SAI GOSHT

This is a speciality of Sind which is now cooked all over Pakistan. Although a special red spinach called kulfa *is frequently used for this dish in Pakistan, any variety of spinach will do. This dish can also be made with shrimp or fish.*

SERVES 4

2 lb boned lamb, cut into 1½ × ½-inch pieces
4 oz ghee or melted butter
1 large onion, finely chopped
2 lb spinach, thoroughly washed
8 fl oz yoghourt
MASALA (SPICE PASTE)
1 large onion, chopped
2-inch piece fresh root ginger, peeled and chopped

3 cloves
1 teaspoon whole black cumin seeds
1 teaspoon whole coriander seeds
1 garlic clove
8 peppercorns
½ mint sprig
½ sprig coriander leaves
2 green chillies
1 teaspoon salt

First prepare the spice paste. Put all the ingredients with 1 to 2 tablespoons of water in an electric blender. Blend the ingredients until the mixture forms a purée.

Combine the meat pieces and the spice paste together in a bowl. Set aside. Heat the *ghee* or melted butter in a large saucepan. Add the onion and fry until golden. Add the meat and spice paste and fry, stirring constantly, for 5 minutes. Add the spinach and cook, stirring, for 2 minutes. Stir in the yoghourt. Bring the mixture to the simmer. Cover the pan, reduce the heat to very low and simmer until the meat is very tender and the spinach smooth and velvety.

Cook uncovered for the last 20 minutes if the dish is too liquid.

Stuffed Wholemeal Fried Bread
BHURÉ PARATHES

Typical fare of rural Punjab, stuffed parathas *are a meal in themselves. They are traditionally eaten with yoghourt and freshly churned butter or with an omelette and a large bowl of grated raw vegetables and fruit.*

MAKES 4

DOUGH
8 oz wholemeal flour
½ teaspoon salt
2 oz ghee or melted butter
4 fl oz water
FILLING
1 oz ghee or melted butter
1 medium-sized onion, finely chopped
8 oz finely minced lean meat
1 teaspoon chopped mint
1 teaspoon chopped coriander leaves
1 green chilli, finely chopped
Salt

Put the flour and salt in a bowl. Add half of the *ghee* or melted butter and rub it into the flour. Add just enough of the water to make a smooth dough. Pat the dough into a ball and turn it out on to a lightly floured surface. Knead the dough well for 10 minutes, or until it is smooth and springy. Return the dough to the bowl, cover it and set it aside while the filling is being made.

To make the filling, heat the *ghee* or melted butter in a small frying-pan. Add the onion and fry it, stirring occasionally, until it is golden.

Add the meat, mint, coriander leaves, chilli and salt to taste and fry until the meat is cooked.

Divide the dough into 8 equal pieces. Shape each piece into a ball and then flatten it. Roll it out, on a lightly floured surface, into a thin round about 6 inches in diameter. When all the dough has been rolled out, divide the filling into 4 equal portions. Place a portion of filling on each round of dough. Spread the filling evenly to within ½ inch of the edge. Dampen the edges with water and place another dough round on top, pressing the edges together to seal them.

Lightly grease a heavy frying-pan or griddle with a little of the *ghee* or melted butter. Place the pan over moderate heat and when it is hot put in one *paratha*. Cook it, moving it constantly in the pan with fingertips, for 2 minutes. Turn the *paratha* over and brush it with a little of the *ghee* or melted butter. Cook as before for 2 minutes. Turn the *paratha* over again and brush it with a little more of the *ghee* or melted butter. Continue cooking the *paratha* in this way until it looks somewhat transparent with brown patches. Serve warm.

Vermicelli Dessert
SEVIYAN

This sweet is served in Muslim homes particularly on the day of the Id festival. This is the most important religious festival among Muslims because it marks the end of a month of fasting and prayer—the month of Ramadan. Friends and relatives visit each other wearing new clothes for the occasion, and the young are presented with money by their elders.

SERVES 8 TO 10

4 oz ghee or melted butter
5 cloves
5 whole cardamom pods
1 lb vermicelli
15 fl oz water
8 fl oz milk
8 oz castor sugar
½ teaspoon saffron threads soaked in 2 tablespoons boiling milk for 20 minutes
10 almonds, blanched and slivered
10 pistachio nuts, blanched and sliced

Heat the *ghee* or melted butter in a deep frying-pan. Add the cloves and cardamom pods and fry, stirring occasionally, until the pods puff up. Add the vermicelli and fry, stirring frequently, over low heat until it is a deep golden brown.

Pour in the water and the milk and stir in the sugar and cook, stirring occasionally, until the vermicelli is soft (but not soggy) and all the liquid has been absorbed.

Turn the vermicelli on to a serving dish. Sprinkle the saffron and the soaking milk over the top and garnish with almonds and pistachios.

Food spicy and subtle, varied and exciting

INDIA IS A VAST COUNTRY and food varies from region to region, as strongly influenced by religion and custom as it is by geography. When the Moguls invaded India in the sixteenth century, they brought with them their Central Asian Muslim cuisine, which is based on meat. Their influence was strongest in North and Central India and it is here that meat cooking is at its best. Farther south, where Mogul influence was slight, the cooking is mainly vegetarian, except in those coastal pockets where Christian, Zoroastrian, Jewish and Muslim influence has predominated.

India's regional cooking is also influenced by the staple food of the area. In the North, where wheat grows, the food is dryer and the sauces thicker than in the South, where rice is the staple diet. This is because Indians eat with their fingers, and with the help of a *chapati*, flat, unleavened whole-wheat bread, it is easier to pick up dry food. The more liquid curries are better eaten with rice, which is more absorbent. Climate, too, plays its part and the South, with its heavy rain-all, grows an abundance of vegetables that make the vegetarian cuisine varied and exciting.

Most of India's large population are Hindus. They never eat beef because they regard the cow as sacred. Although the majority is vegetarian, especially those people who are members of the higher castes, there are exceptions. Influenced by long years of Muslim rule, the Brahmans of Kashmir, for example, eat mutton. The Brahmans of Bengal and the Saraswat Brahmans of Mangalore eat fish because it is plentiful, cheap and delicious. Other than the large Muslim minority there are the smaller minority communities, which include the Catholics of Goa, the Syrian Christians of Kerala, the Parsees and Jews of the west coast and the reformed Hindu community of Jains, each with its own distinctive cuisine.

India is the land of home cooking because restaurants are unable to compete with private homes in the quality of the ingredients used and the care taken in the preparation of each dish. Indians, therefore, rarely eat in restaurants and when they do it is to eat food which is not traditionally made at home. Consequently, a visitor to Bombay, for example, interested in tasting authentic local dishes, may very likely find it impossible.

The brightly lit, air-conditioned restaurants in Bombay serve, besides Chinese and European food, the inevitable *tandoori* dishes of the North, while suburban restaurants often serve *idli* and *dosa*, the rice flour breads of the South. To taste the subtly spiced vegetarian food of the Gujeratis, the more robust food of the Maharashtrians and the exciting, spicy Goan or Parsee dishes, one would have to dine at a private home in Bombay.

Prior to India's Independence in 1947, and the industrial and economic expansion which followed, when cities were less crowded and life more leisurely, the average middle-class family not only never ate in a restaurant, they never bought commercially prepared foods. Great pride was taken by the women in making pickles and preserves at home. Spices were ground and mixed in accordance with old family recipes. Wheat for *chapatis* was ground into flour in a *chakki*, two massive stones, one on top of the other, turned by two servants who squatted on the floor facing each other. Butter was churned from rich, creamy, buffalo milk, while *ghee*, clarified butter, the best and

preferred cooking medium, was invariably made in the home.

Today, the wide variety of commercial pickles and chutneys available in Indian shops shows that fewer women have time to make their own. Itinerant spice-grinders stand on street corners pounding spices in giant mortars, throwing the heavy pestle with skill and ease, making passers-by sneeze as the finely powdered spices fly in the air.

The middle-classes have moved from their spacious bungalows into modern flats, and there is no longer space for the grain mill, nor spare hands to turn it. Instead, grain is taken to the neighbourhood mill—a small *kholi*, a room with a motor-driven mill—where, for a penny, it is ground into flour. *Ghee*, when it is used, is now bought at a dairy but, because it is so expensive, most households use the cheaper *vanaspati*, a hydrogenated vegetable fat.

There are, however, some foods, particularly sweets, which have always been bought in the bazaar. Sweets have always held a special place in India's social and religious life. Every joyous occasion—every holiday, every arrival and departure, a new job or baby, an examination passed or a prize won—is celebrated with sweets. Bright yellow, crumbly chick-pea, flour and sugar balls called *ladus*, creamy white, smooth fudge-like *peras*, *halvas* of every kind, some made with milk and vegetables, others with cornflour or semolina, and those syrup-laden, golden pretzel-shaped confections called *jelabies*, are all so delightful to eat and so tedious to make, that most Indians leave the job to the professionals.

The professional sweet-makers, or *halvais* as they are called, keep the secrets of their trade strictly within the family and hand them down from father to son. Although there are many large chains of shops selling sweets which are neatly and hygienically

wrapped in paper or arranged in glittering pyramids behind glass, there are even more small family businesses. These tiny, open-fronted shops look out on busy streets and the *halvai* squats in front, stirring the milk, which simmers in a large, wide-mouthed pan beside him.

Most Indian sweets are made from milk which is simmered until it condenses into a thick mass called *mawa*. The *mawa* is then further cooked with sugar and such flavourings as coconut, almond, pistachio or *kewra*, a perfumed flower essence.

Other milk sweets, and these are more frequently made at home, are known as *kheer*. Semi-liquid, they usually contain rice, ground rice, vermicelli and sago or almonds. *Kheer* is flavoured with cardamom, garnished with nuts and often covered with thin edible silver or gold leaf.

Milk is also made into a cottage cheese called *chenna*. First mixed with a little flour, the *chenna* is shaped into small balls which are then simmered and served in syrup to make *rasgulla*, the most famous of this type of sweet.

There are also sweets which are made not from milk but from wheat flour, *gram* (chick-pea) flour, semolina or cornflour. In this category are jelly-like *Karachi halva*, made from cornflour, and *suji halva*, made from semolina.

Other foods rarely made in an Indian home, and if they are they never taste as exciting, are the spicy, salty, sweet-and-sour snacks sold in special shops or by street-sellers. These snacks may be just hot roasted *channa*, chick-peas, *kurmari*, puffed rice, or the more tasty *panipuri*, little dough puffs filled with a peppery liquid. But best of all is that special and most delicious of all

Offerings of food are made to the Hindu god, Lord Krishna, in this sixteenth-century Mughal painting.

A unique and distinctive vegetarian cuisine

Indian snacks, *bhel-puri*, a mixture of crushed crisp dough puffs, chopped onion, hot chillies, sour-sweet chutneys, potato, lentils, puffed rice and fragrant coriander leaves.

At lunch-time and in the evenings, street-sellers set up their huge baskets of snacks on the pavements. Small earthenware pots containing glowing charcoal keep the chick-peas hot. Old newspaper, cut into rectangles and deftly twisted into cones, is the only wrapping. Gay little stalls with striped awnings are set up in the evenings on Bombay's beaches, where thousands come to stroll and to escape the heat of the city. Most of the stalls serve their specialities on leaves. The more expensive ones, however, provide plastic plates and spoons for those who do not wish to dirty their fingers.

The heart of all Indian cooking is *masala*, the combination of spices and herbs which gives each dish its individuality. It may be a mixture so mild and delicate that a sensitive palate is subtly aware of the different spices, or it may be so strong and sharp that a tiny taste brings tears to the eyes. The ability to mix and choose the correct spices for each dish is the mark of a good cook, to display virtuosity is the sign of a great one.

Today, spices are used mainly for flavouring, but in the old days they were also used as preservatives and for their medicinal properties. Spices are also used to make food more attractive, by providing colour. Turmeric, which makes food yellow, is used to colour rice and such white vegetables as potatoes. Coriander leaves and green chillies make the famous green curries of the South, while red chillies give the Goan curries of the west coast their vivid colour.

Spices are ground on a flat, rectangular stone with a stone rolling pin, or in a circular, shallow, stone mortar. Great care is taken of the stone and it is regularly resurfaced by itinerant stone workers. The high-pitched banging sound of the stone being chipped is one of the earliest memories of an Indian childhood.

Masalas may be either wet or dry. Wet *masalas*, which must be used immediately, are ground with vinegar, water or coconut milk and form the base of all the spicy dishes cooked in the coastal areas of South India. Dry *masalas*, which do not have to be freshly ground each day, are more commonly used in the North.

The combination of spices is endless and each cook follows his own taste and regional preference. There is only one proviso, the end product—the curry, *korma* or *raan*—must be a perfect blend of all the spices, with no one spice so strong as to dominate the dish, unless, of course, the cook particularly wishes it to do so.

Over a hundred spices are known to Indian cooking. Fortunately, most of the important ones are available in the West, in Indian and Pakistani food shops, and in some of the larger supermarkets. The basic spices for making Indian food are: *haldi* (turmeric), a hard yellow root which is ground into powder and, because of its appetizing flavour, can be used alone as well as in combination with other spices and herbs; *zeera* (cumin seed), a sharp-tasting spice which may be bought whole or powdered; *dhanya* (coriander seed), a delightful spice, also available whole or powdered, which adds both flavour and aroma to a dish; *methi* (fenugreek), a powdered seed used in small quantities because of its strong and distinctive flavour; *soonf* (fennel seed), used in cooking and also chewed after meals as a digestive; *kesar* (saffron), the most expensive spice in the world, made from the stamens of the crocus blossom. Several thousand blossoms are used to make an ounce of saffron, but, fortunately, one pinch of good saffron is all that is required to flavour and give aroma to a whole bowl of rice.

Javitri (mace), *jaiphal* (nutmeg), *elaichi* (cardamom), *laung* (clove) and *dalchini* (cinnamon), are also commonly used, as is black, white and red pepper. Additional distinctive flavours are provided by *rai* (mustard seed), *khus khus* (poppy seed), a white variety, not to be confused with the grey-black poppy seeds used in Western cooking, and *til* (sesame seed).

There is also that combination of ground spices called *garam masala*. No two recipes for making it are the same, but it usually contains black pepper, cardamom, cinnamon, clove and cumin seed. *Garam masala* is generally sprinkled over a dish before

AB GOSHT
Lamb cooke[...]

ZARD[...]
Sweet [...]

MAK[...]
Maiz[...]

CHAPATIS
Whole-whea[...]

SARSON KI SAG
Mustard greens

KABLI CHANNA
Whole Bengal bean[...]

M[...]
B[...]

GURDA KORMA
Curried kidneys

TANDOORI [...]
Spiced chicken

KARHI
Yoghourt and chick[...]

SEEKH KABAB
Cigar-shaped minced
meat kebabs

KOFTAS
Spicy meatballs

R A J A S T H A[...]

BAJRA
KA ROTI
Millet bread

MUTTON PULAO
Rice cooked with lamb

BHINDI KH[...]
Okra with mi[...]

RIVER

serving, or stirred in just before the end of the cooking time.

Chillies are essential to most Indian cooking. Green and red when fresh, a brownish-red when dried, they can be mild or fiery hot, and must be used with discretion. The seeds are the most pungent part of the chilli and may be removed and discarded before the chilli is used. Chillies must be handled with care because the juice is strong enough to make the skin tingle and the eyes burn. Hands must be thoroughly washed after handling chillies.

Even more commonly used as flavourings are garlic and onions, which also give body to a dish. Such fresh herbs as *hara dhanya*

(coriander leaves), *pudeena* (mint), *kari patha* (curry leaves) and *tulsi* (sweet basil) are used in many dishes and to make chutneys and sauces.

Besides vinegar and lemon juice, the most commonly used souring agent is *imli* (tamarind). A bean-like seed pod, *imli* is sold dried or in pulp form. Before the pod is used it is soaked in hot water for an hour, strained and the pulp pushed through the strainer. Only the pulpy water is used. The seeds and pod are discarded. *Anardana* (pomegranate seed) and *amchur* (dried mango powder) are also used to add piquancy to Indian food.

There are many kinds of Indian *roti*, or

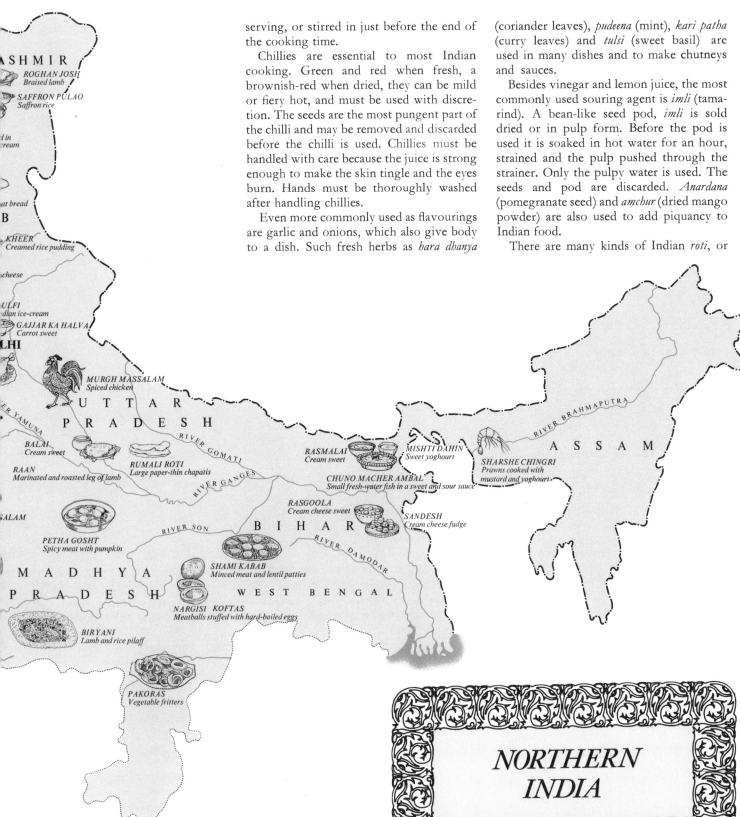

ASHMIR

ROGHAN JOSH
Braised lamb

SAFFRON PULAO
Saffron rice

d in
cream

at bread

B

KHEER
Creamed rice pudding

cheese

ULFI
dian ice-cream

GAJJAR KA HALVA
Carrot sweet

LHI

MURGH MASSALAM
Spiced chicken

U T T A R
P R A D E S H

RIVER YAMUNA

RIVER GOMATI

BALAI
Cream sweet

RUMALI ROTI
Large paper-thin chapatis

RAAN
Marinated and roasted leg of lamb

RIVER GANGES

ALAM

PETHA GOSHT
Spicy meat with pumpkin

RIVER SON

M A D H Y A
P R A D E S H

SHAMI KABAB
Minced meat and lentil patties

B I H A R

RIVER DAMODAR

W E S T   B E N G A L

NARGISI KOFTAS
Meatballs stuffed with hard-boiled eggs

BIRYANI
Lamb and rice pilaff

PAKORAS
Vegetable fritters

RASMALAI
Cream sweet

MISHTI DAHIN
Sweet yoghourt

CHUNO MACHER AMBAL
Small fresh-water fish in a sweet and sour sauce

RASGOOLA
Cream cheese sweet

SANDESH
Cream cheese fudge

RIVER BRAHMAPUTRA

A S S A M

SHARSHE CHINGRI
Prawns cooked with mustard and yoghourt

NORTHERN INDIA

Infinite combinations of herbs and spices

MOTYA
MIRACHANCHI BHAJI
Spiced green peppers

KANTOLI BHAJI
Bitter gourd cooked with spices

MASALA KICHERI
Rice cooked with lentils

• **AHMEDABAD**

KACHURI
Deep-fried pastry with spicy green pea stuffing

G U J A R A T

VALNI DAL
Spiced dried beans

KHANDVI
Chick-pea flour and buttermilk noodles

RIVER NARMADA

M A H A R A S H T R A

JALEBI
Sweets

RIVER MAHANADI

O R I S S A

AKURI
Spicy scrambled eggs

SHRIKHAND
Yoghourt and saffron sweet

SAMOSAS
Stuffed crisp pastry

• **BOMBAY**

BATATA VADA
Potato patties

SHIKAMPURI KABABS
Stuffed meatballs

MASALA MACHEE
Stuffed pomfret

BHELPURI
Sour-sweet snack

SHEERMAL
Thick unleavened bread

NAARHI
Soup made from sheep's trotters

RIVER GODAVARI

DHANSAK
Meat and lentil curry

RIVER BHIMA

HALIM
Wheat, lentils and meat soup

• **HYDERABAD**

A N D H R A   P R A D E S H

MACHEE ACHAR
Fish pickle

SORPATEL
Pork and pig's liver curry

RIVER KRISHNA

STUFFED BANGRA
Small mackerel stuffed with spices and fried

VINDALOO
Vinegar curry

TUNGABHADRA

• **PANJIM**

CASHEW NUT LIQUEUR

GOA

PALM BEER

M Y S O R E

RIVER PENNER

MOLEE
Curry made with fish, meat or poultry and coconut milk

TAYIRCATAM
Rice cooked with yoghourt

RASSAM
Spicy lentil soup

COCONUT RICE

MOOROONGKAI FOOGATH
Drumsticks with spices

APPAM
Rice flour pancakes

BANGALORE

MADRAS •

• **MANGALORE**

KOYKOTAY
Steamed sweet rice flour balls

KUTHERAKAI SAMBAL
Aubergine relish

DOSA
Rice and lentil pancakes

IDLI
Rice and lentil cakes

BANANA CHIPS
Salty, crisp banana wafers

PUTTU
Steamed rice and coconut cakes

T A M I L   N A D U

K E R A L A

RIVER CAUVERY

SAMBAR
Lentils cooked with spices and vegetables

PRAWN AND COCONUT CURRY

TRIVANDRUM •

CENTRAL AND SOUTHERN INDIA

bread. Most are unleavened, are usually made from whole-wheat flour and, with one exception, are round and flat. The most commonly eaten *roti* is the *chapati*.

Some breads are made on a griddle others are stuffed and fried, some are thrown on hot cinders so that they puff up and there are the exceptions, the leavened, flat breads. *Naan*, for example, is a leavened, flat bread made with yeast, or baking powder, and cooked in a *tandoor*, a clay oven. *Paratha* a fried bread, is rolled out and folded a number of times so that when it is cooked it is layered and crisp. It is often stuffed with spicy vegetables or minced meat.

In the North cornmeal is used to make a popular bread called *maki ki roti*, traditionally eaten with mustard greens. Other flours made from millet, barley and chick-peas are

lso used regionally to make *chapatis* of various kinds.

In South India, where rice is the staple food, bread is made from rice flour, and toddy, the fermented juice of coconut palm, is used as leavening.

The long tradition of vegetarianism in India, the abundance and variety of vegetables, the choice of spices and the methods used in cooking have combined to produce a unique and distinctive vegetarian cuisine.

The commonest, simplest and most delicious way of cooking vegetables, known as *bhujia* in the North and *foogath* in the South, is to fry them with spices. There is no sauce and the dish can be surprisingly pungent.

Vegetable curries are made from one or a number of vegetables. A dish of puréed vegetables, delicately spiced, is called *bharta*. Mashed vegetables are shaped into patties or balls, fried and eaten dry or added to a curry sauce. *Sambal*, a South Indian speciality, is a mixture between a relish and a salad and can be served hot or cold. *Raita* is a North Indian salad made from yoghourt to which vegetables or fruit and seasonings are added. It is served as a cooling contrast to hot and spicy dishes.

No Indian meal is complete without a *dhal* of one kind or another. *Dhals*, pulses or lentils, are a tasty and inexpensive source of protein and are the most important part of a vegetarian diet. There are nearly sixty varieties of *dhals* in India. The most common ones, such as *moong*, both green and yellow, *masoor*, Egyptian lentils, and *channa*, split peas, *tur*, pigeon-pea, *lombia*, black-eyed peas and *rajma*, red kidney beans, are all available in the West.

Since the advent of modern methods of egg farming in India, "vegetarian", or unfertilized, eggs are slowly being accepted and eaten by Indian vegetarians.

For those who do eat meat in India, meat usually means mutton. Very little beef is available and pork is eaten mainly by the Christian communities on the west coast.

There are many different ways of cooking meat. Besides curries, there are *kormas*, braised meats that are cooked in yoghurt or cream and sometimes in both. There are kebabs of various kinds and *bhoona*, sautéed and baked meat. *Koftas* are spicy meatballs that may be plain or stuffed and served either dry or in a curry sauce. Roasted meats include those cooked on a spit in a *tandoor*.

Indian chickens, although they are small and scrawny, are very tasty. Indians have

many delicious ways of cooking chicken, from the lightly seasoned dishes of the North to the spicier, coconut-flavoured curries of the South. Chicken cooked in a *tandoor* is a northern dish which is now eaten all over India. The chicken is marinated in spices and yoghourt, threaded on a spit and cooked in a clay oven. The result, a succulent bird with a dry crusty surface, is difficult to achieve in a modern oven.

Duck and goose are also eaten in India, but not as commonly as chicken. Game birds are a delicacy and *teetur*, partridge, is a special favourite.

India boasts a coastline of over two thousand five hundred miles. The Arabian Sea, the Indian Ocean and the Bay of Bengal ride its shores, providing thousands of varieties of fish. It is no wonder, then, that the people of the coastal areas have such a large repertoire of seafood dishes.

Prawns and shrimp, from the smallest and tastiest shrimp to the gigantic prawns which can weigh one pound each, are used in curries, baked with spices or grilled. On the west coast, in Goa and Kerala, they make them into the liveliest of curries. In Bengal they cook them with mustard and yoghourt or coat them in a spicy batter and fry them until crisp. In Bombay, prawns are cooked with onions, tomatoes, green chillies, raw sugar and cumin or they are minced with fresh herbs, mixed with spices and made into patties.

The incomparable Indian pomfret with its fine, firm flesh is cooked in as many ways, too. It is often stuffed with a mixture of onions, coriander leaves, green chillies, garlic and fresh ginger which is fried with a paste made of turmeric, cumin, tamarind and red chillies. The fish is then wrapped in a banana leaf and baked, steamed or fried. The banana leaf imparts an unusual flavour which is lost when foil replaces it in a modern kitchen.

Mention must be made, too, of *bombil*, a fish better known as Bombay Duck. Caught in large quantities, these small almost transparent fish are dried in the sun and provide a cheap form of protein. In the West, Bombay Duck is best known as an accompaniment for curries, but in India it is made into many dishes both in its dried and fresh forms.

In a middle-class Indian home the main meal of the day usually consists of two or three vegetable dishes, one of which will be *dhal*, a meat or a fish dish, if the household is not vegetarian, together with yoghourt, pickles and chutneys. *Chapatis* or rice, sometimes both, are also served. A sweet is often included and eaten with the other dishes, rather than afterwards as is the custom in the West.

All the food is put on the table at the same time. Each person eats what he or she wishes, combining the different dishes to suit individual taste. Generally, the meal is eaten off *thalis*, large, round trays made of brass, stainless steel or, for grand occasions, silver. On the *thalis* are placed a number of small matching bowls called *katoris*. These are filled with the various dishes. The rice is placed in the middle of the *thali* itself, and the chutneys, pickles and such side dishes as *pappadums*, vegetable fritters and fried chillies, to one side.

In South India, banana leaves often replace *thalis*. They are cheap and since each is used but once, hygienic. Even in modern Indian cities, such as Bombay, banana leaves are used, particularly when hundreds of guests have to be served at a wedding banquet or a reception.

In traditional Indian homes, guests and the men of the family eat first, the women later. The food is put on the *thalis* by the woman of the house or by the servants. The diners never help themselves to food because they eat with their fingers, using only the right hand.

No Indian meal is complete without *paan*. *Paan* is *betel* leaf, spread with lime paste and wrapped around chopped *betel* (areca) nut and mixed spices to make a small triangular wad which is chewed as a digestive and mouth freshener. In the old days, the preparation of *paan* after dinner was an elaborate ritual performed by the woman of the house. Today, although it is still frequently prepared by her, it is as often bought already prepared from a shop.

Paan is the perfect ending to a good Indian meal which, well cooked, perfectly balanced and beautifully served, is a pleasurable experience.

A variety of unusual dishes

Spiced Roast Chicken
TANDOORI MURGH

Tandoori *chicken is a North Indian dish, traditionally served, whole or carved, on a bed of thinly sliced onions, tomatoes and chopped, green chillies dressed with lemon juice. Lemon quarters are used as a garnish. In a modern kitchen* tandoori *chicken can be made in the oven or on a revolving spit.*

SERVES 3 TO 4

3 lb chicken, skin removed
½ teaspoon salt
½ teaspoon freshly ground black pepper
½ to 1 teaspoon cayenne pepper
1½ tablespoons lemon juice
MARINADE
3-inch piece fresh root ginger, peeled and chopped
4 garlic cloves
2 teaspoons whole coriander seeds
1 tablespoon whole cumin seeds
2 tablespoons lemon juice
2 tablespoons yoghourt
½ teaspoon cayenne pepper
¾ teaspoon red vegetable colouring
1 oz ghee or melted butter

Wash the chicken thoroughly and pat it dry. Slash the meat on the thighs and breast with a sharp knife. Mix the salt, black pepper, cayenne and the lemon juice together and rub the mixture all over the chicken and into the cuts. Set aside for 30 minutes.

Meanwhile, make the marinade. Place the ginger, garlic, coriander and cumin seeds, lemon juice and yoghourt in the jar of an electric blender. Blend at high speed until the ingredients form a smooth paste. Mix in the cayenne and the food colouring.

Place the chicken in a bowl and coat it with the yoghourt mixture. Cover the bowl and place it in the refrigerator for 24 hours.

Preheat the oven to 400°F (Gas Mark 6).

Place the chicken on a rack in a shallow roasting pan or on the spit. Spoon over any of the juices accumulated in the bowl and the *ghee* or melted butter. Roast for 45 minutes, basting occasionally with the pan juices.

Increase the heat in the oven to 425°F (Gas Mark 7) and, without basting, cook the chicken for a further 10 to 15 minutes. Serve hot.

Fish Coconut Curry
MEEN MOLEE

A molee *is a curry made with partly cooked fish, vegetables or poultry and coconut milk. It is a South Indian dish and is also found in Sri Lanka and Malaya.*

SERVES 4

2 lb thick haddock or cod steaks
1 teaspoon turmeric
1¼ teaspoons salt
2 oz ghee or butter
2 medium-sized onions, finely sliced
4 green chillies, slit lengthwise
½-inch piece fresh root ginger, peeled and finely sliced
8 fl oz thick coconut milk (see page 215)
Juice of 1 lemon

Wash the fish steaks and pat them dry. Rub them all over with the turmeric and 1 teaspoon of the salt.

Heat the *ghee* or butter in a large frying-pan. Add the fish steaks and fry them lightly on both sides. Remove and set aside on a plate.

Add the onions, chillies and ginger to the pan and fry until the onions are golden. Stir in 4 tablespoons of the coconut milk and cook for 1 minute.

Return the fish steaks to the pan and pour over the remaining coconut milk. Bring the mixture to the boil. Cover the pan, reduce the heat to low and simmer the fish steaks for 10 to 15 minutes, or until they are cooked.

Uncover the pan and add the lemon juice. Taste the sauce and add the remaining salt if necessary. Serve hot.

Curried Lamb
KORMA

Constant stirring and careful adjustment of the heat are required during the preliminary frying of the meat with the yoghourt. The mixture must not be allowed to burn, but it must fry. At the end of the cooking time, the sauce must be very thick and the meat very tender. Serve with phulkas.

SERVES 4

2 medium-sized onions
4 garlic cloves
Seeds of 6 cardamom pods
50 almonds
2-inch piece fresh root ginger, peeled and chopped
½ teaspoon cayenne pepper
1 tablespoon whole coriander seeds
1 teaspoon salt
2 lb boned leg of lamb, cut into 1-inch cubes
2 oz ghee or butter
5 fl oz yoghourt
5 fl oz single cream
¼ teaspoon powdered saffron
1 tablespoon chopped coriander leaves

Chop one of the onions and put it into an electric blender with the garlic, cardamom, half the almonds, ginger, cayenne pepper, coriander seeds and salt. Blend at high speed, adding a spoonful or two of cold water, until the ingredients are reduced to a purée.

Place the meat cubes in a bowl and rub the spice purée into them. Cover the bowl and set it aside for 1 hour.

Heat the *ghee* or butter in a heavy casserole. Add the remaining onion, finely sliced, and fry until it is well browned. Add the meat cubes and fry, stirring constantly, until they are browned and dry.

Add 2 tablespoons of the yoghourt and continue frying until it is absorbed. Add the rest of the yoghourt 1 spoonful at a time, allowing the first to be absorbed before adding the next. When all the yoghourt has been added, cover the pan and cook over low heat for 30 minutes, adding a spoonful of water if the meat gets too dry.

Preheat the oven to 300°F (Gas Mark 2). Grind the remaining almonds and mix them with the cream and saffron. Stir this into the meat. Cover and cook gently for 5 minutes.

Place the casserole in the oven for 25 minutes. Garnish with the coriander leaves and serve hot.

Rice

In India there are nearly as many ways of cooking rice as there are varieties of this most subtle of all staple foods. Rice may be boiled, steamed or fried. It may be flavoured with all kinds of herbs and spices, cooked with vegetables and meats and made into *pulaos, biryanis* and *kitcheris*. One of the best varieties of rice for making these dishes, and one that is available in the West, is the delicately flavoured, long-grain *basmati* rice.

To prepare rice for cooking, first pick it over and remove and discard any small stones and husks. Wash it thoroughly under cold running water. When the water runs clear, leave the rice to soak for 30 minutes to 1 hour. Drain well.

BOILED RICE

Bring plenty of salted water to a boil in a large saucepan. Add the rice and, stirring once, boil it for 12 to 15 minutes, or until the grains are tender. Remove the pan from the heat and pour the contents into a colander. Pour over a cup of cold water. This helps to separate the grains. When the rice is thoroughly drained it is ready to serve.

STEAMED RICE

Place the rice and salt in a saucepan. Add enough cold water to cover the rice by a half inch. Bring the water to a boil, cover the pan, reduce the heat to very low and cook for 15 to 20 minutes, or until the rice is cooked and all the water has been absorbed.

Rice may be cooked in advance and reheated just before serving. Reheat cold boiled rice in butter—1 to 1½ ounces of butter is sufficient for 8 ounces of rice. Onions and spices may be added to make the rice savoury. To reheat cold cooked rice another way, bring a saucepan of water to a boil. Add the rice and, when the water comes to a boil again, remove the pan from the heat, drain and serve.

A *pulao* or *biryani* may be reheated in the oven. Cover the dish with aluminium foil or a well-fitting lid and place it in a moderate oven, 350°F, (Gas Mark 4) for 30 minutes.

In India, 8 to 12 ounces of rice is considered enough for an average serving. In the West, 2 to 3 ounces per person is usually sufficient.

Coconut Milk

Coconut milk is an infusion made from grated coconut and hot water. It is an essential ingredient in many Indian dishes and is used, particularly in South India, to flavour and to thicken curries and other dishes. The first infusion is called thick coconut milk and the second, thin coconut milk.

Choose a coconut which is heavy for its size. Shake it. If it is full of liquid it means that it is fresh. Pierce the 3 "eyes" with a skewer. Pour out and discard the liquid. Put the coconut in a fairly hot oven, 375°F (Gas Mark 5), for 15 minutes. Remove the coconut from the oven, and put it on a board or on the floor. While it is still hot, give it a sharp tap with a mallet. The coconut will break in two and the shell will come away from the flesh.

With a sharp parer or knife, remove the brown skin from the white coconut meat. Cut the coconut meat into pieces and grate it into a bowl. Bring water to just under boiling point and pour it over the coconut—1 pint of water is enough to cover the meat of a medium-sized coconut. Set the bowl aside for 30 minutes.

Strain the coconut milk through a strainer lined with cheesecloth or muslin, squeezing the cloth to extract as much "milk" as possible. A second infusion may be extracted in the same way.

If coconuts are not available, coconut milk can be made from commercially prepared creamed coconut. For thick coconut milk, dissolve 3 ounces of creamed coconut in 10 fluid ounces of hot water. For thin coconut milk, halve the amount of creamed coconut.

Yoghourt
DAHIN

Yoghourt, either plain or sweetened, is eaten every day in India. It is used in salads, made into lhassi, *a refreshing drink, used as an ingredient in cooking and as a marinade to tenderize meat. In the tropics, yoghourt sets naturally. In temperate climates it has to be kept warm, from 85°F to 90°F, while it is setting. An electric oven is ideal because it can be set to the correct temperature and is free of draughts and disturbance. Yoghourt will set at lower temperatures but not as well, and it takes a much longer time, sometimes 48 hours or more. Most commercial yoghourts can be used as a "starter". Because they do not all give the same results, some giving a firmer set than others, it is best to experiment until the right one is found.*

MAKES 1 PINT

1 pint homogenized milk
2 heaped teaspoons commercial yoghourt

Bring the milk to boiling point. When it rises in the pan, remove the pan from the heat and place it in a basin, or in the kitchen sink, which is partly filled with cold water. While the milk is cooling, smear the inside of a small bowl with the commercial yoghourt.

When the milk cools to lukewarm (it should feel warm not hot to the touch) pour it into the bowl. Then pour the milk into the pan. Repeat this procedure twice. Stir to mix the milk and the yoghourt thoroughly.

Estimate and set your oven between 85°F and 90°F. Place the bowl in the oven or in a warm place, cover it and leave it undisturbed for at least 6 hours or overnight.

Meatball Curry
KOFTA KARI

This meatball curry should be served with rice and the usual accompaniments of yoghourt, sambals and chutneys. The meatballs may also be served without the curry sauce. They may be added to a plain pulau *as a garnish or added, straight from the frying-pan, to a bowl of cold yoghourt and served with a rice dish or with Indian bread.*

SERVES 4

1½ lb minced meat, lamb or beef
1 medium-sized onion, finely chopped
2 green chillies, finely chopped
1-inch piece fresh root ginger, peeled and
   finely chopped
2 garlic cloves, crushed
1 teaspoon salt
Seeds of 6 cardamom pods, crushed
¼ teaspoon mace
¼ teaspoon black pepper
1½ oz fresh breadcrumbs

1 tablespoon finely chopped mint
6 tablespoons vegetable oil
CURRY SAUCE
4 tablespoons vegetable oil
2 medium-sized onions, finely chopped
2 green chillies, finely chopped
1½-inch piece fresh root ginger, peeled and
   finely chopped
3 garlic cloves, crushed
1 teaspoon turmeric
1 tablespoon ground coriander
1 teaspoon ground cumin
½ teaspoon cayenne pepper
1 teaspoon salt
1 pint thin coconut milk (see above)

Put the meat, onion, chillies, ginger, garlic, salt, cardamom, mace, pepper, breadcrumbs and mint in a large bowl. Knead the ingredients together until they are well mixed. Shape the mixture into small walnut-sized balls.

Heat the oil in a large frying-pan. Add the meatballs and fry them, turning them fre-quently, until they are well browned. Remove the meatballs from the pan and put them aside on a plate covered with kitchen paper.

Now make the curry sauce. Heat the oil in a large saucepan. Add the onions and fry them until they are golden brown. Add the chillies, ginger and garlic and, stirring frequently, fry for 3 minutes.

Mix the turmeric, coriander, cumin, cayenne pepper and salt in a cup with 2 tablespoons of the coconut milk.

Add this spice paste to the pan and fry, stirring well, for 5 minutes. Add a spoonful or two of water if the mixture becomes too dry and begins to stick and burn.

Stir in the remainder of the coconut milk and bring the curry to the boil. Reduce the heat, cover the pan and simmer the curry for 20 minutes. Add a little water if the sauce is too thick.

Add the meatballs and bring back to the simmer. Cover the pan and cook gently for 30 minutes. Taste and season, if required.

A culinary sampling from a vast country

Spiced Lamb Kebabs

BOTI KABABS

Juicy, spicy and tender, these lamb kebabs are the simplest to make. The secret of their succulence lies in the hours of soaking in the yoghourt marinade.

SERVES 4

5 fl oz yoghourt
4 garlic cloves, crushed
1½-inch piece fresh root ginger, peeled and finely chopped
1 tablespoon finely chopped coriander leaves
1 teaspoon ground cumin
1 teaspoon turmeric
1 teaspoon salt
1 teaspoon cayenne pepper
2 lb boned leg or shoulder of lamb, trimmed of fat and cut into 1-inch cubes

GARNISH

Finely sliced onion rings
Lemon quarters

Put the yoghourt into a bowl and beat it well. Mix in the garlic, ginger, coriander leaves, cumin, turmeric, salt and cayenne pepper.

Place the lamb cubes in a large bowl. Pour in the yoghourt mixture and toss the meat cubes in it until they are well coated. Cover the bowl and refrigerate for 24 hours, turning the meat in the marinade 3 or 4 times. Remove the bowl from the refrigerator 1 hour before the kebabs are to be cooked.

Thread the meat on to skewers. Preheat the grill to high. Place the skewers under the heat and cook for 5 minutes. Turn the skewers and cook for a further 4 minutes.

Remove the meat cubes from the skewers and pile them on to a serving dish. Garnish with the onion rings and lemon quarters.

Chicken Cooked with Yoghourt

DAHI MURGHI

This mildly spiced North Indian chicken dish is served with naan.

SERVES 4

4 lb chicken, skin removed and cut into serving pieces
10 fl oz yoghourt
1 teaspoon salt
1½-inch piece fresh root ginger, peeled and grated
2 green chillies, seeded and finely chopped
6 garlic cloves, crushed
2 oz ghee or butter
1 tablespoon chopped chives

Prick the chicken pieces all over with a fork and place them in a bowl. Mix the yoghourt, salt, ginger, green chillies and garlic together. Pour the marinade over the chicken pieces, then toss them in the mixture until they are well coated. Set aside for 4 hours.

Heat half the *ghee* or butter in a large saucepan. When the *ghee* is very hot add the chicken pieces and the marinade. Stirring constantly, cook the chicken pieces, uncovered, until they are tender and most of the marinade has evaporated.

Meanwhile, in a small frying-pan, heat the remaining *ghee* or butter. Add the chives and fry them for 2 minutes. Pour over the chicken pieces, gently turning them in the sauce.

Chicken Pilaff

MURGHI PULAO

This is a Muslim-influenced North Indian dish of rice cooked with subtly-spiced chicken. It may be served with a curry or alone with chutney and a raita.

SERVES 4 TO 6

2 oz butter
2 medium-sized onions, finely chopped
1-inch piece fresh root ginger, peeled and finely chopped
2 garlic cloves, crushed
3 lb chicken, cut into serving pieces
½ teaspoon cayenne pepper
2 teaspoons ground coriander seeds
5 fl oz yoghourt
1 teaspoon salt
½ teaspoon black pepper
Seeds of 6 cardamom pods, crushed
1-inch stick of cinnamon
6 cloves
12 oz long-grain rice, washed, soaked in cold water for 1 hour and drained
¼ teaspoon saffron, soaked in 2 tablespoons of boiling water for 10 minutes
1 pint chicken stock

GARNISH

2 tablespoons oil
1 large onion, sliced
3 tablespoons raisins
3 tablespoons blanched, slivered almonds
2 hard-boiled eggs, quartered

Melt the butter in a large flameproof casserole. Add the onions and fry them, stirring occasionally, until they are golden brown. Add the ginger and garlic and fry for 2 minutes. Add the chicken pieces and fry, turning frequently, until they are lightly browned. Stir in the cayenne pepper and the coriander and cook for a minute. Stir in the yoghourt and salt and cook the chicken pieces, uncovered, over low heat, for about 40 minutes, or until they are tender and all the moisture has evaporated.

Preheat the oven to 300°F (Gas Mark 2).

Stir in the black pepper, cardamom, cinnamon and cloves. Increase the heat to moderate, add the rice and fry, stirring constantly, for 5 minutes. Stir in the saffron and the water in which it has been soaking. Pour in enough of the stock to cover the rice by a half inch. Bring the liquid to the boil, cover the pan and cook over a very low heat for 15 to 20 minutes, or until the rice is cooked and all the liquid has been absorbed.

Place the casserole in the oven for 15 minutes.

While the *pulao* is in the oven, prepare the garnish. Heat the oil in a small frying-pan and fry the onions, raisins and almonds until the onions and almonds are brown.

Serve the rice from the casserole or spoon it on to a large platter. Arrange the egg quarters on top and scatter the fried onions, raisins and almonds over the top.

Stuffed Herrings

MASALA BANGRA

Although bangra *belongs to the mackerel family, it is more like a herring in shape and size. This is the way it is prepared in Bombay and Goa.*

SERVES 4

4 herrings, cleaned and gutted, but with heads and tails left on
3 tablespoons lemon juice
1½ teaspoons salt
1½-inch piece fresh root ginger, peeled and finely chopped or grated
4 garlic cloves, crushed
1 teaspoon turmeric
1 teaspoon cayenne pepper
¼ teaspoon ground fenugreek
1 tablespoon ground coriander
1 tablespoon finely chopped coriander leaves
2 tablespoons vegetable oil
2 medium-sized onions, finely chopped

GARNISH

Lemon quarters

Wash and dry the herrings. Sprinkle 1 tablespoon of the lemon juice and half the salt inside the fish and set aside for 30 minutes.

Meanwhile, mix the ginger, garlic, turmeric, cayenne pepper, fenugreek, coriander, coriander leaves, the remaining salt and lemon juice together to make a paste.

Heat the oil in a frying-pan. Add the onions and fry until golden brown. Add the spice paste and fry, stirring, for 5 minutes, or until the mixture is thick and smooth. Remove the pan from the heat. Spread equal amounts of the spice mixture inside the fish.

Preheat the grill to high. Place the fish on a rack in the grilling pan and grill the fish for 4 to 5 minutes on each side or until they are cooked. Garnish with lemon quarters and serve.

Duck Curry

VATHOO KARI

This is a duck curry from South India that should be served with plain boiled rice. Accompaniments may include poppadums, *chutneys and* sambals.

SERVES 3 TO 4

tablespoons ghee or butter
medium-sized onions, finely chopped
garlic cloves, crushed
-inch piece fresh root ginger, peeled and
  finely chopped
teaspoons turmeric
teaspoons ground coriander
teaspoon ground cumin
to 1 teaspoon cayenne pepper
teaspoon ground fenugreek
pint thin coconut milk (see page 215)
large duck, skin removed and cut into
  serving pieces
teaspoon salt
green chillies, slit lengthways
juice of ½ lemon

Heat the *ghee* or butter in a large saucepan. Add the onions, garlic and ginger and fry, stirring, until the onions are golden.

Mix the turmeric, coriander, cumin, cayenne pepper and fenugreek to a paste with a little of the coconut milk. Add the paste to the pan and fry, stirring, for 8 minutes. Add a little water to the pan if the mixture gets too dry.

Add the duck pieces and fry them, turning them frequently, for 8 minutes. Pour in the coconut milk and add the salt and chillies. Bring the curry to the boil. Cover the pan, reduce the heat to low and simmer until the duck is tender. Stir in the lemon juice and adjust the seasoning.

Egg Curry

ANDA KARI

This is a simple, easily made curry using creamed coconut instead of the purée of fresh coconut that is used in India. Serve the curry with steamed or boiled rice, poppadums, chutneys *and* raita.

SERVES 4

tablespoons vegetable oil
medium-sized onions, finely chopped
-inch piece fresh root ginger, peeled and
  finely chopped
garlic cloves, crushed
teaspoon turmeric
teaspoon ground cumin
teaspoons ground coriander
teaspoon cayenne pepper
teaspoon ground fennel seeds
tablespoon finely chopped coriander leaves
lb tomatoes, blanched, peeled and chopped
teaspoon salt
teaspoon sugar
-inch slice creamed coconut
hard-boiled eggs, cut in halves lengthways
tablespoon lemon juice

Heat the oil in a large saucepan. Add the onions, ginger and garlic and fry until golden brown.

Add the turmeric, cumin, coriander, cayenne pepper and fennel seeds and fry, stirring, for 8 minutes, adding a spoonful or two of water if the spices get too dry. Add the coriander leaves, tomatoes, salt and sugar and bring to the boil. Reduce the heat to low, cover the pan and simmer for 30 minutes.

Stir in the creamed coconut and when it has dissolved add the eggs. Simmer, covered, for 20 minutes. Stir in the lemon juice. Taste and adjust the seasoning. Serve hot.

Potatoes and Spinach

ALU SAGH

Spinach is a favourite vegetable in India, and many varieties are available, each with a distinctive flavour. The following is one of the simplest, but nevertheless, most tasty, ways of cooking spinach. The potatoes may be omitted if preferred.

SERVES 4

2 lb spinach
1½ teaspoons salt
2 oz ghee or butter
2 medium-sized onions, finely sliced
1-inch piece fresh root ginger, peeled and
  cut into thin strips
2 green chillies, finely chopped
1 teaspoon turmeric
1 lb potatoes, peeled and cut into even-sized
  pieces

Wash the spinach thoroughly. Place the spinach and half the salt in a large saucepan. Cook the spinach over high heat for 1 minute, stirring constantly. Reduce the heat to moderate and continue cooking for 5 minutes. Remove the spinach from the pan and drain it. Place it on a board and chop it coarsely.

Heat the *ghee* or butter in a large saucepan. Add the onions, ginger and chillies and fry, stirring, until the onions are golden. Stir in the turmeric and add the potatoes. Reduce the heat to low, cover the pan and cook until the potatoes

are just tender. Add the spinach, increase the heat to moderate and cook, stirring, for 5 minutes, or until all the excess moisture has evaporated. Serve hot.

Moong Lentils

MOONG KI DHAL

There are many ways of cooking dhal, *some taking hours of slow cooking. This is a fairly quick recipe.*

SERVES 4

8 oz yellow *moong dhal*
1 teaspoon turmeric
1 teaspoon salt
2 green chillies, slit lengthways
2 oz ghee or butter
1 teaspoon mustard seeds
1 medium-sized onion, finely sliced
1 garlic clove, finely sliced
½ teaspoon cayenne pepper

Wash the *dhal* thoroughly in cold running water. When the water runs clear, set the *dhal* aside to soak for 4 hours.

Drain the *dhal* and put in a saucepan with the turmeric, salt and green chillies. Add enough water to cover the *dhal* by 1 inch and bring to the boil. Partly cover the pan, reduce the heat to low and simmer for 1 hour, or until the water has been absorbed and the *dhal* is tender but not a mush. Add more water if necessary.

Meanwhile, heat the *ghee* or butter in a frying-pan. Add the mustard seeds and cover the pan. Fry for 2 minutes. Uncover the pan and add the onions and garlic and fry until golden. Stir in the cayenne pepper and cook for 30 seconds. Add the entire contents of the frying-pan to the *dhal*. Stir and cook for 2 minutes. Serve hot.

Innumerable kinds of unusual and delicious vegetables and fruits make India's vegetarian cuisine varied and exciting. Here a proud merchant sits amid his colourful display of fresh fruit, vegetables and nuts.

Relishes, chutneys and breads

All over India, *paanwallahs* sell their wares from open stalls. *Paan*, a mixture of betel nuts, leaves and spices, is chewed after meals as a digestive.

Aubergine Purée
BAINGAN BHARTA

Bharta can be made with any vegetable but the most common and best is made with aubergines.

SERVES 4

3 lb aubergines
3 oz ghee or butter
2 medium-sized onions, finely chopped
2 garlic cloves, crushed
1½-inch piece fresh root ginger, peeled and finely chopped
1 green chilli, finely chopped
1 tablespoon ground coriander
1 teaspoon turmeric
½ teaspoon chilli powder
3 tablespoons chopped coriander leaves
1 teaspoon salt
1 teaspoon garam masala (see page 214)
Juice of ½ lemon

Preheat the oven to 350°F (Gas Mark 4) or preheat the grill to high. Wash the aubergines and dry them. Gash them in several places and put them in a baking dish. Cover the dish with foil and place it in the oven for 1 hour. Alternatively, put the aubergines under a hot grill and, turning frequently, grill for 10 minutes, or until the outer skin is charred and the pulp soft.

When the aubergines are cool enough to handle, cut them in half and spoon out the pulp. Chop the pulp and set aside. Discard the skins.

Heat the *ghee*, or butter, in a large saucepan. Add the onions, garlic, ginger and chilli and fry, stirring, until golden. Add the ground coriander, turmeric and chilli powder and cook, stirring, for 2 minutes.

Add the aubergine pulp, 2 tablespoons of the coriander leaves and the salt. Cook until the mixture is thick and comes away from the sides of the pan.

Stir in the *garam masala* and the lemon juice. Taste the *bharta* and add more seasoning if required. Serve garnished with the remaining coriander leaves.

Rice and Lentils
KITCHERI

Kitcheri is a mixture of rice and lentils cooked with butter—a dish commonly eaten in most of India. The proportion of lentils to rice may vary from equal quantities to one part lentils to four parts rice.

SERVES 4 TO 6

8 oz long-grain rice
8 oz Egyptian lentils
4 oz butter
2 medium-sized onions, finely chopped
½-inch piece fresh root ginger, peeled and finely chopped
1 garlic clove, crushed
1 teaspoon salt
1 teaspoon turmeric
Boiling water
2 tablespoons milk
GARNISH
1 large onion, sliced and fried until golden brown

Wash the rice and the lentils together in cold running water. When the water runs clear, leave them to soak for 1 hour.

Melt the butter in a large saucepan. Add the onions, ginger and garlic and fry, stirring occasionally, until the onions are golden. Drain the rice and lentils thoroughly. Add them to the pan and fry gently, stirring constantly, for 2 minutes. Add the salt and turmeric, toss the mixture lightly to mix and cook for 5 minutes.

Pour in enough boiling water to cover the rice and lentils by a half inch. When the water bubbles vigorously, cover the pan, reduce the heat to very low and cook the *kitcheri* for 15 to 20 minutes, or until the rice and lentils are cooked and all the water has been absorbed.

Spoon the *kitcheri* on to a heated serving dish. Sprinkle the milk on top. Garnish with the fried onions and serve.

Potatoes Cooked with Yoghourt
DAHIN ALOO

A mixture of sweetness, sourness and spiciness makes this North Indian dish unusually tasty. In some recipes the potatoes are fried after being boiled and before they are added to the other ingredients.

SERVES 4 TO 6

3 tablespoons ghee or vegetable oil
1 medium-sized onion, finely chopped
1-inch piece fresh root ginger, peeled and finely chopped
1 tablespoon ground coriander
1 teaspoon turmeric
2 green chillies, finely chopped
3 medium-sized tomatoes, blanched, peeled and chopped
1 teaspoon salt
1 teaspoon sugar
10 fl oz yoghourt
¼ teaspoon ground mace
4 tablespoons raisins
1½ lb small new potatoes, boiled
1 tablespoon chopped coriander leaves

Heat the *ghee* or oil in a large frying-pan. Add the onion and ginger and fry until golden. Add the coriander and turmeric and fry, stirring constantly, for 30 seconds. Stir in the chillies, tomatoes, salt, sugar and yoghourt. Simmer the sauce, uncovered, until it is thick.

Add the mace, raisins and potatoes and cook, stirring, for 5 minutes.

Turn the potatoes out on to a serving dish, sprinkle the coriander leaves on top and serve hot.

Chutneys
Chutneys are as common a part of an Indian meal as salt and pepper.

Tomato Chutney
TAMATAR CHATNI

MAKES ABOUT 1½ LB

1 lb tomatoes, blanched, peeled and chopped or 1 lb canned peeled tomatoes, undrained
1 medium-sized onion, finely chopped
1-inch piece fresh root ginger, finely chopped
4 oz stoned dates
4 oz raisins
4 oz currants
1 teaspoon chilli powder
1 teaspoon salt
4 tablespoons vegetable oil
1 teaspoon mustard seeds

Place all the ingredients except the oil and mustard seeds in a saucepan and bring to the boil, stirring occasionally. Reduce the heat and simmer, uncovered, for 1½ to 2 hours, or until the chutney is thick.

Meanwhile, heat the oil in a small frying-pan. Add the mustard seeds and fry, covered, until they stop popping. Remove the pan from the heat and tip the contents into the saucepan with the chutney. Stir to mix.

Taste the chutney and add more seasoning, if required. Serve cool or cold.

Fresh Coriander Chutney
HARA DHANYA CHATNI

2 heaped tablespoons desiccated coconut
5 fl oz yoghourt
1 bunch coriander leaves and half the stalks
2 green chillies
1 teaspoon salt
1 teaspoon sugar
4 tablespoons lemon juice

Mix the desiccated coconut with the yoghourt and set aside for 1 hour.

Place the yoghourt mixture, coriander leaves and stalks, chillies, salt, sugar and lemon juice in an electric blender. Blend at high speed until the ingredients are puréed. Add more lemon juice, if necessary, to make the purée smooth. Taste the chutney and adjust the seasoning.

Place the chutney in a small bowl and chill.

Onion and Tomato Relish
PEAZ AUR TAMATAR SAMBAL

Sambals *are relishes, usually served cold and, sometimes, hot. They originated in South India.*

SERVES 4

2 medium-sized tomatoes, chopped
1 medium-sized onion, finely chopped
1 green chilli, finely chopped
1 tablespoon chopped coriander leaves
½ teaspoon salt
¼ teaspoon freshly ground black pepper
½ teaspoon sugar
2 tablespoons lemon juice
1 tablespoon freshly grated coconut

Combine the tomatoes, onion, green chilli, coriander leaves, salt, pepper, sugar and lemon juice in a shallow serving bowl. Sprinkle the coconut over the top. Chill thoroughly.

Yoghourt Salad
KHEERA KA RAITA

Usually served as accompaniments, raitas *are cool and fresh tasting and contrast well with pungent and heavily spiced dishes.*

SERVES 4 TO 6

½ cucumber, sliced, unpeeled
2 teaspoons salt
6 spring onions, finely sliced
15 fl oz yoghourt
½ teaspoon freshly ground black pepper
½ teaspoon paprika

Put the cucumber slices in a colander. Sprinkle with 2 teaspoons of salt. Put a plate on top and leave for 30 minutes. Rinse the cucumber slices and pat dry. Mix all the ingredients except the paprika in a bowl. Refrigerate for at least 2 hours. Sprinkle with the paprika and serve.

Whole-Wheat Unleavened Bread
PHULKAS AND CHAPATIS

Phulkas *are small, thin and pancake-like. They are made to puff up in the last stages of cooking. In India, they are thrown on hot cinders to puff up.* Chapatis *are made from the same dough, but are larger, thicker and flat.*

MAKES 12 PHULKAS

8 oz whole-wheat flour
¼ teaspoon salt
6 fl oz water

Put the flour and salt into a bowl. Make a well in the centre and pour in half the water. With your hands, mix the water into the flour to make a dough. If the mixture seems too dry, add more water. Pat the dough into a ball.

Turn the dough out on to a lightly floured surface and knead it for 10 to 15 minutes, or until it is smooth and elastic. Cover the dough with a damp cloth and set it aside for 30 minutes.

Knead the dough again for 5 minutes, then divide it into 12 pieces. Shape each piece into a ball. Flatten the ball slightly and roll it out on a lightly floured surface into a round about 5 inches in diameter.

Heat a lightly greased, heavy frying-pan or griddle. Place a dough round on the pan or griddle and cook it, rotating it with your fingertips, for 1½ to 2 minutes, or until bubbles appear on the top. Turn the dough round over the cook, rotating it, for 1 minute, or until brown spots appear on the underside.

Remove the dough round with a perforated spatula and hold it over the open flame until it puffs up. If the hob is electric, turn the dough round over on the griddle and, with folded kitchen paper or a cloth, press it down firmly. The *phulka* will puff up when the pressure is released. Serve hot.

Deep-Fried Bread
PURIS

Puris *are the light, puffed bread of North and Central India, usually made with whole-wheat flour.*

MAKES 16 PURIS

8 oz whole-wheat flour
¼ teaspoon salt
2 tablespoons ghee or melted butter
4 fl oz warm water
Vegetable oil for deep-frying

Put the flour and salt into a bowl. Add the *ghee*, or melted butter, and rub it into the flour. Make a well in the centre and pour in half the water. With your hands, mix the water into the flour to make dough. If the dough seems too dry, add more water.

Pat the dough into a ball and turn it out on to a lightly floured surface. Knead the dough for 10 to 15 minutes, or until it is smooth and elastic. Cover the dough with a damp cloth and set it aside for 30 minutes. Divide the dough into 16 equal portions. Shape each portion into a ball, flatten slightly and roll out to a round 3½ inches in diameter.

Heat the vegetable oil in a deep frying-pan until the temperature registers 360°F on a deep-frying thermometer. Fry the dough rounds one at a time. Press down on the *puri* with the back of a slotted spoon. Turn the *puri* over and press it down again. Fry it for a few seconds, or until the *puri* puffs up and is a pale golden colour.

Drain the *puris* as they fry and serve warm.

Flat Leavened Bread
NAANS

Traditionally cooked in a tandoor, a large clay oven, this North Indian bread gets its teardrop shape from being stuck on the wall of the oven and stretching while it cooks.

MAKES 4 NAANS

8 oz plain flour
¼ teaspoon salt
1 teaspoon sugar
1 teaspoon baking powder
½ teaspoon bicarbonate of soda
1 egg
4 tablespoons yoghourt
5 tablespoons milk
1 tablespoon sesame seeds
4 tablespoons ghee or melted butter

Sift the flour, salt, sugar, baking powder and bicarbonate into a bowl. In another bowl mix together the egg, yoghourt, 4 tablespoons of the milk and half the *ghee* or melted butter.

Make a well in the centre of the flour mixture. Pour in the liquid mixture and work into the flour until the mixture forms a dough. Knead the dough on a lightly floured surface for 15 minutes, or until it is smooth and elastic. Dust with flour if the dough is sticky. Pat the dough into a ball and put it into a bowl. Cover the bowl with a damp cloth and set it aside in a warm, draught-free place for 3 hours.

With floured hands, divide the dough into 4 equal pieces. Shape them into balls. Flatten the balls and then pat and pull them into flat oval shapes about 6 inches long.

Preheat the oven to very hot, 450°F (Gas Mark 8). Brush one side of the *naans* with the remaining *ghee* or melted butter and the other side with the remaining milk. Sprinkle the sesame seeds over the *naans*. Place the *naans* on baking sheets and bake for 5 minutes or until they are golden and firm to the touch. Remove from the oven, turn the *naans* over and brown them under a hot grill.

Serve hot.

The unusual food of four countries

THE FOOD OF INDOCHINA is as diverse as the people. Composed of North and South Vietnam, Cambodia and Laos, Indochina is set in the southeastern corner of Asia, overshadowed by China to the north, bordered by Thailand and Burma to the west, with the South China Sea to the east and the south. Besides the Vietnamese, Khmers (Cambodians) and Laotians, Indochina is the home of Montagnards, Chams, Meos and numerous other tribes, and substantial numbers of Chinese, Thais and French.

Although other Oriental countries have figured prominently in cook books for many years, Indochina has been largely ignored. The reason for this lies in the idea that Indochina, a melting-pot for so many different cultures, lacks a specific cuisine of its own. Yet its four countries have developed along separate paths, with their own modifications to external influences.

Vietnam has been strongly influenced by China, by whom it was invaded and occupied for nearly ten centuries. Chinese food is, however, heavier and greasier than Vietnamese, and nuoc-mam, the Vietnamese fish sauce, is the salient feature of the cuisine. Laotian and Cambodian food has followed a Thai tradition, while a Malaysian influence can be detected in Cambodia. Both Laos and Cambodia are renowned for hot, dry curries eaten with small, thin, pungent chillies. Garlic and herbs also predominate. In Laos, food is frequently eaten raw. The Laotians, like the Indians, eat with their hands, while the Vietnamese and Khmers use chopsticks and spoons.

The French colonized Indochina for nearly a century and in that time the people came to savour French cuisine, but due to its different style, French cooking had little influence on traditional Indochinese food.

The staple food in Indochina is rice. It is eaten every day, at every meal and is made into desserts, cakes and vermicelli; it is also flattened into rice paper and distilled into alcohol.

Plain, boiled rice is given variety and flavour by the nutritious nuoc-mam, or fish sauce, which is the Indochinese equivalent of salt in the West or soy sauce in China.

Nuoc-mam is made commercially by fermenting fish with salt and filtering the liquid several times; this process can take up to ten years.

Nuoc-mam *is prepared for the table by mixing 4 tablespoons of* nuoc-mam, *or fish sauce, with a small quantity of hot chillies, 2 tablespoons of water, 1 tablespoon of vinegar, a little sugar and garlic and mixing all the ingredients together well.*

Indochinese cooking is time consuming. Garlic and chillies are pounded in a stone mortar, fennel leaves, ginger, basil, shallots are chopped into fine pieces and dried mushrooms and lily flowers are soaked before they are used. Salt, pepper, sugar, pimentos, lemon juice and nuoc-mam are added in varying quantities.

Dishes are served simultaneously, as in China, although soup is often served as a one-dish meal. A rich noodle soup from North Vietnam, pho is a substantial meal in itself.

To make pho *to serve 8, first prepare the stock. Put 2 pounds of beef shin, 1 large marrow bone, 2 large onions, cut in half, a small piece of star anise and a 2-inch piece of peeled, fresh root ginger in a large saucepan or casserole. Add 6½ pints of water and bring to the boil, skimming off the scum as it rises. Cover the pan, reduce the heat to low and simmer the stock for 3 hours. Strain the stock and skim off the fat.*

Meanwhile, boil 2 pounds of dried rice noodles for 5 minutes in salted water. Drain them well and place them in 8 large soup bowls. Finely shred 1 pound of rump steak and scatter a layer on top of the noodles along with 2 finely chopped shallots and a little Vietnamese mint, if available.

Pour the strained stock into a saucepan and bring it to the boil. Stir in a pinch of monosodium glutamate and 3 tablespoons of nuoc-mam. *Pour the stock over the meat and noodles, squeeze a few drops of lemon juice into each bowl and serve.*

Soup is also regarded as a breakfast dish, like the Cambodian soupe chinoise. One of the ingredients used in many soups is citronella or lemon grass, a foot-high grass which, in Cambodia, is grown by every family in a large plant pot. The white stem at the base, chopped like a spring onion, gives a cool, refreshing flavour to spicy soups and hot curries. The green leaves are used by the Khmers to make a kind of tangy tea.

Indochinese cooking differs from region to region. Laos can be divided at Luang Prabang, the royal city. To the north, glutinous rice is preferred to the dry, long-grain rice of the south, and sugar is omitted from the cooking. Ingredients in the north are cooked before adding nuoc-mam, while in the south the sauce is mixed during cooking, giving the dishes a darker colour and more uniform taste.

The Montagnards, who live in the highlands of North and South Vietnam, use salt, rather than nuoc-mam. They grow hill rice or dry rice by the slash and burn method. Areas are cleared for rice planting by burning and are subsequently deserted when the soil is depleted of its minerals. Half of the rice crop is devoted to rice wine, which is kept in large earthenware jars and drunk through hollow bamboo straws. The Montagnards cook rice by filling a piece of bamboo with rice and water, sealing the ends of it with leaves and mud and cooking it under hot cinders. Meat and fish, first wrapped in banana leaves, are cooked in the same way.

In Vientiane, the Laotian capital, ants' eggs, stuffed frogs and a well-reputed Lao caviar are specialities. Less unusual, but delicious is khao poun, the Lao national dish, which is made of vermicelli and vegetables with a spicy fish or chicken stock.

In Phnom Penh, the capital of Cambodia, a speciality is phoat khsat, royal rice, a tasty mixture of chicken, pork, crayfish and rice.

To make phoat khsat *to serve 6, fry 10 finely chopped shallots, 10 crushed garlic cloves and 2 finely chopped fennel sprigs in 6 tablespoons of peanut oil until the shallots are golden. Add 6 ounces each of diced chicken, pork and crayfish and fry, stirring, until the meats are cooked. Stir in 1¼ pounds of boiled rice and 1 tablespoon of dried shrimp. Fry, stirring, until all the ingredients are well mixed and the rice is heated through. Stir in 1 tablespoon of vinegar, and* nuoc-mam, *salt, pepper and sugar to taste. Garnish the rice with a shredded flat omelette made with 1 egg, and a finely sliced green pepper. Sprinkle with the juice of 1 lemon before serving.*

Another popular Khmer dish is a dessert made from black rice, a black glutinous grain found near Battambang and Kompong Cham, which is mixed with coconut milk, jasmine flowers, honey and sugar.

In Saigon and Hanoi there is a great variety of shellfish—succulent lobsters, crayfish, crabs and mouth-watering king prawns from the South China Sea. Bun-bo is a delightful South Vietnamese dish of beef and noodles with cucumber and peanuts.

To make bun-bo *to serve 4, first prepare all the ingredients: cut 2 pounds of frying steak into*

INDOCHINA

strips, crush 3 ounces of roasted peanuts, dice 1 cucumber, finely slice 2 medium-sized onions. Boil 1 pound of rice vermicelli for 5 minutes. Place the pan under cold running water for a second then drain thoroughly.

Arrange the vermicelli in 6 small bowls, and keep hot. Fry the onions in 2 tablespoons of peanut oil until they are golden. Add the beef and salt and pepper to taste. Fry, stirring for a few minutes, until the beef is cooked. Put the diced cucumber over the vermicelli. Arrange the beef and onions over the cucumber and sprinkle a generous layer of crushed peanuts on top. Serve with nuoc-mam.

Food has always held an important place in the history of Vietnam. Ancient literature describes the banquets given in honour of the Vietnamese envoys to the Chinese courts in the early centuries AD. Traditionally, the Emperor of Vietnam savoured "the eight delicacies" of peacock pie, phoenix pie, rhinoceros skin, bear paws, deer tendons, orangoutang lips, elephant soles, and swallows' nests. These delicacies, most of which are no longer attainable, were held to have great medicinal value. Rhinoceros skin was said to ward off rheumatism, and bear paws were remedial for the aged.

Swallows' nests are, however, still used to make soup. The best nests are found on the islands off South Vietnam near Nha Trang. The swallows produce a gelatinous saliva string with which they bind their nests. The best strings are red, but the more common ones are translucent white. The nests are cleaned by a lengthy procedure. First, they are submerged in hot water and after a few hours, when they have begun to unravel, a small quantity of vegetable oil is added and the nests are stirred. After adding more hot water the oil floats to the top bringing with it the impurities. This is repeated many times. The nests are then boiled with rice, vermicelli and chicken or beef stock. Lotus seeds are added. The soup is very sweet and considered a great speciality, given to the sick and elderly and reputed to be an aphrodisiac.

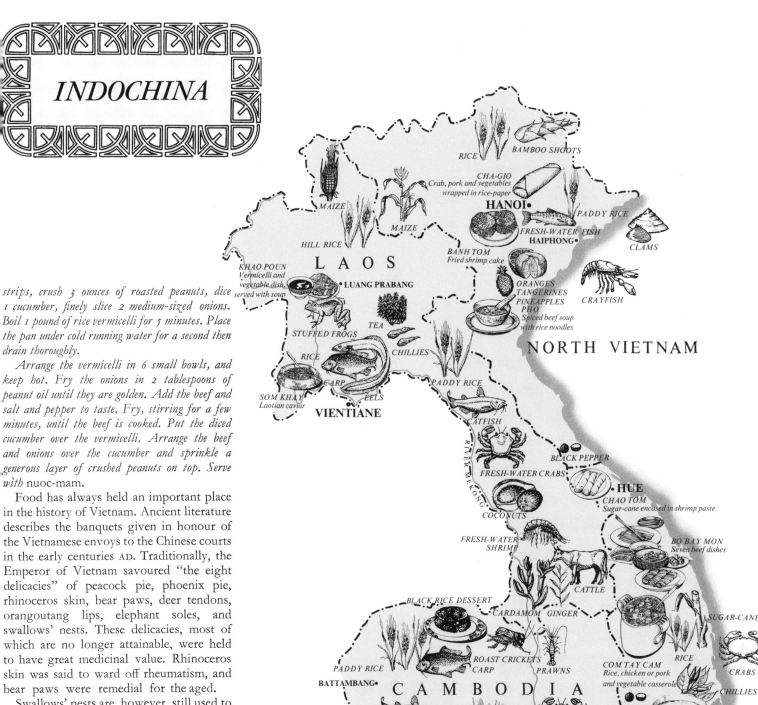

An outstanding cuisine of great subtlety

IT WOULD BE EXPECTED that in a country as enormous as China there would be vast regional differences in its cuisine as well as its culture. China's cultural and culinary unity is, therefore, most striking. There are many dishes which are prepared in virtually the same way all over China. These are best described as Chinese metropolitan dishes and much of the country's haute cuisine falls into this category. Regional characteristics are most pronounced in those dishes which can be called either *cuisine bourgeoise* or *cuisine paysanne*.

Chinese cooking is distinguished above all else by its sheer subtlety and enormous range. This is undoubtedly due in part to the continental size of China, but, more important, it is the result of the complete absence of religious taboos and of food inhibitions. The Chinese can cook and enjoy almost anything edible.

The natural artistry inherent in the Chinese people is obvious in the enormous range of their cuisine. One example of this is the practice of cross-cooking—the use of several different cooking techniques and the unusual combinations of ingredients in the preparation of a single dish.

This tradition of cross-cooking has resulted in an amazing number of dishes. For when one major ingredient is cooked with a group of other ingredients, and the result of this mixing is modified by incorporating a second group of ingredients and this in turn is subtly changed by adding a third group, the variety of dishes which can be based upon the major ingredient is indeed great. Nobody has attempted to count the total number of Chinese dishes, but it must reach into tens of thousands.

The subtle refinement of heat control is essential to Chinese cooking. There are at least forty different established and accepted Chinese methods of heating. In quick stir-fry cooking, for example, a much higher heat is employed than is customarily used by the Western cook. When slow cooking is required a far lower heat and longer cooking time is used than is usual in the West. There is, too, a long tradition of cooking food in earthenware casseroles for five hours or more.

The use of soybeans and such derivatives as soy sauce, soybean paste, soy cheese and fermented salted soybeans is important in Chinese cooking. Chinese food is, however, seasoned just as Western food is, with salt, pepper, vinegar, sugar, mustard and chilli peppers and, consequently, although some dishes may seem unusual or exotic to the average Westerner, there is, nevertheless, a certain familiarity in their flavours.

Another important element in Chinese cooking is the deliberate use of flavoured oil or fat. Oil is flavoured by frying such vegetables and spices as onions, garlic, ginger or scallions (spring onions) in it, often with the addition of dried or pickled ingredients. The oil is then used to fry or stir-fry the main ingredient.

When meat is larded with fat it is cooked in such a way that the fat does not flow out during cooking, but becomes, instead, a part of the meat's texture, adding to its succulence and flavour. This appreciation of well-cooked and well-flavoured fat extends even to the skin. To the Chinese, pork skin, when well cooked and well flavoured, is a great delicacy.

In Chinese cooking, many of the ingredients are used primarily for texture. Water chestnuts, for example, are coarsely chopped and added to meatballs and prawn balls to give them crunchiness. In the same way, such raw vegetables as cucumbers, scallions (spring onions) and radishes are often added or are served with noodles. Tree ears and other fungi are used in soft-fried dishes, principally for their slippery-crunchy texture.

A Chinese meal consists of many dishes and it is carefully planned so that contrasts of textures and even of colours, as well as a variety of flavours, are achieved. For a formal Chinese meal more than one soup is often served. Quick-fried dishes are balanced with others which are steamed, casseroled and crisply deep-fried. Nothing delights the Chinese gourmet more than a dish or a meal in which flavour, texture, colour and content are harmoniously and excitingly combined.

Most impressive is the voluptuousness of good Chinese food—its great range and variety as well as the sheer quantity and beauty of a meal as it is served and displayed on the table. For those who can afford it, a family meal will consist of four or five dishes and a soup. For a banquet or party the number of courses or dishes served rises to a dozen or more. For the Chinese gastronome, who is accustomed to being served at least twelve dishes at a dinner party, a three-course meal can never be really satisfying. No matter how good the main course may be, there is not that overture of slowly moving into the fray, the evolving expectation, the surprises, the rest periods between courses which can spread over a period of several hours, thus providing interesting conversation and entertainment. To a Chinese, the Western meal is comparable to a short story, while the best Chinese meal runs the length of *War and Peace*.

In the sections which follow, most of the recipes are designed to be served as part of a meal for four to six people. The food and cooking of China have been divided into five main regions—Peking and North China; Shanghai and East China; Szechwan Hunan and West China; Canton and South China; Fukien and Coastal China. Together they can be compared only with the cuisine of France as the greatest and most important contribution to the world of food.

MAIZE

CATTLE

DEER

SOYA BEANS

DEER

SHEEP

POMEGRANATES

HWANG HO

CATTLE

PERSIMMONS

PEKING

PACIFIC PRAWNS

SHEEP

CHINESE TURNIPS

PHEASANT

DUCKS

GRAPES

PEARS

WHEAT

WALNUTS

PINE

GARLIC

APPLES

MAIZE

CHESTNUTS

KERNELS

CHINESE CABBAGE

HONEYDEW MELON

CATTLE

PUMPKINS

SPRING ONIONS

CHILLIES

DEER

CHICKENS

PEACHES

GEESE

CHINESE TURNIPS

CARP

POMEGRANATES

CARROTS

CHICKENS

EGG

DUCKS

LOBSTER

PLANT

GEESE

PIGS

SWEET CORN

RICE

WINTER

NANKING

SHANGHAI

PIGS

MELON

SHRIMPS

SHELLFISH

PINE

PIGS

WHEAT

CABBAGES

CRAB

KERNELS

WUHAN

PINE KERNELS

FRESHWATER

YANGTZE KIANG

CRAB

SHRIMPS

PUMPKINS

LOTUS

YELLOW FISH

CHUNGKING

CABBAGES

ROOTS

SWEET CORN

CHICKENS

BAMBOO

TEA

LOTUS SEEDS

WHEAT

RICE

RICE

SHOOTS

LYCHEES

PEPPERS

PIGS

APPLES

PIGS

APPLES

BEETROOT

FROGS

SCALLOPS

PEARS

WINTER

POTATOES

APPLES

MUSHROOMS

MELON

MUSHROOMS

DUCKS

TS'ANG FISH

TEA

RICE

INKFISH

CIVET

PIGS

DEER

CHICKENS

GINGER

PINEAPPLES

ROOT

LOTUS

LYCHEES

SEEDS

ORANGES

BANANAS

SI KIANG

BANANAS

SUGAR-CANE

SNAKE

BANANAS

PIGS

CANTON

LOBSTER

LYCHEES

SCALLOPS

MUSSELS

PINEAPPLES

223

The techniques of Chinese cooking

MORE TIME IS SPENT in a Chinese kitchen in the preparation of ingredients than in cooking them. All the ingredients are usually cut to the same size and shape, not only for the appearance, but because in that way all the ingredients will cook in the same amount of time. Ingredients used in a Chinese dish are diced, cubed, sliced, shredded, cut into wedges or are coarsely or finely ground. The Chinese cook uses a light, sharp cleaver for cutting everything, except to cut through bones when a heavy cleaver is used. The traditional Chinese chopping board is a thick cross section of a tree trunk.

Chinese cooking utensils are few but practical. They are designed for the most economical and efficient use of heat. The most commonly used pan in a Chinese kitchen is a *wok*—a large frying-pan with a rounded bottom. A *wok* works best on a traditional Chinese stove. In a Western kitchen it is more efficiently used on a gas stove than on one which is electric, although *woks* are now sold with a metal ring which holds the pan securely on the burner.

The other important utensil of the Chinese kitchen is the bamboo steamer. Made in tiers, so that a number of dishes can be cooked at the same time, the steamer has no bottom and is designed to fit on a *wok*. The dishes which require the least cooking go in the highest sections of the steamer, and those which require the most cooking are put in the lower tiers.

The Mongolian hot-pot is a most unusual and useful cooking pot. It has a central chimney surrounded by a covered moat in which the food is cooked. The pot fits on to a brazier which burns charcoal. To cook Chinese food the only other utensils which are necessary are ladles, strainers, chopsticks, sieves and spatulas or fish slices.

Smoking
Smoking is a popular Chinese method of flavouring rather than cooking fish, poultry or meat. Tea leaves, sugar or sawdust are left to smoulder over hot charcoal and the ingredients are placed in a container over the smoke. In the West a convenient way to smoke food is to line a large pan with aluminium foil. Sprinkle the base with tea leaves, sugar or sawdust and place the pan over high heat. Put the food on a rack and place it in the pan. When the tea leaves, sugar or sawdust begin to smoke heavily, cover the pan, turn off the heat and leave the ingredients to smoke for 10 to 15 minutes.

Red-Cooking
Braising in a mixture of soy sauce, stock and wine is called red-cooking because the soy sauce darkens the food. Red-cooking is slow and takes up to four hours. The ingredients—usually large pieces of meat or whole chickens—are first fried and browned before being added to the simmering sauce. The principal technique is to keep the heat steady and low throughout the cooking so the liquid in the pan does not evaporate completely and the meat remains moist and juicy and should be tender enough to be cut without chopsticks.

Long, slow red-cooking produces a delicious gravy which is quite thick and highly flavoured. Perfect as it is, this gravy requires neither dilution nor thickening.

Properly cooked, red-cooked dishes are the high point of Chinese culinary creations. Several types of Chinese steamed buns, such as steamed flower rolls and silver thread steamed buns, are specially designed to soak up the gravy of red-cooked dishes.

Quick Stir-Frying
Quick stir-frying is the most widely practised method of Chinese cooking. Because the cooking is rapid, seldom taking longer than five minutes and occasionally taking as little as fifteen seconds, the ingredients—meat, poultry, fish or vegetables—are cut into small, even-sized pieces. The *wok* is put over high heat and a little oil is poured into it. As soon as the oil is very hot, a tablespoon or two of a flavouring vegetable, such as onion or garlic, is added and stirred for a few seconds. The meat is then added and stirred, turned and tossed in the flavoured oil for a minute or two. The meat is then removed and set aside. The vegetables are then added to the pan in order of toughness—those requiring longer cooking going in first. When all the vegetables have been stir-fried the meat is returned to the pan. At this point a little wine, sugar, monosodium glutamate and seasoning is added. The dish must be served immediately because stir-fried food loses all character if it is served lukewarm.

Steaming
Steaming is a method of cooking far more generally used in China than in the West. This is because quantities of rice are cooked every day and the steam from this cooking is utilized to cook other foods. By placing several basket steamers, each on top of another, over a large rice pan, a whole array of dishes can be made ready at the same time as the rice is cooked.

All the ingredients and materials in the dishes are pre-set, pre-arranged, pre-seasoned and marinated before they are put into the steamer. As opposed to stir-frying, the cooking is entirely static and what will emerge as the finished dishes will appear largely as they were arranged when put into the steamer.

To steam Chinese dishes without a traditional steamer an aluminium steamer can be used or a successful substitute can be improvised by putting a dish or bowl on a rack in a large covered pan of water. The dish or bowl must be above the water. Boiling water must be added as the water in the pan evaporates.

Deep-Frying
There is no special pan for deep-frying in China because the *wok* makes an excellent and economical deep-fryer which requires using less oil than the equivalent Western pan. Ingredients for deep-frying are usually cut into small pieces and then coated in batter. Sometimes the ingredients are deep-fried in stages—immersed in the hot oil until just golden, removed and then later returned to the reheated oil to be cooked through. For some dishes the ingredients are first steamed and then deep-fried to make them crisp and brown. Whole birds and large pieces of meat are often cooked in this way.

Crystal-Boiling or Clear-Simmering
This is a method of cooking in which the ingredient is boiled in stock or water for a minute. The pan is covered, the heat turned off and the food left to cook in the heat which is retained in the pan. Chicken cooked this way is sometimes left for 20 minutes and then the liquid is brought to a boil again. This process may be repeated again. Meat or poultry cooked in this way is rarely over-cooked or tough.

A Chinese meal is usually composed of many dishes all served at once and, consequently, most of the recipes in this section do not indicate the number of servings. To serve six people, five dishes and a soup is considered adequate. For additional guests, increase quantity of each dish.

Many of the ingredients required for Chinese cooking can be bought in any supermarket, but some are only available at Chinese food stores.

Abalone is a shellfish used extensively in Chinese cooking. It is available in cans. Once the can is open, abalone will keep at least 4 days if stored in the can liquid in a tightly shut jar in the refrigerator.

Bamboo shoots are the ivory-coloured crunchy shoots of the tropical bamboo. They are available canned. Rinse them before use and store them in water in a covered bowl or jar. Change the water every day, and the shoots will keep for a week in the refrigerator.

Bean curd is available fresh in cakes. It is the purée of soybeans pressed and set in custard-like squares. Highly nutritious, it is an important ingredient in Chinese cooking.

Bean paste (sweetened) is made from red soybeans. It is used as a filling or spread for desserts.

Bean paste (savoury) is used instead of soy sauce when a thick sauce is required. It is sold in cans and jars.

Bean sprouts are the white shoots of mung beans. They are available fresh and canned. When fresh, the Chinese prefer to husk the beans, but this is not absolutely necessary. Rinse the shoots in water and discard any which are discoloured. Use them on the day of purchase or store them in a plastic bag in the refrigerator for no longer than two days.

Bêche-de-mer is also called sea slug or sea cucumber. Sold dried, it keeps indefinitely.

Black beans are salted, strongly flavoured, fermented black soybeans. They are available in cans. Stored in well-covered jars in the refrigerator, they will keep for at least 4 months.

Bok choi is a cabbage with deep green leaves and yellow flowers. The entire vegetable is used in Chinese cooking.

Celery cabbage is a long, pale green cabbage with a white stem. It has a delicate flavour and a crunchy texture.

Chilli sauce is a hot red sauce made from small chillies. If it is not available, Tabasco sauce may be substituted, although the flavour is different.

Cloud ears are a greyish-black dried fungus. They must be soaked in water for 15 minutes before use.

Dried Chinese mushrooms are blackish-brown in colour and have a strong, distinctive flavour. They must be soaked for about 20 minutes before use.

Five-spice powder is a mixture of star anise, anise pepper, cloves, cinnamon and fennel. It is sold ready mixed.

Ginger root is sold fresh and dried. When fresh it is a khaki-coloured knobby root which will keep for weeks if enclosed in a plastic bag and refrigerated. Peeled and chopped, it is an essential flavouring for Chinese food.

Golden needles, or tiger-lily buds, are the dried stems of the lily plant. They have a pleasant, musty taste. Sold in bundles, they must be soaked before use.

Glutinous rice is a short-grained variety of rice which becomes sticky when cooked.

Hoisin sauce is a sweetish dark brown sauce made from soybeans, spices and garlic.

Lotus leaves are the leaves of the water-lily. Used for wrapping around food, they impart a fragrance. They are usually sold dried and require soaking before use.

Lotus roots are the roots of the water-lily. They are used in Chinese cooking for their crunchy texture. They are available in cans.

Oyster sauce is a thick brown sauce made from oysters and soy sauce. It has a strong flavour and is used in various meat and poultry dishes.

Pea-starch noodles are also called cellophane noodles. They are fine, transparent noodles sold looped in packets.

Plum sauce is made from plums, apricots, chillies and vinegar. It is sold in cans and bottles.

Red dates are small dried dates which must be soaked before use. They have a prune-like flavour and a tough skin which must be discarded.

Sesame oil is made from roasted sesame seeds. It imparts a nutty flavour and aroma to food.

Sesame seeds are used to flavour cakes and desserts.

Shark's fin is actually the dried cartilage from the fin. When cooked it becomes gelatinous and translucent. It is considered a delicacy in China.

Soy sauce is made from fermented soybeans. There are many varieties, the best being available at Chinese or Japanese food stores.

Star anise is a spice shaped like an eight-pointed star. It is sold whole and must be used sparingly as it has a strong flavour.

Tangerine peel is used dried to flavour chicken, duck and meat dishes. The flavour is increased if the peel is soaked before use.

Tree fungi, or wood-ears, are ear-shaped after soaking. Grey in colour, they have a crunchy, slippery texture.

Water chestnuts are small bulbs with brown stems and white, crunchy meat. They are used mainly for their texture.

The culinary arts exquisitely refined

It has been said that a great school of cooking comes into being and develops only when within the society there is a large, self-indulgent bourgeoisie bent on feeding themselves lavishly and vying with one another in the refinement and pretension of their entertainments. Prior to the Second World War, the Cantonese were probably the most self-indulgent people in China and the most refined in the culinary arts.

The culinary refinement and general self-indulgence of the Cantonese can be attributed in large part to the favourable geographical situation of Canton on the Si Kiang in the province of Kwangtung, which is agriculturally one of the most fertile and productive areas of China. Unlike the lower reaches of the Hwang River, the Si Kiang does not cause periodic havoc and devastation by flooding. Owing to this good fortune, the communities along the banks of the Si Kiang have always been well off. Added to this geographical good fortune was the wealth which filtered in through trade with the West, and remittances from the overseas Chinese, the bulk of whom had their roots in this area, and who migrated abroad during the nineteenth and twentieth centuries.

The climate of Canton is subtropical and the trees and shrubs are laden with fruit. As a result, fruits and fruit juices are used more in the meat and savoury dishes of Canton than anywhere else in China. There are such dishes as chicken wings in tangerine-peel sauce, hundred-flower chicken and prunes steamed with spareribs, and the many sweet and sour dishes which make use of a wide variety of fruit juices.

Kwangtung has a coastline of more than a thousand miles and from these waters a vast harvest of seafood and marine produce is reaped. Oyster sauce is widely used in the preparation of many meat and some vegetable dishes. Prawns and crabs are used as stuffings for meat or as ingredients in meat dishes. The yellow of crab (crab eggs) is often cooked with such vegetables as asparagus and Chinese cabbage. Dishes which include sharks' fins, abalone, squid and hair vegetables, a variety of seaweed, are common. There is an abundance of freshwater as well as salt-water fish, which are often cooked and flavoured with salted black beans which have been fried with onion in ginger-flavoured oil.

Lobsters, crabs and snails are as highly prized in Canton as they are in Europe. A typical way of cooking crabs and lobsters is to fry them explosively. After a preliminary frying of the flavourings and of the shellfish, the heat is increased until the ingredients are almost red hot. At this point, a cup or two of sauce is poured over, causing a near explosion which makes the flavoured oil penetrate the cracked shells of the crabs or lobsters, thus flavouring the meat and creating a delectable sauce. A lightly beaten egg is added in a thin stream to the sauce, enhancing and augmenting it. To suck this sauce from the shells is one of the high points of Cantonese gastronomic pleasure.

Two other favourite methods used by the Cantonese to cook very fresh shellfish and fish are steaming and quick-dip boiling in water or broth. The raw ingredients used for quick-dip boiling are served in all their original freshness after instant cooking; the seasoning, which consists of vinegar, chilli sauce, *hoisin* sauce (a mildly hot vegetable sauce), mustard, tomato ketchup, chopped ginger, garlic and scallion, and the best soy sauce, in various combinations, is left to the diners.

Before fish is steamed, it is usually rubbed with ginger and salt, marinated for a short time in a mixture of soy sauce, sugar and wine, and covered with raw and dried vege-

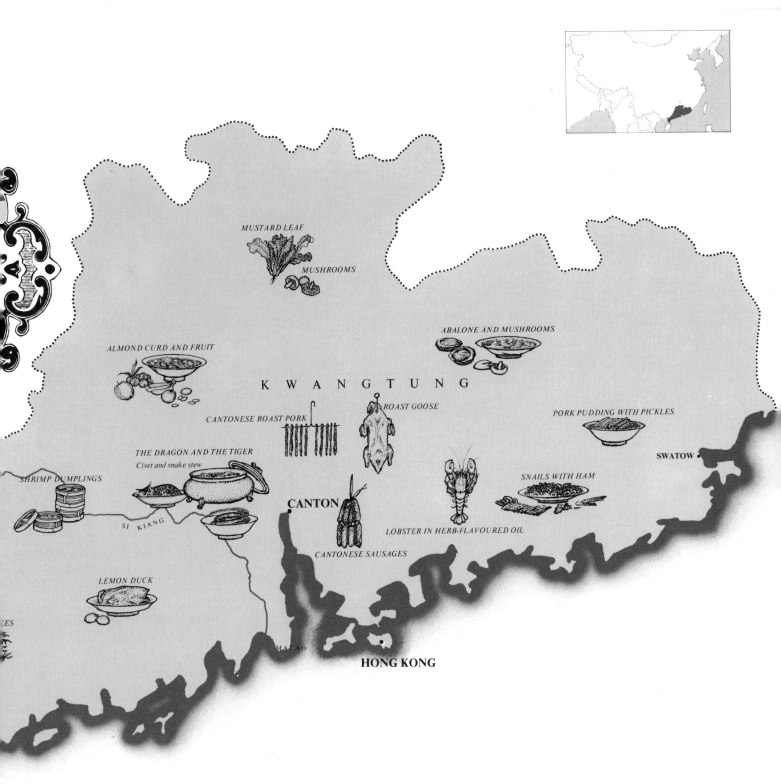

MUSTARD LEAF

MUSHROOMS

ABALONE AND MUSHROOMS

ALMOND CURD AND FRUIT

K W A N G T U N G

ROAST GOOSE

CANTONESE ROAST PORK

PORK PUDDING WITH PICKLES

THE DRAGON AND THE TIGER
Civet and snake stew

SWATOW

SHRIMP DUMPLINGS

SNAILS WITH HAM

CANTON

SI KIANG

LOBSTER IN HERB-FLAVOURED OIL

CANTONESE SAUSAGES

LEMON DUCK

MACAO

HONG KONG

tables and strips of bacon or pork fat. It is then given a short steaming lasting from ten to twenty-five minutes, depending upon cut, thickness and the quality of the fish. The finished dish is unbelievably tasty.

Another favourite method of Cantonese cooking is *cha shao*, barbecue or lacquer roasting. The meat or poultry is first marinated in a mixture of soy sauce, soy paste, soy cheese, oil, sugar or honey. It is then hung in the oven and roasted. The meat or poultry is removed from the oven two or three times and brushed over with the marinade until its surface becomes glossy and lacquered. Meat cooked in this way is often served cold and is sliced across the grain

into quarter-inch slices. Duck or chicken is usually chopped into large bite-sized pieces. The drippings, which are caught in a pan placed under the roast in the oven, are made into a rich gravy by the addition of a little stock, wine and a pinch of monosodium glutamate.

The Cantonese are not particularly well known for their soups, and do not seem to give them the same attention as they do other dishes. This is, too, the only cuisine in China in which dog meat and snake feature as possible gastronomic delights.

Quite a number of Cantonese dishes use milk, an unusual ingredient in Chinese cooking, and others are called toasts, tarts and

pies. This is undoubtedly due to the "foreign devils" who have been sailing up the Si Kiang for nearly two hundred years, and whose culinary creations and gastronomic habits have influenced the methods and practices of the local population. While this is to be expected, the blatant and unabashed way in which these foreign dishes have been accepted as if they were Cantonese creations is surprising. They seem to have incorporated all that is offered from abroad without a second thought or acknowledgement.

The Cantonese, because of their geographical position, natural wealth and affluence, have developed a self-assured way of life which is reflected in their cuisine.

Shellfish and pork unusually prepared

Pork and Watercress Soup

In China this soup is designated Ching T'an, *which means that it is considered to be clear, pure and simple.*

3 oz lean pork, cut into thin slices
½ teaspoon salt
2 teaspoons cornflour
2 pints well-flavoured chicken stock
½ teaspoon monosodium glutamate (optional)
1 bunch watercress
Freshly ground black pepper

Rub the pork slices with the salt and the corn-flour.

In a large saucepan bring the stock to the boil. Add the monosodium glutamate, if using, and the pork slices. Reduce the heat and simmer, uncovered, for 10 minutes.

Add the watercress and pepper to taste. Simmer for 3 minutes more.

Pour the soup into a tureen and serve immediately.

Abalone and Fish-Ball Soup
CHING P'OW YU YUAN

Although this dish from Kwangtung is called fish-ball soup, it is not necessarily a soup; the fish balls may be eaten separately as part of a main course, omitting the broth altogether.

10 oz canned abalone, drained, thinly sliced and then shredded
10 oz crab meat, minced
2 oz pork fat, minced
3 egg whites, beaten until nearly stiff
1½ tablespoons cornflour
2 tablespoons finely chopped lean cooked ham
2 tablespoons finely chopped coriander leaves
2 pints chicken stock
Salt
Black pepper
¼ teaspoon monosodium glutamate (optional)

In a bowl, combine the abalone, crab meat, pork fat, egg whites and cornflour. Mix the ingredients well together and form into walnut-sized balls. Sprinkle the top of each ball with a little of the chopped ham and coriander.

Place the balls in a large, deep-sided heat-proof dish and place the dish in a steamer. Steam the balls for 12 minutes.

Heat the stock in a large saucepan. Season with salt and pepper to taste and the mono-sodium glutamate, if used. When the stock is hot, pour it into a tureen and add the fish balls. Serve immediately.

Deep-Fried Oysters in Crispy Batter
CH'AO SEN HOU

These oysters are served with a selection of savoury dips and sauces.

20 oysters, shelled
Salt
1 teaspoon finely chopped fresh root ginger
6 oz plain flour, sifted
1 tablespoon baking powder
10 fl oz water
2 tablespoons vinegar blended with 2 tablespoons soy sauce
4 fl oz tomato ketchup
2 teaspoons black pepper
Vegetable oil for deep-frying

Put the oysters in a shallow bowl and sprinkle with salt and ginger. Set aside to marinate for 30 minutes. Drain off any excess liquid.

Sift the flour and baking powder into a mixing bowl. Gradually stir in the water to make a smooth batter. Set aside.

To make the sauces, divide the vinegar mix-ture between the two small bowls. Divide the ketchup between two similar bowls.

Heat 1 tablespoon salt and the pepper in a small frying-pan for 2 minutes over high heat. Divide the mixture between the two very small bowls and set aside with the other dips.

Heat the vegetable oil in a large saucepan. When it is hot, dip a few of the oysters in the batter to coat them thoroughly and lower them into the hot oil. Deep-fry for 3 minutes and drain. Fry the remaining oysters in the same way.

Place all the fried oysters in a wire basket and lower them into the oil again. Deep-fry for 30 seconds and drain thoroughly.

Arrange the oysters on a warmed serving dish and serve immediately with the sauces.

Quick-fried Crab Meat with Mushrooms
HSIA JOU P'A HSIEN KU

3 tablespoons chicken stock
½ teaspoon sugar
¼ teaspoon monosodium glutamate (optional)
1 tablespoon soy sauce
2 tablespoons dry sherry
¼ teaspoon black pepper
2 tablespoons vegetable oil or lard
1 garlic clove, crushed
1 teaspoon shredded fresh root ginger
1 small onion, shredded
½ teaspoon fermented, salted black beans, soaked in cold water for 10 minutes and drained
Salt

12 oz crab meat
¾ oz butter
12 oz small button mushrooms, cleaned and sliced

In a small bowl, combine the stock, sugar monosodium glutamate if used, soy sauce sherry and black pepper. Set aside.

Heat the oil or melt the lard in a large frying-pan. Add the garlic, ginger, onion, beans and salt and stir-fry for 30 seconds. Add the crab meat and stir-fry for 45 seconds. Remove the pan from the heat and keep warm.

Melt the butter in a small saucepan. Add the mushrooms and cook, stirring, for 2 minutes.

Add the mushrooms and cooking liquid to the frying-pan and return the frying-pan to the heat. Pour in the stock mixture and stir-fry over high heat for 1½ minutes.

Serve immediately.

Crab with Black Beans and Green Pepper
KU CHIAO KUO HSIA

Although it is said that crabs are only poor man's lobster, a great many Chinese actually prefer them.

This dish is comparatively simple to pre-pare, and it is very effective.

4 tablespoons vegetable oil
2 teaspoons fermented, salted black beans, soaked in cold water for 10 minutes and drained
2 garlic cloves, crushed
1 tablespoon finely chopped fresh root ginger
1 medium-sized onion, thinly sliced
1 lb fresh crab meat
1 large green pepper, seeded and cut into 2-inch by ¼-inch strips
Salt
Black pepper
1 cup chicken stock
½ chicken stock cube, crumbled
1 tablespoon cornflour blended with 3 tablespoons cold water
2 tablespoons dry sherry
1½ teaspoons sesame oil

Heat the oil in a large frying-pan. Add the beans, garlic, ginger and onion. Stir-fry for 45 seconds over high heat. Add the crab, green pepper, salt and pepper and stir-fry for 2 minutes. Add the stock and chicken stock cube and stir well to mix.

Cover the pan and cook for 2 minutes. Stir in the cornflour mixture and sprinkle with the sherry and sesame oil.

Remove the pan from the heat and transfer the mixture to a heated serving dish. Serve immediately.

Steamed Prawns
CHENG HSIA

To eat this dish, traditionally, the diner picks up a prawn with his chopsticks, dips it into the spicy sauce and bites through the shell, sucking out the flesh.

2 spring onions, finely chopped
2 teaspoons finely chopped fresh root ginger
1 garlic clove, crushed
3 tablespoons soy sauce
1 tablespoon hoisin sauce
1 teaspoon Chinese chilli sauce or Tabasco sauce
1 tablespoon dry sherry
1½ lb prawns, in their shells, washed, drained and heads removed

In a bowl, combine the spring onions, ginger, garlic, soy sauce, *hoisin* sauce, chilli sauce or Tabasco sauce and sherry. Divide the mixture between two small sauce dishes and set aside.

Put the prawns in a heatproof dish and put the dish in a steamer. Steam for 10 minutes. Remove the dish from the steamer and serve with the sauce.

Cantonese Lobster
HSIANG YIU KUO LUNG HSIA

This dish, which is also known as lobster in aromatic oil, should be eaten immediately after it has been cooked.

1 large live lobster
1 tablespoon soy sauce
2 tablespoons dry sherry
1 teaspoon sugar
10 fl oz chicken stock
2 spring onions, cut into ½-inch lengths
4 tablespoons vegetable oil
2 teaspoons fermented, salted black beans, soaked in cold water for 10 minutes and drained
1 garlic clove, crushed
1 medium-sized onion, chopped
2 teaspoons chopped fresh root ginger
4 oz lean pork, coarsely minced
Salt
Black pepper
¼ teaspoon monosodium glutamate (optional)
1 tablespoon cornflour blended with 3 tablespoons cold water
2 eggs, well beaten

Kill the lobster by severing the vein in the base of the neck. Put the lobster on its back and holding it by the head slit the body and the tail in half lengthways. Cut off and discard the head. Remove and discard the hard sac near the eyes and the intestinal tract. Using poultry shears,

cut off the claws and split them in half. Cut the body and tail into pieces. Set aside.

In a bowl, combine the soy sauce, sherry, sugar, chicken stock and spring onions. Set aside.

Heat the vegetable oil in a large frying-pan over high heat. Add the beans, garlic, onion and ginger and stir-fry for 6 seconds. Add the pork and stir-fry for 2 minutes. Add the lobster pieces and stir-fry for 2 minutes. Slowly pour in the chicken-stock mixture and season with salt and pepper to taste and the monosodium glutamate, if used. Let the liquid come to a rolling boil, cover the pan and cook for 1 minute. Uncover and add the cornflour mixture. Cook, stirring, for 1 minute. Slowly pour the beaten eggs over the back of a fork in a thin stream into the pan.

Remove the pan from the heat and transfer the lobster and sauce to a deep serving dish. Serve immediately.

Stir-Fried Sliced Beef with Oyster Sauce
HAO YIU NIU JOU

The combination of fresh oysters with meat is quite common in the southern coastal provinces of China.

1 lb frying steak, cut diagonally into very thin 2- by 1-inch slices
½ teaspoon salt
¼ teaspoon black pepper
1 tablespoon soy sauce
1½ tablespoons dry sherry
4 tablespoons vegetable oil
1 tablespoon cornflour
½ medium-sized onion, thinly sliced
2 teaspoons finely chopped fresh root ginger
6 oysters, shelled
1½ tablespoons oyster sauce
1 tablespoon cornflour blended with 3 tablespoons chicken stock
4 lettuce leaves

Put the beef in a shallow bowl. Mix together the salt, pepper, soy sauce, sherry and 1 tablespoon of the vegetable oil and pour over the beef. Toss well to mix and marinate for 1 hour.

Drain the beef and rub with the cornflour.

Heat the remaining oil in a large frying-pan. Add the onion and ginger and stir-fry over high heat for 30 seconds. Remove the onion and ginger from the pan and discard them. Add the beef and oysters and stir in the oyster sauce. Stir-fry for 1½ minutes. Add the cornflour mixture and stir-fry for 1 minute longer.

Remove the pan from the heat. Line the bottom of a serving dish with the lettuce leaves and spoon the beef mixture on top.

Serve hot.

Spareribs with Plums

2 lb meaty pork spareribs, chopped into 1½-inch lengths
1 teaspoon salt
3 tablespoons vegetable oil
1 tablespoon chopped fresh root ginger
1½ tablespoons fermented salted black beans, soaked for 15 minutes and mashed
1 lb plums, peeled, stoned and halved
3 teaspoons sugar
2 tablespoons soy sauce
2 tablespoons sherry
1 tablespoon cornflour

Rub the spareribs with the salt.

Heat the oil in a heavy frying-pan. When the oil is very hot add the ginger and black beans and fry, stirring constantly, for 1½ minutes. Add the spareribs and fry over high heat, stirring constantly, for 5 minutes.

Transfer the spareribs to a large bowl. Add the plums, sugar, soy sauce, sherry and cornflour and mix gently but well. Place the bowl in a steamer and steam for 30 minutes.

Serve hot.

Barbecued Roast Pork
CHA SHAO JOU

2½ lb pork fillet, cut along the grain into long strips 3 inches wide and 1 to 2 inches thick

MARINADE 1

2 teaspoons shredded fresh root ginger
1 medium-sized onion, shredded
2 garlic cloves, crushed
6 tablespoons soy sauce
4 tablespoons sherry or red wine

MARINADE 2

1 tablespoon honey or sugar
1 tablespoon soy sauce
1 tablespoon dry sherry
1 tablespoon vegetable oil

Put the pork strips in a large shallow bowl. Combine the ginger, onion, garlic, soy sauce and sherry or red wine and pour over the pork. Marinate for several hours or overnight.

Preheat the oven to 375°F (Gas Mark 5).

Drain the pork strips and put them on a rack in a large roasting pan. Add 5 fluid ounces of water to the pan. Roast for 20 minutes.

Meanwhile, in a small bowl, combine the honey or sugar, soy sauce, sherry and vegetable oil. Remove the pork strips from the oven and, using a pastry brush, coat the strips with the honey mixture. Return the pork strips to the rack in the roasting pan and bake for a further 15 minutes.

Cut the pork across the grain into thin slices and arrange the slices on a serving dish. Serve hot or cold.

A collection of exotic dishes

Sweet and Sour Spareribs

3 lb meaty pork spareribs, chopped into
   1-inch pieces
1 teaspoon salt
3 tablespoons vegetable oil
2 tablespoons chopped onion
1 teaspoon finely chopped fresh root ginger
1 garlic clove, crushed

SAUCE

2 tablespoons sugar
2 tablespoons vinegar
1½ tablespoons soy sauce
2 tablespoons tomato purée
2 tablespoons fresh orange juice
1½ tablespoons cornflour blended with
   3 tablespoons water

Sprinkle the spareribs with the salt. Put all the
ingredients for the sauce in a bowl and mix
until they are well blended and the mixture is
smooth.

Heat the oil in a frying-pan. When the oil is
hot add the spareribs and fry over high heat,
stirring constantly, for 5 minutes. Add the
onion, garlic and ginger.

Reduce the heat and continue to stir-fry for
5 more minutes.

Stir the sauce quickly and pour it over the
spareribs. Continue to cook, stirring constantly,
for 1 minute.

Serve hot.

Crystal Pork Pudding
SIU CHING K'O JOU

2½ lb pork belly, with skin
1 lb cucumber, cut into ¼-inch thick slices
2 oz sugar
2 tablespoons vinegar
3 tablespoons soy sauce
Vegetable oil for deep-frying
1 medium-sized onion, thinly sliced
2 oz soft brown sugar

Put the pork in a large saucepan with water to
cover. Boil the pork for 25 minutes. Drain and
cut into pieces 1¼ inches by 2¼ inches.

Put the cucumber in a shallow bowl and
sprinkle with the sugar, vinegar and half of the
soy sauce.

Marinate for 30 minutes.

Rub the pork pieces with the remaining soy
sauce.

Heat the vegetable oil in a large saucepan.
When the oil is hot, add the pork pieces and
deep-fry them for 3 minutes, in two batches if
necessary. Drain the pork and put the pieces,
skin side down, in a heatproof bowl, inter-
leaving them with the cucumber slices. Pour
the marinade over the pork and cucumber. Put
the onion slices on top.

Place the dish in a steamer and steam for
35 minutes.

Reverse the contents of the bowl on to a
warmed serving dish, like a pudding. Sprinkle
with the brown sugar and serve.

Beef with Green Peppers and Tomatoes

1 lb round steak
4 tablespoons cooking oil
1 garlic clove, crushed
1 teaspoon salt
½ teaspoon pepper
1 teaspoon grated fresh root ginger
4 tablespoons soy sauce
¼ teaspoon sugar
2 green peppers, cut into strips
2 tomatoes, quartered
3 tablespoons cornflour blended with
   ¼ cup cold water
2 young spring onions, cut in 1-inch pieces

Slice the steak in thin, short strips. Heat the oil
in a heavy frying-pan. When the oil is very hot
add the garlic, salt, pepper and ginger and
stir-fry for 3 seconds. Add the beef slices and
stir-fry for 2 minutes.

Add the soy sauce, sugar and green pepper,
cover the pan and cook for 4 minutes. Add the
tomatoes and cook for 2 minutes longer. Add
the cornflour mixture and cook, stirring constantly, until the sauce thickens.

Sprinkle with the spring onions and serve.

Beef with Ginger

20 thin slices fresh ginger
6 tablespoons salt
1 lb round steak, trimmed and thinly sliced
6 tablespoons cooking oil
1 garlic clove, crushed
3 tablespoons soy sauce
3 teaspoons sherry
2 teaspoons sugar
¼ teaspoon pepper
2 tablespoons cornflour blended with
   5 fl oz cold water

Mix the ginger and the salt together and let
stand for 15 minutes. Rinse the ginger under
cold running water. Drain well.

Heat the oil in a heavy frying-pan. When the
oil is hot add the garlic and ginger. Cook for 5
seconds, stirring constantly. Add the beef and
fry, stirring constantly, for 3 minutes. Add the
soy sauce, sherry, sugar and pepper. Cook for 1
minute, stirring constantly. Add the cornflour
and water mixture and cook, stirring, until the
sauce has thickened.

Serve hot.

Bean Sprouts with Beef

*Pork, chicken or duck can be substituted for the
beef in this recipe.*

1 lb lean beef, shredded
4 tablespoons vegetable oil
½ garlic clove, crushed
2 teaspoons salt
½ teaspoon grated fresh root ginger
1 lb canned or fresh bean sprouts,
   rinsed and well drained
2 tablespoons soy sauce
4 fl oz beef stock
3 teaspoons cornflour blended with
   4 tablespoons cold water
2 young spring onions, cut in 1-inch pieces

Heat the oil in a heavy frying-pan. Add the
garlic, salt and ginger and stir-fry for 2 seconds.
Add the beef and stir-fry for 2 minutes. Remove
the beef with a slotted spoon and keep hot.

Add the bean sprouts, soy sauce and beef
stock. Bring to a boil, reduce the heat, cover and
cook for 3 minutes. Add the cornflour mixture
and cook, stirring constantly, until the sauce
has thickened.

Sprinkle with the spring onions and serve
immediately.

Crab Fu-Yung

*This dish, which combines crab, egg and a dash of
sherry, is a Cantonese favourite.*

6 eggs
1 teaspoon salt
Black pepper
2 medium-sized tomatoes, blanched,
   peeled and cut into eighths
1 medium-sized onion, chopped
1 garlic clove, crushed
2 slices fresh ginger, shredded
4 tablespoons vegetable oil
6 oz crab meat
2 tablespoons dry sherry

Beat the eggs with half of the salt and a dash of
pepper until the eggs are foamy.

Heat 2 tablespoons of oil in a frying-pan. Add
the onion and stir-fry for 1 minute. Add the
garlic and ginger and stir-fry for 30 seconds.
Add the crab meat and the remaining salt and
stir-fry for 1 minute. Remove the pan from the
heat.

Heat the remaining oil in another frying-pan.
Add the tomatoes and pour in the beaten eggs.
Shake and tilt the pan so the egg coats the
bottom evenly and does not stick. When the
egg begins to coagulate scramble it lightly. Pour
in the contents of the other pan and scramble
the ingredients together. Add the sherry and
toss lightly.

Serve immediately.

Salt-Baked Chicken

YEN KUO CHI

This is an unusual recipe. When the chicken is cooked, the salt is scraped off and the skin underneath is browned and crisp and, surprisingly, not very salty.

3 lb chicken, washed and dried
5 lb coarse-grained sea salt
1 oz lard
2 whole spring onions, chopped
2 tablespoons salt
4 tablespoons prepared mustard
4 tablespoons sesame oil

Put the chicken in a colander in an airy place for 3 hours so that it will dry completely.

Preheat the oven to 375°F (Gas Mark 5).

Cover the bottom of a large flameproof casserole with 1 pound of the sea salt. Place the chicken on the salt, breast side up, and cover with the remaining sea salt. Pack the salt firmly over and around the chicken. Cook over moderate heat for about 8 minutes.

Transfer the casserole to the oven and bake for 1¼ hours.

Meanwhile, melt the lard in a small pan, add the spring onions and, stirring, cook for 1 minute. Put in a saucer for use as a dip.

Combine the 2 tablespoons of salt, the mustard and sesame oil together and put in small saucers to use as a dip.

Remove the chicken from the casserole and scrape and shake off the salt. Chop the bird into 16 to 18 pieces and place them on a heated serving dish. Serve with the dips.

Crackling Fried Chicken

1 chicken
2 teaspoons salt
2 tablespoons finely chopped fresh root ginger
½ tablespoon sugar
1½ tablespoons white vinegar
1½ tablespoons light soy sauce
2 tablespoons water
1½ tablespoons sherry
3 tablespoons cornflour
Vegetable oil for deep-frying

Mix the salt and ginger together and rub the chicken thoroughly inside and out with the mixture. Put the chicken in a colander and leave in an airy place for 3 to 4 hours.

Chop the chicken into 16 to 20 pieces with a very sharp, heavy cleaver. Mix together the sugar, vinegar, soy sauce, water, sherry and cornflour. Rub the chicken pieces with half of the paste. Put them on a large platter or baking sheet and let them dry in an airy place for 2 hours.

Rub the chicken pieces with the remaining paste and leave to dry for 1 hour more.

Heat the oil in a deep pan. Put half of the chicken pieces into a deep-frying basket and when the oil is very hot deep-fry the chicken for 3 minutes, or until the pieces are very crisp. Repeat with the remaining chicken pieces. Serve hot.

Lemon Duck

NING MUNG YA

5 lb duck, cleaned
2 small lemons
1½ pints water
1 large onion, thickly sliced
1 small piece fresh root ginger, peeled
1 teaspoon salt
¼ teaspoon monosodium glutamate (optional)
10 fl oz white wine

Preheat the oven to 375°F (Gas Mark 5).

Place 1 lemon inside the cavity of the duck. Cut 4 slices from the other lemon and squeeze the juice from the two ends into a cup and reserve.

Put the duck in a flameproof casserole. Add the water, onion, ginger, salt and monosodium glutamate, if used. Bring the liquid to the boil.

Cover the casserole, transfer it to the oven and cook for 1¼ hours.

Remove the casserole from the oven. Lift out the duck. Strain the cooking juices and skim off the fat. Return the strained juices and the duck to the casserole. Pour the wine over the duck. Return the casserole to the oven and roast for 30 minutes, or until the duck is cooked.

Sprinkle the duck with the reserved lemon juice, garnish with the lemon slices and serve from the casserole.

Pigeons Braised in Fruit Juice

HSI TSE' KUO YU K'E

2 tablespoons soy sauce
2 tablespoons dry sherry
2 young pigeons
2 tablespoons orange juice
2 tablespoons lychee juice
1 tablespoon lemon juice
2 tablespoons tomato purée
1 tablespoon hoisin sauce
1 tablespoon soy sauce
2 teaspoons sugar
¼ teaspoon monosodium glutamate (optional)
2 tablespoons chicken stock
Vegetable oil for deep-frying
2 tablespoons lard
1 medium-sized onion, thinly sliced

In a small saucer, combine the soy sauce and sherry. Rub this mixture all over the pigeons, inside and out, and set them aside to marinate for 1 hour.

In a small mixing bowl, combine the orange juice, lychee juice, lemon juice, the tomato paste, *hoisin* sauce, soy sauce, sugar, monosodium glutamate, if used, and the chicken stock. Set aside.

Heat the vegetable oil in a large saucepan. When the oil is hot, add one of the pigeons and deep-fry for 4 minutes. Drain thoroughly. Fry the other pigeon. Chop each pigeon into four pieces.

Melt the lard in a large frying-pan. Add the onion and stir-fry for 1 minute. Add the fruit-juice mixture and the pigeon pieces and cook over medium heat for 5 minutes, stirring constantly. Cover the pan and cook for 10 minutes. Transfer the pigeon pieces to a heated serving dish and keep them hot.

Continue cooking the sauce, uncovered, for 2 minutes. Pour the sauce over the pigeons and serve.

Fried Chiu-Chow Rice-Stick Noodles

CH'AO MI-FEN

2 tablespoons vegetable oil
1 medium-sized onion, thinly sliced
2 oz lean pork, coarsely chopped
4 dried Chinese mushrooms, soaked in cold water for 30 minutes, drained, stalks removed and caps shredded
12 oz Chinese rice-stick noodles, boiled for 12 minutes, rinsed in cold water and drained
2 tablespoons soy sauce
2 tablespoons lard
4 oz leeks, trimmed and finely sliced
1 garlic clove, crushed
4 oz fresh crab meat
8 oysters, shelled
Salt

Heat the oil in a large frying-pan. When the oil is hot, add the onion and stir-fry over medium heat for 1 minute. Add the pork and mushrooms and stir-fry for 2 minutes over high heat. Reduce the heat to medium, add the noodles and stir-fry for 3 minutes. Add the soy sauce and simmer gently over low heat.

Melt the lard in another frying-pan. Add the leeks and garlic and stir-fry over high heat for 2 minutes. Add the crab and oysters. Sprinkle with salt to taste. Stir-fry for 1½ minutes.

Mix half of the leek and crab mixture into the noodle mixture and cook for 30 seconds. Transfer to a heated serving dish and garnish with the remaining leek and crab mixture. Serve hot.

The spicy food of a fertile region

THE PROVINCE OF SZECHWAN, situated in the upper basin of the Yangtze River, is unique. None of the great rivers of the world—the Mississippi, the Nile nor the Amazon—has an upper basin quite as large, fertile or populous. The area was first written about in the Chinese classics at about the time of the birth of Christ. A celebrated prime minister of the day, in a famous letter to his king, described Szechwan as "heaven's own country, a homeland where fertile plains run in stretches of a thousand miles".

Hunan is a smaller basin of a tributary of the Yangtze called the Han. The two provinces share a climatic characteristic in common; they both enjoy long, hot, steamy summers.

Their cuisines, which are similar, have one particular quality in common—most of their dishes are hot to the taste. This is achieved in Szechwan by the use of fagara, Szechwan pepper, a piquant spice which is strong and very hot, or by stir-frying chilli peppers in oil or fat together with a liberal amount of chopped onion, garlic and ginger. This hot sauce is then stir-fried or cross-cooked with other ingredients. When salted black beans are added the dishes produced are called fish fragrant, although no fish is involved in any part of the cooking. What are involved are simply the ingredients which are usually used in the cooking of fish.

A special Hunan method of cooking is p'un, which can best be described as explosive braising and is similar to the Cantonese method of explosive frying.

One popular Hunan dish consists of stir-fried, shredded dried squid with shredded meat or vegetables. The dried squid imparts an anchovy-like flavour to everything cooked with it.

In the past, the social structure of Szechwan was decidedly more feudal than that of the coastal provinces and consisted mainly of landlords and peasants, ruled by warlords or mandarins. This social situation is reflected in the cuisine of the region, which falls into two categories—*cuisine paysanne*, and *cuisine mandarine* or *officiale*, which is very much like the Palace cuisine of Peking and North China.

The peasants of Szechwan have, for example, a whole series of dishes known as three steamed dishes and nine turn-out dishes, which they serve when entertaining on occasions of weddings, funerals, birthdays and other anniversaries, which occur with great frequency. The steamed dishes are all served in bowls rather than on plates. Steamed chopsuey, one of the most popular steamed dishes, is very different from the chopsuey which is so famous in the United States.

Favourite turn-out dishes are pork pudding and chicken pudding, both of which consist of cooked meat or poultry chopped into bite-size pieces and packed into heat-proof bowls, with potatoes or dried beans, liberally seasoned with flavourings and sauces and turned out on to a serving dish.

Many of the Mandarin dishes of Szechwan bear close resemblance to the original Palace or Mandarin dishes of Peking. These dishes are usually less hot than those which are native to Szechwan. Peking stir-fried diced chicken in bean-paste sauce is cooked in a similar manner in Szechwan, but it is made with a liberal amount of hot chilli pepper oil which gives the food a pinkish colour. Fish fragrant quick-fried shredded pork is another typical Szechwan dish and makes liberal use of the Szechwan hot sauce. The aromatic and crispy duck of Szechwan is much like Peking duck, and sour and pepper fish soup is similar to chrysanthemum fish soup hot-pot.

The Szechwanese are very fond of the *fu-yung* dishes (those which include beaten egg white), which are also favourites in Peking. There are other classical dishes with slight local or provincial touches which in many cases are an improvement on the original. These include butterfly bêche-de-mer, sweet and sour crispy fish and green jade shrimp, as well as the Szechwan interpretations of the sharks'-fins and birds'-nest dishes.

In Szechwan, venison is used in many dishes, as are many varieties of mushrooms and fungi, and bamboo shoots, which grow in greater profusion in Szechwan than in the more barren, drier north.

The Szechwanese also frequently use smoking and barbecuing as methods of cooking. They are famous for their smoked spareribs and spit-roast rib-squares. Splash-

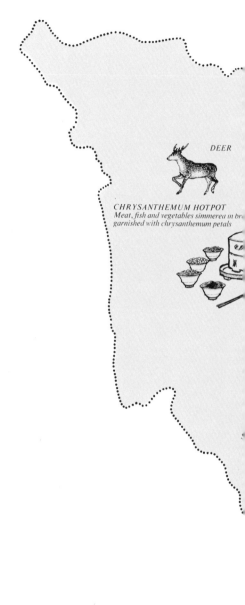

DEER

CHRYSANTHEMUM HOTPOT
Meat, fish and vegetables simmered in bro garnished with chrysanthemum petals

frying, a method of frying common in Szechwan, is also used in Peking, Hopeh and Shantung. The ingredients are hung over a pot of boiling oil and constantly splashed with the oil until cooked.

Until recently the cuisines of Hunan and Szechwan were unknown outside China, although both were among the five early styles of Chinese cooking. Today, restaurants specializing in Szechwan cooking are flourishing in New York and interest in this highly spiced food of China continues to grow.

HWAN

REE KINDS OF MUSHROOMS

SZECHWAN PICKLED GREENS

SMOKED RIBS

YANGTZE KIANG

FIVE KINDS OF FISH

TRIPE HOTPOT

•CHUNGKING

BLES

shrooms

SMOKED CHICKEN IN TANGERINE-PEEL SAUCE

SEA CUCUMBER IN SOYA BEAN SAUCE

STEAMED PORK WRAPPED IN LOTUS LEAVES

SPECIAL SAVOURY RICE WITH PORK
AND BEANS WRAPPED IN LEAVES

HUNAN

FRIED MUSHROOMS, BEAN CURD, PORK AND CHILLIES

TUNG AN CHICKEN
Chicken with hot sauce

•HENGYANG

SZECHWAN
AND
HUNAN

Fragrant and flavourful fish and meats

Hot and Sour Soup
SUAN-LA T'ANG

Pork is the meat normally used in hot and sour soups, but in this Szechwan recipe beef is used instead.

1½ pints good beef stock
1 tablespoon soy sauce
Salt
Black pepper
¼ teaspoon Chinese chilli sauce or
   Tabasco sauce
6 medium-sized Chinese dried mushrooms,
   soaked for 30 minutes, drained, stalks
   removed and caps sliced
2 small bamboo shoots, shredded
¼ lb lean beef, finely shredded
¼ lb uncooked shrimp, shelled and deveined
2 cakes bean curd, each cut into 12 pieces
2 spring onion stalks, cut into small pieces
2 tablespoons cornflour, mixed with
   6 tablespoons cold water
1 egg, lightly beaten
2 teaspoons sesame oil

Heat the beef stock in a large saucepan. Add the soy sauce, salt, pepper, chilli sauce or Tabasco sauce, mushrooms and bamboo shoots and simmer for 3 minutes. Add the beef, shrimp, bean curd and spring onions. Simmer for 1 minute. Add the cornflour, stirring constantly until the soup thickens. Trickle the egg in slowly, stirring constantly. As soon as the egg has set, sprinkle the soup with sesame oil and serve.

Chrysanthemum Fish Soup
CH'U HUA YU KENG KUO

Unlike the hot-pot used in Peking, which uses charcoal for heating and has a funnel, the pot used in Szechwan is large and wide, like a casserole, and heated by a spirit burner. In a modern household, a casserole with a lid may be substituted.

1 lb fish bones
1 fish head
1½ pints chicken stock
1-inch piece fresh root ginger, shredded
Salt
Black pepper
Vegetable oil for deep-frying
2 oz chicken liver, cut into thin slices
3 oz pork tripe, cut into thin strips (optional)
1 oz transparent pea-starch noodles
1 oz lard or oil
2 tablespoons shelled peanuts
1 medium-sized onion, sliced
4 oz cabbage heart, cut into 8 pieces
4 oz spinach leaves, chopped
2 oz shelled green peas
8 oz white fish fillets, cut into 2- by
   1½-inch slices

4 oz chicken breast, cut into 2- by 1½-inch
   slices
1 tablespoon chopped coriander leaves
1 large chrysanthemum, separated into
   petals

Place the fish bones and head, stock, ginger, salt and pepper in a large saucepan and bring to the boil over high heat. Reduce the heat to low and simmer for 30 minutes. Strain the stock through muslin and set aside.

Heat the vegetable oil in a deep saucepan and add the liver slices and tripe, if it is used. Fry for 2 minutes, drain and set aside. Add the pea-starch noodles to the oil and fry for 1½ minutes, or until they are crisp. Drain and set aside.

In a large casserole, melt the lard or heat the oil over medium heat. Add the peanuts and stir-fry for 1 minute. Add the onion and stir-fry for 1½ minutes. Add the cabbage, spinach and peas and pour in the stock. Bring the mixture to a boil and add the fish, chicken, liver and tripe. Cook for 3 minutes.

Light the spirit burner and place it on the table. Transfer the casserole to the burner. Sprinkle the fried noodles and the coriander leaves on top of the soup.

Arrange the chrysanthemum petals over the soup and simmer for a few minutes before serving.

Dry-Fried Shredded Beef
KAN PIEN NIU JOU

This is a dish usually served at the beginning of a multi-course dinner party to encourage the flow of wine. The beef is shredded and stir-fried over high heat until it is dry and chewy.

4 tablespoons vegetable oil
1 lb round steak, cut into shreds 2½ inches
   long
Salt
Black pepper
2 tablespoons soy sauce
2 tablespoons soybean paste (optional)
2 teaspoons Chinese chilli sauce
1½ teaspoons sugar
2 tablespoons dry sherry
2 teaspoons shredded fresh root ginger
2 small carrots, shredded
3 celery sticks, shredded

Heat the oil in a large frying-pan over high heat until it is very hot. Add the beef and sprinkle with salt and pepper. Stir-fry for 4 to 5 minutes, or until most of the moisture in the beef has evaporated.

Add the soy sauce, the soybean paste, if it is being used, the chilli sauce, sugar and sherry. Stir well to mix and add the ginger, carrots and celery. Stir-fry for 2 minutes. Serve on a heated serving dish.

Smoked Spareribs
YEN HS'UN P'AI KU

Chinese smoked dishes are usually lightly smoked so that the smoking adds only a touch of flavour. In the West, this smoking is best done by putting 2 tablespoons each of sugar, dry tea or pine needles on a sheet of aluminium foil placed inside a very large, old saucepan with a tight-fitting lid. The food to be smoked should be placed on top of a wire rack standing over the foil. Heat the pan over medium heat for 1 minute, or until the sugar, tea or pine needles begin to smoke. Remove the pan from the heat and set aside, covered, to smoke for 15 minutes. Smoked food may be served hot or cold.

4 tablespoons vegetable oil
3 large onions, thinly sliced
2 garlic cloves, chopped
1 tablespoon fermented salted black beans,
   soaked for 20 minutes, drained and
   mashed
2½ to 3 lb pork spareribs, separated into
   individual ribs and cut into 1½-inch pieces
Salt
Black pepper
4 tablespoons soy sauce
⅔ cup chicken stock
2 teaspoons Chinese chilli sauce
3 tablespoons dry sherry
1 tablespoon sugar
Vegetable oil for deep-frying
1 tablespoon sesame oil

Heat the 4 tablespoons of vegetable oil in a large, heavy casserole. Add the onions, garlic and beans and stir-fry for 2 minutes. Add the spareribs, salt and pepper and stir to mix. Fry for 5 minutes, stirring occasionally.

Add the soy sauce, stock, chilli sauce, sherry and sugar and bring to a boil, stirring. Reduce the heat to low, cover the casserole and simmer for 40 minutes, or until the ribs are cooked and the liquid has evaporated. Remove the pan from the heat.

Heat the oil for deep-frying in a large saucepan. When hot, add the ribs and deep-fry, a few at a time, for 3 minutes.

Drain the ribs well and smoke them as described in the introduction.

Brush with the sesame oil and serve hot or cold.

Stir-Fried Fish Fragrant Shredded Pork

A dish is called "fish fragrant" in Szechwan when it is cooked with ingredients which are normally used in cooking fish. There is a whole series of dishes made in this way. This is one of the best of them.

½ teaspoons salt
tablespoon cornflour
oz lean boned pork, shredded
teaspoons sugar
½ tablespoons soy sauce
½ tablespoons wine vinegar
tablespoon dry sherry
vegetable oil for deep-frying
½ oz lard
-inch piece fresh root ginger, shredded
chillies, seeded and shredded
garlic cloves, crushed
oz green part of leek, shredded

Rub the salt and cornflour into the pork shreds
and set aside.

In a small bowl, combine the sugar, soy
sauce, vinegar and sherry.

Heat the vegetable oil in a large saucepan.
When the oil is very hot, add the pork and deep-
fry for 2 minutes. Drain the pork and set aside.

Melt the lard in a large frying-pan. Add the
ginger, chillies, garlic and leeks and stir-fry for
minutes. Add the pork and stir-fry for 1½
minutes. Stir in the sherry mixture and stir-fry
for a further 1½ minutes. Transfer to a heated
serving dish and serve immediately.

Double-Cooked Pork
HUI KUO JOU

2½ pints water
2 lb pork belly or leg
tablespoon salt
large onion, quartered
3 tablespoons vegetable oil
2 spring onions, finely chopped
teaspoon chopped fresh root ginger
2 garlic cloves, finely chopped
2 teaspoons fermented salted black beans,
    soaked in water for 30 minutes, drained
    and mashed
2 tablespoons soy sauce
2 to 3 teaspoons Chinese chilli sauce
1 tablespoon tomato paste
2 tablespoons beef stock
2 teaspoons sugar
2 tablespoons dry sherry
2 teaspoons sesame oil

Heat the water in a large saucepan. Add the
pork, salt and onion. Bring the water to the
boil, cover the pan, reduce the heat and simmer gently for 40 minutes. Remove the pork.
Discard the liquid and the onion. Cut the pork
into thin slices about 2 inches by 3 inches.

Heat the oil in a large, heavy frying-pan. Add
the spring onions ginger and garlic. Stir-fry over
medium heat for 1 minute. Add the black beans
and continue to stir-fry for 2 minutes. Add the
soy sauce, chilli sauce, tomato paste, stock, sugar
and sherry. Stir and mix for 2 minutes. Add
the sliced pork. Turn the slices in the sauce until

every piece is well coated. Sprinkle with the
sesame oil. Serve on a heated serving platter.

Quick-Fried Diced Chicken with Chilli Pepper

*This dish is cooked quickly, and it should be
eaten immediately. The use of chillies, as opposed
to the soybean paste used in a similar Peking
dish, is typical of Szechwan cooking.*

8 oz boned chicken breast, cut into cubes
Salt
2 tablespoons dry sherry
1 egg white, well beaten with 2 tablespoons
    cornflour
½-inch piece fresh root ginger, shredded
2 spring onions, very finely chopped
1 garlic clove, chopped
1 tablespoon wine vinegar
1½ tablespoons soy sauce
2 tablespoons chicken stock
2 teaspoons cornflour
3 tablespoons lard or vegetable oil
2 red chillies, seeded and shredded

Put the chicken, salt and half the sherry in a
mixing bowl, stir well and set aside for 5
minutes. Add the egg white mixture and mix it
in so that the chicken pieces are well coated.

Combine the ginger, spring onions, garlic,
vinegar, soy sauce, stock, the remaining sherry
and cornflour in a bowl and mix well.

Melt the lard or heat the oil in a large frying-
pan over high heat. Add the chillies and stir-fry
for 1½ minutes. Add the chicken and stir-fry for
1 minute. Pour in the ginger and sherry mixture
and stir-fry for a further 1½ minutes, or until the
chicken is cooked.

Serve immediately, in a heated serving bowl.

Beaten Chicken
K'UNG K'UNG CHI

*This is a famous Szechwan dish, which is really
a "crystal-boiled" chicken. It is eaten by dipping
the meat into various traditional dips and sauces.
"Crystal-boiled" means that the chicken has been
boiled at different temperatures and for varying
lengths of time. This is done by adding cold water
to the pan at specified intervals. The best thing
about this dish is the contrast of sharp, spicy
sauces and simply cooked chicken.*

3 tablespoons vegetable oil
2 red chillies, seeded and chopped
3 spring onions, chopped
4 tablespoons soy sauce
1 tablespoon sugar
3 tablespoons toasted sesame seeds
2 tablespoons sesame paste blended with
    1 tablespoon sesame oil

2 tablespoons peppercorns, crushed
4 lb chicken

GARNISH

2 spring onions, chopped

First prepare the accompanying dip. Heat the
oil in a small frying-pan. Add the chillies and
stir-fry for 4 minutes. Remove the pan from
the heat.

In a small serving bowl, combine half of the
spring onions, the soy sauce, sugar, half of the
stir-fried chillies and the oil, one-third of the
toasted sesame seeds and half of the sesame
paste. This is the principal dip to be placed in the
centre of the dining-table. Place the remaining
spring onions, stir-fried chillies and the oil,
sesame seeds, crushed peppercorns and sesame
paste separately into small sauce dishes. These
are placed in front of each diner.

Bring 4 quarts of water to the boil in a large
saucepan. Put the chicken in the water and boil
for 10 minutes. Pour in 1 pint of cold water and
bring to the boil again. Boil for 10 minutes.
Pour in another pint of cold water, bring to the
boil and boil for another 10 minutes.

Drain the chicken. Cut off the wings and legs.
Chop the body into 6 pieces. Using a mallet or
rolling pin, gently beat each piece for a few
minutes.

Arrange the beaten chicken on a warmed
serving dish. Sprinkle with the chopped spring
onions and serve immediately, with the accompanying dips.

Szechwan Chicken "Pudding"
K'O CHI

1 tablespoon salt
2 pints water
3 lb chicken, chopped into 16 pieces
1 teaspoon peppercorns
2 tablespoons soy sauce
2 large onions, shredded
1-inch piece fresh root ginger, shredded
1½ lb sweet potatoes, peeled, sliced and cut
    into triangular 1½-inch wedges

Add the salt to the water and bring to the boil.
Add the chicken, reduce the heat to moderate
and cook for 15 minutes. Drain the chicken.

In a small frying-pan, cook the peppercorns
over moderate heat for 1 minute. Set aside. Pack
the chicken pieces, skin side down, in a thick
layer in the bottom of a large heatproof dish.
Sprinkle with the peppercorns, soy sauce, onions
and ginger, and cover with the potatoes, packing
them down tightly.

Cover the dish with aluminium foil and steam
in a steamer for 1 hour, or bake in an oven preheated to 375°F (Gas Mark 5) for 1¼ hours.

Hold a large round serving plate over the dish
and reverse the two.

Serve hot.

Dishes planned for texture and taste

Yunnan Distilled Chicken
CH'I KUO CHI

This is an unusual dish, where the chicken is placed in a Yunnan pot—an earthenware or porcelain pot which has a chimney in the centre to let in the steam from the saucepan of water in which it is boiled. A lid is fitted over the pot covering the chimney. The steam condenses as it hits the lid, and it is this "distilled" water which eventually forms a soup in the pot, although the ingredients were originally packed dry into the pot. The pot is brought to the table and the soup is served first and the chicken and vegetables later.

Since the chicken is simply cooked, it is usually dipped into good-quality soy sauce, or such other dips as chilli sauce, mustard or ketchup before eating. Owing to the sense of purity given by the "distilled water", the dish is treated with some reverence.

1 spring chicken, cut into 8 pieces, blanched and drained
4 dried Chinese mushrooms, soaked for 30 minutes, drained and stalks removed
2 oz bamboo shoots, cut into 1½-inch wedges
2 leeks, cut on the diagonal into 3-inch lengths
½-inch piece fresh root ginger, shredded
Salt
3 tablespoons white wine

Arrange the chicken pieces in the bottom of a Yunnan pot. Place the mushrooms, bamboo shoots, leeks and ginger over the chicken. Sprinkle with salt and the white wine.

Put the lid in place and put the pot on a wire rack inside a large saucepan. Pour in enough cold water to come 1 inch up the sides of the pot. Cover the pan and bring the water to a rolling boil. Boil, adding more water if necessary, for 1 to 1¼ hours.

Remove the pot from the saucepan and serve immediately.

Tangerine-Flavoured Peppered Chicken

This dish has a strong flavour and is typical of Szechwan cooking. Dried tangerine peel is available at most Chinese food stores.

2 spring onions, cut into ¼-inch lengths
2½ tablespoons soy sauce
2 teaspoons sugar
1½ tablespoons vinegar
2 tablespoons chicken stock
2 tablespoons dry sherry
Vegetable oil for deep-frying
3 lb chicken, chopped into 20 pieces
2 tablespoons sesame oil
2 teaspoons peppercorns

½-inch piece fresh root ginger, shredded
1 dried red chilli, seeded and finely chopped
Salt
1 piece dried tangerine peel, broken into small pieces

In a small mixing bowl, combine the spring onions, soy sauce, sugar, vinegar, stock and sherry.

Heat the oil in a large saucepan. When the oil is very hot, add the chicken pieces, a few at a time, and fry for 4 minutes, or until they are brown.

Heat the sesame oil in a large frying-pan. When the oil is hot, add the peppercorns, ginger, chilli, salt and tangerine peel and stir-fry for 1½ minutes. Add the chicken pieces and stir-fry for 2½ minutes. Add the spring onion and sherry mixture and stir-fry for a further 3 minutes.

Serve hot in a heated serving bowl.

WHY WINE-DRINKING has never caught on in China, or anywhere in Asia, is one of the historical mysteries. Adequate red and white wine is made in small quantities in Shantung province, but in no sense is it the people's drink of the People's Republic. Meals are washed down with lemonade or rice beer or tea.

The true drink of China is tea, which is processed in different ways in different districts to give drinks of completely different character—fermented or unfermented, scented or unscented smoked or unsmoked.

The natural unprocessed tea, for which the leaves of the tea bush (a member of the camellia family) are dried but not fermented, is green tea. Tea for this purpose is grown in most parts of China, but particularly in Chekiang, Anhwei and Kwantung provinces. It is the mildest tea, little drunk in the West except in Chinese restaurants.

Formosa specializes in a half-fermented style known as Oolong. Scented tea (jasmine is the commonest blossom to add for its scent) is normally made with Oolong or the similar Lo Cha.

Fully-fermented leaves give black tea, which is much more pronounced in flavour. Keemun, from Anhwei, is the best-known of the black teas. But strongest-flavoured of all is smoked black tea—the Lapsang Souchong of Hunan. A mere pinch of smoked tea in a blend is enough to give its character to the whole pot.

Crispy and Aromatic Duck
HSIANG SHU YA

In this dish, the meat of the duck is chopped and either wrapped in pancakes, as is Peking duck or served with steamed buns, using shredded cucumber and chopped scallions to add texture and a little sweetened bean paste to increase the spiciness.

2 teaspoons peppercorns, crushed
2 garlic cloves, crushed
2 medium-sized onions, chopped
1 tablespoon fresh chopped ginger
1 tablespoon mixed dried herbs or ¼ teaspoon five-spice powder
Salt
2 tablespoons dry sherry
3 lb duck
2½ tablespoons soy sauce
Vegetable oil for deep-frying

In a small bowl, combine the peppercorns garlic, onions, ginger, herbs or spice powder salt and sherry. Rub this mixture into the duck inside and out. Set aside to marinate overnight

Place the duck in a deep heatproof dish in a steamer. Steam for 1 hour.

Drain the duck and pour any liquid in the bottom of the dish into a large saucepan. Add the soy sauce and bring to a boil. Add the duck, and, basting with the liquid, cook over fairly high heat until the duck is evenly browned Drain the duck on a wire rack.

Heat the oil in a large saucepan. When the oil is hot, lower the duck into it and deep-fry for 8 minutes, or until the skin is crisp.

Drain the duck and cut the meat and skin off the bones. Arrange the meat and skin separately on a heated dish and serve.

Smoked, Steamed, Fried Marinated Duck
CHANG CH'A FEI YA

This is a slightly complicated dish and takes a long time to prepare, but it has a delicious flavour, typical of dishes of West China, and is worth the effort.

If sweetened soybean paste is not obtainable, a substitute may be made by heating 2 tablespoons of sesame oil, 1 tablespoon of sugar, 1 tablespoon of flour and 2 tablespoons of soy sauce over low heat, stirring, until the mixture forms a thick paste. The mixture is served in a small bowl, and the fried duck pieces are dipped into it before being eaten.

4 teaspoons salt
2 large onions, finely chopped
2 teaspoons peppercorns, crushed
2 tablespoons dry sherry

lb duck
vegetable oil for deep-frying
spring onions, chopped
tablespoons sesame oil mixed with
2 tablespoons sweetened soybean paste

OR SMOKING

large lump burning charcoal
tablespoons jasmine tea leaves
r
tablespoons dried pine needles
r
tablespoons sawdust

n a small bowl, combine the salt, onions, peppercorns and sherry. Rub the mixture into the duck, inside and out, and set it aside in a cool place to marinate overnight.

Place the lump of burning charcoal in the bottom of a large earthenware pot or flame-proof casserole. Sprinkle the tea leaves, pine needles and sawdust over the charcoal. As the smoke rises, place the duck on a wire rack and place the rack in the pot. Cover with aluminium foil and smoke for 10 minutes. Turn the duck over and smoke for a further 10 minutes.

Remove the duck from the rack and place it on a heatproof dish. Place the dish in a steamer and steam for 1½ hours, or until the duck is cooked. Remove the duck from the steamer and, using a cleaver, chop it into about 20 pieces.

Heat the vegetable oil in a large saucepan. When the oil is hot, add the duck pieces a few at a time and fry for 4 minutes.

Arrange the duck pieces on a heated serving dish and sprinkle the spring onions over the top. Put the sesame-oil mixture in a small bowl and serve with the duck.

Braised Bean Curd with Mushrooms and Hot Meat Sauce
MA-P'O TOU-FU

2 tablespoons vegetable oil
1 medium-sized onion, thinly sliced
2 garlic cloves, crushed
¼ lb minced pork or beef
4 medium-sized Chinese dried mushrooms, soaked for 30 minutes, drained, stalks removed and caps sliced
6 tablespoons beef stock
3 tablespoons soy sauce
Black pepper
¼ teaspoon Chinese chilli sauce or Tabasco sauce
2 tablespoons dry sherry
5 cakes bean curd, each cut into 20 pieces
1 tablespoon cornflour mixed with 2 tablespoons cold water
1½ teaspoons sesame oil

Heat the oil in a large, heavy frying-pan. Add the onion and garlic and stir-fry over moderate

heat for 2 minutes. Add the meat and mush-rooms and continue to stir-fry for 3 minutes. Pour in the stock and add the soy sauce, pepper, chilli or Tabasco sauce and sherry. Cook, stir-ring frequently, for 3 more minutes. Add the bean curd and mix with the other ingredients. Pour the cornflour mixture evenly over the ingredients and cook, stirring constantly, for 1 minute. Sprinkle with sesame oil and serve immediately.

Hunan Steamed Rice

The proper way to cook rice is a controversial subject because there are so many different methods of doing it. Rice should be dry, fluffy and even in texture. All the moisture should have been ab-sorbed by the rice grains, and none left between the grains. In China, rice is generally steamed, which is probably the best way to cook it.

Hunan is often referred to as the rice-bowl of China. The Hunan method of cooking rice is to boil it first and then steam it. The water used to boil the rice may be used as a base for soups.

1 pint water
6 oz long-grain rice, washed and drained

Bring the water to the boil in a saucepan. Add the rice and bring the water to the boil again. Cook, stirring with a wooden spoon to prevent the grains from sticking, for 5 minutes. Drain the rice. Spread the rice out on a large, flat heatproof dish. Place the dish in the steamer and steam for 25 to 30 minutes, or longer if you want the rice to be very tender.

Orange Soup with New Year Yuan-Hsiao Dumplings
YUAN-HSIAO CH'U KENG

Yuan-hsiao is a special type of sweet dumpling which is made by rolling a ball of sweet stuffing in ground rice or rice flour repeatedly until a thick layer of rice surrounds it. The dish is served in Chinese homes during the New Year.

Sweet soups such as this one are often served to provide variety and as intervals between savoury courses at a meal.

2 oz finely chopped walnuts
2 oz ground almonds
2 tablespoons watermelon seeds
2 tablespoons sesame seeds
5 tablespoons castor sugar
1½ tablespoons softened lard
1½ lb Rice flour

SOUP

15 fl oz fresh orange juice
15 fl oz water
1½ tablespoons castor sugar

Place the walnuts, almonds, melon seeds, sesame seeds, sugar and lard in a medium-sized mixing bowl. Knead the mixture well and form it into balls about ½ inch in diameter.

Spread half of the rice flour in a deep-sided tray in a ¼-inch-thick layer. Dip the balls quickly into cold water and place them on the tray. Roll the balls by tipping and rotating the tray until they are thoroughly coated.

Wet the balls again and spread the remaining rice flour over the tray. Roll the balls until they are thickly coated with flour and are perfectly round.

Bring a large saucepan of water to the boil and gently drop the balls into it. When the water comes to the boil again, boil the dumplings for 1 minute.

With a slotted spoon, remove the balls from the water and divide them between the soup bowls. Keep the dumplings hot.

Put the orange juice and water in a large saucepan. Stir in the sugar and when it has dissolved bring the liquid to the boil.

Pour the soup over the dumplings and serve.

Festival Sweet Rice Porridge
LA PA CHOU

Sweet rice porridge is usually eaten in China as a snack, but it may also be eaten during a multi-course meal to break the monotony of savoury and fried dishes.

SERVES 12

4 tablespoons vegetable oil
6 walnuts, blanched and chopped
3 oz glutinous rice, washed and drained
3 oz long-grain rice, washed and drained
2¾ pints water
1½ oz red beans, washed and drained
12 dates, stoned
2 tablespoons sugared lotus seeds
2 tablespoons watermelon seeds, blanched
2 crab apples, peeled, cored and sliced
4 tablespoons castor sugar
3 tablespoons raisins
4 tablespoons chopped candied fruits

Heat the oil in a small frying-pan. When it is hot, add the walnuts and fry, stirring, for 2 minutes. Drain and set aside.

Place the glutinous and long-grain rice in a large, heavy-based saucepan. Add the water and bring to the boil. Simmer gently over very low heat for 1½ hours.

Half fill another large saucepan with water and bring to the boil. Add the red beans, dates, lotus seeds and watermelon seeds. Boil gently for 20 minutes. Drain and add to the rice, with the crab apples. Simmer the rice mixture for a further 30 minutes. Stir in the sugar.

Divide the mixture equally between 12 warmed bowls. Garnish with the walnuts, raisins and candied fruits and serve hot.

A cuisine centred on a cosmopolitan city

NEARING THE END OF ITS JOURNEY, the Yangtze, China's longest river, runs through its lower reaches in lush rice-growing country and then flows into the sea just north of Shanghai—a great port and one of the largest cities in the world. Bitterly cold in winter, hot and sticky in the summer but delightful in the spring and autumn, Shanghai is a city of delicate and delicious food and sweet wine. During the second quarter of the twentieth century, with a population of seven million, Shanghai was one of the wealthiest and most cosmopolitan cities in China. Hundreds of restaurants did a thriving business, serving excellent European as well as fine Shanghai food.

Just north of the river is the city of Yangchow, renowned for its cuisine, as the many dishes named after it confirm. South of the river and farther upstream is Nanking, many times the capital of China. To the east are the silk cities of Soochow and Wuhsi, where the people are naturally refined and particular about their food. In the same region are the towns of Shao Xing, famous for its rice wine, and Ching Hua, well known for its ham. Just south of where the Yangtze flows into the sea is Hangchow Bay and the city of Hangchow, famous for its scenic West Lake, the freshness of its shrimp and other fresh-water fish, as well as its soy duck, which is said to rival Peking duck in popularity.

In such a well-watered area as the Lower Yangtze, the cuisine is naturally inspired by the produce of the region—a great range of vegetables and a fine selection of fresh-water fish, shrimp and crabs which are considered more delicate in taste than those from the sea. The dishes of this area are delicately seasoned and the sauces are light. Sugar is used fairly liberally. Chingkiang vinegar, the most fragrant vinegar in all China, is used both as a dip and as an ingredient to add piquancy to sauces and dishes.

In this region, more than in any other, food is cooked in such a way as to bring out the natural flavour of the main ingredient, rather than to blend its flavour with other ingredients or to mask it with seasonings. This is usually achieved by steaming in a closed vessel—a practical way of cooking as the steam is usually provided by the boiling of the rice. The result is a semi-soup dish, the main ingredient cooked and served in a well-flavoured broth. Fish is often cooked in meat broth. Typical dishes are carp cooked in mutton broth and trout in salt pork broth. Meat is frequently simply boiled, steamed or simmered in soy sauce. Spareribs are fried and seasoned only with salt and pepper. These simple methods of cooking, however, require ingredients which are fresh and of the highest quality. The hearts of vegetables are commonly used.

In this region, when stir-frying is the method of cooking there is only the minimal addition of sauces and seasonings. The results are the so-called crystal dishes, which are very much in contrast to the Cantonese versions, in which the strong taste of salted and fermented black beans is always present; or with similar dishes from Szechwan, where garlic, ginger, scallions and chilli peppers are frequently added in some strength.

A well-known dish from this area is the pressed duck of Nanking. The duck is seasoned, marinated, pressed and dried, then soaked for two to four hours before it is slowly brought to a boil and then left to cool in the liquid for twenty minutes before the process is repeated. By never bringing the liquid to a full boil, very little of the nutritious and delectable elements are lost in the cooking. The duck is often served cold, but it can also be cross-cooked with other ingredients.

One of the favourite fresh-water fish of this area is eel, which is often deep-fried and then quickly cooked in a thick sauce made with rice wine, soy sauce, soy paste, sugar and five-spice powder. The sauce is thickened through rapid cooking rather than with the use of a thickening agent.

The people of Shanghai have a sweet tooth, and in many recipes of the area crystal sugar (large lumps of unrefined sugar crystals) is generously used in the preparation of pork, ham and even of fish. Shrimp and crab dishes, too, are often sweeter than those of most other parts of China.

In this area, where there has always been a profusion of vegetables, vegetarianism was often indulged in as a fad by the rich in much the same way as today the wealthy in Western society take to health farms and health foods. Consequently, vegetarian food had a certain snob appeal and the creation of vegetarian dishes was regarded as the greatest test of a cook's gastronomical knowledge and ability. Mushrooms and fungi of countless varieties are used to produce some delicious soups. Many of these vegetarian dishes are imitations of non-vegetarian dishes. Among these are vegetarian roast duck, vegetarian stir-fried shrimp, vegetarian stir-fried crabs, vege-tarian ham, vegetarian braised eel and sweet and sour vegetarian whole fish.

In China, rice is seldom cooked and served in any other way except plain boiled or steamed, but in this area there is an unusual rice dish called vegetable rice. A vegetable is seasoned and lightly fried. It is then buried in rice and cooked while the rice is boiled or steamed, thus imparting a pleasant flavour to the rice. Handmilled rice has an earthy fragrance when it is cooked and when this fragrance combines with the green taste of vegetables. Together they reflect the main products of the region—rice and vegetables.

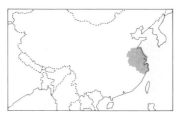

LIONS' HEADS
Large meatballs

PRESSED DRIED DUCK

SPRING ONIONS

CHINESE CHIVES

NANKING •

GARLIC

CHINESE CABBAGES

SWEET POTATOES

VINEGAR

POTATOES

BEAN CURD AND
DRIED BEAN CURD

SALTED PRESSED
PORK

SNAILS

SHELLFISH

WHEAT FLOUR
BALLS

PORK BELLY

BROAD BEANS

PEACHES

FRESH-WATER
CRAB

• **SHANGHAI**

SPARERIBS

LU
FISH

LOTUS
SEED

EELS

BEAN CURD

DEEP FRIED
SQUIRREL-FISH

WATER
CHESTNUTS

LOTUS FLOWER

LEG OF PORK BRAISED
WITH CRYSTAL SUGAR

WATER
NUTS

YAMS

LOTUS LEAF
Wrapper for
steamed pork

EIGHT JEWEL
STEAMED RICE PUDDING

KWEI FISH

LOTUS ROOT

YANGTZE KIANG

SPRATS

SMOKED CHICKEN

SHRIMPS

SALT-WATER
FISH

C H E K I A N G

NINGPO

TEA

SHAO-HSIN
RICE WINE

LILY ROOT
AND FLOWER

CURED HAM

BAMBOO SHOOTS

PAPER-WRAPPED CHICKEN

Light sauces and dishes delicately seasoned

The Squirrel Fish
SHUNAG SHU YU

This dish is called the squirrel fish because the fish curls around like the tail of a squirrel when it is deep-fried, and squeaks when the sweet and sour sauce is poured over it. If sea bass is not available, carp or pike may be substituted.

2 to 3 lb sea bass, cleaned and gutted
4 tablespoons flour
3 tablespoons wine vinegar
3 tablespoons chicken stock
2 tablespoons sugar
1 tablespoon tomato purée
1 tablespoon soy sauce
1 tablespoon cornflour, blended with
    4 tablespoons water
Vegetable oil for deep-frying
1½ tablespoons vegetable oil or lard
1 medium-sized onion, thinly sliced
4 dried Chinese mushrooms, soaked for
    30 minutes in cold water, drained, stalks
    removed and caps shredded
2 medium-sized tomatoes, blanched, peeled
    and coarsely chopped
2 oz bamboo shoots, thinly sliced
¼ teaspoon monosodium glutamate
    (optional)

Using a sharp knife, cut off the head of the fish. Slit the fish into two halves leaving the tail intact. Cut out the backbone. Open out the fish and score the flesh side to within ¼ inch of the skin with criss-cross cuts about 1 inch apart. Dredge the fish with the flour and set aside.

In a small bowl, combine the vinegar, stock, sugar, tomato purée, soy sauce and cornflour mixture. Set aside.

Heat the vegetable oil for deep-frying in a large saucepan. Deep-fry the fish for 5 minutes. Remove the pan from the heat and set aside.

In a small saucepan, heat the oil or melt the lard. Add the onion, mushrooms, tomatoes and bamboo shoots. Stir-fry over medium heat for 2 minutes. Add the soy sauce mixture and the monosodium glutamate, if being used, and cook the sauce, stirring constantly, until it is thick. Remove the pan from the heat and keep the sauce hot.

Return the fish to high heat and deep-fry for a further 2 minutes, or until the fish curls up.

Drain the fish and place it on a heated serving dish. Pour over the sauce (which should make the fish squeak) and serve immediately.

Stir-Fried Shrimp with Green Peas
CHING TOU CH'AO HSIA JEN

2 tablespoons vegetable oil
1 teaspoon finely chopped fresh root ginger
12 oz uncooked shrimp, shelled
1 oz butter
2 oz bamboo shoots, diced
1 lb fresh, shelled, or frozen green peas
2 tablespoons chicken stock
1 tablespoon soy sauce
1 tablespoon dry sherry
¼ teaspoon monosodium glutamate
    (optional)
Salt
1½ teaspoons sugar

Heat the oil in a large, deep frying-pan. When the oil is hot, add the ginger and stir-fry for 10 seconds. Add the shrimp and stir-fry over moderate heat for 1½ minutes, or until they change colour. Remove the pan from the heat.

In a small saucepan, melt the butter over moderate heat. Add the bamboo shoots and peas and stir-fry for 2 minutes.

Add the pea mixture to the shrimp and return the frying-pan to the heat. Add the chicken stock, soy sauce, sherry, monosodium glutamate, if being used, salt to taste and sugar and stir-fry over low heat for 2 minutes. Transfer the mixture to a warmed serving dish and serve.

Paper-Wrapped Chicken
CHIH PAO CHI

Cooking food wrapped in a paper parcel is an interesting method of preparation. It can be applied to almost any food which needs only a short cooking time. The wrapping is broken with chopsticks before eating.

8 oz boned chicken, cut into 1½-inch strips
2 tablespoons soy sauce
1 tablespoon dry sherry
1 tablespoon sugar
2 teaspoons finely shredded fresh root ginger
4 medium-sized dried Chinese mushrooms,
    soaked in cold water for 30 minutes,
    drained, stalks removed and caps
    shredded
3 spring onions, cut into 1½-inch lengths
16 6-inch squares of cellophane or wax paper
Vegetable oil for deep-frying

Put the chicken, soy sauce, sherry and sugar in a mixing bowl, stir well and marinate for 1 hour.

On each square of paper put some chicken, ginger, mushrooms and spring onion. Fold each square like an envelope, tucking in the flap. Arrange the parcels, flap side down, on a plate.

Heat the oil in a large saucepan. Put half of the parcels in the oil and deep-fry for 3 minutes or until they are light brown. Drain. Fry the remaining parcels in the same way. Return all the parcels to the oil and deep-fry for a further 1½ minutes. Serve immediately.

Stir-Fried Beef with Spring Onions
YANG CH'UNG CH'AO NIU HOU SSU

Salt
Black pepper
1 tablespoon cornflour
1 lb lean beef, cut into 3-inch matchstick
    strips
3 tablespoons vegetable oil
2 teaspoons finely shredded root ginger
1 tablespoon lard
10 spring onions, cut into 3-inch lengths
2½ tablespoons soy sauce
2 tablespoons dry sherry
2 tablespoons beef stock
1½ teaspoons sugar
¼ teaspoon monosodium glutamate
    (optional)

Combine the salt, pepper and cornflour, and rub the mixture into the shredded beef.

Heat the oil in a large frying-pan. Add the beef and ginger and stir-fry over high heat for

... minutes. Add the lard and, when it has melted, add the spring onions and stir-fry for 30 seconds. Add the soy sauce, sherry, stock, sugar and monosodium glutamate, if being used, and stir-fry for 30 seconds. Transfer to a warmed serving dish and serve.

Red-Braised Hand of Pork with Crystal Sugar
PING TANG YUAN TI

3 pints water
3-3½ lb hand of pork, meat scored with deep vertical cuts
1 medium-sized onion, thinly sliced
2 teaspoons coarsely chopped fresh root ginger
6 tablespoons soy sauce
3 tablespoons crystal sugar or brown sugar
2 tablespoons lard or vegetable oil

Bring the water to the boil in a large flameproof casserole. Add the pork and, when the water returns to the boil, partly cover, reduce the heat and simmer gently for 30 minutes.

Preheat the oven to 350°F (Gas Mark 4).

Skim all the fat and scum off the top and pour off half of the liquid. Add all the remaining ingredients. Cover the casserole and transfer it to the oven. Bake for 2 hours, turning the meat every 30 minutes.

Transfer the casserole to the top of the stove and cook, uncovered, over high heat until the liquid has reduced to about half a cupful.

Put the pork in a warmed serving dish, pour the sauce over it and serve.

Salt and Pepper Spareribs
CHIAO YEN P'AI KU

This dish derives its name from the fact that the cooked spareribs are eaten hot with a dry-fried salt and pepper mixture, as well as with a soy sauce and sherry dip.

1½ lb pork spareribs, divided into ribs and chopped into 2-inch lengths
1 tablespoon dry sherry
2 tablespoons soy sauce
1½ tablespoons cornflour
1 tablespoon salt
1½ tablespoons black pepper

DIP
1 tablespoon vegetable oil
1 tablespoon soy sauce
1 tablespoon sugar
1½ tablespoons vinegar
1 tablespoon sherry
¾ tablespoon cornflour, blended with 4 tablespoons water
Vegetable oil for deep-frying

Put the spareribs in a shallow bowl. Mix together the sherry and soy sauce and rub the mixture over the ribs. Marinate for 1 hour then pat the ribs dry with kitchen paper and dust them evenly with the cornflour. Set aside.

In a small frying-pan, heat the salt and pepper over moderate heat for 3 minutes, stirring and shaking the pan constantly. Put the mixture in a small serving bowl and set aside.

Next make the dip. Heat the oil in a small saucepan over low heat. Add the soy sauce, sugar, vinegar, sherry and the cornflour mixture. Cook, stirring constantly, until the sauce thickens and becomes translucent. Pour into a small serving bowl and set aside.

Heat the oil for deep-frying in a large saucepan over fairly high heat. When the oil is hot, place half of the spareribs in a wire basket and lower them into the hot oil. Deep-fry for 1½ minutes and drain. Repeat with the other spareribs. Now put all the spareribs together in the basket in the oil and deep-fry for 1½ minutes. Drain and serve immediately with the dip and the salt and pepper mixture.

Stir-Fried Mange-Tout
CH'AO HSUEH TOU

The addition of lard in this recipe makes the vegetables glisten.

2 tablespoons vegetable oil
1 lb mange-tout, washed, dried and stringed
4 tablespoons chicken stock
½ chicken stock cube, crumbled
1 tablespoon lard, cut into small pieces

Heat the oil in a large frying-pan. Add the mange-tout and fry over low heat for 30 seconds, stirring constantly. Add the stock, the stock cube and salt to taste and stir-fry for a further 30 seconds. Remove the pan from the heat and stir and turn the vegetables for 1 minute.

Return the pan to the heat and cook, stirring, until most of the liquid has evaporated. Add the lard and cook, still stirring, until it melts and the mange-tout glisten. Serve hot.

Stuffed Steamed Marrow
TUNG KUA CHUNG

To serve this dish, the marrow is placed on the table and the diners help themselves by dipping into it with spoons.

1 round marrow, about 8 inches in diameter, washed
¼ lb cucumber, trimmed and coarsely chopped
2 spring onions, cut into 1-inch lengths

4 oz bamboo shoots, diced
8 oz Chinese straw mushrooms or canned drained button mushrooms
8 oz fresh or canned crab meat
1 teaspoon shredded fresh root ginger
Salt
1 tablespoon sesame oil
2 tablespoons white wine
6 tablespoons chicken stock
1 tablespoon soy sauce

Using a sharp knife, cut off the upper quarter of the marrow to make a lid. Scoop out and discard the soft pulp and seeds, leaving the firm flesh. Set aside.

Place the remaining ingredients in a saucepan and, stirring constantly, bring to the boil. Pour into the marrow and replace the lid. Put the marrow into a heatproof bowl and put the bowl in a steamer. Steam for 1 hour. Serve hot in the bowl.

Fruit-Filled Watermelon
SHIH-CHIN KUO PIN

1 small watermelon
1 small can lychees
1 small can mandarin oranges
6 preserved kumquats, chopped
4 oz green grapes, peeled and seeded
3 peaches, peeled, stoned and chopped
2 pears, peeled, cored and chopped
2 medium-sized apples, peeled, cored and chopped
¼ teaspoon almond essence

Cut off the top third of the melon. Scoop out and discard the seeds. Scoop out the flesh and cut it into 1-inch cubes. Place the melon cubes in a large mixing bowl and add the remaining ingredients. Stir well and put the mixture into the melon shell. Replace the lid and refrigerate for at least 2 hours before serving.

A tradition distilled from three sources

BARBECUED LAMB

MANDARIN HOTPOT
Meat, fish and vegetables simmered in broth

PEKING DUCK WITH PANCAKES

MAIZE WINE

MONGOLIAN LAMB HOTPOT
Lamb cooked in boiling broth

MUSHROOMS

PEKING

DRY-FRIED PRAWNS

TIENTSIN.

FISH IN VINEGAR AND CHILLI SAUCE

.PAO TING

CHESTNUTS AND CHINESE CABBAGE   H O P E H

BARBECUED MUTTON

DRAWN-GLASS-THREAD APPLES
Toffee apples

GRAPE WINE

APPLES

PEACHES

GRAPES

PEARS

DUMPLINGS AND STEAMED BREAD

CHICKEN

.TSINAN

WATER-MELON

TSING TAO .

CAKES

HWANG HO

S H A N T U N G

YELLOW RIVER SWEET AND SOUR CARP

STEAMED DUMPLINGS

PEKIN

THE CUISINE OF PEKING AND NORTH CHINA derives its character from three distinct sources—Chinese Moslem, Palace or Mandarin dishes and the indigenous cooking of North China.

Chinese Moslem cooking originated in the great grasslands and steppes of western China, where the population was predominately Mongol. It was brought to the north after the conquest of Peking and all of China by the Golden Horde of Genghis Khan in the thirteenth century. Barbecuing, spit-roasting, long, low-heat simmering of large chunks of meat and deep-frying were the methods of cooking used by the Mongols. Many centuries of adaptation by the Chinese refined the techniques of the Mongol herdsmen. Peking duck, for example, one of China's finest dishes, which did not finally become established in Peking until the middle of the nineteenth century, evolved from primitive spit-roasting.

Quick-dip boiling is the basis of Peking hot-pot. A pot of broth is kept at a rolling boil in a charcoal-burning hot-pot. Paper-thin slices of lamb are dropped into the broth and cooked instantly, to be retrieved with chopsticks and dipped in various sauces before eating. The dish, also known as the Mongolian hot-pot, is a favourite in Peking during the winter.

The barbecues of the steppes became the table-barbecued meats of Peking. A large charcoal-burning brazier blazes in the centre of a plain wooden table. Each diner uses extra-long chopsticks to pick up the thinly sliced beef or lamb and barbecues them on top of the brazier. The slice of meat is dipped into a bowl of beaten egg, then into various piquant sauces and eaten with aromatic hotcakes or buns. Sometimes the meat is mixed with noodles, lettuce, cabbage hearts, mushrooms, bamboo shoots and a little wine and cooked for a few minutes in a small casserole.

The Imperial Palace contributed less to the cuisine of Peking than did the Mongols. This was, perhaps, because the last family to occupy the throne of China came from Manchuria, where no distinctive style of cooking seems to have existed. Although the Manchus were great fighters when they first moved into China over three hundred years ago, they did not have the time or inclination to develop a distinctive cuisine of their own.

During the Manchu dynasty all Manchurians were pensioned from birth. The result of such pampering was the degeneration of a vigorous tribal people into weak, ineffectual courtiers. But as they declined in martial prowess, their interest and taste in food grew, and almost all of the more refined Palace dishes were created or developed during the second half of the Manchu rule, especially after Emperor Ch'ien-lung's visit to South China. Some of these truly excellent dishes, which seem to reflect southern influence, include *chi ting hsia jen*, mixed fry of diced chicken with shrimp, *t'ang ts'u ying t'ao jau*, sweet and sour cherry-coloured pork, *li tzu pai ts'ai*, braised cabbage with chestnuts, and *kuei fei chi*, royal concubine chicken.

The indigenous cuisine of North China is based principally on the produce and cooking methods of the provinces of Hopeh, in which Peking is situated, and Shantung, where Confucius was born. The people of these areas eat steamed buns and noodles rather than rice. Their favourite noodle dish, *ch'a chiang mein*, can almost be described as a version of *spaghetti bolognese*. The principal difference between the Chinese and the Italian versions is that the Chinese add raw shredded vegetables, bean sprouts and pickles to the noodles, thus providing textural contrasts and greater piquancy. *Man tou*, steamed buns, plain and solid, are the principal bulk food of North China.

A favourite cooking ingredient of the region is *t'sing*, soybean paste, which can best be described as soy sauce in solid form. It is used extensively in stir-frying pork or chicken pieces and minced meats. It is also an ingredient in the sauce brushed on the pancakes in which pieces of Peking duck are wrapped. This paste, used in judicious quantities, brings out the savouriness and flavour of the ingredients with which it is cooked.

The Pekingese use liberal amounts of vinegar and pepper in their soups. Sliced fish-peppered soup is certainly very peppery. They have their own version of hot and sour soup, which is said to have originated in Szechwan, but is now part of the Pekingese cuisine. This way of taking over provincial dishes and regarding them as their own seems to be a prerogative of the Pekingese, since many such provincial dishes became established and famous only after their arrival in the capital.

When beaten egg white and minced chicken or minced white fish are blended together, it is called *fu-yung*, the original and correct use of the term. Today, in many overseas Chinese restaurants, any dish with egg added is loosely termed *fu-yung*, a sad misnomer. As a result, many Westerners think that *fu-yung* means omelette.

Beaten egg white is used in *kao li tou shahm*, a Pekingese dessert best described as meringue balls stuffed with sweetened bean-paste and deep-fried. The other well-known Peking dessert is *pa ssu ping kou*, sometimes called toffee apples in the West. Properly translated it should be drawn glass-thread apples, which describes what happens when the pieces of apple are drawn from the molten sugar, before they are plunged into cold water.

All three strands of Peking cooking comprise a varied cuisine of highly individual character, giving it a unique position among the regional cuisines of China.

Classic dishes of a varied cuisine

Minced Duck Soup with Crackling Croûtes
YA NI MIEN PAO T'ANG

This soup gets its name from the fried bread squares, or croûtes, which crackle as the hot soup is poured over them.

1 pint good stock
4 medium-sized dried Chinese mushrooms, soaked for 30 minutes, drained, stalks removed and caps finely chopped
4 oz shelled green peas
4 oz cooked duck meat, minced
1½ tablespoons cornflour mixed with 4 tablespoons water
2 tablespoons soy sauce
4 tablespoons white wine
Salt
Black pepper
2 teaspoons chicken fat
½ chicken stock cube, crumbled
Vegetable oil for deep-frying
1 large slice white bread, crusts removed, cut into small cubes

Heat the stock in a large saucepan. Add the mushrooms, peas and minced duck and simmer for 5 minutes. Add the cornflour, soy sauce, white wine, salt, pepper, chicken fat and stock cube and bring to a slow boil, stirring constantly until the soup has thickened. Remove the pan from the heat and keep the soup hot.

Heat the oil in a medium-sized saucepan over fairly high heat. When the oil is very hot, add the bread cubes and fry for 2 minutes, or until they are crisp and golden.

Drain the bread cubes on absorbent paper and place them in a heated soup tureen. Pour in the soup and serve immediately.

Dry-Fried Giant Prawns
KAN SHAO TA HSIA

Pacific prawns are used for this dish in Peking, but any giant prawns which are 5 to 6 inches in length may be substituted.

8 giant prawns, washed
Salt
2 tablespoons chicken stock
1½ tablespoons soy sauce
1½ tablespoons dry sherry
1 tablespoon vinegar
1½ tablespoons tomato purée
½ teaspoon Chinese chilli sauce
2½ tablespoons vegetable oil
2 tablespoons chopped onion
½-inch piece fresh root ginger, sliced
1 garlic clove, crushed
1 teaspoon castor sugar
¾ oz lard

Cut off the heads of the prawns. Slit them up the back through the shell and remove the dark vein. Rub the prawns all over with salt and set aside.

In a small mixing bowl, combine the chicken stock, soy sauce, sherry, vinegar, tomatoe purée and chilli sauce and set aside.

Heat the oil in a large frying-pan over moderate heat. Add the onion, ginger and garlic and stir-fry for 30 seconds. Remove and discard the ginger. Add the prawns and stir-fry for 1 minute. Add the sherry mixture and the sugar and increase the heat to high. Stir-fry until most of the liquid has evaporated. Add the lard and when it has melted remove the pan from the heat, stir well and turn the mixture out on to a heated serving dish. Serve immediately.

Fried and Braised Carp
KAN SHAO CHI YU

It is said that in the eighteenth century, this dish was served to the Emperor Ch'ien-lung by a famous Soochow chef, when he visited the area south of the Yangtze.

1½ lb carp, cleaned and gutted
Salt
1½ tablespoons cornflour
4 spring onion stalks, cut into ½-inch pieces
1-inch piece fresh root ginger, finely chopped
3 tablespoons soy sauce
2 teaspoons castor sugar
3 tablespoons yellow wine or dry sherry
1 tablespoon wine vinegar
2 tablespoons good stock
Vegetable oil for deep-frying
1 oz lard

Rub the fish all over with salt and cornflour. Set aside.

In a small bowl, combine half of the spring onions, half the ginger, the soy sauce, sugar, yellow wine or sherry, vinegar and stock. Set aside.

Heat the oil in a large saucepan. Put the fish in a deep-frying basket and lower it into the hot oil. Fry for 5 minutes and drain.

Melt the lard in a large frying-pan. Add half of the sherry mixture and stir well. Put the fish in the pan and pour the remaining sherry mixture over it. Cook the fish, basting it frequently and turning it over once, until it is cooked and the liquid has evaporated.

Remove the pan from the heat and transfer the fish to a heated dish. Sprinkle the remaining spring onions and ginger over the top and serve.

Hot and Sour Peppered Fish

This is a dish which the Chinese call a main-course soup dish. It is not a conventional fish dish, nor is it a soup in the Western sense; at a Chinese dinner party, it is left on the table and eaten throughout the meal, with the diners helping themselves to the soup or fish whenever they like.

Vegetable oil for deep-frying
3 lb whole fish, preferably carp, bream or sole, cleaned and gutted
¾ oz lard
1 medium-sized onion, coarsely chopped
1-inch piece fresh root ginger, coarsely chopped
2 teaspoons peppercorns, crushed
1 pint chicken stock
Salt
½ chicken stock cube, crumbled
3 tablespoons sherry
3 tablespoons wine vinegar
2 spring onions, cut into 1-inch pieces
2 tablespoons chopped fresh coriander leaves
2 teaspoons sesame oil

Heat the vegetable oil in a large saucepan. Place the fish in a deep-frying basket and lower it into the oil. Deep-fry for 4 minutes and drain thoroughly.

Melt the lard in a large casserole. Add the onion, ginger and peppercorns and stir-fry over high heat for 2 minutes. Add the chicken stock, salt to taste, stock cube and fish. Simmer over low heat for 20 minutes. Add the sherry, vinegar, spring onions, coriander leaves and sesame oil and simmer for a further 5 minutes.

Remove the casserole from the heat and serve.

Mongolian Sliced Lamb Hot-Pot
SHUANG YANG JOU

The hot-pot used in cooking and serving this dish is a decorative piece of brassware. It is made in three parts: a charcoal-burning pot that fits beneath a round, squat funnel, about 4 inches wide, which extends upwards for about a foot from the base. Around the funnel is a circular "moat", about 4 inches wide, in which the food is cooked. It must have liquid, usually stock, in it before the burner, filled with hot, glowing charcoal, is placed in position. The lid of the hot-pot encircles the funnel.

This dish is often served with steamed buns as a one-dish meal.

SERVES 6 TO 8

3 to 4 lb boned leg of lamb, thinly sliced and each slice cut into 3-inch by 1½-inch strips

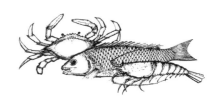

3 tablespoons wine vinegar
6 tablespoons soy sauce
2 tablespoons sesame oil
2 tablespoons dry sherry
1 tablespoon soft brown sugar
2 tablespoons peanut butter
1½ tablespoons Chinese chilli sauce
2 teaspoons prepared mustard
2 teaspoons red bean-curd cheese (optional)
8 oz spinach, trimmed, washed and shaken
   dry
8 oz Chinese cabbage or heart of celery
   cabbage, trimmed, washed and shaken
   dry
2 oz transparent pea-starch noodles, soaked
   in warm water for 5 minutes and drained
3 pints hot chicken broth
2 spring onions, coarsely chopped
2 garlic cloves, chopped
1-inch piece fresh root ginger, coarsely
   chopped

Put the lamb strips in a single layer in 6 or 8 small, flat dishes. Put the dishes on the dining-table in front of each diner.

In a small mixing bowl, combine the vinegar, soy sauce, sesame oil, sherry, sugar, peanut butter, chilli sauce, mustard and the bean-curd cheese if it is used. Divide the mixture equally among 3 or 4 small bowls. Put the bowls on the table between the diners.

Arrange the prepared vegetables and noodles on a large platter and put it on the table.

Put the hot-pot in the centre of the table. Pour the hot broth into the hot-pot and place the burning coals beneath. Cover the pot. When the broth comes to the boil again, add half of the spring onions, garlic and ginger and 4 to 5 of the more fatty strips of the lamb. Cover, bring to the boil again and remove the lid. The diners, using chopsticks, dip the strips of lamb into the broth for 15 to 20 seconds, then take them out of the broth and dip them into the spicy soy-sauce mixture before eating.

When half of the meat has been eaten in this way, a little of the spinach, cabbage and noodles are added to the pot and eaten with the rest of the meat as they cook.

When most of the meat and vegetables have been eaten, all the leftovers are added to the pot—the remaining dip, garlic, meat, vegetables and noodles. The mixture is simmered for 5 to 6 minutes and then ladled into serving bowls and served as a soup.

Sesame Seed Hot-Cakes
SHAO PING

These easy-to-make hot-cakes or buns are traditionally served with a Mongolian hot-pot.

4 oz sesame seeds
1 teaspoon salt
2 teaspoons castor sugar
1½ lb plain flour
1½ teaspoons baking powder
10 fl oz water
1½ tablespoons sesame oil

Spread the sesame seeds out on a tray or baking sheet and set aside.

In a large mixing bowl, combine the salt, sugar, flour and baking powder. Gradually add the water, stirring with a wooden spoon to make a smooth dough. Add the sesame oil and mix it in. Turn the dough out on to a lightly floured surface and knead it for 5 minutes.

Shape the dough into a long roll about 1½ inches in diameter. With a sharp knife, cut the roll into 1½-inch pieces. Pat each piece into a ball and flatten each ball into a cake about ⅓ inch thick. Moisten one side of each cake with a little cold water and press the wet side into the sesame seeds to coat it thoroughly.

Heat a griddle or a large frying-pan over moderate heat. When the griddle or frying-pan is hot, place the cakes, sesame-coated sides uppermost, on it and cook for 5 minutes.

Arrange the cakes, seed-coated sides uppermost, on a baking sheet and put the sheet under a preheated grill. Grill for 4 to 5 minutes, or until the sesame seeds begin to turn brown and become slightly aromatic.

Serve the cakes hot.

Onion Pancakes
TS'UNG PING

These aromatic onion pancakes are served hot with meat or stir-fried dishes.

12 oz plain flour
8 to 12 fl oz hot water
1½ oz lard
4 tablespoons chopped spring onions
¼ teaspoon salt
3 tablespoons sesame oil

Sift the flour into a mixing bowl and gradually stir in the water until a dough is formed. Knead the dough for a few minutes until it is smooth, then cover the bowl with a cloth and set aside for 30 minutes.

Shape the dough into a roll about 2 inches in diameter and cut it into 1¼-inch pieces. Make an indentation with your thumb in the centre of each piece and fill each indentation with ½ teaspoon of lard, 1 teaspoon of chopped spring onion and ⅛ teaspoon of the salt. Fold and pinch the sides up and over to enclose the filling and roll the dough into a ball. Flatten the balls into cakes about 3 inches in diameter.

Heat the sesame oil in a large, heavy frying-pan over moderate heat. Reduce the heat to low and place the pancakes in the pan. Cook, turning the pancakes over every 30 seconds, for 4 minutes.

Red-Cooked Hand of Pork
HUNG MEN CHOU TZU

This dish is usually served with plain boiled rice, or steamed buns or dumplings.

4 pints water
6 lb hand of pork
4 fl oz soy sauce
8 fl oz red wine
2 tablespoons castor sugar
1 piece dried orange peel
6 peppercorns
Bouquet garni

Preheat the oven to 375°F (Gas Mark 5). Bring the water to the boil in a large flameproof casserole. Add the pork and boil for 10 minutes, turning the meat over once. Pour out all but 15 fluid ounces of the liquid.

Add the soy sauce, wine, sugar, orange peel, peppercorns and *bouquet garni* and bring to the boil, stirring.

Place the casserole in the oven for 3½ hours, turning the pork over every 30 minutes.

Remove the casserole from the oven. Lift the pork out of the casserole, break the meat into chunks with chopsticks or cut into slices with a knife and transfer to a heated serving dish. Strain the gravy over the pork and discard the orange peel, *bouquet garni* and peppercorns.

Serve immediately.

Imperial influences on peasant food

Egg-Flower Pork
MU-SHU-JOU

Egg-flower pork is sometimes served wrapped in pancakes, but more commonly it is served plain as part of a selection of dishes to make a complete meal.

3 tablespoons vegetable oil
8 oz lean boned pork, sliced and shredded
5 medium-sized dried Chinese mushrooms, soaked for 30 minutes, drained, stalks removed and caps sliced
3 tablespoons dried tree ears, soaked for 30 minutes and drained
2 spring onion stalks, cut into 1½-inch lengths
3 stalks golden needles soaked for 30 minutes, drained and cut into 1½-inch lengths (optional)
2 tablespoons soy sauce
2 tablespoons good stock
½ oz lard
1½ tablespoons sesame oil
4 eggs, well beaten with 1 teaspoon salt
2 tablespoons dry sherry

Heat the oil in a deep frying-pan. Add the pork and stir-fry over high heat for 2 minutes. Add the mushrooms, tree ears, spring onions and golden needles, if used, and stir-fry for 2 minutes. Add the soy sauce and stock and stir-fry for a further 1½ minutes. Remove the pan from the heat and keep hot.

Heat the lard and sesame oil in a small frying-pan. When the lard has melted, pour in the beaten eggs. Swirl the eggs around so that they cover the bottom of the pan completely. Cook the mixture over low heat until the eggs have set in a thin, flat omelette.

Remove the pan from the heat, lift out the omelette and cut it into thick strips. Add the strips to the pork and mushroom mixture and return the pan to the heat. Stir in the sherry and gently mix the ingredients over high heat until hot.

Turn the mixture out on to a warmed serving dish and serve immediately.

Lion's Head Casserole
SHA KUO SSU TZU T'OU

1½ lb boned pork, coarsely minced
1 large onion, finely chopped
1-inch piece fresh root ginger, finely chopped
Salt
4 tablespoons soy sauce
4 tablespoons dry sherry
1½ tablespoons cornflour
4 tablespoons lard or vegetable oil
10 fl oz water
1¼ lb spinach, trimmed and washed

In a large mixing bowl, combine the pork, onion, ginger, salt to taste, 2 tablespoons of the soy sauce, 2 tablespoons of the sherry and the cornflour. Knead the mixture well and shape it into 4 large balls.

Preheat the oven to 375°F (Gas Mark 5). Melt the lard or heat the oil in a large frying-pan. Add the meatballs and fry until they are evenly browned.

Remove the frying-pan from the heat and transfer the meatballs to a flameproof casserole. Set the frying-pan aside. Add the remaining soy sauce, sherry and the water to the casserole and bring to the boil.

Place the casserole in the oven for 25 minutes. Turn the meatballs over and bake for a further 15 minutes.

Meanwhile, return the frying-pan to high heat and, when the fat is hot again, add the spinach. Cook, stirring, for 3 minutes. Lift the meatballs out of the casserole. Put the spinach in the casserole and place the meatballs on top. Return the casserole to the oven and bake for a further 15 minutes. Serve from the casserole.

Diced Chicken Cubes Quick-Fried with Soy Paste
TSIANG P'AO CHI TING

1¼ lb boned chicken breast, cut into ½-inch cubes
1 tablespoon cornflour
3 tablespoons vegetable oil
1½ tablespoons sesame oil
2 teaspoons finely chopped onion
½ garlic clove, crushed
2 tablespoons soybean paste
1 tablespoon castor sugar
1 tablespoon sherry

Rub the chicken cubes all over with the cornflour.

Heat the oil in a large frying-pan. When the oil is hot, add the chicken cubes and stir-fry over high heat for 1 minute. Remove the chicken from the pan and keep hot.

Add the sesame oil to the pan. Add the onion and garlic and stir-fry for ½ minute. Add the soybean paste, sugar and sherry and remove the pan from the heat. Stir the mixture until it forms a thick paste. Return the chicken to the pan and return the pan to the heat. Stir-fry for 1 minute.

Turn the mixture out on to a warmed serving dish. Serve immediately.

Quick-Fried Diced Chicken with Shrimp
CHI TING CH'AO HSIA JEN

This is another dish which is said to have struck Emperor Ch'ien-lung's fancy when he visited the south.

8 oz boned chicken breast, cut into ¼-inch cubes
12 oz shelled and deveined cooked shrimp
Salt
1 tablespoon cornflour
2 tablespoons light soy sauce
2 tablespoons dry sherry
1½ teaspoons castor sugar
3 spring onions, cut into ½-inch pieces
2½ tablespoons sesame oil
½-inch piece fresh root ginger, finely chopped
2 garlic cloves, crushed.
Pepper

Rub the chicken and shrimp all over with salt and cornflour. Set aside.

In a small bowl, combine the soy sauce, sherry, sugar and the green part of the spring onions. Set aside.

Heat the oil in a large frying-pan. Add the ginger, garlic and the white part of the spring onions and stir-fry for 15 seconds. Add the chicken and stir-fry for 1½ minutes over high heat. Add the shrimp and stir-fry for 1 minute. Add the sherry mixture and the pepper and stir-fry for 1 minute.

Turn the mixture out on to a well-heated dish and serve.

Royal Concubine Chicken

KUEI FEI CHI

This recipe is not dissimilar to the coq au vin *of France, and it is one of the few dishes in which the Chinese use wine in any great quantity.*

1-inch piece fresh root ginger, finely chopped
1 small onion, finely chopped
2 tablespoons soy sauce
1 tablespoon dry sherry
3 lb chicken
Vegetable oil for deep-frying
Salt
Black pepper
1 pint chicken broth
2 spring onions, cut into 1-inch pieces
15 fl oz white wine

In a small mixing bowl, combine the ginger, onion, soy sauce and sherry. Rub this mixture over the chicken, inside and out, and set aside for 2 hours.

Preheat the oven to 375°F (Gas Mark 5). Heat the oil in a large saucepan. Add the chicken and deep-fry for 7 minutes. Drain the chicken and dip it into a large pan of boiling water for 1 minute. Drain and dry well.

Place the chicken in a flameproof casserole and add salt and pepper to taste. Pour in the chicken broth and bring to the boil.

Place the casserole in the oven for 1¼ hours, turning the bird over once.

Remove the casserole from the oven and skim off any fat. Sprinkle the spring onions on top

...nd pour in the wine. Return the casserole to the oven and cook for a further 25 minutes. Serve from the casserole.

Peking Duck
PEI CHING K'AO YA

Peking Duck is probably the best-known Peking dish in the West. In Peking the ducks used for this dish are specially reared. The duck is traditionally prepared and cooked in a very elaborate way. This recipe is rather simplified, but, nevertheless, preparation takes two days.

To eat Peking duck, the diner places a slice of duck skin, a slice of meat and a little spring onion and cucumber on a pancake which has been heavily brushed with sauce. The pancake is rolled up and eaten with the hands. The crunchiness of the raw vegetables, the crackling of the duck skin, the tenderness of the meat and the piquant sauce combine to make this dish very special and memorable.

4 lb duck, cleaned
1 tablespoon honey mixed with 4 fl oz water
5 tablespoons soybean paste
1½ tablespoons castor sugar
2 tablespoons sesame oil
10 spring onions, slit in half lengthways and cut into 2½-inch pieces
½ cucumber, quartered lengthways and cut into 2½-inch pieces

Put the duck in a large bowl. Pour over enough boiling water to cover the bird. Drain the bird. Tie a string around its neck and hang it in a cool, airy place overnight to dry. Rub the honey and water mixture into the duck skin. Hang the duck up again until it is completely dry (about 10 hours).

Preheat the oven to 400°F (Gas Mark 6). Put the duck, on its breast, on a rack placed inside a roasting tin. Place the tin in the oven and roast the duck for 15 minutes. Reduce the temperature to 375°F (Gas Mark 5) and roast, without basting, for 1 hour, or until the duck is cooked and the skin is crisp.

While the duck is roasting, make the sauce. Place the soybean paste, sugar and sesame oil in a small saucepan and cook over moderate heat for 4 minutes, stirring. Pour the sauce into two small bowls and keep warm.

Remove the duck from the oven and, using a very sharp knife, slice off the skin and arrange it on a warmed serving dish. Carve the meat into thin slices and arrange them on another warmed serving dish. Serve with chopped spring onions, cucumber, sauce and pancakes.

Pancakes for Peking Duck
PO-PING

These pancakes are served with Peking Duck. The cooked pancakes may be wrapped in foil, stored in the refrigerator for a few days and steamed to reheat.

SERVES 4

8 oz plain flour
6 to 8 fl oz boiling water
2 tablespoons sesame oil

Sift the flour into a mixing bowl. Gradually add the water, stirring constantly with a wooden spoon until a dough is formed.

Turn the dough out on to a working surface and knead for 8 minutes. Return the dough to the bowl, cover with a damp cloth and set aside for 15 minutes.

Shape the dough into a long roll approximately 2 inches in diameter. Using a knife, slice the roll into ½-inch-thick pieces. Pat each piece into a circle 3 inches in diameter. Brush the top side of each circle with a little of the sesame oil and place two circles together, greased sides facing inwards. Roll the double layer out into a circle 6 inches in diameter.

Heat a large, heavy frying-pan or griddle over moderate heat for 30 seconds. Place one double pancake in the pan or griddle and cook for 2 to 2½ minutes, or until brown specks begin to appear on the underside. Turn the pancake over and cook for a further 2 to 2½ minutes. Cook the remaining pancakes in the same way, then set them aside to cool slightly.

Carefully separate the pancakes and fold each one in half. Pile them on to a warmed serving dish and serve.

Braised Chestnuts with Chinese Cabbage
LI TZU PAI TS'AI

1½ oz lard
2 tablespoons vegetable oil
2 tablespoons dried shrimp
½-inch piece fresh root ginger, chopped
12 oz shelled and skinned chestnuts, boiled for 25 minutes and drained
4 medium-sized dried Chinese mushrooms, soaked for 30 minutes, drained, stalks removed and caps quartered
1¼ lb Chinese cabbage, washed, drained and each leaf cut into 4 pieces
8 fl oz chicken stock
4 tablespoons soy sauce
2 tablespoons dry sherry
½ chicken stock cube, crumbled
1½ tablespoons castor sugar

Heat the lard and the oil in a large saucepan. Add the shrimp, ginger, chestnuts and mushrooms and stir-fry for 2 minutes over medium heat. Add the cabbage and cook, stirring, for 1 minute. Pour in the stock, soy sauce and sherry, add the stock cube and sugar and cook over low heat for 25 minutes, stirring.

Transfer the mixture to a heated, deep serving dish and serve.

Flower Rolls
HUA CHUAN

A flower roll is a steamed roll which is made of many layers of dough. The rolls may be eaten with hot-pots, or stir-fried with red-cooked dishes.

½ oz fresh yeast
15 fl oz lukewarm water
1 tablespoon castor sugar
1¼ lb plain flour, sifted
1 teaspoon salt
1 tablespoon vegetable oil

In a large mixing bowl, mash the yeast in 2 tablespoons of the water. Add the remaining water, with the sugar and flour, and mix into a dough.

Turn the dough out on to a working surface and knead it for 12 minutes, or until it is smooth and elastic. Return the dough to a clean bowl, cover with a damp cloth and leave to rise for 3 hours in a warm, draught-free place.

Knead the dough thoroughly and divide it in half. Roll each half into a sheet about 16 inches wide and 18 inches long. Rub the surface of each piece of dough with the salt and vegetable oil. Roll the dough pieces up like a Swiss roll and, using a sharp knife, cut the rolls into 3-inch pieces. Using a pair of thick chopsticks, press each cut-dough roll in the middle, pushing down the layers, to make a depression. This makes the two ends open up slightly, like a bow tie.

Place the flower rolls, well spaced, on a large heatproof dish and cover with a cloth. Place the dish in a steamer and steam the rolls in two batches if necessary, for 15 minutes.

Almond "Tea"
HSING JEN CHA

Almond "tea" may be served as a snack or at the end of a multi-course meal.

6 oz rice
3 oz blanched almonds
1 pint water
6 tablespoons castor sugar
¼ teaspoon almond essence

Put the rice and almonds in a large mixing bowl. Add enough cold water to cover and soak overnight. Drain the rice and almonds and grind in an electric blender.

Place the ground mixture in a heavy saucepan and add the water. Bring to the boil, stirring constantly.

Pour the mixture into a double boiler and cook over fairly low heat, stirring occasionally for 30 minutes. Add the sugar and almond essence and stir until the sugar has dissolved. Serve hot, in individual bowls.

The home of a distinct culinary culture

THE DIFFERENCE between the cooking of Fukien and that of Canton is one of degree. The two areas have many similarities; they are both coastal, and their climates are subtropical. The major difference is that Kwangtung province, of which Canton is the capital, is more fertile, well-watered and productive than Fukien.

The Fukienese bourgeoisie, too, could not be compared in number or wealth with those of Kwangtung, and were recognizably different in their cultural interests and culinary achievements. In Foochow, the capital city of the province, they pride themselves, for example, on having produced more successful candidates for the former Imperial Examinations than anyone else in the whole empire.

Where literary and cultural preoccupation exist, gastronomic and culinary preoccupation usually coexist. This was always particularly so in China, where men of letters were usually gourmets and food critics. In the southern part of the province, where the thriving cities of Amoy, Changchow, Chuanchow and Hingchua are situated, the considerable wealth was derived mainly from the remittances from overseas Chinese, especially from those living in Indonesia, Borneo, Malaysia and the Philippines.

In an area which is bounded by mountains to the west and north, and by the Formosa Strait and the China Sea to the east, and where, until very recently, communication with the outside world was never easy, a distinct culinary culture was bound to evolve.

All Chinese gastronomes agree that Fukien produces some of the best soy sauce in the land. Because of this their cuisine specializes in "red cooking", stewing or braising in soy sauce, which imparts a red colour to the sauce. In flavouring, Fukien cooking also makes extensive use of shrimp sauce and shrimp paste, which are used for all kinds of dishes, from soups and noodles to vegetables.

Unlike the Cantonese, whose soups are indifferent, Fukienese clear soups rank among the best in the country. Fukien clear broth is produced not only by simmering chicken, knuckle of pork and ham bones together for a long time, but, ten minutes before the soup is cooked, chopped raw chicken bones are added for a short period of slow cooking, after which the broth is strained. The addition of raw chicken bones gives the broth a freshness and savouriness which is rarely equalled in any other regional cooking. Because the Fukienese make excellent soups they often serve two or three soups at one meal, to the consternation of visitors from other provinces.

Another special method of Fukien cooking involves the use of *hung chiao*, a red-coloured, savoury wine sediment paste, which is made from the lees of wine. It is used, in much the same manner as soy paste is in the north, for stewing, braising, quick stir-frying, roasting or preserving. Only those who have tasted food cooked with *hung chiao* can say that they know what Fukien cooking is all about.

Two other distinctive features of Fukien

cooking are *jou shun*, meat wool, and *yen pi*, a dough skin made partly of meat. The dried meat wool is produced by stir-frying small, regular-sized pieces of meat over low heat in a small amount of oil, with soy sauce, sugar and *hung chiao*. The stir-frying is kept up continuously until the meat has become completely dehydrated and every fibre is light and crisp, resembling fluffy wool. Meat wool, when properly made, is not only tasty but highly digestible. Served with plain soft rice it is a favourite dish of the very young, elderly and invalid.

Yen pi looks like an ordinary thin sheet of pastry or dough skin. It is used for making meat-stuffed dumplings. It is sometimes cut into strips and stuck on to meatballs to resemble a lion's mane. *Yen pi* is made by pounding together finely chopped lean meat with flour and cornflour for a long time until a completely homogenous substance results. When this dough is rolled out into a thin skin it is more firm and transparent than an ordinary dough skin made from water and flour. When *yen pi* is used for making *wuntuns* or *chiao t'zu*—Chinese ravioli—it gives the dish a quality which is practically unknown outside the province.

In a coastal, subtropical region such as Fukien, it is natural that the abundant seafoods and fruit play an important part in cooking. Such dishes as lychee pork, crystal chicken in scallop broth, rice-buried steamed crab, fish in its own habitat, shrimp in snow mountain, tangerine-flavoured eels, kidney flowers in sesame sauce and frogs' legs braised with wine sediment paste, demonstrate the richness of Fukien cuisine.

Fukien is also the land of water chestnuts and sugar-cane. During the summer both are displayed, peeled and gleaming white, on roadside stalls for the hungry or thirsty to chew. Sugar-cane is the source of brown sugar, which is a constituent of many things, including soy sauce. Water chestnuts are chopped coarsely and are used to add crunchiness to many dishes.

Fukien province is famous for olives. Although they are seldom incorporated as an ingredient in a dish, they are salted, spiced, marinated, pickled and presented in a number of different forms and flavours for eating as tidbits and appetizers. They are usually served skewered on a sliver of bamboo.

Although less wealthy and pretentious than their neighbours, the Fukienese nevertheless have a cuisine that is both distinctive and by no means negligible.

FUKIEN

TEA

CHICKEN IN CRYSTAL JELLY

LYCHEES AND PORK

• NAN PING

SHRIMP PEONY SOUP

PORK IN MEAT-AND-DOUGH WRAPPERS
LOBSTERS

SHRIMP IN SNOW MOUNTAIN
Shrimps in savoury meringue

SCALLOPS

FOOCHOW

EEL AND ORANGES

F U K I E N

FISH SOUP WITH FIVE KINDS OF VEGETABLES

FROGS' LEGS

FISHBALL SOUP

STEAMED SNOWFLAKE CHICKEN
Egg, chicken and rice wrapped in leaves

CRAB

AMOY •

Tasty dishes of an ancient cuisine

Fish-Ball Soup

There are two special qualities about this soup. First, the fish is chopped, ground or beaten until its consistency is so fine that it can float on water. Second, a very special cooking stock is made for the soup. To make the stock, simmer equal amounts of chicken bones and pork spareribs weighing 12 ounces together in 3 pints of water for 1½ hours, or until it has reduced to 1 pint of stock. Skim off any excess grease or scum from the broth and add 4 tablespoons of ground chicken meat. Simmer for 3 minutes and strain the stock. It is now ready for use.

Cod, halibut, turbot or bream are the most suitable fish for this soup.

12 oz skinned and boned white fish, finely
 ground
1 teaspoon salt
½ teaspoon black pepper
2 oz cooked pork fat, finely minced
1½ tablespoons cornflour
1 pint stock
2 lettuce leaves, shredded
1 spring onion, chopped
1 teaspoon sesame oil

Put the fish, salt, pepper and 6 tablespoons of water in an electric blender and blend at slow speed for 4 minutes. Add the pork fat and cornflour and blend for 1 minute more.

Scrape the paste out of the blender and with wet hands shape the mixture into walnut-sized balls. Set aside.

Heat the stock in a large saucepan. When it is hot, add the fish balls, one at a time, and simmer over fairly low heat for 8 minutes. Add the lettuce, spring onions and seasoning and simmer, stirring, for 1 minute. Taste the soup and add more salt and pepper if necessary.

Pour the soup into a warmed soup tureen, sprinkle with the sesame oil and serve.

Shredded Fish Quick-Fried with Shredded Meat and Vegetables
CH'AO YU SSU

This dish combines contrasting textures of fried and boiled ingredients, as well as a variety of flavours. Sole, cod, bream or halibut are the most suitable fish to use. Lemon juice may be sprinkled over the finished dish, although this is not strictly authentic.

12 oz fish, skinned, boned and shredded
4 oz lean and fat pork, shredded
Salt
1 tablespoon cornflour
10 fl oz good stock
½ chicken stock cube, crumbled

3 celery sticks, shredded
4 large dried Chinese mushrooms, soaked in
 cold water for 30 minutes, drained, stalks
 removed and caps shredded
½-inch piece fresh root ginger, shredded
2 oz transparent pea-starch noodles, soaked
 in warm water for 10 minutes and drained
1 tablespoon soy sauce
Vegetable oil for deep-frying
4 spring onion stalks, cut into 2-inch pieces
2 teaspoons sesame oil
2 tablespoons dry sherry

Rub the fish and pork all over with salt and the cornflour and set aside.

Heat the stock in a large saucepan and, when it is hot, add the stock cube, celery, mushrooms and ginger. Simmer for 3 minutes. Add the noodles and soy sauce and stir to mix. Simmer for a further 3 minutes. Remove the pan from the heat and keep the mixture hot.

Heat the oil in a large saucepan. When the oil is hot, add the pork and deep-fry for 4 minutes, or until it is crisp. Drain and keep warm. Add the fish and fry for 2 minutes. Drain the fish and add, with the pork, to the stock mixture.

Return the pan to the heat and add the spring onions, sesame oil and sherry. Cook, stirring and tossing the mixture, for 30 seconds over high heat.

Transfer the mixture to a warm, deep serving bowl and serve.

Shrimp in Snow Mountain
HSUEH SAN TAN HSIA

This is a rather unusual dish, popular in Fukien. Plain-fried shrimp are enclosed in a mountain of beaten egg white, the top of which is sprinkled with chopped ham and coriander leaves.

8 oz shelled and deveined shrimp
Salt
10 egg whites
1 tablespoon cornflour
Vegetable oil for deep-frying
2 oz cooked ham, finely chopped
1½ tablespoons finely chopped coriander
 leaves

Rub the shrimp all over with salt.

In a large mixing bowl, beat the egg whites until they are stiff. Add the cornflour and beat for a further 30 seconds.

Heat the oil in a large saucepan. Add the shrimp and deep-fry for 1 minute. Drain the shrimp well.

Place half the egg-white mixture on a round, greased plate. Spread the shrimp over the top and cover with the remaining egg white. Slide the egg white "mountain" into the hot oil and fry for 2½ to 3 minutes, ladling the hot oil over the "mountain".

Using a large spatula, remove the "mountain" from the oil and transfer it to a warm serving dish. Sprinkle with the chopped ham and coriander leaves and serve.

Eight-Treasure Crab Rice
PA PAO HSIN FAN

In this dish the crabs are buried in rice, as if they were buried in sand. Other ingredients are sprinkled on top and add interest and flavour to the finished dish.

1 lb glutinous rice, washed and drained
6 fl oz good stock, warm
1 oz lard, cut into small pieces
3 tablespoons dry sherry
2 oz lean ham, diced
2 oz dried mushrooms, soaked and diced
2 oz bamboo shoots, diced
1 oz dried shrimp
1 oz blanched almonds, slivered
2 medium-sized cooked, shelled crabs,
 chopped, shells and claws reserved
Salt
2 spring onions, finely chopped
1 oz peanuts, chopped
½-inch piece fresh root ginger, finely
 chopped

Place the rice in a medium-sized heavy saucepan and add the same volume of cold water. Bring the water to the boil, cover the pan and simmer over very low heat for 15 minutes. Turn off the heat and leave the rice for 10 minutes.

In a small mixing bowl, combine the stock, lard and sherry. Set aside.

Stir the ham, mushrooms, bamboo shoots, shrimp and almonds into the cooked rice and transfer the mixture to a large heatproof serving bowl. Bury the crab pieces in the rice and arrange the reserved shells and claws on top in the shape of crabs. Sprinkle the top of the rice with salt, spring onions, peanuts and ginger, Pour the stock and lard mixture over the top.

Place the bowl in a steamer and steam for 35 minutes. Alternatively, place all the ingredients, in the same way, in a large casserole and bake, covered, for 25 minutes in an oven preheated to 375°F (Gas Mark 5). Serve hot.

Drunken Spareribs

These spareribs are not as "drunk" as in some parts of China, where they are soaked in wine for several days. Here they are only cooked for a little while in a sherry-flavoured sauce.

1½ lb pork spareribs, chopped into 1½-inch pieces
1 egg white, well beaten with 1 tablespoon cornflour
1½ teaspoons salt
½ teaspoon black pepper
6 fl oz vegetable oil
1½ tablespoons soy sauce
3 tablespoons dry sherry
1 tablespoon sesame oil
1 medium-sized onion, thinly sliced
2 garlic cloves, crushed
4 tablespoons stock
2 teaspoons sugar
2 teaspoons wine vinegar
1 teaspoon dry mustard
1 teaspoon curry powder
2 tablespoons tomato purée
2 tablespoons sesame paste or peanut butter
1 teaspoon Chinese chilli sauce

Put the spareribs in a shallow bowl and rub them all over with the egg-white mixture and salt and pepper.

Heat the vegetable oil in a large saucepan over high heat. When the oil is hot, add the spareribs and fry, turning frequently, for 8 minutes. Drain off as much oil as possible and reduce the heat to low. Pour in the soy sauce and sherry and cook, stirring, for 1 minute. Arrange the spareribs in a heated serving dish and pour any cooking liquid over them. Keep hot.

Heat the sesame oil in a small saucepan over moderate heat. Add the onion and garlic and stir-fry for 3 minutes. Add the stock, sugar, vinegar, mustard, curry powder, tomato purée, sesame paste or peanut butter and chilli sauce and cook the mixture, stirring, for 2 minutes.

Pour the sauce over the spareribs and serve hot.

Fukien Double-Cooked Pork
CHA LI JOU

This dish is made with thick slices of pork, red-cooked and then coated with breadcrumbs and deep-fried.

2 tablespoons vegetable oil
2 lb boned leg of pork, cut into 4-inch by 2-inch pieces about 1 inch thick
3 tablespoons soy sauce
1 tablespoon sugar
2 teaspoons mixed herbs
2 teaspoons vinegar
2 tablespoons dry sherry
10 fl oz good stock
1 egg, lightly beaten
6 oz dried white breadcrumbs
Vegetable oil for deep-frying
8 oz young carrots, scraped and cut into matchsticks

Heat the oil in a large casserole. When the oil is hot, add the pork slices, the soy sauce, sugar, mixed herbs, vinegar and sherry. Fry over moderate heat for 4 to 5 minutes, turning the pork over occasionally, until it becomes a deep red-brown colour. Pour in the stock and, when it comes to a simmer, reduce the heat to low and cook for 10 minutes, or until most of the liquid has evaporated.

Remove the casserole from the heat. Lift the pork pieces out of the casserole and set them aside to cool. When the meat is cool, coat the slices first with the beaten egg and then with the breadcrumbs.

Heat the oil in a large saucepan over moderate heat and, when it is hot, add half of the pork pieces and deep-fry for 3 minutes. Drain and fry the remaining pork pieces.

Cut the pork pieces into ¼-inch slices and arrange them in the centre of a large oval dish. Arrange the carrots decoratively around the pork.

Serve immediately.

Snow-White Chicken

Snow-White Chicken is so-called because it is coated with rice and steamed.

2 whole chicken breasts, skinned and boned
Salt
Black pepper
2 tablespoons dry sherry
8 oz glutinous rice, soaked in cold water for 1 hour and drained
2 egg whites, well beaten with 1 tablespoon cornflour

Cut the chicken breasts into ¼-inch-thick slices.

Using the point of a sharp knife, score criss-cross lines across both sides of the meat. Cut the meat into 1-inch squares and place them in a shallow bowl. Add salt, pepper and the sherry and toss well. Set aside for 5 minutes.

Spread the rice out on a baking sheet or tray. Dip the chicken pieces into the egg-white mixture and then press them into the rice to coat them thoroughly.

Arrange the rice-covered chicken pieces on a heatproof dish and place the dish in a steamer. Steam for 45 minutes.

Serve hot.

Red-Braised Lamb in Wine Sauce
KANG TS'AO YANG JOU

2 pints water
Salt
1 large onion, thinly sliced
2½ lb boned lamb, cut into 1¼-inch cubes

RED WINE PASTE

1½ tablespoons vegetable oil
¼-inch piece fresh root ginger, finely chopped
2 garlic cloves, crushed
2 medium-sized onions, finely chopped
1 tablespoon flour
3 tablespoons tomato purée
1½ tablespoons soy sauce
3 fl oz red wine
2 teaspoons sugar
2 tablespoons brandy
1 pint good stock
2 teaspoons cornflour blended with 2 tablespoons water

Bring the water to the boil in a large saucepan. Add salt, the onion and lamb and boil for 3 minutes. Drain the lamb and discard the water and onion.

Now make the red-wine paste. In a small frying-pan, heat the oil. Add the ginger, garlic and onions and stir-fry for 2 minutes. Add the flour and stir-fry for 1 minute. Add the tomato purée, soy sauce, red wine, sugar and 1 tablespoon of the brandy and cook, stirring occasionally, until the sauce has reduced by about half the original quantity.

Meanwhile preheat the oven to 400°F (Gas Mark 6).

Heat the stock in a large flameproof casserole. Add the lamb and bring the stock to the boil. Stir in the red-wine paste and put the casserole in the oven. Bake for 1½ hours, stirring the stew every 30 minutes.

Remove the casserole from the oven and stir in the cornflour mixture. Cook over moderate heat for 4 minutes, stirring until the mixture thickens.

Sprinkle the remaining brandy over the top and serve.

Simple food served with natural grace

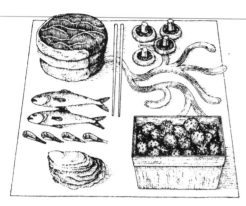

OF ALL THE WORLD'S GREAT CUISINES, Japan's must be the most elegantly simple. It is the taste for natural things which is the essence of Japanese culture. Japanese tradition prefers pottery to porcelain, soft reed mats to carpets, iron to bronze and wood to ivory.

Pure Japanese cuisine, too, is highly idiosyncratic, although there are detectable early influences from Korea and Portugal and many later ones from America and Europe. Between 1600 and 1868, Japan closed her ports to foreigners and it was during this time that the tea ceremony and *kaiseki*, its attendant, delicate cuisine, was evolved. It is *kaiseki*, a meal of several light courses served in the tea house on fine lacquer and pottery dishes, that epitomizes the "exquisite" school of Japanese food. It would be wrong to imagine, however, that it represents Japanese cuisine as a whole.

A Japanese meal, by tradition, is plain and frugal. Four hundred years ago, with the powerful emergence of the *samurai* warrior class, excesses of any kind, including eating, were considered vulgar. This philosophy was also practical since the *samurai* were often poor. Their diet, of rice, pickles and dried fish, was little better than that of the farmers. Even the Emperor or the Shogun, the military governor of Japan, would not have eaten in luxurious abundance. The banquet, as it is known in most of the world, is foreign to Japan.

Today in Japan, the philosophy of frugality remains as an ideal, but the practice is rather different. After 1868, the Japanese became interested in everything Western, including Western food and drinks. And although the period after the Second World War led to a great abundance of food, the change in eating habits had started long before.

The modern Japanese enjoys Western food both at home and in restaurants, at steak bars, hamburger joints and *bierkeller*. But at home, at least one meal of the day is cooked and served Japanese style. Most Japanese families still sit around the traditional low table, which is about one foot from the floor. The dishes are all placed on the table at one time and there is little formality about the order in which they are eaten. The tradition of Japanese food preparation is naturally graceful and the simple elegance and beauty with which each dish is presented seems to be achieved without conscious effort. The food itself is simple, delicious and satisfying.

The staple foods of Japan are rice, soybeans, fish and seaweed. Every traditional Japanese meal in these affluent times uses all these ingredients in some form. Soybeans are fermented into *miso*, bean paste, salted and boiled, sweetened and mashed. They are made into *shoyu*, the light Japanese soya sauce, or formed into *tofu*, a creamy bean curd. Rice, the main staple of the Japanese diet, is also the basis of *sake*, Japanese rice wine, and *mirin*, its sweetened form.

The eating of meat was considered contrary to the teachings of Buddhism, and it was not until the beginning of Japan's industrial revolution, in the latter half of the nineteenth century, that this prohibition was lifted and meat was introduced. Today Japan is world-famous for the tenderness of its beef and for the extraordinary lengths to which Japanese farmers go to maintain its quality, such as massaging the cattle with *shochu*, Japanese gin.

Fish is so abundant in Japan's coastal waters that even the introduction of meat has not diminished the importance of fish to the Japanese diet. Tuna, cod, horse mackerel, bass, flounder, *ayu*, or sweet fish, carp and squid are most popular, but there are also many varieties of subtropical fish that are edible and delicious.

Raw fish and shellfish, the greatest of Japanese delicacies, demand perfect freshness. Lobsters and prawns are always kept alive until the last minute before serving, and tuna and other fish that are eaten raw are kept miraculously fresh in deep tubs of water at air-temperature.

Katsuo, dried bonita, a fish of the mackerel family, is a basic ingredient of *dashi*, the distinctive and aromatic Japanese stock, together with *konbu*, dried kelp. Other varieties of seaweed are used as flavourings or as vegetables in soups.

An essential part of every Japanese meal is *o-cha*, the ubiquitous green tea that comes in many varieties, classed according to where it is grown and whether it has been smoked. Such is its appeal, complexity and promise that green tea has evolved its own connoisseurs, who exhibit the same passion and interest as connoisseurs of wine.

The variety of vegetables grown in Japan today is astonishing and includes almost every vegetable grown in the West. The indispensable, traditional vegetables, however, are *negi*, a thin Japanese leek, *daikon*, a giant white radish, *hakusai*, Chinese cabbage, lotus roots and shoots, *wasabi*, Japanese horseradish, edible chrysanthemum leaves, burdock, bamboo shoots, spinach, ginger root, many varieties of aromatic mushrooms, edible ferns, peas and beans.

Fruit is abundant in Japan, and includes many fine varieties of apples and pears, grapes, plums, cherries, melons and two crops a year of delicious strawberries. But most typical of Japan are the varieties of fragrant orange, including *mikan*, the sweet mandarin orange, and the golden persimmon, which seems to grow in everyone's backyard.

A semi-formal Japanese meal usually begins with a prolonged course of such appetizers as quail eggs, roe, grilled vegetables or fish, fish paste, steamed chicken or game or raw fish. They are accompanied by *sake*, which is no longer drunk once rice appears on the table.

JAPAN today is in the act of embracing wine as a principal drink for the first time in her history. Knowing the thoroughness with which the Japanese do such things the rest of the wine-drinking world waits with apprehension. The memory of what happened to prices when the United States became interested in wine is still fresh.

Wine has been made from grapes grown in Japan for a number of years, but with only limited success. Japan's humid climate is seemingly ideal for the fungal enemies of the vine. Imported grape juice (much of it from Australia) has played a large part in the more successful wines bearing the label "Made in Japan".

Japan's traditional alcoholic drink is sake, a sort of wine made by fermenting rice to about the strength of sherry. Sake is served warm in little porcelain cups with the profusion of appetizers at the beginning of the meal. It has no particular flavour, but is slightly sweet and agreeably effective.

Next there is a setting of soup and side dishes, which include a boiled dish, usually vegetables, a serving of braised or grilled meat or fish and a small dish of raw vegetables or fish dressed with vinegar or pounded sesame seeds. The meal is invariably concluded with a bowl of rice, some pickles and green tea. The Japanese eat fruit after a meal, rather than puddings or desserts.

There are some Japanese dishes, notably *sukiyaki* and *tempura*, that are rules unto themselves; they are virtually one-dish meals. Although both seem entirely Japanese in context, they are mavericks in the world of Japanese cuisine. The origin of *sukiyaki* is disputed, but it dates from the nineteenth century and probably derived from the peasant's way of roasting game on a convenient spade or hoe. *Tempura*, deep-fried fish and vegetables, is said to have been introduced by the Portuguese traders and missionaries in the sixteenth century.

Cooking Japanese food in the Western kitchen is simple and satisfying, and it is worth taking the trouble to obtain the few basic ingredients necessary from a Japanese food shop.

After a meal, Japanese guests make the traditional salute to the cook—"*Gochiso-sama desh'ta*", "Thank you for going to so much trouble."

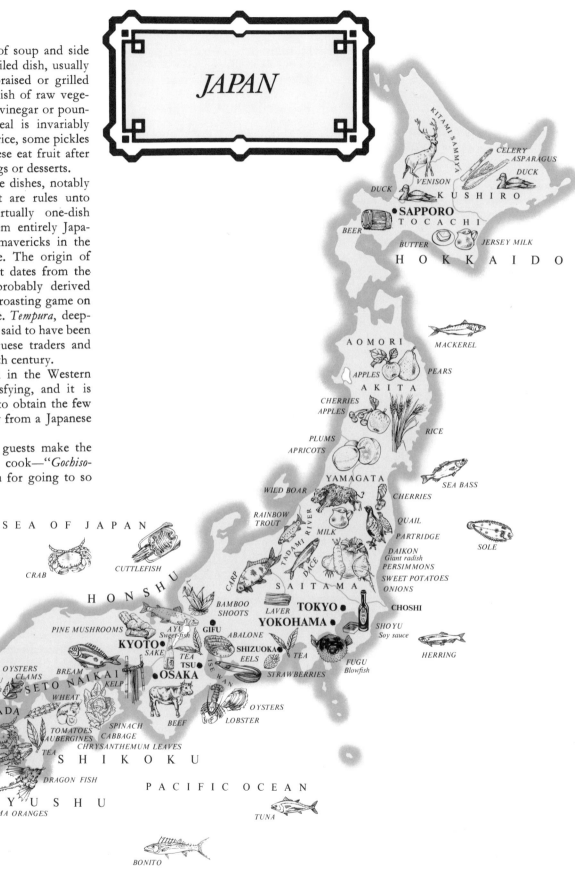

JAPAN

KITAMI SAMMYA

CELERY
ASPARAGUS
DUCK
VENISON
DUCK
K U S H I R O
BEER
•SAPPORO
T O C A C H I
BUTTER
JERSEY MILK
H O K K A I D O

A O M O R I
MACKEREL
APPLES
PEARS
A K I T A
CHERRIES
APPLES
RICE
PLUMS
APRICOTS
YAMAGATA
SEA BASS
WILD BOAR
CHERRIES
RAINBOW
TROUT
QUAIL
MILK
PARTRIDGE
DAIKON
Giant radish
PERSIMMONS
SWEET POTATOES
ONIONS
SOLE

SEA OF JAPAN

CARP
DACE
TADAMI RIVER
S A I T A M A
CHOSHI

CRAB
CUTTLEFISH
H O N S H U
BAMBOO
SHOOTS
LAVER
TOKYO •
YOKOHAMA •
SHOYU
Soy sauce
PINE MUSHROOMS
AYU
Sweet-fish
GIFU
ABALONE
HERRING
KYOTO•
SAKE
TEA
SHIZUOKA•
EELS
TEA
FUGU
Blowfish
OYSTERS
CLAMS
BREAM
TSU
•OSAKA
KELP
STRAWBERRIES
FUGU
Blowfish
S E T O N A I K A I
WHEAT
ISE WAN
OYSTERS
COCKLES
S U O
N A D A
BEEF
OYSTERS
LOBSTER
TOMATOES
AUBERGINES
SPINACH
CABBAGE
CHRYSANTHEMUM LEAVES
GRAPES
PEACHES
CRAB
TEA
S H I K O K U
LEMONS
PRAWNS
DRAGON FISH
PACIFIC OCEAN
K Y U S H U
LYCHEES
SATSUMA ORANGES
TUNA
BANANAS
BONITO

253

Delicacies from an Oriental kitchen

Japanese Stock
DASHI

The flavour and aroma of dashi, *an essential ingredient in many Japanese dishes, reflect the essence of Japanese cuisine.*

3-inch strip of kombu (dried kelp)
3 to 4 tablespoons katsuobushi (dried bonito flakes)

Pour 2 pints of water into a saucepan. Add the *kombu* and bring to the boil slowly. As soon as the water boils, lift out the *kombu* and remove the pan from the heat.

Sprinkle the *katsuobushi* over the surface of the water and return the pan to low heat. As soon as the stock boils again, turn off the heat. Let the *katsuobushi* sink to the bottom of the pan, then strain the *dashi* and use as required.

Japanese Boiled Rice
GOHAN

Japanese rice has a short grain and is cooked to a slightly sticky texture so that it can be eaten neatly with chopsticks. Californian rice and Australian long-grain rice work very well. Patna and quick-cooking American rice are not suitable.

To cook Japanese rice to serve 2 to 3, put 6 ounces of rice in a large bowl and wash under cold running water until the water runs clear. Leave the rice to soak for at least 30 minutes, then drain.

Put the rice in a heavy pan. Add 10 fluid ounces of water. Cover the pan tightly and bring it to the boil over high heat. Just as the water is on the point of boiling over, reduce the heat to very low and leave the rice to simmer for 15 minutes, or until the bubbling sounds have subsided.

Without removing the lid, turn the heat up for a few seconds. Then remove the pan from the heat and leave the rice to steam in its own vapour for about 15 minutes.

Deep-Fried Fish and Vegetables in Batter
TEMPURA

A complete tempura dinner consists of a selection of tempura, misoshiru, *bean-paste soup, rice,* tsukemono, *pickles, and fruit. Small portions of* tempura *make an excellent side dish or first course served with other Japanese dishes.* Tempura *is eaten either with a dipping sauce or more simply with salt and a squeeze of lemon.*

SERVES 4

8 large prawns
1 small squid

½ small daikon (Japanese radish), grated
4 fillets of sole or plaice, cut in half lengthways
4 Japanese dried mushroom caps, soaked, or 4 large fresh flat mushroom caps, wiped dry
1 small sweet potato, unpeeled and cut into ¼-inch-thick slices
1 small aubergine, unpeeled and cut into ¼-inch-thick slices
1 green pepper, with seeds and white pith removed, cut into pieces
4 parsley sprigs, washed and dried
Vegetable oil or tempura oil for deep-frying

BATTER
8 fl oz iced water
5 oz plain flour
1 large egg

DIPPING SAUCE
5 fl oz dashi
3 tablespoons shoyu (Japanese soy sauce)
1½ tablespoons mirin (sweet sake)

Peel and clean the prawns without removing their tails. Slit them halfway through under the belly.

Clean the squid by emptying out the bag and removing the hard transparent part. Rub off the loose outer skin under cold running water. Flatten the body out into a sheet and cut it into 2-inch squares.

Put the grated *daikon* in a small serving bowl and set aside. Arrange the prawns, squid, fish, mushrooms, sweet potato, aubergine, green pepper and parsley on a large plate or board ready for frying.

Next make the batter. Sift the flour into a bowl and beat in the iced water and egg until just blended.

Mix together the ingredients for the dipping sauce and divide between 4 shallow serving dishes.

In a large saucepan heat the vegetable oil or tempura oil until the temperature reaches 375°F. Test it by dropping in a teaspoonful of batter. If it sinks and then rises rapidly to the surface, the temperature is about right. Maintain the same temperature throughout the cooking of the *tempura,* removing any pieces of batter.

Tempura should be eaten as soon as it is cooked. Start with the prawns, fish fillets and the squid. Dip each ingredient in batter and deep-fry, a few at a time, until the batter just starts to change colour. It should not brown.

When the seafood has been eaten, cook the vegetables and the parsley sprigs in the same way.

Each person mixes some grated *daikon* into his bowl of dipping sauce and coats each piece of *tempura* with this mixture before eating it.

Bean-Paste Soup
MISOSHIRU

This thick soup, richly flavoured with miso, *red bean paste, is particularly good served with grilled fish and* tempura. *The Japanese do not use spoons for soup. The garnish is picked out with chopsticks and the soup is drunk from the bowl.*

SERVES 4

2 pints dashi
1 to 2 tablespoons miso (red bean paste)

GARNISH (CHOICE OF ONE)
1 block tofu (bean curd), 2 large fish fillets, ½ pint small clams, 4 oz button mushrooms or 8 chicken or pork meatballs
Dashi to cook garnish

First prepare the garnish. The *tofu* should be cubed. Cut each fish fillet into 4 pieces. The meatballs are made from a mixture of 8 ounces minced lean pork or chicken breast worked to a smooth paste with 1 beaten egg and a pinch of salt. Precook the chosen garnish in a little *dashi* until it is just cooked.

To make the soup, bring the *dashi* to the boil. Press the *miso* through a fine-meshed sieve into the *dashi.* The *miso* is very salty, so adjust the quantity to taste.

Divide the garnish between 4 individual soup bowls and pour in the soup. Serve immediately.

Fish or Beef in Sweet Shoyu Glaze
TERIYAKI

Teriyaki is one of Japan's most famous dishes. In a Japanese meal it is served with rice, soup and a shrimp and green bean sunomono.

SERVES 4

2 lb tuna or salmon in one piece, or 2 lb lean frying steak
Oil for frying
TERIYAKI GLAZE
2 tablespoons shoyu (Japanese soy sauce)
1 tablespoon mirin (sweet sake)
½-inch piece fresh ginger, peeled and finely chopped (optional)

First prepare the glaze by mixing together the *shoyu, mirin* and the ginger, if used, in a large, shallow dish.

If using fish, bone and slice into fillets. Cut the fillets into ¾-inch chunks. The steak may be left whole, unless chopsticks are to be used, in which case cut it into strips.

Put the fish or steak in the glaze, turning the pieces to coat them evenly. Leave them to marinate for at least 30 minutes.

Teriyaki fish should be fried in a little oil until the fish is just cooked and the glaze is reduced but not completely evaporated. The steak may be either fried, grilled or barbecued over a moderately high heat.

Roast Beef on a Hoe
SUKIYAKI

The origin of Sukiyaki *is disputed, but it probably derived from the peasant's way of roasting game on a convenient spade or hoe.*

SERVES 4

1½ lb tender, lean sirloin or rump steak in one piece

3 young leeks, trimmed and thinly sliced on the diagonal

8 oz button mushrooms, washed

½ large Chinese cabbage, cut into chunks

2 blocks fresh tofu (bean curd), drained and cut into 1-inch cubes

8 oz shirataki noodles or Chinese vermicelli, boiled in unsalted water and rinsed in cold running water

4 eggs

A piece of fresh beef suet

COOKING SAUCE

4 fl oz shoyu (Japanese soy sauce)

5 tablespoons dashi

2 tablespoons sugar

Put the beef in the ice-making compartment of the refrigerator or the freezer for 45 minutes to make it easier to slice. With a very sharp knife slice the beef horizontally against the grain as thinly as possible. The "sheets" of beef may be quite large.

Mix the ingredients for the cooking sauce together in a small jug, and put it on the dining-table, together with 4 bowls, each containing an unbroken raw egg.

A cooking pan, approximately 12 inches in diameter and 2 to 3 inches deep, should be placed on the table over a portable gas ring or electric hot plate—an electric frying-pan is also suitable, provided it is deep enough. Arrange the beef, vegetables and noodles together on a large platter on the table.

To cook *sukiyaki,* make the pan very hot and wipe it around with the lump of suet until it is well greased and smoking. Add a quarter of the meat, followed immediately by a selection of vegetables. Pour over enough of the cooking sauce to moisten the contents of the pan, and add some noodles and *tofu.* Stir and cook just long enough to cook the beef through and soften the vegetables slightly.

While the *sukiyaki* is being cooked, each person breaks an egg into his bowl and beats it well with chopsticks. Pieces of beef and vegetables are taken from the pan and dipped in egg before being eaten. The *sukiyaki* pan should be kept bubbling with sauce, meat and vegetables until everything is finished.

Salted Pickles
TSUKEMONO

These pickles are a refreshing accompaniment served with rice at the end of every Japanese meal. A little shoyu *may be poured over them just before they are eaten.*

Cucumber, aubergine, medium-sized daikon (Japanese radish) or turnip

Crushed sea salt

Lemon juice (optional)

Hot dried chilli peppers (optional)

Prepare the vegetables. Cucumbers and aubergines, both left unpeeled, are washed, quartered lengthwise and the quarters cut into pieces ¼ inch thick. The *daikon* or turnip should be thinly peeled, cut across into slices ½ inch thick and then quartered.

The ideal pickling crock is a pottery one with a flat base and straight sides, but a pottery or glass bowl makes a good substitute.

Drop the vegetables into the crock and sprinkle them with some crushed sea salt— 1 teaspoon is sufficient for an average-sized cucumber, aubergine or turnip, or for a small *daikon. Daikon* and turnip also benefit from a sprinkling of lemon juice, which helps to preserve their colour, and another good addition for turnip is ½ hot dried chilli pepper, sliced into thin rings.

Cover the vegetables with a plate slightly smaller in diameter than the crock, and place a heavy weight on top. The pickles are ready after 1 hour and will keep for 2 days in a cool place.

Serve one, or several, pickles on tiny individual dishes, grouping them attractively by colour.

"Swimming" Trout
SHIOYAKI

This is a popular Japanese side dish, served with misoshiru, *bean-paste soup, a* sunomono *of vegetables or fish, rice and* tsukemono, *pickles.*

1 small trout per person, cleaned

Fine sea salt

Beni shoga (vinegared ginger) or lemon wedges, to garnish

With a long skewer, pierce each fish through the head near the eye. Push the skewer through the body and out behind the dorsal fin, about halfway down the body, and in again just next to the tail. Seen from above, the fish will appear to be swimming.

Sprinkle each fish liberally with sea salt, rubbing it well into the skin. Rub a little into the fins and tail as well.

Preheat the grill to moderate. Arrange the trout on their bellies in the grilling pan. Grill the trout for about 7 minutes. Turn them on to their backs and grill for a further 7 minutes, or until the flesh can be gently separated from the bone and the skin is crisp and brown.

Carefully withdraw the skewers. Lay the fish on a serving dish and serve them garnished with *beni shoga* or lemon wedges.

Vinegared Vegetables or Seafood
SUNOMONO

Sunomono *is a side dish which complements one or two other dishes of fish, vegetables or meat. The dressing may be poured over most vegetables and fish, cooked or raw.*

SERVES 4

½ daikon (Japanese radish), finely grated

1 large carrot, finely grated

8 oz scallops, cooked and shredded

½ cucumber, cut in julienne strips

4 oz prawns, poached

8 oz green beans, cut into 2-inch lengths and cooked

1 to 1½ lb spinach or 8 oz broccoli, lightly cooked and well drained

DRESSING

6 tablespoons su (rice vinegar)

2 tablespoons sugar

1 to 2 teaspoons shoyu (Japanese soy sauce)

Salt

First make the dressing. In a small bowl, combine the *su,* sugar, *shoyu* and salt to taste. Pile the cooled vegetables and prawns into small individual serving bowls. Pour a little of the dressing over the ingredients in each bowl.

A little *katsuobushi* (dried bonito flakes) may be sprinkled over each bowl to add texture and a subtle flavour.

255

Good food in the Spice Islands

Map labels: STRAIT OF MALACCA · SOUTH CHINA S · TURTLES' EGGS · BAMBOO SHOOTS · CRAB · MALAYSIA · LUMPIA *Pancakes stuffed with meat, fish or vegetables* · FRIED SHARKS' FINS · PASSION FRUIT · MALAYA · KUALA LUMPUR · CHINESE C · PRAWNS · CRAYFISH · PISTACHIO NUTS · CATTLE · SINGAPORE GARUPA · PEANUTS · SHEEP · SARAWAK · LAOS · DRIED S. · CHILLIES · SUMATRA · POMFRET · BORI · KALIMA · DURIAN · CITRUS LE · TEA · LEMON GRASS · SATE *Charcoal-grille served with spic* · COCONUT · POMEGRANATES · PALEMBANG · GREATER SU · KRUPUK *Deep-fried dried shrimp wafers* · UDANG BUMBU GORENG *Spiced fried shrimp* · CORIANDER ROOT · CUSTARD APPLES · INDONES · SHRIMP · OTAK-OT. *Stuffed fish* · DJAKARTA · TAMARIND · ABALONE · SWEET CO · NASI GORENG *Fried rice with chicken and prawns* · RICE · MADU · BEAN SPROUTS · INDIAN OCEAN · MANGOSTEEN · JAVA · SUGAR-CA · COFFEE · FRIED SWE

STEPPING OUT of an air-conditioned plane at Kamajoran Airport in Djakarta, the capital of the Republic of Indonesia, to be greeted by an upsurge of damp heat, is likely to make the thought of food as remote as it would be in a Turkish bath. Yet, remarkably quickly, the sights and smells and sounds of these rightly named Spice Islands, which together comprise the fascinating country of Indonesia, will awaken a gourmet interest in, and sensual enjoyment of, the highly seasoned, and often hot, national dishes.

Driving from the airport to a hotel in the centre of town, the first impression is likely to be of the sheer numbers of people on the streets. Most of the men in the cities have adopted a Western style of dress, tropical white cotton suits, or white shorts with coloured shirts. But the women make the streets gay with their colourful sarongs of locally produced batik, worn with thin, flowered *kebayas*, long jackets with close-fitting, wrist-length sleeves.

After dark the street restaurants are more immediately noticed. Lit by gas flares, these are small stalls comprising two or three glowing charcoal buckets on which there are steaming bowls of rice, grilled *saté*, skewered, marinated pieces of beef, lamb, chicken or pork, accompanied by small bowls of peanut sauce into which the *saté* is dipped; and, of course, *sambals*, made by pounding together basic ingredients of chillies, garlic, onions and tomatoes. Even the smell of spices, and, perhaps, fried coconut, from these stalls kindle an appetite.

The Indonesian Archipelago consists of more than three thousand islands stretching more than three thousand miles along each side of the Equator, forming a long series of stepping stones between Asia and Australia. Java, Sumatra, Kalimantan (previously Borneo), Silawesi (Celebes) and Bali are among the largest and best-known islands.

It is a land of old and rich cultures. The earliest known visitors came from India in about the fifth century BC. From the first century AD, Hindu and Chinese traders began to call at the islands, and to settle on some of them. Then, in about 1300, Arabian merchants came, bringing with them an evangelical zeal as well as trade. A vast majority of Indonesians adopted, by conversion or expediency, the Islamic faith.

There were, however, a few examples of a heroic resistance. Madjopahit, the king of the last great Hindu-Javanese Empire, in 1478, committed suicide rather than surrender to the enveloping tide of Islam. His son fled to Bali, together with many members of the court, priests, men of letters and artists. To this day Hinduism flourishes in Bali, as does an extraordinary, virile artistic tradition.

Bali is fiercely individualistic in the most delightful way. It is an island of thousands of temples, and a profusion of festivals and ceremonies. To the Balinese, the social religious and artistic aspects of life are inextricably interwoven. Music, dancing, painting and wood-carving are as natural as sleeping, breathing and eating. There are Balinese dishes which are not available in other parts of Indonesia.

The first European known to have se foot in Indonesia was Marco Polo in 1290 He was followed by many Portugues traders who went as far east as the Moluccas But it was the Dutch who, in 1596, began the founding of their East Indies Empire and who ruled these islands for more than three centuries, with a brief interruption of three years of British rule from 1811 to 1814 It is the Dutch who adopted Indonesian food, so that today one can eat a mos memorable Indonesian meal in Amsterdam as well as in Cape Town, Durban or Johannesburg. After a troubled period of Japanese occupation during the Second World War when the Dutch were driven out, the Indonesians declared themselves an independent Republic in August 1945.

CHICKEN CURRY

ASSAVA

ONIONS

BLACHAN
Shrimp paste

SAMBALS
Hot spicy pickles

SOYA SAUCE   CELEBES

I S L A N D S

LIMES

SOUR SOP

ROAST STUFFED SUCKING PIG

RED SNAPPER   TUNA

MBOK

E S S E R   S U N D A

RAMBUTAN

CASHEW NUTS

SWEET POTATOES

SAGO

M O L U C C A S

LYCHEES

BANANAS

WEST IRIAN

PINEAPPLES

INDONESIA

Eighty per cent of Indonesia's population is engaged in some form of agriculture. Its abundant rainfall and rich alluvial soil combine to make it one of the most fertile countries in the world. The most important food crop is rice, the staple food.

Coffee, the favourite drink of the people, is grown in Java, Sumatra and Bali. Java and Sumatra have plantations producing excellent tea, but this is mostly exported. Other important food crops, mainly for domestic consumption, are cassava, corn, sweet potatoes, peanuts, soybeans and sugar-cane. There are a few places, in Madura, for example, and on some of the islands east of Bali, where the conditions are less good for rice crops and corn is also an important part of the diet. And in the Moluccas Islands, sago, which comes from the inside of the trunk of the sago palm tree, is the staple food and rice is reserved for special occasions.

Many familiar vegetables such as cabbage and tomatoes, as well as bean sprouts and bamboo shoots are available. Fruit abounds, including paw paw, pineapple, bananas in many varieties, custard apples, passion fruit, pomegranates, lychees and Chinese gooseberries.

Main dishes in Indonesia usually consist of rice, vegetables and fish, chicken or meat. Meat is eaten sparingly and a little is made to go a long way. Dried salted fish is popular because it is cheap and tasty. Fresh sea fish and shellfish are difficult to get except near the sea shore, but most villages have their fish ponds, and fish are also bred in the flooded rice fields.

The famous *rijstaffel*, which in Dutch means rice table, is not a single dish, but a feast of representative Indonesian dishes served with a huge bowl of dry white rice. A successful *rijstaffel* requires the careful planning of from twenty to thirty different dishes, selected to create an interplay of flavours, including bowls of fresh pineapple slices, fresh and fried bananas, dried shrimp, peanuts, pistachios, crisp fresh coconut, cucumbers, gherkins, mango chutney, a selection of *sambals* and *krupuk*, pounded

dried shrimp which, fried in very hot olive oil, swell up in seconds into light curly flakes.

Essential in the choice of dishes for a *rijstaffel* is at least one kind of *saté*, a good chicken and vegetable bouillon, a *nasi goreng*, fried rice with chicken, shrimp, vegetables and spices, a hot curry and a heavily spiced fish.

Indonesia and Malaysia share a similar cooking tradition. The Malays and the Indonesians have a common ethnic origin and, to a considerable extent, the same climatic conditions govern their agricultural produce. The differences that exist result principally from the cultural and economic influences of historical factors, such as the long periods of colonization by the Dutch in Indonesia, and the British in Malaysia. Moreover, the Chinese make up roughly half the population of Malaysia, and the Indians another ten per cent. This is reflected in eating habits. In Indonesia, however, the Malayan racial group predominates and, therefore, the food tends to be more authentically their own.

Piquant dishes to suit every palate

Spiced Fried Shrimp
UDANG BUMBU GORENG

Serve this dish piping hot with plain boiled rice.

SERVES 4

2 garlic cloves, crushed
1-inch-piece fresh root ginger, peeled and
    finely chopped or grated
2 teaspoons ground coriander
1 tablespoon vinegar
2 teaspoons brown sugar
½ to 1 teaspoon chilli powder
Salt
Pepper
1 lb large, shelled and deveined uncooked
    shrimp
4 tablespoons peanut or vegetable oil

Combine the garlic, ginger, ground coriander, vinegar, sugar, chilli powder and salt and pepper to taste. Slit the shrimp down the back. Rub the spices into the shrimp and set aside to marinate for 4 hours.

Heat the oil in a large frying-pan until it is very hot. Add the shrimp and fry them, turning them once or twice, for about 5 minutes until they are pink and lightly browned.

Chicken Bouillon
SOTO AJAM

In Indonesia, soups are not served at the beginning of a meal but as part of it. This chicken soup when served with the garnish is substantial enough to be served as a main dish—among others —in an Indonesian meal.

SERVES 6 TO 8

3 tablespoons peanut or vegetable oil
2 medium-sized onions, finely chopped
1 garlic clove, crushed
1 teaspoon grated fresh root ginger
½ teaspoon cayenne pepper
½ teaspoon ground coriander
¼ teaspoon sereh (powdered lemon grass) or 1
    teaspoon grated lemon rind
3 lb chicken
4 pints water
Salt
Pepper
GARNISH
2 carrots, coarsely grated
2 leeks, finely sliced
2 celery sticks, finely sliced
2 hard-boiled eggs, sliced
4 oz cooked rice

Heat the oil in a large saucepan. Add the onions, garlic and ginger and fry, stirring occasionally, until the onion is soft but not brown. Stir in the cayenne pepper, coriander and *sereh* or grated lemon rind. Cook for 1 minute. Add the chicken and pour in the water. Add salt and pepper to taste. Bring the water to the boil, cover the pan and simmer for 1 hour, or until the chicken is tender.

Remove the chicken from the pan and set aside. Strain the stock and return it to the pan. Bring the stock to the boil again, lower the heat and cook, uncovered, for 30 minutes, or until the stock is reduced to about 2½ pints. Taste the stock and adjust the seasoning.

Meanwhile, skin and bone the chicken and slice the meat finely.

Place the sliced chicken in individual soup bowls with the grated carrot, sliced leeks, celery and hard-boiled eggs. Pour in the hot bouillon and serve with rice in a separate bowl.

Liver Bali Style
HATI BUMBU BALI

A quick and easy dish to make, hati bumbu bali *must not be overcooked because the liver will become tough and rubbery.*

SERVES 4

2 tablespoons peanut or vegetable oil
1 medium-sized onion, finely chopped
1 garlic clove, crushed
½ teaspoon turmeric
½ teaspoon brown sugar
1 tablespoon ground peanuts, cashew nuts or
    crunchy peanut butter
1 teaspoon chilli powder
Salt
Pepper
1 lb liver, thinly sliced
8 fl oz thick coconut milk (see p. 215)
1 curry leaf or bay leaf
GARNISH
1 medium-sized onion, thinly sliced and
    fried until crisp

Heat the oil in a frying-pan and fry the onion and garlic until the onion is golden. Stir in the turmeric, sugar, ground peanuts, chilli powder, and salt and pepper to taste. Cook for 2 minutes stirring constantly. Add the liver and cook, turning the pieces over, for 1 minute. Pour in the coconut milk and add the curry or bay leaf. Cook, stirring frequently, for 2 to 3 minutes, or until the sauce is thick and the liver cooked.

Spoon the liver and sauce on to a heated serving dish. Garnish with the fried onion and serve.

Chicken Saté
SATE AJAM

Traditionally, satés *are served as snacks but they make an excellent first course. Serve saté* ajam *with individual cucumber and onion salads.*

SERVES 8 AS A FIRST COURSE

4 whole chicken breasts (8 pieces)
MARINADE
3 tablespoons dark soy sauce
1 tablespoon treacle
1 tablespoon brown sugar
2 garlic cloves, crushed
2 tablespoons water
1 tablespoon lime or lemon juice
SAUCE FOR THE SATE
6 tablespoons ground peanuts or crunchy
    peanut butter
1 garlic clove, crushed
8 fl oz coconut milk (see p. 215)
1 teaspoon chilli powder
1 tablespoon soy sauce
1 teaspoon brown sugar
1 bay leaf
Freshly ground black pepper
Salt

Skin and bone the chicken breasts and cut the meat into 1-inch cubes. Combine all the ingredients for the marinade in a shallow bowl. Thread the chicken pieces on saté sticks or skewers and place them in the marinade for 30 minutes, turning and basting frequently. If it is more convenient, put the chicken pieces in the marinade first, threading them on the skewers after they have marinated.

Meanwhile make the sauce. Combine all the ingredients for the sauce in a small saucepan. Cook over low heat, stirring constantly, until the sauce is thick and smooth. Keep the sauce hot while the chicken is grilled.

Grill the chicken pieces over a charcoal fire or under a hot grill, turning the skewers occasionally, for 5 minutes, or until they are crisp and golden brown.

Serve immediately with the sauce served separately in small individual saucers.

Fried Rice
NASI GORENG

One of the best-known Indonesian rice dishes, nasi goreng *is traditionally served with fried eggs and sliced tomato.*

SERVES 4 TO 6

3 fl oz peanut or vegetable oil
3 eggs, lightly beaten with salt to taste
4 medium-sized onions, chopped
2 large garlic cloves
2 red chillies or 1 teaspoon chilli powder
1 teaspoon blachan (shrimp paste), optional
8 oz shelled and deveined uncooked shrimp
8 oz cooked diced chicken, turkey or veal
12 oz cooked long-grain rice
2 tablespoons soy sauce
1 teaspoon brown sugar
Juice of ½ lemon
Freshly ground black pepper

Salt
8 oz cooked ham, shredded

Heat 2 tablespoons of the oil in a small frying-pan. Add the beaten egg and let it set like a thin pancake. Cook until golden. Slide the omelette on to a plate. Cut it into strips. Set aside and keep warm.

Place the onions, garlic, chillies and *blachan,* if available, in an electric blender and blend the mixture to a purée, or finely chop and mix the ingredients together.

Heat the remaining oil in a large, deep frying-pan. Add the onion purée and fry, stirring constantly, until it is golden brown. Stir in the shrimp and fry, stirring, until they are pink. Stir in the diced chicken, rice, soy sauce, sugar and lemon juice. Season to taste with pepper and salt. Fry the mixture, stirring constantly, until it is heated through and the rice grains are coated. Add more oil if necessary.

Spoon the rice mixture on to a heated platter. Garnish with the shredded ham and omelette strips and serve with a side dish of fried onions mixed with unsalted peanuts.

Vegetable Salad with Peanut Sauce
GADO-GADO

Gado-gado is a popular salad in Indonesia and Malaysia. It is a mixture of cooked and raw vegetables attractively arranged in layers on a large platter and served with a spicy peanut sauce.

SERVES 4

2 large potatoes, boiled and sliced
8 cabbage leaves, blanched and shredded
3 carrots, sliced lengthways and parboiled
8 oz green beans, cut into 1-inch pieces and parboiled
8 oz bean sprouts, washed
8 oz kang kung (Chinese spinach) or spinach, coarsely chopped and blanched
2 bean curd cakes, cubed and fried in oil until golden
1 small cucumber, sliced
2 hard-boiled eggs, sliced
2 medium-sized onions, finely sliced and fried until brown and crisp
SAUCE
8 oz shelled, unsalted, roasted peanuts
2 tablespoons peanut or vegetable oil
1 medium-sized onion, finely chopped
2 garlic cloves, crushed
4 green chillies, seeded and finely chopped
1 teaspoon blachan (shrimp paste)
1 tablespoon brown sugar
4 tablespoons tamarind water or 2 table-spoons lemon juice
15 fl oz thick coconut milk (see p. 215)
8 fl oz water
1 teaspoon salt

First make the sauce. Put the peanuts in an electric blender or a food mill and grind them coarsely. Set aside.

Heat the oil in a frying-pan. Add the onion, garlic and chillies and fry, stirring, until the onion is golden. Add the *blachan* and mix it well with the other ingredients. Add the ground peanuts, sugar, tamarind water or lemon juice and cook, stirring, for 1 minute. Pour in the coconut milk and water and add the salt. Stir to mix and bring to the boil. Reduce the heat to low and, stirring occasionally, simmer the sauce until it is smooth, but not too thick to be poured. Taste the sauce and adjust the season-ing. Pour the sauce into a sauceboat.

Arrange the vegetables on a platter in layers beginning with the potatoes and continuing with the cabbage, carrots, green beans, bean sprouts, spinach, bean curd, cucumber and, last, the hard-boiled eggs.

Scatter the fried onions on top and serve with the sauce.

Fried Noodles
BAMIE GORENG

Use Chinese noodles—also called mie *or* mee— *for this dish. The cooking instructions will be on the packet.*

SERVES 4

3 tablespoons peanut or vegetable oil
1 garlic clove, crushed
½-inch-piece fresh root ginger, peeled and finely chopped
8 oz diced uncooked chicken
8 oz chopped uncooked shrimp
4 large white cabbage leaves, shredded
1 celery stick, chopped
3 carrots, sliced thinly, lengthways
8 oz thin egg noodles (mie or Chinese noodles), boiled
Salt
Pepper
8 fl oz chicken stock, boiling
1 tablespoon light soy sauce
GARNISH
1 onion, finely sliced and fried until brown and crisp
1 to 2 red chillies, finely chopped

Heat the oil in a large, deep frying-pan or *wok.* Add the garlic and ginger and fry for 30 seconds. Add the diced chicken and shrimp and fry, stirring, until the chicken becomes opaque and the shrimp pink. Add the cabbage, celery and carrots and fry, stirring, for 3 minutes. Add the noodles and salt and pepper to taste and fry, stirring constantly, until the noodles are well coated. Pour in the boiling stock and cook for 1 minute. Remove the pan from the heat and stir in the soy sauce.

Heap into a heated bowl and garnish with the onions and chillies.

Sambals

Sambals are relishes or condiments used in or served with Indonesian dishes. They can also be served as interesting accompaniments to such Western dishes as boiled beef, boiled chicken and roast duck.

Spicy Soy Sauce
SAMBAL KETJAP

2 fl oz soy sauce
1 teaspoon crushed chilli
1 garlic clove, crushed
1 teaspoon treacle

Combine all ingredients and serve.

Spicy Fresh Tomato Chutney
SAMBAL TOMAT

2 crushed red chillies (or 2 teaspoons of ground chilli)
2 medium-sized tomatoes, blanched, peeled and chopped
1 teaspoon shrimp sauce
1 teaspoon salt

Soak the crushed chilli in a tablespoon of water for 10 minutes. Mix and mash it with the other ingredients, preferably in a mortar. Serve.

Spicy Garlic Sauce
SAMBAL DJELANTAH

1 garlic clove, crushed
1 tablespoon crushed chilli
1 teaspoon salt
1 teaspoon shrimp sauce
1 tablespoon vegetable oil

Combine all ingredients and cook over a low flame for 2 minutes.

Spicy Pepper Sauce
SAMBAL BADJAK

2 tablespoons chopped onion
2 tablespoons vegetable oil
4 garlic cloves, crushed
2 tablespoons crushed chilli
1 small tomato, blanched and peeled
1 teaspoon salt
2 teaspoons brown sugar
1 teaspoon shrimp sauce

Fry the onion in the oil over low heat. Add the garlic. Cook until golden brown. Add the remaining ingredients. Stir and mix for 10 minutes. Chopped fresh shrimp may be added if desired.

259

Superb raw ingredients used imaginatively

ASKED which aspect of New Zealand most impressed him, the Victorian novelist and traveller Anthony Trollope said, "The work-worn hands of its women." For society women in the nineteenth century, emigration to Australia or New Zealand meant the sudden end of that below-stairs scurry of servants that kept the tables of their English counterparts groaning with traditional English food. Instead of loftily supervising the cook, pioneer wives had to prepare their food themselves, often under the most primitive conditions. It is not surprising that necessity, practicality and simplicity should have left a strong mark on the cooking of both Australia and New Zealand.

Many Australian and New Zealand

women of the older, pioneer-minded tradition still spend the blazing hot days of February red-faced in their kitchens, stirring vast amounts of jam and preserves, often using the large preserving pans their grandmothers brought out from England. All this activity is due to the seasonal abundance of fruits and vegetables, often grown in their own gardens.

Their pride is measured in the rows of jars on the pantry shelves in which they have bottled vegetables and pickles, meat and fish, beans, corn and tomatoes. And there are usually several dozen jars of Golden Queen peaches and small sweet apricots, not tossed in casually, but layered in neat, overlapping rows in their glistening syrup.

Some women take preserving jars on

camping holidays and, with the aid of a cut-down kerosine can over a campfire, they will trim, scale and preserve trout, snapper and mussels minutes after they are caught. Many younger women, however, reject the idea that rows of filled jars are the symbol of a successful Down-Under housewife.

Yet every summer the backyard trees groan with grapefruit and lemons and the rich garden soil of the average quarter-acre section, compost-fed, produces far more beans, peppers, tomatoes, cauliflowers, sweet corn and potatoes than any one household could possibly consume in a year. The less traditionally minded housewife, faced with this seasonal glut and mindful that shops, especially in New Zealand, are closed for two full days at the weekends and for

three or four days at a time for other holiday periods, finds deep-freezing the answer.

Large freezers are fairly commonplace in basements and garages in Australia and New Zealand, while a small refrigerator in the kitchen holds everyday supplies. A freezer might contain a side of beef together with sides of springtime bargain lamb bought wholesale.

The women are ardent bulk buyers, perhaps because they have large families and because every family is likely to own a car. They will buy ten-pound commercial packs of frozen beans and peas, and they will drive out to the country on a Saturday morning for half a dozen dressed chickens, a case of apples or to pick their own strawberries (for which they pay bargain prices) at the height of the season.

There is one time of the year, however, when in most homes convenience is overcome by sentiment. At Christmas even third and fourth generation Australians and New Zealanders watch the satellite-relayed Queen's Speech on television and talk nostalgically of "home". And the cook says "I know it's silly" as she produces, on a brilliant summer day, roast lamb and turkey, mince pies and Christmas pudding, topped with a sprig of plastic holly. Everyone agrees it is silly, but Christmas is Christmas and tradition has to be satisfied.

Most families try to combine the best of both old and new Christmas traditions. They drink ice-cold beer with fruit cake on the Australian Gold Coast, or they have a picnic lunch with Christmas crackers and funny hats under the midsummer blaze of the scarlet pohutukawa trees of New Zealand. There is, too, a popular recipe for a Yule pudding which consists of mixed dried fruit set in a sherry or port jelly in a deep bowl. It is turned out and decorated with whipped cream. Some sentimental cooks put lucky coins in it. Christmas Down Under remains an uneasy compromise.

Completely indigenous Australian and New Zealand recipes are almost nonexistent, unless you count the bushman's damper (flour and water wrapped around a stick and baked in a fire), or his billy tea, which is made by throwing a handful of tea leaves into a billy can of boiling water. The billy is then boiled for as long as it takes to round up the sheep. The result is powerfully strong and black.

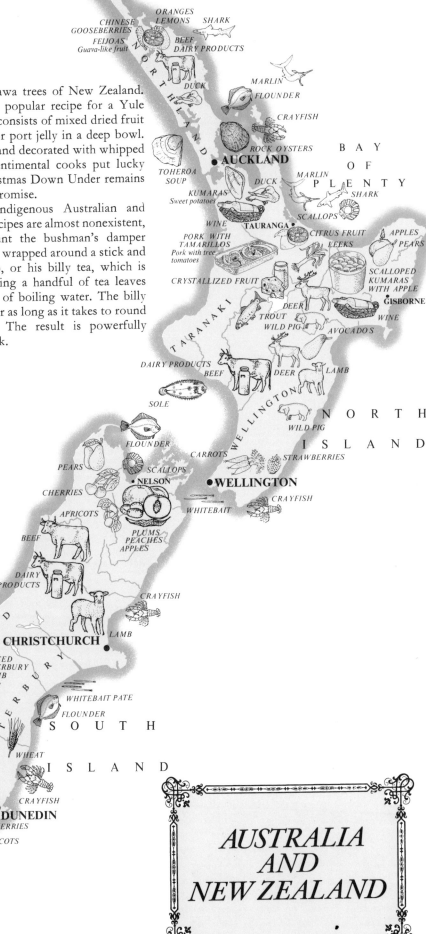

AUSTRALIA AND NEW ZEALAND

Flavourful creations of resourceful people

The Australian Aborigines may have been the first to anticipate the current interest in clay-casserole cooking. For centuries they have wrapped edible snakes and lizards in damp clay and left them in the embers for hours before breaking open the hardened container. Fortunately, visitors to Australia are seldom offered this sort of clay-baked dish as a national speciality. The New Zealand Maoris have always used the deep-earth oven method of cooking pork and fish at their *hangis* or feasts. The Maoris are of Polynesian ancestry and this method of cooking, known in Hawaii, for example, as the *luau*, is common throughout Polynesia.

Australia popularized a meringue dessert by naming it Pavlova in honour of the dancer's visit. New Zealand's pioneers, homesick for English poultry, gave the name of colonial goose to boned and stuffed leg of mutton. Kangaroo tail soup is certainly an Australian speciality, but only because of its main ingredient. It is prepared in a similar way to ox-tail soup. And, the pride of New Zealand, toheroa soup, owes its fame to the rarity of this shellfish, which tastes like oysters fed on asparagus. The same recipe can also be used for mussels.

The barbecue, more than anything else, must epitomize the Australian and New Zealand way of eating. A barbecue can be a formal affair at which a whole lamb, fragrant with herbs, turns on a mechanical spit watched by champagne-sipping guests in evening dress. More often, however, a barbecue is an impromptu gathering of family and friends on the beach or around a patio.

Immigration has brought about many changes in the traditional eating patterns Down Under. The influx of Italians and Greeks has brought more variety and subtlety to the average menu. It has also resulted in an astonishing growth in the number of good restaurants during the last ten years.

Australians and New Zealanders travel a good deal and inevitably bring back new ideas to their own countries. But the image of the practical, inventive cook remains a true one, especially since most people still prefer to do almost all their formal entertaining at home.

With its growing range of imaginative ways of dealing with their superb raw ingredients, Australian and New Zealand cooking have now progressed far beyond being poor colonial cousins of British food.

Kangaroo Tail Soup

Having caught your kangaroo, this is one of the best ways to enjoy its gamy flavour. Ox-tail may be substituted.

SERVES 6

2 oz beef fat
3 large brown onions, sliced
4 carrots, peeled and sliced
2 turnips, peeled and sliced
4 celery sticks, chopped
1 kangaroo tail, skinned and jointed
5 pints beef stock
4 tablespoons barley, washed
2 bay leaves
2 blades mace
1 whole nutmeg
Salt
Cayenne pepper
6 tablespoons claret
Chopped parsley

Melt the fat in a large saucepan. Add the vegetables and fry gently for 10 minutes, or until browned.

Add the tail joints, stock, barley, bay leaves, mace and nutmeg and bring the mixture to the boil. Reduce the heat to low, cover the pan and simmer for 3 hours.

Cool the stock and remove the scum and fat from the surface. Strain the soup and return it to the rinsed and dried pan. Season to taste and bring it back to the boil. Stir in the wine and remove the pan from the heat. Pour the soup into a tureen, sprinkle with parsley and serve.

Lamb Stew with Plum Jam

After beef, lamb is the favourite meat in Australia. Only young lamb is eaten—those reared for the pot rarely exceed 8 months in age.

SERVES 4

2 lb boned leg of lamb, cut into cubes
Seasoned flour
1 oz butter
1 tablespoon oil
2 medium-sized onions, sliced
6 carrots, sliced
2 large potatoes, cubed
6 celery sticks, sliced
2 cooking apples, peeled and sliced
Salt
Freshly ground black pepper
15 fl oz light stock
2 tablespoons plum jam

Roll the lamb cubes in the seasoned flour. In a large casserole, melt the butter and heat the oil. Add the lamb cubes a few at a time and brown them quickly. Remove them as they brown and set aside.

Add the onions, carrots, potatoes, celery and apples and fry, stirring, until they are lightly browned. Season well with salt and pepper. Stir in ½ tablespoon of seasoned flour. Add the stock and stir to mix. Return the meat to the pan and bring to the boil. Cover the casserole, reduce the heat to low and simmer for 1 hour, or until the lamb is tender.

Stir in the plum jam. Taste the sauce and adjust the seasoning. Serve immediately.

Carpet Bag Steak

The best of Australian beef and seafood are combined in this dish.

SERVES 4

4 thick fillet steaks
Salt
Freshly ground black pepper
8 oysters, shelled
Melted butter
1 tablespoon finely chopped parsley

With a sharp knife carefully make a horizontal slit in each steak to make a pocket. Rub a little salt and pepper inside each pocket. Insert 2 oysters into each steak pocket. Sew up the slits with a large needle and strong thread or secure with small skewers.

Preheat the grill to high. Brush each steak liberally with melted butter and sprinkle with pepper. Grill the steaks for 4 to 6 minutes on each side, depending on whether the steaks are to be rare or medium rare. Brush the steaks with more butter when they are turned.

To serve, put the steaks on a heated serving platter, sprinkle with the parsley and pour over them the juices accumulated in the grilling pan.

Pineapple and Cabbage Salad

Australians make use of their many tropical fruit in salads as well as in desserts. This salad may be served in hollowed-out pineapple halves.

SERVES 4 TO 6

1 large ripe pineapple, peeled, cored and cubed
1 grapefruit, peeled and segmented
1 orange, peeled and segmented
½ white cabbage, finely shredded
½ cucumber, sliced unpeeled
1 large red pepper, seeded and sliced
8 oz cooked ham, diced
Grated rind of 1 orange
4 tablespoons olive oil
2 tablespoons wine vinegar
2 tablespoons mayonnaise
2 tablespoons double cream
Salt
Sugar

In a large salad bowl combine the fruit, vegetables and ham. In a small bowl, mix together the grated orange rind, oil, vinegar, mayonnaise and cream, salt and sugar to taste. Pour the dressing over the salad. Mix well and chill thoroughly before serving.

Grape and Apricot Cream

This cool and creamy dessert is an unusual blend of two popular Australian fruits.

SERVES 6

8 oz dried apricots
4 oz seedless grapes, peeled
2 tablespoons brandy
Piece cinnamon bark
2 egg yolks
2 tablespoons castor sugar
10 fl oz milk
20 black grapes, seeded
½ oz gelatine
10 fl oz double cream, whipped

Soak the dried apricots in cold water for 1 hour; drain and reserve 5 fluid ounces of the soaking water.

Place the peeled grapes in a bowl and sprinkle with the brandy. Set aside.

Place the apricots, cinnamon and the reserved water in a saucepan. Cook over low heat until the apricots are soft. Remove and discard the cinnamon. Drain and purée the fruit in a food mill or an electric blender.

Beat the egg yolks with the sugar until pale and creamy. Scald the milk and pour it on to the egg mixture, stirring constantly. Dissolve the gelatine in a little water over low heat. When it is dissolved and slightly cooled, stir it into the custard. Strain the custard mixture into a clean bowl.

When the custard is cool and thick, fold in the apricot purée and the black grapes. Fold in the whipped cream. Spoon the mixture into a chilled mould.

Place the mould in the refrigerator and chill for at least 3 hours. Unmould on to a chilled plate, decorate with the brandied grapes and serve.

Pavlova

This is a sweet, airy and calorie-laden dessert with a firm exterior and a marshmallow-like centre.

SERVES 6

4 egg whites, at room temperature
½ teaspoon salt
8 oz castor sugar
2 teaspoons cornflour
2 teaspoons vinegar
1 lb sliced fruit such as bananas, pineapple, strawberries, Kiwi- or passion-fruit
10 fl oz double cream, whipped

Preheat the oven to 300°F (Gas Mark 2). Grease an 8-inch round cake tin and cover the bottom with a round of greaseproof paper. Grease the paper and dust lightly with cornflour.

Beat the egg whites in a large mixing bowl until they are foamy. Add the salt, and continue to beat until the egg whites are stiff and form peaks. Add the sugar gradually, beating well after each addition. When the meringue is glossy, combine the cornflour with the vinegar and fold it into the meringue. Spoon the mixture into the prepared cake tin and smooth it towards the edges, hollowing the centre slightly.

Place the tin in the oven and reduce the temperature to 250°F (Gas Mark ½). Bake for 1¼ hours. Remove the meringue from the oven and let it cool in the tin. Carefully remove the meringue and place it on a serving dish. Drain the fruit and spoon it on to the meringue. Cover with whipped cream and serve immediately.

Toheroa Soup
TOHEROA SOUP

The toheroa is a rare shellfish which must be dug, by hand, from the black sand of New Zealand's North Island and South Island beaches. This soup has a delicate flavour.

Toheroa are available canned, or clams may be substituted.

SERVES 4

1 tablespoon butter
1 tablespoon flour
15 fl oz fish stock
5 fl oz milk
4 oz toheroas or clams, minced
¼ teaspoon grated nutmeg
Lemon juice
Salt
White pepper
Single cream
Chopped parsley

Melt the butter in a saucepan and stir in the flour. Add the fish stock gradually, stirring constantly. Bring the milk to the boil separately and add it together with the toheroas or clams, to the fish stock mixture. Stir until smooth. Add the nutmeg and the lemon juice, salt and pepper to taste. Stir in a little cream just before serving, and sprinkle lightly with chopped parsley.

Canterbury Lamb with Honey

Wild New Zealand honey is best for this method of cooking young lamb. The honey settles to the bottom of the pan and caramelizes.

SERVES 4

2 lb boned leg of lamb
1 garlic clove, cut in half
2 oz butter
Salt
Freshly ground black pepper
2 tablespoons honey
1 oz flour
1 pint water or stock
4 medium-sized tomatoes, blanched, peeled and chopped
3 medium-sized carrots, sliced
1 small onion, chopped
2 teaspoons grated fresh root ginger

Preheat the oven to 350°F (Gas Mark 4).

Rub the lamb all over with the garlic. Cut the lamb into 2-inch cubes.

Melt the butter in a large, heavy pan. Add the lamb cubes and sauté, turning them frequently. Season with salt and pepper and stir in the honey. When the meat is well browned, sprinkle with the flour and cook for a further few minutes, stirring constantly. Add the water or stock, tomatoes, carrots, onion and ginger. Bring the mixture to the boil. Cover the pan, place it in the oven and cook for 45 minutes to 1 hour, or until the lamb is tender.

ONE OF THESE DAYS AUSTRALIA is going to take the world by surprise. For the moment she lets it go on thinking that the relative merits of Swan and Foster's lager are the sum total of her gastronomic concern. Meanwhile she nurtures wines of a standard which will eventually turn the French green with envy, if not white with fright. Australia's best Rieslings, Cabernets and Shiraz reds are already very fine wines indeed. Her bulk everyday wine still trails behind California's, but her best wines are as good or better.

South Australia is the centre of the wine industry and Adelaide its natural capital, but important wine areas are scattered from the Hunter Valley northwest of Sydney, through Victoria, right across to Perth. The cooler climate of the extreme south is drawing more experimental plantings that way every year.

By comparison, New Zealand is merely dabbling in wine-making. It is very early days yet in her infant industry, and the puritan instincts of the average New Zealander combine with stringent licensing laws to make wine seem an exotic, however favourable natural conditions may be.

A tropical profusion of fish and fruit

A FAMOUS GASTRONOMIC ERROR occurred in the Pacific Islands about a hundred years ago when some Fijians cooked and ate a missionary named Baker without first removing his rubber boots. Even today you can embarrass a Fijian by commenting that something is "as tough as Baker's boots". Although missionaries (or "long pig" as the cannibals preferred to call their victims) are no longer on the menu, strange stories are still occasionally heard of feasts in the wild New Guinea highlands.

Right across the broad sweep of the southern Pacific Ocean, from Guam to Tonga to the Marquesas, real pig remains the Islanders' favourite meat, especially when it is cooked in the steam and smoke of an earth oven and served on banana leaf platters. Other feast delicacies include taro, the root vegetable which is the staple food of the area, sweet yams, prawns, chicken, baby octopus, various kinds of fish and *palusami*, a savoury meat and onion mixture cooked in coconut cream and wrapped in taro leaves.

Coconut, the Islanders' universal food, is used in hundreds of different ways in the Pacific. The "water", or clear juice of the coconut, is obtained by simply punching a hole in two of the three "eyes" in the hard inner shell. Coconut milk and cream are made by grating the fresh white coconut flesh and adding hot water before squeezing the mixture through a cloth.

Very similar ways of using pork, chicken, taro and coconut are found throughout the islands, but foreign influences have created interesting regional differences. Tahiti and New Caledonia had the gastronomic good luck to become territories of the French. The Pacific Chinese prepare local vegetables in their special way, and Fiji's large Indian population has taught the native Fijians to enjoy curry. The Fijians prefer a mild curry. They use only the smallest amount of chillies and stir coconut cream into the curry to give it a rich, creamy texture.

Unwary tourists may venture to sample the explosive local toddy, which is based on fermented coconut water. There is, however, a safer drink, which tends only to weaken the knees a little. It is the ceremonial drink *yaqona*, a muddy-coloured, toothpaste flavoured liquid made from the roots of the pepper plant.

Most of the menus of the better Pacific Island hotels are based on the local fish and fruit. These naturally include pineapples, oranges (especially from the Cook Islands), bananas, pawpaws (papayas) and mangoes which are delicious in champagne. Seafood includes giant prawns, turtles, clams, rock snails, sea urchins and *bêche-de-mer*, as well as such fish as trevalle, bonito, mullet and shark. Soft vegetables like lettuce and tomatoes would wilt under the Pacific sun but there are interesting local alternatives as well as taro and yams, which are eaten at every meal. There is cassava, breadfruit and *duruka*, the Fijian name for a milky pale asparagus-like shoot.

Other than pork and poultry, the only meat most Islanders eat in quantity is bully beef, which they still import more than two hundred years after the first Europeans in the Pacific shared their ship's rations with them.

Shrimp Palusami

This is a Samoan recipe, sometimes made without the shrimp as a vegetable side dish. The Fijians and Cook Islanders like to make it with corned (bully) beef.

SERVES 6

Several taro leaves (or substitute cabbage)
1 lb shrimp, cooked, peeled, deveined and chopped
1 medium-sized onion, finely chopped
Salt
Pepper
6 fl oz coconut cream (see p. 265)

Preheat the oven to 350°F (Gas Mark 4). Wash and drain the taro or cabbage leaves. Cut six 8-by 10-inch rectangles of aluminium foil, one for each leaf.

Chop two or three of the remaining leaves and place them in a mixing bowl. Add the chopped shrimp, onion, salt and pepper to taste and mix well.

Spoon equal quantities of this mixture on to the leaves and top each with 2 tablespoons of the coconut cream. Fold the leaves over the filling. Wrap and seal each stuffed leaf in foil.

Arrange the packages in a baking dish with a little water in the bottom, and bake for 1 hour. Serve hot.

Roast Suckling Pig

In Tahiti a pig is roasted in a pit over heated stones covered with palm fronds and banana leaves. Baked at the same time are chunks of plantain, sweet potato, peeled breadfruit and taro root wrapped in banana leaves as well as fish wrapped in ti *leaves and* pota, *a mixture of chicken, salt pork and seasonings also wrapped in* ti *leaves. This recipe is an adaptation for the modern kitchen.*

SERVES 8 TO 10

12 lb suckling pig, weighed when dressed
6 tablespoons brown sugar
8 fl oz dark soy sauce
Coarse rock or sea salt
Freshly ground black pepper
4 large garlic cloves, crushed
6 tablespoons vegetable oil
GARNISH
Butter
6 ripe plantains, cut into 2-inch chunks

2 lb sweet potatoes, boiled, peeled and cut into 2-inch chunks
1 lemon or lime

Wash the pig thoroughly and dry it. In a small bowl, dissolve the sugar in the soy sauce. First rub the pig all over, inside and out, with the salt, pepper and garlic and then with half the soy sauce mixture. Set the pig aside to absorb the seasoning for 3 hours.

Preheat the oven to 450°F (Gas Mark 8). Put a small block of wood or a ball of crumpled foil in the pig's mouth to keep it open. Tie or skewer the legs, bending the back legs in a crouching position and front legs straight out in front. Place the pig on a rack in a large roasting pan. Mix the remaining soy sauce mixture with the oil, and brush the pig all over with it. Cover the ears and the tail with foil to prevent them from burning.

Roast the pig for 15 minutes. Reduce the heat to 325°F (Gas Mark 3) and roast, basting regularly, for 4½ to 5 hours or until the pig is cooked through. Test by piercing the thigh with a sharp knife. If the juices run clear the pig is cooked. If there is not enough basting liquid, make some more.

Towards the end of the cooking time prepare the garnish. In a large frying-pan, melt enough

THE SOUTH PACIFIC ISLANDS

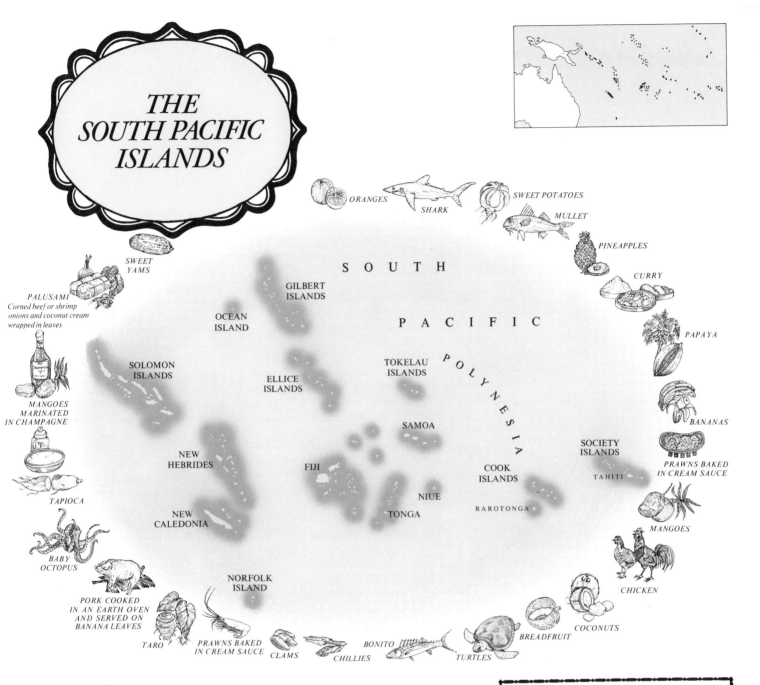

ORANGES · **SHARK** · **SWEET POTATOES** · **MULLET** · **PINEAPPLES** · **CURRY** · **PAPAYA** · **BANANAS** · **PRAWNS BAKED IN CREAM SAUCE** · **MANGOES** · **CHICKEN** · **COCONUTS** · **BREADFRUIT** · **TURTLES** · **BONITO** · **CHILLIES** · **CLAMS** · **PRAWNS BAKED IN CREAM SAUCE** · **TARO** · **PORK COOKED IN AN EARTH OVEN AND SERVED ON BANANA LEAVES** · **BABY OCTOPUS** · **TAPIOCA** · **MANGOES MARINATED IN CHAMPAGNE** · **PALUSAMI** Corned beef or shrimp onions and coconut cream wrapped in leaves · **SWEET YAMS**

SOUTH PACIFIC · POLYNESIA

GILBERT ISLANDS · OCEAN ISLAND · SOLOMON ISLANDS · ELLICE ISLANDS · TOKELAU ISLANDS · SAMOA · NEW HEBRIDES · FIJI · COOK ISLANDS · SOCIETY ISLANDS · TAHITI · NIUE · TONGA · RAROTONGA · NEW CALEDONIA · NORFOLK ISLAND

---

butter to cover the bottom of the pan. Add the plantain chunks and fry, stirring constantly, until golden. Remove from the pan and keep warm. Add more butter to the pan if necessary and fry the sweet potatoes, turning the pieces over until they are golden.

Transfer the pig to a large platter. Remove the foil. Replace the block of wood with the lemon or lime.

Arrange the plantain and sweet potato chunks around the pig and serve.

Baked Fruit Pudding
TAHITIAN POE

Poe *is Tahitian dessert made from tropical fruit pounded to a purée, mixed with arrowroot and baked.*

SERVES 6

1 large ripe papaya, halved, seeded, peeled and chopped
4 large ripe bananas, peeled
3 ripe mangoes, peeled, seeded and chopped
1 pineapple, peeled, cored and finely chopped
6 oz brown sugar
1 teaspoon vanilla essence
3 fl oz pineapple juice
2 oz arrowroot
8 fl oz thick coconut cream or double cream

Preheat the oven to 400°F (Gas Mark 6). Generously butter a shallow baking dish. Purée the papaya, bananas and mangoes and pineapple in a blender or put through a food mill. Put the fruit purée in a large bowl. Beat in the sugar and the vanilla essence. Dissolve the arrowroot in the pineapple juice and mix it in.

Pour the mixture into the prepared baking dish and bake for 1 hour, or until the top is golden brown. Let the *poe* cool, then refrigerate it.

Serve very cold with the coconut cream or whipped double cream served separately.

Coconut Milk and Cream

Select a mature coconut that is heavy for its size. Using a skewer, punch out 2 of the 3 "eyes" and pour away the liquid inside. Tap the coconut sharply all over with a hammer and split it in half. Cut out the meat with a sharp, strong knife and pare the brown skin. Grate the coconut by hand or in an electric blender.

Put the grated coconut in a bowl and pour in an equal amount of boiling water. Leave it to infuse for 30 minutes, then pour it through a strainer lined with a double thickness of cheesecloth. Squeeze the cloth to extract as much milk as possible. 1 cup of grated coconut and 1 cup of water makes 1 cup of coconut milk.

To make coconut cream, first make coconut milk with triple the amount of grated coconut to water. When the coconut milk is cool, refrigerate it for 4 hours. When the "cream" rises to the top skim it off. 3 cups of grated coconut and 1 cup of water will make 1 cup of coconut cream.

The evolution of a national cuisine

THE COOKING OF CANADA, like that of the United States, reflects the mixed heritage of its many settlers, originally the French and English of Eastern Canada, with later scatterings of Scots, Irish, Germans, Poles, Ukrainians, Russians, Scandinavians and Icelanders. These varied ethnic cuisines became harmoniously interwoven with the indigenous foods of the country—fish and shellfish, corn and wild rice, game, wild berries and mushrooms.

Even today, the style of cooking remains fluid, as further influxes of migrating Europeans colour and change the eating habits of the cities. Add to this the wilderness stretches of the Northwest Territories and the Yukon, where life retains a frontier freedom, and the picture is that of a country still evolving a national cuisine. What Canada does have, and in abundance, are great resources of natural foods that make this, perhaps, one of the last outposts of the kind of unprocessed, unpackaged sustenance the world enjoyed in the past.

Mainly farmers and seafaring folk, the first Canadian settlers cooked simply and ate heartily, a pattern that still continues outside the major cities—in the prairie and the Maritime and northern provinces. Depending on foods they could catch, hunt, raise and store, the settlers concentrated on nourishing stews, thick soups of dried beans and peas, salt cod and a sufficiency of starch, in the form of cakes, pies, biscuits, breads, muffins and pancakes.

In many ways the cooking of Canada resembles that of the northern American states to which it was historically linked. Not only do the Maritimes and New England, British Columbia and Washington and Oregon share many of the same natural foods, but there was also a constant interchange of population, especially after the American Revolution, when a steady exodus of Loyalists streamed into British Canada.

Although Canada has not been French since the Peace of Paris ceded the colony of

New France to England in 1763, the oldest and most enduring dishes are those of the first settlers of Quebec, mostly fishermen and farmers from the French sea-coast provinces of Normandy, Brittany and Poitou. It is their tastes and traditions that prevail in the distinctive and delicious food known today as French Canadian. There are many unusual pies: the pork *tourtière* served on Christmas Eve; *cipâte* or *cipaille*, layers of pastry interleaved with a filling of game, poultry, pork and vegetables; *cipâte aux bleuets*, a three-crust blueberry pie with a pastry heart softened by the oozing juice.

From Acadia, as Nova Scotia was known, come *pâté à la râpure*, Anglicized to rappie pie, in which potatoes are grated (in French, *râpé*), squeezed to fluffy dryness, then cooked in boiling chicken broth and layered in a pan with poached chicken; and *pâté aux bucardes*, clams baked in a biscuit dough.

There is always a liberal and thrifty use of every part of the pig, from pork chops and roasts, ham and sausages, to salt pork, head cheese, or brawn, pork galantine and *ragoût de pattes*, pork hocks. French Canadians love their pork down to the last lingering mouthful of *graisse de rôti*, the fat and jelly from roast-meat drippings spread on bread.

Habitant pea soup is named for the *habitants*, farmers, of French Canada. This famous yellow pea soup has become almost synonymous with French Canadian cooking.

To make 6 to 8 servings of habitant pea soup, soak 1 pound of yellow split peas in cold water overnight. Next day, drain them and put them in a heavy, 4½-quart casserole, or soup kettle, with 1 large, thinly sliced onion, 1 pound lean salt pork, or 2 pounds smoked ham hocks, 3 tablespoons chopped celery leaves, ½ teaspoon dried savory, ¼ teaspoon dried thyme, 1 tablespoon chopped fresh parsley and 3½ pints of cold water.

Bring to the boil over high heat. Cover, reduce heat and simmer slowly, stirring frequently, for 2 to 3 hours, or until the peas are soft and the soup is creamy. Taste the soup and add freshly ground pepper and salt if necessary.

The forbidding rocky coasts of Canada's Maritime Provinces, New Brunswick, Nova Scotia, Newfoundland and Prince Edward Island, bear witness to the hardiness of the people, a tough and resilient mixture of English, Scots, Irish, French, New Englanders and Germans who make their living, as they have always done, chiefly by fishing and farming.

Maritime dishes are simple and sustaining. Fish is turned into chowders, stews and hashes and a rather Spartan concoction

known as fish and brewis, made with fresh or salt cod, hardtack biscuits, onions, potatoes and salt pork.

Prince Edward Island, Canada's smallest province, is noted for shellfish and even more for potatoes grown in the rich red soil of this fertile garden spot. There they make a delicious warm potato salad which is very good with cold meats.

To make 6 to 8 servings of potato and bacon salad, boil 8 medium-sized potatoes in their jackets until tender but still firm. Drain well and dry in the pan over low heat, shaking the pan. When the potatoes are cool enough to handle, peel and slice them 1 inch thick.

Fry 6 slices of bacon and drain on kitchen paper, leaving the fat in the pan. Crumble the bacon.

In a salad bowl, put the sliced potatoes, 2 sticks diced celery, 1 medium, thinly sliced onion, ½ teaspoon celery seed and the bacon and toss just to combine.

Mix into the bacon fat 4 fluid ounces of cider or wine vinegar, 4 fluid ounces dry white wine, 1 teaspoon prepared mustard, 1½ teaspoons salt, ½ teaspoon black pepper. Heat through. While hot, pour over the vegetables and toss well. Sprinkle with 2 tablespoons chopped parsley and serve.

Fiddleheads, the tender, curled shoots of the ostrich fern, are a New Brunswick delicacy which the rest of the world must buy canned or frozen. Briefly cooked in a little salted water and dressed with butter, they capture the flavour of the wilds.

Of all the Canadian provinces, Ontario, stretching one thousand miles from east to west, produces the greatest variety of foods and has the least traditional cooking. The fish come from almost three-quarters of a million lakes.

One of Ontario's most unusual pockets of regional cooking is in Kitchener, settled by a community of Mennonites who brought with them the typical foods of the Pennsylvania Dutch. Stuffed goose is one of their special dishes, and the goose fat and meat scraps go into a superb, smooth, rich spread.

The western prairie provinces of Manitoba, Saskatchewan and Alberta were settled late in the nineteenth century by different ethnic groups, all of whom brought with them the cooking practices of their homelands. Here you find the bannock of Scotland co-existing with Russian *kasha*, Ukrainian *medivnyk*, German Mennonite rivvel soup, chicken soup with tiny dumplings, Western chuckwagon stew, corned beef and cabbage and such native Indian foods as succotash and wild rice.

CANADA

The lakes and forests of northern Saskatchewan harbour pickerel and whitefish,
game, wild berries like the saskatoon, which
looks something like a blueberry but has a
taste all its own, and the tiny pinchberry,
which makes a wonderful tart jelly to serve
with game. The southern part of the province is a tamed and cultivated bread basket,
where rippling fields of wheat, maize, oats
and barley extend to the horizon.

Alberta, expansively Western in size and
spirit, grows prize-winning wheat and
raises grain-fed turkeys and Canada's finest
lamb and beef. The eating here is plain and
filling, Western-style, with steaks, beef and
beans, hash and pancakes.

British Columbia, the most westerly of
Canada's provinces, is well named, for the
atmosphere and ambiance are decidedly
English. The climate is well tempered, the
gardens and orchards well tended and the
delightful turn-of-the-century capital of
Victoria, with its afternoon tea ritual and
long-established chocolate shops, seems to
belong to a vanished age of sedate pleasures.

The Fraser River is the spawning ground
of the great Pacific salmon, the king or
Chinook, coho, chum and the dark red,
oily sockeye, excellent for canning. From
the Pacific waters come halibut, black cod
(technically, not a cod but sablefish), which
when smoked, poached in milk and
smothered with butter makes one of the
world's finest breakfasts, and an unequalled
range of shellfish.

The fruits of British Columbia are equally
celebrated—big juicy raspberries, strawberries, loganberries, wild blackberries and
huckleberries. Apricots, cherries, peaches,
plums, pears and apples ripen to luscious
perfection in the sheltered Okanagan Valley.

To the north lie the Yukon and the North-
west Territories, lands of wilderness and
water, of Eskimos and reindeer, moose,
caribou, snow geese, ptarmigan, hare, seal,
wild berries and the famous Arctic char, a
fish of the salmon family with exquisitely
delicate flesh. The names of the traditional
Yukon dishes recall the gold rush days, the
rough-and-ready food of the camps—hooli-
gan, slumgullion and sourdough pancakes.

This is a last frontier of food, to be
savoured before it, too, becomes engulfed
by the supermarket culture.

A cornucopia of foods, an inventive cuisine

THE UNITED STATES is a vast pantry. Its rich soil, its broad plains, its lush orchards and the seas lapping at its shores provide a breathtaking array of food in huge abundance. Enormous herds of beef cattle roam American grasslands that are as large as some of the countries of the world. A veritable cornucopia of fruit and vegetables of countless varieties springs from its earth. A profusion of lobsters, crabs, clams, oysters, shrimp and fish is drawn from its waters. Its amber waves of grain overlap endless horizons.

If America is a pantry, the American kitchen is a laboratory. It is equipped with a galaxy of culinary machines and gadgets designed to simplify the task of preparing the products of nature's generosity for the dinner-table. America's obsession with labour-saving tools and mechanical devices was translated, first, into such simple gadgets as apple peelers and hand-cranked ice-cream freezers, and later into space-age ovens, high-speed blenders, electric juicers and an extensive catalogue of other implements that have transformed the process of cooking.

Ironically, this amalgam of abundance and mechanics has not resulted in an ornate American cuisine. There are, indeed, such intriguing anomalies as the daring culinary improvisations of California, the imaginative delicacies of New Orleans Creole cooking, the exotic ethnic influences in mid-Atlantic kitchen lore and the craving for pungent flavours prevailing in the Southwest. But, generally, American cooking is unsophisticated and straightforward, concerned with content rather than form.

The best-known and most popular American foods are grilled steaks, hamburgers, fried chicken, boiled lobster and fried fish. All of these dishes can be delicious and none requires any cooking flair. Some recipes for Southern fried chicken, however, are jealously guarded family secrets and a pure beef hamburger with onions and relish on a fresh sesame-seed roll can taste good enough to be a product of culinary magic.

The simplicity of most cooking in the United States is deceptive. Although the American cook may not spend long hours over a hot stove, and, due to a highly efficient food distribution system, big-city cooking tends to be the same across the country, the variety of regional foods in America is formidable. New England and Pennsylvania Dutch cooking have little in common. Neither do a Montana rodeo roast

and a magnificent traditional Hawaiian *luau*.

Clam chowder, pepperpot soup, jambalaya, red-flannel hash, sour milk pancakes, Kentucky burgoo, shoo-fly pie, Caesar salad, flapjacks, cherry cobbler—there is poetry in even an abbreviated list of America's culinary specialities, and there is drama in the story of how the American cuisine, in all its varied forms, developed.

Indian influences in what was frontier land, Mexican influences in the Southwest, and French-Spanish influences in Louisiana are still apparent. But the settlers from England and Holland, who tamed the Atlantic coast, and from a dozen other countries as well, who gradually pushed the frontier back across the continent to the Pacific Ocean, had little time or inclination for ceremony or ritual in cooking.

The first problem was survival, which was not always easy. The suggestion that the wholesome food they cultivated could be much improved by fancy shenanigans in the kitchen was a presumption few of them would have entertained. They held that if the ingredients were good and properly cooked, whether fried, baked or boiled, that's all that could, or should, be desired.

Over the decades, this no-nonsense approach to cooking sank deep into the American culture, although even on the frontier a woman could gain fame for the lightness of her corn biscuits or the delicacy of her hot berry pie. Gradually, however, regional distinctions began to emerge and flourish so that, for example, ham became one thing in one place and something different elsewhere—fried Kentucky ham with red-eye gravy, smoked Pennsylvania Dutch ham with dried apples, cornmeal-coated Texas ham, thinly sliced Virginia ham with hot biscuits, Missouri baked glazed ham. Similarly, clam chowder was given a milk base in New England, a tomato base in the mid-Atlantic region and the clams in the chowder sometimes gave way to oysters in the South.

Aside from regional differences, there were lessons learned from late arrivals from Europe who brought with them to America a taste and a skill for a different kind of kitchen craft—for sauerbraten in Milwaukee, for Polish sausage in Chicago, for gefilte fish and for a dozen different spaghetti sauces in New York.

There is a versatility and ingenuity to the American cuisine which belies its basic simplicity. It is as varied, inventive and ultimately indefinable as America itself.

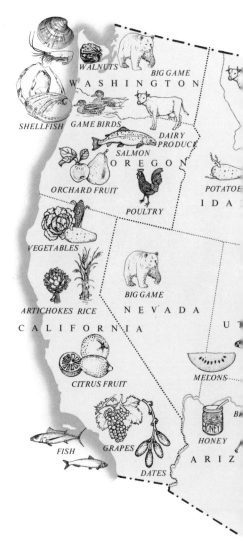

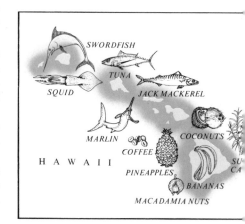

WALRUS

REINDEER
ALASKA
YUKON CARIBOU
DAIRY PRODUCE
VEGETABLES
SALMON HERRING
KING CRAB SHRIMP
SEAL HALIBUT
A L E U T I A N   I S L A N D S

BIG GAME
BIG GAME
BIG GAME POTATOES
MONTANA WHEAT NORTH DAKOTA GAME BIRDS MINNESOTA WILD RICE TROUT CATFISH
VEGETABLES CATTLE GAME BIRDS DAIRY PRODUCE SWEET CORN CARP VT. MAINE
SOUTH DAKOTA WISCONSIN MICH. PIKE DAIRY PRODUCE N.H. LOBSTER
FRUIT CORN SMALL GAME SWEET POTATOES BASS VEGETABLES MAPLE SUGAR MASS.
WYOMING SHEEP NEBRASKA IOWA VEGETABLES CRANBERRIES FRUIT NEW YORK GRAPES SHAD
POTATOES HOGS ILL. APPLES OHIO GAME BIRDS CONN. R.I. CLAMS
CATTLE DAIRY PRODUCE ORCHARD FRUIT PA. POULTRY SCALLOPS
COLORADO SUGAR-BEET IND. MUSHROOMS N.J. OYSTER
CATTLE POULTRY W.VA. TROUT MD. SWORDFISH
KANSAS OHIO HOGS DE. BASS
WHEAT KY. SWEET POTATOES SMALL GAME VA. FLOUNDER
SHEEP MISSOURI STRAWBERRIES ORCHARD FRUIT PERCH
NEW MEXICO POULTRY OKLAHOMA SHEEP TENN. FRUIT NORTH CAROLINA RICE CRAB
ARK. PEACHES SOUTH CAROLINA
RIO GRANDE VEGETABLES PECANS WATER MELONS
PEPPERS CATTLE MISS. PEANUTS GEORGIA RED SNAPPER
HOGS TEXAS SMALL GAME ALA. CATFISH CATTLE CRAB
GAME BIRDS SHRIMP
RICE SUGAR-CANE LOUISIANA OYSTER FLORIDA
SMALL GAME FISH SHRIMP POMPANO CITRUS FRUIT
SHELLFISH
CITRUS FRUIT

THE AGRICULTURAL REGION
OF THE UNITED STATES

Spring wheat region
Winter wheat region
Corn belt
Dairy farming
Rice, sugar and citrus fruits
General farming region
Fruit and market gardens
Rice and sorghums

Culinary treasures in the New World

To GRASP THE KEY to New England cooking, it must be understood that New England is, for the most part, an austere place. It has a rugged, windswept shore, dense, brooding forests and an extensive scattering of cold lakes and streams. Much of it is mountainous. Its winters are long and hard.

Moulded in such a setting, New Englanders tend to be candid and unpretentious. Their taste in all things, food in particular, is direct and to the point.

The New England personality has been shaped, too, by the character of the people who crossed the stormy Atlantic from England more than three centuries ago—with a cargo of salt-pork, hardtack and cheese for sustenance—to settle in New England and open wide the gates of the New World.

The Pilgrim Fathers were austere sober and frugal, and so were their wives. To indulge in elaborate sleight-of-hand in food preparation would have offended their sense of fitness.

Nevertheless, the early New Englanders were astounded by the culinary treasures they stumbled across. One settler wrote, "This country aboundeth naturally with a store of roots of great variety and good to eat. Our turnips, parsnips and carrots are bigger and sweeter than in England. Here are pumpkins, cucumbers and other things of that nature which I know not. Also diverse excellent potherbs grow abundantly among the grass ... pennyroyal, winter savory, sorrel, liverwort, carvel and water-cresses.

"The abundance of seafish is almost beyond believing. There is a fish called a bass, a most sweet and wholesome fish as ever I did eat. We take plenty of skate and thornbacks and abundance of lobsters. I was soon cloyed with them, they were so great and fat and luscious. Also here is abundance of herring, turbot, sturgeon, cusks, haddock, mullet, eels, crabs, mussels and oysters. Here are likewise abundance of turkey, exceedingly fat, sweet and fleshy."

That exceedingly fat and fleshy bird became the centrepiece of Thanksgiving, originally the Pilgrims' ceremony of gratitude for survival in their new and bounteous land. At a Thanksgiving dinner today, succulent roast turkey, with chestnut stuffing, is served with sweet potatoes, corn, brussels sprouts, squash, succotash, creamed onions and cranberry sauce, and topped off with pumpkin pie. The first Thanksgiving dinner, however, was an even more elaborate affair which also included roast duck and geese, lobsters and eel pie, as well as mounds of venison provided by friendly Indians.

But the early New Englanders, whose puritanical inclinations kept them even from celebrating Christmas, declined to make a habit of feasts and convivial gatherings. Instead, they, and those who followed them to New England and who pushed into its vast woods, turned diligently to the task of building their homes and their communities, without pomp or festivities. A meal was simply intended to provide sustenance and nourishment. The easiest way to prepare a meal was to put a pot over a fire and fill it with whatever was immediately available, fish, vegetables and meat which was often so tough that prolonged boiling was required.

Baking in an untended oven was another simple way to prepare food, but if bread or popovers were being baked, there was no sense letting all that oven heat go to waste. So huge pots of beans were put in alongside the bread dough and out came enough New England baked beans—later called Boston baked beans—to provide dinner that night, as well as lunch with codfish cakes the next day, to be served with stew the next night and to find their way into a half-dozen other meals before the week was out.

These terse cooking traditions were handed down through the generations. Although some are now neglected and others have been altered, they still dominate the New England cuisine, the high points of which remain New England boiled dinners, New England stews and boiled lobsters with butter sauce. There is also the inimitable clambake, in which seaweed is laid over hot stones, chicken is laid over the steaming seaweed, trays of corn, sweet potatoes and onions over the chicken and trays of lobsters and clams over the vegetables to provide a sprawling feast on the spot for waiting guests.

From the local Indians, New Englanders learned how to tap maple trees. The sap boiled down to make maple syrup, a rich thick, incomparable liquid used in dozens of different delicious ways—for cake baking for meat basting, for drenching pancakes, for maple syrup fudge. When the first boiling-off of the sap comes in contact with the snow, it turns into a chewy candy-like substance much in demand among the children who turn up for the occasion.

The climate is milder farther south in the mid-Atlantic, and garden produce plays a much bigger role in its cuisine. But the fruit of the nearby ocean—lobsters, other crustaceans and fish—is almost as crucial an ingredient in mid-Atlantic cooking as it is in New England.

Many people consider Long Island's blue point oysters the tastiest in the world. Little neck and cherrystone clams are much acclaimed delicacies and mid-Atlantic razor clams are known to be "good to stew, good to fry and good to make into a good clam pie".

Like the New Englanders, the people along the mid-Atlantic coast do not tinker much with their seafood, but when they do it is with ingenuity and zest, producing such splendours as crab Imperial, a hot, spicy creation, and lobster Newburg.

But seafood is only part of the mid-Atlantic cuisine which is, in fact, a medley of cooking styles. In this part of the United States, there is a greater *mélange* of identifiable foreign influences than anywhere else in the world, all intriguing and all now part of the mid-Atlantic way of life.

Superimposed on a cuisine of seafood dishes, the inevitable hamburger and the thick steak, are Italian, Jewish, Chinese, German, Puerto Rican and other cuisines. Pastrami, tasty, spiced beef, is originally Romanian, but the pastrami sandwich served in Jewish delicatessens is as much part of New York City as the Empire State Building. Pizza is served in more mid-Atlantic restaurants than in all of Italy.

Corned beef and cabbage, the frankfurter hot dog, sauerkraut, baked lasagne and lox and bagels all have origins elsewhere but are now as much a part of the mid-Atlantic food culture as Long Island scallops or Philadelphia scrapple.

New Jersey is called the Garden State with good reason. It has a prolific harvest of

MID-ATLANTIC AND NEW ENGLAND

MAINE

APPLE PAN DOWDY
Deep dish apple pie with
biscuit topping

ANADAMA
CORNMEAL
BREAD

JOLLY BOYS
Small doughnuts

BLACKBERRY PIE

PUMPKIN PIE

CORN
CHOWDER

STEAMED LOBSTER

VERMONT

SUCCOTASH
Steamed corn
and lima beans

AUGUSTA

MAPLE
SUGAR
CANDY

GREEN SAGE
CHEESE

MONTPELIER

CLAMBAKES
Shellfish, fish, chicken,
sausages and corn steam-baked

CHEDDAR CHEESE

COLE SLAW

BEARBURGERS

RED-FLANNEL
HASH
Sautéed left-over
meat and beetroot

CHEDDAR
CHEESE

CONCORD

LOBSTER STEW

LAKE ONTARIO

LOBSTER
NEWBURG

N. H.

CRANBERRY
MUFFINS

SAUTEED CODS'
CHEEKS AND TONGUES

APPLE PIE

GRILLED
SHAD

ALBANY

MASS.

BOSTON CREAM PIE
Cream-filled sponge cake
with chocolate icing

LAKE ERIE

DILL
PICKLES

NEW YORK

CLUB
SANDWICH

BOSTON
BROWN
BREAD
Steamed dark bread

BAKED
BEANS

BOSTON

CHICKEN A LA KING

LEMON
MERINGUE PIE

PARKER HOUSE ROLLS

SEVEN SWEETS AND
SEVEN SOURS
Sweet and sour pickles

PENNSYLVANIA

HARTFORD

R. I.

PROVIDENCE

MORAVIAN CANDY
Assorted mints, marzipan,
molasses and
candied popcorn

ROAST
TURKEY

ROCK
CORNISH
HENS

OHIO
RIVER

WALDORF
SALAD

CONN.

GRILLED BAY
SCALLOPS

CLAM CHOWDER

DANDELION
SALAD
Salad with hot
bacon dressing

SCHNITZ N KNEPP
Ham and dried apple

CIDER
PIE

CHEESECAKE

LOX AND BAGELS

CHICKEN WITH
DUMPLINGS

CORNED BEEF
AND COLE SLAW
SANDWICH

NEW YORK

MANHATTAN
CLAM CHOWDER

PITTSBURGH

HOT PASTRAMI
Spiced beef

APPLE
BUTTER

HARRISBURG

SHOOFLY PIE
Molasses pie

CLAMS ON THE
HALF SHELL

POTATO
SALAD

STICKY
BUNS

TRENTON

OYSTER
PAN ROAST

PHILADELPHIA

PEACH PIE

FRIED FLOUNDER

SCRAPPLE
Pork and cornmeal loaf,
sliced and fried

FASTNACHTS
Doughnuts

BLUEBERRY
MUFFINS

ATLANTIC CITY

PEPPERPOT SOUP
Tripe and vegetable soup

NEW
JERSEY

DOVER

DELAWARE

tomatoes, cucumbers, onions, asparagus, peas, beans, cranberries, cantaloupe melons and a long list of other fruit and vegetables that lend stimulating diversity to the mid-Atlantic menu.

The Pennsylvania Dutch, most of whose forebears came from Germany, planted their roots in America when it was still a British colony. Many of them still cling tenaciously to their old traditions, dressing as their ancestors did, painting huge murals on their barns and shunning such new-fangled instruments as electricity and mechanically-driven vehicles. Through diligence and

hard work, they are, nevertheless, the most productive farmers in the United States.

Pennsylvania Dutch cooking is noted for good peasant food, in the best sense of the word—unembellished, filling and honest. Many dishes still bear old German names, like boova shenkel, which are filled noodles, and schnitz und' gnepp, a savoury concoction of ham, apples and dumplings. The Pennsylvania Dutch cuisine contains

lots of starch and boiled dishes thickened with gravy, like flour-thickened goose stew and fried pork with corn meal.

Much of this food is bland, but it is accompanied by a picturesque selection of pickled vegetables and fruit, spiced preserves, salads and apple butter to bring out the heartiness of the ingredients that make up a Pennsylvania Dutch meal.

There is nothing frivolous about this cooking, but there is nothing dreary about it either, as anyone who has ever tasted shoo-fly pie, a hot molasses pastry, can testify.

271

Where a meal is a ritual and a social event

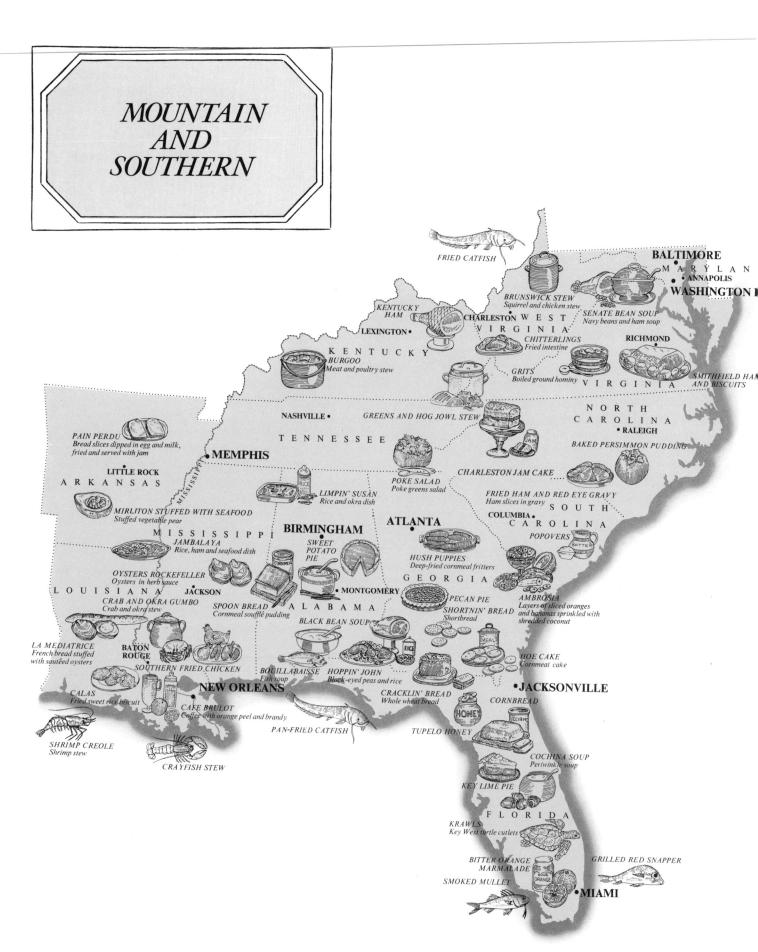

MOUNTAIN
AND
SOUTHERN

FRIED CATFISH

BALTIMORE
MARYLAN
• ANNAPOLIS
WASHINGTON

BRUNSWICK STEW
Squirrel and chicken stew

SENATE BEAN SOUP
Navy beans and ham soup

KENTUCKY
HAM

CHARLESTON WEST
VIRGINIA

LEXINGTON •

CHITTERLINGS
Fried intestine

RICHMOND

KENTUCKY

BURGOO
Meat and poultry stew

GRITS
Boiled ground hominy

VIRGINIA

SMITHFIELD HAM
AND BISCUITS

NASHVILLE •

GREENS AND HOG JOWL STEW

NORTH
CAROLINA
• RALEIGH

TENNESSEE

PAIN PERDU
Bread slices dipped in egg and milk,
fried and served with jam

BAKED PERSIMMON PUDDING

• MEMPHIS

LITTLE ROCK

POKE SALAD
Poke greens salad

CHARLESTON JAM CAKE

ARKANSAS

LIMPIN' SUSAN
Rice and okra dish

FRIED HAM AND RED EYE GRAVY
Ham slices in gravy

SOUTH
CAROLINA

MIRLITON STUFFED WITH SEAFOOD
Stuffed vegetable pear

COLUMBIA •

POPOVERS

MISSISSIPPI

BIRMINGHAM

ATLANTA

JAMBALAYA
Rice, ham and seafood dish

SWEET
POTATO
PIE

HUSH PUPPIES
Deep-fried cornmeal fritters

OYSTERS ROCKEFELLER
Oysters in herb sauce

GEORGIA

LOUISIANA

JACKSON •

• MONTGOMERY

PECAN PIE

AMBROSIA
Layers of sliced oranges
and bananas sprinkled with
shredded coconut

CRAB AND OKRA GUMBO
Crab and okra stew

SPOON BREAD
Cornmeal soufflé pudding

ALABAMA

SHORTNIN' BREAD
Shortbread

BLACK BEAN SOUP

LA MEDIATRICE
French bread stuffed
with sautéed oysters

BATON
ROUGE

HOE CAKE
Cornmeal cake

SOUTHERN FRIED CHICKEN

BOUILLABAISSE
Fish soup

HOPPIN' JOHN
Black-eyed peas and rice

• JACKSONVILLE

CALAS
Fried sweet rice biscuit

NEW ORLEANS

CRACKLIN' BREAD
Whole wheat bread

CORNBREAD

CAFE BRULOT
Coffee with orange peel and brandy

HONEY

PAN-FRIED CATFISH

TUPELO HONEY

SHRIMP CREOLE
Shrimp stew

COCHINA SOUP
Periwinkle soup

CRAYFISH STEW

KEY LIME PIE

FLORIDA

KRAWLS
Key West turtle cutlets

BITTER ORANGE
MARMALADE

GRILLED RED SNAPPER

SMOKED MULLET

SOUR
ORANGE

• MIAMI

When people from America's Southern states rave about Southern cooking, they are not merely boasting about Southern fried chicken, pecan pie or other individual delicacies. The Southern cuisine is not only distinctive and eminently palatable; it plays a central role in a complex way of life.

No people in the United States are more conscious and proud of their regional identity than Southerners. They are proud of their closely knit family structure, which has always been the basis for social life in the South and which, in turn, revolves to a great extent around the dining-table. A meal is more than something to be eaten. It is a family ritual and social event for which the standards of cooking and baking must be appropriately high.

It is not an accident that the first American cookbook, *The Compleat Housewife*, was published in 1742 in Williamsburg, Virginia. Nor is it merely by chance that Southern women are particularly dubious about claims that packaged foods can be as good as home cooking. Brought up in a food-conscious context, Southern women consider that recipes they inherit from their mothers are treasures which they will hand on to their daughters—the mysteries of a distinctive terrapin stew, a sweet potato pie or light-as-a-feather shortnin' bread.

The original English, Scotch-Irish and French culinary tastes, moulded by the skills of slaves from Africa, set the framework of Southern cooking, as did the abundance of corn, fish and fowl. The early settlers found pigs easier to raise than cattle or sheep. The result is a cuisine heavily larded with cured ham, spareribs, sow belly, crackling, fatback and chitterlings.

The many uses to which corn and corn meal are put also testify to the inventiveness of the Southern cuisine. Among them are corn fritters, corn bread, corn biscuits, corn pudding, hoe cakes, and hominy or corn grits, with butter for breakfast.

The cooking in the region near Chesa-peake Bay and other coastal areas of the South inevitably takes full advantage of available seafood, the stone crabs of Florida, Carolina shrimp, Chesapeake Bay oysters, blue crab, shad and green sea-turtle.

Along the Southern coastline, a gastro-nomic free-for-all called an oyster roast is more popular. So is the so-called fish muddle, a stew of various kinds of fish seasoned with onions, potatoes and pepper. She-crab soup, with crab roe, is a North Carolina speciality.

The craggy mountain region of Arkansas, Kentucky, Tennessee and West Virginia is a land of legend—once the home of the back-woodsman, with his coonskin hat and long-barrelled rifle, and of clannish hill-billies with their rich, racy humour.

It is a region of great natural beauty, but it offers little opportunity for extensive agricultural cultivation or cattle raising and has known very hard times. Mountain cooking is based on what can be shot, hooked out of a mountain stream or extracted from stubborn, often sharply inclined hillside soil.

Much resourcefulness goes into convert-ing wild roots and tough meats into stews, pies and pickled foods. Among the best-known mountain dishes is Kentucky bur-goo, a well-simmered stew based originally on squirrel, cabbage and potatoes, but now sometimes sufficiently refined with beef, chicken and more subtle vegetables to make its way down into the bluegrass flatlands as a speciality at the annual Kentucky Derby.

Mountain people have a great fondness for hush puppies, fried cornmeal cakes, which get their name from the tradition of throwing some to the dogs to keep them quiet when the fragrance of cooking excites them.

No city in the United States has a greater and more deserved reputation for the quality and vivacity of its cooking than New Orleans, the centre of Creole cuisine. Creole cooking blends a French genius for flavour nuances, the Spanish love for a strong seasoning, the native Choctaw Indian knowledge of roots and herbs and the culinary skills of the slaves of the early settlers.

The result is that a Creole meal is a celebration, not just a means of stilling hunger pangs. The Creole cuisine can be as subtle as oysters Rockefeller, as fragrantly explicit as jambalaya or as down-to-earth as a dish of red kidney beans and rice.

The nineteenth-century English author, William Makepeace Thackeray, a great gourmet, called New Orleans the city "where you can eat and drink the most and suffer the least". Food preparation is treated with such respect and care that, un-like the situation which prevails in most American cities, the quality of New Orleans restaurant fare generally matches the best of its home cooking.

New Orleans was Spanish before it was French, and French before it was American. The Europeans who settled in Louisiana found awaiting them not only the Indians, whose *filé*, the ground powder of the sassafras leaf, is one of the key ingredients of some Creole gumbos, but also immense areas of inland waterways and estuaries fingering down to the Gulf of Mexico. They were, and still are, alive with crayfish, shrimp, crab and fish in dozens of different tantalizing varieties. The Louisiana swamp-land was full of wild game.

The settlers seized on what they found and produced a cuisine based on exceedingly good taste, enough culinary confidence to experiment in food preparation and an acute sense of the value of spices.

Food itself has long been a way of life in Creole country, with such strong æsthetic overtones that it was in New Orleans that raw, hard liquor was transformed into the more sophisticated cocktail. The simple cup of coffee was turned into café Brûlot, spiced with cinnamon, cloves and lemon peel and flambéed with cognac.

Such dexterity in the cuisine produced the many-faceted family of gumbos. Gumbo is a soup and a stew, yet too unique to be classified as either. It starts with a base of highly-seasoned roux, scallions and herbs and then the dish takes off, serving as a vehicle for oysters, crabs and shrimp, or chicken, ham and veal, or combinations thereof.

Fish gumbo is only one example of the satisfying games that are played with sea-food in the Creole kitchen. Oysters, more than palatable raw and unadorned, are sautéed and packed into hollowed-out French bread, or baked on the half-shell and served with any of an assortment of garnish; chopped shallots, celery, tomatoes, onions, spinach, sorrel, or a mixture of them. Shrimp, crayfish and crab are similarly starting-off points for the Creole cook who might have croquettes in mind, or a pie, or an omelette, or a stew.

Homespun dishes and hearty eating

THE MIDWEST is America's centre of gravity. It is the country's heartland, its granary and its repository of traditional values. Its people live simply, they eat simply and they work hard.

Abraham Lincoln came from the Midwest, as did Mark Twain and Henry Ford. But although it has produced a formidable list of illustrious figures, the Midwest is not a home of heroes.

Midwesterners are profoundly, methodically egalitarian. They are contemptuous of privilege and social distinctions. They are so unmoved by boasting, affectations and special claims that the words, "I'm from Missouri", have entered the lexicon as a catch-all expression of cynicism and disbelief. A pompous food recipe is likely to draw a frown and a raised eyebrow rather than humble respect.

Midwesterners are independent and direct. It is not style they are after, it is substance. The buffet dinner—a cousin of the Scandinavian smörgåsbord—is a symbol of the Midwestern code. The buffet table is loaded down with ham, chicken, pork, potatoes, bread, pies and chocolate cakes, with everybody taking as much as he wants as often as he wants, and with plenty held in reserve.

The buffet tradition stems from the days when teams of itinerant farm labourers worked their way through the Midwest at harvest time to help bring in the crops. Farmers' wives would prepare enormous spreads of meats, pies, cakes, jams and jellies to cope with the towering hunger long days in the fields evoked.

Midwesterners are hospitable people and they have a tradition of also welcoming unexpected guests to their tables, a tradition of "pot luck"—sharing already prepared meals with visitors, with perhaps some extra preserves brought up from the basement and some extra vegetables from the garden thrown into the pot.

This is blunt, uncomplicated Middle America and proud of it. It has as little use for frills in its cuisine as it has in its pattern of behaviour. Home cooking could not be more unadorned—a steak and hashed-brown potatoes, roasts on Sunday, spareribs and turnips, country sausage, fried chicken, chicken salad, cold cuts, cole-slaw, home-grown tomatoes, wheat cakes, corn fritters, corn pudding, brownies and apple pie.

When Midwestern cooking ranges into more complicated elements, it is generally only as far as such homespun dishes as pot roast, chicken fricassee, fried smelts and such originally foreign delicacies as Swedish meatballs, Polish stuffed pike and German hot potato salad.

The population of the rural Midwest can be divided into two strands. There are those of German, Scandinavian, Polish, Bohemian and other European origin whose forebears, mostly within the last century, went directly from Europe to the Midwest and settled there. They had heard of fertile land available for the taking. They faced many hungry years before their motivating vision, in which success rewarded honest work, became a reality.

The other major Midwestern population strand is descended from those who took part in an immigration within America, the movement of people from New England and the mid-Atlantic states away from what they considered the unappealing comparative sophistication and rapid tempo of those areas.

Both strands were made up largely of people who deliberately chose to stop at America's midland rather than pursue excitement farther West, as thousands of others were doing at the time. They were not adventurers then and they still are not.

People here tend to remember that food was not always plentiful. Wasting it still goes against the Midwestern ethic—not so much a crime as a sin. During "hawg killin'" time in late fall in Missouri, ribs and sliced sides of the pig are fried, the liver, heart and kidneys are boiled together and much of the remaining meat is ground down for sausages.

Out of the Midwest came John Kellogg's and C. W. Post's remarkable discovery, later to become a huge international industry, that a satisfying breakfast could be made of nothing more complicated than a bowl of dry cereal, milk and sugar.

Nevertheless, Midwesterners tend to be hearty eaters and a Midwestern breakfast can

still consist of a stack of pancakes soaked in syrup, three fried eggs, a quarter pound of bacon, fresh cornbread and a half pot of coffee. Paul Bunyan, the legendary giant of Minnesota's timber country, is reputed to have had an appetite so immense that men tied sides of bacon to their feet and skated across the griddle used to cook his breakfast pancakes in order to grease it properly.

This is a continent within a continent bounded by the Rocky Mountains, the Appalachian Mountains, the Great Lakes and the Ozark Hills. Fanning out within these frontiers is an intricate system of waterways, based on the meandering Missouri, Mississippi and Ohio Rivers. They provide arteries of fertility, nourishing the wheat belt of the Great Plains and the corn belt stretching out from Iowa.

The Dakotas, Minnesota, Wisconsin and Michigan—the Midwest's northern arc—are dotted with deep forests and tens of thousands of lakes. Fish and game are not as plentiful as they once were, but the hunter and fisherman are still tempted out into the wilds by a goodly number of deer, Canada geese and ring-necked pheasant, as well as the stubborn, elusive Muskellunge pike (the Midwestern angler's dream) and the hard-fighting, cannibalistic bull trout.

People in the Midwest are partial to cheese, and their dairy farms, particularly in Wisconsin, produce a large assortment, not only for Midwestern consumption but also to satisfy a nationwide appetite for toasted cheese sandwiches, cheeseburgers, ham and cheese sandwiches, pizza topping and low calorie cottage cheese. Many of the Midwestern cheeses are copies of such European favourites as Edam, Gouda, Cheddar, mozzarella, blue and Brie. Some are as good as the original; some fall far short, although Wisconsin dairymen, exaggerating only a little, unblushingly call their Swiss cheese better than Switzerland's. Liederkrantz and brick are native American cheeses. American munster cheese is in an exalted class of its own.

Despite the inroads of industrial development, the Midwest remains primarily an agricultural area, America's breadbasket. It has long expanses of prairie, virtually endless fields of grain and lush, rolling pasture land. Its countryside is dotted with homey simple farmhouses—cool in the summers, comfortable in the punishing winters—and large sturdy barns and silos; although there have been harvests when there was so much corn in Iowa and wheat in Kansas that it

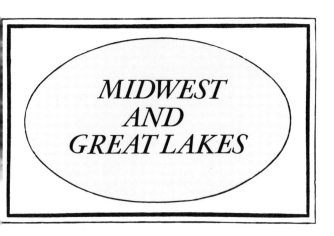

MIDWEST AND GREAT LAKES

WILD RICE CASSEROLE

N. D.

COFFEE CAKE WITH FRUIT FILLING

OLD HEIDELBURGER CHEESE

ROAST VENISON

• BISMARCK

TURKEY WITH WILD RICE STUFFING

BRAISED PHEASANT

CHEESE FONDUE

FRIED BASS

SOYA BEAN HAMBURGERS

ROAST GOOSE WITH RED CABBAGE

CHERRY COBBLER

MEAT LOAF

M I N N.
MINNEAPOLIS •

WISCONSIN CHEDDAR CHEESE

TURKEY CROQUETTES

BLUEBERRY PANCAKES

S. D.

• PIERRE

CHICKEN PIE WITH BISCUIT TOPPING

ST. PAUL

BAKED GLAZED HAM

FROGS' LEGS

W I S.
MILWAUKEE

SMOKED CARP

APPLE JONATHAN
Apple and batter pudding

GRILLED WALL-EYED PIKE

KOLACES
Fruit-filled pastries

MACARONI AND CHEESE

DEEP-FRIED SMELTS

MADISON •

M I C H.
LANSING •
DETROIT •

FRIED PERCH

BAKED POTATOES WITH SOUR CREAM DRESSING

POPCORN

I O W A

CHICAGO •

LIMBURGER CHEESE

CLEVELAND

N E B.

BRAISED ANTELOPE

OMAHA •

DES MOINES •

CORN CHOWDER

HOT FUDGE SUNDAE

GRILLED BEEF STEAK

CANDIED APPLES

LINCOLN •

BROWNIES

ROOT BEER FLOAT

COLUMBUS

NAVY BEANS WITH HAM HOCKS

CORN FRITTERS

CORN PUDDING

I L L.

BAKED APPLES

APPLE SAUCE

O H I O

BOILED POKE GREENS

INDIANAPOLIS •

CINCINNATI

ROAST DUCK

FRIED RABBIT

M O.

• SPRINGFIELD

WILD PLUM JAM

SWISS STEAK

K S.

KANSAS CITY •

SUNFLOWER SEEDS

DRIED CORN CASSEROLE

I N D.

ASPIC SALAD

TOPEKA •

FRIED CATFISH

BAKING POWDER BISCUITS

ST LOUIS •

CORN BREAD

WICHITA •

ICE-CREAM CAKE

FRIED OPOSSUM

WILTED LETTUCE SALAD

STUFFED PORK CHOPS

CREAMED CORN

overflowed all the available storage space.

Modern agricultural technology has meant that most of the small farms, that were once the heart of the Midwest and of the country, have merged into larger, more efficient units. The village general store, with its pot-bellied stove, once the centre of Midwestern social life, has now largely given way to antiseptic supermarkets.

But, aside from such metropolitan centres as Chicago, Detroit, Minneapolis and St Louis, the Midwest retains a flavour of small-town America, with uncluttered Main Streets, tidy wooden homes, state fairs, church socials and cooking contests, which

are likely to focus on baked hams, chicken pies, fruit pies, jellies and preserves. Much of the Midwest's big city industry is food-oriented as well—for example, flour milling, beer brewing and meat processing, which helped make cities like Milwaukee and Chicago famous.

When the early settlers moved into the Midwest, they were baffled by the thick, tangled grasslands which stretched out to the horizons. They had been city folk or small farmers and could not decipher exactly what was to be done with an infinity of high, untamed, matted grass. After laboriously hacking out clearings on river

banks, they only gradually came to realize that the relatively small fertile plots they cultivated for survival amounted to only a promise of the vast fertility which stretched as far as the eye could see.

Goaded on by such promise and displaying an inventiveness that has since become part of the Midwestern character, they contrived ploughs to conquer the tough grass roots and to help them build their farms. Over the decades, they invented reapers, binders, tractors and harvesters to master the soil and the crops and convert the Midwest into the most fertile grain-producing area in the world.

Food substantial and memorable

THE AMERICAN WEST is a land of wide open spaces. It is a land of spectacular soaring mountain ranges, narrow mountain passes, long high plateaus, sprawling ranches and eerie deserted mining towns. It is a land of winter blizzards, parched summers and breathtaking sunsets. It is a land of rolling wheat fields and pasture land, of cattle, sheep and wild game and of awesome stretches of barren wasteland.

This is cowboy country, the home of bow-legged cattle herders with their ten-gallon hats, rodeos, round-ups and flapjacks "rustled up" over open fires. It is a place where steers are roasted whole for large, social occasions, as an example of the ingenuousness of Western cooking and eating habits.

Although modern, thriving cities and towns punctuate the map of the West, its rugged, haunting landscape retains a sharply defined atmosphere of space and solitude. Outside the cities Westerners tend to live scattered. The nearest neighbour may be miles away. For many, there is nothing unusual about a one-hundred-mile journey to do some shopping, to visit with friends for a few hours or to get in some early morning fishing.

During winter blizzards, when the snow is often packed roof-high, weeks may pass without contact with anyone from outside the house or ranch. Months might pass without a chance to stock up on supplies at the store. A winter could howl by without outsiders being able to get through to put right any problems that might arise.

Consequently, Westerners are self-reliant, self-sufficient and resourceful. They do their own providing and fixing. Making do with what is available is so much a part of their lives that it has pervaded their culinary habits, as well as their general attitude towards what constitutes the good life.

Their forebears came originally from many places—from England, Scandinavia and central Europe mostly—all areas with distinctive national styles and cuisines. For the most part, however, the crisp, majestic Western context has overawed the origins that might otherwise distinguish Westerners from one another.

Their food, like their lives, is untheatrical and uncomplicated. They do not need much that they cannot provide for themselves. Beef cattle and sheep are often home-slaughtered. Preserves and dried fruit are prepared in the summer and put by for use during the long winter. There is a lot of homemade bread, biscuits and pastries. Moose, white-tail deer and various other species of game still contribute significantly to the Western cuisine, accounting for as much as one-third of the diet in some remote areas. Braised pronghorn antelope, rabbit stew, roast wild turkey, pheasant, fried rainbow trout and bass are popular dishes.

The huge herds of buffalo which once roamed the West have long been decimated, and the survivors are protected by law. But periodic culling processes take place to keep the remaining herds manageable, and buffalo steak, though hard to come by, is still one of the West's delicacies.

The old necessity for the cowboy or prospector to make camp under an open sky has been handed down as a recreation to modern Westerners. Others, elsewhere, may flock to beaches or big cities at vacation time, but Westerners prefer packing up and going off to spend their free time in the hinterland, with a sleeping bag, a rifle, a fishing rod, a dutch oven, a coffee pot, some coffee, water, salt and, perhaps, some biscuit mix.

There is more beef eaten in the West and Southwest than in any other part of America. There are various ways to barbecue beef and these people know them all. They spit barbecue, pit barbecue and grill.

Lamb, generally roasted or stewed, plays a respectable role in the Western cuisine. But, although there is an abundance of sheep, this is essentially cow country and game country, in eating habits as well as in statistical fact and in the American imagination.

Like many other parts of the United States, the Southwest is a melting pot of diverse influences. The habits and tastes of Mexico, of the Indians, of the frontiersmen and of the cowboys blend together in a setting of remarkable natural contrasts.

The subtropical shore of the Gulf of Mexico boasts sandy beaches, palms and citrus groves. The Arizona desert is so barren that astronauts trained there in preparation for the terrain they expected to find on the Moon. The vast Texas grasslands, home of the world's largest cattle herds, are internationally renowned, as are the rows of oil derricks pumping "black gold" from otherwise inhospitable topography. The Grand Canyon, the Petrified Forest and the Painted Desert are among the area's natural splendours and tourist attractions.

The pioneers who descended on the Southwest in search of land and room to breathe carried with them the relatively unembellished culinary inclinations they had acquired in New England, the mid-Atlantic and the South. But they soon succumbed to local Mexican and Indian preferences for spicier, sharper flavours, for chilli peppers, frijole beans and tamales, and for the wondrous effects of oregano, garlic, cumin and rosemary.

There are, however, more cattle than people in Texas, and beef was and remains a focus of the cuisine. Livestock breeding and crossbreeding has been raised to a fine art in the Southwest to provide the leanest beef and tenderest cuts available anywhere.

Before the days of refrigeration, it was a common practice of cowboys on the range to slaughter a fat heifer at sundown for dinner with pinto beans, for breakfast with hot biscuits and for as many more meals as the animal provided.

The incalculable wealth and extravagance of some of the cattlemen and oil magnates of the region is world famous. They sometimes indulge in huge barbecues for hundreds of guests, in which dozens of oxen and javelina pigs are turned on spits and served with corn and squash.

But although Southwestern tycoons sometimes import European chefs to signify how far they have come from the "rough and ready" frontier days, and although Texas cowboys are now more likely to be "riding herd" in a car than on horseback, the standards and customs of the frontier have not completely vanished. There are still cowboy singing-jamborees, hog-calling contests and square dances.

Skinned rattlesnakes and armadillos, extracted from their armoured shells, are occasionally brushed with hot sauce and grilled or barbecued much the same as they were out on the range in the old days. There is also a cowboy concoction irreverently called "son-of-a-bitch stew", a mixture of

MONTANA

GUACAMOLE
Spicy avocado dip

GREAT FALLS

HELENA

SOUR DOUGH BISCUITS

YELLOWSTONE RIVER

BAKED RICE PUDDING

BRAISED ELK

BAKED POTATOES

IDAHO

W Y.

CORN-ON-THE-COB

FRIED RAINBOW TROUT

BOISE

CHILLI DOGS
Frankfurters with chilli sauce

FRIED SQUIRREL

CHARCOAL-GRILLED LAMB CHOPS

ROAST BUFFALO

BARBECUED LAMB KEBABS

SAGEBRUSH HONEY

AVOCADO STUFFED WITH SHRIMPS

N E V A D A

CHEYENNE

HASH BROWN POTATOES
Diced, fried potatoes

SALT LAKE CITY

ROAST GOOSE

C O L O R A D O

CARSON CITY

U T A H

DENVER

DRIED FRUIT COMPOTE

CHERRY PIE

FRIED RABBIT

BRAISED ANTELOPE

BAKED SWEET POTATOES

DATE BREAD

FRIJOLES
Mexican beans

BARBECUED SPARERIBS

JAVELINA HAM
Wild boar ham

ARKANSAS RIVER

RASPBERRY VINEGAR

RED BEANS AND RICE

O K L A H O M A

LAS VEGAS

VENISON SAUSAGE

ENCHILADAS
Baked, stuffed tortillas

PEPITAS
Salted roast pumpkin seeds

PANOCHA
Sweet corn pudding

MEATBALL SOUP

OKLAHOMA CITY

TAMALES

SANTE FE

LAMB STEW

ALBUQUERQUE

N E W   M E X I C O

CHOCOLATE LAYER CAKE

COWBOY BEANS
Beans in spicy sauce

TACOS
Fried tortillas

TAMALE PIE
Meat and cornmeal casserole

CHILLIES RELLENOS
Fried stuffed peppers

MELON FRUIT CUP

PHOENIX

TEXAS GUMBO
Okra and shellfish stew

DALLAS

A R I Z O N A

BARBECUED BEEF

CHILI CON CARNE

ROAST WILD DUCK

COLACHE
Spicy vegetable stew

BARBECUED ARMADILLO

SOUR MILK PANCAKES

ROAST LEG OF MUTTON

TORTILLAS
Unleavened cornmeal bread

MOLE
Meat in chilli and chocolate sauce

FRIED SQUASH BLOSSOMS

THREE BEAN SALAD

AUSTIN

HOUSTON

T E X A S

SAN ANTONIO

CACTUS SALAD

BLACK BEAR STEAKS

RIO GRANDE

SHRIMP AND RICE PILAF

calf's intestinal and stomach tracts and other innards, a tribute to the sturdiness of the cowboy's digestive system.

But the Mexican influence is all-pervasive. Chilli pepper and frijole beans are as much a part of the Southwestern scene as the charm of the Spanish architecture and the tumbleweed of the Arizona wastelands. The peppers provide the pungency for which Southwest cooking is known, and the beans are likely to turn up at lunch or dinner and sometimes warmed up for breakfast, too.

Purist Mexicans across the border disclaim any responsibility for chili con carne, a dish much appreciated in many parts of America. It is, in fact, a native Southwestern

contrivance, conceived from Mexican influences and subject in preparation to varying degrees of sharpness, depending either on taste or recklessness.

Another speciality of the region is chiles rellenos, in which a large spicy chilli pepper is wrapped around a square of Cheddar cheese, which is then dipped in batter and deep-fried.

The cuisine of the Southwest can be potent, substantial and memorable. The way the "anglos" have blended the Mexican with their own is an indication of either the wisdom or the resilience of the people who settled in this part of the country.

Foods unusually and excitingly combined

THE PACIFIC STATES constitute the least homogeneous region in America. They are grouped together only through proximity. As far as similarity of mood and life-style is concerned, California and the Northwest states of Oregon and Washington might just as well be in different parts of the country. Alaska and Hawaii are exotically different from each other and from every other part of the United States.

Ever since the great nineteenth-century gold rush, California has been an Eldorado of one kind or another—for Midwesterners weary of harsh winters, for Oklahomans escaping from recurring, devastating sandstorms, for Chinese and Japanese seeking a new world, for people from the mid-Atlantic region chasing after a less frenzied existence, for Mexicans looking for work.

Everything about California is superlative. What is good there is the best in the world. What is bad is the worst anywhere. Its cuisine is unfettered by any laws of cooking, unrestrained by a hard core of tradition, untrammelled by convention.

All kinds of fruit and vegetables thrive in California's rich soil and glorious climate—okra, kale, shallots, Chinese cabbage, mangoes, avocados, loquats, papayas, limes, pomegranates, dates and figs, not to mention more conventional oranges, lemons, grapefruit, grapes, lettuce and tomatoes.

The Pacific Ocean and the lakes and streams of the area provide an equally impressive assortment of ingredients, including abalone, shad, salmon, tuna and lobsters.

There is an obsession in California with unusual food combinations—artichoke hearts and crab, chicken and anchovies, turkey and cheese, peppers and oranges. This kind of inspired recklessness has produced superb creations, including Caesar salad, celery Victor and the variety of cream-based dips which are now party favourites across the country.

There is nothing extravagant or audacious about the Pacific Northwest, except its setting of snow-capped mountains, stark, rugged shore, vast forest and the mighty Columbia River, from which some of the finest salmon in the world are hauled.

The wide range of ingredients that goes to make up California's exotic cuisine is available here as well. A magnificent selection of fruit and vegetables—some home-grown, some from California—is available in markets in Oregon and Washington.

But these states are tempered by a harsher

ALEU

climate than California's. Their population is far less diverse and restless. There is little of California's persistent, ravenous hunger for novelty. Their cuisine relies heavily on steaks, chops and other standard American foods. It is, however, considerably enlivened by game from the forest and mountain districts and by the seafood extracted from the Pacific and Northwest waterways and lakes, including Dungeness crab, Columbia River salmon, butter clams, sand dabs and Olympia oysters.

For most people, the image of Alaska is of ice, blizzards and unendurably frigid, interminable winters. In fact, that picture is accurate only for that part of the state situated within the Arctic region.

In the southern part of Alaska, the fertile Mantanuska Valley is a patchwork of efficient dairy and vegetable farms, producing crisp, delicious lettuce, some of the largest cabbages in the world, barley and oats.

Sourdough, the nickname for the old-time Alaskan pioneer, once was merely a rough, fermented portable dough used by gold prospectors as leaven for making bread out in the forbidding frigid wilderness. Now, however, it is an Alaskan speciality, replete with a score of different recipes for making such things as sourdough poppy-seeded potato bread, sourdough caraway-studded rye, sourdough whole-wheat bread and sourdough French loaf.

There is little stylized food preparation in Alaska, although it does have a distinctive cuisine, built largely around seafood and game, including salmon, king crab and herring, moose and elk. Caribou sausage

POI
Pounded taro root

LOMI LOMI
Salmon, tomato and onion salad

BARBECUED SWEET AND SOUR SPARE RIBS

HONOLULU•

GRILLED TUNA

BAKED YAMS WITH PINEAPPLE

CHICKEN LUAU
Chicken and taro leaf stew

HAUPIA
Coconut pudding

BUTTERFLY SHRIMP
Fried shrimp

H A W A I I A N   I S L A N D S

TERI YAKI STEAK
Soya sauce-marinated steak
HILO•

HAM WITH PINEAPPLE

LUAU
Pit-roasted whole pig with side dishes

and reindeer steak are Alaskan specialities.

Mark Twain called Hawaii "the loveliest fleet of islands that lies anchored in any ocean". It has since become fashionable in some quarters to dismiss Hawaii, with its wonderful climate and magnificent beaches, as merely a playground for tourists. It is, however, much more than that. It has a rich Polynesian history, an engagingly un-frenzied atmosphere, and a remarkably assimilated population of Japanese, Chinese, Polynesian, Filipino, Korean, Puerto Rican, European and mainland American origin.

The most famous single item in the specifically Hawaiian cuisine is the *luau*, in which a whole pig and chickens are cooked for hours in an underground oven lined with banana leaves and corn husks and then served with various other delicacies, in-cluding a salty clam-like mollusc called opihi.

Pineapples grow in abundance in Hawaii and pineapple slices are commonly served with ham steaks—an Hawaiian contribution to international cuisine. Other Hawaiian specialities reflect the wealth of marine life in the seas around Hawaii—boiled cuttlefish, squid, boiled convict fish (so called because of its vertical black stripes), marinated bone fish and steamed crabs.

A key component of the Hawaiian cuisine is *poi,* a thickish paste made from ground and cooked roots of the taro plant. *Poi* has a starchy, mild taste and, although it is Hawaii's staple food, it seems strangely incongruous in an area which boasts an abundance of such tasty natural products as fresh lychees, coconuts, avocados, papayas, macadamia nuts and guavas.

Traditional cooking from the Atlantic coast

MID-ATLANTIC AND NEW ENGLAND

Scalloped Oysters

Originally, oysters were to be found in abundance in America—a situation that is, alas, no longer true—and they were cooked in just about every way an ingenious cook could devise. Scalloped oysters, a dish in which the oysters are extended with layers of crushed cream crackers, has always been extremely popular.

SERVES 4 TO 6

4 oz melted butter
2 oz coarsely crushed cream cracker crumbs
1 pint shelled oysters
Salt
Pepper
Nutmeg
4 fl oz oyster liquor
5 fl oz double cream
Tabasco sauce
2 oz buttered breadcrumbs

Preheat the oven to 375°F (Gas Mark 5).

Brush melted butter liberally over the bottom and sides of a 2½-pint baking dish or casserole. Cover the bottom with a third of the biscuit crumbs and cover with half the oysters. Season them with a little salt, pepper and freshly grated nutmeg. Cover with another third of the cracker crumbs and sprinkle with half the melted butter. Make another layer of the remaining oysters, season lightly, cover with the remaining crumbs and melted butter.

Combine the oyster liquor, cream and a dash of Tabasco sauce. Pour this over the layers, top with the buttered breadcrumbs. Bake for 35 minutes.

Fish Chowder

Chowders, the traditional soups of New England, are eaten in homes and restaurants from the Canadian border to Connecticut. With the exception of corn chowder, most chowders are based on fish or shellfish and always include salt pork, onion, potato and milk (or cream, for a richer soup). Manhattan clam chowder, a later version heavy with vegetables, especially tomatoes, is scorned by New England purists as little more than a clam-flavoured vegetable soup. While clam chowder is the best known of the New England chowders, many people prefer the one made with the local haddock or cod.

SERVES 6 TO 8

4 lb haddock or cod, skinned and filleted (reserve bones, head and tail for stock)
1½ pints water
4 oz lean salt pork, cut in ½-inch dice
1 small onion, finely chopped
1½ lb potatoes, peeled and diced
Salt
Freshly ground black pepper
1½ pints hot milk or single cream
1 oz butter

Put the fish bones, head and tail in a pan with the water. Bring to the boil, skim, reduce the heat and simmer for 30 minutes. Strain the stock and set aside.

Meanwhile, render the salt pork in a large heavy pan until browned and crisp. Add the onion and fry until limp. Add the fish stock, potatoes and salt and pepper to taste. Simmer until the potatoes are half cooked. Add the fish fillets and simmer for about 10 minutes, or until they can be flaked with a fork. Add the milk or cream and heat through, but do not boil. Taste for seasoning. Lastly, add the butter and let it melt into the soup. Serve in soup cups or bowls.

Boston Baked Beans

Baked beans have been a Saturday night and Sunday morning tradition in New England for generations. For Saturday supper, they would be accompanied by steamed brown bread and home-made piccalilli and at Sunday breakfast they would be served, reheated, with codfish cakes. In Massachusetts the beans are flavoured with molasses. In Vermont, maple sugar is the customary flavouring.

SERVES 12

1 lb pea or navy beans (small white beans)
2½ pints boiling water
1 large whole onion (optional)
2 teaspoons salt
1 teaspoon dry mustard
2 fl oz molasses
3 tablespoons light brown sugar firmly packed
8 oz salt pork

Wash and pick over the beans, discarding any that are shrivelled. Place them in a large saucepan, cover with the boiling water and cook for 2 minutes after the water returns to the boil. Remove from the heat, cover and let stand for 1 hour. Return the pan to the stove, reheat quickly to boiling point, then reduce the heat and simmer the beans for about 1 hour, stirring occasionally. Remove from heat.

Preheat the oven to 350°F (Gas Mark 4).

Put the beans and cooking water in a bean pot, or a heavy casserole. If using the onion (some people don't like the onion flavour in their beans; this is a matter of choice), bury it in the beans. Mix the salt, mustard, molasses and brown sugar into the beans. Cut through the rind of the pork and push it down into the beans so the rind barely shows on top.

Cover and bake for 1 hour, stirring gently from time to time and adding more water if necessary. Uncover and bake for 1 hour longer.

Pumpkin Pie

Traditional for Thanksgiving dinner, this pie is popular throughout the autumn and winter months. Fresh pumpkin is rarely used today because the canned variety is more consistent in flavour and quality.

SERVES 6

2 medium-sized eggs, lightly beaten
6 oz sugar
12 oz cooked pumpkin purée
1 teaspoon ground cinnamon
¼ teaspoon ground allspice
10 fl oz milk
1 9-inch unbaked pie shell

Preheat the oven to 450°F (Gas Mark 8).

In a medium-sized bowl, beat the sugar and eggs together until light and lemon coloured. Stir in the pumpkin, spices and milk. Pour into the pie shell.

Place the pie on the middle shelf of the oven for 10 minutes. Reduce the heat to 350°F (Gas Mark 4) and continue baking until the custard is firm, and a table-knife blade inserted in the centre emerges clean. Cool the pie on a rack. Serve warm or cool.

Lindy's Cheesecake

The United States has dozens of different cheese-cake recipes, but none more famous than this one. It originated in Lindy's Restaurant, a New York establishment, that in its heyday was a favourite with stage, screen and radio stars and with the tourists who came to see them. The restaurant is gone but the cake survives in this recipe.

SERVES 12

BISCUIT DOUGH PASTRY

4 oz sifted plain flour
2 oz sugar
1 teaspoon grated, fresh lemon rind
1 egg yolk
¼ teaspoon vanilla essence
4 oz butter cut into small pieces

CHEESE FILLING

2½ lb cream cheese, at room temperature
14 oz sugar
3 tablespoons plain flour
1½ teaspoons grated fresh orange rind
1½ teaspoons grated fresh lemon rind
¼ teaspoon vanilla essence
5 eggs
2 egg yolks
2 fl oz double cream

In a small bowl, combine the flour, sugar and lemon rind. Make a well in the centre and place the egg yolk, vanilla essence and butter in it. Using fingertips, mix the ingredients together until the dough comes away from the sides of the bowl and forms a ball. Wrap the dough

tightly in aluminium foil and refrigerate for about 1 hour.

Preheat the oven to 400°F (Gas Mark 6). Lightly grease the bottom of a 9-inch spring-form pan.

Place half the dough on a lightly floured board and roll it out to $\frac{1}{8}$ inch thick. Place the dough on the bottom of the pan and trim the edges. Add the trimmings to the rest of the dough in the refrigerator. Place the bottom crust on the middle shelf of the oven and bake for about 20 minutes, or until it is pale gold.

Remove from the oven and place on a rack to cool. When the bottom crust is cool, grease the sides of the pan and lock it on to the base. Roll the remaining dough into 2 strips about $\frac{1}{8}$ inch thick and long enough to line the sides of the pan. Fit them into the pan, pressing the ends together to seal. Trim and discard excess dough.

Reset the oven to 450°F (Gas Mark 8).

Beat the cream cheese with a wooden spoon. Blend in the sugar, flour, orange and lemon rind and vanilla. Beat in the eggs one at a time, and then the egg yolks. Stir in the cream. Pour the mixture into the assembled crust and place it in the oven for 15 minutes. Reduce the temperature to 200°F (Gas Mark $\frac{1}{4}$) and bake for 1 hour more.

Remove the cheesecake from the oven and place it on a rack to cool. Let it cool for at least 2 hours before removing the sides of the pan.

AMERICA's old drinking pattern was simple. You had three or four shots of hard liquor—all you needed (or could take) in the way of alcohol. Then you sat down to eat, with nothing more interesting than cold milk or iced water in your glass. Then, often in mid-meal, along came a great breakfast-cup of weak coffee.

All this is changing. What is causing the change is wine. Ten years ago wine was an exotic concept, almost a subversive one, to the average American. Today it is benignly influencing all his mealtime habits. Most of the wine in question is Californian. California makes precisely the strong, clean-flavoured, not over-subtle wine American food demands.

What still needs to change is the coffee. The small cups of strong coffee that Europe drinks after a meal with wine are still almost unobtainable in the United States. A "demi-tasse" is the same watery coffee in a half-size cup. American coffee, after a meal with wine, leaves the drinker feeling as though he has just swallowed his bath water.

Chocolate Chip Cookies

These crisp, lightly browned biscuits were first made and served at the Toll House Restaurant in Whitman, Massachusetts, and, consequently, are often called Toll House Cookies, but they are equally well known as chocolate chip cookies. If packaged chocolate bits are not available, substitute 6 ounces of plain chocolate broken into $\frac{1}{4}$-inch pieces.

MAKES ABOUT 48 BISCUITS

5 oz sifted plain flour
$\frac{1}{2}$ teaspoon bicarbonate of soda
$\frac{1}{2}$ teaspoon salt
4 oz butter
4 oz firmly packed light brown sugar
2 oz granulated sugar
1 teaspoon vanilla essence
1 egg
6 oz plain chocolate bits
3 oz coarsely broken walnuts or pecans

Preheat the oven to 375°F (Gas Mark 5).

After sifting the flour, measure it and sift again with the bicarbonate of soda and salt. Cream the butter and the sugars. Mix in the vanilla and egg. Work in the dry ingredients, one-third at a time. Stir in the chocolate bits and nuts.

Drop in slightly rounded teaspoons on to greased baking sheets, leaving about $\frac{3}{4}$-inch in between to allow the biscuits to spread. Bake for 10 to 12 minutes, or until the biscuits are set and lightly browned.

With a spatula, remove the biscuits while hot and place them on racks. Cool before serving.

MOUNTAIN AND SOUTHERN

Black Bean Soup

America has a wealth of beans of all kinds which have contributed many delicious dishes to its cuisine. Among the soups, the bean soup served in the dining-room of the United States Senate, and the rich, smooth black bean soup of the South are justly celebrated. This recipe comes from The Coach House, a restaurant in New York City, where some of America's outstanding foods and dishes are a regular part of the menu.

SERVES 8

1 lb black beans
2 oz butter
2 large onions, coarsely chopped
2 garlic cloves, crushed
2 leeks, well washed and coarsely cut
1 celery stalk, finely chopped
2 tablespoons flour
$6\frac{1}{2}$ to 8 pints water
$1\frac{1}{2}$ lb smoked ham hocks with bone and rind
3 lb beef bones
2 bay leaves

2 cloves
8 peppercorns
Salt
Freshly ground black pepper
4 fl oz Madeira
GARNISH
2 hard-boiled eggs, finely chopped
Thin slices of lemon

Soak the beans overnight in water to cover. Next day, melt the butter in a stock pot, add the onions, garlic, leeks and celery and fry for 3 minutes. Blend in the flour and cook gently for 2 minutes, then stir in the water. Add the ham hocks, beef bones, bay leaves, cloves and peppercorns. Bring the water to the boil, skim off the scum, reduce the heat and simmer for 4 to 6 hours, partially covered, skimming off the scum from time to time.

Drain the beans and add them to the stock. Simmer for $2\frac{1}{2}$ hours, stirring occasionally. Add more liquid if the mixture gets too thick or the beans are not covered. Remove and discard the ham hock and rind and the beef bones. Put the soup through a food mill to purée the beans and vegetables. Taste for seasoning. Add salt, if needed (this depends on the saltiness of the ham), and freshly ground pepper. Return the soup to the pot, add the Madeira and bring to the boil. Serve in soup dishes with the garnishes.

Oysters Rockefeller

The richness of the sauce inspired the name of this dish, which originated at New Orleans' famous old restaurant, Antoine's. Their recipe is kept secret, but this is one of the many versions that have been developed. Serve as a first course.

SERVES 4 TO 6

6 spring onions, chopped
1 stick chopped fennel or celery
3 oz butter, melted
2 tablespoons chopped parsley
8 oz spinach, chopped
$\frac{1}{2}$ teaspoon Pernod
$\frac{1}{4}$ teaspoon lime juice
1 or 2 dashes Tabasco sauce
$\frac{1}{2}$ oz breadcrumbs
Salt
Freshly ground black pepper
24 fresh oysters on the half shell

Fry the spring onions and fennel or celery in half the butter until just soft. Stir in the parsley and spinach and cook, stirring, until the spinach wilts. Transfer to a blender. Add the Pernod and lime juice and purée. Remove and mix with the Tabasco sauce, breadcrumbs, salt and pepper to taste and the remaining melted butter.

Spread some of this sauce over each oyster and grill under very high heat for about 4 to 5 minutes or until the topping is lightly browned.

A pride in unpretentious cooking

Creole Jambalaya

America's jambalaya evolved in Louisiana and no one knows to what extent early Spanish explorers figured in its invention. It resembles a Spanish paella, a rice, seafood and meat casserole, the contents of which vary from cook to cook and day to day.

SERVES 4

6 oz long-grain rice
1 large onion, chopped
2 fl oz olive oil
1 garlic clove, crushed
1 medium-sized green pepper, stemmed, seeded and chopped
12 oz cooked ham, cubed
1 14-oz can peeled tomatoes, including the juice
8 fl oz water
½ teaspoon dried thyme
Salt
Pepper
A few drops of bottled red pepper sauce
12 oz peeled, raw, medium-sized shrimp

Fry the rice and onion in the oil in a large skillet until the rice is pale gold. Add the garlic, green pepper, ham, tomatoes, water, thyme and seasoning. Bring to a boil, cover tightly and simmer for 30 to 40 minutes or until rice is tender and most of the liquid has been absorbed. Add the shrimp 5 minutes before the jambalaya is done, cover and continue cooking.

Southern Fried Chicken

Fried chicken is one of the best-known of all American dishes. It is eaten from coast to coast, but perhaps most of all in the South. Traditionally the chicken is fried in lard or vegetable shortening, but a light cooking oil or a combination of shortening and bacon fat gives a browner, crisper crust. Often, as in this recipe, cinnamon is used to season the flour.

SERVES 4

3 lb frying chicken, cut in pieces
Salt
1 teaspoon ground cinnamon
8 tablespoons flour
8 oz fat (lard, vegetable shortening or ⅔ vegetable shortening and ⅓ bacon fat) or vegetable oil
8 fl oz single cream or milk

Preheat the oven to 200°F (Gas Mark ¼). Salt the chicken pieces lightly. Combine the cinnamon and 6 tablespoons of flour in a paper bag, drop in the chicken pieces and shake until coated.

Melt the fat or heat the oil in a deep, heavy frying-pan, large enough to hold the chicken pieces in one layer. The fat should be ¼-inch deep. Add the chicken, skin side down. Brown on both sides, turning with tongs. Reduce the heat, cover and continue cooking until tender. The breast section will be done before the legs and thighs. As the pieces cook, remove them and drain on absorbent paper. Keep warm in the oven.

When all the chicken is cooked, drain off all but 2 tablespoons of fat from the pan. Blend in the remaining 2 tablespoons of flour, then gradually stir in the cream or milk and cook, stirring, until the sauce has thickened. Season to taste with salt and pepper. Serve the sauce separately.

Baked Ham

So many different types of ham are sold in the United States that most come with cooking directions on the wrappings. This Southern recipe is for a smoked ham that has not been precooked.

SERVES 12 TO 14

10 to 12 lb smoked ham
Water
15 fl oz cider
Whole cloves
6 oz light brown sugar
1 teaspoon dry mustard

In a pot just large enough to hold the ham, simmer it in water to cover for about 20 minutes per pound. Add half the cider during the last half hour of simmering.

Cool the ham in the cooking liquid until it can be handled. Preheat the oven to 425°F (Gas Mark 7).

Transfer the ham to a cutting board, discard the liquid and remove skin. Trim the fat if necessary to leave an even layer ½ to ¾ inch thick. Score the fat in diamond shapes and stud with cloves at the points of the diamonds. Cover with a thin layer of the sugar mixed well with the mustard. Bake for about 15 to 20 minutes in the oven to set the coating. Reduce the heat to 325°F (Gas Mark 3) and bake for 30 to 45 minutes more, basting occasionally with the remaining cider.

Pecan Pie

Both the South and Southwest claim this rich and very sweet dessert as their speciality. Pecans grow wild over a large area that extends as far west as Texas.

SERVES 6

3 eggs
8 oz sugar
8 fl oz light corn syrup
6 oz pecan halves, coarsely broken
1 teaspoon vanilla essence
1 8-inch unbaked pie shell

Preheat the oven to 425°F (Gas Mark 7). In a small bowl, beat the eggs and sugar together until thick and lemon coloured. Stir in the corn syrup, pecans and vanilla. Pour the mixture into the pie shell and place it on the middle shelf of the oven. After 10 minutes reduce the oven temperature to 325°F (Gas Mark 3) and continue baking for about 35 to 40 minutes, or until the filling is set and the crust is lightly browned. If the edges of the crust begin to brown too much before the filling is set, cover the edges with aluminium foil.

MIDWEST AND GREAT LAKES

Old-Fashioned Chicken Pie

Chicken is a favourite food in the Middle West, America's vast heartland, where it is cooked in all the time-honoured ways—fried, roasted, stewed, fricasseed or made into a creamy pie like this one.

SERVES 6

4 lb chicken
1 onion, stuck with 2 cloves
1 celery stick
2 parsley sprigs
2 teaspoons salt
6 peppercorns
12 small white onions
12 tiny carrots or 2 large carrots, cut into 1-inch dice
3 oz butter
6 tablespoons flour
4 fl oz double cream
1 recipe baking powder biscuit dough

Put the chicken in a large pot with the clove-stuck onion, celery, parsley, salt, peppercorns and enough water to cover. (For a richer stock, use half water, half chicken stock.) Bring to the boil and skim off the scum. Reduce the heat and simmer gently, partly covered, for about 1 to 1½ hours, or until the chicken is tender.

Add the 12 small onions and carrots to the pot for the last 20 minutes of the cooking time.

Transfer the onions and carrots to a bowl. Remove and discard the clove-stuck onion, celery and parsley. Cool the chicken in the stock. When it is cool enough to handle, remove and discard the skin and bones and cut the meat into large pieces. Strain the stock and skim off the fat. Measure 1 pint of the stock for the sauce.

Preheat the oven to 450°F (Gas Mark 8).

Melt the butter in a heavy saucepan, stir in the flour and, stirring constantly, cook until golden and bubbling. Gradually mix in the 1 pint of stock and cook, stirring, until the sauce is smooth and thickened. Add the cream and heat through. Taste and correct the seasoning. Mix the chicken, onions and carrots with the sauce and put it in a deep, round, 2½-quart baking dish.

Make the biscuit dough. Roll out the dough to ½ inch thick and cut into 2½-inch circles with a floured cutter. Place the biscuits on top of the chicken and gravy and bake for 15 to 20 minutes, or until the biscuits are golden brown.

Baking Powder Biscuits (Soda Scones)

Hot, freshly made biscuits, which are really scones, are a staple of the American table, served from breakfast through the day. In the Middle West, they are always eaten with fried ham and red gravy or cream gravy, made by stirring water or milk into the pan juices. This was said to be a favourite breakfast of Abraham Lincoln. Baking powder biscuits should be very light, golden brown on the outside and soft and flaky inside. The trick is to mix quickly and handle the dough very little.

MAKES 10 BISCUITS

8 oz plain flour, sifted
1 tablespoon baking powder
1 teaspoon salt
3 oz butter
5 fl oz milk

Preheat the oven to 425°F (Gas Mark 7). Sift the flour, baking powder and salt together into a bowl. Cut in the butter with a pastry blender or two knives, or crumble with your fingers until you have coarse crumbs. Add the milk all at once and mix quickly to a smooth dough with a wooden spoon. Do not overmix. Turn out on to a lightly floured board, knead a couple of times and roll or pat into a circle ½ inch thick.

Cut into circles with a floured 2½-inch cutter or the rim of a glass. Arrange on a baking sheet, ½ inch apart. Bake for 12 to 15 minutes, or until the biscuits are golden brown.

Wild Rice Stuffing

Wild rice is the Rolls-Royce of grain. It is the long, narrow, dark brown grain of a native American grass, Zizania aquatica. The Indians have harvested this rice-like grain for centuries and, because it has not yet been domesticated, it commands prices far greater than those of true rice, Oryza sativa. It is traditionally used as a stuffing for Rock Cornish hen or game.

MAKES ABOUT 5 CUPS

6 oz wild rice
1½ pints chicken stock
1 medium-sized onion, chopped
2 celery sticks, chopped
½ green pepper, chopped
2 oz butter
8 oz mushrooms, sliced
¾ teaspoon dried marjoram
⅛ teaspoon dried thyme
Salt
Pepper

Wash the rice thoroughly. Bring the chicken stock to the boil. Add the rice and, when the stock returns to the boil, cover the pan and simmer for 35 to 40 minutes, or until the rice is tender, the grains have opened and the stock has been absorbed.

While the rice cooks, fry the onions, celery and pepper in the butter until soft but not brown. If using fresh mushrooms, cook them with the vegetables. If using canned mushrooms, drain them well and stir into the vegetable mixture after it is cooked. Combine the vegetable mixture and seasonings with the cooked rice and cool it before using to stuff poultry.

Apple Jonathan

This is one of the many apple desserts that are found throughout the Middle West, especially in the states where Johnny Appleseed travelled in the frontier days, distributing his apple seeds.

SERVES 4

6 to 8 green cooking apples
4 tablespoons maple syrup
1½ oz butter
4 oz sugar
1 egg, beaten
4 oz plain flour
2 teaspoons baking powder
½ teaspoon salt

Preheat the oven to 400°F (Gas Mark 6). Peel, core and thinly slice the apples. Layer them in a shallow 2½-quart glass baking dish. Pour the maple syrup over them, letting it dribble down between the layers.

Cream the butter and sugar and mix in the beaten egg. Sift together the flour, baking powder and salt and mix with the butter and sugar to make a stiff batter. Spread this over the apples. Let it stand for 5 minutes to settle. Bake in the centre of the oven for 35 to 40 minutes, or until the apples are cooked through and a cake tester or skewer inserted in the centre comes out clean.

Serve hot or at room temperature with cream.

Brownies

This is an all-time American favourite, with infinite variations. Every good cook prides herself on her brownie recipe. This one has a rich moist texture, almost like a fudge cake.

MAKES 30 BROWNIES

7 oz plain flour
¼ teaspoon salt
4 oz softened butter
1 lb icing sugar
4 eggs

4 oz plain chocolate, melted
1 teaspoon vanilla essence
6 oz chopped walnuts

Preheat the oven to 350°F (Gas Mark 4). Lightly grease a 10 × 12-inch baking tin.

Sift the flour and salt together. Beat the butter and sugar together until light and fluffy, then beat in the eggs, one at a time, until the mixture is light. Beat in the melted chocolate and vanilla. Quickly stir in the sifted flour and salt, and then the chopped nuts.

Spread the batter evenly in the prepared tin and bake for 25 to 30 minutes. Cool in the tin for 10 minutes and then cut into squares with a sharp knife. Allow to cool completely before removing the squares from the tin.

WEST AND SOUTHWEST

Barbecued Spareribs

Although in this recipe the spareribs are baked in the oven, they qualify as barbecued because they are basted with a spicy barbecue sauce. When cooking the ribs, it is advisable to bake some of the fat out first. Be sure to use an American or Mexican chili powder compound, not ground chilli peppers.

SERVES 4

4 lb pork spareribs
2 tablespoons vegetable oil
1 medium-sized onion, chopped
2 garlic cloves, minced
2 fl oz vinegar
4 fl oz tomato ketchup
3 fl oz Worcestershire sauce
1 teaspoon salt
½ teaspoon freshly ground black pepper
½ teaspoon dry mustard
¼ teaspoon Tabasco sauce
2 tablespoons brown sugar
2 teaspoons chili powder compound
1 lb canned tomatoes, drained

Preheat the oven to 450°F (Gas Mark 8).

Place the ribs, meaty side up, on a rack in a large, shallow roasting pan containing ½-inch water. (The water should not touch the meat.) Bake for 20 to 30 minutes, or until most of the fat has cooked out. Remove and discard the fat and water from the pan. Reduce heat to 350°F (Gas Mark 4).

Meanwhile, heat the oil in a heavy frying-pan. Add the onion and garlic and cook, stirring, until the onion is limp. Mix in all the remaining ingredients and simmer, uncovered, for 10 to 15 minutes, until the flavours are well blended.

Return the ribs to the roasting pan, without the rack, pour the barbecue sauce over them and bake in the oven, uncovered, for 1 to 1½ hours, basting frequently. If the sauce gets too thick, add water. Cut the spareribs into serving portions.

Flavours of the West and the Pacific

THE GAUGE OF American food is rightly said to be the snack. In the same way America's great original contribution to drink is the bottle of pop, available at the drop of a dime anywhere, any time. If Coke is the pop to end all pops there are scores of others of more limited local, age-group, traditional or even racial appeal—such fizzy waters as root beer and Dr. Pepper, which only America drinks.

In a sense even beer is a form of pop to Americans. It is drunk casually, without thought, often from the can, so iced that its flavour is completely masked—a drink for refreshment, not gastronomy.

America drinks crazes, too. Suddenly a few summers ago in the Midwest a peculiar mixture of sweet pink sparkling wines called Cold Duck took off like a prairie fire. Within months every winery in the United States was launching a Cold Duck. The makers had stumbled on a new pop which happened to be made of wine.

Historically, Cold Duck may have been a very important craze indeed—no less than the weaning of middle America from pop to wine.

Tamale Pie

This Southwestern adaptation of a Mexican dish is popular from Texas to California, which contributes the ripe olives that are an essential part of the recipe. Be sure to use an American or Mexican chili powder compound, not ground chilli peppers.

SERVES 6

2 pints water
10 oz yellow cornmeal
2½ teaspoons salt
2 oz butter or margarine
1 lb sausage meat
1 to 2 tablespoons chili powder
½ teaspoon ground cumin
2 medium-sized onions, finely chopped
1 large garlic clove, finely chopped
1 green pepper, seeded and chopped
1 lb minced beef
1½ lb canned tomatoes, drained
1 lb canned whole-kernel corn, drained
3 oz stoned black olives
4 to 6 oz grated Cheddar cheese

Bring the water to the boil in a large pan. Gradually, so that the water does not stop boiling, stir in the cornmeal and 1½ teaspoons of salt. Reduce the heat and keep the mixture simmering while stirring in the butter or margarine. Continue cooking slowly, stirring constantly, until the mixture is thick and mushy.

Preheat the oven to 325°F (Gas Mark 3).

Cook the sausage meat in a large frying-pan, mashing it with a fork or wooden spoon. Add the chili powder compound and cumin and cook, stirring, for 5 minutes. Add the onion, garlic and green pepper and cook, stirring, until the vegetables are limp. Drain the excess fat from the pan, add the beef and cook, breaking it up with a wooden spoon, until the redness of the meat disappears. Add the tomatoes, the remaining 1 teaspoon of salt and the corn and simmer for 20 minutes, until the mixture is well blended and the liquid has reduced slightly.

Rub a large (about 10 × 14 inches) baking dish with butter or oil. Spread two-thirds of the cornmeal mush over the bottom and sides of the pan. Spoon the meat filling into the dish and dot with the olives. Cover with the remaining cornmeal mush and sprinkle the cheese over the top. Bake for 1 hour.

Chili Con Carne

This is one of the most famous dishes of the Southwest, and there are innumerable versions of it. Although obviously influenced by Mexico, this belongs to the category of cooking known as Tex-Mex. While chili con carne is often made with minced beef, purists prefer to have the beef cut in small cubes. Nor will they permit beans to be introduced to their chili, which you mostly find as a meat-stretcher in the canned version, chili con carne with beans. Use American or Mexican chili powder compound, not ground chillies.

SERVES 6

6 tablespoons rendered beef or bacon fat, or vegetable oil
3 lb top side, rump or chuck, cut into ½-inch dice
2 medium-sized onions, chopped
2 garlic cloves, chopped
2 tablespoons tomato paste
1 teaspoon ground cumin
1 teaspoon dried oregano
3 to 4 tablespoons chili powder compound
1 teaspoon salt
1 lb canned tomatoes, drained
15 fl oz hot beef stock

Heat the fat or oil in a heavy pot and brown the beef cubes on all sides, a few at a time. They should sear, not stew. Remove the cubes as they are browned. Add the onions and garlic and cook gently until the onion is limp. Mix in the tomato paste, cumin, oregano, chili powder, salt and tomatoes. Mix in the beef stock and stir over a medium heat until it comes to the boil. Reduce heat, add meat and simmer, covered, for 2 to 4 hours, or until the beef is very tender and the liquid is reduced to a thick, soupy consistency. The longer it cooks, the better the flavour.

Devil's Food Cake with Fudge Icing

Richly iced layer cakes are long-time dessert favourites in the farm and ranch country of the West and Southwest. This cake cuts more easily and improves in flavour if it is baked and iced one day before serving.

MAKES ONE 9-INCH CAKE

8 oz sifted plain flour
1 teaspoon bicarbonate of soda
½ teaspoon salt
4 oz butter or margarine
11 oz castor sugar
2 eggs
3 oz plain chocolate, melted and cooled
8 fl oz milk
1 teaspoon vanilla essence

Preheat the oven to 350°F (Gas Mark 4). Lightly grease and dust with flour two 9-inch cake tins.

Sift the flour before measuring. Add the bicarbonate of soda and salt and sift together twice more.

Cream the butter or margarine and beat in the sugar until the mixture is light and fluffy. Beat in the eggs one at a time. Add the chocolate and blend in well. Add the flour mixture alternately with the milk, beginning and ending with flour and beating well after each addition. Stir in the vanilla essence.

Divide the batter between the two cake tins. Bake on the middle shelf of the oven for about 30 minutes, or until the top springs back when touched lightly with a finger and the cake shrinks slightly from the sides of the tin. Remove the cake layers from the oven and let them stand for about 10 minutes before turning them out on to racks to cool.

FUDGE ICING

3 oz plain chocolate
8 fl oz plus 2 tablespoons milk
1½ lb castor sugar
Pinch of salt
1 tablespoon golden syrup
1½ oz butter
1½ teaspoons vanilla essence

Place the chocolate and milk in a saucepan over a very low heat. Stir constantly until the chocolate has melted and the mixture is smooth. Add the sugar, salt and syrup and stir constantly until the sugar dissolves and the icing boils. Boil, stirring occasionally, until a small amount dripped into cold water will form a soft ball when rolled between the fingers, or the temperature on a sugar thermometer registers 232° to 234°F.

Remove the pan from the heat, add the butter and vanilla and cool to lukewarm. Then beat the icing until it is thick enough to spread. If the icing thickens too rapidly, place the pan over a pan of hot water to keep it soft. Spread on tops and sides of the cooled cake layers.

Crab Louis

This is a great West Coast salad that has always been popular in San Francisco, Portland and Seattle, where it is made with the superb Dungeness crab.

SERVES 4

8 fl oz mayonnaise
2 tablespoons chilli sauce
1 tablespoon grated onion
2 teaspoons lemon juice
2 tablespoons finely chopped parsley
4 fl oz whipped cream
Dash of cayenne pepper
1½ lb fresh crab meat

GARNISH

Shredded lettuce
Ripe olives
Hard-boiled eggs

Mix the mayonnaise with the chilli sauce, onion, lemon juice, parsley, whipped cream and cayenne pepper. Add the crab meat and toss.

Serve on a bed of shredded lettuce, garnished with ripe olives and quartered hard-boiled eggs.

Cioppino

Every restaurant on San Francisco's famed Fisherman's Wharf has its own version of this seafood soup-stew that resembles Italian bourrida. *Olive oil, garlic, onion and tomatoes are basic to the dish, but the seafood content varies with each day's catch. Cioppino is said to have originated with early San Francisco fishermen, many of whom were of Italian birth. Crusty sourdough bread and butter are traditionally served with this dish to sop up any remaining sauce.*

SERVES 6

3 tablespoons olive oil
1 medium-sized onion, chopped
4 garlic cloves, chopped
1 medium-sized green pepper, seeded and chopped
6 spring onions, green and white parts, chopped
1¼ lb canned tomatoes, drained
10 oz tomato puree
8 fl oz dry white wine
⅛ teaspoon dried basil
Salt
Pepper
1½ lb firm, white-fleshed, salt-water fish, cut in large chunks
1 lb medium-sized uncooked shrimps, shelled and deveined
2 lb clams or oysters in shells, well scrubbed
3 small or 1 large crab, split or disjointed

Place the olive oil, onion, garlic, green pepper, spring onions, tomatoes and tomato purée in a large saucepan and simmer, covered, for about 1 hour. Add the wine, basil, salt, pepper and fish. Cover and cook for about 10 minutes. Add the shellfish and cook for 10 minutes more. Discard any clams or oysters that have not opened. Serve in soup bowls with spoons and forks.

Caesar Salad

A salad which has become an American classic, Caesar Salad is believed to have originated with a restaurant owner in Tijuana, Mexico, the border town below San Diego. In California-style, this is usually eaten as a course on its own, before the entrée, and it also makes a good main-dish luncheon salad. The order in which the ingredients are added is all-important, as the lettuce leaves should be well coated with oil before anything else goes in.

Some people use a raw egg, but the texture of the dressing is pleasanter if the egg is coddled, or slightly cooked, first.

SERVES 4 TO 6

Olive oil
3 garlic cloves
4 large thick slices bread, trimmed and cut into ½-inch cubes
2 heads cos lettuce, washed, dried and chilled
1 egg
Juice of 1 lemon
16 anchovy fillets, cut in pieces
Freshly ground black pepper
2 oz grated Parmesan cheese
Salt

Heat 4 tablespoons of olive oil in a frying-pan with 2 crushed garlic cloves. Add the bread cubes, and brown quickly on all sides, adding more oil as needed. Remove the bread cubes and drain on absorbent paper. Discard the garlic and oil. Crush the remaining garlic clove and rub it around the salad bowl.

Tear the lettuce into bite-size pieces and drop them into the salad bowl. Pour on 8 tablespoons of olive oil and toss until the lettuce is well coated.

Cook the egg in boiling water for 1 minute. Break the egg over the lettuce, add the lemon juice, anchovies, ½ to ¾ teaspoon pepper, according to taste, and the cheese.

Toss until the leaves are thoroughly coated. Taste for seasoning and add salt if needed. Add the croûtons, toss again, and serve immediately while the croûtons are crisp.

Hawaiian Banana Bread

This is a moist, sweet breakfast or tea bread that is also very good toasted. The addition of maca-damia nuts, which are grown in Hawaii, makes it even better.

MAKES 1 LOAF

4 oz butter
6 oz granulated sugar
3 medium-sized ripe bananas, mashed
2 eggs, beaten
6 oz plain flour
1 teaspoon salt
1 teaspoon baking powder
3 oz chopped macadamia nuts (optional)

Preheat the oven to 300°F (Gas Mark 2).

Cream the butter and sugar. Mix in the banana pulp and then the eggs. Sift the flour with the salt and baking powder. Mix into the banana mixture, just enough to combine. Do not over-mix. Fold in the nuts, if used, and pour into a buttered loaf tin.

Bake for 1 to 1¼ hours, or until a cake tester or skewer inserted in the centre comes out clean.

Strawberry Shortcake

One of the most universal and popular of all American desserts, strawberry shortcake deserves the biggest, ripest berries. The shortcake part is actually sweetened baking powder biscuit dough.

SERVES 6 TO 8

8 oz plain flour
3 teaspoons baking powder
3 tablespoons sugar
½ teaspoon salt
4 oz butter, cut into small pieces
6 fl oz milk
1 lb ripe firm strawberries
Sugar
Whipped cream

Preheat the oven to 450°F (Gas Mark 8). Lightly grease an 8-inch layer cake tin with butter.

Sift the flour, baking powder, sugar and salt into a bowl. Work in the butter with fingertips until the mixture resembles coarse cornmeal. Make a well in the centre, pour in the milk and mix quickly with a wooden spoon to form a soft dough. Do not overmix.

Turn the dough on to a floured board and knead lightly, then pat it into the cake tin. Bake for 12 to 15 minutes, or until golden. Turn out on to a rack and split horizontally while hot.

While the shortcake is baking, slice half the strawberries into a bowl (reserve the most perfect berries for the top) and sprinkle with sugar to taste.

Arrange the bottom half of the shortcake on a serving dish and cover it with the sliced, sugared berries. Top with the other half of the shortcake and garnish with the whole strawberries.

Serve with whipped double cream.

The colourful vitality of an ancient cuisine

MEXICAN CUISINE is of great antiquity and retains a strong stamp of its early beginnings. Agriculture began in the Valley of Mexico about 7000 BC, at the same time as it did in the Middle East. The early Mexicans cultivated peppers, squashes and avocados. By 5000 BC, corn (maize) and many varieties of beans were being grown. But perhaps the greatest achievement of these early farmers was the successful cultivation of the tomato, in about AD 700. These foods, and several others that were introduced as a result of Cortés's conquest in 1521, still play a dominant role in Mexican cuisine.

The cooking style of the Spaniards at the time of the conquest was deeply influenced by hundreds of years of Moorish occupation. Because of this, and as a direct result of Spanish settlements in the Far East, they introduced Mexico not only to the foods of Europe, but also to the foods of the Middle East and Asia. It says a great deal for the

MEXICO

CHIHUAHUA

FRIJOLES
Fried mashed beans

MENUDO ESTILO SONORA
Tripe stewed with maize kernels and chilli

FRIJOLES MANEADOS
Beans with cheese

ABALONE

FLAN DE ALMENDRA
Almond caramel custard

PASTEL PERDIDO
Pork and chilli casserole

CARNITAS DE CARNERO
Steamed and fried lamb pieces

SONORA

MOCHOMOS
Pork with avocado salad

COAHUILA

SOPA DE ALETA DE TIBURON
Shark's fin soup

CABRITO AL HORNO
Roast marinated kid

GUACAMOLE
Avocado sauce

TAMALES NORTEÑOS
Pork and chilli tamales

TORTILLAS DE HARINA
Flat wheat bread

SOPA DE CAGUAMA
Turtle soup

CALDILLO DURANGUEÑO
Beef stewed with chillies

SINALOA

AGUJAS
Grilled beef spareribs

DURANGO

BARBACOA NORTEÑA
Spit-roast lamb

CABRITO AL HORNO
Roast marinated kid

MEXICO

NUEVO LEON

SQUID

CAMARONES RELLENOS
Stuffed jumbo prawns

CARNE ASADA A LA TAMPIQUEÑA
Grilled fillet steaks

TAMAULIPAS

GUL

TORTUGA A LA BAJA CALIFORNIA
Turtle in almond sauce

OSTIONES AL HORNO
Baked oysters

ASADO DE VENADO
Roast venison in sour cream sauce

BIRRIA
Spiced lamb casserole

FIAMBRE
Garnished cold meats

SOPA DE JAIBA
Crab soup

SAN LUIS POTOSI

ZACATECAS

QUESADILLAS POTOSINAS
Cheese and tomato stuffed turnovers

SCALLOPS

CABRITO AL HORNO
Roast marinated kid

GROUPER
PESCADA A LA VERA
Red snapper in tomato an

CLAMS

GUANAJUATO

PACIFIC OCEAN

NAYARIT

HIDALGO

MUC
Chick

ABALONE

CALDO MICHE
Catfish soup

FRESAS PRENSADAS
Condried strawberries

TACOS DE CARNITAS
Tortillas stuffed with fried pork pieces

ASADO AL PASTOR
Spit-roast lamb with pulque sauce

CAZON
Dogfish i

PICO DE GALLO
Jicama with oranges and chilli

OSTIONES ESTI
Oysters in tomato -

JALISCO

CHARALES
Lake fish

BARBACOA
Lamb cooked in an earth oven

PUEBLA

VERACRUZ

COLIMA

ATES DE FRUTAS
Fruit pastes

MEXICO CITY

JAIBA
Crab w

MICHOACAN

MORELOS

CHILES EN NOGADA
Stuffed green peppers in walnut sauce

CALDILLO DE MARISCOS
Seafood soup

GUERRERO

MOLE POBLANO DE GUAJOL
Turkey in chilli and chocolate sauce

MOLE NEGRO OAXAQUENO
Turkey in dark chilli sauce

TORTILLAS
Flat maize bread

CO
Stu

SEVICHE
Raw pickled fish

OAXACA

TAMALES ESTILO OAXACA
Banana-leaf tamales

CALDO DE CAM
Dried prawn soup

strength of the indigenous cuisine that it survived this assault and emerged dominant.

It is interesting that while Mexico was enthusiastic about the foods introduced by the conquerors, Europe and the rest of the world were slow to accept the splendid offerings from this cradle of agriculture. Indeed, Cortés destroyed a glittering Aztec court, where fine food was commonplace.

Although there is great diversity in the Mexican cuisine, it has a national character. There are special dishes of the north, where wheat is grown and cattle raised, and of the rich, agricultural central area, where all manner of fruits and grains and livestock flourish. These differ from the specialities of the coasts, with their magnificent harvest of fish and shellfish, and of the tropical regions lavish with pineapples, bananas, coconuts, mangoes and other tropical fruits. But the whole country has a common cooking tradition arising from the achievements of these early agriculturists.

The peppers of Mexico are legion. They

range in size from a tiny one-eighth of an inch to a bold, fat eight inches. In colour they vary from light to deep shiny green; from yellow to orange; from bright red to brick red, and to reds and greens so dark they are almost black. They are round or tapering, wide or narrow. And they may be sweet, pungent or hot, with a whole orchestra of flavours in between. Peppers are known by dozens of names, but generally, the mild ones are called sweet peppers and the hot ones, chillies. In Mexico both fresh and dried chillies are used.

Mollis, or *moles*, are an integral part of Mexican cuisine. Meat or poultry is cooked and then steeped or simmered in a sauce made from chillies or sweet peppers, or a combination of several varieties. These sauces are modified by other ingredients and are not necessarily hot.

The Mexican green husk tomato, a small pale green or yellow fruit covered with a papery husk, whose flavour develops only when it is cooked, as well as the common red tomato, is used a great deal in sauces. The thickening agent may be ground, toasted pumpkin seeds, nuts—almonds, walnuts, pecans or peanuts—or the special corn flour that is also used to make *tortillas* and *tamales*.

The Mexican method of sauce-making differs radically from European techniques. Dried peppers, either mild or hot, are soaked, seeded and ground to a paste. Herbs, spices and vegetables are ground and mixed with the chillies. A little of the stock in which the meat or poultry has been cooked is added to make a fairly heavy paste or purée. This is fried in lard, or vegetable oil, then thinned to a medium consistency and added to the drained meat or poultry.

The dish is usually simmered to blend the flavours. In Mexico, because of the high altitude, boiling point is reached at a lower temperature than at sea level. Consequently, food may be simmered very slowly indeed with little danger of overcooking. This slow cooking gives Mexican stews a unique character.

Mexican corn dishes are cooked in equally distinctive ways. Dried corn is boiled with lime and the husks are removed. The cooked corn is then ground to make the *masa*, or dough, for *tortillas* and *tamales*. Mexican housewives can buy cooked, ground corn today, called *masa harina*, literally dough flour. It is mixed to a dough with water and rolled into little balls which are flattened into thin pancakes, four to six

inches in diameter, with a *tortilla* press. The pancakes are baked briefly on a *comal*, a griddle. For *tamales*, the same flour is beaten with lard and stock until it is very light. The mixture is then spread on corn husks or banana leaves, topped with whatever meat, poultry or sweet filling is being used, folded over into a neat package and steamed.

The *tortilla* itself is put to many uses. Besides being eaten as bread, it may be filled with a mixture of fried, spicy *chorizo* sausage and cubes of fresh cheese, and topped with *guacamole*, avocado sauce or salad. It is sometimes filled with leftover meat or poultry in a little thick sauce; mashed beans, cheese and one or other of the chilli sauces; or shredded chicken breast mixed with cream cheese and *salsa verde*, green tomato sauce. The fillings are endless, depending only on the ingenuity of the cook.

Crisply fried *tortillas* may be covered with layers of lettuce, onion, mashed beans, *guacamole*, cheese or chilli sauce; these are called *tostadas*.

Dried beans are another important feature of the Mexican cuisine. There are many varieties to choose from. Cooked beans, which are rather soupy, are traditionally served, in separate bowls, after the main course and before the sweets at the main meal of the day. They may also be mashed and fried in lard or oil to make a smooth paste, and are then called *frijoles refritos*, refried beans. They are often used in this form in the *tortilla* dishes.

Guacamole, an ancient Mexican dish, is a mixture of mashed avocado, tomato and onion. It is served with everything except dessert, and is eaten in Mexico as regularly as the fresh hot sauces, *salsa cruda*, made from chilli pepper, onion and tomato, and *salsa verde*, which consists of chilli pepper, onion and Mexican green tomato.

The Mexican cuisine is rich in soups, and in rice, pasta or tortilla dishes, which are served after the soup. This course is known, curiously, as the *sopa seca*, dry soup.

The Aztecs had few desserts beyond sweet tamales. They relied on the vast array of fresh fruits available all year. The puddings and sweets of modern Mexico were created in the convents and the lavish use of egg yolks and sugar shows a strong Portuguese influence.

Mexico has a richly varied cuisine that still carries on the Aztec tradition of dazzling culinary skill.

Chillies and chocolate from Aztec royalty

Turkey in Chilli Sauce from Puebla
MOLE POBLANO DE GUAJOLOTE

This is Mexico's most festive and famous dish. Although it is said to have been invented by Sor Andrea, Sister Superior of the Santa Rosa Convent in the city of Puebla, it is clearly pre-Columbian, and, since it contains chocolate, a royal dish. The Aztecs, however, would have used allspice instead of cinnamon and cloves. The peppers used are dried red ones. If all three varieties are not available, substitute ancho chillies for the others. A picante version of this recipe adds 3 very hot chipotle chillies. Serve the turkey with hot tortillas, guacamole, frijoles, beans, and rice.

SERVES 8 TO 10

6 ancho chillies
2 pasilla chillies
6 mulato chillies
8 lb turkey, cut into serving pieces
Salt
4 oz lard
2 medium-sized onions, chopped
3 garlic cloves, chopped
¼ teaspoon anise seeds
¼ teaspoon ground cloves
½ teaspoon ground cinnamon
2½ oz sesame seeds
4 oz blanched almonds, chopped
2½ oz seedless raisins
1 lb tomatoes, blanched, peeled, seeded and chopped
2 stale 4-inch tortillas or 2 slices toast
1½ oz plain chocolate

Remove the stems from the chillies, shake out and discard the seeds. Tear the chillies into pieces and put them to soak in about 15 fluid ounces of hot water.

Place the turkey pieces in a large casserole, cover with salted water, bring to the boil and simmer for 1 hour. Drain, reserving the stock. Rinse and dry the casserole.

Pat the turkey pieces dry with kitchen paper. In a large, heavy frying-pan brown the turkey in the lard, a few pieces at a time. Transfer the turkey pieces to the casserole. Reserve the lard.

In an electric blender purée the chillies, the water in which they were soaked, the onions, garlic, anise seeds, cloves, cinnamon, 4 tablespoons of the sesame seeds, almonds, raisins, tomatoes and toast. Do this in several batches and be careful not to overblend. The purée should be heavy and quite coarse.

Reheat the lard remaining in the frying-pan and cook the chilli mixture, stirring constantly with a wooden spoon, for 5 minutes. Add 15 fluid ounces of the turkey broth, chocolate and salt to taste and cook, stirring, until the chocolate has melted. Pour the sauce over the turkey pieces. Cover the casserole and simmer very gently for 30 minutes.

Cook the remaining sesame seeds in a frying-pan without any fat. Sprinkle them over the turkey just before serving.

Mexican Rice
ARROZ A LA MEXICANA

Rice was introduced to Mexico in the mid-sixteenth century and it is very popular. It is often served as a separate course, the oddly named sopa seca, *dry soup, that follows the soup and comes before the fish in a formal meal. This is the most popular way to serve rice as a separate course.*

SERVES 6 TO 8

12 oz long-grain rice
1 medium-sized onion, chopped
1 garlic clove, chopped
1 lb tomatoes, blanched, peeled, seeded and chopped
2 fl oz vegetable oil
1¼ pints chicken stock
Salt
4 oz cooked green peas

GARNISH

Hot red chillies, sliced from tip to stem end into 4 or 5 sections to form flowers
Fresh coriander or flat-leaf parsley sprigs
1 large avocado, peeled, stoned and sliced

Place the rice in a bowl. Pour in enough hot water to cover the rice and leave it to soak for 20 to 30 minutes. Drain and rinse the rice in cold water. Leave the rice in the strainer to dry a little.

Put the onion, garlic and tomatoes in an electric blender and reduce to a purée. Set aside.

In a heavy saucepan, heat the oil. Add the rice and fry, stirring, over low heat until the oil has been absorbed. Be careful not to let the rice burn. Add the tomato purée and stock. Season to taste with salt and bring to the boil. Cover the pan and cook, over the lowest possible heat, for about 15 minutes, or until the rice is almost tender.

Fold in the peas and continue cooking for 5 minutes longer, or until all the liquid has been absorbed and the rice is tender.

Serve garnished with the chillies, coriander or parsley sprigs and avocado slices.

Tortillas

Tortillas, corn pancakes, the bread of pre-Columbian Mexico, accompany most dishes. Tacos are tortillas stuffed with any of a large number of fillings and rolled. They may be fastened with cocktail sticks and fried crisp or, more usually, left unfried. Tostadas are fried, then filled but not rolled. They make admirab[le] hors d'oeuvre, or a light meal. Once made tortillas can be kept warm for a short perio[d] wrapped in paper towels or a cloth. Wrapped i[n] aluminium foil, they can be kept warm for severa[l] hours in a cool oven, 150°F. To serve the tortillas wrap them in a napkin and place in a basket. They must be kept covered to remain soft an[d] warm.

MAKES 12 TO 16 SMALL TORTILLAS

8 oz masa harina (tortilla flour)
10 fl oz warm water

In a bowl, mix together the *masa harina* and the water to form a soft dough. If the weather is very humid use less water as the cornmeal picks up moisture from the air. Traditionally, no salt is used, but add 1 teaspoon of salt to the flour, i[f] desired. Form the dough into balls the size o[f] small eggs and flatten on the *tortilla* pres[s] between 2 sheets of greaseproof paper to form thin pancakes about 4 inches across. If the dough is too moist the *tortilla* will stick. Scrape it off, add a little more *masa harina*, and start again. The dough is not hurt by handling. Cook on an ungreased griddle for about 1 minute on each side. The *tortillas* should be very lightly and patchily browned. They are ready to turn when the edges lift slightly. Sometimes they puff up during cooking.

MEXICAN DRINKS have their own mystique. Perhaps the whole notion of cactus whisky—a fair definition of tequila—needs softening to the average drinker of good wholesome American grain liquor.

Tequila is distilled from the sap of one of the agave family of long-spiked succulents. But as far as flavour is concerned, it could be made from corn or molasses—there is only the faintest hint of anything exotic about it. What makes it exotic in practice is the habit of drinking it with salt, either (the original way) licked from the back of the hand, or by dipping the rim of the glass in salt before filling it. The margarita is a tequila sour made with lime juice and sipped over salt—an original and excellent conception.

Tequila's country cousin, mezcal, is a more sultry number altogether, with enough of the drug mescaline in it to induce, reputedly, very sweet dreams. Mezcal, however, is little known in polite society, any more than pulque, the cactus-sap beer which is a staple in country districts.

Taco Fillings

Left-over cooked chicken, turkey or pork, shredded and mixed with cream cheese, *salsa verde*, green sauce, or *salsa cruda*, uncooked tomato sauce, are popular fillings for *tacos*. Chopped boiled ham or left-over *mole poblano* may also be used, or perhaps *chorizo* (Spanish hot sausage), skinned, chopped and fried, mixed with cubed boiled potatoes, and *salsa cruda*, or *chorizo* mixed with cubed cheese such as Münster.

Any *taco* may be garnished with guacamole, avocado sauce or salad, and *frijoles refritos*, fried beans, are always a welcome addition. Within the framework of Mexican food, anything may go into a *taco*.

Beans
FRIJOLES

No Mexican meal is complete without beans.

SERVES 6

¼ lb red kidney, pink, pinto or black beans
1 onion, chopped
1 garlic clove, chopped
2 tablespoons lard
Salt

Wash the beans thoroughly, but do not soak them. Put the beans into a pot, preferably earthenware, with the onion and garlic and enough cold water to barely cover. Bring the mixture to the boil. Reduce the heat to low, cover the pan and simmer for 20 minutes, or until the beans begin to wrinkle. Add the lard, cover and continue cooking. Add a little hot water from time to time as needed.

When the beans are tender, add salt to taste and continue cooking, uncovered, for 30 minutes longer.

Mash about 3 tablespoons of the beans with a little of the bean liquid to form a smooth purée. Stir this into the beans to thicken the liquid. The beans should be slightly soupy, but there should not be a great deal of liquid.

Fried Beans
FRIJOLES REFRITOS

SERVES 6

3 oz lard
1 onion, finely chopped
1 recipe cooked beans

In a large, heavy frying-pan heat 2 tablespoons of the lard over moderate heat and fry the onion until it is tender but not browned. Add the beans and broth a tablespoonful at a time and mash them into the onion. Gradually add the remaining lard until the beans form a smooth, heavy paste. Spoon the beans into a heated serving bowl. Sprinkle, if desired, with crumbled fresh cheese and serve with quartered *tortillas*, fried crisp (*tostaditas*).

Green Sauce
SALSA VERDE

MAKES ABOUT 10 FLUID OUNCES

10 oz can Mexican green tomatoes, drained
1 small white onion, finely chopped
2 or more canned or fresh hot serrano chillies (small, tapering green chillies)
2 tablespoons chopped fresh coriander leaves
Salt to taste

Combine all the ingredients in an electric blender and blend at high speed for 2 or 3 seconds. Taste for seasoning and serve at room temperature.

Uncooked Tomato Sauce
SALSA CRUDA

This sauce, with its culinary companion, salsa verde, *green sauce, is as common on Mexican tables as is salt and pepper. Both sauces enliven dishes from breakfast to dinner and are always used in* tacos.

MAKES ABOUT 8 FLUID OUNCES

2 large, ripe tomatoes, blanched, peeled and chopped
2 or more canned or fresh hot serrano chillies (small, tapering green chillies)
1 small white onion, finely chopped
1 tablespoon chopped fresh coriander leaves or flat-leaf parsley sprigs
Salt
Freshly ground black pepper
Pinch of sugar

Mix all the ingredients together. Taste for seasoning and serve at room temperature.

Avocado Sauce or Salad
GUACAMOLE

Guacamole *appears on Mexican tables with almost the same frequency as do* salsa cruda *and* salsa verde. *It is eaten spread on* tortillas *before or with a meal or as a side salad. It is everybody's favourite, and everybody has a favourite recipe, although the variations from one to another are slight.*

MAKES ABOUT 12 FLUID OUNCES

2 large, ripe avocados
1 medium-sized tomato, blanched, peeled, seeded and chopped
½ small white onion, finely chopped
2 or more canned or fresh hot serrano chillies (small, tapering green chillies)
2 or 3 sprigs fresh coriander or flat-leaf parsley sprigs, finely chopped
Salt

Halve the avocados and remove the stones. Scoop out the flesh with a spoon and mash it with a fork. Add the rest of the ingredients, mixing well. Cover tightly with plastic wrap and refrigerate. Use as soon as possible as the sauce discolours quickly.

Almond Caramel Custard
FLAN DE ALMENDRA

Although it originated in Spain, flan *is Mexico's favourite dessert. There are many variations of plain* flan *of which this is one of the most popular.*

SERVES 6

10 oz castor sugar
1½ pints milk
8 egg yolks
1 teaspoon vanilla essence
Pinch salt
3 oz blanched, ground almonds

First caramelize the mould. In a small, heavy saucepan heat 4 ounces of the sugar, stirring constantly with a wooden spoon, until it melts and turns a rich golden brown. Have ready a 2½-pint mould, warmed by standing in hot water. Pour the caramel into the mould, turning the mould in all directions so that the caramel covers the bottom and part of the sides. Set aside.

Preheat the oven to 350°F (Gas Mark 4). Scald the milk, remove from the heat and cool. Beat the remaining sugar with the eggs to form a ribbon. Gradually add the milk, vanilla, salt and almonds, mixing well. Pour the mixture into the caramelized mould. Place the mould in a pan filled with water reaching halfway up the mould.

Bake for 1 hour, or until a knife inserted into the custard comes out clean.

Cool the custard, then chill in the refrigerator. To unmould, run a knife between the custard and the mould, then place a serving dish upside down over the custard and invert quickly.

The seven cuisines of seven countries

SWEET
POTATOES

RICE

AGOUTI

BELIZE

BELMOPAN

SUGAR-
CANE

SOUPA DE HESS
Conch soup

GULF
OF
HONDURAS

BANANAS

COCOA

CHILES RELLENOS
Stuffed sweet peppers

CODFISH HOLIDAY
Salt cod and vegetables with rice

PICADO DE RABANO
Radish salad

GUATEMALA

MEXICAN GREEN
TOMATOES

MAIZE

SUGAR-
CANE

EMPANADAS
Maize flour turnovers

PAPAYA

TOMATOES

HONDURAS

TAMALES DE COCO
Sweet coconut tamales

MANGOES

COFFEE

CARNE EN JOCON
Beef in tomato and chilli sauce

GUATEMALA

CASSAVA

BANANAS

TAPADO DE
CARNE SALADA
Salt-beef stew

COCOA

PAN DE BANANO
Banana bread

DRIED
BEANS

TEGUCIGALPA

RED SNAPPER

GALLO EN CHICHA
Chicken in a spicy sauce

SAN SALVADOR

PINEAPPLES

NACATAMALES
Banana-leaf tamales

RICE

EL SALVADOR

SWEET
POTATOES

POTATOES

PACIFIC
OCEAN

BUDIN DE PLATANOS
Banana pudding

SHELLFISH

NICARAGUA

CANGREJOS A LA
SALVADOREÑA
Stuffed crab

CITRUS FRUIT

SOPA DE CHAYOTE
Chocho soup

GUAVAS

CUSTARD
APPLES

MANAGUA

RIVER FISH

LAKE
NICARAGUA

VEGETABLES

CITRUS FRUIT

COSTA RICA

CARIBBEAN
SEA

SALPICON
Minced beef in
lemon sauce

PAN DE YUCA
Cassava-flour bread

SAN JOSE

CUSTARD
APPLES

FRITURAS DE PLATANO
Banana fritters

COFFEE

PANA

PAT
PLATAN
Fried green

CENTRAL AMERICA

FOOD IN CENTRAL AMERICA reflects the history of British Honduras, now called Belize, Guatemala, Honduras, El Salvador, Nicaragua, Costa Rica and Panama, the seven small countries that make up the land bridge between North and South America.

Guatemala and its neighbour Honduras were part of the old Mayan Empire and the pre-Columbian past of both countries is detectable, to some extent, in their cuisines. Some of the dishes are not unlike those of that part of Mexico which was once Maya territory. But the great Maya civilization was already in decline by the time of the Spanish conquest and only echoes remain of what must have been a delicate and attractive cuisine.

As a result of the conquest, the cooking of Guatemala and Honduras shows a strong Spanish influence. There are also strong cosmopolitan influences, mainly British and German, in the major cities, where it is difficult to find anything but international food.

Workers from the Caribbean have subtly enriched the cuisine, too. They come to the banana plantations and, because raw materials are the same, they are able to make their favourite dishes. Just as it is easy for

Caribbean dishes to take root, so it is difficult to disentangle the many strands that go to make up these small cuisines.

An echo from the Mayan culture, *annatto*, the seeds of small, flowering tropical trees, which give food a rich yellow colour and a delicate flavour, are as widely used in Guatemala and Honduras as in the Yucatán Peninsula. *Tortillas* are as much a part of the cuisine as they are in Mexico.

In Guatemala a wonderful selection of fresh green vegetables is served. They are beautifully fresh and often native to the region, like *chayote*, a squash which originated in Mexico and was cultivated by both the Aztecs and the Mayas long before Columbus.

In Nicaragua, *chayote* is made into an elegant soup which is enhanced by the addition of shredded chicken breast.

To make sopa de chayote *to serve 6, peel and slice 3 medium-sized* chayotes *and simmer in salted water for about 20 minutes, or until tender. Purée the* chayotes *in an electric blender with 15 fluid ounces of the cooking liquid.*

In a frying-pan, fry 1 finely chopped onion and 1 chopped garlic clove in 1 ounce of butter until the onion is tender. Stir in 1 tablespoon of flour and cook, stirring, for 1 minute. Add 1½ pints of chicken stock to the pan and cook, stirring, until the mixture is smooth.

Combine the stock and the puréed chayotes *in a saucepan and cook for 5 minutes, stirring occasionally. Add 1 whole cooked and shredded chicken breast and cook just long enough for the chicken to heat through. Season to taste with salt and white pepper. Garnish with croûtons and serve.*

Mexican green, husk tomatoes, *tomatillos*, are used a great deal, often in combination with red tomatoes. Stale *tortillas* are used to thicken sauces, although *masa harina*, the special cooked corn flour that is used to make *tortillas,* is a good substitute and is in the Mayan tradition.

Carne en jocon, beef in jocon sauce, is a

Guatemalan recipe which shows strong Mayan influence.

To make carne en jocon *to serve 6, heat 4 tablespoons of peanut oil in a heavy casserole and in it fry 1 finely chopped onion, 2 chopped garlic cloves, 2 seeded, sliced sweet peppers and 1 seeded and chopped chilli until the onion is translucent and tender.*

Add 3 pounds of stewing beef, cut into 2-inch cubes, the contents of an 8-ounce can of Mexican green tomatoes, 3 medium-sized tomatoes, blanched, peeled and coarsely chopped, 1 bay leaf, 2 cloves, ½ teaspoon dried oregano, 4 fluid ounces of beef stock and salt and freshly ground pepper to taste. The liquid should barely cover the meat. Add a little more stock if necessary. Cover and simmer gently for 2 hours, or until the beef is tender.

Soak 2 stale tortillas *in cold water, squeeze out and crumble (or use 2 tablespoons of* masa harina*). Add to the casserole and cook, uncovered, until the sauce is thickened.*

Serve over *arroz Guatemalteo*, rice Guatemala-style, which traditionally accompanies *carne en jocon.*

To make arroz Guatemalteo, *heat 2 tablespoons of peanut oil or butter in a heavy saucepan with a well-fitting lid. Add 6 ounces of rice and 8 ounces of mixed vegetables (carrots, celery and sweet red pepper, finely chopped, and green peas) and sauté lightly, stirring constantly to prevent the rice from burning. Season to taste with salt and pepper.*

Add 15 fluid ounces of water and bring to the boil. Cover the pan, reduce the heat as low as possible and cook for about 20 minutes, or until the rice and vegetables are tender and all the water has been absorbed.

El Salvador, also Mayan territory, was invaded by the Aztecs as well as by the Spanish. The cooking traditions of both cultures are evident in the cuisine. As in Mexico, the emphasis is on corn, tomatoes, chillies and sweet peppers, and *tamales* are a favourite dish. The most popular Spanish contribution is *arroz con pollo*, chicken and rice.

Nicaragua, Costa Rica and Panama have been strongly influenced by the cooking traditions of Colombia. In each of these countries bananas, plantains and coconuts play a considerable role in the cuisines, and fish is cooked in coconut milk, green plantains are sliced and fried and *sancocho*, a stew of pork and tropical root vegetables, is a speciality.

The seven cuisines of Central America form a culinary bridge between Mexico and Colombia, two cultures with totally different cooking styles.

ALBACORE

CORVINA AL HORNA
Sea bass baked in coconut milk

PANAMA
PANAMA CANAL

ROMPOPE
Egg and rum cream

SANCOCHO
Pork, salt-beef and root vegetable stew

MANGOES

PAPAYA

GULF
OF
PANAMA

AVAS

The golden foods of the sun-worshippers

CHIPI-CHIPI
Tiny tropical clams

•CARACAS

AREPAS
Maize buns

CAROATAS NEGRAS
Black beans

HALLACAS
*Maize pasties steamed
in banana leaves*

GEORGETOWN • *PRAWNS*

AVOCADOS

PAWPAWS

FOO-FOO
Pounded plantain balls

CRABS

MANGROVE OYSTERS

FRENCH
GUIANA

COFFEE

SALSA DE AJÍ
Chilli sauce

PABELLÓN
Beef, rice, plantain and black bean dish

BUÑUELOS DE YUCA
Cassava fritters

CALLALOO
Taro-leaf soup

PARAMARIBO •

CAYENNE •

SOBREBARRIGA BOGOTANA
Stuffed, simmered flank steak

VENEZUELA

CURRIES

PAPAS CHORREADAS
Potatoes with cheese sauce

•BOGOTA

GUYANA

RIVER FISH

PEPPERPOT
*Meat stew with
cassareep*

SOPA DE AGUACATE Y PAPAS
Avocado and potato soup

BANANAS

AJIACO BOGOTANA
Chicken stew

FLAN DE PIÑA
Pineapple custard

DULCE DE COCO
Coconut dessert

PLANTAINS

AGOUTI

SURINAM

SEA BASS

ECUADOR

QUITO •

COLOMBIA

SANCOCHO ESPECIAL
Mixed boiled meats and vegetables

LLAPINGACHOS
Potato cakes

CHICHARRÓN CON YUCA
Pork cracklings with cassava

MAÍZ MORADO
Purple sweet corn

PERU

CUSTARD APPLES

PRAWNS

SEVICHES
Seafood "cooked" in lime juice

VIZCACHA
Peruvian hare

LIMA BEANS

SWEET PEPPERS

PICARONES CON MIEL
DE CHANCACA
Sweet fritters with sugar syrup

AJÍ DE GALLINA
Chicken in chilli sauce

ANTICUCHOS
Skewered beef hearts

CHUPE DE CAMARONES LIMEÑO
Thick prawn and potato soup

PALTAS RELLENAS
Stuffed avocados

EMPANADAS SALTEÑAS
Small meat pies

•LIMA

CORVINA A LA CHORRILLANA
Sea bass with vegetables

ARROZ CON PATO
Duck with rice

CAUSA A LA LIMEÑA
*Mashed potatoes with prawns
and vegetables*

JOJOTO EN HOJAS
*Maize, tomatoes and sweet peppers
steamed in corn husks*

OCOPA AREQUIPEÑA
*Potatoes with peanut,
chilli and cheese sauce*

•LA PAZ

CHAIRO COCHABAMBINO
Highly seasoned meat, vegetable and chuño stew

LAKE FISH

BOLIVIA

CHUÑO
Freeze-dried potatoes

TROUT

SOUTH AMERICA 1

GEOGRAPHY, AS MUCH AS HISTORY, is responsible for the cuisines of this vast continent. South America, with the exception of the Guianas, Brazil, Uruguay and Paraguay, is dominated by the Andes, the four-thousand-mile mountain system that runs parallel to the Pacific coast from Venezuela to the tip of the continent.

The cold Humboldt current and the lofty mountains conspire to turn the coasts of Peru and Chile into deserts, but give both countries an incredibly rich harvest of fish and shellfish. There is an immense diversity of foods available. At sea level, tropical fruits and vegetables flourish, and crops that need cooler climates grow at various levels on the mountain plateaus.

At one time the mountains kept many of the South American countries so separated that their cuisines developed independently not only of each other, but within themselves. Coastal Colombia, Ecuador and Peru all have sea-level as well as high-plateau cuisines, although with modern methods of transport these distinctions are becoming blurred.

In many ways the most interesting of these cuisines is that of Peru. Here the Inca and pre-Incaic people, who were brilliant botanists, developed over a hundred varieties of the potato as early as 2500 BC. They invented a method of freeze-drying to preserve potatoes—freezing them in the bitter cold Andean night air, and squeezing out the moisture when they had thawed in the sun, until the potatoes, now called *chuño*, were more like stones than vegetables and would keep almost indefinitely.

Although Peruvian cuisine was greatly influenced by the Spanish conquest, the indigenous cooking style was never totally eclipsed. Peru still has many dishes that have direct culinary links to the pre-Columbian past. Foods are combined in unusual ways, but the cuisine is in no way bizarre.

Possibly because the Incas were sun-worshippers, Peruvian food is often predominantly yellow. A herb, *palillo*, is made into a yellow powder that colours food a pure and lovely shade. Since it does not have much taste it seems to be used more for appearance than for flavour.

As a result of this use of yellow, many dishes are exceedingly attractive. *Causa à la chiclayana*, for example, consists of a heaped mound of mashed, seasoned yellow potatoes surrounded by lettuce leaves. Pieces of boiled, white cassava root, boiled sweet potatoes, strips of cheese, slices of fried ripe plantain and corn on the cob, pieces of fried fish and black olives are arranged on top of the potatoes. The dish is served with an onion and chilli vinaigrette.

The mountain ranges left Inca farmers with little flat land for cultivation, so they terraced the mountainsides, often working at what must have been a precarious angle. On the way to the mountain-top ruins of Machu Picchu, the remains of this ancient terracing can still be seen. On the way, when the train stops at Ollantaytambo, hungry travellers can buy hot corn on the cob that is sold by the wayside. This corn, which has huge white kernels, is the type used to make the special flour for *arepas*, the corn buns of Colombia and Venezuela. It testifies to the botanical genius of the Incas who first brought corn from Mexico.

There is also a purple corn, *maíz morado*, that has a flowery, delicate fragrance and flavour when cooked. It is used to make *mazamorra morado*, a delightful fresh fruit dessert that is refreshing and original. The same purple corn is used to make *chicha de maíz morado*, and it gives this slightly fermented drink, which is rather like an alcoholic fruit cup, a lovely purple colour.

Ecuador, once part of the Inca Empire, has a small, distinctive cuisine. Its most glorious speciality is *seviche*, made from bass, shrimp, lobster, crab or conch. The fibres of the fish, or shellfish, are broken down through being soaked or "cooked" in lime juice. This technique is believed to have come from Polynesia. It is popular in all Latin America, but the Ecuadorian *seviche* is considered the finest. The secret of its superior flavour is the use of Seville (bitter) orange juice in the spicy sauce in which it is served.

Potatoes are cooked in many imaginative ways in Ecuador. They are made into *locro*, a thick potato and cheese soup that is sometimes served with avocado slices.

Another popular dish is *llapingachos*, fried potato and cheese cakes traditionally served with *salsa de mani*, peanut sauce.

Annatto is the delicately flavoured seed of the tropical tree *Bixa orellana*. The pulp which surrounds the seeds colours foods a deep orange-red. *Annatto* is sold in liquid form.

Several Spanish dishes were assimilated into the Ecuadorian cuisine, but, as in Peru, the cooking strongly reflects the country's pre-Columbian past.

Bolivia is landlocked and much of the country is at a great altitude. This, naturally, has had its effect on the cuisine since at high altitudes the boiling point is reached at a lower temperature than at sea level, thus slowing down the cooking process.

Bolivia has fine lake and river fish, such as *surubi* and *dorado*, as well as trout and smelt. Food is highly seasoned. *Locoto*, a type of chilli pepper which adds both heat and flavour, is used lavishly with meat and vegetable dishes.

Picante de pollo, a chicken stew made with onions, garlic, sweet red peppers, hot chilli pepper, tomatoes, parsley, thyme, marjoram and black pepper is typical of this high-plateau cooking. The *chupes*, a type of pot-au-feu in which meats and poultry are cooked with a variety of both root and green vegetables, make satisfying one-dish meals which keep out the cold in the chilly uplands.

Colombia and Venezuela have cuisines best described as a wedding of indigenous foods and Spanish cooking. Colombian food is subtly seasoned. Although hot chilli pepper sauce is present on the table, it is used with discretion.

Food cooked in coconut milk is characteristic of the coastal areas which are rich in fish and shellfish. *Arroz con coco y pasas*, rice with coconut and raisins, *arroz con coco frito y pasas*, rice with fried coconut and raisins, and *sopa de candia con mojarras*, okra and pompano soup, are typical coastal dishes.

Specialities of the highland cuisine include *papas chorreadas*, potatoes with cheese sauce, and *sobrebarriga bogotana*, stuffed flank steaks.

In Venezuela the beef is of excellent quality. It is often cooked, as it is in Argentina, on a type of grill called a *parrilla*. It is served with *guasacaca*, an avocado sauce, and a hot chilli pepper sauce.

Arepas, corn buns made from large-kernel white corn, cooked and ground, are the country's most original speciality. They

Exotic ingredients in a melting-pot of cuisines

are superb served with fresh cream cheese. There are many types of *arepas,* some very hearty baked ones; others, which are more delicate, are flavoured with cinnamon and fried. *Pabellon,* spiced shredded beef, the national dish, is served with white rice, fried plantain and *caraotas negras,* black beans, a culinary mixture of the Old World and the New.

In the low-lying Guianas, fish, shrimp and crab are plentiful. The cuisine is a mixture of dishes introduced by the colonists and indigenous Amerindian foods. The great Amerindian contribution is *cassareep,* seasoned, bitter cassava juice, boiled down and used to flavour meat and poultry stews. The pot is kept going day after day by the addition of fresh meats and more *cassareep.* *Rijstaffel,* Indonesian dishes served with rice, was introduced by the Dutch colonists. Lamb, shrimp and chicken curries were brought in by Indian migrants. Garlic pork has found its way here from Portugal, and there is an interesting black pudding served with sweet potatoes. Altogether, this is an eclectic cuisine.

Brazil's cuisine is as diversified as its climate and the ethnic mixture of its population. Each district has its own distinctive food. In the tropical north, and especially in the state of Bahia, Amerindians and Africans, using the cooking techniques and foods of Portugal, as well as their own, have created a unique cuisine. One of their most exciting dishes is *vatapá de galinha,* chicken in a shrimp and almond sauce. The chicken, cooked in a rich tomato sauce, is boned and skinned and added to a sauce made of dried, pulverized shrimp and almonds, puréed with chicken stock and thick coconut milk. *Dendê* oil, which has a fine nutty flavour and is also used to colour foods a vivid and vibrant yellow, is added.

Fresh shrimp are superlative in this area and the stuffed crabs, *siri recheado,* are always good. There are two kinds of hot peppers here, the tiny, exceedingly hot *malagueta* peppers and the larger hot peppers. Both are used to make the *môlhos de pimienta,* pepper sauces, that are always on the table.

Xinxin de galinha, chicken cooked in a dried shrimp and peanut sauce with ginger and *dendê* oil, and the fish, chicken or shrimp stews called *muquecas,* made with tomatoes, hot chillies, *dendê* oil and, sometimes, coconut milk, are typical of this extraordinary northern cuisine.

Fejoada completa, a regional dish from Rio de Janeiro, is now considered the Brazilian national dish. It is a complicated mixture of meats with black beans, served with rice and cooked kale or collard greens, *farofa de mandioca,* cassava meal, *môlho de pimenta e Limão,* chilli pepper and lime-juice sauce, and sliced oranges.

Black beans, cassava meal and rice are the three basic ingredients of the Brazilian cuisine. Hot chilli pepper is the most important flavouring, and hearts of palm are a favourite vegetable and salad ingredient. Everywhere in Brazil cassava meal, which looks rather like grated Parmesan cheese, is routinely sprinkled over fish, meat and poultry dishes.

The south is famous for its beef. The most popular cuts are those which can be broiled or grilled. *Churrascarias,* restaurants which specialize in grilled meats, are found all over the country.

São Paulo is the gastronomic centre of Brazil and the home of *cuscuz paulista,* an adaptation of *couscous,* which is made of steamed cornmeal instead of wheat. A round colander, called a *cuscuzeiro,* is lined with such ingredients as tomatoes, eggs, olives and shrimp. Layers of special cornmeal and layers of meats and vegetables are added until the *cuscuzeiro* is full. It is steamed and turned out on to a platter with the decorative pattern of tomatoes, eggs, olives and shrimp on top.

In contrast to Brazilian cuisine, which has strong African and Amerindian influences, the cuisines of Chile, Argentina and Uruguay are quite European.

Chile has the most unusual seafood in the world. *Erizos,* giant sea urchins, are an exquisite delicacy, served raw with a little chopped onion, lime juice, salt and pepper. They are used in omelettes or, covered in white sauce, as a filling for crêpes.

Another of Chile's exotic shellfish is *picorocco,* beaked creatures that, when cooked, taste like crabs. *Locos,* abalone,

when properly prepared, are as tender as chicken. Mussels, crabs, clams, shrimp and small, sweet oysters abound, particularly in the south. Among the best seafood dishes are *paila,* a seafood stew, *chupe de mariscos,* a seafood casserole thickened with breadcrumbs, and *fruta de mar,* shrimp and crab on a bed of rice and corn kernels with a tomato-flavoured mayonnaise.

Congrio is a favourite fish in Chile. Although its name means eel in Spanish, it is a fish with a huge head, a tapering body and firm, well-flavoured flesh. It is served in many ways, but one of the best is *caldillo de congrio,* a fish stew with potatoes, tomatoes, onions and seasonings.

There are some traces of the indigenous cuisine in such dishes as *porotos granados,* cranberry beans cooked with pumpkin, corn and tomatoes. The Spanish influence is detectable, too, in such dishes as *pollo en escabeche,* chicken cooked in an oil and vinegar mixture.

No great Indian civilization existed in Argentina and Uruguay and the cooking of these countries has long been influenced by Europe. First, there was the Spanish conquest. Then, after independence, a wave of immigrants, especially Spanish and Italian, introduced their own dishes which were adapted to local ingredients.

Argentinian beef is world famous and plays a dominant role in the cuisine. Restaurants have huge charcoal *parrillas,* grills, where steaks are cooked to order. But Argentinian cuisine is not limited to beef. *Empanadas,* flaky pastry turnovers stuffed with meat or poultry combined with peaches, pears or quinces, are a speciality. Splendid pumpkins, more like Hubbard squash than the American pie pumpkin, are found all over South America and in Argentina are used to make *carbonada,* a stew of beef, squash, corn and peaches, all cooked and served in the hollow pumpkin shell.

Other local dishes are *vizacha en escabeche,* hare in seasoned oil and vinegar, *cazuela de humitas,* a thick corn and squash soup, and *almendrado,* an exceptional ice-cream cake dessert which is served with a hot chocolate and almond sauce.

The cuisine of Uruguay is similar to that of Argentina. *Mondongo,* tripe cooked with tomatoes, sweet peppers, oregano and chickpeas, is a speciality. The steak, shellfish and fish, particularly *brotola,* which is large, firm-fleshed, with few bones, all have splendid flavour.

MOLHO DE ACARAJE
Black-eyed pea fritter sauce

RIVER AMAZON

SIRI RECHEADO
Stuffed crabs

MANAUS

ABARA
Steamed black-eyed peas

CITRUS FRUIT

AVOCADOS

FAROFA DE AZEITE DE DENDE
Cassava meal cooked in palm oil

SALADA DE PALMITO
Hearts of palm salad

BRAZIL

MAIZE

ACARAJE
Black-eyed pea fritters

CASSAVA

CHILLIES

XINXIM DE GALINHA
Chicken in prawn, peanut and ginger sauce

VATAPA DE GALINHA
Chicken in prawn and almond sauce

COZIDO A BRASILEIRA
Meat stew

TUTU A MINEIRA
Mashed black beans with eggs and meat

BRASILIA

QUINDINS DE YAYA
Coconut dessert

MUQUECA DE CAMAROES
Prawn stew

COFFEE

COUVE A MINEIRA
Kale fried with garlic

PARAGUAY

PUDIM DE ABOBORA
Pumpkin pudding

CUSCUZ DE GALINHA
Steamed chicken, cornmeal and vegetables

FEIJOADA COMPLETA
Bean and meat national dish

CHILE

SO' O-YOSOPY
Thick minced beef soup

SAO PAULO

RIO DE JANEIRO

LOCOS
Giant abalone

CATTLE

ASUNCION

CUSTARD
APPLES

SOPA PARAGUAYA
Cheese and maize bread

CATTLE

PAILA
Seafood stew

PEBRE
Chilli sauce

MATAMBRE
Stuffed flank steak

PARANA

ORCHARD
FRUIT

MUQUECA DE PEIXE
Fish stew

VALPARAISO

SANTIAGO

CARBONADA A LA CRIOLLA
Meat stew with fruit

SWEET POTATOES

ROSARIO

MONDONGO
Tripe

CHUPE DE MARISCOS
Thick seafood soup

PASTELILLOS DE FRUTILLA
Strawberry tartlets

BUENOS
AIRES

MONTEVIDEO

URUGUAY

EMPANADAS
Beef and fruit in pastry

ASADO A LA PARRILLA
Beef and sausage mixed grill

MAR DEL PLATA

ERIZOS
Giant sea urchins

VIZCACHA EN ESCABECHE
Hare cooked in seasoned oil and vinegar

PUMPKINS

CONGRIO CON SALSA DE MARISCOS
Local fish with shellfish sauce

ARGENTINA

SOUTH AMERICA 2

In river-rich, landlocked, subtropical Paraguay there are two official languages: Guarani, the language of the Indians of the region, and Spanish; and the cuisine, too, is Spanish and Guarani.

Local river fish, particularly *surubi* and *dorado* and river shrimp are delicious. The beef, although not quite up to Argentinian standard, is still good and is used in the country's most unusual dish *so'o-yosopy*, which is made from ground lean steak mashed in a mortar until it is pulverized. It is cooked with a *sofrito* of tomatoes, and stirred continuously to form an homogenous mixture. The other outstanding speciality is *sopa paraguaya*, which is not a soup but a rich cheese and cornmeal bread, which is always served with steak.

A melting-pot of cultures and communities, of the ancient and the new, of indigenous food and introduced dishes, the cuisine of this mountain-dominated continent is exciting, diverse and, above all, delicious.

295

Dishes that graced the Incas' tables

Meat Soup
SO'O-YOSOPY

This unusual meat soup from Paraguay can also be served as a main dish.

SERVES 6

2 lb lean sirloin or round steak
2 tablespoons vegetable oil
2 medium-sized onions, finely chopped
1 green pepper, seeded
    and finely chopped
4 medium-sized tomatoes, blanched, peeled
    and chopped
3 oz rice
Salt
2 tablespoons chopped parsley

Have the butcher mince the meat twice, then pound it in a mortar to make sure it is completely pulverized. Set aside.

Heat the oil in a frying-pan and fry the onions and pepper until the onions are tender, but not browned. Add the tomatoes and cook for 5 minutes longer. Remove the pan from the heat and set aside to cool slightly.

Combine the meat and the tomato and onion mixture in a saucepan. Stir in 3¼ pints of cold water. Bring the mixture to a boil over moderate heat. Add the rice and cook, stirring constantly with a wooden spoon, for about 15 minutes or until the rice is tender. Season to taste with salt.

Garnish with the parsley. Serve with a baked sweet potato, or a slice of boiled cassava root, or with water biscuits on the side.

Shrimp Soup Lima Style
CHUPE DE CAMARONES LIMENO

Soups that are almost too thick to be regarded as soups are popular in many South American countries. Chile has a number of chupes, some of them thickened with breadcrumbs. This chupe, from coastal Peru, reflects the richness of the harvest from the sea.

SERVES 6 TO 8

8 oz butter
1 medium-sized onion, finely chopped
1 lb tomatoes, blanched, peeled and chopped
2 sweet red peppers, seeded and chopped
1 lb potatoes, peeled and cubed
8 oz shelled peas
2½ pints milk
3 oz rice, washed
Salt
Freshly ground pepper
½ teaspoon dried oregano or marjoram
2 lb fillets of bass, or similar white fish, cut
    into 1-inch pieces
2 eggs, lightly-beaten
1 lb peeled, raw, medium-sized shrimp

8 oz fresh cheese, or Münster, cut into
½-inch cubes

In a large, heavy saucepan or casserole, heat the butter and fry the onion until it is very lightly browned. Add the tomatoes and the sweet peppers and cook, stirring occasionally, for 2 to 3 minutes. Add the potatoes and the peas and just enough water to allow them to cook. Cover the pan and cook until the potatoes are tender.

Add the milk and the rice and stir to mix well. Season with salt, pepper and the oregano or marjoram. Cover the pan and simmer gently for 15 minutes.

Stir in the beaten eggs, add the fish and continue cooking for about 10 minutes, or until the fish has lost its translucent look.

Add the shrimps and cook for 3 to 5 minutes, or until they are pink. Remove the pan from the heat and stir in the cheese.

The soup should be very thick but still soupy. If necessary add a little more milk during cooking.

Seviche of Striped Bass
SEVICHE DE CORVINA

Many Latin-American countries, especially Mexico and Peru, have very good seviches—fish or shellfish "cooked" in lime or lemon juice. It is generally acknowledged that the seviches of Ecuador are the best. This recipe comes from Ecuador.

SERVES 4

1½ lb fillets of striped bass, or similar white
    fish, cut into 1-inch pieces
12 fl oz lime or lemon juice
8 fl oz Seville (bitter) orange juice, or sweet
    orange juice
8 fl oz salad oil
1 hot red chilli, seeded and finely chopped
1 medium-sized onion, finely sliced
1 clove garlic, chopped
Salt
Freshly ground pepper

Place the fish in a bowl and pour on the lime or lemon juice. If there is not enough juice to cover the fish, add a little more. Cover the bowl and refrigerate for 3 to 4 hours, turning the fish once or twice. At the end of this time the fish will be opaque, "cooked" by the lime juice.

Drain the fish, discarding the juice. Combine the remaining ingredients and toss the fish gently in the mixture.

Pickled Fish
PESCADO EN ESCABECHE

This speciality from Uruguay is an excellent first course.

SERVES 8 AS A FIRST COURSE

2 medium-sized onions, thinly sliced
1 garlic clove, chopped
2 fl oz vegetable oil
2 lb fillets of white fish
2 eggs, well beaten
Salt
Fine breadcrumbs
2 red peppers, seeded and sliced
1 clove
1 bay leaf
Freshly ground black pepper
2 fl oz vinegar
2 fl oz water

In a large frying-pan, fry the onions and garlic in the oil until the onion is tender. With slotted spoon remove the onion and garlic and set aside.

Dip the fish fillets into the beaten eggs seasoned with salt, and then into the bread crumbs. Fry the fish in the oil remaining in the pan, adding a little more if necessary. Arrange the fish in a deep glass dish, together with any oil from the pan.

Combine the onion and garlic in a small saucepan with the peppers, clove, bay leaf black pepper to taste, the vinegar and the water. Simmer gently for 5 minutes. Remove the pan from the heat and pour the mixture over the fish. Serve cold.

Meats and Black Beans
FEJOADA COMPLETA

This dish of meats and black beans originated in Rio de Janeiro but is now recognized as the national dish of Brazil. It is traditionally served with boiled rice, sliced oranges, cassava meal kale or collard greens and a mõlho de piment e limas.

SERVES 8 TO 10

1 lb piece jerked or dried beef
1 smoked beef tongue, about 3 lb
1 lb linguica sausage
8 oz piece lean bacon
1 lb fresh pork sausages
1½ lb black beans
1 lb piece chuck steak
2 medium-sized onions, finely chopped
2 garlic cloves, chopped
1 oz lard
2 medium-sized tomatoes, blanched, peeled,
    seeded and chopped
1 red chilli, seeded and chopped
    or ¼ teaspoon Tabasco sauce
Salt
Freshly ground black pepper

Place the jerked or dried beef in a bowl, cover with cold water and leave overnight. Drain the beef, put it in a saucepan with water to cover.

and bring to the boil. Reduce the heat. Cover the pan and simmer the beef for 30 minutes. Drain and set aside.

In another saucepan, simmer the beef tongue, in water to cover, for 2½ hours. Cool in the stock, lift out and remove and discard the skin, and any bones and gristle. Set aside.

Simmer the *linguica* sausage and the bacon in water to cover for 15 minutes. Add the pork sausages and simmer 15 minutes longer. Drain and reserve the meats.

Pick over and wash the beans in cold water. Place the beans in a large casserole with enough cold water just to cover them, and simmer, covered, for 1 hour, adding hot water as needed. At the end of that time, add the dried beef, tongue, bacon, *linguica* and pork sausages, together with the chuck steak to the beans and cook for 1 hour longer, or until the beef and beans are tender. Add a little more hot water during the cooking time, if necessary.

In a frying-pan, fry the onions and garlic in the lard until the onions are tender but not browned. Add the tomatoes, chilli or Tabasco sauce, and salt and pepper to taste. Simmer until the sauce is thick and well blended.

Meanwhile, lift out the meats from the casserole, slice them and arrange them on a platter. Keep warm. Remove a cup of the beans and mash them into the onion and tomato sauce. Stir the mixture into the beans.

Ladle the beans into a tureen and serve with the meat.

Toasted Cassava Meal
FAROFA DE MANDIOCA

8 oz cassava (manioc meal)

In a large frying-pan, toast the cassava meal over low heat, stirring with a fork, until it begins to turn a very pale brown. Stir frequently so that it does not burn. Transfer to a serving bowl. Sprinkle over the *fejoada*.

Pepper and Lime Sauce
MOLHO DE PIMENTA E LIMAO

4 green chillies, chopped
1 medium-sized onion, chopped
1 garlic clove, chopped
½ teaspoon salt
½ cup lime juice

Purée the ingredients in an electric blender. Add about 4 fluid ounces of the bean liquor to the sauce, if desired.

Kale Minas Gerais Style
COUVE A MINEIRS

Kale or collard greens are traditionally served with Fejoada *or with its Minas Gerais variation,* Tutu a Mineira, *mashed black beans with eggs, pork and* linguiça *sausage.*

SERVES 8 TO 10

2 lb kale or collard greens
Salt
2 oz bacon fat
1 garlic clove

Wash the kale or collard greens thoroughly under cold running water. Trim the leaves from the stems and shred the leaves finely. Place the greens in a large bowl and pour boiling, salted water over them. Let them stand for 3 minutes, then drain thoroughly.

In a heavy frying-pan, heat the bacon fat with the garlic clove. Remove and discard the garlic. Add the greens and fry, gently, stirring frequently for about 15 minutes or until they are tender. Season to taste with salt. Serve in a separate bowl with the *fejoada*.

Skirt Steak Bogotá Style

This Colombian dish is typical of the highland cuisine and is traditionally served with papas chorreadas, *potatoes with cheese sauce, and a simple avocado salad, the avocado cubed and tossed with an oil and vinegar dressing. It is a hearty and warming food, very good in Bogotá's alpine climate.*

SERVES 6

2 lb skirt steak, with fat left on
1 medium-sized onion, coarsely chopped
2 medium-sized tomatoes, chopped
Thyme sprig
Parsley sprig
1 bay leaf
1 head garlic, peeled
Salt
Freshly-ground pepper
15 fl oz beef stock
2 tablespoons softened butter
Fresh breadcrumbs

Put the steak into a large casserole with the onion, tomatoes, thyme, parsley, bay leaf, garlic, salt and pepper to taste and stock to cover. Cook, covered, at a gentle simmer for about 2 hours, or until the steak is tender.

Lift out the steak and pat dry with kitchen paper. Reserve the cooking liquid. Arrange the steak fat side up, in a grilling pan. Spread with the butter and cover thickly with the breadcrumbs. Place the steak under the heat and grill until the crumbs are golden brown.

Slice the steak and arrange the slices on a heated serving dish. Strain the cooking liquid into a sauceboat and serve with the steak.

Meat Stew with Peaches and Pears
CARBONADA A LA CRIOLLA

This is one of the most characteristic dishes of the Argentinian criolla *kitchen. It is sometimes*

---

cooked and served in a whole, large pumpkin shell making it a beautiful party dish. The pumpkin used is the zapallo, *very like West Indian pumpkin, but quite different from the pie pumpkin of the United States.*

SERVES 6 TO 8

4 tablespoons olive oil
1 medium-sized onion, finely chopped
2 lb beef, cut into 1-inch cubes
3 medium-sized tomatoes, blanched, peeled, seeded and chopped
1 bay leaf
½ teaspoon dried oregano or marjoram
1 tablespoon tomato paste
1 teaspoon sugar
1½ pints beef stock
1½ lb sweet potatoes, peeled and cubed
1½ lb potatoes, peeled and cubed
1 lb pumpkin or Hubbard squash, peeled and cubed
Salt
Freshly ground black pepper
3 small peaches, peeled, halved and stoned
3 small pears, peeled, halved and cored
3 ears of sweet-corn, cut into 1-inch slices

Heat the oil in a heavy, flameproof casserole. Add the onion and fry until it is lightly browned. Push the onion to one side of the pan. Add the meat and brown lightly all over. Add the tomatoes, bay leaf, oregano or marjoram, tomato paste, sugar and the stock and stir to mix. Cover and simmer for 1 hour.

Add the sweet potatoes, potatoes and pumpkin. Season to taste with salt and pepper, cover and cook for 15 minutes. Add the peaches and pears, cover and cook 10 minutes longer. Add the corn and cook for 5 minutes.

Hot Chilli Pepper Sauce
SALSA DE AJI

A freshly-made hot pepper sauce is as commonplace on Latin-American tables as are salt and pepper. Each country has its own sauce, which differs slightly from the others. They have one thing in common—they are all extremely picante *and are to be used with discretion. This is a Colombian recipe.*

8 oz hot green chillies
1 medium-sized onion, finely chopped
1 teaspoon salt

Remove and discard the stems from the chillies. Chop the chillies and put them through a food mill with the onion and salt. Be careful to wash your hands after handling chillies. If accidently rubbed into the eyes it can be painful.

Transfer the sauce to a small bowl and serve with any meat, fish or poultry dish.

Exotic ingredients in a melting-pot of cuisines

Chilean Sauce
SALSA CHILENA

This tasty Chilean sauce can be served with any grilled, roasted or cold meat, fish or poultry.

MAKES ABOUT 1 PINT

2 fl oz plus 1 tablespoon salad oil
15 fl oz beef stock
1 medium-sized onion, finely chopped
2 medium-sized tomatoes, blanched, peeled and chopped
Juice of 2 lemons
Salt
Freshly ground black pepper

In a saucepan, combine the tablespoon of oil, stock and onion and simmer until the onion is tender. Push through a sieve and set aside.

Purée the tomatoes in an electric blender or in a food mill. In the same saucepan, cook the tomato purée until it is thick then mix in the onion and beef stock, lemon juice and salt and pepper to taste. Gradually beat in the 2 fluid ounces of oil. The sauce should be thick. Beat in more oil if necessary.

Peanut Sauce
SALSA DE MANI

1 tablespoon annatto (achiote) seeds
2 tablespoons lard or oil
1 medium-sized onion, finely-chopped
1 garlic clove, chopped
1 lb tomatoes, blanched, peeled, seeded and chopped or 14 oz can peeled tomatoes and the liquid
6 oz peanuts, finely ground
Salt

In a small, heavy frying-pan, combine the *annatto* seeds and lard or oil and cook over medium heat for a few minutes, or until the seeds have given up their rich orange colour. Do not overcook as the colour fades. Strain and discard the seeds.

Reheat the lard or oil and fry the onion, garlic and tomatoes until the onion is tender. Stir in the ground peanuts and cook for 3 or 4 minutes longer, or until the sauce is smooth. Season to taste with salt if necessary. The sauce should be thin enough to pour.

Potatoes with Cheese Sauce
PAPAS CHORREADAS

This is a typical Bogotá recipe, part of the highland cuisine.

SERVES 6

6 large potatoes, scrubbed

1 tablespoon butter
1 tablespoon lard
1 medium-sized onion, finely chopped
3 medium-sized tomatoes, blanched, peeled, seeded and chopped
Salt
Freshly ground black pepper
¼ cup heavy cream
1 cup grated Münster cheese

Put the potatoes into a large, heavy saucepan, with water to cover, and boil until they are tender. Drain the potatoes and peel them. Keep them warm.

In a frying-pan, melt the butter and lard. Fry the onion until it is tender but not brown. Add the tomatoes, and salt and pepper to taste. Simmer, stirring occasionally, for 5 minutes, or until the mixture is smooth and well blended. Stir in the cream and cheese and cook over very low heat, stirring, until the cheese melts. Pour over the potatoes.

Seasoned Shredded Steak with Rice and Black Beans
PABELLON CRIOLLO

This is regarded as the national dish of Venezuela. The beef is cooked in much the same way as the Spanish ropa vieja, *old clothes. If the* pabellon *is served with* tajadas de plátano, *(1-inch diagonal slices of ripe plantain fried in oil), it is called* pabellon con baranda, *flag with a railing.*

SERVES 6

2 lb skirt or flank steak
15 fl oz beef stock or water
1 medium-sized onion, finely chopped
1 garlic clove, chopped
2 fl oz olive oil
4 medium-sized tomatoes, blanched, peeled and chopped
Salt
Freshly ground pepper

Put the steak in a heavy saucepan or casserole with stock or water to cover. Simmer, covered, for 1½ to 2 hours, or until the steak is tender. Leave the meat in the stock until it is cool enough to handle.

Lift out the meat and reserve the stock for another use. Cut the meat into pieces about ¼ inch wide and 1 inch long.

In a large, heavy frying-pan, fry the onion and garlic in the oil until the onion is limp but not brown. Add the tomatoes, season to taste with salt and pepper and cook for 5 minutes longer.

Add the steak and simmer in the sauce until it is heated through.

Mound the beef in the centre of a heated platter and surround it with a ring of white rice, and mounds of cooked black beans, *caraotas ras.*

Cranberry Beans with Pumpkin and Corn
POROTOS GRANADOS

This Chilean dish has decided Indian overtones, since tomatoes, beans, corn and marrow all originated in Mexico and gradually spread over the whole South American continent.

SERVES 6

1 lb shelled fresh cranberry (shell) beans, or 8 oz dried cranberry beans or navy beans
2 tablespoons sweet paprika
2 fl oz olive oil
2 medium-sized onions, finely chopped
2 green chillies, seeded and chopped
Kernels from 2 large ears of fresh corn or 8 oz frozen or canned sweet-corn kernels
1 lb pumpkin or winter squash, cut into 1-inch cubes
1 lb tomatoes, blanched, peeled and chopped
½ teaspoon dried oregano
Salt
Freshly ground black pepper

Cook the fresh beans in unsalted water for about 45 minutes, or until tender. If using dried beans, soak them for 3 to 4 hours, and cook in unsalted water for 1½ to 2 hours, or until tender. Set aside.

In a heavy, deep frying-pan, mix the paprika with the oil and fry the onions until they are tender. Add all the remaining ingredients and simmer for 5 minutes.

Drain the beans, reserving the liquid. Add the beans to the tomato mixture with a little of the bean liquid if the purée is very dry. Cover the pan and simmer gently for 15 minutes to blend the flavours. The squash will disintegrate and thicken the sauce. Serve in soup plates.

Potato Cakes
LLAPINGACHOS

The potato, that supreme achievement of Inca and pre-Incaic civilization, is as highly esteemed in Ecuador as it is in nearby Colombia and in Peru, its native land. These potato cakes may be served as a main dish or as an accompaniment to fish or meat. In Ecuador they are traditionally accompanied by salsa de mani, *peanut sauce. Use firm, floury potatoes, since not all varieties remain in neat cakes when fried, even after chilling.*

otherwise, the cakes may be placed on a buttered baking sheet and browned in a hot oven, or under the grill.

SERVES 6

1 lb potatoes
Salt
3 medium-sized onions, finely chopped
3 oz butter
3 oz Münster Cheese (Emmenthal, Gruyere or Cheddar), shredded
Oil, lard or butter, for frying

Boil the potatoes in their jackets in salted water until tender. Drain, peel and mash them, and put them aside.

In a heavy frying-pan, fry the onions in the butter until soft and golden. Add the onions, the butter and the cheese to the mashed potato. Mix well and season to taste with salt if necessary. Divide the mixture into 12 balls. Flatten them into cakes and chill them thoroughly in the refrigerator.

Using just enough lard, oil or butter to coat the bottom of a frying-pan, fry the potato cakes until they are golden brown on both sides. Serve with *salsa de mani*.

Stuffed Avocados
PALTAS RELLENAS

The avocado, called aguacate *in Spanish, a word of Nahuatl origin, is known as* palta *in many South American countries. The avocados of Bolivia are small and round. It is not possible to give exact quantities for this Bolivian recipe because the sizes of avacado vary tremendously. These amounts are, therefore, approximate.*

SERVES 6

6 small avocados
8 oz cooked, chopped shrimp, fish, chicken or turkey
1 lettuce heart, finely shredded
8 fl oz mayonnaise
2 hard-boiled eggs, sliced

Carefully peel the avocados. Cut them in halves and remove and discard the pits. Combine the cooked shrimp, fish, chicken or turkey with the lettuce and mayonnaise. Fill the cavities of the avocados with the mixture and garnish with the sliced egg. Serve a whole avocado per person.

Potatoes with Fish
CAUSA A LA CHICLAYANA

This sea-level Peruvian dish, with others just as hearty, is described as an entrada, *an appetizer or first course. It is, however, a main course for modern appetites. The* quesco fresco, *fresh cheese, used is the* queso blanco *of Spain. Either*

mozzarella *or* Münster *may be used as substitutes. Peruvians like their dishes very* picante. *Personal taste should dictate the amount of chilli pepper used.*

SERVES 6

SAUCE

1 medium-sized onion, finely chopped
4 fl oz lime or lemon juice
Cayenne pepper
Salt
Freshly ground pepper
8 fl oz olive oil
6 large potatoes, scrubbed

GARNISH

2 ears sweet-corn
1 lb sweet potatoes, peeled and sliced
1 lb cassava root, peeled and sliced
3 ripe plantains or large bananas
Oil for frying
1½ lb fillets of bass, or similar white fish, cut into 2-inch pieces
Flour
3 medium-sized onions, thickly sliced
2 hot, red chillies, seeded and cut into strips
4 fl oz white vinegar
4 fl oz olive oil
Lettuce leaves
3 hard-boiled eggs, halved
6 large black olives, stoned
8 oz fresh cheese, cut into 6 wedges

In a bowl, combine the finely chopped onion with the lime juice, cayenne and salt and pepper to taste. Mix well then beat in the oil. Set aside.

Boil the potatoes and when they are tender, peel and mash them. Mix the sauce into the potatoes. Mound the potatoes in the centre of a large serving platter and keep warm.

Drop the ears of sweet-corn into boiling salted water and cook for 5 minutes. Drain and cut each ear into 3 slices. Keep warm.

Drop the sweet potatoes and cassava root into salted water, bring to a boil and cook for about 15 minutes or until they are tender. Drain and keep warm.

Peel the plantains or bananas. Slice them lengthwise, then crosswise. Heat a little oil in a frying-pan and fry the pieces on both sides for about 5 minutes or until they are lightly browned. Lift out the pieces, drain on paper towels and keep warm with the other vegetables.

Season the fish with salt and pepper, dust with the flour and fry lightly on both sides in the frying-pan, adding a little more oil if necessary. Lift out, and keep warm.

In a small saucepan, combine the thickly sliced onions with the chilli strips, cover with salted water, bring to a boil and drain. Add the oil and vinegar and bring to a boil. Remove the pan from the heat, and pour the mixture over the mashed potatoes.

To assemble the dish, arrange the lettuce leaves around the edge of the platter. Place the fish, eggs, root vegetables, plantains or bananas, sweet-corn, black olives and cheese wedges in a decorative pattern on the lettuce leaves and the edge of the potatoes. Serve immediately.

Milk Pudding
DULCE DE LECHE

This pudding is made in every country of Latin America. It may be eaten as a dessert by itself, as a sauce on cake or over ice-cream, or with fruit. Recipes differ slightly from country to country, as do the names. In Chile it is manjar blanco, *in Colombia* arequipe, *and in Peru* natillas piuranas. *This recipe is Argentinian.*

SERVES 4 TO 6

1½ pints milk
8 oz sugar
1 teaspoon vanilla essence
¼ teaspoon bicarbonate of soda

Combine all the ingredients in a heavy saucepan and bring to just under boiling point. Cook over very low heat, stirring occasionally until the mixture begins to thicken, then stir continuously until the mixture is thick.

ONE BOTTLE IN EVERY TEN of the world's wine is grown in South America and one bottle in every twenty is grown in the single state of Mendoza, Argentina's vast irrigated plain of vineyards under the shadow of the Andes.

Argentina's wine remains largely unknown to the outside world, although the industry is one of the world's largest and most modern. In general style and standard it resembles a great deal of Spanish wine—little of it, that is, would cut much of a figure on the international stage.

In contrast, Chile's better wines, from vineyards not one hundred and fifty miles from Mendoza, but the other side of the Andes, must be compared with French wine, more specifically Bordeaux. What the Atlantic is to Bordeaux, the Pacific is to the vineyards of Chile. The potential for superlative quality can be seen in the trickle of wine which Chile exports.

None of the wine of Brazil, Uruguay or Peru is exported, except in the form of Pisco Brandy, which makes a good sour with lemon and lime juice.

A paradise of culinary delights

THE CARIBBEAN

SNAPPER

TARPON

YAMS

GRO

COQUIMOL
Coconut cream sauce

CUBA

SOPA DE FRIJOL NEGR
Black bean soup

BLUEFISH

LANGOSTA ENCHILADA
Spiny lobster in pimento sauce

SW

GRAND CAYMAN

SALTFISH AND ACKEE

STAMP AND GO
Codfish cakes

CHRISTOPHER COLUMBUS discovered the West Indies in 1492. He was seeking a route to India when, thousands of miles off course, he sailed into the Caribbean and the most beautiful chain of islands in the world. There were so many islands, each one more beautiful than the next, that it was not surprising that he thought he had discovered Paradise. Today, as then, the sea is crystal clear and brilliantly blue, the sand shimmering white, the slopes wooded, the flowers scarlet and the fruit exotic.

The islands of the Caribbean stretch for two thousand five hundred miles in a great arc from Florida in the north to the Venezuelan coast in the south, separating the Caribbean Sea from the Atlantic Ocean. For convenience this green garland of islands and islets is divided into the Greater Antilles—Cuba, Jamaica, Hispaniola (Haiti-the Dominican Republic), and Puerto Rico—and the Lesser Antilles—the Leeward and Windward Islands, Trinidad, Tobago, Barbados, Curaçao, Aruba and Bonaire.

Many of the islands are wholly independent, others are associated politically with Great Britain, France, the Netherlands or the United States. Consequently, the islands fall into English-, Spanish-, French- or Dutch-speaking groups. The Dutch islands have a second language, Papiamento, a mixture of Spanish, Dutch and English, peppered with African, Portuguese and French words. In the French islands, Créole, a mixture of French and African languages, is also spoken.

The first people to settle in the islands were the gentle Arawaks and the warlike Caribs, Amerindian groups from the mainland of South America. From them the cuisine of the islands has inherited little except the use of allspice as a seasoning and of cassava, or manioc, meal in such dishes as the *matoutou de lambis* of Martinique-Guadeloupe, a stew made of conch and cassava meal.

Cassava was first cultivated in Brazil in 1500 BC. The first settlers, therefore, probably brought the cassava root with them when they set off in canoes on their voyages of discovery. It is known that they used vast quantities of chilli peppers in their food. These were introduced either by man or nature from Mexico, where all peppers originated. The Caribbean chilli pepper is very hot, full of flavour and as popular today as it was when the Arawaks and Caribs used it so lavishly.

The Arawaks were excellent farmers. In addition to cassava they grew yams, sweet potatoes and corn, or maize, which they may also have introduced from nearby Yucatán. Peanuts, which were used widely, may have been introduced by the Arawaks or, much later, by African slaves.

The arrival of Columbus opened the Caribbean to the world. Spain, Portugal, the Netherlands, France, Britain, Africa, Denmark, the United States, the Indian subcontinent and China have all contributed to the island cuisines. After Columbus, during the turbulent centuries when the European powers fought for control of the area, the Caribbean islands changed hands with great frequency, some as many as sixteen times. Each conquering nation arrived with its own cuisine and cooking techniques and introduced food plants and livestock. African slaves and, later, indentured labourers from the Indian subcontinent, brought their favourite foods with them.

The Africans introduced okra, probably some varieties of yam and akee, a strangely beautiful, yellow, black and red fruit.

Akee grows on a tree that would be cultivated for its handsome looks even if it bore nothing useful. Cooked and eaten as a vegetable the only edible part of the fruit is the yellow section, which resembles scrambled egg. The Indians brought curry, and the French brought their genius for selecting the perfect seasoning. Out of this mixture of cooking traditions, a rich and varied cuisine that can properly be described as Caribbean is emerging.

There are a few island dishes, known as nationality dishes, that remain firmly in their home island. The *keshy yena* of Curaçao, a whole Edam or Gouda cheese stuffed with shrimp, chicken or fish, and baked in a casserole, is an example. Curiously, this has migrated to the states of Chiapas and Yucatán in Mexico where, suitably enough, since it was originally a Spanish dish, it is called *queso relleno*, Spanish for stuffed cheese. The two glories of the Jamaican cuisine, akee with either saltfish or shrimp,